THE PUBLISHER GRATEFULLY ACKNOWLEDGES THE GENEROUS CONTRIBUTION TO THIS BOOK PROVIDED BY THE JUDY AND BILL TIMKEN ENDOWMENT FUND IN CONTEMPORARY ARTS OF THE UNIVERSITY OF CALIFORNIA PRESS FOUNDATION.

true to life

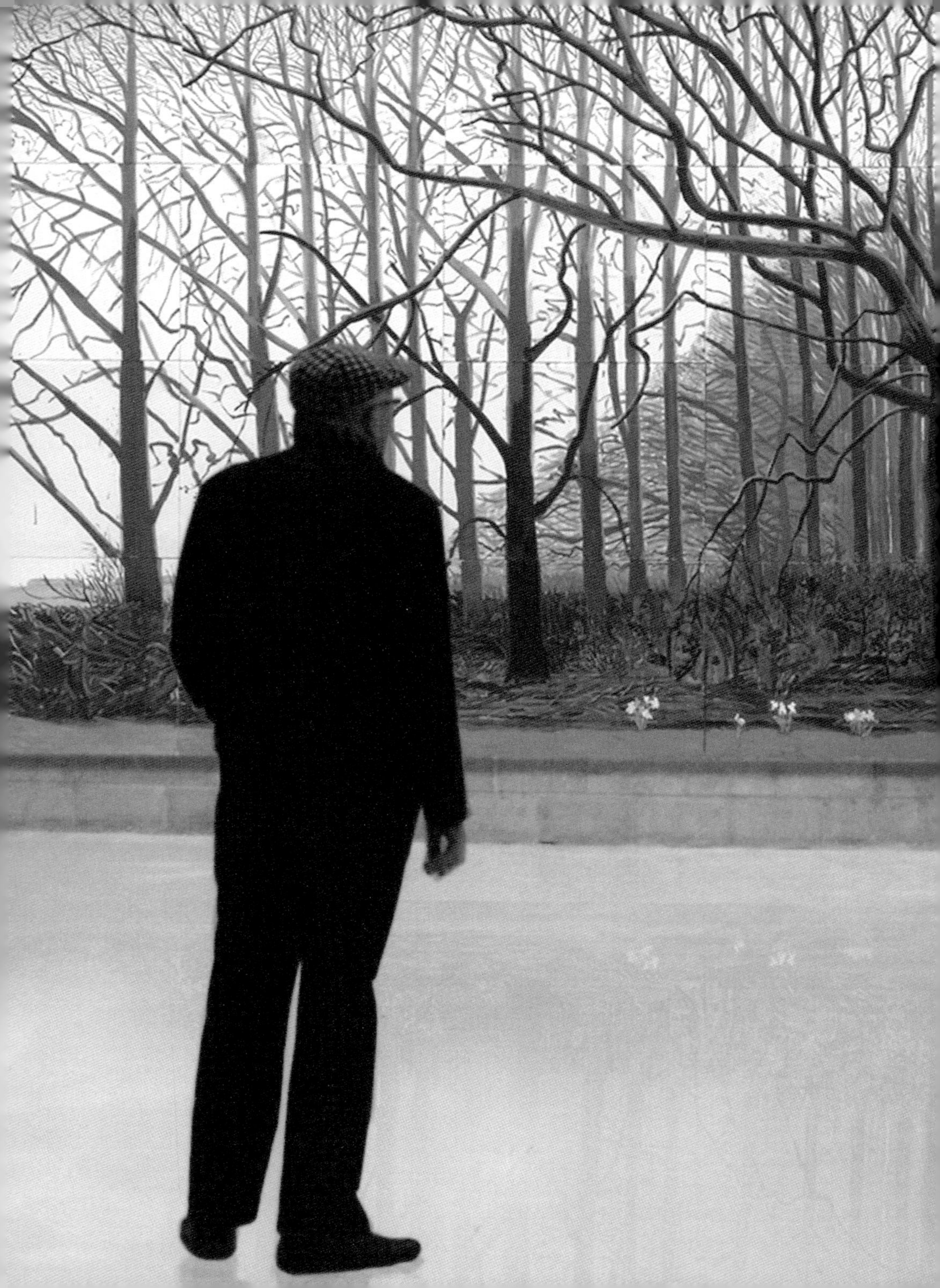

true to life

TWENTY-FIVE YEARS OF CONVERSATIONS WITH DAVID HOCKNEY

LAWRENCE WESCHLER

PUBLISHED WITH THE ASSISTANCE OF
THE GETTY FOUNDATION

UNIVERSITY OF CALIFORNIA PRESS

Frontispiece. Detail of photo composite, 2008 © David Hockney. Photo: David Hockney and Jonathan Wilkinson.

University of California Press, one of the most distinguished university presses in the United States, enriches lives around the world by advancing scholarship in the humanities, social sciences, and natural sciences. Its activities are supported by the UC Press Foundation and by philanthropic contributions from individuals and institutions. For more information, visit www.ucpress.edu.

University of California Press
Oakland, California

Library of Congress Cataloging-in-Publication Data

Weschler, Lawrence.
True to life : twenty-five years of conversations with David Hockney / Lawrence Weschler.
p. cm.
Includes bibliographical references and index.
ISBN 978-0-520-24375-0 (cloth : alk. paper)—ISBN 978-0-520-25879-2 (pbk. : alk. paper)
1. Hockney, David—Interviews. 2. Artists—England—Interviews. I. Hockney, David. II. Title.
N6797.H57A35 2008
760.092—dc22 2008009383

26 25 24 23 22 21
10 9 8 7 6 5 4

The paper used in this publication meets the minimum requirements of ANSI/NISO Z39.48–1992 (R 1997) (Permanence of Paper).

In memory of
my mother,
FTW
&
for Bob

contents

illustrations

FIGURES

COLOR PLATES

All works by David Hockney except where noted

SECTION ONE

SECTION TWO

SECTION THREE

follows page **218**

a prefatory note on david hockney and robert irwin

At one level the reader is invited to read this book as he or she would any other—which is to say, in this instance, as the chronicle of coming on twenty-five years of conversations between its author and the artist David Hockney.

But actually, there's a second book tucked into the pages that follow, or anyway another way of reading them, and perhaps the best way to get at that second text is to recount how the whole project began in the first place.

Back in 1982, I published my first book, a midlife portrait of the California Light and Space artist Robert Irwin, entitled *Seeing Is Forgetting the Name of the Thing One Sees,* a title that paradoxically, in this instance, said it all. Which is to say that the book surveyed all the things that Robert Irwin, sequentially over a period of about two decades (1958–1978), had had to bracket out of his practice—figure, image, line (which is to say associations of any kind), focus, any made or permanent object, signature, and presently even exhibition itself—before he was able to arrive at what he came to comprehend as the true subject of art: the sheer wonder of perception itself or, as he sometimes parsed matters, "all the marvels inherent in our perceiving ourselves perceiving."

Shortly after that book's publication I got a call from another artist famously associated with California, David Hockney, a painter I'd never met but one whose work I naturally knew well. He invited me up to the Hollywood Hills home into which he'd recently moved, and, after cordially offering me tea and making me feel quite at ease, he began by telling me he'd recently finished reading my book about Irwin, and though he disagreed with almost every single thing in it, still, he couldn't get it out of his head, such that he thought it might be a good idea to discuss the thing with me.

"I've never met Irwin," he noted, "though I've of course been quite aware of his work, as what artist, especially here in L.A., wouldn't be?" Already then, Irwin was regarded as one of the most significant artists and thinkers on artistic practice anywhere in the country, at least among fellow artists (though his reputation was considerably less well established among the public at large); within a few months he would become the first visual artist to be awarded one of the MacArthur Foundation's so-called genius awards. "I mean," Hockney continued, "I've observed his progress, though at times that was by no means easy, and for the longest time I felt that his position on the photographing of his work"—a flat prohibition, as it happens (which is one of the principal reasons he was so much less well known among the public at large)—"was pretty preposterous, and somewhat fetishistic." Irwin for his part accounted for that absolutist injunction by arguing that a photograph could capture everything that the work was not about (which is to say its image) and nothing that it was about (which is to say its presence), so why bother?

Hockney paused and took a drag on a cigarette before going on to confound me entirely: "The thing is," he now said, "with time I've come to see that Irwin was right about that ban on photographing his work; I wish I'd imposed a similar ban regarding my own from the outset." (This from an artist whose work was more photographed and more ubiquitously visible in the world than that of just about anybody else, with the possible exception of Andy Warhol!) "I mean, no one can come upon one of my paintings in a museum, say, and simply see *it;* instead they see the poster in their college dorm or the dentist's office or the jacket on the book they are reading, all sorts of second-rate mediations getting in the way of experiencing the work as if from scratch."

Our conversation went on from there, and gradually Hockney proceeded to lay out the profound divergence from Irwin he nevertheless felt, which essentially came down to a radical disagreement over the true significance of the cubist achievement and how one ought to be required to proceed as an artist if one were going to take that achievement seriously.

For Irwin, cubism represents the culmination of a five-hundred-year-long process of flattening, as it were, in the subject deemed worthy of artistic attention (from Christ, to this king, to this burgher, to his maid, to her red shawl, to the color red, to the process of seeing the color red); and if one were to take seriously its greatest accomplishment—which is to say the so-called marriage of figure and ground—one couldn't very well go on making paintings, which would necessarily have to read as figures to the wall's ground, thereby undermining the whole point of the artistic project.

Hockney emphatically disagreed with this assessment, and as he insisted to me a few weeks later (for in the meantime he'd invited me to start visiting more regularly so that I might compose a text for a planned coffee-table book surveying the Cameraworks series on which he'd only just embarked), "No! Cubism was precisely about *saving the possibility of figuration,* this ages-old need of human beings, going all the way back to Lascaux, and saving that possibility at the moment of its greatest crisis, what with the onslaught of photography with all its false claims to be able to accomplish such figuration better and more objectively. It was about asserting all the things photography couldn't capture: time, multiple vantages, and the sense of lived and living experience."

He went on to acknowledge that ever-greater degrees of abstraction constituted one possible path out of cubism. But he for one was sure that Picasso and Braque, from early on, would have realized that such a path would only lead into a dead end or, as he put it, "an empty room." That last comment seemed a direct dig at Irwin (who for his part disagreed completely—I know, because he subsequently told me so, characterizing Picasso and Braque's failure to pursue such a path as a failure of nerve), and in a sense that entire first Hockney essay of mine could be read as a refutation of the earlier Irwin book. Just as the essay I subsequently wrote for the 1993 Irwin retrospective at the Museum of Contemporary Art in Los Angeles would come to stand quite consciously as, among other things, a refutation of my intervening Hockney writings.

Indeed, for some twenty-five years now, whenever I have written about one or the other of these two giants of contemporary art (arguably the two most significant artists to come out of the late twentieth-century California art milieu), the other one has called to tell me, "Wrong, wrong, wrong." The two have never met or conversed in person (straddling that Southern California scene like Schoenberg and Stravinsky before them, each seemingly oblivious of the other's existence though in fact deeply seized by the work); instead they have been carrying on this quite vivid argument for over two decades, *through me,* as it were.

Such that the reader is invited to explore this book in a second way, as a companion (or counterpoint) to the new edition of my Irwin biography, coming out roughly simultaneously, which will in turn include over twenty-five years of my parallel conversations with him.

And the truly odd thing about all this is that the longer this metaconversation goes on, and the more at odds the two artists continue to imagine themselves ("Oh, naah," Irwin averred when he happened to reach me on my cell phone a few months back just as I was about to go onstage to address a museum auditorium full of visitors to Hockney's touring portrait show in Boston. "No, no, I don't disdain him at all, you've got me all wrong, I think he's an excellent *practitioner*"—an evaluation he delivered with truly withering hauteur), the more it seems to me (the mere conduit, sounding board, tuning fork) that at a deeper level, the two of them have in fact been engaged in an exploration, an activity of "pure inquiry," as Irwin would parse the task at hand, that is entirely convergent and indeed now virtually congruent.

CHAPTER 1

cameraworks

STARING DOWN A PARALYZED CYCLOPS (1983)

Aboard the jetliner that was flying me out to Los Angeles a few months back, I was browsing through a recent book by David Hockney, the forty-six-year-old British-transplant Californian whose newest work I was heading out to see. Or not so much a book as a pamphlet, the artist's textual accompaniment to an exhibition he'd organized at the National Gallery in London back in 1981. The National Gallery has lately been sponsoring a series of exhibitions under the rubric The Artist's Eye, in which contemporary artists are invited to select a group of masterworks from the museum's own bounteous collections and to comment on why these particular paintings have been especially important to them. For his turn, Hockney selected a Vermeer, a Piero della Francesca, a Van Gogh, and a Degas. A few years earlier, Hockney had composed a painting of his own (Plate 2) in which he portrayed his friend, the curator Henry Geldzahler, thoughtfully looking at reproductions of these very paintings taped to a screen in his studio, and he now included this work in his small show as well. In his catalogue essay, Hockney celebrated the exquisite richness of the experience of looking at such paintings, especially when compared with the damning poverty of the experience of looking at most ordinary photographs. With a certain irony, he suggested that the only thing photography was much good at conveying—or at any rate, conveying truthfully—was another flat surface, as, for example, in the reproduction of a fine painting. "About sixty years ago," he concluded, "most educated people could draw in a quite skillful way. Which meant they could tell other people about certain experiences in a certain way. Their visual delights could be expressed. . . . Today people don't draw very much. They use

---

This essay was originally composed as the text for David Hockney's coffee-table volume *Cameraworks* (New York: Knopf, 1984), in which color versions of virtually all the images described can still be found.

the camera. My point is, they're not truly, perhaps, expressing what it was they were looking at—what it was about it that delighted them—and how that delight forced them to make something of it, to share the experience, to make it vivid to somebody else. If the few skills that are needed in drawing are not treated seriously by everybody, eventually it will die. And then all that will be left is the photographic ideal which we believe too highly of."

Hmmm, I remember thinking as the seat belt signs came on and I stowed my satchel for the descent into Los Angeles, that last comment seemed a bit odd, since about the only thing Hockney had been doing in the two years since was taking photographs—tens of thousands of photographs—and it was indeed Hockney's *photographic* work which this jet, landing, was now delivering me to see.

I rented a car at the airport, drove to my hotel at the base of the Hollywood foothills, deposited my bags, phoned Hockney, and within the hour was driving up Laurel Canyon toward the artist's home. At the top of the canyon, the road intersects Mulholland Drive, onto which I now turned—a long meandering avenue that casually skirts the crest of the Hollywood Hills, heading west to east, bobbing in and out of canyons where dusty chaparral outcroppings give way to wide valley vistas far below (a drive vividly evoked, as it happens, in one of the last major paintings Hockney had undertaken before being swallowed into his photographic passion (Plate 1). About two miles east of Laurel Canyon, I veered onto Hockney's side street and quickly parked the car. The home where Hockney has been living since 1979 is nestled below street level, and one arrives at the front door by walking down cement steps shaded in foliage. As I rang the doorbell, I could see through a narrow window into the living room–studio—a delirious clutter. Poster boards were leaning against every available vertical, their faces brimming with layers upon layers of photoprints. Hockney was standing in front of a large table, a thick deck of photoprints in his hand, staring down at a poster board collage-in-the-making, lost in thought. He'd posit a print, look at it for a moment, move it over, finger another print a few inches to the side, pick it out of the jumble and relegate it to one of the many piles of photoprints surrounding the board. Then he'd revert to his even concentration, his game of photo solitaire, utterly oblivious. I rang the bell again, and again, until finally he looked up, awakened, and came to the door, smiling, to let me in.

"I'm sorry," he said with genuine concern. "Were you waiting here long?" His face was friendly and congenial, his round features reemphasized by round glasses (the left frame gold, the right one black). Pyroxide blond hair shagged out from beneath a yellow-and-red checkered cap across which was emblazoned the word CALIFORNIA. He wore a skinny loosened burgundy tie, a red-striped shirt, a green smock, a pair of well-worn gray wool slacks, and black-and-white checkered slippers over mismatched yellow and red socks. He was of average height but, as he led me now through the living room, I noticed that he lumbers along with the comfortable slouch of a tall man. Leaving the entry foyer, I peered down the hallway into the next few rooms, noting how each wall had been painted a different brilliant color. The afternoon sun streamed in, bouncing hue off hue, to simultaneously cooling and luscious effect. Hockney mentioned that the rooms had only recently been painted and then excused himself for a moment, returning to his collage. He made a few more adjustments, lifted another print out of the middle, set it aside, slid in a replacement, and said, "There, that will do for the time being." He then looked up and led me out through the sliding glass door onto the shaded blue-painted wood deck.

Only here does one get a sense of the layout of the house—a curving amphitheater of rooms overlooking (in place of the stage) a modest bean-shaped pool. A few months back, Hockney drained the pool and applied playful navy blue brushstrokes to its aqua bottom: this afternoon, refracted, the strokes seemed to lollygag on the surface of the water—hedonist amoebas. Beyond the pool, high ferns and bushes blocked any view of the neighboring houses.

Leaning now against the deck railing, looking back through the sliding glass doors at the piles of photos scattered about the room, I mentioned my airplane reading and asked Hockney what he was doing at this point taking photographs *at all.* "Ah well," he replied impishly. "You mustn't overinterpret those comments. It's not that I despised photography *ever,* it's just that I've always distrusted the claims that were made on its behalf—claims as to its greater reality or authenticity. Actually, I've taken photographs for years—snaps, I'd call them, pictures of friends and of places we'd visit. When I'd get home I'd put the pictures in albums. Since the midsixties I've managed to fill several each year. During some periods I was more involved than others. I mean, clearly, all along I've had an *ambivalent* relationship to photography—but as to whether I thought it an art form, or a craft, or a technique, well, I've always been taken with Henry Geldzahler's answer to that question when he said, 'I thought it was a *hobby*.'"

Beginning in 1968, Hockney often used photography as an aide-mémoire in his painting. Several of his most famous portraits—for example, *Christopher Isherwood and Don Bachardy*, 1968, or *Mr. and Mrs. Clark and Percy*, 1970–71—were preceded by dozens of photographic studies, alongside the many pen-and-ink sketches. He'd photograph the furniture, the walls, the way light fell across the room at different times of day; details of faces, hands, limbs; impressions of stances and postures. Photorealism had come into vogue during that period, but Hockney wasn't interested in achieving a photographic likeness—a painting which would look "as real as a photograph" (many photorealist paintings had in fact been traced onto the canvas from the projected slide of a photograph). Rather, he was using the photographs to jog his memory; the confluence of dozens of discrete recollections and observations would form the eventual painting, which would distill the essence of all the studies that had preceded it. By using photographs in this way Hockney, if anything, came to distrust their purported reality all the more.

"I mean, for instance, wide-angle lenses!" Hockney exclaimed as we stood that afternoon on the deck overlooking his pool. "After a while I bought a better camera and I tried using a wide-angle lens because I wanted to record a whole room or an entire standing figure. But I hated the pictures I got. They seemed extremely untrue. They depicted something you never actually saw. It wasn't just the lines bending in ways they never do when you look at the world. Rather it was the falsification—your eye doesn't ever see that much in one glance. It's not true to life."

To get around this problem, Hockney began making "joiners." For example, when he needed a photo of his friend Peter Schlesinger standing, gazing downward, as a study for his *Portrait of an Artist (Pool with Two Figures)*, 1972, he took five separate shots of Peter's body—head and shoulders, torso, waist, knees, feet—and spliced the prints together, effecting the closest possible overlap (Figs. 1 and 2). "At first I was just going through all this because the result, the depiction of the

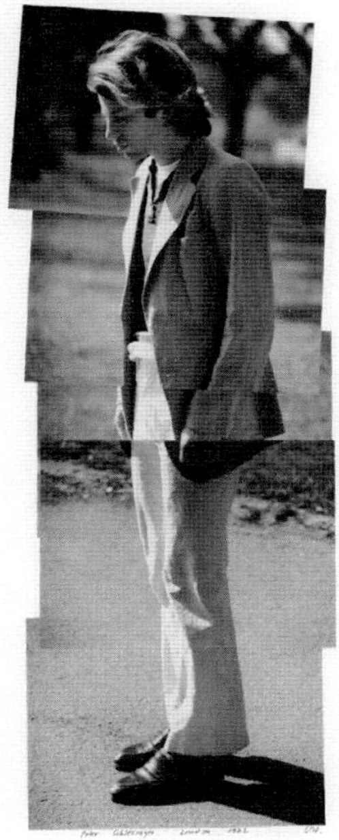

FIG 1 David Hockney, *Peter Schlesinger, London, 1972.*

FIG 2 David Hockney, *Portrait of an Artist (Pool with Two Figures)*, 1972.

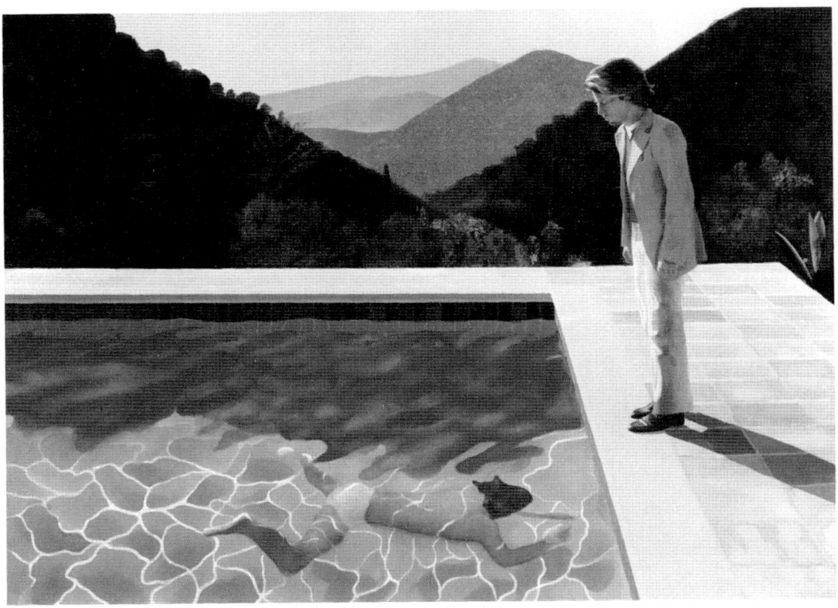

particular subject, came out looking clearer and more true to life than a single wide-angle version of the same subject," Hockney explained. "However, fairly early on I noticed that these joiners also had more presence than ordinary photographs. With five photos, for instance, you were forced to look five times. You couldn't help but look more carefully."

Throughout the seventies, Hockney continued to take photos, as studies or mementos, but with little interest in the medium itself. Dutifully, he'd have his assistants enter the prints into his ever-expanding shelf of albums (by the early eighties more than 120 of them), but he was utterly careless with the negatives, tossing them, unsorted, into boxes. Hockney's apathy notwithstanding, other people were becoming quite interested. "The Pompidou Center in Paris kept nattering away at me for years to do a show of the photos," Hockney recalled, "and I kept putting them off. I wasn't interested: most photo shows are boring, always the same scale, the same texture. But they kept insisting—they said they wanted to do it *because* I was a painter, and so forth. Finally, in 1981, I gave in, but I told them they'd have to come and make the selection themselves because I didn't have a clue. So, early in 1982, the curator Alain Sayag arrived here and spent four days looking through the albums, making his selection, and for four nights we sat here arguing about whether photography was a good medium for the artist.

"My main argument was that a photograph could not be looked at for a long time. Have you noticed that?" Hockney led me back into the studio and picked up a magazine, thumbing through randomly to an ad, a photograph of a happy family picnicking on a hillside green. "See? You can't look at most photos for more than, say, thirty seconds. It has nothing to do with the subject matter. I first noticed this with erotic photographs, trying to find them lively: you can't. Life is precisely what they don't have—or rather, time, lived time. All you can do with most ordinary photographs is stare at them—they stare back, blankly—and presently your concentration begins to fade. They stare you down. I mean, photography is all right if you don't mind looking at the world from the point of view of a paralyzed cyclops—*for a split second.* But that's not what it's like to live in the world, or to convey the experience of living in the world.[1]

"During the last several months I've come to realize that it has something to do with the amount of time that's been put into the image. I mean, Rembrandt spent days, weeks, painting a portrait. You can go to a museum and look at a Rembrandt for hours and you're not going to spend as much time looking as he spent painting—observing, layering his observations, layering the time. Now, the camera was actually invented long before the chemical processes of photography—it was being used by artists in Italy in the seventeenth and eighteenth centuries in the form of a camera obscura, people like Canaletto, who used one in his paintings of Venice. His students would trace the complicated perspectives of the Grand Canal onto the canvas, and then he'd paint the outline in, and the result would appear to confirm the theory of one-point perspective. But in terms of what we've been talking about, it didn't really matter, because the entire process still took time, the hand took time, and though a 'camera' was used, there's no mistaking the layered time. At a museum you can easily spend half an hour looking at a Canaletto and you won't blank out.

"No, the flaw with the camera comes with the invention of the chemical processes in the nineteenth century. It wasn't that noticeable at first. In the early days, the exposure would last for several seconds, so that the photographs were either of people, concentrated and still, like Nadar's, or of *still* lifes or empty street scenes, as in Atget's Paris. You can look at those a bit longer before you blank out. But as the technology improved, the exposure time was compressed to a split second. And the reason you can't look at a photograph for a long time is because there's virtually no time *in it*—the imbalance between the two experiences, the first and second lookings, is too extreme.[2]

"Anyway," Hockney concluded, "Sayag and I spent four nights having these arguments, and in the daytime he made his selection." The trouble came when it was time to find the negatives amid the many boxes so that proper reproductions could be made. "There was no way they were going to find them in four days, so instead we went down to the store and bought several cases of Polaroid SX-70 film and came back up and photographed the prints Sayag had selected so that he could go back to Paris and prepare the show." The curator left, the negatives were eventually ferreted out, and by summer 1982 the Pompidou Center was indeed running a highly successful show entitled David Hockney Photographs.[3] Meanwhile, back in Los Angeles Hockney was left with several dozen packs of unused Polaroid film.

He began almost immediately. The morning after Sayag left, Hockney loaded

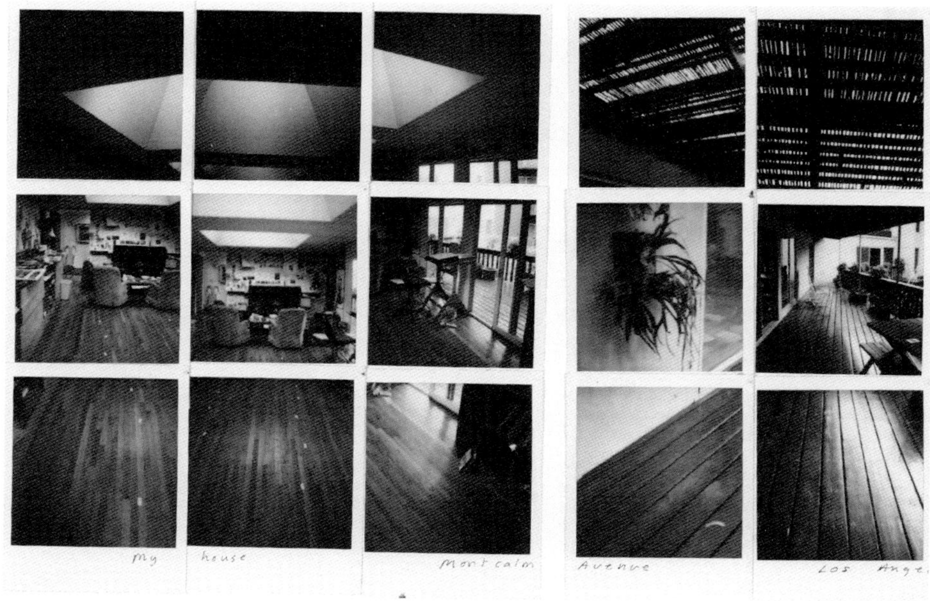

FIG 3 David Hockney, *My House, Montcalm Avenue, Los Angeles, Friday, February 26th, 1982.*

his Polaroid and started on a tour of his house, snapping details (Fig. 3). Beginning in the living room (which at the time was much less cluttered—indeed, one imagines that this was to constitute a record of the very last time it would be that uncluttered), he cast three views of the floor, moving left to right, then three views of the middle distance, and then three views of the ceiling with its lovely skylight. There was no attempt to effect the exact matching that had characterized his earlier joiners. Indeed, the two chairs that appeared in one of the middle-distance shots appeared again in the next, but as if closer and from a slightly different angle. (The parallel beams of hardwood in the floor emphasized the different perspectives.) The third middle-distance view included the sliding glass door and, through it, the deck. He then went out onto the deck, repositioned himself, and shot another series of images with new perspectives but similar repetitions. In the corner of the rightmost of these middle-distance images could be seen the top of a staircase leading downward. Repositioning himself once again, leaning out over the edge of the

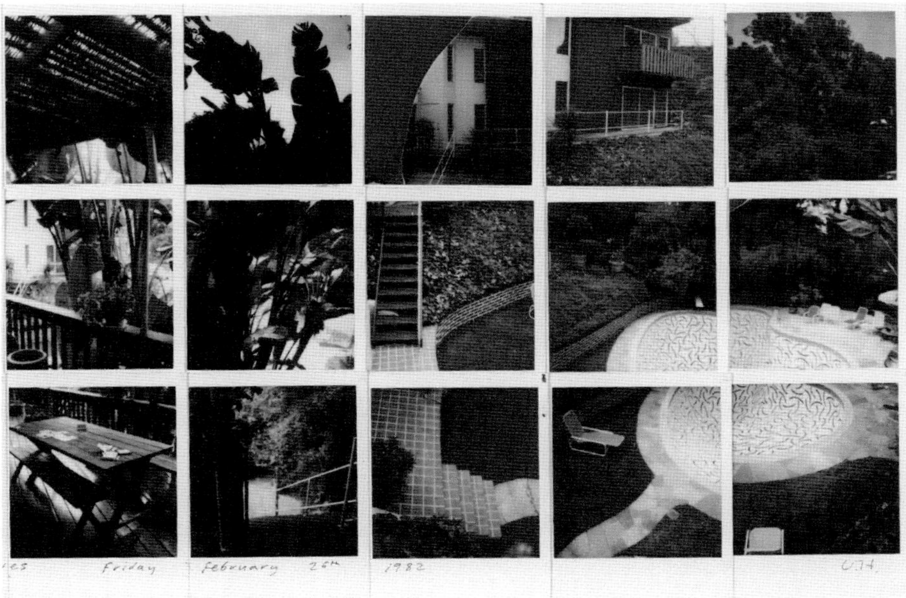

balustrade, he shot still another series, this time of the steps and the garden and pool toward which they led.[4]

Already as he was shooting the individual Polaroids, he was arranging them into a composition, laying the square SX-70 prints side by side, reshooting perspectives where the images didn't quite meld or where the articulation of space became confused. "Very early on," Hockney subsequently reported, "I realized that if the pictures weren't clear enough, and if their relationship to each other wasn't clear enough, the collage ended up looking like a jigsaw puzzle and your eyes literally couldn't stay on it." By the time he was through, he'd created a rectangular panel consisting of thirty individual square images, arrayed in a grid (three high and ten wide), which uniquely conveyed the experience of walking through that house from the living room onto the deck, down the stairs and toward the pool. Yet this movement was not conveyed in traditional comic-book style or in the staccato-cinematic mode of Eadweard Muybridge, where each new frame implied a new episode or another staggered step. Rather, the entire panel reads as an integrated whole, as a house, a home, through which the viewer was invited to move, from inside to outside and then back. Indeed, that's what this collage finally looked most like—the very experience of looking as it transpires across time.

Hockney glued the thirty Polaroids down onto a panel and then inscribed a title across the white borders of the bottom ten squares: *My House, Montcalm Avenue, Los Angeles, Friday, February 26th, 1982.* And he was off: during the next three months he would compose over 140 Polaroid collages. By summertime they would be the focus of three separate exhibitions—in New York, Los Angeles, and London. A couple of them would even be included at the Pompidou Center show in Paris.[5]

"From that first day," Hockney recalls, "I was exhilarated. First of all, I immediately realized I'd conquered my problem with time in photography. It takes time to see these pictures—you can look at them for a long time, they invite that sort of looking. But, more importantly, I realized that this sort of picture came closer to how we actually see, which is to say, not all at once but rather in discrete, separate glimpses, which we then build up into our continuous experience of the world. Looking at you now, my eye doesn't capture you in your entirety, but instead quickly, in nervous little glances. I look at your shoulder, and then your ear, your eyes (maybe, for a moment, if I know you well and have come to trust you, but even then only for a moment), your cheek, your shirt button, your shoes, your hair, your eyes again, your nose and mouth. There are a hundred separate looks across time from which I synthesize my living impression of you. And this is wonderful. If, instead, I caught all of you in one frozen look, the experience would be dead—it would be like . . . it would be like looking at an ordinary photograph."

No sooner had Hockney achieved his breakthrough with his tour-of-the-house collage than he began training his Polaroid on people. Indeed, people, carefully observed, became his preferred subject—or rather, perhaps, continued to be his preferred subject. "There are some lines in Auden's 'Letter to Lord Byron,'" Hockney commented to me that afternoon, as we began looking through a box of 8-by-10-inch reproductions of his Polaroid collages, "which I've always particularly fancied:

> To me art's subject is the human clay,
> Landscape but a background to a torso.
> All of Cézanne's apples I would give away,
> For a small Goya or a Daumier.

I mean, I don't know about those *particular* apples—Cézanne's apples *are* lovely and very special—but what finally can compare to the image of another human being?"

By the end of his first week of voracious experimentation, Hockney had already achieved what would prove one of the most fully realized collages in the entire series, a warmly congenial portrait of his friends Christopher Isherwood and Don Bachardy (Plate 3). The two emerge from a grid of sixty-three Polaroid squares, nine high by seven wide. Isherwood, the aging master, is seated, a wineglass in his hand and a cheerful gleam in his eye, which is trained upon the camera. The younger Bachardy stands, leaning against the wall and looking down affectionately at his long-time friend. Isherwood's head is basically captured in one square still, but Bachardy's hovers, in a play of movement that fans out into five separate squares—that is, five separate vantages, five separate tilts of the head, five distinct moments of friendly concentration. Bachardy's five heads give the impression of a buzzing bee bobbing about Isherwood's still flower of a face. Yet the five vantages read, immediately, as one head; and indeed, a head no larger than Christopher's. If anything, Isherwood's face is the center of attention, the fulcrum of the image.

"With this one of Christopher and Don I started with their faces, just as I always do in drawings and paintings," Hockney recalls. "But I've noticed with these collages that you almost always end up throwing out the first pictures of faces: they're too self-conscious and stiff. Afterwards, when you've been spending time snapping elbows and legs" (the vantages that include Bachardy's legs seem tilted so as to emphasize his height—one square foreshortens his leg from knee all the way to floor, whereas another, a few squares over, consists of nothing but Isherwood's huge kneecap), "then you can go back to the face, which in the meantime has calmed to a more natural aspect. In this case at first they were both looking at me, but as the minutes passed, I noticed that Don spent more and more time gazing down at Christopher with that fond, caring look that so characterizes their relationship. So the piece changed as I was making it."

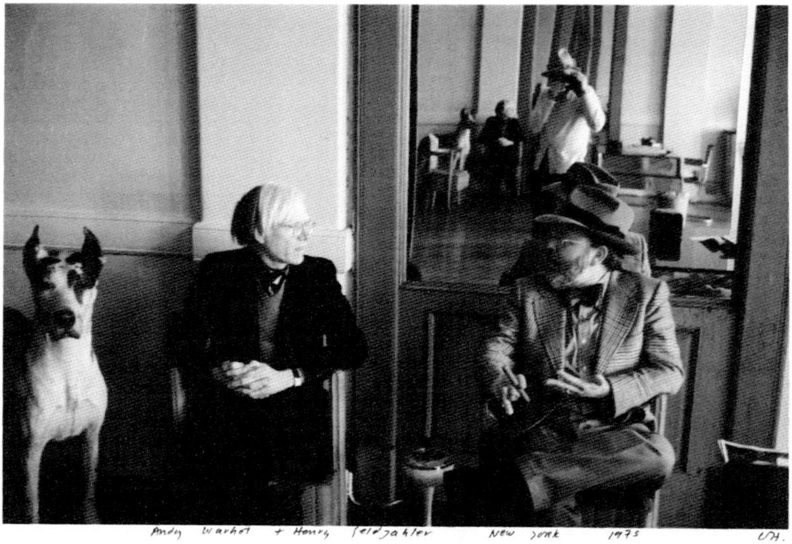

FIG 4 David Hockney, *Andy Warhol and Henry Geldzahler, New York, 1975.*

Back in 1975, by way of contrast, Hockney had snapped a photo of his friend Henry Geldzahler, cigar in hand, making an animated point in a conversation with Andy Warhol (Fig. 4). The two were seated, facing each other, and a Great Dane stood guard at Warhol's side, facing the camera. Behind Warhol and Geldzahler was a mirror, in which you can see Hockney standing, taking the picture. Behind Hockney was another mirror, where again you can see the conversationalists and the dog, only smaller. Strangely, it's only in this second reflection that you notice that the dog is not real: it's stuffed. And looking back at the figures of Geldzahler and Warhol, you can't really tell the difference. "That's the whole point," Hockney confirms. "In ordinary photographs, everybody's stuffed." In this new portrait, however, Isherwood and Bachardy are anything but stuffed. Theirs is a living relationship: it's living right there before your eyes.

"It took me over two hours to make that collage," Hockney explained. "I'd snap my details, spread them out on the floor while they developed, and go back for more. Christopher said I was behaving like a mad scientist, and there *was* some-

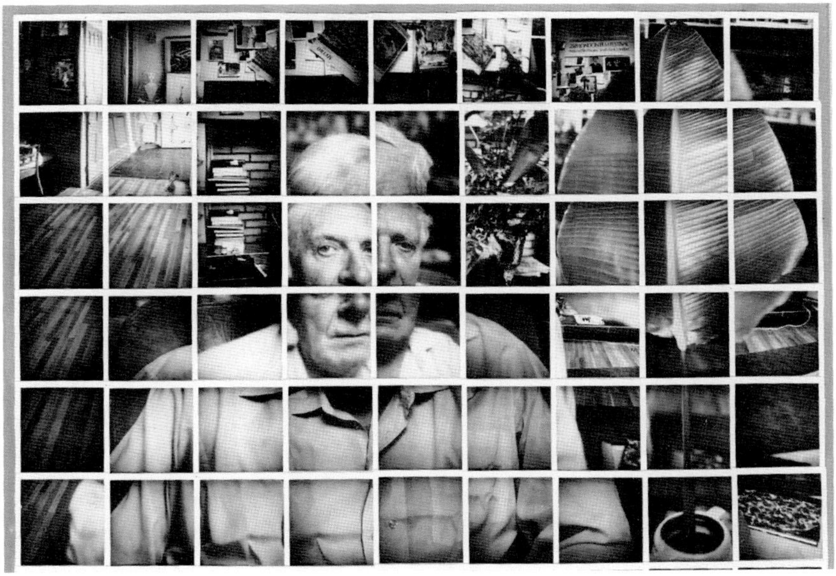

FIG 5 David Hockney, *Stephen Spender, April 9th, 1982* (detail).

thing mad about the whole enterprise. Looking back at the completed grid, it seems as if each shot were taken from one vantage point—there is, as it were, a general vantage—but if you look more closely, you can see that I was moving about all over. The lens on a Polaroid camera is fixed: you can't add close-up or zoom lenses or anything. So that to get a close-up of the floor, I had to get close up *to* the floor. In this other one here, of Stephen Spender" (Hockney pulled out a reproduction of a remarkable composite portrait with the writer seated in the foreground and the living room–studio receding into the background), "I spent so much time in the back of the room, *behind* Stephen's chair, that finally he exclaimed, 'Are you still taking *my* picture, David?' [Fig. 5]. Or, in this one here" (Hockney showed me the reproduction of a collage of his darkened bedroom in the morning, the light just beginning to filter through the Levellor shades, all seen, apparently, from a vantage point at the head of the bed, the viewer still under the covers, a magazine by his side), "it looks like I just woke up, rubbed my eyes, picked up the camera and started snapping away, never leaving the cozy sheets; but in fact I had to get up and walk over to the bookshelves, the window, all around, to slowly build up the image.[6]

"This one here," he said, pulling out a reproduction of a smallish collage, a grid five by five, of his London dealer John Kasmin, smoking a cigarette, "took a very long time to shoot. Kas ended up having to smoke ten cigarettes! I kept on getting the line of his face wrong. It didn't look like him—or my sense of him. I took more than twice as many pictures as I finally used. Similarly, with this other one here of Kas sitting in a blue chair, I kept having to rephotograph the chair to get it right. As it turned out, the chair looks much larger than it actually is, but that's because it seemed that way, with Kas sitting in it. The same thing happens with the leafy tropical plant next to Stephen Spender in the other collage: it's much larger than it actually is, but that's because I got interested in it. Relative importance, not accuracy, was what I was trying to convey. Which is to say, the entire process was just like drawing."

The exhibitions of these Polaroid collages, when they were mounted a few months later, would be called Drawing with a Camera. Assay and correction, approximation and refinement, venture and return. "The camera is a *medium* is what I suddenly realized," Hockney explained. "It's neither an art, a technique, a craft, nor a hobby—it's a tool. It's an extraordinary drawing tool. It's as if I, like most ordinary photographers, had previously been taking part in some long-established culture in which pencils were used only for making dots—there's an obvious sense of liberation that comes when you realize you can make lines!" And for all their beauty as color-saturated objects (Hockney, as ever, is an extraordinary colorist; he somehow manages to coax colors out of the Polaroid film you'd never have imagined were in there), these collages are principally about line. An internal sleeve crease, for example, aligns in the next frame with the outer sleeve contour, and contours generally jag from one frame to the next, a series of locally abrupt disjunctions merging into a wider coherence.

There is in some of these collages, as in some of Hockney's finest pencil drawings, a remarkable psychological acuity at work. In the Spender combine, for example, the face itself develops out of six squares—three tall and two wide—alert, inquisitive, probing to the left, and to the right, tired, weary, resigned. Spender, Hockney seems to suggest, contains both aspects. About the same time, Hockney

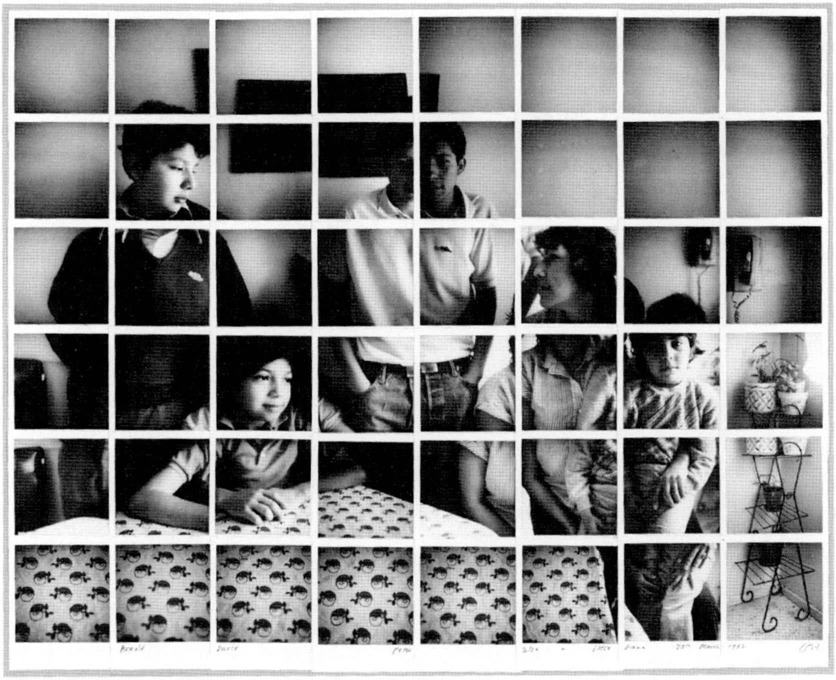

FIG 6 David Hockney, *Arnold, David, Peter, Elsa, and Little Diana, 20th March 1982.*

contrived a poignant study of his housekeeper Elsa with her four children, grouped around the kitchen table (Fig. 6). Little Diana peers out at the camera, adorably, from her mother's lap. Her mother, meanwhile, is looking over to the side at her second-oldest son, who is looking back benignly at her. Her youngest son is looking calmly out into space, a hint of a smile playing across his cheeks. Each of the faces exists serenely whole, centered in its respective square: a great, soft, uncomplicated calm recirculates lovingly among them. Only the oldest son, standing in the middle, his lean body taut and his hands shoved in his pockets, seems to exist apart: his face is divided between two squares, and his gaze seems more complex, anxious, intent, as if in growing, he is growing out of this simple household. He is as divided as his face.

In another treatment of the same theme of mother and children Hockney trains

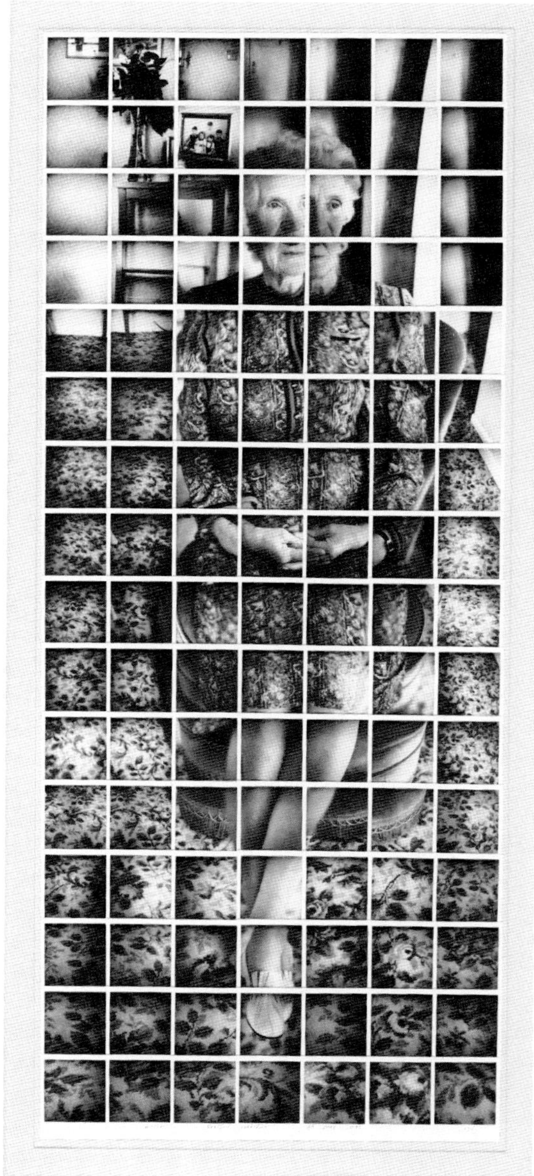

FIG 7 David Hockney, *Mother, Bradford, Yorkshire, 4th May 1982.*

his gaze on his own mother as she sits in the living room of her home in Bradford, Yorkshire (Fig. 7). (The grid consists of 112 squares, sixteen tall by seven wide.) Her paisley dress seems to blend into the floral rug: she almost disappears into the camouflage, except for her hands, folded mildly in her lap, and her thoughtful face, which emerges from a six-square rectangle (three tall by two wide)—you can almost see the thoughts moving slowly from one square to the next. Just over to the side of her head, resting on a table in the back of the room, bounded in a single square of this massive collage, is a framed photograph of her five children as youngsters (David among them). The photograph reads almost as a caption bubble: what she is thinking.

In other collages, there is an almost puckish sense of play. This is especially true of Hockney's repeated treatments of his pool, where more than anywhere else, his collage technique reveals its elastic possibilities: Silly Putty vision. Since he can frame as many details as he likes on his way to making his collages, he can alter the shape and size of the pool at will. In one collage, *Nathan Swimming,* the lima bean shape is smoothed out to a more regular ovoid, and Nathan's arms push forward in an aerodynamically sleek reach. His activity of swimming seems to take up the entire collage: it's as if the pool is only one lazy push-and-stroke from end to end. In the huge collage *Gregory Swimming,* by contrast, Hockney has ballooned the turquoise waters to Olympic proportions. (The collage consists of 120 squares in a rectangle eight high by fifteen wide, and on all sides the pool extends right up to the edge.) Gregory, naked, is everywhere—arms, legs, head, bottom—a polymorphous carousel of sensuality, a carp pool boiling over with delight. "I sort of see this one as my version of a Tiepolo ceiling," Hockney says, smiling, "you know, those baroque vaults with all the little chubby angels ascending high into the blue, blue sky."

Although within days of setting out, Hockney was already making some of the finest collages in the series, there was still a progression in his technique and style across the three months of his Polaroid passion, which was perhaps most evident in the size of the collages. Starting out fairly small (that first panel had consisted of a mere thirty squares), he quickly progressed to collages of over a hundred squares, and the complexity of vision had everything to do with the scale of the collages. (The largest of all, *The Printers at Gemini,* consisted of 187 squares—eleven tall by seventeen wide—and took more than three hours to complete. It portrays seven figures and, along the wall in the background, some of the lithographs these artisans produced, including works by Roy Lichtenstein, Jasper Johns, James Rosenquist, and Hockney himself.)

By the end of the Polaroid series, however, Hockney had so mastered his technique that he could radically reduce the scale of his collages while sustaining the complexity of images he'd attained in the largest works. Thus the masterpiece of the entire series is arguably one of the last collages, a composite of Noya and Bill Brandt consisting of forty-nine squares, seven by seven (Plate 5). In early May, encountering the distinguished British photographer in a London restaurant, Hockney invited him and his wife to pay a call at his Pembroke studio. A few days later, when the couple took up the invitation, Hockney attempted a portrait. The collage, as usual, changed as it went along: as Hockney completed each new shot, he'd place the square on the floor before the seated couple, slowly building up his collage. The two sitters became increasingly absorbed in the process and the portrait turned into a celebration of their intent concentration. Brandt's soft, intelligent face appears in profile across two squares, leaning further and further forward. His hands seem to start by his shoulder, resting on the high armrest, then slide slowly down the armrest into an almost prayerful clasp just above his knee and then on down his leg to a balancing clutch above the ankle. (Seven hands in all appear, reading as one gesture.) Brandt's entire posture seems cusped, nestled in the larger arc of his wife's seated figure. (She, closer to us, likewise gazes down at the developing collage.) "As I was finishing this piece," Hockney recalled while we examined a reproduction of the collage, "Brandt asked me, 'Couldn't you be in the picture, too?' So I turned the camera back on myself, snapped several shots, replaced the collage at their feet with these shots of my face, and took some more pictures of this new array on the floor. Thus, although they now seem to be looking at a collage of me, what they were actually looking at when I photographed them was the picture of themselves, coming into being."

As Hockney spoke, I was reminded of a passage from his essay in the National Gallery booklet in which he referred to his own painting of Henry Geldzahler looking at the screen with the reproductions of masterworks by Piero, Vermeer, Van Gogh, and Degas. That painting, Hockney had written, "was about the pleasure

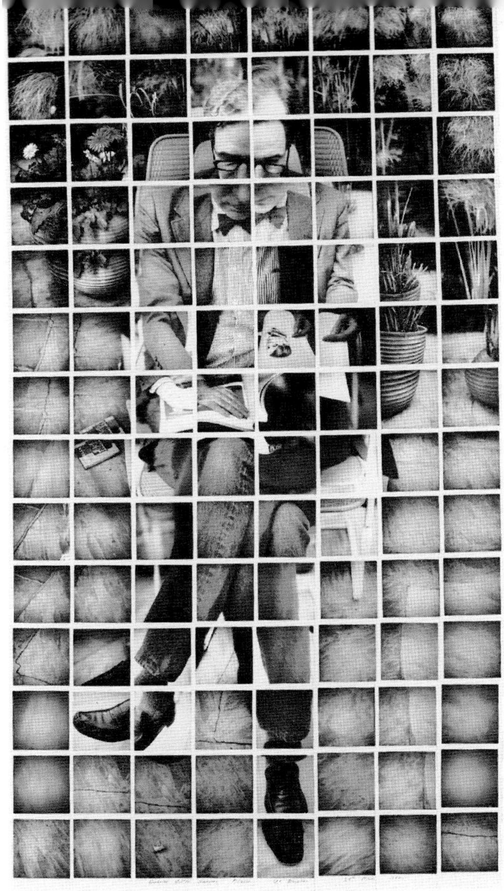

FIG 8 David Hockney, *Nicholas Wilder Studying Picasso, Los Angeles, 24th March 1982.*

of looking. I painted a picture of Henry, who loves pictures, looking at them . . . [so] that you could identify with him and his pleasure, because you were doing exactly the same thing, looking at it." I mentioned the line to Hockney and he concurred. "Yes," he said, "I think some of the most effective collages in both the Polaroids and my more recent series involve the theme of looking—of looking at people looking. There's a kind of doubling, an intensification of the experience. Take this one for instance." He pulled out the reproduction of a collage of the art dealer Nick Wilder, seated by the pool outside, poring over a volume of Picasso drawings and paintings. "See how Nick has put his hand over the upper half of the picture he is looking at, as we often do when we are looking at paintings, trying to fathom the composition and structure and so forth [Fig. 8]. Well, the Polaroid squares themselves make you look at this picture of Nick in much the same way. The grid guides your eye, summoning up countless varied details and relationships in an almost mathematical profusion. Each middle square is surrounded by eight others, corners are surrounded by three, side squares by five, and so on. Your eye fixes on such groups, then moves beyond them to others. You end up looking at the collage in much the way he is looking at the Picasso reproduction.

"For that matter," Hockney continued after a pause, "looking itself has been the central subject of all of these collages. Ordinary photography, it seems to me, is obsessed with subject matter, whereas these photographs are not principally about their subjects. Or rather, they aren't so much about things as they are about *the way things catch your eye.* I don't believe I ever thought as much about vision, about how we see, as I have during the last several months." And Hockney's collages are in turn a school for vision. Ordinary photographs present a whole, from which details can be elicited. Hockney seems to suggest that this is the opposite of how we actually see the world. For him, vision consists of a continuous accumulation of details perceived across time and synthesized into a large, continuously metamorphosing whole. "Working on these collages," Hockney explains, "I realized how much thinking goes into seeing—into ordering and reordering the endless sequence of details which our eyes deliver to our mind. Each of these squares assumes a different perspective, a different focal point around which the surroundings recede to background. The general perspective is built up from hundreds of micro-perspectives. Which is to say, memory plays a crucial role in perception. At any given moment, my eyes catch this or that detail—they really can't keep any wide field in focus all at once—and it's only my memory of the immediately previous details which allows me to form a continuous image of the world. Otherwise, for instance, turning my head the world would black out at the sides—but it doesn't! Which is really quite remarkable when you think about it. And which, again, is a part of the visual experience that gets falsified in ordinary photography."[7]

One of the most striking things about these Polaroid grids is the way they meld and confound the distinction between the rational and the sensual. The grid bestows an evenness, an equivalence over the entire visual field, and yet within this field a thousand details are endlessly divulging themselves. There is a saturation, almost an oversaturation of pleasure, tempered to a serenity by the democratic matrix of the grid.[8]

Looking, for Hockney, is interest-ing: it is the continual projection of interest. "These collages only work," Hockney explains, "because there is something interesting in every single square, something to catch your eye. Helmut Newton, the photographer, was by here the other day, and I said, 'Everywhere I look is interesting.' 'Not me,' he replied, 'I bore easily.' Imagine! I've always loved that phrase of Constable's where he says, 'I never saw an ugly thing,' and doing these collages I think I've come to better understand what he means: It's the very process of looking at something that makes it beautiful."

Hockney paused, suddenly very tired. "Of course," he said, "thinking intensively about looking forced me to think more carefully about cubism, because looking—perception—was the great theme of cubism. But let's talk about that tomorrow. I'm afraid I'm getting sleepy. My friends have been amused at my pace these past several months—they say I've become like a child, playing for hours on end and then just suddenly conking out. The truth is, I'm not sleeping very well: I keep waking myself up with ideas!"

Driving back up toward Hockney's the next morning, weaving in and out of the gullies along Mulholland ridge, I noticed the way each new outbound furl of the road would present me with a new view of the same valley—or, rather, the same view only slightly altered, moved over just a bit. I realized that this drive, which Hockney had been taking almost every morning for several years now, must itself have been preparing in him a special "view" of vision.

The door at Hockney's house was ajar and I entered quietly. Hockney was once again at his worktable, this time leaning down with his face very close to the splay of photoprints in the new combine he was arranging. He nudged one picture over slightly and then slowly stood upright, continuing to look down at the collage, until finally, rubbing his face and breaking the spell, he turned. "Ah," he said, "hallo," with that upward lilt in his voice which I was beginning to associate with the onrush of his enthusiasm. "Have you ever noticed," he continued, as if there hadn't been the slightest interval since the close of our conversation the night before, "how when you look at things close up, you sometimes shut one eye—that is, you make yourself like a camera. Otherwise, things start to swim; it becomes difficult

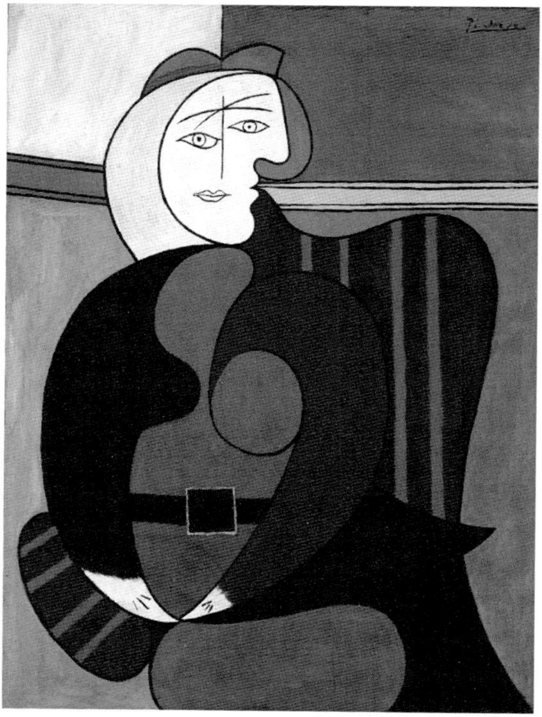

FIG 9 Pablo Picasso, *The Red Armchair,* 1931.

to hold them in visual space. The cubists, you know, didn't shut their eyes. People complained about Picasso, for instance, how he distorted the human face. I don't think there are any distortions at all. For instance, those marvelous portraits of his lover Marie-Thérèse Walter which he made during the thirties [Fig. 9]; he must have spent hours with her in bed, very close, looking at her face. A face looked at like that *does* look different from one seen at five or six feet. Strange things begin to happen to the eyes, the cheeks, the nose—wonderful inversions and repetitions. Certain 'distortions' appear, but they can't be distortions because they're reality. Those paintings are about that kind of intimate seeing."

Among Hockney's Polaroid collages there's an especially luscious portrait of his friend and frequent model Celia, which seems intended as an homage to these Picasso portraits of Marie-Thérèse (Plate 4). She is wearing a white lacy blouse, one arm thrown languorously behind her head, her cheek resting calmly against the other hand. Her eyes seem to float—there are three of them, two mouths, two noses, and a frond of curls on her forehead that drifts away into the dark surround—a smoky wisp, a whisper of desire.

"Analytic cubism in particular," Hockney continued, referring to the work Picasso and Braque undertook between 1909 and 1912 (paintings characterized by especially dense visual composition, usually in monochrome grays or browns), "was about perception—about the difficulty of perception. I've recently been reading a lot of books about cubism, and I keep coming upon discussions of intersecting planes and so forth, as if cubism were about the structure of the object. But really, it's rather about the structure of *seeing* the object. If there are three noses, this is not because the face has three noses, or the nose has three aspects, but rather because it has been seen three times, and that is what seeing is like. When I showed some of my Polaroid collages in England last year, one critic came up to me and told me that I was completely misinterpreting cubism; I replied, 'Well, that may be, but if so, it's only the four hundred and seventy-eighth misinterpretation this year. Only, I don't think I am misinterpreting cubism, and I'm absolutely certain that it's cubism today that remains to be dealt with."[9]

Hockney's love of Picasso is of long standing, although only recently has it taken on this sort of urgency. Hockney visited the Museum of Modern Art's 1980 Picasso extravaganza eight times and subsequently bought the Zervos catalogues, the thirty-two-volume catalogue raisonné of Picasso's lifework. He even acquired a small Picasso painting (Fig. 10). "I'd originally seen it in Paris," Hockney recalled that morning, "a lovely rendition of his familiar theme of the artist and his model, seemingly simple but at the same time extraordinarily supple and inventive. A few months later, a dealer offered to trade me that painting for one of my own. I mean, it's an indication of the present foolishness of the art world that I can be offered a Picasso in exchange for just one of mine. Well, I'm not a collector by nature—postcards will usually do for me (I tack them on the wall)"—Hockney gestured toward the walls about him, which were festooned with dozens of postcards (Piero della Francesca's *Baptism of Christ,* Caravaggio's *Last Supper,* Toulouse-Lautrec's *Couple in Bed,* a Van Gogh self-portrait, Vermeer's *Lute Player,* a Cézanne landscape, a Gauguin beach scene)—"but I was thrilled by the offer and I accepted. I keep the painting

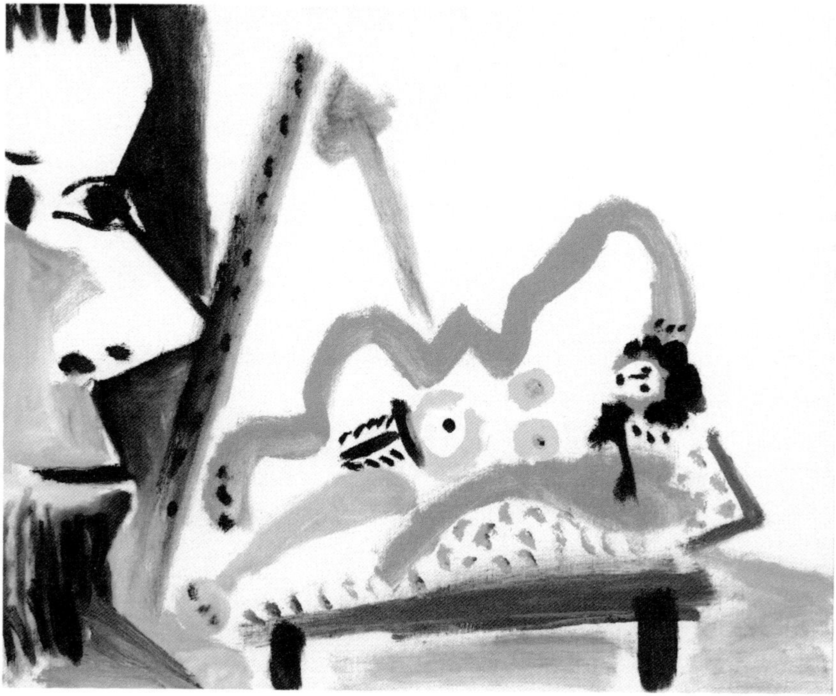

FIG 10 Pablo Picasso, *Artist and Model Reclining Nude and Man in Profile,* March 29, 1965.

in my bedroom. I study it. I'm continually discovering new things in it. It must have been made very quickly. I mean, it can't have more than—well, I've counted: it has fifty-two strokes."

On several occasions recently in Los Angeles, Hockney has delivered a lecture he calls "Major Paintings of the Sixties." The audiences are invariably surprised when he starts out by proclaiming that the most important art of the sixties did not occur in New York or California or London, nor was it a part of any abstract expressionist, minimalist, or pop movement; rather, it came into existence over a period of ten days in March 1965 in the south of France in an eruption of creativity during which Pablo Picasso created thirty-two variations on the theme of the artist and his model. (One of these is indeed the piece Hockney owns—he discovered the others while researching his own in the Zervos catalogues.) The claim is doubly heretical: other artists are usually considered to have been doing much more interesting work during the sixties, and Picasso himself is thought to have done much more important work earlier in his career. "The sophisticated art world tends to act as if Picasso died about 1955, whereas he lived for almost twenty years after that," Hockney argues. "Common sense tells you that an artist of that caliber—the only people you can compare him to are Rembrandt, Titian, Goya, Velázquez—does not spend the last twenty years of his life repeating himself. It's harder to see what he's doing, perhaps. But he remains to the end far and away the greatest draughtsman of the twentieth century, the artist with the most sensitive and inquiring eye, and the most supple and inventive hand. Those thirty-two paintings are simply richer and more engrossing than anything else that was being done at the time—still, at that age, at eighty-four, Picasso was finding new ways to see, new ways to express his visions!"[10]

Hockney's Polaroid collages came into being very much under the thrall of Picasso.[11] The portrait of Celia is but one example. Another portrait, of the curator Geldzahler, seated on a rickety stool, legs outspread, cleaning his glasses, echoes Picasso's 1910 portrait of the dealer Ambroise Vollard. There are allusions to *Les Demoiselles d'Avignon* in other collages, and there are even two still lifes—witty riffs on the old cubist themes of guitar, tobacco can (Half and Half, half in one square and half in the other), wine bottle, and daily journal (in this case, the *Los Angeles Times*). (When the cubists insisted they were putting time into painting, they'd sometimes show it to you right there, in bold typeface: TEMPS.)

By mid-May 1981, however, Hockney had stopped producing his Polaroid collages. This was partly, perhaps, because the passion had simply spent itself. (He had created over 140 collages in less than three months!) It was partly, no doubt, because he was now needing to redirect his energies from making collages to preparing them for exhibition—the three shows were all on the verge of opening late that spring. But an additional factor was also beginning to make itself felt: Hockney was beginning to sense an interior flaw in the Polaroid medium. Just as cubes are not the point of cubism, squares were not the point of Hockney's activity. But the square matrix-grid seemed an insurmountable requirement with these collages: one cannot cut the white border from a Polaroid picture the way you might slice off the crust from a piece of bread (with Polaroids, if you slice into the tile, it literally comes apart in your hands; the various layers of chemical pigment come unfixed). While the vision evoked in these grids seemed more true to life than ordinary photography, the white grid itself in a very real sense constricted all that burgeoning life. It wasn't just that people began focusing on the grid (seeing Hockney's as yet another in a series of modernist variations on the grid theme—Eva Hesse, Sol LeWitt, Agnes Martin, and so forth). Rather, it was that the rectangular grid remained trapped in the aesthetic of the view out a window that had been one of the principal targets of the entire cubist movement.

"It can't just be a coincidence that cubism arose within a few years of the popularization of photography," Hockney surmises. "Picasso and Braque saw the flaw in photography—all the sorts of things about time and perception which I've only recently begun to appreciate—the flaw in the camera; but in doing so, they also recognized the flaw in photography's precursor, the camera obscura. Now, the camera obscura was essentially a room—*camera* means room—it had a hole in it, and the hole was a window. You're looking out a window, that was the idea. In fact, that's why you get easel painting, which arose around the same time: the resultant canvas was meant to be a kind of window you could slot into your own wall. This idea of looking out a window dominated the European aesthetic for three hundred years. Interestingly, by the way, Oriental art never knew the camera obscura, and their art instead looks out of *doors*. The difference between a window and a door is you can walk through a door toward what you are seeing. Much Oriental art takes the form of a screen which, like a door, stands on the floor. You cannot do that with a window: a window implies a wall, something between you and what you're looking at. A lot's been written about the influence of Oriental art during the last half of the nineteenth century—Manet's appropriation of Japanese motifs, Van Gogh's use of the bold solid colors, Monet's gleanings of atmospheric perspective, and so forth—but I suspect the Oriental alternative was especially important for the cubists. Because what they were up to, in a word, was breaking that window. Cézanne was getting there: in his still lifes he observed that the closer things are to us, the harder it is for us to place them; they seem to shift. But he still looked through a window at those cardplayers grouped around that café table. Whereas, as has often been said, Picasso and Braque wanted to break that window and shove the café table right up to our waist, to make us part of the game."

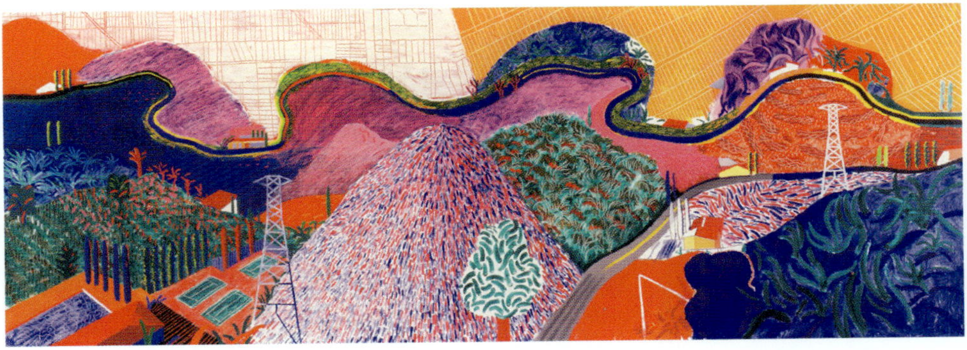

1 *Mulholland Drive: The Road to the Studio*, 1980.

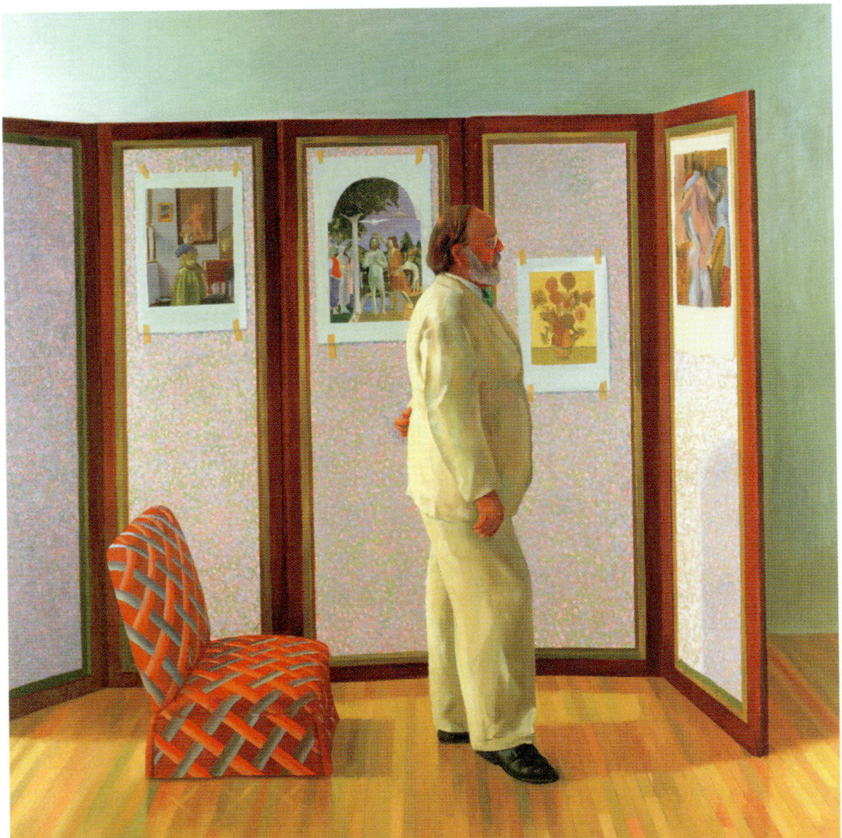

2 *Looking at Pictures on a Screen*, 1977.

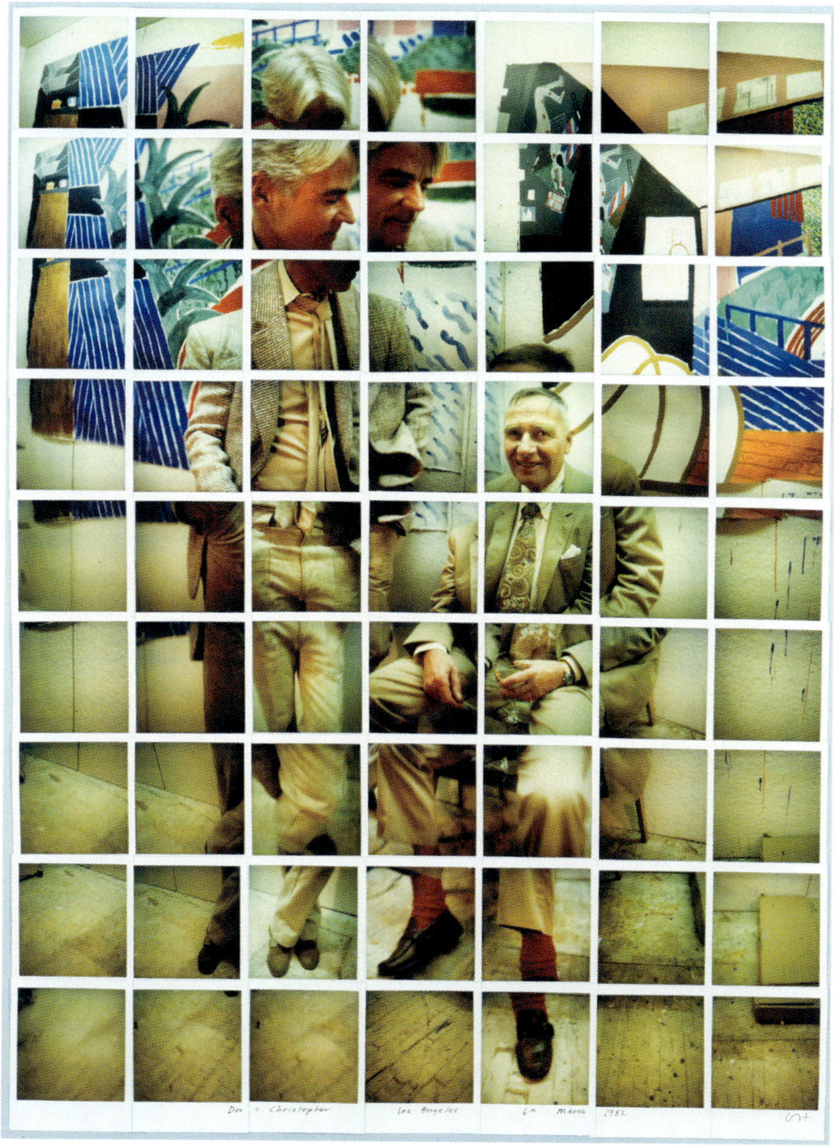

3 *Don + Christopher, Los Angeles, 6th March 1982.*

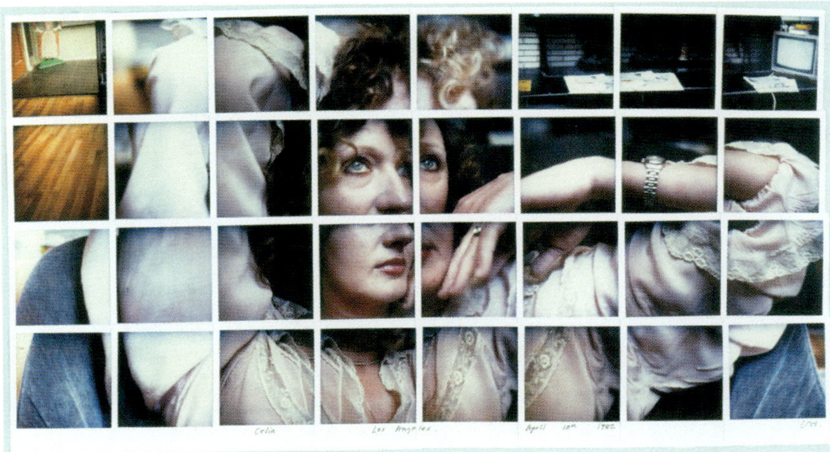

4 *Celia, Los Angeles, April 10th, 1982* (detail).

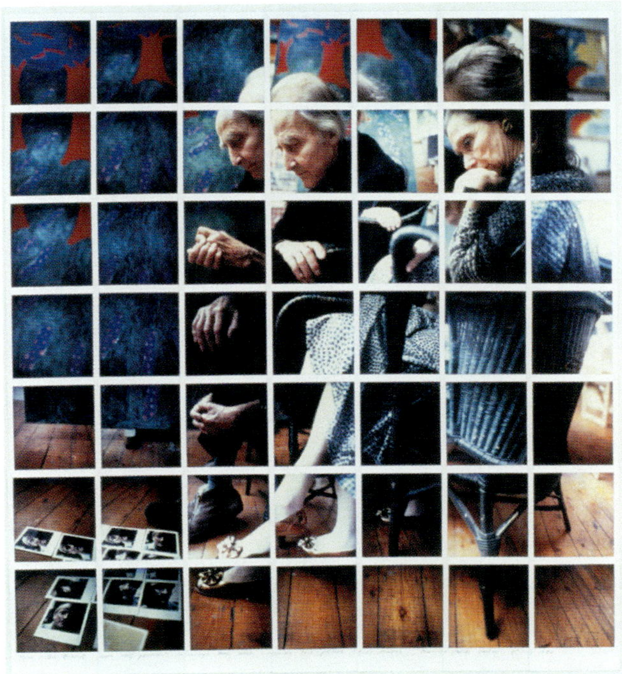

5 *Noya and Bill Brandt with Self-Portrait (although they were watching this picture being made), Pembroke Studios, London, 8th May 1982.*

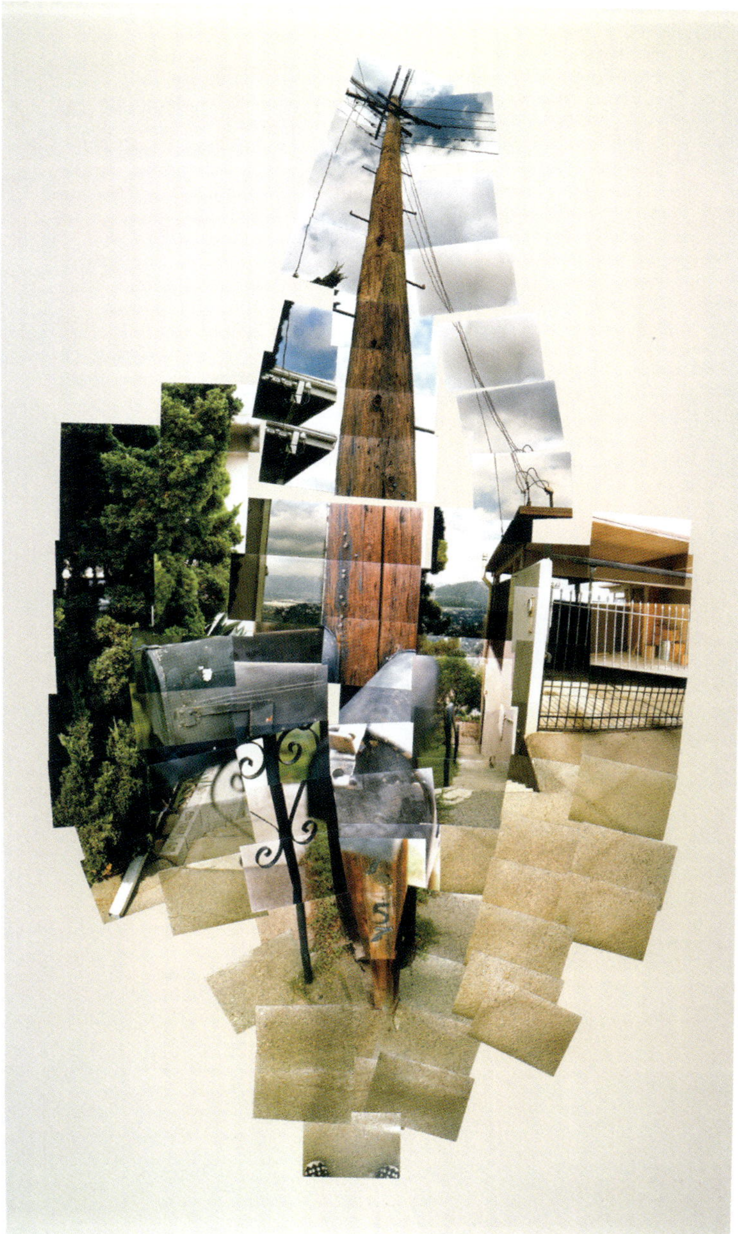

6 *Telephone Pole, Los Angeles, Sept. 1982.*

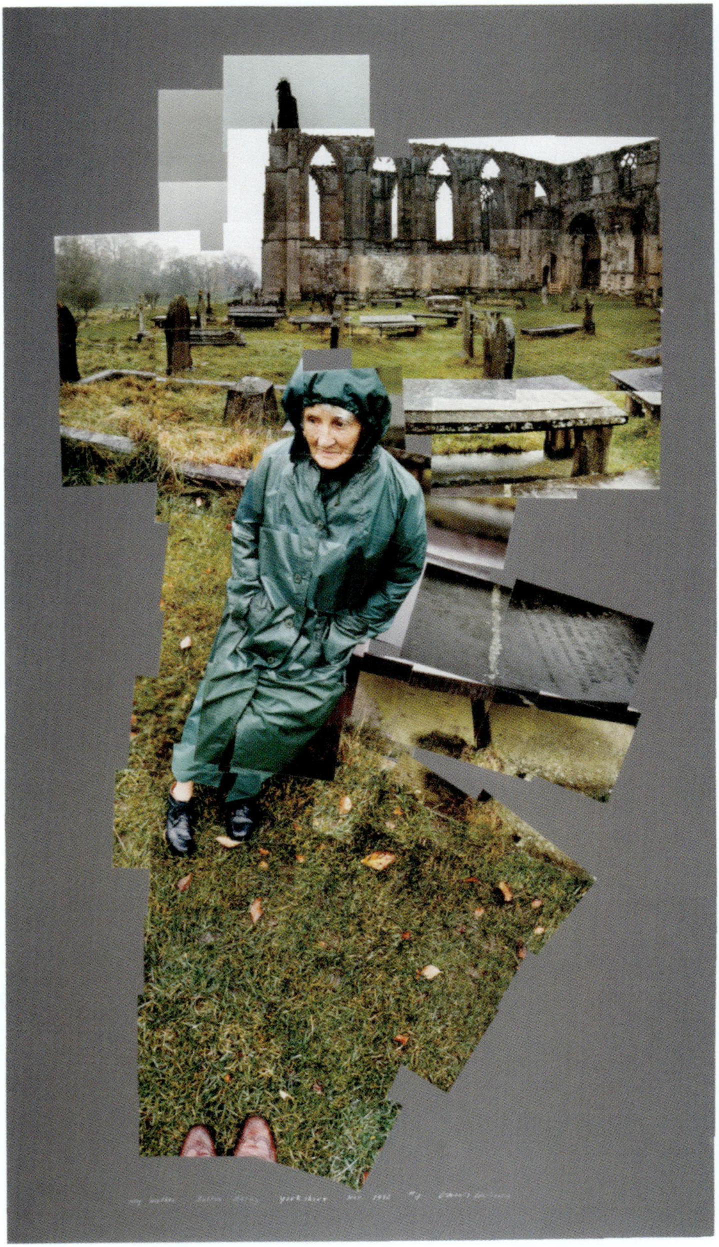

7 *My Mother, Bolton Abbey, Yorkshire, Nov. 1982.*

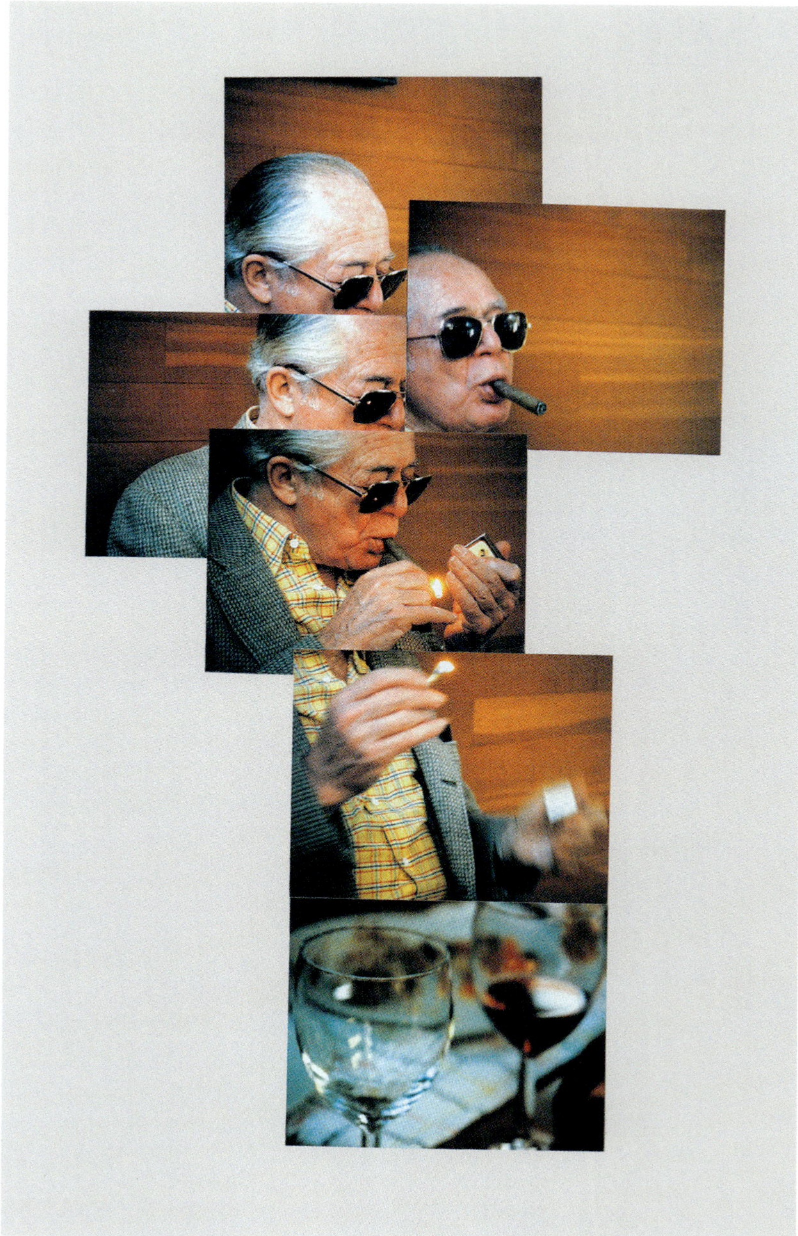

8 *Billy Wilder Lighting His Cigar, Dec. 1982.*

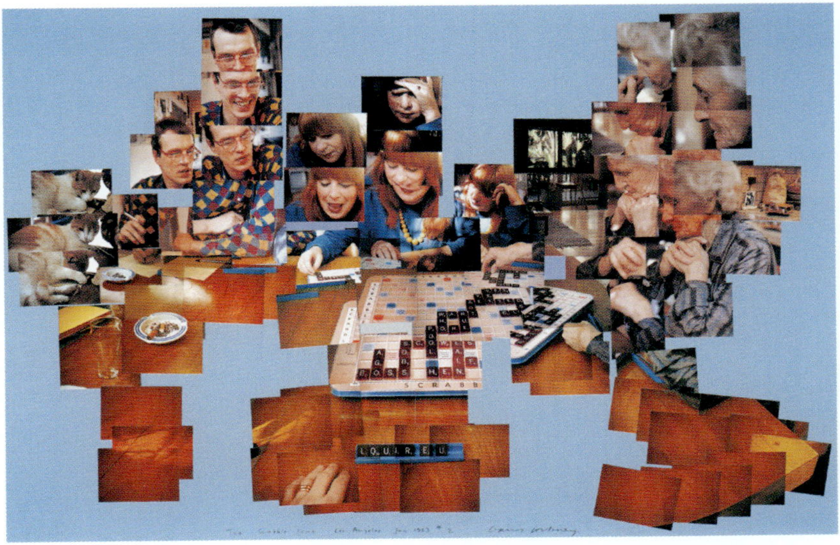

9 *The Scrabble Game, Jan. 1, 1983.*

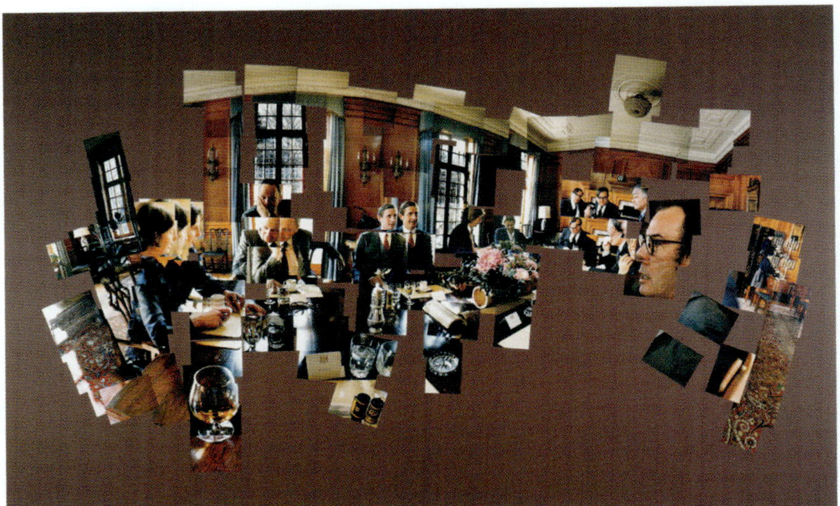

10 *Luncheon at the British Embassy, Tokyo, Feb. 16, 1983.*

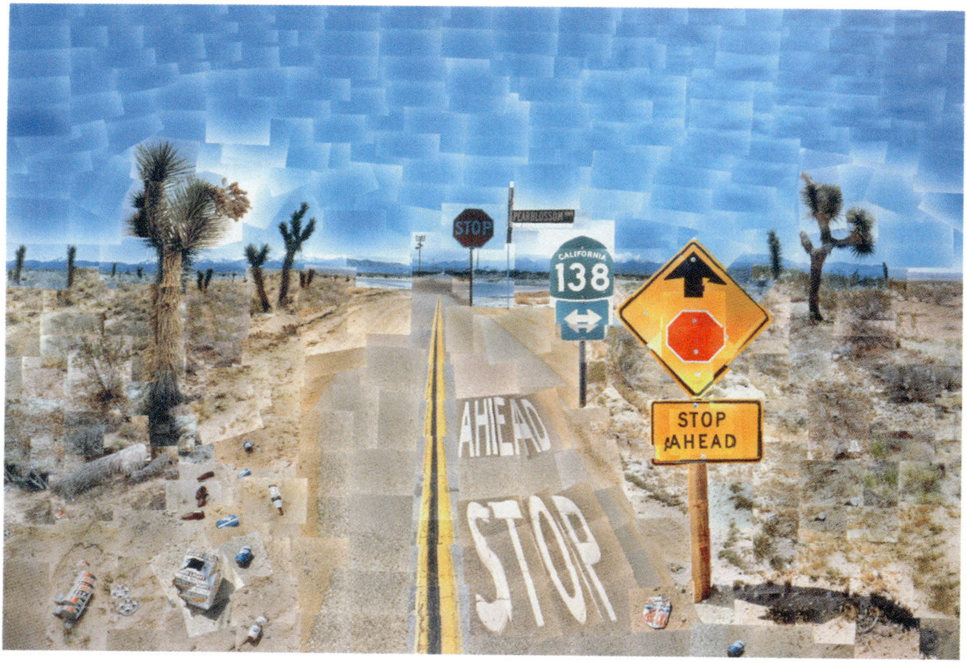

11 *Pearblossom Hwy., 11–18th April 1986 (Second Version).*

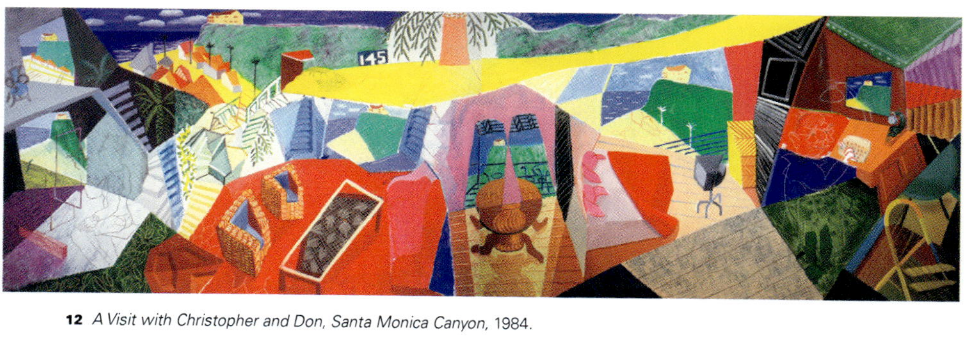

12 *A Visit with Christopher and Don, Santa Monica Canyon,* 1984.

For all the Polaroids had taught Hockney about time and vision, they weren't going to be able to help him break that window: on the contrary, that quaint white grid made them look even more windowlike than most conventional paintings.

At first, it seemed Hockney had sworn off photography altogether—or, at any rate, had reverted to a decidedly off-again mode. In mid-May he drove north to help supervise the installation of his sets for the San Francisco Opera Association's production of *The Rake's Progress,* by Stravinsky. On the way, he veered briefly into Yosemite Valley, where, using a 35 mm camera, he took one sequence of nine shots of Yosemite Falls—not nine separate shots of the entire waterfall but rather a vertical sequence of nine segmented sections, starting with the sky, trilling down the falls, into the far valley, across a river, up from the near shore, all the way to his own foot, clad in a tennis shoe (Fig. 11). Coming back to the car, he threw the camera into his pack; he wouldn't develop the film until early in the fall.

During the summer, he traveled to Paris (for the opening of the Pompidou show) and to London (to work in his Pembroke studio), as well as to Martha's Vineyard and Southampton for a vacation with Henry Geldzahler. He filled three notebooks with drawings, and he started painting again. The principal work of this period (produced at the Pembroke studio) was an eight-panel unfinished painting of four of his friends (the eight panels are divided into four long, narrow bands), clearly a work influenced by his Polaroid excursion: David Graves's face exists at once frontally and in profile, and he has four arms and three legs; Ian Falconer, on the other side, has two eyes, two noses, two mouths, and three legs. "And yet," as Hockney pointed out that morning, pushing aside the clutter to reveal the abandoned painting, which he'd brought back with him to Los Angeles, "they don't read as monsters. They're clearly and simply individuals in the midst of living. I've made something of a leap here: never again will anyone I'm painting have to 'sit' for me, in the traditional sense—frozen still for hours. I can deal now with their liveliness." Late in the summer, Hockney and his friend Gregory Evans traveled by car through the Southwest, to Zion, Bryce, and the Grand Canyon National Parks. He was again taking pictures. They weren't Polaroids (which are notoriously inadequate for capturing long-distance vistas), although as in the Polaroid collages, he was compiling dozens

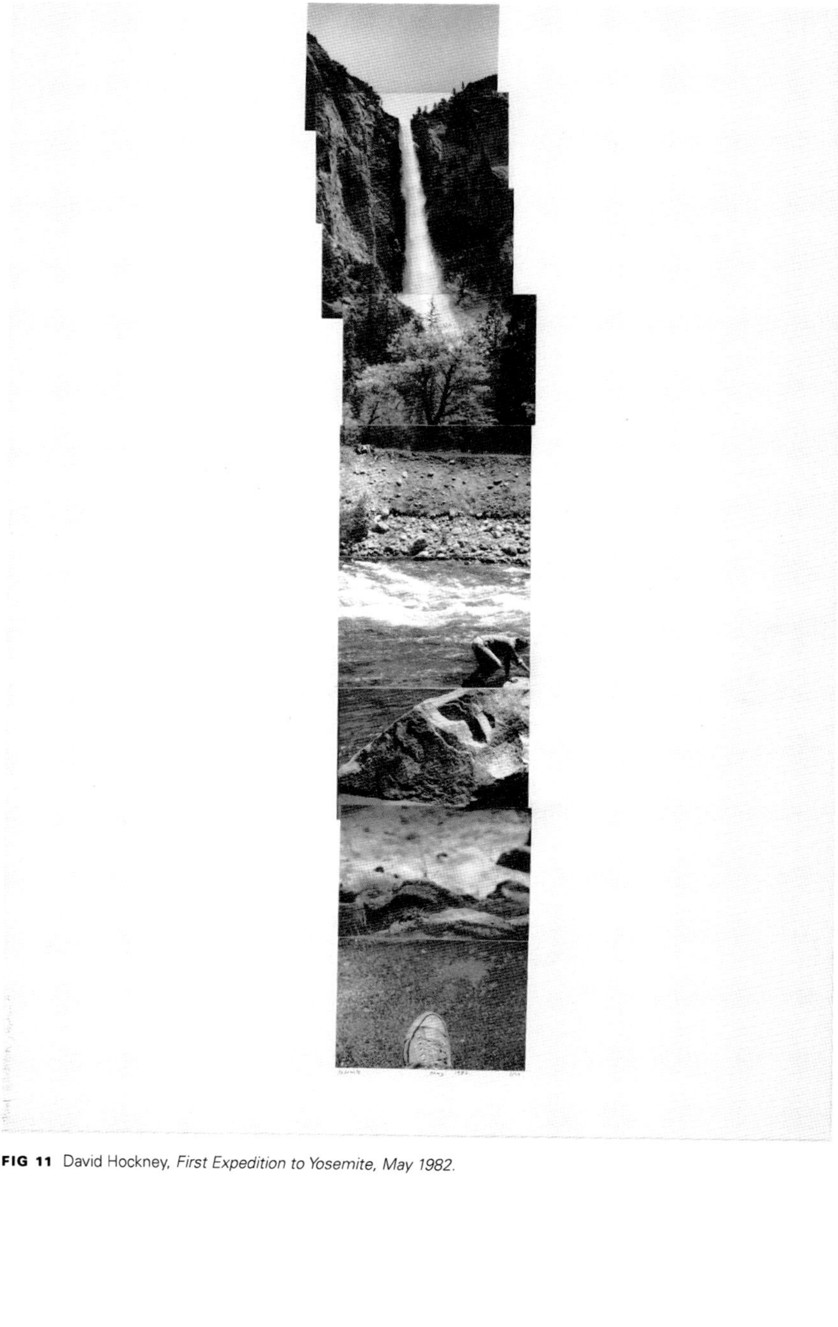

FIG 11 David Hockney, *First Expedition to Yosemite, May 1982.*

of details rather than single wide-angle swaths. He wasn't sure what, if anything, he was up to, and he wouldn't have an inkling until early in the fall, when, returning to Los Angeles, he had the film developed. Once he'd gotten the prints back, however, he quickly assembled a few collages and realized, with a great new wave of excitement, that he was on the verge of another breakthrough.

These new pieces were different from the Polaroids in many ways. With those Hockney would establish a general perspective but had to move all over the room to compile the details. With the new collages he could stay in one spot, using the camera's lens to zoom in for details at various distances. (Hockney now alternated between a Nikon 35 mm camera, with its fairly elaborate host of optional lenses, and a much simpler Pentax 110 single-lens reflex camera, which he preferred. Though not much larger than a cigarette pack, it featured a remarkable optical sophistication, and he could slip it into his pocket and carry it around all the time, pulling it out whenever the fancy took him.) The Polaroids took hours to make, but when he'd finished shooting, he'd also finished the collage. With the new pictures, the actual shooting could be completed in a few minutes (as fast as he could reload the camera), but the assembly of the collage occurred only when he got the prints back, days or weeks later, and began building the piece on his worktable in the living room–studio. This second stage of the process could take hours. With the Polaroids, he had had to deal with those white borders, whereas these new photos were printed without borders, hence no white window grid.

"I take dozens of pictures at any given site," Hockney explains, "and then I just take the exposed rolls down to one of the local places here to have them developed—usually I go to Benny's Speed Cleaning and One-Hour Processing. It took me a long time to convince them that I truly wanted them to 'print regardless,' and I still get these wonderful standardized notices back with my batches of prints, patiently explaining what I am doing wrong, how I should try to center the camera on the subject, focus on the foreground, and so forth. Once I've got the prints, I start building the collages, keeping to one strict rule: I never crop the prints. Somehow this seems important to the integrity of the enterprise: the evenness of time seems to be tied up with a regularity in the print size, and things would get all messed up whenever I trimmed the prints. This, in turn, forces me to be aware of how I'm framing the shots as I take them; in effect I end up 'drawing' the collages twice."

Given the dissimilarity of the two processes, it is striking how similar the earliest of these new collages were to their Polaroid antecedents. (For the sake of convenience, I will refer to all the collages in this later series as "photocollages," as opposed to "the Polaroid collages" of the earlier phase.) They seemed to come as close as one could imagine to the original rectangular grid of the Polaroids: only the white borders were missing. There was little overlap of prints. (Later it would be rare not to find overlaps.) It seemed as if Hockney, given a vista—say, the Grand Canyon, looking north—had simply framed a detail, taken a shot, moved the viewfinder over from the previous detail, refocused, and taken a new one, again and again and then down, zigzagging in rows, back and forth. The resultant collage formed a perfect rectangle and, still, a sort of window. "It's incredible how deeply imprinted we are with these damn rectangles," Hockney commented as we looked at one of these early Grand Canyon collages on its cardboard panel. "Everything in our culture seems to reinforce the instinct to see rectangularly—books, streets, buildings, rooms, windows. Sam Francis once told me how odd the American Indian initially found the white settlers: 'these people who insist on living in rectangular-shaped buildings.' The Indians, you see, lived in a circular world.

"But these early collages were really more like studies: you did them, just as you do a drawing sometimes, to teach yourself something; it doesn't matter what they look like when you're finished, that's not why they were made. In this case, in retrospect, I realize I was training my visual memory, and this took a lot of time." Since these prints, unlike the Polaroids, weren't developing right before his eyes, Hockney had to be aware of which areas he'd already covered and which ones he hadn't. Even in a rectangular format this exercise required intense concentration. Presently when he'd begin tilting the camera and anticipating intricate overlaps, he would have to hone these skills considerably further.

As soon as he put together the first of these new collages, in September, Hockney realized he was on to something, and within a few days he was on the road again, back to Utah and the Grand Canyon, this time by himself. "I've always loved the wide-open spaces of the American West," Hockney explains. "But I was never able to capture them in photography, to convey the sense of what it's actually like to be there, facing that expanse—that incredible sense of spaciousness, which is somehow as elusive to ordinary photography as time is. I thought that, among other things, this new kind of photography might be able to capture that sense of vast extent."

Hockney took thousands of pictures during the next three or four days, enough, in fact, to compose twenty-five collages (although it would take over a month to assemble them once he got home). A few of them were intimate: one collage in particular wittily celebrated the possibilities of the new medium by affording an otherwise impossible continuous rendition of the view from the driver's seat in Hockney's car. But most of the collages from this trip concerned wider vistas, portrayed with astonishing clarity. Ordinarily, the photographer of such a vista has to choose one point of focus, with the result that things closer or farther or to the sides are progressively more out of focus—this, according to Hockney, is another way in which photography falsifies the experience of looking. "Everything we look at is in focus as we look at it," he explains. "Now, the actual size of the zone the eye can hold in focus at any given moment is relatively small in relation to the wider visual field, but the eye is always moving through that field and the focal point of view, though moving, is always clear." The experience of this kind of looking is preserved in the collages, where each frame of distant butte or nearby outcropping is in focus and comprises just about as much of the field as the eye itself could hold in focus at any one moment in the real world.

The pictorial rigor and clarity of these panels recalls the treatment of space in paintings by Van Eyck, say, or Piero della Francesca, two of Hockney's favorites (Figs. 12 and 13). These artists, too, went to great lengths to record each "object" at its moment of clearest focus—every object on the canvas, "near" or "far," can bear the weight of focused attention, just like the real world, and precisely unlike the world as portrayed in conventional photography. "I've always loved the depiction of space in early Renaissance pictures," Hockney explains. "It's so *clear.* I think that clarity is something that has to exist in all good pictures. The definition of a bad picture for me is that it's woolly—those paintings aren't ever, no matter what's portrayed. If it's a mist, it's a clear mist and not a woolly mist. There has to be this clarity, which is the clarity of the artist who did it, the clarity of his vision, his sense of being."

The major breakthrough in these new photocollages had less to do with the early Renaissance, however, than with high cubism. For the first time, on this second

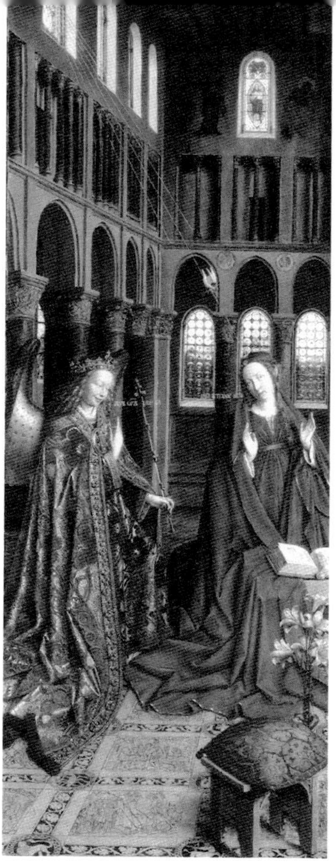

FIG 12 Jan van Eyck, *The Annunciation*, ca. 1434/1436.

FIG 13 Piero della Francesca, *The Baptism of Christ*, ca. 1450.

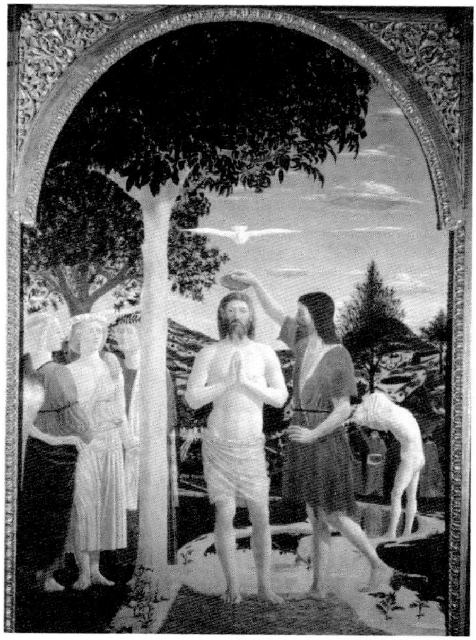

trip to the Southwest, Hockney was beginning to break the window. Looking at that set of collages from his first trip, Hockney had quickly realized what was wrong: there was an arbitrariness to the edge, particularly the bottom edge. To a great extent, conventional photography is about edges, about how to frame the object of vision. Indeed, that is the ordinary photographer's main contribution to the moment of seeing, his sense of composition, how he chooses to frame the world within four perpendicular edges. "But I wasn't interested in that," Hockney insists. "Already with the Polaroids, that sort of composition wasn't an issue: I could have added a strip of squares to the left or the right, or removed one, without really affecting the experience of seeing those collages. The cubists had a lot of problems with their edges—sometimes they tried to solve these by creating circular paintings—and it's easy to see why: there are no edges to vision, and certainly no rectangular edges." For Hockney, to stop at some arbitrary middle distance was completely alien to the kind of vision he was now attempting. Looking at those first collages of the Grand Canyon, he immediately realized that he had to bring the picture right up to the viewer, that he had to bring the distance right up to his own feet and include the ground right in front of him, as well as the canyon beyond.

"Cubism, I realized during those few days," Hockney continued, "is about our own bodily presence in the world. It's about the world, yes, but ultimately about where we are in it, *how* we are in it. It's about the kind of perception a human being can have in the midst of living." A few months after this conversation, *Vanity Fair* highlighted some of these collages in its May 1983 issue, suggesting that they somehow blended "NASA spaceship photography with cubism." And there was a certain striking similarity: just as the telescopic photographs of distant nebulae that were popularly reproduced around the time Jackson Pollock produced his lush optical fields might be seen as having influenced them, so Hockney's work can be seen as having come into existence under the sign of NASA—the sequential shutter-streams of overlapping photographs recording lunar and Martian landscapes, for example, or Saturnine rings. But it's precisely the connection with cubism that upends this false analogy: Hockney's collages, like cubism, are a record of *human* looking. It is exactly the point that an automatic machine could not possibly have generated them.

From this point on, Hockney usually included photos of his own feet in these collages. In effect, they stood in for him; they planted him as they plant any subsequent viewer. Indeed, standing there, facing forward into the world before them, the world of vision, these feet seem transposed figures for the eyes themselves. Several of the Grand Canyon collages are huge and spectacular, long banners of looking made up of hundreds of prints. The horizon line curves, but not as in the artificial distortion caused by wide-angle lenses; rather, the gentle swell seems to suggest the curvature of the earth; even more to the point, it replicates the actual movement involved in looking at a long horizon line, how, as Hockney points out, "your head starts out low, looking far to the side, then rises slowly on the neck joint as it moves toward that part of the horizon directly before you, falling again as it moves on to the other side." Sometimes in these collages there is an almost vertiginous sense of depth. In one, for example, the horizon line stretches across the very top row of photos; as the viewer's eyes descend the collage, they descend into the canyon (the

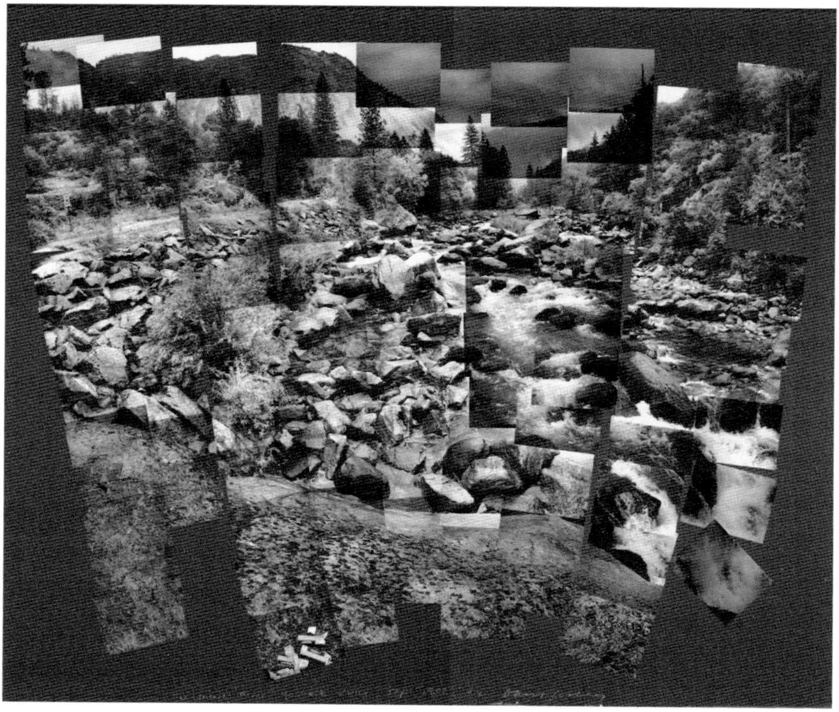

FIG 14 David Hockney, *Merced River, Yosemite Valley, California, Sept. 1982.*

falling flanks of several buttes guide one's viewing): only, as one's eyes descend still further, to the bottom of the collage, they quickly ascend back up the nearer rim to the foreground, which is as high as the horizon at the top. At the heart of this collage, perception itself seems to bend, much as it seems to when one is actually standing at the canyon ledge.

But Hockney took one of the most noteworthy of the collages from this period along the Merced River in Yosemite Valley, which he visited on his return drive, somehow managing in them to convey how the sound of a rushing stream *looks* (Fig. 14). The rectangular grid of the earliest photocollages seems to shake apart before our very eyes amid the surging onrush of the cold tumbling mountain water. "I'm not sure in which of these collages I actually moved beyond the gridlike place-

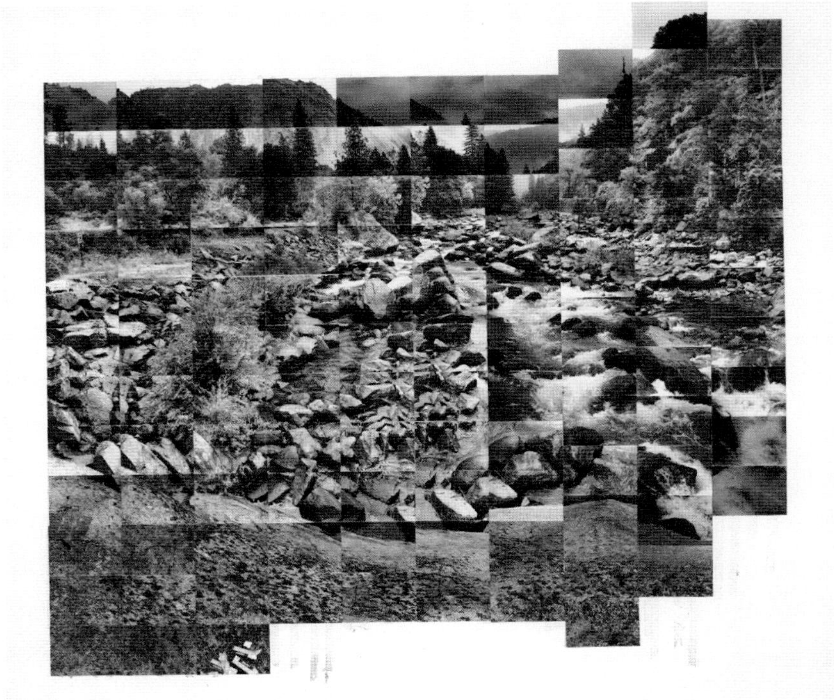

FIG 15 David Hockney, *Merced River, Yosemite Valley, Sept. 1982.*

ment of the prints," Hockney explained as we looked at this panel that afternoon in his studio. "I was doing several of them at once. But with this one, after I'd assembled the collage in this new jumbled sort of format, I went back and took another set of the same prints and reassembled them in the stricter perpendicular grid of the earlier photocollages. You can see the difference." He pulled out a panel with the second version (Fig. 15) and set the two side by side. The one in the grid format flattens space to equivalence and stillness; the jumbled version, with its angles and overlaps, allows for a greater sense of depth (the stream receding into the distance) and movement (the stream cascading into the foreground), giving the viewing experience a topography of highs and lows, of concentration and release.

The photos which were to compose perhaps the finest of all of these early photocollages were taken not on the road but rather just down the road. One afternoon back home in the midst of a long siege of composition and collation, Hockney took a break and went out for a walk, the little Pentax, as usual, in his pocket. He came upon a telephone pole. This was along a stretch of canyon road where the houses are cantilevered over a precipitously falling slope (driveways seem to leap off the roadway into levitating garages). There were houses on either side with, between them in the distance, a beautiful view of the valley and, between them in the foreground at street level, this looming wooden telephone pole. Just in front of the telephone pole were two metal mailboxes on posts. Charmed, Hockney began snapping. The collage he put together a few days later (Plate 6) constituted his most radical break yet with the window-rectangle aesthetic. One sequence of prints scales the telephone pole to the top; another follows the cement steps as they wend down the sides of the houses, so that your eye has no sooner descended the towering pole than it's sliding right down the mountain face. Hockney's compositional delight is almost palpable: "There," he seems to be taunting conventional photographers, "top that!" The rendering of the mailbox closest to the viewer is extraordinary: through the subtlest of juxtapositions and edge-notchings, Hockney lets us sense the space immediately *behind* the mailbox, how it gives out onto the view of the valley—while at the front of the mailbox, the latch seems to jut right out into our hand: we can barely keep ourselves from reaching out with our index finger and popping the door open. The entire collage, meanwhile, constitutes a playful homage to the cubist guitar, the pole reading as the guitar's long neck, the cables as its taut strings, the lineman's rungs as its measured frets, the wrought-iron curlicues on the mailbox post as the design work on the instrument's front panel, and the arched mailbox door in the middle of the collage as its sounding hole.

Hockney spent much of the fall of 1982 and the winter of 1983 traveling. Early October found him still in California, but by November he'd journeyed to England, where he visited with his mother in his childhood hometown of Bradford, in Yorkshire. On the way back, later in the month, he stopped in New York City to assist John Dexter and the Metropolitan Opera in their restaging of *Parade.* By mid-December he'd returned to California, where his mother joined him for Christmas. In January, he traveled to Minneapolis, where he worked with Martin Friedman of the Walker Art Center on an upcoming exhibition of his stage designs, and then he was off again to London. Early in February he was back in Los Angeles, but by the end of the month he'd left for Japan to participate as a panelist at a paper conference. Everywhere he went he snapped pictures, and whenever he was back in Los Angeles he'd assemble the harvest into collages in his living room. It was an extraordinarily productive period: even with all the interrupting travel, between September 1982 and March 1983 Hockney managed to complete almost two hundred photocollages.

As with the Polaroid series, landscapes soon gave way to his truer passion: people. Many of these middle-period photocollages (those taken between mid-October and Christmas) are noteworthy. A series of figure studies in the pool, taken in early October, revel in the possibilities of the new medium: for starters, Hockney this time is *in* the pool, along with his subjects. The collages of people floating languidly are built up from shots taken both above and below the waterline—it takes the viewer a moment to realize how improbable a feat this would be for most ordinary cameras or, for that matter, the unassisted eye. By focusing in a little tighter for the underwater shots, Hockney renders the body below the waterline somewhat larger, more buoyant, than the head above: what is depicted here is the *feeling* of floating.

Another theme carried over from the Polaroid series is that of looking at people looking. When David Graves sits looking out a window onto a wet London street, every shot, indoors and out, is in focus, except for those describing Graves's head, which blur in sympathy with the outwardness of his looking—his even concentration seems to encompass everything except his own activity of concentrating. We say, "He is lost to himself."

Hockney's mother is the subject of several of these collages as well. In one, taken during his November trip to England, Hockney portrays her in a blue-green raincoat on a slate gray afternoon in the cemetery outside Bolton Abbey, in Yorkshire (Plate 7). The grass in the foreground is wet and marvelously described—a rich pelt of individual green blades. In the background rise ancient gravestones: his mother sits leaning against one of them. There is a blank rectangle, a lacuna in the middle of the collage immediately above her head—an empty plot, her consciousness perhaps of her own mortality? It is at any rate a portrait brimming with remembrance: Bolton Abbey, Hockney explains, is one of the places his late father and his mother used to go sixty years ago, when they were courting.

These and the countless other photocollages of this middle period constitute an exploration of how people are couched in space and how that space is couched in time, the time of looking. The viewer, looking, experiences a living relationship, in time, and yet it's a strangely unreciprocated one: the people in the picture, suspended, don't quite live back at us. It was this fixity that Hockney, by mid-December, would be seeking to shatter.

A poster commission for the 1984 Winter Olympics proved the occasion for one of Hockney's first efforts in the new direction. "I decided to do a study of an ice skater," Hockney recalls, "and I invited a skater friend to join me at a rink in New York City. I watched him for some time, and I noticed something very odd: you never see the blur. The convention of the blur comes from photography; it's what happens when motion is compressed onto a chemical plate. We've seen so many photos of blurs that we now think we actually see them in the world. But look sometime: you don't. At every instant the rapidly spinning skater is distinct. And I wanted somehow to convey this combination of speed and clarity." The resultant collage has a lot of spin—legs flying, skates scraping, shirt billowing, head turning, arms rising, everything converging on and moving out from the focused center, the waist—but no blur.

A series of studies Hockney undertook a few days later, back in his Los Angeles home, during a particularly gemütlich dinner with his friends Billy and Audrey Wilder, proved both simpler and more successful. At one point, following dessert, Hockney noticed that Billy Wilder was fixing to light his cigar, and he immediately reached for his Pentax. In the resultant collage (Plate 8), a flourish consisting of merely six overlapping prints (and the bottom one, with only the two beautifully described wineglasses on the table in the foreground, doesn't really count), Hockney shows Wilder striking his match, bringing it up to his face, inhaling, momentarily distracted from the conversation, which he already seems bent on rejoining; the last print finds him looking up, puffing contentedly, obviously framing some repartee. (I say that the bottom one doesn't really count, but then look again, for those two wineglasses both establish a sense of conviviality and Hockney's own presence at the table and give a wider sense of spaciousness, grounding the whole scene. Block out that print with your hand and you will see all that gets lost.) The prints fold one on top of another: the entire piece reads as one carefree, casual gesture—a toss-off.[12]

On the first day of the new year, Hockney, his mother, and his friend Ann Upton sat down at the wooden table in his living room to play a game of Scrabble, with David Graves keeping score (Plate 9). "The game lasted two hours. I was clicking away the whole time," Hockney boasts, "and I still came in second! Naturally, my mother won." And looking at the picture, you can see she's going to: her face appears a half dozen times, in different degrees of close-up, and every shot captures the visage of a shrewd, veteran contender. BOSS HEN reads the bottom file of words as the board faces Hockney. (The words SCOWLS, SOBS, and POOL are also floating in there.) The plastic board is mounted on ball bearings so that it can be rotated from one player to the next. Hockney has taken his details of the board at various moments of the game and cleverly interwoven them in the center of the collage so that it's possible, with a little study, for the viewer to reconstruct the entire game, or at least its key moments. We watch as Mrs. Hockney concentrates and then scores a handsome windfall by centering VEX over a double-word square—a neat twenty-six points. The board presently comes around to Ann, affording her access to a triple-word corner slot—she ponders and ponders (five separate faces) and finally ventures the truly pathetic NET (three lower-scoring letters could not have been found). David Graves, keeping score, looks over her shoulder, considers her predicament, and then breaks into a grin at her solution: three times one times three—nine points. A cat on the side of the table looks up, rummages around, and falls back to sleep. Hockney's own tiles are arrayed on their stand before him: LQUIREU. "He was trying for 'LIQUOR,'" one cognoscente hypothesized at the opening in New York, the day this collage was first exhibited, "only he kept his 'Q' way too long into the game. You can't just hold onto those big letters, endlessly waiting for the right vowels to come along." "I don't know about that," replied her friend. "What about 'LIQUEUR'—that would have given him a fifty-point bonus for using all his letters, if he could have attached it to an 'S.'" And the extraordinary thing about this collage is that it lends itself to that kind of second-guessing—it opens out onto that kind of storytelling. Indeed, it simultaneously tells a story and presents a group portrait. Dozens of hands, eyes, faces, a spinning board at countless

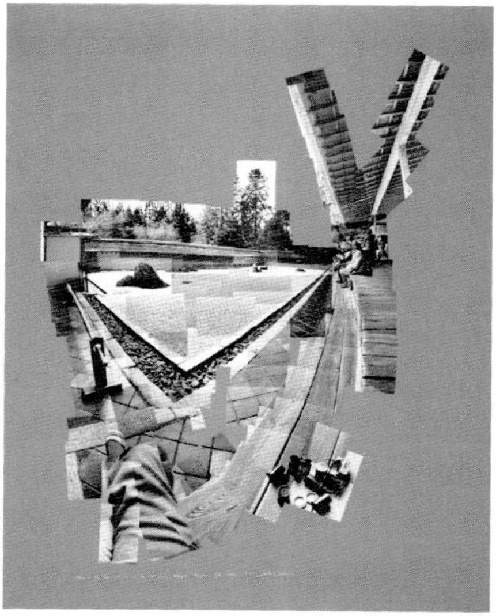

FIG 16 David Hockney, *Sitting in the Zen Garden at the Ryōanji Temple, Kyoto, Feb. 19, 1983.*

FIG 17 David Hockney, *Walking in the Zen Garden at the Ryōanji Temple, Kyoto, Feb. 1983.*

angles: and yet at all times a recognizable picture of a group of three (implicitly four) individuals engaged in an immediately recognizable activity.

These increasingly sophisticated collages built toward the series Hockney undertook on his February trip to Japan. Indeed, the Japanese collages offer perhaps the finest elaboration of many of the themes we have been considering thus far.

The rock garden at the Ryōanji Temple in Kyoto, for example, the subject of several drawings by Hockney during earlier trips to Japan, became on this trip the site for further research into the dissolution of the rectangle. "What I began to realize in putting some of these recent ones together," Hockney explained as we looked at the first of two studies of the Ryōanji rock garden, "is that it's the solid, no matter what shape, that constitutes the rectangle and constrains like the rectangle. You have to open it up, put holes in the middle, and stretch bands off to the side to get away from the window aesthetic." In the first Ryōanji collage (Fig. 16), Hockney sits on a wooden step, looking out from a corner of the Zen garden. The garden itself is a large outdoor rectangular field, covered with meticulously raked white pebbles and punctuated by occasionally obtruding half-buried boulders. The dimen-

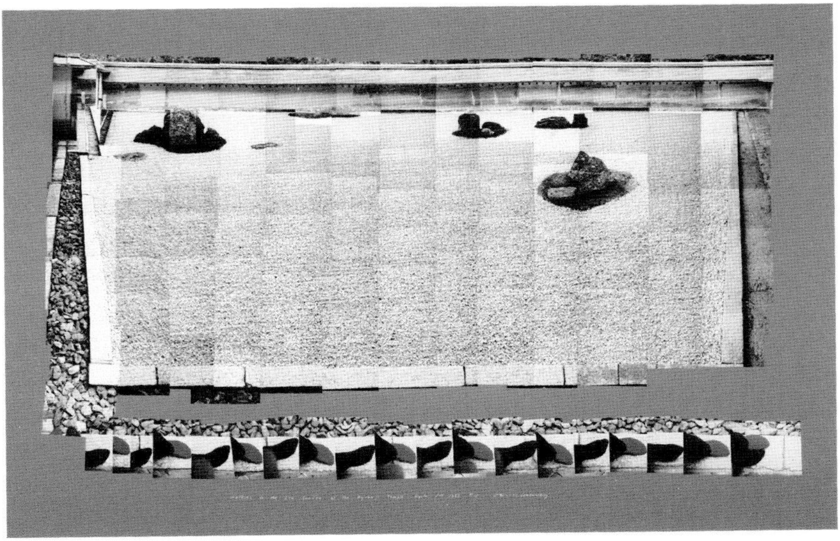

sions, the spacing of the boulders, the pattern of the raking—everything has been exquisitely calibrated to encourage calm meditation and spiritual renewal. (The rocks rise like islands in the sea of pebbles, the mossy patches spread like miniature forests over the rocks.) Hockney's collage includes the wooden eave floating disembodied above him, receding into the distance where it eventually joins the back wall, and below the eave, the deck with people sitting and standing, looking out, watching. The Zen garden branches out in a seeming V from the corner where Hockney sits. A narrow band of black tile pavement between the wood deck and the white curbstones skirts the gravel field, further emphasizing the way space recedes along both sides of the V. A low yellow wall bounds the rectangular field on the far sides. In the middle of the collage is an irregularly shaped blank that exists partly, Hockney explains, because he was interrupted as he was taking his pictures and simply failed to record these middle frames. But the hole also works to further sabotage the window illusion, reading (like the boulders in the field of white gravel) as a zone of nothingness, of serene nullity in the heart of being.

In his second collage of the rock garden of Ryōanji, Hockney decided to attempt movement in his point of view (Fig. 17). Almost all of his collages up to this point had presupposed a fixed vantage point, a still center from which viewing took place (even if, as in the case of the Polaroids, this fixed point was sometimes an elaborate fiction). Now he was beginning to wonder how he might account for his own movement in the world, as well as that of his subjects. So he got up and began walking along the white curbstones skirting one side of the rectangular garden. Every couple of steps, he'd stop, face the garden, and take a row of shots extending from the space at his feet all the way back to the yellow wall. Then he'd move on a few steps and repeat the procedure. The resultant collage proved to be a nearly perfect rectangle yet had nothing whatsoever to do with the window aesthetic. "In fact," Hockney noted as we looked at this second collage, "the only time you actually see rectangles in the world as truly rectangular is when you're moving in relation to them. Otherwise, they always present themselves as at least slightly foreshortened in some way." To underline his movement, Hockney included a row of shots at the bottom of this collage detailing his feet advancing forward, one step at a time, red sock then black sock then red sock, forming a rhythmic, seemingly Oriental pattern. The dozens of shots that make up the field of white gravel in this collage have been exactly rendered, pebbles matching pebbles from one frame to the next. "This one," admits Hockney, "was a real headache to put together."

Hockney also composed some of his finest portrait collages during this trip. There are several lovingly intimate studies of his friend and traveling companion Gregory Evans. In one, Gregory is seated, hunched over a camera he is loading for David. His hands converge efficiently over the camera on his lap—five hands and, over to the side, on the wooden deck beside him, an empty glove. His head, bending down in quiet concentration, stretches across several pictures, the soft dark curls of his hair flowing sensuously from one print to the next; the viewer must look several times to notice that he has three thighs, which mysteriously taper down to two feet, something like the famous optical illusion of the impossible triple-pronged magnet.

While in Japan, Hockney gave a slide lecture on his photographic work up to the present. In advance of that lecture, back at the hotel, his friend Paul Cornwall-Jones, the director of the Petersburg Press, ran through a carousel of slides for the benefit of the woman who would be serving as Hockney's translator, Mie Kakigahara. Hockney sat opposite them, his back to the screen, snapping away. The re-

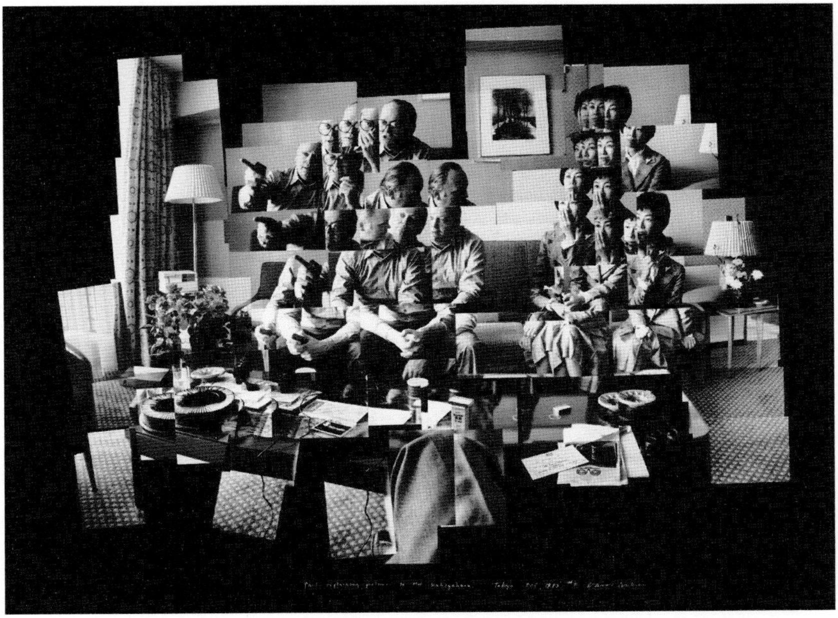

FIG 18 David Hockney, *Paul Explaining Pictures to Mie Kakigahara, Tokyo, Feb. 1983.*

sultant collage (Fig. 18) provides perhaps the most intricate example yet of his growing skill in capturing the multifaceted nature of human personality. The space in the room is presented fairly straightforwardly, but the two people, sitting on a long yellow couch, are veritable explosions of liveliness. Cornwall-Jones's face appears twelve times, Kakigahara's thirteen. (She holds on to the couch with her left hand as if to keep from blowing away.) Cornwall-Jones is animated, his hands pointing, returning to his lap, pressing the remote-control button, his face looking at the screen and then over at her. She is quiet, reserved, by turns enchanted and perplexed. The two conglomerations of details are modeled into general shapes congruent with their subjects' respective bodies: Cornwall-Jones round and stocky, Kakigahara long and thin (a totem pole of response). The two of them exist in time. The etching on the wall between them, a study of trees lining a stream, Hockney presents straight on, without any faceting or repetitions—the art seems to exist out of time, to be timeless.

On the table between Hockney and the two slide-watchers is an invitation to a luncheon at the British embassy. This luncheon was to prove the occasion for what may be Hockney's most successfully integrated photocollage to date (Plate 10). In it all of the artist's ambitions are realized simultaneously: the depiction of real space and real time, the rendering of people in the fullness of their living, the breaking of the rectangle. Ten people sit around a long elegant table in a beautifully appointed dining room, partaking of good food and talk. Hockney himself is represented this time by neither his feet nor his hands but rather by a place card, a telltale pair of exposed film rolls, and a half-empty snifter of brandy. To his left, the ambassador's wife converses with Paul Cornwall-Jones—she shy and soft-spoken, he polite and slightly bored. To Hockney's far right, at the head of the table, the ambassador holds forth, a study in casual erudition. It's indicative of the sophisticated treatment of visual space in this collage that the ambassador at the far end of the table draws our attention, and we hardly even notice the looming face of the man seated directly next to the artist. This face is far and away the biggest single physical presence in the collage—it takes up three full prints. (The ambassador's entire body, by contrast, never takes up more than a quarter of each of the several prints in which it appears.) Yet the neighbor's face recedes to equivalence with all the others: he's big only because he's closest; our attention is mainly elsewhere. Hockney defuses his neighbor's presence by couching it in a field of peripheral vision. Floating almost free in a cloud of prints behind him, at the far right-hand side of the collage, is a servant preparing a tray. Dressed in a kimono, geisha-like, she is utterly quiet and self-effacing. Indeed, she seems to have no legs: where her legs should be, we see clear through to the back of the room. We sense that she is so unobtrusive that her feet don't even touch the ground—but only sense this, for these details barely skim our consciousness: even though the photoprints that make up the servant girl are as large and real as all the others, Hockney has found a way to suggest the peripheralness of peripheral vision.

"The visual pleasure here is a sensuous exploration of surfaces," the art critic Christopher Knight wrote in a recent article in *Aperture,* describing one of Hockney's Polaroid collages with words that might apply equally to his *Luncheon at the British Embassy.* "The artist moves around the room, approaching the object of

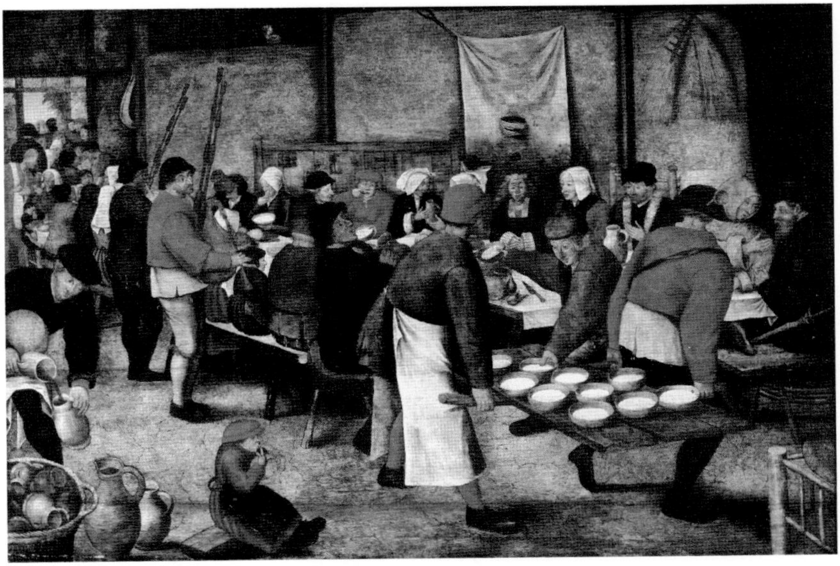

FIG 19 Pieter Brueghel the Younger, *The Peasant Wedding Dinner.*

desire, embracing it at a distance as the shutter clicks and the electronic motor purrs, then retreating and moving on to the next. The composite image is reconstructed from a composite of sensory experiences, of surfaces seen and collected. The wholly mundane compendium of objects in the room assumes the dimensions of a spectacle."[13]

Flowers, silver saltshakers, glass ashtrays, Persian carpet, ceiling molding, wall sconces, faces, shirts, ties, hands, eyes. . . . The *Luncheon at the British Embassy* is a feast of vision. In this it is reminiscent of that other celebration of visual bounty, Brueghel's painting *The Peasant Wedding Dinner* (Fig. 19). Indeed, William Carlos Williams's poem about that painting,[14] with its extraordinarily precise evocation of the way our eyes move about the canvas—move and catch, catch and hold, and then move on again—provides one of the best intimations I can imagine of what it's like to look at some of these late Hockney collages, particularly this *Luncheon at the British Embassy:*

Peasant Wedding

Pour the wine bridegroom
where before you the
bride is enthroned her hair

loose at her temples a head
of ripe wheat is on
the wall beside her the

guests seated at long tables
the bagpipers are ready
there is a hound under

the table the bearded Mayor
is present women in their
starched headgear are

gabbing all but the bride
hands folded in her
lap is awkwardly silent simple

dishes are being served
clabber and what not
from a trestle made of an

unhinged barn door by two
helpers one in a red
coat a spoon in his hatband

With these late collages, Hockney was becoming increasingly interested in the depiction of movement through space—not just the movement of people's heads and limbs as they sat talking but rather their movement as they walked, the movement of cars and trains, and his own movement, walking or driving through the field of vision. In one collage taken from the bridge over a narrow canal in Kyoto, for example, the traffic on the road gets minced into dozens of narrow, clipped details—car windows, fenders, hoods, headlights. This noisy jumble of traffic plays off against the imperturbable verticals of the telephone poles, and details from the same cars seem to move forward in a stuttering progression from one frame to the next. Similarly, as Gregory looks out the window of a train moving through suburban Tokyo, he seems to be surveying a sprawling city: it takes a moment to realize that most of this "city" is made up of the same house, seen over and over again, at different distances as the train rolls by, and that this sleight of collage is one of the things that gives this piece its internal sense of movement.

"At the time I did *The Scrabble Game,*" Hockney recalled as we reviewed some of these moving images, "Ann said, 'It's better than a movie.' And in a way it was. You see, I think we overrate the cinema in much the same way we do photography. The increasing popularization of movies may have been one of the reasons for the lapse in the progress of cubism after the First World War. The movie must have appeared to be the most vivid and accurate depiction of reality possible—it seemed to address many of the same concerns as cubism (the need to include time, for instance), so that many artists just gave up the terrain of depiction and took off on this journey toward abstraction. The problem, though, is that the movie too is flawed. For one thing, we're back with the camera obscura—now all of us literally sit inside the dark room, staring through the rectangular hole in the wall. Furthermore, a movie must traffic in literal time and can only go forward. Even when it pretends to go back, the spool is moving forward, forcing us to keep to an established, dictated pace. There's no time for looking, as there always is in the world. I'm not saying that it's not a good medium, only that it's not what we think or thought it was. So that recently I've been trying to figure out ways of telling stories in which the viewer can set his own pace, moving forward and back, in and out, at his own discretion."[15]

As the occasion for one of the first of these "line narratives," Hockney decided to photograph the noted photographer Annie Leibovitz, who'd come out to California, on assignment from *Vanity Fair,* to photograph him. "She's a lovely bright woman," Hockney recounts, "and we had some wonderful conversations about the issues I was grappling with. When it came time for her to take my portrait, she said, 'I just want it to be natural, I don't want to lay anything on it,' whereupon she packed me and her assistant into a station wagon and drove for two hours into the high desert: she wanted a plain, flat horizon. It turned out there was snow on the desert when we got there, but that didn't seem to matter. So we parked, and she and her assistant unloaded all these lamps and cables, opened her hood to attach the wires to the car battery, dragged the equipment a few dozen yards into the desert, where they established this elaborate setup, and then finally took their supposedly spontaneous, natural pictures. Well, all the while I was snapping my snaps, and a few days later I put together this collage." Hockney produced a board depicting the entire production—the parked station wagon, Leibovitz and her assistant deploying their paraphernalia, the open hood, the cables, the dirty footprints in the slushy snow, the huge arc lamps—both Leibovitz and her assistant appearing at several places in the collage, wrestling with all the equipment. And then, off at an inverted angle over to the right of the collage, Hockney had included Leibovitz's portrait of him in his red pants, green smock, blue-striped shirt, red polka-dot tie, purple and black cap, his right hand extended, wielding the tiny Pentax. Click: counterclick! "I asked Annie if I could include her photo of me in my collage and she agreed. She came over here, a few days later, to look at the result and she said, 'Yeah, I had a feeling *you* got the picture that day.'"

Hockney proceeded to show me several of his other narrative pieces—one of a friend bringing him a cup of tea by the pool, another of David Graves and Annie Upton getting married in Hawaii—and it occurred to me that while he had indeed been deploying all his cubist innovations in making these late narrative pieces, the resultant collages seemed to draw even more directly on a much earlier source, the tradition of medieval painting in which one character moves through several incidents in his life across a single continuous landscape. Christ thus appears overturning the tables in the Temple, sharing his last supper with his disciples, being tried before Pontius Pilate, scourged in the streets, and then crucified outside the walls of Jerusalem—all in a single panel. Or, as in the late medieval Italian painting by Sassetta on view at the National Gallery of Art in Washington, D.C., St. Paul is shown at the top of the panel, walking alone along a path that presently brings him to a centaur in the upper right-hand corner, whom he converts, and then through a forest down to a meeting with St. Anthony, whom he embraces in the center foreground of the picture. In effect, Hockney was blending a narrative mode in common currency before the invention of the camera obscura with a visual grammar, developed some five hundred years later, one of whose principal ambitions is to break the hegemony of the camera obscura that had risen up in the meantime.

A month later, back in New York City, I ambled over to the André Emmerich Gallery on Fifty-seventh Street to meet up with Hockney just before the opening of his first comprehensive show of these photocollages. It was now two in the afternoon—the official reception was set for four. On my way into the building I ran into a friend on her way out. I asked how she'd liked the show. "You want to know the truth?" she replied. "At first I was really liking it a whole lot but within about ten minutes I ended up fleeing in terror: it was too much like being inside somebody else's eyeballs."

Upstairs a considerably calmer crowd was previewing the exhibition, and Hockney himself was making a final, quick inspection tour. I joined him by one of the most recent pieces, yet another rendition of an evening with Christopher Isherwood and Don Bachardy. "They're seated in the same room and seats I photographed them in back in 1968, when I was making studies for my painting of them," Hockney commented. "But this picture makes the 1968 photo look like 1868."

A first-year art student came up to him, beaming with enthusiasm. "You know what I like about these things?" he offered. "I've always been fascinated by insects' eyes. I've got a big blow-up of a pair of mosquito's eyes in my room. You know how each of the eyes is made up of thousands of little eyes. This is great! This is what the world must look like to a fly!" Another visitor, this one a man pushing a perambulator, commented on how much the collages reminded him of children's drawings: "For one thing, there's the way the same people recur from one collage to the next—just like the way a child is always drawing the people in his immediate, intimate surroundings. But it's even more reminiscent of the way a child will include *everything* in the room in his picture, even though he'd never be able to see all that stuff in a single glance." A third person came up to Hockney, introducing himself as a perceptual psychologist. "I study photographs and how people see them," he said, "and I've never seen anything like this. These pictures are *supervivid*." "Gee," Hockney replied, smiling. "I mean, I've always said they were vivid, but. . . ." In no time Hockney was holding forth on time and perception for a small cluster of gallery visitors.

After a while he broke off and came over to me, asking if I'd like to join him for a brief visit to the Museum of Modern Art—he would have to get back to his studio in Los Angeles almost immediately after the reception, and there were a few paintings he wanted to look at again before he left town.

On our way over to the museum, walking the few blocks, Hockney spoke about some of the larger issues raised by his photocollages. "What's at stake for me in this sort of work," he insisted, "is the revitalization of depiction. The great misinterpretation of twentieth-century art is the claim advanced by many people, especially critics, that cubism of necessity led to abstraction, that cubism's only true heritage was this increasing tendency toward a more and more insular abstraction. But on the contrary, cubism was about the real world. It was an attempt to reclaim a territory for figuration, for depiction. Faced with the claim that photography had made figurative painting obsolete, the cubists performed an exquisite critique of photography; they showed that there were certain aspects of looking—basically the *human* reality of perception—that photography couldn't convey, and that you still needed the painter's hand and eye to convey them. I mean, several paths led out from those initial discoveries of Picasso and Braque, and abstraction was no doubt one of them. In that sense, it's a legitimate heir. I've always felt that what was wrong with Tom Wolfe's polemic against the American abstract expressionist movement in *The Painted Word* was that he never did understand that those people were *sincere.* But still you have to ask yourself, why didn't Picasso and Braque, who invented cubism, ever follow that path? And I suspect that it's because sitting there in Paris back in the early 1910s, playing out the various possibilities in their minds, they could already see that abstraction led into a cul-de-sac, eventually even just an empty room, and they didn't need to do it to find out.

"I mean, the urge to depict and the longing to see depictions is very strong and very deep within us. It's a five-thousand-year-old longing—you see it all the way back to the cave paintings, this need to render the real world. We don't create the world. It's God's world, he made it. We depict it, we try to understand it. And a longing like that doesn't just disappear in one generation. Art is about correspondences—making connections with the world and to each other. It's about love in that sense—that is the origin of the erotic quality of art. We love to study images of the world, and especially images of people, our fellow creatures. And the problem with abstraction, finally, is that it goes too far inwards and the links become tenuous, or dissolve, and it becomes too hard to make those connections. You end up getting these claims by some of the formalist critics that art just isn't for everybody—but that's ridiculous.

"The revival of the figure with many of the young painters today testifies to the enduring longing for depiction, although the crude character of much of this so-called neo-expressionist drawing testifies to the deterioration in basic training which we've seen during the last couple generations. I mean, training people to draw is basically training them to look. I'm convinced you can teach people to draw as well as Augustus John, although admittedly you can't teach them to draw as well as Picasso or Matisse. If you don't know how to draw, you end up drawing expressionist, anxious-looking faces. The original expressionists knew how to draw and what they chose to draw was anxiety and anguish; hence the drawing had an authority, a lasting power which is often missing in the work you see currently. The other trouble with not knowing how to draw is that you draw yourself into certain highly mannered corners which you can't then draw yourself out of. I think a lot of work you see currently has drawn itself into those kinds of corners.

"The strange thing about the legacy of cubism is that it did exert an influence on abstract artists during the thirties and forties and fifties but was virtually ignored by the realists. Its lessons are very hard: few people besides its originators—Picasso, Braque, Gris, Léger—have been able to deal with them successfully. Most midcentury realists went on as if cubism had never happened. I mean, I don't mind things looking as though something never happened. In fact there is a certain perversity in that which I sort of like. I just think that now, as the cul-de-sac of abstraction has become increasingly self-evident, that for painting to go forward, we have to go back to cubism. It still has very important lessons left to teach us."

Hockney's passionate monologue had spirited us from the elevator at the Emmerich Gallery, across several bustling city blocks, all the way into the elevator at the Museum of Modern Art, whose doors now opened, delivering us into the temporary exhibition space in the museum's basement. Immediately before us were some Cézanne landscapes, and to the side a Picasso and a Braque. Hockney was suddenly struck speechless.

"Oh dear," he sighed finally, taking a deep breath, "I truly *must* get back to painting."

CHAPTER 2

a visit with david and stanley

HOLLYWOOD HILLS (1987)

For a long time his cameras had been getting smaller and smaller. Polaroid. Nikon. Pentax. A little tiny pocket job, James Bond style. "More and more lifelike," is the way David Hockney had put it to me a few years back when he had been describing his ongoing explorations and I was preparing the introductory essay for the *Cameraworks* volume, which was going to document some of those investigations. "More true to life. I mean, one's own eye doesn't hang out of one's face, monocular, drooping at the end of some long tube. No, it's nestled in its socket, rolling about, free and responsive. And I feel a camera should be as much like that as possible."

Deploying his increasingly tiny cameras, he'd been generating increasingly mammoth collages: dozens, hundreds, presently thousands of snapshots shingled one upon another, resolving into ever more intricate and lovely portraits and vistas. An explosion of perspectives—and in the process the utter subversion of the tyrannical hegemony of traditional one-point perspective.

"*Wider* perspectives are needed now," Hockney would proclaim as he pulled a camera the size of a cigarette pack out of his pocket and started up once again, snapping away.

So you can perhaps imagine my surprise recently, when Hockney invited me out to his home and studio in the Hollywood Hills above Los Angeles to have a look at some of his current work, at finding him hunched over his latest camera: a full-ton monster—a huge blinking box—a Kodak Ektaprint 222 *office copying machine.* Hockney looked up for a moment, beckoned me in, and returned to his labors: snapping, as ever, away.

This essay was written for the catalogue of the retrospective exhibition held at the Tate in London and the Metropolitan Museum of Art in New York, in 1987.

Hockney's studio is built up over the former tennis court above his amphitheatric home, and the copying machines (for there were two, a Canon NP 3525 as well) actually occupied only half the court. The other half was taken up with a large three-dimensional model of his stage designs for an upcoming production of Richard Wagner's *Tristan und Isolde.* Indeed Hockney's workday that month seemed to consist in a regular volleying, as it were, between Wagner and Xerox. That particular afternoon, however, he mainly seemed interested in talking about his explorations into the artistic possibilities of copying machines.

"A while back," he told me, "as you may remember, I used to enjoy confounding people by declaring that the only thing a photograph might be able to convey with some degree of truthfulness would be a flat surface, as in the reproduction, say, of a painting. When it attempted to depict space, that's when photography seemed to me to get into trouble. The camera, although people think it sees everything in front of it, cannot see the main thing we get excited about in front of us, which is space. The camera cannot see it. Only human beings maybe, or anyway only living beings, can see space. That's part of what I was exploring with all those photocollages: how a camera might be transformed to convey space after all, which means how it might be forced to acknowledge time. But it's only just now that I've been returning to my initial insight, which is how good a camera is at conveying a flat surface and the possibilities which that particular sort of effectiveness might afford.

"Because an office copier *is* a camera," Hockney continued, patting his giant beast of a colleague. "When you use it to copy a letter, you're basically getting a photographic reproduction of the letter. It's a camera, and it's also a machine for printing. Over the years, I've made a lot of prints working in several different master printshops. It's an exciting process, but I've always been bothered by the lack of spontaneity: how it takes hours and hours, working alongside several master craftsmen, to generate an image. How you're continually having to interrupt the process of creation from one moment to the next for technical reasons. But with these copying machines, I can work by myself—indeed you virtually have to work by yourself; there's nothing for anyone else to do—and I can work with great speed and responsiveness. In fact, this is the closest I've ever come in printing to what it's like to paint: I can put something down, evaluate it, alter it, revise it, reexamine it, all in a matter of seconds. Actually I've been trying to come up with a name for what to call these things"—he gestured toward a wall where several of his photocopied creations were hanging on display—"and I've hit on the phrase 'Home Made Prints.'"

To understand how Hockney was generating these Home Made Prints of his, it's useful to keep in mind the model of a self-contained print studio. The prints are wonderfully colorful and various; yet within each edition they are consistent from one "pressing" to the next. But Hockney was not simply producing a finished image, hundreds of color copies of which he was then proceeding to mass-produce out of his copying machine. Rather he was working in *layers,* as in a standard print workshop. Much of his activity over the past several months, he now informed me, had consisted in exploring what things look like when they're photocopied, how the machine sees them; and to find out, he'd been photocopying everything in sight: leaves, maps, grass, towels, shirts, Plasticine models, painted images, gouaches, washes, ink-thatches. He'd explored how the machine reads these various subjects at various settings and in various colors. He'd even been in touch with some of the technicians at Canon in Japan, having them brew him up some new colors, specifically a yellow for which no previous customer had ever seemed to have any call.

He photocopied everything, and then he cut and collaged. The prints he was eventually creating were thus the culmination of several dozen different operations. By the time he was ready to make an edition of any specific print—say, the charming portrait of his new intimate companion, a dachshund puppy named Stanley, which he was "editioning" the afternoon I came to visit (Plate 25)—he might have six or ten or fifteen different sheets of paper, layers of the image, which he would now begin successively "combining" inside the photocopier. He'd load the machine's paper feed bin with high-quality Arches paper, the sort used by the finest print studios, lay his first image on the glass screen, select a color and a setting, run a few copies, recalibrate the settings, and then shoot a hundred sheets, say, through the machine. He'd then take those hundred sheets, evaluate their consistency, reject any copies that failed to pass muster for one reason or another, and then put the remaining sheets back in the feed bin, replacing the first image on the screen with a second and repeating the process. (In this particular instance, a soft light brown wash was being superimposed on the witty, crisp black-ink outline of the first pressing—or rather Hockney now replaced the machine's black pigment with brown from one of several canisters he kept alongside the copier; the actual image on the sheet Hockney was photocopying was the palest gray watercolor. Hockney explained that the machine seemed to read the white-gray contrast better than it would a white-brown.) By the end of this particular run, only thirty sheets survived all the operations, and they came to constitute the complete edition of that particular print. Everything else was fed into a nearby paper shredder, which digested the debris into exceptionally high-quality confetti.

It was not only the spontaneity of the process that Hockney seemed to be enjoying in his newly discovered medium. There were certain ancillary benefits he'd come upon along the way as well—for one thing, the blacks. "I've never been able to generate such blacks before," he declared, pointing to the incredibly luscious black tree trunk, set off by a simple, almost luminous green leaf in one of the prints tacked to the wall. "I think it has something to do with the process by which the pigment is made to adhere to the page. In almost every other printing or painting process the pigment is conveyed to the page through a liquid medium of some sort, which then both evaporates into the atmosphere and is absorbed into the page, in either case leaving a sort of visual residue. No matter how black, there's always a trace of reflectivity, a sheen, and you don't get that pure sense of void. With photocopying, however, the powdered pigment is conveyed onto the page by a heat flash rather than a liquid. And there's therefore no subsequent reflective sheen. Just this rich, wonderful black."

Most of these prints seemed to have an uncanny presence and clarity, a startling immediacy. "Somebody the other day was telling me how one of these images just seemed to pop off the page for him," Hockney commented. "But I think that that formulation is subtly wrong. In most other printing processes there are several intervening, intermediary stages in the production, and in a way you can see them in the finished product. The image seems to be hanging back, to be subsumed, as it were, a few millimeters beneath or behind or below the surface of the sheet of paper. But here the process has been more direct—no negatives, no apparatus, just paper to paper—so that if anything, the image can be said to have popped *onto* the surface of the page.

"In general," Hockney continued, "it seems to me that most reproduction in the past has tried to behave as if the page were not there, as if you were looking through the page to the image which was just beyond it, as if the page were like a pane of glass. I'm reminded of those extraordinary George Herbert lines, which have fascinated me for years:

> A man may look on glass,
> On it may stay his eye;
> Or if he pleaseth through it pass
> And there the Heaven espy.

But what I've been trying to get in some of these recent prints is the beauty of the surface itself, of color on paper, the Heaven that's there. Heaven isn't far away; it's right there on the surfaces before us."

In other words, it was a typical visit to Hockney's studio: the still young, not-*that*-young artist utterly engrossed in and possessed by some new passion, relentlessly pursuing it through all its myriad permutations. Hockney is an awesome worker: the sheer amount of his production—its variety and the density within that variety—is staggering. And all the more so because that sheer intensity of labor runs so contrary to his public persona as a ubiquitous presence in society, an endlessly vacationing, lotus-languid bon vivant. Few artists, with the possible exception of Andy Warhol (for whom such exposure was itself, in a sense, near the core of his artistic vocation), have so often found their countenances gracing the pages of fashion magazines and artsy journals. It's David Hockney here and David Hockney there. Indeed in this regard Hockney sometimes reminds me of Kierkegaard or at any rate of the perhaps apocryphal stories about Kierkegaard, who, it was said, used to disguise his own ferocious productivity—particularly during the 1840s, when he was penning a whole series of volumes under countless pseudonyms (each "author" seeming to attack all the others)—by continually traipsing about Copenhagen behaving like the most flamboyant and unregenerate of dandies. He'd make a particular point, or so the stories went, of showing up each evening at the opera, making a grand entrance into the concert hall, sitting through the overture, and then ever so quietly, without provoking the slightest notice, exiting the hall and hurrying back to his desk and his countless pseudonymous tasks. (Indeed the exercise was essential to the success of the whole pseudonymous venture; everyone was avidly wondering who all these wildly contentious new authors were, but nobody ever so much as suspected that idle dabbler Søren Kierkegaard.)

I mentioned that story to Hockney now, as I gingerly moved him away from the force field of his photocopying machines and over to a set of easy chairs in the studio's midcourt, and he started to laugh before I could even complete the analogy. "Ah, yes," he said, "I see what you're getting at. I mean, I don't really care what people think, but it *is* funny. A few months ago, for instance, in New York, a friend of mine urged me to come along to the Palladium. I didn't want to, I don't like discos, and I can't stand the music, but in the end I went as a sort of favor to her. And sure enough, there were all these people there photographing other people, and they all photographed me, so that even though I only stayed for about half an hour, the photos were appearing for weeks thereafter. I can see how it could give someone the impression that I'm out partying every night, even though, in fact, I hardly ever go out. But I don't care. In fact, there are certain advantages to people's not taking you too seriously."

Like what?

"Well, think of it the other way. If you're taken very, very seriously, you run the risk of becoming bogged down in another direction, which I wouldn't like. One's freer this way. I mean, I take my work seriously, I don't take myself too seriously, but if you spend your whole life doing it, you're obviously taking it seriously in a way. You don't choose to do all that work as a mere dalliance, as nothing at all."

He went on to point out how, for instance, some people, observing his photo albums, imagine he's on vacation all the time. "The thing is," he said, "that's what makes those albums utterly ordinary. Everybody's photo albums document them with their friends and when they go on holiday. People don't spend much time photographing the street they live on. Although, actually, my backyard has been the subject of most of my work. People see me as some sort of hedonist because I always seem to be portraying either my California home or my various travels. But I never traveled out of boredom or the need for new impressions. I've always realized that the bored person will be bored anywhere. The reason I moved from one place to another was to find peace actually, peace to work. It was the nattering that usually got me down. I fled for peace and quiet in each case." It occurred to me, as Hockney said this, that the reason we think he's always on holiday—in Mexico or Provence or China or Japan or the Southwest and so forth—is because of all the work he brings back from these travels. He portrays others lounging about sleepily—sometimes in his drawings it seems that all the world's a nap—but he's wide awake and deep at work.

"That's why I settled here in California in 1979, for that matter," he continued. "It suits me here. You can live more privately here than anywhere else and yet still be in a city. In a way I moved here for the isolation."

It's not just the locales portrayed that often give people the wrong impression about Hockney's intentions. "I mean," he continued, "it's like people say, 'Ah yes, you paint swimming pools.' But I must admit, I never thought the swimming pool pictures were at all about mere hedonist pleasure [Fig. 20]. They were about the surface of the water, the very thin film, the shimmering two-dimensionality. What is it you're seeing? For example, I once emptied out my pool and painted blue lines on the bottom. Well, now, when the water's still, you see just clear through it and the lines are clean and steady. When somebody's been swimming, the lines are set to moving. But where are they moving? If you go underneath the surface, no matter how turbulent the water, the lines are again steady. They are only wriggling on the surface, this thinnest film. Well, it's that surface that fascinates me; and that's what those paintings are about really."

The same as with the Xeroxes.

Spend any amount of time with Hockney and you quickly realize that he's an intensely cerebral artist, extraordinarily well read and deeply involved in that reading and extraordinarily thoughtful in those terms about the wider implications of his artistic endeavor. He is endlessly struggling with issues of representation, perception, reality, worldview, the transcendence of constrictions. Curiously, however, most of those implications pass most of the fans of his art right by. What makes Hockney such an iconic presence in contemporary popular culture, it seems to me—all the Hockney posters on living room walls, the Hockney reproductions on the jackets of novels and the covers of records, and so forth—is the sunny benevolence of the subject matter and the unfailingly endearing charm of its rendering. I asked Hockney whether he ever became bothered by the misreading—or anyway, the half-reading—of his work. "I suppose even in the experimental work I have to do

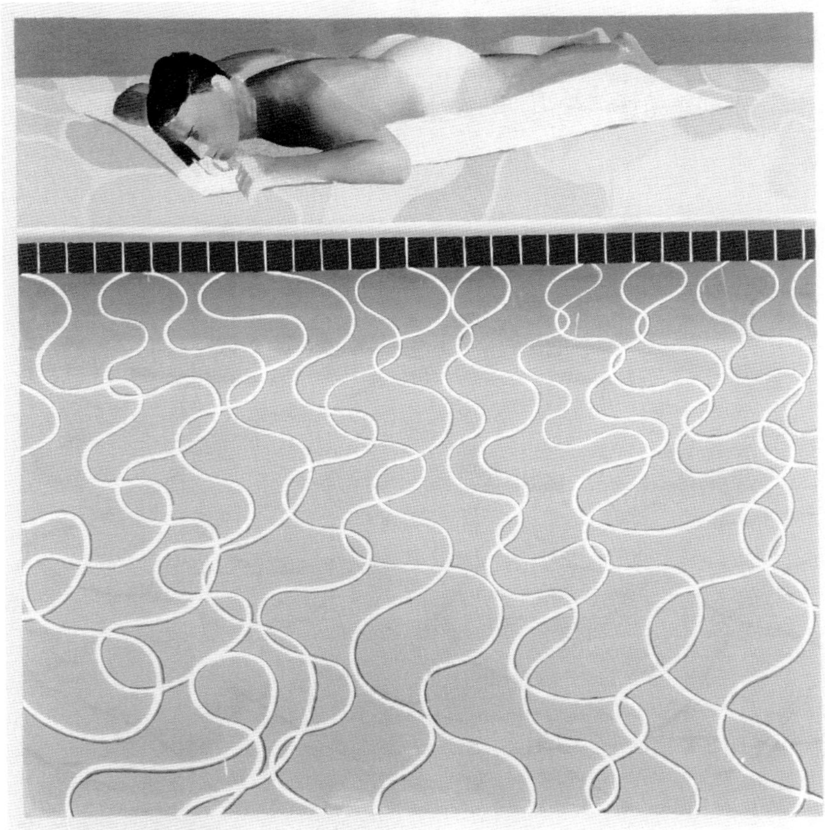

FIG 20 David Hockney, *Sunbather*, 1966.

it in a charming way," he replied. "That's just my personality. I can't not do it that way, you see. When people say, 'Ah, but it's much too charming,' I don't really care, because I know something else is going on as well."

I asked him about the roots of that charm. "I think ultimately what it is, is that I'm not a person who despairs. I think that ultimately we do have goodness, really, in us. For instance, with the Ravel opera [*L'Enfant et les sortilèges,* for which he did the stage designs in 1980], I totally responded to that story and the music particularly. And what was it saying? That kindness is our only hope. I think that was in every note of that music. Stunning. And I loved it. I did what I could to make it alive in the theater because basically I believe that. And if I do believe that, that's what I should express. That's where my duty lies. I mean, I'm not naive. I have moments—I don't think happiness is . . . We just get glimpses, tiny moments, that's all. But they're enough. At times I feel incredibly lonely, especially when I'm not working. The impulse can go away, just dry up. But the moment I get to work, the loneliness vanishes. I love it in here, on my own, painting. You know all that stuff about angst in art: I always think Van Gogh's pictures are full of happiness. They are. And yet you know he wasn't happy. Although he must have had moments to be able to paint like that. The idea that he was a miserable wretch and mad is not true. When he was mad, he couldn't paint, actually.

"I guess basically I'm an optimistic person," he continued. "I ultimately think we will move on to a higher awareness, that part of that road is our perceptions of the world as they change, and I see art as having an important role in that change."

A somewhat subtler misperception about Hockney's art is that he is essentially a painter and that all the rest—the theater work, the photocollages, the lithographs, the paper-pulp pools, the Home Made Prints—are somehow secondary, incidental, or tangential, a series of holding actions or at best experiments leading back to the more serious work of painting. Various commentators have expressed exasperation over Hockney's propensity for such side trips, and they've wondered when he was going to return to the more essential labor. Occasionally Hockney himself has reinforced that sense of priority. "Oh, dear," as he'd said to me the day of the New York opening of his photocollage show back in 1983, when we'd walked from the gallery over to the Museum of Modern Art and were suddenly delivered before Cézanne, Braque, and Picasso. "Oh, dear, I truly *must* get back to painting." More than three years had now passed, and although he had, in fact, produced a few new paintings—including the major two-panel rendition of *A Visit with Christopher and Don* (1984; see Plate 12)—he seemed to be as consumed as ever with his experiments in photography, printing, theater design, magazine layout, and so forth. I asked him whether that hierarchy of expectations mattered in any way to him.

"Less and less," he replied, "if at all. I mean, they're all tending toward the same set of issues—the clear depiction of space in time, the widening of perspective, and so forth—just in different media is all. And they all influence each other. Discoveries in one area move the other along. Just today I made a breakthrough with the design for *Tristan* based on some of the negative-positive contrasts I've been able to generate with the photocopying machines. Both the Xeroxes and the photocollages have been moving more and more to the condition of painting—you can see that especially with that recent *Pearblossom Highway* collage [1986, Plate 11], which is the most painterly of any of those I've done. At one point somebody did criticize the photographs for being less like art than the others, and I must admit I couldn't care less in a sense whether they are art or not. I mean, it's not up to me to say, and maybe it's not up to him either. It's certainly interesting where they're leading and where they've led, and you don't stop in the middle of it all because, you know, 'Gee, I'm not sure if this is art anymore.' There's a wonderful quote of Picasso's, which I keep referring to, where he says he never made a painting as a work of art; it was always research and it was always about time. On another occasion somebody was giving him a hard time about something—I forget what the argument was, but Picasso's reply was, 'Ah, then what you're talking about is *mere* painting.' Meaning, of course, that it's always about something else, something bigger. All of this work is undertaken in a spirit of research. I'm not so much interested in the mere objects I'm creating as in where they're taking me, and all the work in all the different media is part of that inquiry and part of that search."

Such probably would not have been his answer to that question back in the early seventies, when painting was still clearly central to his prodigious production. Ironically though, it was a sort of crisis in the paintings of that period—a sense of dead-endedness that persisted through much of the rest of that decade—which launched him into the other media. The blockage with those paintings provoked questions—at first barely articulated—which provided the contours for much of the research that was to follow

"Actually it was only a relatively short period," Hockney recalls, "from 1969 to 1972 or so, where I did a number of paintings in a naturalistic style with a very clear one-point perspective. In fact, it was so clear that the vanishing point was bang in the middle of the canvas. In the 1969 portrait of Henry Geldzahler [Fig. 21] there's an absolute vanishing point for everything there just slightly above his head. What

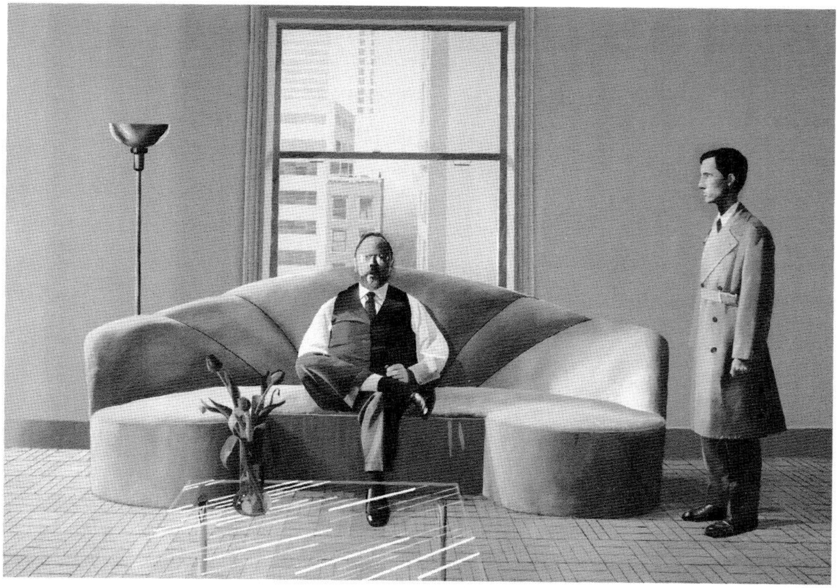

FIG 21 David Hockney, *Henry Geldzahler and Christopher Scott*, 1969.

I wanted to do, what I was struggling to do, was to make a very clear space, a space you felt clear in. That is what deeply attracts me to Piero, why he interests me so much more than Caravaggio: this clarity in his space that seems so real. Well, I just couldn't achieve that clarity, frankly; it was a hopeless struggle, and the painting I eventually gave up on was the double portrait of George Lawson and Wayne Sleep (1972–75), which I never exhibited, though it has been reproduced; it's a very dull picture."

It was reproduced in the 1977 volume *David Hockney by David Hockney*, where, interestingly, Hockney gives a different account of his reasons for abandoning the picture, as he understood them at the time, citing his growing dissatisfaction with acrylic versus oil paints and a growing disillusionment with "naturalism." Henry Geldzahler in his introduction to the volume, speculates—no doubt basing his speculations partly on contemporaneous conversations with Hockney himself—that "in the early 1970s Hockney's technical facility grew to such a degree that it frightened him into pulling back. . . . The double portrait *George Lawson and Wayne Sleep,* abandoned in 1973 and resumed in late 1975, achieved such heights of naturalism and finish that a sentimental and anecdotal quality in the subject matter threatened to undermine the painting's formal strengths."

Ever since his remarkable debut as an artist in the late fifties Hockney's work had been characterized by a youthful zest, a fresh sense of freedom, a playfulness. I started to make this point, but Hockney interrupted me. "If art isn't playful, it's nothing. Without play, we wouldn't be anywhere. Play is incredibly important; it's deeply serious as well. It's hardly a criticism of my work to call it playful; on the contrary, it's flattering!" I asked him whether there was a sense back there in the early seventies in which the growing technical mastery was no longer allowing the earlier playfulness, and he agreed. "Yes, yes, it's true. I couldn't play in that space, and it's only by playing with the space in the years since then that I've been able to make it clearer. Everything since then has been a progression toward a playful space that moves about but is still clear and not woolly."

At the time, back there in the midseventies, all he realized, in his own words, was that "'No, no, you cannot go anymore in this direction.' I knew that. I didn't know how to deal with it, so I just slowed down, and I moved into the theater. The first opportunity to do the staging for an opera came up about this point, Stravinsky's *The Rake's Progress* at the Glyndebourne Festival in the summer of 1975. I took this opportunity to work in a different medium when they asked me, and immediately everything became fresher."

In retrospect Hockney recognizes that one of the ways in which things became fresher was that stage design sprang him into a world of multiple and moving perspectives—sprang him, that is, clear of the constricting ensnarements of traditional one-point perspective. One painting he did during this period as a sort of spinoff from the opera, a product of his extensive researches into Hogarth's original *Rake's Progress* engravings, was a color rendition (1975) of the black-and-white engraving that Hogarth had provided as the frontispiece for an obscure treatise on perspective by one John Kerby (Fig. 22). "The original etching [*sic*] was a kind of visual joke, all about common mistakes in perspective," Hockney recalls, "and I found it vastly amusing. The perspective was, of course, all wrong, but what was fascinating was that it still worked as a picture. So I made my painting, although at the time I did it, I did not yet realize what that painting was all about. It took

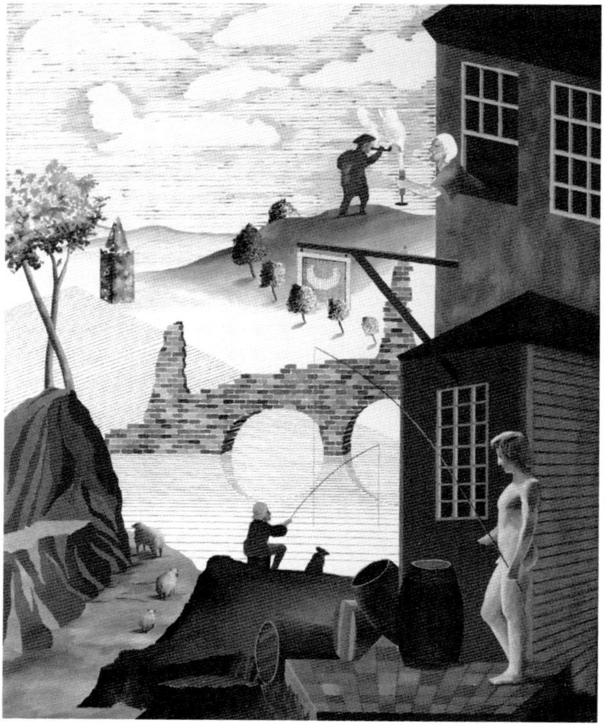

FIG 22 David Hockney, *Kerby (After Hogarth) Useful Knowledge,* 1975.

me almost ten years to understand how, for instance, the reverse perspective in the foreground, far from being a mistake, gives the image greater reality."

The mid- and late seventies were the period when Hockney was becoming increasingly involved with Picasso and with cubism, but that involvement was only gradually and grudgingly revealing its lessons. In the meantime Hockney was continuing to try to make his paintings work.

"I'd moved to Los Angeles and was working on a painting of the view outside my studio on Santa Monica Boulevard," Hockney recalls. "And it wasn't working [Fig. 23]. It was still stuffy, still asphyxiated by that sense of supposedly 'real' perspective. Eventually I gave it up. At the same time, though, I'd now moved up here to this house in the Hollywood Hills, and I began a painting depicting the drive down to the studio. (This was before we built this studio up here, so I was work-

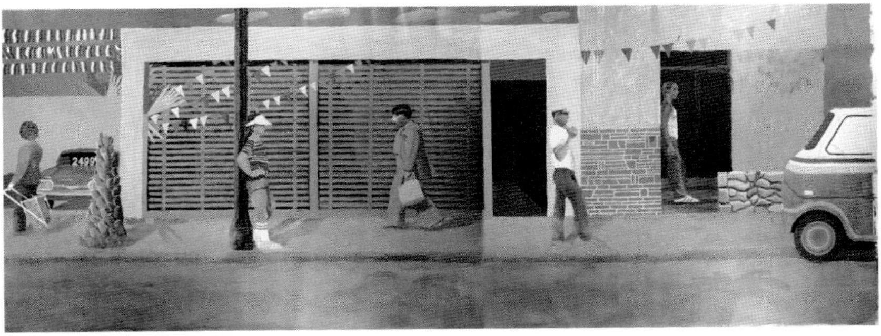

FIG 23 David Hockney, *Santa Monica Blvd.,* 1978–80.

ing down there and driving there each morning.) The moment I moved up here into the hills, wiggly lines began appearing in my paintings. The only wiggly lines that I'd had in my L.A. paintings before that were those on water. Buildings, roads, sidewalks were all straight lines, because that's what L.A. looks like in the flatlands: long straight roads, right angles, cubes. So anyway, I now began to paint this *Mulholland Drive* too, down there in the studio (see Plate 1). The one which I could see right out the window wasn't working, but this other one which I was painting from memory—the memory of the drive down—was beginning to work. You see, it was all about movement and shifting views—although at the time I didn't yet fully understand the implications of such a moving focus."

In *Mulholland Drive,* "drive" is a verb.

"So that *Mulholland Drive* was working," Hockney continued, "whereas *Santa Monica Boulevard* was not. And with *Santa Monica Boulevard,* I now understand, the problem was photography. I think it was necessary for me in a sense to destroy photography—or anyway what I thought photography was—to refute the claims it was making in order to be able to change for myself the whole notion of a painting's being real, of what is real in the world of a painting. It's taken a long time; it took me over five years. I had no idea it would take so long, not that I minded. I mean when people said I was wasting my time, I could care less. What I was learning was amazing to me. I realized more and more what you could do, how you could chop up space, how you could play inside the space, that only by playing could you make it come alive, and that it only became real when it came to life."

"We've spoken about a lot of this before," Hockney pointed out, referring to our conversations at the time of the *Cameraworks* volume. "So we needn't go over it all again. But the principal point, I suppose, is that the major problem with traditional perspective, as it was developed in fifteenth-century European painting and persists to this day in the approach of most standard photography, is that it stops time. For perspective to be fixed, time has stopped and hence space has become frozen, petrified. Perspective takes away the body of the viewer. You have a fixed point, you have no movement; in short, you are not there, really. That is the problem. Photography hankers after the condition of the neutral observer. But there can be no such thing as a neutral observer. For something to be seen, it has to be looked at by somebody, and any true and real depiction should be an account of the experience of that looking. In that sense it must deeply involve an observer whose body somehow has to be brought back in."

As far as Hockney is concerned, the initial cubist achievement was to make this case with devastating finality at the very moment of photography's apparent triumph. It has taken years for the implications of that achievement to filter through, and indeed most cultural observers, not to speak of the vast majority of average citizens in the world of vision, have still failed to grasp those implications. "Most people, when you say, 'realism,' still think you're talking about a certain way of seeing from a distance and in good, orthodox perspective," Hockney explains. "When you say, 'cubism,' they think you're talking about a particular historical style, a kind of painting, say, that was popular for a few years over half a century ago. I think one could mount a certain case against the Museum of Modern Art for helping to perpetuate that fallacy, for diluting the effects of cubism's visual revolution by encapsulating it, confining it inside the walls of a museum (and even then, only certain walls in certain rooms, devoted to a particular historical moment), as if it need have no effect outside, as if movies or television or photography or politics or life could simply go on without someday having to be cubified. A while back, I was reading Hilton Kramer's review in the *New Criterion* of the core installation at the new MoMA, and at one point he described the room containing both Picasso's *Demoiselles d'Avignon* [1907] and his *Boy Leading a Horse* [1905–6] and almost in passing he referred to the *Boy Leading a Horse* as 'more realistic' [Figs. 24 and 25]. Well, that's, of course, what most people think. (You can

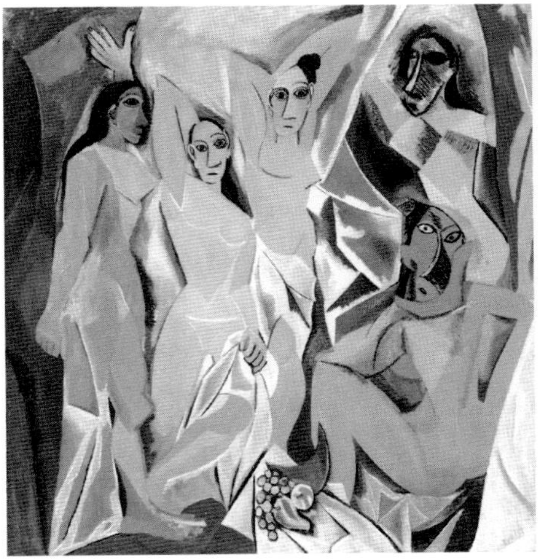

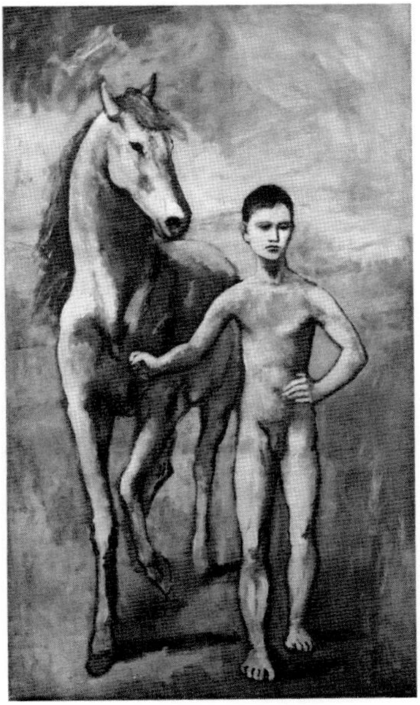

FIG 24 Pablo Picasso, *Les Demoiselles d'Avignon*, 1907.

FIG 25 Pablo Picasso, *Boy Leading a Horse*, 1905–6.

imagine if even Hilton Kramer talks like that, what some high school teacher in Kansas is telling his students.) But it isn't actually. That's the point. It isn't. And of course, this obviously means it's still hard to see. No matter how much *Les Demoiselles,* for example, gets praised as 'a great revolution in painting,' the revolution has still not truly arrived yet in the sense that it's still not readable as being the more realistic painting, which it undoubtedly is. Juan Gris said that cubism wasn't a style, it's a way of life, and I subscribe to that."

Hockney then referred, as he is given to doing often, to a book he'd been reading recently, in this case Pierre Daix's *Le Cubisme de Picasso.* Daix makes a similar point about the need to avoid seeing cubism in terms of "ephemeral fashions and short-lived schools" and then goes on to relate the power of its revolution "to the fact that physics was simultaneously destroying our three-dimensional space-time perception."[1] During the latter stages of his photocollage activity, Hockney now explained, he had himself been increasingly drawn to the terrain of modern physics.

"I was at a friend's house in Canada," he recalled, "and I was just browsing through some of his books about physics, and in one of them there were just two or three sentences that got me going. Coming back, I picked up several other books, and I found to my amazement that I could read them and follow their arguments. I mean, quantum physics is something way outside my ordinary understanding or involvement, but I quickly found incredible connections with the sorts of things I was concerned about. For instance, in the old Newtonian view of the world, in Newtonian physics, it's as if the world exists outside of us. It's over there, out there, it works mechanically, and it will do so with or without us. In short, we're really not part of nature; it virtually comes to that. Whereas modern physics has increasingly thrown that model into question and shown how it cannot be. Mr. Einstein makes things more human by making measurement at least relative to us, or anyway, to some observer; the supposedly neutral viewpoint is obliterated. There can be no measurement without a measurer. Heisenberg's Uncertainty Principle is, of course, highly technical and specialized. It deals with a paradox in particle physics, showing how if you attempt to measure the velocity of a given particle you won't be able to identify its exact location and vice versa. Previous to this, of course, science believed that given enough technical advancement, it would eventually be able to measure anything, but Heisenberg showed that this was not just a problem of not yet having the right measuring devices but that the problem was inherent in the nature of physical reality itself. The old conception of scientific inquiry had gone on as though we could measure the world as if we weren't in it. Heisenberg showed that the observer, in effect, affects that which he is observing, so that some of those old borders and boundaries begin to blur, just as they do in cubism.

"But perhaps my greatest excitement along these lines," Hockney continued, "came from reading a fairly recent book by a physicist named David Bohm, entitled *Wholeness and the Implicate Order.* Just a second."

Hockney bounded out of his easy chair—out of the studio, down to his house, returning a few minutes later flipping through an obviously well-thumbed copy of the book. "Here, listen to this." He proceeded to read a long passage from Bohm's introduction.

"The notion that the one who thinks (the Ego) is at least in principle completely separate from and independent of the reality that he thinks about," Bohm writes (and Hockney read), "is, of course, firmly embedded in our . . . tradition. . . . General experience . . . along with a great deal of . . . scientific knowledge . . . suggests . . . that such a division cannot be maintained consistently."

After he'd read several paragraphs further into the text in a state of growing animation,[2] Hockney put down the book, thoroughly invigorated. "You can see why I was so excited," he said. "This insistence on the need to break down borders, to entertain the interconnectedness of things and of ourselves with things: the notion that in science today it is no longer possible to have ideas about reality without taking our own consciousnesses into account. And beyond that, just the language, which Bohm shares with a lot of other physicists. They're always talking about 'overall worldview,' the need for 'new horizons' or 'wider perspectives' or 'a new picture of reality'—all these visual metaphors which a painter of pictures can understand and which have relevance for how he thinks about his own pictures. There's that famous phrase of Gombrich's about the triumph of Renaissance perspective—'We have conquered reality'—which has always seemed to me such a Pyrrhic victory, again, as if reality were somehow separate from us and the world now hopelessly dull because everything was known and accounted for. These physicists, by contrast, were suggesting a much more dynamic situation, and I realized how deeply what they were saying had to do with how we depict the world, not what we depict but the way we depict it."

I asked Hockney whether he'd shown much interest in science in his school days.

"Not particularly," he replied. "Not really. I was good at mathematics, but I think it was just the playfulness that attracted me. I didn't do too much with it though. I think I took a rather general view of the sciences as somewhat cold and objective. I was going to be an artist, not a scientist, and those were two completely different categories. Finding out that they're not that different has been *very* exciting for me. The more I've read of mathematicians and physicists, the more engrossed I've become. They really seem like artists to me. One's struck how it's almost a notion of beauty which seems to be guiding them, how at the frontiers of inquiry, contemporary physics even seems to be approaching and acknowledging eternal mysteries. Science is moving toward art, not art toward science. Of course, in an earlier time one spoke of the arts and sciences together, in one breath. Nowadays in the paper you get 'Arts and Leisure.' That just shows how far behind the paper is, as usual. But scientists and artists have all kinds of things to say to each other now."

He suddenly laughed. "There's something else I want to show you," he said, getting up and walking over to a long countertop over to the side, rummaging around for a bit, and returning with another book, this time *The Renaissance Rediscovery of Linear Perspective,* by Samuel Y. Edgerton Jr.

"Here. I was just reading this this morning. Listen to this." He read another long passage,[3] in which Edgerton started out by suggesting that the invention of linear perspective had been partly responsible for setting the context in which Newtonian physics could both flourish and then, with the invention of progressively more "complex machinery" (also made possible in part by the existence of linear perspective), be superseded by "the new era of Einsteinian outer space." Edgerton concluded by predicting that this new era might one day come to invalidate linear perspective itself: "Surely in some future century," Hockney read, "when artists are among those journeying throughout the universe, they will be encountering and endeavoring to depict experiences impossible to understand, let alone render, by the application of a suddenly obsolete linear perspective."

Hockney set the book down. "A lot of good stuff there," he said. "The reason I laughed, though, is that last paragraph. I mean, I guess I hold with Buckminster Fuller's comment, you know, when as an old man he was asked if he was sorry that he would never live long enough to experience travel in outer space and he replied, 'Sir, we *are* in outer space.' The idea that outer space is over there and we're not part of it is silly. We're already journeying throughout the universe. It's like how I can never seem to get interested in space movies, because they always seem to me to be about transport and nothing else. Well, transport is not going to take us to the edge of the universe, though an awareness in our heads might. Transport won't be able to do it; it's like relying on buses. But the Einsteinian revolution, like the cubist, has already done it. Now we just have to open our eyes and see."

Hockney's comments, especially about Heisenberg, reminded me of a point the late anthropologist Jacob Bronowski made in his TV series, *The Ascent of Man.* Crouching down in an open field at Auschwitz, digging with his arm into the muck and mud of the place, he pointed out that in one sense Heisenberg during the 1930s had been proving the impossibility of absolute certainty and conversely the need for tolerance of multiple viewpoints (Bronowski even called Heisenberg's the Principle of Tolerance) at the very moment that Hitler was propounding his dogma of absolute certainty.

I mentioned Bronowski's formulation to Hockney, who was silent for a moment and then took it a step further. "It's not just that," he said, "because Heisenberg's and Einstein's physics actually led in two distinct directions. One of them, the more creative aspect, advanced this wider vision, the tolerance for multiple perspectives, which we've been discussing; at the same time though the other, the older, more straightforwardly technical side, was utilizing some of the ideas simply to make bigger and bigger weapons for our old myopic viewpoint of the world.

"Cubism is important for a lot of reasons," he continued, "not the least of which is that it points the way to a greater tolerance and interdependence of perspectives in a world where failure to learn such lessons could have terribly dire consequences."

From twentieth-century physics it was an obvious progression to fourteenth-century Chinese scrolls, obvious to Hockney anyway. "I want to show you something else," he said, returning to the long countertop, rummaging about again, and coming back with another book and a long rectangular box.

"Around the same time I was beginning to get into all the physics books," Hockney recounted, "I happened to be browsing in the bookshop at the Walker Art Center in Minneapolis—let's see, this would have been late 1983 or so—and I came upon a book called *The Principles of Chinese Painting,* by George Rowley, very dull cover. I thought, 'Well, most Chinese painting looks the same to me.' But I opened it, noticed the chapter headings, and one of them was called 'Moving Focus.' So I started to read it, bought the book, brought it back to the hotel, and got more and more excited."

What was exciting him about it?

"Well, the attack on perspective. You realized it was an attack on perspective—it was all about the spectator's being in the picture, not outside it—an attack on the window idea, that Renaissance notion of the painting's being as if slotted into a wall, which I'd always felt implied the wall and hence separation from the world. The Chinese landscape artists, with their scrolls, had found a way to transcend that difficulty. In my own photocollages, some of the ones I'd done on my trip to Japan earlier that year, I'd been pushing the notion of the observer's head swiveling about in a world which was moving in time, but I'd really only just begun to try and deal with how to portray movement of the observer's whole body across space. And that's precisely what these Chinese landscape artists had mastered, according to Rowley. Here, listen."

Hockney proceeded to read me a passage that was indeed highly suggestive.[4]

"You can see how relevant that sort of talk was to my concerns at that point. A short while later I happened to be in London, and I went to see some of the scrolls at the British Museum. And then I came back to New York to work on some prints up at Ken Tyler's studio up in Bedford Village, about fifty miles north of New York City, and I'd occasionally come into the city and visit the Chinese scrolls department at the Metropolitan. There was a very nice curator there named Mike Hearn, who was assigned to show me some scrolls. That first day I got very excited and was telling him why, and that was getting him excited because normally, he said, he's only showing scrolls to people in the Chinese scroll business, and I was talking about something altogether else. Most of them, the connoisseurs in that field, talk about the exquisite brushwork and the hand. Perfectly good things to talk about—in fact, I saw a direct connection in that regard to the late Picasso, in which all the activity of painting is made visible, not hidden in layers as in a Dufy, but all very clear and transparent—but it was the way of seeing that fascinated me. Meant the viewer participated. Here, look."

Hockney reached for the rectangular box. "This is a reproduction of a Chinese scroll, which the Japanese have started to make recently. You'll see why they have to make a reproduction, because it's not possible to see this in a book, or for that matter in a museum, where it's all spread out and the effect is destroyed. You have to be able to unroll it in your own hands over time. This would have been a beautiful ivory or ebony box; in reproduction you get wood. Once you open it, instead of an elaborate silk thing covering it, you get this bit of nylon. And then here is the scroll: something, you realize, is going to unroll. Instead of an electric motor, I will provide the energy, and I can go back and forth. This is a reproduction of a fourteenth-century landscape done in what the Chinese considered all-color, which is black and white." Hockney held the two staffs of the scroll about eighteen inches apart and began unfurling, loosening one side and picking up the slack with the other. "The point is, your body moves. See, you start here looking down on a village from a hilltop. And then, as you alter the edges of the picture, you've moved on in time, and see, here, now, we've moved down into the valley, skirting the edge of the village, and now here we're looking up toward a mountaintop and, here, moving further—without any break, without panels, rather in a continuous flow of lines—we're now on top of that mountain looking down onto this lake. . . ." Hockney continued for a while, narrating the journey.

"There you are," he said, concluding the demonstration. "You've walked *through* a landscape. It's a profoundly different experience from a Western landscape, which is still based on your standing stock still, really.

"Anyway, you can see why I became so fascinated. Mike Hearn showed me thirty or forty of them. The people there at the Met were themselves getting overjoyed, you know, at a practicing contemporary artist taking an interest in their arcane discipline. I ended up giving a little lecture to the staff there, you know, just twenty people or so. I think they believe they're in a backwater in a sense; I mean, obviously loving it but suspecting that everybody else thought it was a backwater, and I think they almost did themselves. And here I was telling them that these scrolls had the greatest possible relevance to the most contemporary of concerns."[5]

One thing that began to form in my mind as Hockney spoke was an analogy to the initial situation of the cubists. Back in 1907, when Picasso and Braque had wanted to break free of the tyranny of European Renaissance perspective, they'd drawn on non-European African sources. Here Hockney at a similar moment in his career was drawing on non-European Chinese sources.

"Yeah," Hockney concurred, when I tried the notion out on him. "They're actually the same source in a way though. If you think about the beginning of 'modern' painting, with Manet, what you see there is the beginnings of the influence of the East: Japanese prints being seen in Paris around that time and the artists being exposed to another way of seeing. Perspective was driving them crazy in a sense at the Academy and with academic narrative painting. Perspective was making it ridiculous. And here they were exposed to another way of measuring, of seeing, and they got excited: Manet, Van Gogh, and so forth. And the Japanese after all derive from the much older Chinese traditions. A generation and a half later the cubists were similarly drawn to the Africans. So that the beginnings of modern art in Europe are fundamentally anti-European."

I pointed out that ironically this was happening at the very moment of peak European colonization and subjugation of those non-European cultures.

"Wasn't it Ruskin who'd said just a couple generations earlier that there wasn't a piece of art in the whole of Africa outside Egypt?" Hockney responded. "Well, obviously Picasso didn't think so. Everything outside Europe now began to have a major influence on the trajectory of European art. They saw a fresher way, a way of making the observer participate more. *Les Demoiselles d'Avignon,* with that strange evocation of those African masks, draws you into the picture: you as the observer have to start doing things to reconstruct the space. You are getting a more vivid depiction of the *experience* of reality. And yes, for me, those Chinese scrolls at that moment helped me clear to a new way of constructing such experience into my own work.

Hockney came back to Los Angeles and in rapid succession produced a large gouache on paper portraying a visit to the Echo Park home of his friends Mo and Lisa McDermott (1984) and then the major two-panel oil painting of a visit with his friends Christopher Isherwood and Don Bachardy in Santa Monica (Plate 12), both works heavily influenced by the Chinese scrolls and saturated with the temper of Uncertainty.

"In retrospect the gouache was still somewhat crude," Hockney explains, "but with both of these works I was trying to create a painting where the viewer's eye could be made to move in certain ways, stop in certain places, move on, and in so doing, reconstruct the space across time for itself. I was combining lessons from both the Chinese scrolls and my study of cubism. I mean, unlike the scrolls these were going to be large images meant to be seen all at once, but the thing was, what I was aiming for was that in another sense they wouldn't be able to be seen all at once after all. They were filled with incident, but whenever you focused on any single detail everything else blurred into a sort of complex abstraction of shapes and colors, and the image as a whole was always primarily abstraction. This sense of multiple simultaneous perspectives was something I'd, of course, honed during my work on the photocollages.

"As I say," Hockney continued, "the *Visit with Christopher and Don* was considerably more complex." We were looking up at a large photographic reproduction of the two-paneled canvas (the original was then in storage in New York). Following the usual disclaimers regarding the hopeless inadequacy of any photographic reproduction's conveying the experience of a large work, Hockney proceeded to use the photo as the basis for his description. "You see, it's meant to be read from left to right unlike the Chinese scrolls, although there's a kind of tribute to the scrolls in a sort of prologue, the yellow strip at the top of the canvas, moving from right to left, which represents Adelaide Drive in Santa Monica. When I drive up there, I always know when to stop because of the big palm tree, and then there, at the number 145, there's the little driveway where they park their two cars—or anyway, used to. (Dear Christopher has passed on in the meantime.) From that position you look out over Santa Monica Canyon, which is painted in reverse perspective, so it clearly places you up there looking down. You then come down the steps, and they're painted that way because it's not you looking at the steps from afar, you are actually moving down them as you approach the entryway. You come into the living room, and there are those two wicker chairs, which you might perhaps recognize from the double portrait I did of Christopher and Don back in 1968 or from some of the more recent photocollages. Anyway, from the living room you can look out the window and you see the view of the canyon again, which means you've moved, you have to have, to be seeing it. We then make a little detour here to the left into Don's studio, and there's Don drawing. You can go upstairs and downstairs; you see the same view again from two different windows. Then coming back across the living room, moving rightward, you walk down a corridor, past the bedroom. If you notice, the television set, everything, is actually in reverse perspective, meaning you're moving past it, seeing first the front and then the back. And then you walk right to the end, into Christopher's studio and even past him, to the very end, at which point you're looking back on Christopher at his typewriter. You know you're looking back because he's looking out through his window, and it's the same view of the canyon. So there, you've reconstructed the space, and now your eye is free to roam about from room to room, taking in more details.

"It was a very difficult painting to accomplish," Hockney continued. "The problem was how to prevent the eye from stopping, from getting stuck. For instance, that's why both Don and Christopher are rendered transparently. When you look at Christopher, you see him, but when you move along to the bedroom and you're looking at the bed, he dissolves in a sense into patterns of green and blue and red paint. If they'd been rendered solidly, your eye would have tended to fixate on them. Similarly I had to work through several versions before I came to understand that you couldn't have too many verticals or horizontals. (There are too many in the other one, the gouache of Mo and Lisa's; that's one of the problems with it.) In fact, every time a right angle appeared, it seemed to stop the eye's moving. It's all very carefully constructed, even though it might look like chaos at first."

I returned to an earlier question. Didn't this particular oil painting, for example, represent a culmination of sorts, a more significant achievement than some of the same period's works in other media?

"I don't know," Hockney replied. "I don't think so. I mean, you're asking me a question I wouldn't normally think about too much. What you're aware of, I suppose, as the years pass, you might recognize that certain works were key works in that you realized that you really discovered something there.

"For instance, the photocollage of walking in a Zen garden, from 1983. It was the most radical one up to that point, and it's the most radical one in the *Cameraworks* volume. I'd first done that earlier version of sitting in a Zen garden [see Fig. 16], where the sense of perspective was very strong—the rectangle of the rock garden almost read like a triangle, the perspectival V was so strong. And I started gnawing on this question of how one might present the garden as the rectangle it actually was. I mean, in drawing it would have been easy, and I suppose that with a camera one could have rented a helicopter and shot it from above looking down, but any picture you got that way would have mainly been about being in a helicopter, and I wanted to do something about the rectangular quality of this garden. And then it dawned on me that if I moved along the length of one rim of the garden and snapped a row of shots every few steps, scanning from my feet on upward toward the far rim, I'd eventually be able to solve my problem. And as you know, when I got back to L.A. and had the shots developed and assembled the collage [see Fig. 17], I grew very excited. My first thought was that I'd made a photograph

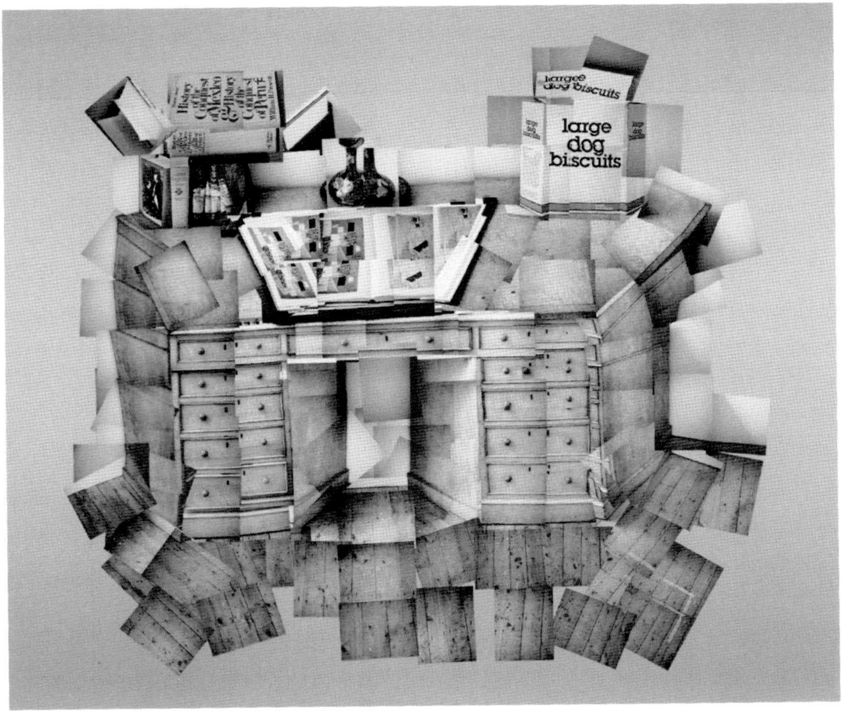

FIG 26 David Hockney, *The Desk, July 1st, 1984.*

without perspective. Comparing it with the earlier collage of sitting in a Zen garden, this one of walking seemed to me truer, not the truth, but truer. And I also realized that with this one the viewer was moving through space."

Were there other breakthroughs?

"Well," Hockney continued, "the Zen garden collages came before the Chinese scrolls. A year later, after the scrolls, I did *The Desk* [1984, Fig. 26], and that was a very important piece for me because there I was really learning to establish an object in space." He pointed to the poster version of the desk collage tacked to the wall. "As you can see, it's in reverse perspective, which means you're moving about it, seeing it from one side, then the other, coming up close and looking down on it, and this opened up all sorts of possibilities for me. I'd done a space, which was the Zen garden, and now a solid object, this desk, and now the challenge was to find some way of putting them together: the object inside the space. That took time too, but in a way that's what the *Visit with Christopher and Don* painting is about and then later the big *Pearblossom Highway* photocollage as well."

Hockney continued looking up at the poster of *The Desk.* "The thing about reverse perspective . . ." he began and then paused. "I mean, my argument has always been that in traditional perspective infinity is a long way away and you can never meet up with it. Whereas if you reverse perspective, infinity is everywhere and you are part of it. There's a vast difference in the two viewpoints, a totally different way of looking at the world. You haven't just reversed a little game, you've reversed a whole attitude toward life and physical reality.

"Furthermore," he continued, "the traditional Renaissance way is by no means the natural one. You have to be rigorously trained into accepting its conventions; the misperceptions have to be drilled into you. Look at how a child draws a house—you get the front, the sides, the back, the backyard tree, everything all jumbled together—and then the teacher comes and says, 'Wrong, wrong. You can't see all those things at once. Do it this way instead.' But in a sense the child was right in the first place; his version was more alive, and the teacher's is a more impoverished rendition. Or, for instance, a child draws a landscape, and he draws the earth at the bottom of the piece of paper, a brown line, and the sky at the top, a blue line, and a tree in the middle, perched on the brown line of the earth. And the teacher comes along and says, 'No, no. Wrong. You don't need two lines because, well, there's only one line, in the middle, where the sky and the earth meet.' Which is true in a way, but it also fails to acknowledge the piece of paper. What the child has done is taken that piece of paper and said, 'When you look up at the sky, that's the top of the page, and down at the ground is the bottom. And that is an exact translation of sky and earth made onto a piece of paper. The other way you're looking through the piece of paper, as if it weren't there. But the child knows it is there and is dealing with that surface, at least until the teacher teaches him not to see it."

As Hockney was speaking, I was again reminded of the childlike quality of much of his early work from his Boy Wonder period in the late fifties and early sixties. I asked him whether he'd been dealing with these sorts of issues even then. "Not in so many words," he replied, "not in these terms. But I have recently been looking back over some of that work, and there are certain striking continuities, things which I've only just now become able to see.

"One of them, for instance, occurred to me a while back when I was reading David Bohm's book, where he talks about how borders must be broken—'for every border is a division or break'—and it occurred to me that probably the most consistent theme in my work is actually that. For instance, there's a little painting from 1962. What happened was that a friend of mine had bought this very elaborate little wooden frame, and I said, 'What are you going to do with that?' He said he was going to put a mirror in it or something, and I said, 'Oh, don't do that. I'll make a painting for it; it seems such a shame, such a beautiful frame.' But what I painted in the frame was a little man, wedged in tight, who's touching all four sides of the picture, and he's shouting, 'Help!' In short, he's really trying to get out of the picture frame [Fig. 27].

"Or think of all those early paintings of curtains. People say, 'Oh, they're about the theater.' But you can also read them in another way, for the figures are standing in front of the curtain, which means, again, you're breaking an edge. There's the edge around the four sides, but there's also the implicit edge in front, the glass separating the painting world from the world of the observer. And in some of those early paintings—for instance, *Play within a Play,* from 1963—the figures in the painting are desperately trying to cross over that boundary [Fig. 28].

"The theme occurs throughout my work," Hockney went on. "For instance, in the stage designs. In the last piece of theater work I did before this *Tristan,* the Stravinsky triple bill back in 1981 at the Met, we did *The Rite of Spring* followed by *Le Rossignol* followed by *Oedipus Rex.* And what we did was, *The Rite of Spring* was staged way at the back of the stage; *Le Rossignol* was almost like Italian theater, with the proscenium all around it; and by the time we got to *Oedipus* to make it like Greek theater, we lit up the proscenium, which had the effect of making that into the set; the whole theater becomes the set, which again is breaking a border, breaking an edge. And you begin to realize what edges do: they're not just showing us things; they're cutting off far more than they're showing us. The edge is the

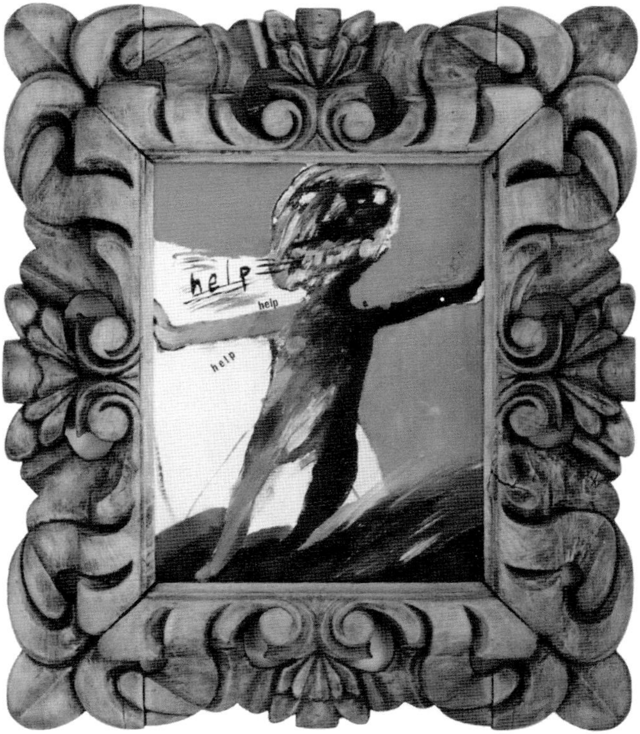

FIG 27 David Hockney, *Help*, 1962.

problem. It's the major problem we have to deal with. I mean, it will always be there, but it can be softened with different ways of looking, a more complex image, and that's what we now need to do."

Back in *Play within a Play*, what Hockney had been playing with was the notion of a figure—the painted rendition of a character looking remarkably like himself—trying to step out from the rigidly perspectival world (note the floorboards) of the painting. He can't do it; his face literally gets smudged up against the imaginary glass of the Renaissance windowpane. In his latest work, though, it's as if Hockney had reversed the terms of the problem. The world of the painting no longer has to get out to reach the observer, because the observer has gone in.

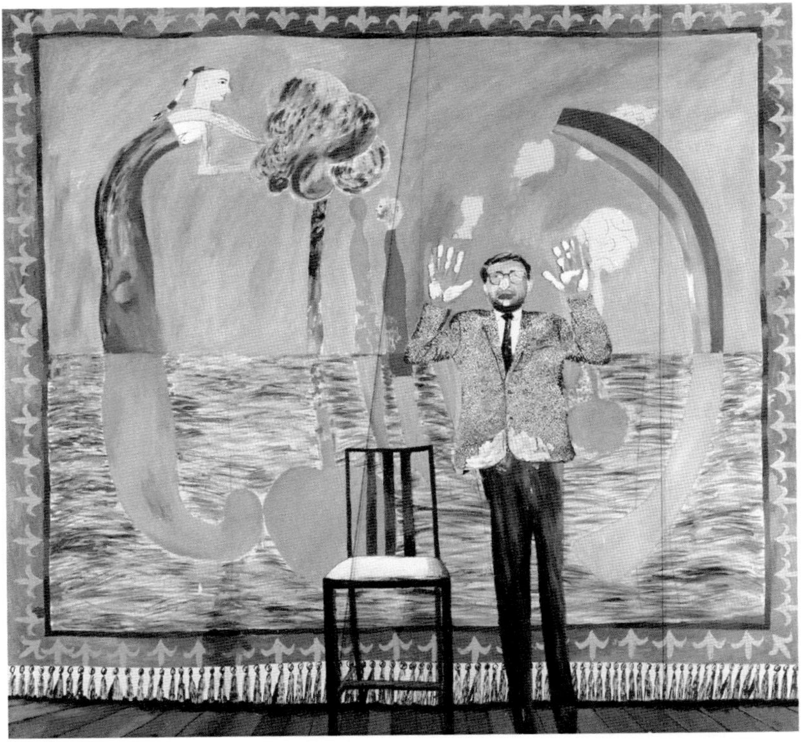

FIG 28 David Hockney, *Play within a Play,* 1963.

"In *Pearblossom Highway,*" Hockney now commented, "which is far and away the most complex and the most successful of the photocollages I've done so far (see Plate 11)—it took me over nine days just to photograph and another two weeks to assemble—the results are quite powerful, I think, in the sense that you're deeply aware of the flat surface but at the same time you start making a space in your head. And yet the space is not the illusionistic kind where you feel, 'Oh, I could walk into that,' which is the old type of illusion and sort of a cheat or a contradiction anyway. You're saying, 'Oh, I could walk into that'—only if you tried, you'd kill yourself or you'd hurt yourself anyway; you'd be walking into a brick wall. No, here you don't feel you need to walk into it because you're already in it.

"That's what my most recent work has been about essentially," he continued, "*Pearblossom Highway,* the Home Made Prints, the paintings which I've been able to do the last few weeks based on some of the lessons about surface I've gleaned in doing the photocopy prints. Take a look at *Pearblossom,* and then take a look at a standard photographic rendition of the same scene [Fig. 29], and you realize that you're beginning to deal with a more vivid way of depicting space and rendering the experience of space."

I'd been meaning to ask Hockney something almost since the moment of my arrival (although I had been a bit shy about doing so), for there had been a striking change in his physical appearance since the last time I'd seen him several years earlier; he was conspicuously wearing a hearing aid. Actually he was wearing two hearing aids, one in each ear. And now I did ask.

"Well," he replied, "I first realized I was losing my hearing back in 1979. I was giving a seminar in San Francisco, and I kept having to tell the people in the back of the room to repeat their questions; I couldn't hear them. I could see that everybody else could hear them, and I thought, this is strange. I went to have my hearing checked, and they told me I'd already lost twenty percent. They gave me a little hearing aid, but I didn't use it much, didn't think about it much, and eventually even lost the thing. But the hearing loss was having an effect apparently—I was getting more antisocial, in a way, because I just couldn't hear people—and it was getting worse. Sounds were getting both dimmer and more blurred. So in 1984 I went to some specialists, and they all told me the same thing, that it would continue to get gradually worse, there was nothing you could do to arrest it really, but that a more sophisticated hearing aid would help. So I got one, and the moment I put it on, it was like a big muffler had been taken off my head. The guy had said either ear would do since they're both the same. So I went back, and I said, 'I think I'll take two actually.' He said not too many people put two on; they think it looks too bad, makes you look old. I said, 'I don't really care what it looks like. I'd rather hear.' I mean, I'm not vain in that way. I wanted him to make me a red one and a blue one."

Mismatched, like his socks.

"I mean," he continued, "you'd have to be daft to think that nobody's going to

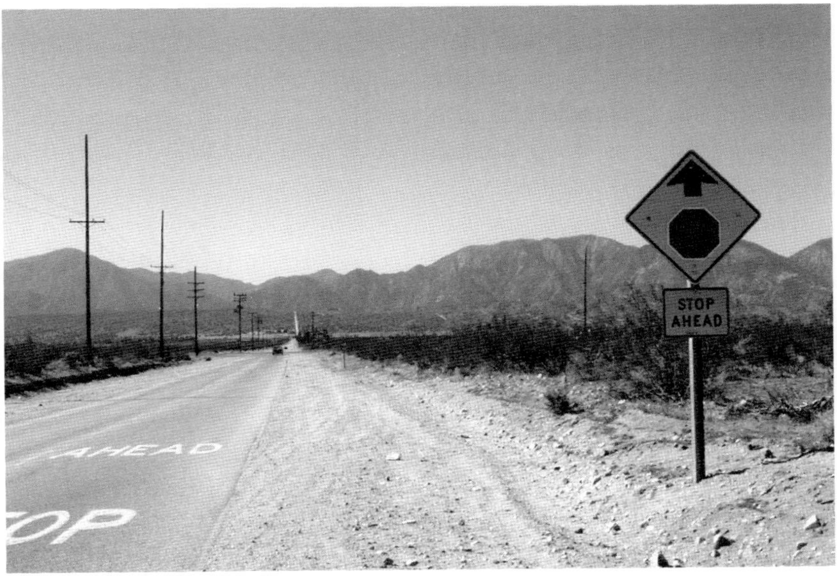

FIG 29 Pearblossom Highway, Palmdale, California, April 1986.

notice it. But who cares? People come up to me now, and they ask, 'Have you got hearing problems?' and I say, 'Well, I used to have, but I don't now.' It's made a world of difference. Everybody comments on how my body movements have changed: I don't lean over, I can lie back and listen, I don't have to be watching people's faces, lip-reading."

The first half of the 1980s, the period when Hockney was struggling with his hearing, also happens to be the time when he was becoming increasingly consumed by his renewed investigations of visual space. I asked him whether he thought there was a relation.

"Well," he said, "of course, hearing is spatial. It is spatial in its essence. It helps you define space—somebody is speaking behind you, there's a noise over to the side—it helps give you your bearings in the physical world. Surely as my hearing began to grow muffled, I was having to rely more on my vision. There's the old truism regarding blind people that they use their hearing to help locate themselves and that therefore they probably develop more acute hearing. Well, the reverse must also be true: a loss of hearing ought to lead to more acute vision and in particular visual perception of space. Ordinarily nobody would know, nobody could see the change, unless you were somebody who used vision in some particular way, say, as an artist. So, sure, I think that has been an important influence in the past several years."

At this point in our conversation Stanley came barging in. Well, "barging" is a bit strong. Trotting? Scampering? Slip-and-sliding? There was a lot of yelping involved. He was still a pup, and coordination was not his strong suit. Hockney scooped the baby dachshund into his arms, nuzzled him close to his cheek, and then carried him back over to the photocopying machine to have a look at the just completed portrait.

"This is little Stanley," he explained, "named after the Great Stanley, of course." David cocked his head in the direction of a small oil portrait, hanging on the wall, of Laurel and Hardy. That portrait was the work of David's father, who'd been a huge fan. "Everybody's been surprised I got a dog. All my friends are shocked. I don't know why. But one reason I never had animals was that for many years I lived like a gypsy—I was always going off—and you can't, for example, take a dog in and out of England. Even the queen can't. So I didn't even entertain the thought. But recently my friend Ian got a little pup, which I loved—did a portrait. And then a few months later, Ian said, 'He's going to have some little brothers in another litter.' And suddenly I thought, maybe I'll get a dog. So I went over, picked Stanley out—he was only about this big—brought him home. He looked frightened to death. I put a rubber ball in front of him, he just stood there looking at it, and I did a painting of that. At first I thought, 'Oh my God, what have I done? I've made a terrible mistake. I'm going to have to fuss around. I won't be able to go anywhere.' But the problem is, within three days you've fallen in love with this little creature, you realize how, you know, he's relying on me, he wants to sleep in the bed, he puts his little head on the pillow next to mine. Clearly he either thinks I'm a big dog or he's a little person. I don't know which. But I love him actually."

It was interesting, I pointed out, reflecting on Hockney's comment about his former gypsy life and recalling his earlier allusion to Buckminster Fuller, that at the very moment his work was shooting off into outer space, as it were, he was taking on anchors that were going to tie him down to home.

"That's it," Hockney agreed.

And Stanley was the icon that represented . . .

"That makes me stay here."

He was able to deal with Stanley because he'd achieved that centeredness?

"I've got an excuse to people: Stanley is here. I can't possibly leave Stanley. And actually I've got a lot to do. There are a hundred things I want to be doing. I'm going back into painting; I can feel it coming on strong. I want to stay in one place now. It's mad to always be going off. I'm going to be fifty next year . . ."

Was turning fifty going to be important for him? The retrospective was going to be touring during his fiftieth year.

"Well, I don't see it as a retrospective. I just see it as work done up till now, that's all. Fifty doesn't make any difference to me, although I did laugh at Nick Wilder's comment the other day. He went to somebody's fiftieth birthday, and they said to him, 'Oh, come on, fifty's only middle age,' and he said, 'How many do you know of a hundred?'

"But I'd rather be isolated to do what I want to do now. There's a point when you're young and you need other artists; you feed off other people's ideas as well. But there comes a point when you have to sort stuff out for yourself; you don't need the stimulus anymore. You've had enough actually. I'm aware of that now. I've quite enough stimulus these days from myself. I also enlighten myself. I don't mind if I never go out. I don't mind if I never get invited anywhere. I amuse myself. Especially with Stanley. Because I need to talk to myself out loud, and before I felt a bit of a fool. So naturally Stanley can hear all the lectures now. He listens, and he keeps coming back for more.

"Like I say, one of the main reasons I used to travel was to get away from all the nattering. But I won't have to be worrying about the natterers anymore. Stanley's going to growl at them when they come to the door."

CHAPTER 3

liebestod

A FINAL *TRISTAN*

(1996)

We are nearing the end of act 3 of Wagner's *Tristan,* and David Hockney has the volume jacked way up.

Intently hunched over the control panel, facing his intricately fashioned miniature stage model—one of three such lightboxes (one for each of the three acts, on a scale of one to twelve, or one inch to the foot) mounted atop adjoining flatbed tables in the hangarlike space of his otherwise darkened Santa Monica Boulevard studio—Hockney is deep in preparation for the upcoming revival of his 1987 production of *Tristan und Isolde* at the L.A. Opera (slated for nine performances in the Dorothy Chandler Pavilion this January and February), and as his hand glides expertly up and down the dozens of slide knobs on his command console (each pegged to its own miniaturized bulb inside the box), he is matching Wagner's motif shifts, uncannily, light for leit (Plates 13–15).

Indeed the experience is like nothing so much as one of those "Parsifal drives" on which Hockney famously used to take visitors to his Malibu outpost, one at a time, about a decade ago, around the time of his first *Tristan*'s vernissage. You'd be sitting there in his glass-enclosed porch, sipping tea and gazing out over the roiling surf as the late afternoon sun arced toward the horizon, when Hockney, glancing up at the clock, would suddenly announce, "It's time: Let's go."

You'd follow him out to the garage, climb into the passenger seat of his fire engine red Mercedes convertible as he slid behind the wheel, lowered the top, and presently eased the car out into the flow of upstream traffic on the Pacific Coast Highway, at which point he'd take to punching a set of mysterious buttons arrayed

---

A version of this piece originally appeared, under the title "The Colors of Silence," in the *Los Angeles* magazine issue of February 1997.

along the dashboard. Suddenly music would come welling up all around you (for typically, Hockney's Mercedes was one of the very first vehicles anywhere to be fitted with what was then an experimental onboard CD player, its ten-deck platform secreted in the trunk of the car): a rousing Sousa march for starters and then (as Hockney's fingers raced authoritatively across the buttons) Bernstein, Gershwin, the "Blue Danube"—brief perfectly chosen passages from each until he veered off the main highway onto one of those steep side roads that wend their way high into the Santa Monica mountains, at which point (another hand pass over the buttons, a downshift of the gears) the music would segue into Wagner, as up and over that initial incline you'd be cruising and then down upon the first unexpected valley vista: the Entrance of the Gods into Valhalla. And so on, across that valley and up its far purpled slope, through one perfectly chosen Wagner passage after another, Hockney pacing the car just right so that Wagner's transitions seamlessly matched the road's own curves and croppings, and the constrictions and the dilations of the endlessly changing view. Mainly orchestral passages from *Parsifal,* as you looped in and among the canyons and then finally back up the main spine of the mountains for the return toward the shore. And if Hockney had managed to time things just right—and usually he had—the music itself would now be reaching its most thrilling climax yet (Siegfried's funeral), exactly one hour and twenty minutes into the drive, just as the car rounded a final bend, suddenly divulging a stupendous sudden view of one last valley at the very moment the sun was sinking behind the far darkened slope.

So that it can get to be like that, sitting beside Hockney at his control panel as he whizzes along, putting his miniature set through its lighting paces—only, louder: much louder. Tristan in his death throes swells ever more deliriously. ("What," he is singing, uncannily, "do I *hear* the light?") Louder and louder and louder. But not loud enough.

For now Hockney is really going deaf.

And after over twenty years of repeatedly taking entire auditoriumsful of opera lovers throughout the world on the sensory rides of their lives, these upcoming nine performances at the Dorothy Chandler Pavilion may well come to constitute Hockney's last such forays ever.

Tristan und Isolde: Beethoven meets Matisse.

A few minutes earlier, on the neighboring lightbox, Hockney had been demonstrating the effect he was aiming at for the incomparable love duet at the center of act 2. Tristan, King Mark's most loyal and beloved knight, has fallen hopelessly in love with the king's bride, Isolde, as she has with him, and the two contrive a secret rendezvous just outside the castle walls in the middle of the night while the rest of the royal party is off on an all-night hunt in the encircling forest. Night, in Wagner's conception throughout this opera, is the realm of true passion, blissfully oblivious to the duties of the day. And in Hockney's version, as the lovers initially approach one another, tiny lights begin to flicker all about them in an otherwise pitch-black surround: they are, we are given to feel, as if lost in a universe of their own. (Later, as the dawn begins to rise, the twinkling lights will gutter out as the deep expanse of castle wall and girdling forest gradually make themselves evident, an astonishingly beautiful and satisfying space, in Hockney's magical rendering, but at the same time one that is somehow claustrophobic, constrictive, and saturated with threat, since we all realize that at any moment the king and his party may come barging in from out of the forest onto this daytime-scandalous scene.)

"I can't *hear* the low notes anymore," Hockney sighed, disconsolate, at one point. "The cello: I know it's there, I *remember* it, but I can't hear it." Hockney's condition is genetic, progressive, and inexorable—his father gradually went stone-deaf, and his older sister has likewise been doing so, just ahead of him: there's nothing to be done. For years now Hockney has been sporting hearing aids in both ears, but their effectiveness is beginning to fall off precipitously. "I really noticed it a few weeks ago in Australia," he recounted, referring to a visit to Sydney, where he'd been supervising a revival of his 1992 staging of Richard Strauss's *Die Frau ohne Schatten.* "Whole swaths of the music: gone. And coming back, what with all those hours spent in the pressurized cabin of the jetliner, I couldn't hear a thing for a whole day. I just went to bed."

Earlier he'd shown me a suite of recent self-portraits, quick-study paintings he'd been producing over just the last few days, and they were, for Hockney, uncharacteristically glum (Fig. 30). Or not glum, exactly: dumb, or rather dumbfounded, questioning, stock-stilled, slack-jawed, stumped. I'll be stumped, they seem to say, and the stump in question is specifically the ear, one of which is conspicuously missing, as if sheared off the side of his head.

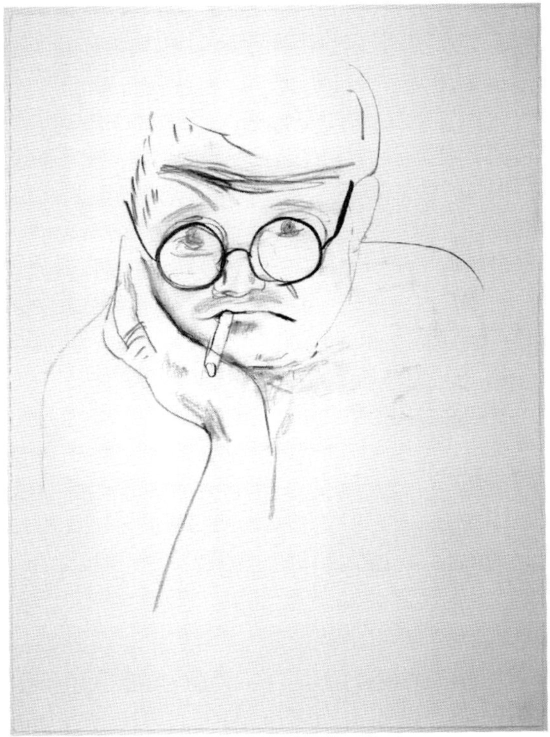

FIG 30 David Hockney,
Self-Portrait with Cigarette, 1983.

And yet such desolation—the sense of being, in a way, in a sense, at a loss—is usually a passing mood with Hockney: his is a celebratory sensibility, little given over to brooding despair. In Wagnerian terms, it is the daytime duties that truly seem to vivify him; if anything, his is more of a Mozartian presence. (One is reminded of his crisply playful staging of *The Magic Flute,* one of his first such efforts—in Glyndebourne, back in 1978—another tale of the passage from night to day, though with all the polarities reversed, such that daytime there implied not a reversion to bland conventionality but rather the hard-won achievement of blessed enlightenment.)

Beyond that, it's as if everything for Hockney—even any given diminishing sensory capacity—feeds the wider creative enterprise. It was not lost on Hockney, as early as ten years ago, around the time of the first *Tristan,* how, with hearing being spatial, a loss of hearing ought to lead to more acute vision, in particular, visual perception of space.

He made a similar point on this visit, noting how he'd recently been reading the second volume of John Richardson's biography of Picasso and had even sent Richardson a note, speculating about the possibility that Picasso may have been tone-deaf. "I mean," he explained to me, "he didn't go to concerts—Braque, by contrast went to concerts and band performances all the time—he didn't respond to music, couldn't fathom its greatness, meaning he couldn't *hear* it, it didn't *mean* anything to him. And I just find myself wondering whether such tone-deafness might help account for the amazingly confident grasp he had of chiaroscuro, as opposed to, say, Braque—the deeper sense of pictorial space in his cubism than in Braque's."

If hearing is spatial, it's temporal as well—by definition, and in a sense more radically so than vision. And if the challenge Hockney's been setting himself in almost all of his labors over the past few decades has been how to evoke (whether through photocollages, on the canvas, or across the stage) a lived sense of deep space and deep time, it's perhaps not so surprising that throughout this process, his studio work and his stage work have been in a constant state of interpenetration.

Opera, of course, has been wonderfully evocative for him in this regard—"Naturally," Hockney agrees. "After all, it is an art of time"—though his earliest stagings, back in the late seventies, still tended to a certain stylized flatness. In fact it was only with the original *Tristan* production, undertaken as his neocubist photocollage explorations were reaching their peak, that Hockney seemed to punch through to a new sense of spatial and temporal depth. He started approaching the entire project more as a lighting designer than as a set or costume man. The focus was no longer so much on creating spellbinding sets—flats, as they're called—as on raking lights across them through time, in time, of course, with the music, in an art of startling synesthesia. (There were moments in *Tristan,* and in *Turandot* after that, when the entire stage seemed to *blush,* and you, in the audience, in physiological response to the sudden barometric shift in sight and sound, blushed right back.)

All the while Hockney has been trying to find ways of introjecting this new sense of spatial depth back into his studio work. One of his more intriguing efforts in this regard was on display earlier this year at the André Emmerich Gallery in

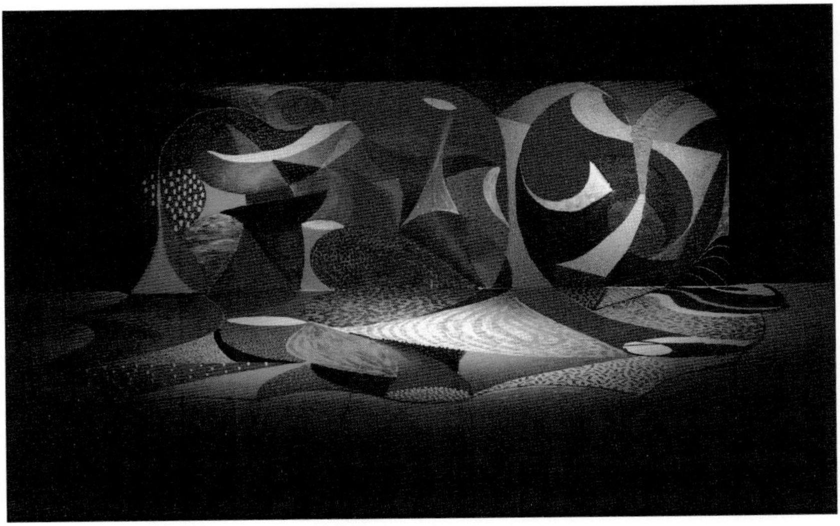

FIG 31 David Hockney, *Snails Space with Vari-lites, "Painting as Performance,"* 1995–96.

New York, a room-size installation in which Hockney had luxuriantly painted both the far wall and the intervening floor with sworls of brightly colored abstract landscapes, set against an otherwise blackened surround (Fig. 31). A bank of four highly sophisticated stage lights, recessed into the ceiling on computerized pivots, individually panned the space, their colors and densities endlessly changing in infinitesimal patterns, across a meticulously programmed ten-minute loop. Hockney dubbed the piece *Snails Space*—a marvelous pun, slurring as it does the distinction between space and pace, between three dimensions and four. An opera without sound, I remember thinking, delighted, at the time. Or else: Music for the deaf.

Hockney's most recent paintings, apart from the self-portraits, have been a series of cut-flower groupings (Plate 16), couched in a luminously clear and deepening space, and he's been talking about them as exercises leading toward a return to the two-figure paintings that once constituted the core of his work but which he largely abandoned, many years ago, in frustration over his inability at the time to break free of the straitjacket of conventional photographic space. Tristan and Isolde

(I now found myself thinking, as he described these ambitions to me), alone on the stage.

In all of these endeavors, though, Hockney has increasingly been like a man who has been forced to look listeningly. And who has heard.

The first time around with *Tristan* somebody had the bright idea of pairing Hockney as designer with his compatriot and virtual contemporary Jonathan Miller, the neurologist and theatrical polymath, as director. (The L.A. Opera's general director, Peter Hemmings, takes both the credit and the blame.) It was a mismatch almost from the start. Although neither man is a raving prima donna, both are perennial boy wonders with often overpoweringly headstrong and definitive visions. In this instance, Miller soon came to realize that faced with Hockney the celebrity, working on his home turf, he wasn't going to get a concept in edgewise. ("I'd clearly been brought in as a sort of real estate agent," Miller jokes about the experience nowadays, "my brief being limited to showing people about the premises.")

Going into his collaboration with Hockney, Jonathan Miller had been struck by the strangely static quality of the opera's action: "The challenge is to figure out some way to galvanize the stage," Miller noted, when I reached him by phone at his London home, "for hardly anything actually happens. The music, of course, is quite moving, but in the famous duet scenes, for instance, there's hardly any love at all—you can't have them thrashing about, screwing, because there is none of that in the text, though it does get alluded to. It's about something odder, deeper, stranger: this peculiar protofascist feeling that pervades the whole, like some SS officer's wet dream. That's what it's about, really, this strange anthropophagus woman swallowing up, unmanning this dutiful knight with her magic potion, and then all that weird stuff about Tristan's endlessly dying, through the entirety of act 3, from the septic wound he contracts at the end of the second act. What's all that about? Not that it's fascist in itself, but it belongs in that sort of world, against that kind of backdrop—you can see what appealed to the budding Nazis. You can just hear them humming the music in their heads. I was even thinking of trying to set the opera in the world of Germany of the late twenties or early thirties."

You can see how Jonathan Miller's and David Hockney's conceptions were never going to converge.

This time around, Hockney himself, his encroaching deafness notwithstanding, is listed as both the designer and the director (although he is being assisted in the latter capacity by Stephen Pickover, who will be credited with "staging"). Hockney insists that the two roles are really one in any case, and that in both instances he's simply trying to serve the music itself.

"One of the first things Jonathan Miller did when he arrived here to begin work on the opera"—David Hockney still can't get over this; he loves regaling people with the tale to this day—"was to announce, confidentially, 'Silly story!' Which, I mean, is amazing. Because the story isn't the words—though the librettos are what most directors seem to spend most of their time mucking about with, plumbing them for motivation and so forth—*it's the music.* It's *in* the music. When I start work on an opera, I maybe read the libretto once, but then I set it aside and hardly ever go back to it: I just listen to the music over and over and over again. And the story *Tristan*'s music tells is anything but silly. It's overwhelmingly moving, really. It's ravishing."

Ravishing is a good word, and it set me to recalling something my mother once told me about *her* Viennese grandmother, how from certain dainty late-life conversations she'd had with the banker's widow about marital duty and marital relations, she'd become convinced that the old dowager had never in her life experienced an orgasm while engaged in physical relations with her husband (the only man, for that matter, she'd ever had such relations with)—"Just the way she talked about things," my mother would recall, "the curl of distaste, of put-upon, vaguely contemptuous, indulgence." Not that my great-grandmother had failed ever in her life to experience physical ecstasy, my mother continued: like many of her contemporaries among the high bourgeois wives of Vienna at the turn of the century, she was a Wagner fanatic—she claimed to have witnessed *Tristan* alone almost a hundred times, often by herself or else accompanied by other women friends at matinees while their husbands were off at work (or, perhaps, frequenting brothels?)—and from the way she talked about *that,* my mother was convinced that she was regularly being ravished, to the point of physical climax, right there in the august, chandelier-decked vault of the theater.[1]

For all his demurrals, Hockney never had an approach as purely aesthetic, music-centered, or otherworldly as he himself avers, either at the time of its first production or this time around. This realization came back to me with renewed force now as, watching David coax his lightbox through the last minutes of act 3, I was reminded once again of the world of those first performances back in 1987.

If *Tristan*'s second act traces the progress through a single love-besotted night, from oblivious darkness into the glaring revelations of dawn (culminating as the scandalously discovered, death-seeking Tristan throws himself onto the outthrust sword of King Mark's other dutiful knight, Melot), act 3 by contrast traces the progress of a single day, from dawn through scalding noon to long-sought fall of night, as Tristan, returned to a stark promontory overlooking the waves near his home castle in Brittany, thrashes in fevered anguish, deliriously awaiting the seaborne arrival of Isolde, who either is or isn't coming with the medicinal balm that alone can salve his gaping wound. (Through wonderfully subtle and cadenced changes of lighting, played out across his parched, upthrust cliffscape, Hockney continually cues the audience, if only subliminally, to the day's fateful passage.) Finally, with nightfall, Isolde arrives (it is her call from offstage that Tristan, by now entirely demented, greets by asking how he can possibly be hearing the light)—but she is too late: Tristan expires in her arms. And presently she herself, in an exaltation of grief and longing, literally sings herself to death with her celebrated *Liebestod,* her love-death, joining him at last.

This climax would be overwhelming in virtually any rendering at virtually any time, but during the winter of 1987, with the devastating scourge of AIDS rampaging through the gay and arts communities, Hockney's *Tristan* must have had an impact all the more powerfully cathartic. By then Hockney himself had lost several of his closest friends to the plague, and several others—including many in the opening-night audience—were HIV-positive, some of those wracked by advanced stages of the illness. Hockney has occasionally been criticized over the years for not confronting the issue of AIDS head-on in his work, but as he has said, "I mean, you shouldn't have to scrawl the word itself all over the wall in order to register a statement." In any case, the charge itself is preposterous. How else are we to interpret the sudden upwelling of the motif of empty (vacated) rooms in his paintings around this time, or the gradual disappearance of variously lollygagging youths as a central motif in his work (the tender, loving gaze instead seeming to transfer over to the dachshund puppies he'd first acquired around this time)? But perhaps Hockney's single most affecting confrontation with the AIDS scourge came here, in the immediate wake of Isolde's dying swoon, as Wagner himself launches the orchestra into that final incomparable chord, the music rising, subsiding, rising, and subsiding again atop an incandescently sustained solitary oboe line: the apotheosis of love and unity beyond death. Perfectly rhyming his effect to the music, Hockney now turned his entire cliff pitch nighttime black, starkly silhouetting it against the engirdling sky, which suddenly swelled up blindingly bright, with rich blue stage lights cast upon the cobalt blue surround.

"The transcendental dawn," Hockney now pronounced, having just re-created the effect that even inside the narrowed confines of his miniature model suggested an infinitely pearlescent expanse. "Because, of course, the thing is, *Tristan*'s ending isn't the tragedy it might at first appear," he continued. "That last chord: despite the bodies' lying there littered all about the stage, the music somehow lifts you up and out of all that and onto another plane altogether, one of ineffable joy and affirmation, a kind of rapture." Hockney paused, sighing, as if himself recalling the death-glutted context of those first performances. "When you suddenly find yourself surrounded by so much suffering," he resumed, "you begin to think of death differently—I know I did: before I hadn't really thought about death at all. It loses some of its terror, and it even begins to feel like a deliverance toward something else. I mean, I think for instance of Nathan and René"—two of his closest friends, both of whom attended the premiere and both of whom would be dead within two years—"death ended up *joining* them really, as they'd both fervently desired. That's the higher possibility Wagner's music holds out and that I too was trying to suggest, whiting out the backdrop sky like that."

Hockney shook his head, sighing again. "But it's really something: I can't hear the low notes anymore. I mean I remember them, so I can sense myself filling in the blanks. But I can also feel all that sound just bleeding away."

It occurred to me that perhaps *that* was going to be the subtext for this upcoming series of performances—the whiting-out, as it were, of an entire swath of Hockney's own creative horizon: the bleeding away of sound, and of the possibility of any future such operatic collaborations on his part.

There was something deeply poignant and almost tragic about that prospect. And yet . . . For one thing I was reminded of something my grandfather, the composer Ernst Toch, used to say when people would provoke him with the hackneyed observation about how tragic it was that Mozart died so young. "For God's sake," he'd exclaim, "what more did you want from the man?" And indeed, what more—after the past twenty years and their entirely unexpected bounty of *The Rake's Progress* and *The Magic Flute,* the French triple bill and the Stravinsky triple bill, *Tristan* and *Turandot* and *Die Frau ohne Schatten*—what more do we want from our man?

Beyond that, I don't know, maybe I was still in thrall to the Tristanian ethos, but this didn't seem an entirely desperate ending: there remained the distinctly happy possibility of transfiguration on the far side. I'd been struck by Hockney's use of the phrase "whiting out" to describe his staging of the opera's final moments—actually he'd used the phrase several times over the past few hours—when, of course, there was nothing the least bit white about that rapturously blue finale. Nonetheless, what in fact does await Hockney on the far side of these final upcoming performances is a virtually infinite expanse of empty white canvases. And as he'd also mentioned several times in passing, with an almost palpable eagerness and anticipation, "Enough of this already: it's really time for me to be getting back to painting."

CHAPTER 4

wider perspectives

PAINTING YORKSHIRE AND THE GRAND CANYON (1998)

A few years ago, David Hockney extracted a paragraph from the late astronomer Carl Sagan's book *Pale Blue Dot:*

> In some respects, science has far surpassed religion in delivering awe. How is it that hardly any major religion has looked at science and concluded, "This is better than we thought! The universe is much bigger than our prophets said—grander, more subtle, more elegant. God must be even greater than we dreamed"? Instead they say, "No, no, no! My god is a little god, and I want him to stay that way." A religion, old or new, that stressed the magnificence of the universe as revealed by modern science might be able to draw forth reserves of reverence and awe hardly tapped by conventional faiths. Sooner or later, such a religion will emerge.[1]

He photocopied it and embedded the text, beneath Sagan's name, in a simple color drawing of a headstone on a rock-strewn plain, copies of which he proceeded to mail to friends. In the version I saw, he'd hand-scrawled, in the lower right-hand corner of the image, the simple injunction, *"Love life!"*

That drawing was very much on my mind, recently, as I flew out to the north of England to meet up with David in Bradford, his childhood hometown and the site of the Salts Mill, a mammoth old dilapidated Victorian textile mill complex entirely reclaimed over the past several years by his dear friend Jonathan Silver and the home now, among other things, of the 1853 Gallery, the world's vastest emporium of Hockneyana. After a few hours touring the mill, David and I set out in his red roadster convertible—the top down, the footspace heater turned full up—

This text was originally composed for the catalogue to the Looking at Landscape/Being in Landscape exhibit of Hockney's East Yorkshire and Grand Canyon paintings at the LA Louver Gallery in September 1998.

through the rolling Yorkshire countryscape to the modest seaside resort of Bridlington, on the North Sea coast, where David keeps an attic studio in his sister's house, a few doors away from the nursing home where his ninety-year-old mother now resides. Our conversation took place there.

LW: David, I've been thinking the past several days about that paragraph you embedded in your drawing of the Carl Sagan tombstone.

DH: Actually, when I made the drawing, Sagan was still alive—I don't think I even knew he was in the process of dying of cancer at the time—and I'd intended the image more as a sort of tablet, a commandment. Though I can see how in retrospect the text might read as an epitaph.

LW: It's interesting, I suppose, that I had that mistaken impression, but the larger point I'm getting at is still valid, because I'm struck by your response, over the past decade and a half or so, to what has truly been for you a death-permeated, death-haunted world. You have lost so many dear friends: your dealer Nathan and the countless others who've died of AIDS; Henry Geldzahler; and now Jonathan Silver. And your response, it seems to me, time and again, has been an almost defiant throwing in the face of death this love of life. Whether it is the flower paintings or the *Tristan* opera staging, the dog paintings, or now these landscapes. I mean, this refusal to be cowed and how, if anything, over and over again, you keep returning to magnificence and awe and—might the proper word be reverence?—as responses to all this devastation.

DH: Well, we all have a fear of death, of course. But, its opposite is surely the love of life. Which, I think, is a much greater force really. Or should be. I mean, Jonathan, a week before he died, said to me, "Paint those pictures, David. Keep on painting them. Life is a celebration, really." I mean, here he was dying—he knew he was dying—and he understood that. And, ever since he died, actually, I've done nothing but work. Been just working away like mad.

LW: Can you talk about Jonathan a little?

DH: Jonathan was a fellow Bradford lad, though about twelve years younger than me. He first contacted me when he was editing an alternative magazine at my old high school to ask if I'd contribute a drawing. A brash, cheeky sort of thing

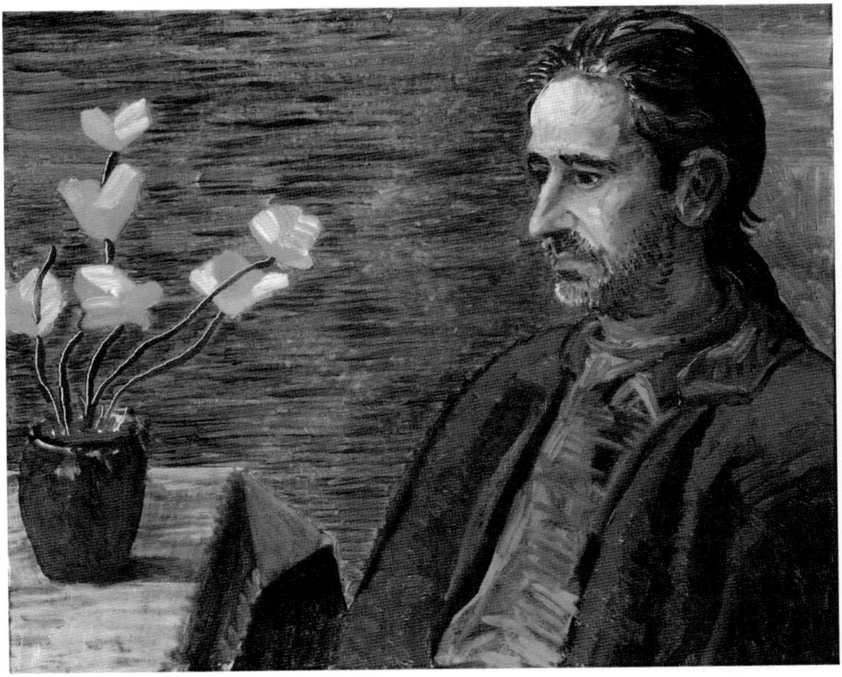

FIG 32 David Hockney, *Jonathan Silver,* 1996.

to do—which I liked. And over the years I kept up friendly relations with him and presently his wife and their two lovely daughters. In 1987 he somehow acquired the abandoned old mill at Saltaire from the town of Bradford and set to reviving it—letting space to software companies, launching restaurants and bookstores along with that gallery devoted mainly to my work. He was wonderfully bright, cultivated, energetic, funny—we were in regular phone contact. And after Henry died in 1994, of a very rare form of pancreatic cancer, I found myself relying more and more on Jonathan for that sort of telephonic companionship.

Then, exactly a year later—actually, I saw it first in my rendering of him [Fig. 32]—I could see it even before he told me, giving the drawings a second look later, after I'd finished them: Jonathan came down with cancer, too. And the very same kind as Henry's! Incredibly bizarre. He fought it valiantly, even looked for a while like he had it beat: he ended up lasting two years. But by the summer of 1997, the cancer had come surging back.

LW: It must have been a terrible time.

DH: I was home in California, and everybody was saying, "Why don't you go back? You're too worried here. You're going a bit mad." Richard [Schmidt] said that. Gregory [Evans] said that. "We can see you're always on the phone. Why don't you go and see him?"

So I came back at the end of July. And I realized when I saw him—I could see he was deteriorating, he was very ill. I mean, you saw it in the face. After all, I'd seen this before. I realized, I can't just fly back to L.A. What would I do there? So, I decided, well, I'll stay here. And actually, I was quite comfortable here.

LW: Here in Bridlington.

DH: Yes, with my sister and her companion, Ken. And, I felt, well, if I'm going to stay here, I might as well get working. I have to do some work or something. I'd been here maybe three weeks, which is the longest I'd been here for a long time—

LW: Meaning, you were driving back and forth each day through East Yorkshire.

DH: To just east of York, actually—not quite as far as Bradford—where Jonathan and his family were now living. By August he wasn't really going to the mill anymore.

LW: Maybe a forty-five-minute drive.

DH: Yes, and as you saw, quite attractive. I kept just going to his house. And one day, driving, I recalled how he'd always been saying to me, "Hey, why don't you paint Yorkshire?"

LW: And why hadn't you painted Yorkshire?

DH: Well, before, I'd simply never stayed long enough to even look at it that much. I'd come for a week and leave—not enough time to notice things, really.

Now, just before that, in June and July, back in America, I'd made two long driving trips from L.A. to Santa Fe and back, and I'd been contemplating doing some sort of big landscape of the West. Big spaces: that's what was getting into my head. I was experiencing a growing claustrophobia or something—

LW: A fear of being in closed spaces, or more the love of being in open spaces?

DH: Yes. That's it: the agoraphilia was stronger, the longing for big spaces.

LW: Could that be related to your progressive loss of hearing, the way the world of sound, for its part, has been closing in on you?

DH: It could be. It could be, but then I often think, you know, Why did I go to California all that time ago in the first place? At the time, I always said I'd gone because it was sexy, it was sunny. But Los Angeles is also the most spacey city in the world. You feel the most space. I was always attracted to its spaces as well. Always.

LW: And now East Yorkshire was turning out to be spacious in a similar way?

DH: Well, it was only after driving back and forth like that, through that actually very attractive space, where at times you could see a long way away—from the top of Garrowby Hill, you see the whole plain of York—that it began to occur to me how it does have some connection to the American West in that way.

LW: Can you describe for people who haven't been here what East Yorkshire is like?

DH: Well, first of all, there are not many people who live here. Historically, it is beyond the Roman wall. The Romans built the town of York—they called it Eboracum—but this area was beyond that. And just to the south there is a wide river, the Humber, which they've only just recently built a first bridge over. So that no main road runs through this part of the country. You don't come through Bridlington on your way to anywhere. You have to decide to come here. Which, come to think of it, may be one of the reasons this region has been so relatively little painted, historically.

But you have the Wolds, chalk hills with these tiny little valleys without rivers running through them. Strange: not caused by water or rivers. A bit like Normandy where Monet painted; that must be chalk there, too.

LW: A wonderful sense of scale. You have these little gullies that hardly deserve the name valley, they're so tiny, but they have a sense of being big valleys.

DH: Right. I've been coming here for quite a long time, and it has hardly changed at all. But driving through the Wolds, virtually every day, I mean, I began really to look at them, you see. Also, it is agricultural country.

LW: I was going to say, in the context of the comparison with the American West, which is also quite underpopulated—but there one has the sense of nature in the raw, of a human confrontation with something alien, vast and other, whereas here we are speaking of a distinctly human space, a space inhabited and domesticated to the human scale.

DH: Well, *husbandry* is the word that comes to mind, if you think about it, a good medieval word. Biblical word from my youth. My mother's quite religious, I was brought up a little religious, but then wandered off from it. But you do remember the language of the King James Bible.

LW: Husbandry, implying being husband to the land, in some intimate relation.

DH: Yes, and a changing one. Meaning the surface of the land is constantly changing, as I came to realize on those drives in my open car. I arrived at the end of July as they were just about to begin harvesting, so the corn was just turning to gold. The big machines were around, getting ready. They told me it rained all of June and July. The moment I came, it seemed to clear up. So this is August really, three weeks into August, and I'm going back and forth, watching, in a sense, the surface changing. I begin to notice how last week that was golden, now it has all these little dots on it from those machines, which were like pregnant insects laying eggs.

LW: The harvesting machines with their little rolls of hay.

DH: Yes, in the evening shadows. One field would be green and another would have these drops on it, another would have sheep, and the surface of the land was constantly changing. Also, I was driving over to see a friend who I was well aware then was in the process of dying. I didn't say it, but deep down, that's why I was staying.

LW: The sense of him near the end of his life and the bringing in of the harvest must have—

DH: Yes, the living aspect of the land, how they bring in the harvest: something dies, it grows up again. I began to see all that far more intensely than I would have if I'd just come for a weekend.

LW: And, on top of everything else, this person who was dying had specifically asked you to do portraits of the land.

DH: Well, Yorkshire has the biggest spaces of England, as I came to see, and I thought, maybe I can deal with those issues here. Also, I was pressed for time,

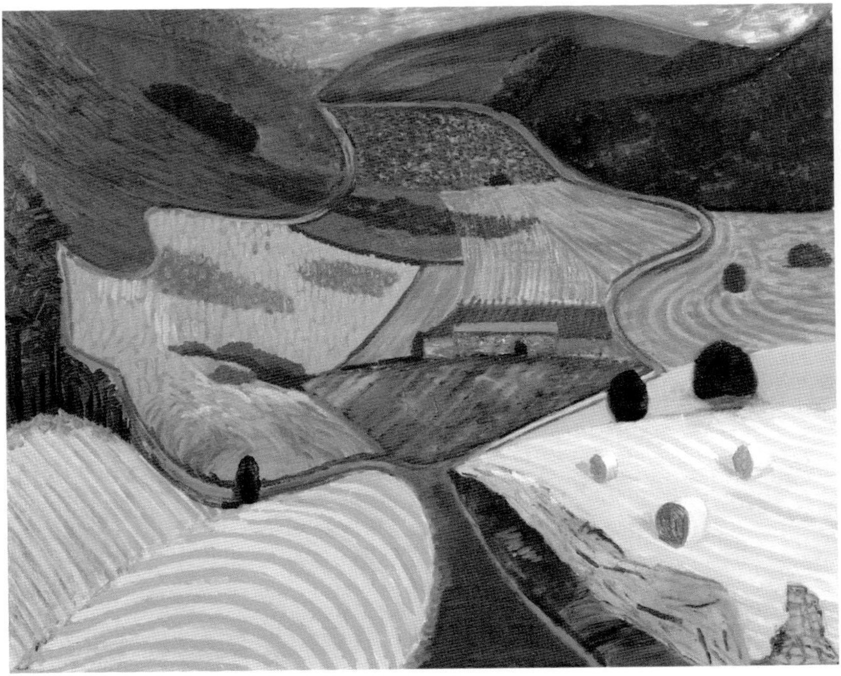

FIG 33 David Hockney, *North Yorkshire*, 1997.

in a sense, observing Jonathan's decay. So, the first one I did was this sort of round trip . . .

LW: The one called *North Yorkshire* [Fig. 33].

DH: Yes, and of course it's a trip, a hundred and fifty miles, actually, up there and back. But the first thing I drew was the outline, which, actually, happens to approximate the shape of Yorkshire on a map.

LW: It also reads to me as alternatively a head or a tree.[2]

DH: Yes. Well, I began playing with such ideas, but I was aware that it was also a map.

LW: And there is no way to look at that painting without driving around inside it.

DH: Yes.

LW: Your eyes go on a ride.

DH: They go on a ride because *I* had been on a ride.

Now, the second one, *The Road through Sledmere,* I was painting at about the same time as *The Road across the Wolds* [Plates 17 and 18].

LW: And all these pictures, you were doing in this attic studio here?

DH: Right. Sledmere is a village that is around fifteen miles from here that, to my knowledge, has not changed one bit in fifty years. Those Edwardian red brick houses, with red paint on them, glorious in their redness those sunny days of late August, September. So one was getting marvelous greens, washed greens, the land changing, the very rich soil; and, in Sledmere I would drive up here, turn the corner, go back through here, around and off down there.

LW: I can say, as someone who has now been on this drive with you, that there is no place, no vantage, from which you could take this photograph. This is not intended as a reproduction of a single-point perspective.

DH: That was the point.

LW: But it does capture what it is like to drive through a place, as opposed to what it is to be frozen in place.

I notice, incidentally, how in all of these, there's hardly any sky—I mean, in contrast to much of the rest of the great English landscape tradition. People like Constable and Turner. Or some of the Dutch painters, whose landscapes were often half-skyscapes.

DH: Yes, I suppose so, but when you're driving you don't really look at the sky, do you? You keep your eye on the road. And in fact, with some of these—*The Road across the Wolds,* for instance—I was consciously piling horizons one atop the next, such that when you were at one place in the painting, that's the horizon you'd see, whereas a bit further along, you'd see this other horizon line. They're fairly complicated paintings, actually.

So, anyway, I was painting away, and people in London would ask me, "When are you coming around? How long are you going to be staying up there?" And I'd say, "I'm painting some pictures of Yorkshire, actually." And I remember someone said, "Aren't they going to be a bit sad?" And I said, "No, I'm painting them for Jonathan. They're going to show all the joy about the world I can. I'm going to take them over for him. Why on earth would I paint it gloomy, anyway?"

LW: I have to tell you, this whole series for me has the quality of a love song.

DH: Well . . .

LW: A quality, too, which may derive from the fact that alongside the death and last-things undercurrent you've evinced in these paintings, they were also constituting a sort of return to first things for you.

DH: Well, yes, as I told you on the drive over, I've really known this countryside quite intimately since the early fifties, when I came here to work during breaks from school—helping with the harvesting of corn. Wheat. Barley. I used to sack them for transport into Bridlington.

LW: And indeed there's a certain T. S. Eliot "Little Gidding" from the *Four Quartets* quality to these paintings—"We shall not cease from our exploration / And the end of all our exploring / Will be to arrive where we started / And know the place for the first time." I'm reminded, too, of Czeslaw Milosz's recent return-tramps through Lithuania.

Can you talk a little about the use of reverse perspective in these paintings?

DH: As you know, the tyranny of vanishing-point perspective is something I've been obsessed about for years now—what it does to us—it's gotten so as I can't even watch television anymore because of the way the box focuses one's gaze down that narrowing—

LW: Like a funnel.

DH: Yes, when all I want to do is just the opposite. Did I ever tell you the story about the time when I was in Milan, doing *The Magic Flute* at La Scala, and I took a drive to Zurich with Ian Falconer? And they'd just built this tunnel under the St. Gotthard Pass. The tunnel is about twenty-three kilometers long, of which about nineteen kilometers are a straight line. And, when we entered it, we were the only car entering. So all you saw was this rectangle ahead of you tapering relentlessly down to a single point in the middle, way up ahead. We were going on and on like this, and I said to Ian, "This is like living in one-point-perspective hell, this tunnel. Never have I experienced anything like this." One found oneself longing so powerfully for the opposite, which at last one finally got, emerging from the tunnel.

LW: A sort of opening out.

DH: Exactly. Oh, I loved it. I love it. I love it, and I've never, ever forgotten that.

In painting, reversing the perspective both brings the distant back up close to you, and also tends to undercut the illusion of being planted in a single space and time. It affords a sense of motion, of liveliness.

LW: So we've talked about the first three paintings. What did you work on next?

DH: Once I'd finished the first three, we rented a van and took them over to Jonathan—he was pleased, he immediately said, "Oh, they go back to your *Grimm's Fairy Tales* etchings—the little Gothic towers."

And, I thought, Well, I'll paint Saltaire: the mill itself with the workers' village all about it. This would be the earth altered even more: architecture, another big subject of mine, going way back, the apartment buildings in L.A., for instance, or the Mexican hotel courtyard painting from a while back. And, in this instance, I'd known the building since my childhood. I mean, I first probably walked down those roads when I was five years old—not more than three miles from our house.

So I drove over and walked around the streets again. I probably took a few little photographs, but this is not a view you could get—you can't really find a view like this at all. And I said to Jonathan, "I'm going to paint Saltaire." All he said to me was, "Show how big the mill is." I said, "Yes, that's the subject. How big, how great the mill is."

I came back here and began working on it—put together two canvases. And I thought, "Well, I can play with these spaces now in an interesting way." I'd take drawings and photos of the developing canvas over to Jonathan each day, and he immediately realized how if you hung this picture at the mill, people would understand what you were doing with the space.

So I was painting away, and I found it quite difficult, really. I mean, the mill itself, actually, is not a subject I normally would have dealt with. And on top of everything, I was working against the clock. Meaning, I knew he was getting worse and worse.

LW: Did you make it?

DH: Actually, it was finished about a week before he died. I think, maybe ten days before he died [Fig. 34]. I'd been showing him the snapshots as the painting developed, and actually he was quite talkative. But it was during that time that he told me not to worry so much about him, to get back to work, that life

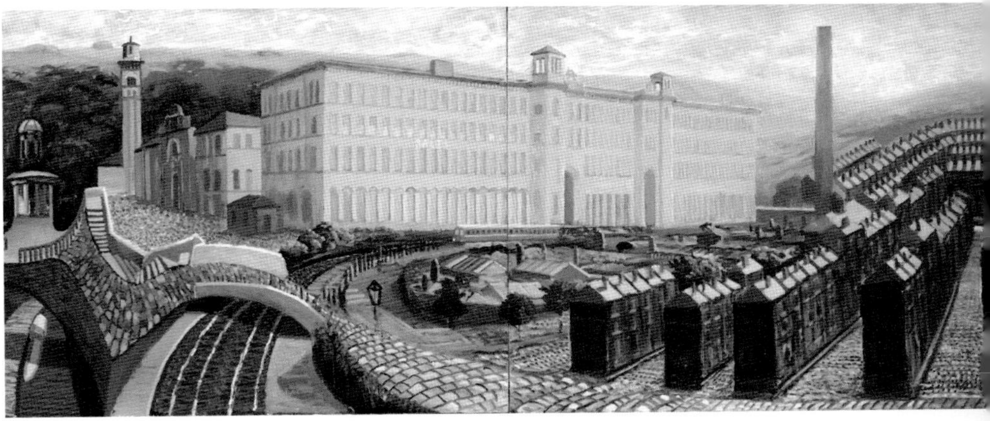

FIG 34 David Hockney, *Salts Mill, Saltaire Yorks.*, 1997.

is—"You just paint those pictures, David. Don't do anything else. Don't bother with anything else now. You paint those pictures. Celebrate life." I mean, he was fading away, in terrible . . . You know, the face begins to cave in. I'd seen it before. And I was in a turmoil, really. I mean, I was pleased I'd done these for him. But . . .

LW: Looking at the Saltaire painting now, do you see Jonathan's death in it?

DH: No, I see his life in it, actually. I see his life.

LW: Strangely, a few minutes ago you described how you only first became aware of Jonathan's illness—of the death in him—looking afterward at the drawings you'd been doing of him. And now here, in the painting you were doing as he was actually dying, what comes through is the opposite of his death.

DH: Because, why not? I mean, you don't think of your friends now as they were when they were dying; you think of them as they were when they were alive. Always. That's how I think of Henry. Jonathan.

So, but . . . he died just after. And I stayed a little bit. They had a very quiet funeral. And then I went back to L.A. It took a while to sink in, what happened. And I started on the next one.

LW: The double canvas: *Double East Yorkshire* [Plate 19].

DH: Which is more, as you see, the autumn. The plowing. The harvest is done.

LW: Your friend has been harvested.

DH: All's been harvested. These were the colors of a much later summer.

LW: This strikes me more as a picture about rhythm than about death.

DH: Rhythms of the landscape around here, yes. And the way you see these patterns, and the plowing. In a way, I realized I hadn't finished with Yorkshire, really.

LW: Or with Jonathan.

DH: No. And then I came back to Bradford: we did a memorial for Jonathan. We put the pictures up, these pictures, in a room at the mill, and we had an afternoon where I spoke, a few people spoke about him. From there I went on to Cologne, where they were preparing a show, came back to L.A., continued finishing the harvest painting, and then went on to . . .

LW: To *Garrowby Hill.*

DH: *Garrowby Hill,* yes, which I'd wanted to do. It was in me. I probably painted it in three weeks, though, of course, I'd been planning it for much, much longer [Plate 20].

LW: Can you talk about it a little bit because to my mind, it's the culmination of the whole series—the one that really brings things all together.

DH: Well, it was the very last one of the Yorkshire pictures, and the one that anticipates the big vistas up ahead.

LW: First of all, can you describe—where was this?

DH: Well, Garrowby Hill is the hill that—York is a city nestled in a great big plain. The Vale of York. The rivers from West Yorkshire meet in York and go on out on the Humber. It is a very flat area. And Garrowby Hill, on the eastern edge of the vale, is the hill where the chalk wolds rise up. And you go from, probably, sea level, to about eight hundred feet.

LW: So, each morning coming over from Bridlington, this would have been your view.

DH: I must have driven up and down that hill—probably sixty times in the previous few months. So it was very strong for me. A very powerful feeling. On clear days, you could probably see fifty, sixty miles, which is a long way for England. And there, on the horizon, you could make out the cathedral, York Minster—twelfth century, huge building.

LW: But the main thing from Garrowby Hill is the sense of scale.

DH: And it also imparts this marvelous feeling, how you're about to take off and fly. A momentary sense of soaring.

LW: Can I try a few associations that I get from the picture on you? First of all, there is no question in this picture that you're driving. You are not just standing there, you are driving into this vista. Not only are you driving, but somehow it is clear—somehow you have conveyed this—you have just come over the hill. In fact, your back wheels are still on the other side of the hill, and the front wheels are only just beginning to start down. And I in turn have two sets of associations to that sense of dynamic. One is to what it was for you to be coming over the hill of this terrible thing you'd just been going through. Coming out the other side, as it were, onto the wide expanse of life remaining for you and the work remaining for you, all the fields remaining for you to go after. But also there's a kind of magisterial quality of what it is or was for Jonathan—

DH: Jonathan.

LW: For him to have come over the hill of his life, and of his final illness, out into this kind of openness, which is where I come back to the Carl Sagan quote. Or phrased differently, maybe: this whole painting seems about *overcoming*. You are coming over the hill. You are overcoming.

DH: That's very good. Yeah. Overcoming.

LW: Which is why this picture feels so much to me like the culmination of that whole body of work.

DH: And it was painted in California without any references, really, at all. And most of those fields keep opening out, you see.

LW: Again: that reverse perspective.

DH: Always opening, as if you were coming out of this tunnel. Which, in a way, I suppose, I was.

LW: Let's gradually go from talking about painting things that generally had not been painted before to painting things that people said were unpaintable. You were telling me the story about an ad for the Santa Fe Railroad.

DH: Well, I went to the Thomas Moran show in Washington, D.C., last December, in the middle of all this, just before I began moving toward my Grand

Canyon paintings, and in the catalogue they featured an early ad for the Santa Fe Railroad, which characterized the Grand Canyon as "the despair of the painter"—meaning, it was too difficult to paint. And I must say, I'd always thought the Grand Canyon was unphotographable, in a sense, as well—by any conventional means, at any rate. In fact, generally, I've long felt that the one aspect of photography that seems to have let us down is, actually, landscape.

LW: How so?

DH: Photography seems to be rather good at portraiture, or can be. But, it can't tell you about space, which is the essence of landscape. For me anyway. Even Ansel Adams can't quite prepare you for what Yosemite looks like when you go through that tunnel and you come out the other side.

LW: Is that why, back in 1982, you headed out to the Grand Canyon almost immediately as you moved from your Polaroid collages to working with a more ordinary camera?

DH: Exactly. I wanted to try to photograph the unphotographable. Which is to say, space. I mean, there is no question—for me, anyway—that the thrill of standing on that rim of the Grand Canyon is spatial. It is the biggest space you can look out over that has an edge. I mean, of course space is bigger if you turn your head and look up, but that space is incomprehensible to us, really.

LW: And indeed it seems to me that each time you're on the verge of some sort of breakthrough, pictorially, you return to the Grand Canyon to see whether you can lick your chops on that.

DH: Well, I must admit I'm always thrilled by it. I mean people go to *look* into it, don't they? Very few actually go *down* into it. And actually, you can peer into it for an awful long time. And you look all over. I mean, it is the one place, I think, where you become very aware of how you move your head, your eyes, everything.

LW: In a way what you're saying is, it is the one place where everybody *actually* peers at the world the way you are suggesting one should peer at the world all the time.

DH: Well, the way we *do* look at the world all the time.

LW: But you become aware of doing so at the Grand Canyon?

DH: You become very aware of it there. I think so.

LW: Actually it was delving once again into those photocollages of the Grand Canyon from the mideighties that proved the immediate occasion for the current series of paintings, wasn't it?

DH: Well, the Ludwig Museum in Cologne was preparing a retrospective of my photographs around this time, and I'd gone over to look at the space, and there was going to be this very large room with a large wall at the end of it. And this afforded me the opportunity to try something I'd wanted to do back in the mideighties—to blow up one of those photocollages into a wall-size mural—something that would have been prohibitively expensive to do back then, but in the meantime, what with laser reproduction, had become entirely feasible. The Grand Canyon seemed the ideal subject for such an exercise—the right scale—and I began reviewing some of those collages, eventually choosing one I'd photographed in 1982 but had actually only put together in 1986, at the time of the ICP retrospective in New York.

LW: When was this?

DH: Well, I was now back in L.A. as we were blowing up the negatives. This would have been January, while I was starting on *Garrowby Hill.* And then I went back out to Cologne to supervise the installation of the wall mural, and it turned out well enough—I mean, people liked it—but what I noticed was how the image did not read from a great distance. It seemed to lose its presence, its impact, as you stepped back [Plate 21].

LW: Why, do you suppose?

DH: Well, for starters, photographic ink, photographic printing, any kind of printing, is not like paint. This is one of the lessons I took from the Vermeer show: the colors! The vibrancy of the colors after all these years. I spent hours in those rooms in The Hague, just studying how he did it, how he made those images *glow* like that. Just technically—the layering, the building-up of thin layers of colors one atop the next, the foreplanning. I joked that Vermeer's colors will last a lot longer than MGM's, but it's true. And I applied those lessons to the flower paintings I did immediately thereafter—people would say, "What do flowers have to do with Vermeer?" and I'd say, "I'm not talking about subject matter"—and then in the Yorkshire landscapes as well. And the photocollage mural in Cologne, as impressive as it was, couldn't hold a candle to that kind of presence. I turned to Richard and said, "I should *paint* the Grand Canyon; I'm going to have to paint the Grand Canyon now."

I decided to do a large wall piece across a grid of sixty small canvases (the same number as there were individual snaps in the photocollage)—in part because it would be more manageable, working in the studio, but also because, as with the photocollages, such a cubist method, as it were, would allow sixty separate vantages, sixty separate vanishing points; it would undermine the one-point perspective and help entice the viewer's eyes to rove about.

LW: Just like at the canyon itself. How would that have differed from, say, Thomas Moran's approach?

DH: I should say, incidentally, that I thought that that was a marvelous exhibition, very enjoyable. Moran was actually an Englishman himself, born exactly one hundred years before me not forty miles away from Bradford. And he, too, obviously, developed a taste for the American West. He went along on Powell's 1873 expedition into the canyon, but almost under a government commission, with the intention, the assignment, of conveying information—about topography, geology, and so forth—as accurately as possible. As I say, that's not my interest. I'm trying to convey *the experience of space.*

LW: Moran also seemed fascinated by atmospherics, by weather and microclimates. There's no sense of haze in your version.

DH: And I didn't want any. I didn't want to use any atmospheric color—the colors on those canvases are very vivid, pure—which in turn was one of the reasons why, even when you were looking at the various studies, and then the developing canvas, from the far side of the studio, it was still as if you were at the very edge of the canyon. In fact, I realized that the further back you got, the stronger the image read [Plate 22].

It was reminiscent of something I'd learned doing *Tristan.*

LW: I was going to say, this image itself is reminiscent of your staging of *Tristan:* the ship's prow, the cliffscape. And perhaps that is not surprising, since the photocollage it's based on was put together in 1986, only a year before you first designed those *Tristan* sets.

DH: Well, onstage, the thing is, if you put a real tree there, if you're sitting in the front row, you'll feel near to it, while if you're sitting in the back row, you'll feel far away. Whereas, for instance, the wiggly lines I painted in on the mast of the ship in *Tristan* made it such that it didn't really matter where you sat: you felt you were on the ship even if you were in the back row. And I've noticed how all the paintings I've done since 1988 share that feature: they read across the room. Especially this Grand Canyon.

LW: Making distance intimate. Indeed, I noted, when I went to see this recent *Bigger Grand Canyon* of yours during its premiere showing in Washington—in fact, right next door to where the Morans are usually hanging at the Smithsonian—everybody seemed to be pushing back, as far away as possible: there was a whole group pressing themselves against the far wall. By no means in revulsion. I was assuming this was because they were trying to get it all in their visual field at once.

DH: In part, perhaps. But it's also the case that the more the viewer pushes back, the more the image pulls him in. It becomes clearer and clearer, stronger and stronger.

LW: The way the sky works seems important in that regard here as well. Again, you have virtually no sky presented, just a thin sliver at the top, and, yet, there's a huge feeling of the sky above you.

DH: Well, because everything above the painting can be the sky.

LW: The blank of the wall . . .

DH: . . . can read as an infinite sky.

LW: Whereas if the sky went halfway down the picture, as it does, say, in a Moran, that would be all the sky there is.

DH: That is it. Exactly.

LW: This way, the white of the wall above the canvas, and specifically above the point on the canvas representing the farthest horizon from you, can read as sky, going up and up, along the ceiling and then, over the top, even behind you—while the bottom of the image, the rim of the canyon, likewise bleeds into the lower wall and then the floor and on under you. The two vectors, as it were, meeting behind you and drawing you in.

DH: And all the more tautly the further back you stand. That's why you feel sucked in, as if there's no gap between you and it.

LW: You were telling me a story about Ed Ruscha . . .

DH: Yeah, I met him at a party one evening as I was working on the big painting, and I was leaving early. I said, "Well, I'm going home. I go to bed early. I get up very early. I'm doing this large painting of the Grand Canyon." And, he said, "Well, in miniature, of course." Which I thought was very witty. For, of course, whatever size we do it, it will be a miniature.

LW: To what extent as you were painting this painting do you suppose Jonathan's deathbed injunction—that you should go out and celebrate life—was still reverberating in your mind?

DH: Well, actually, yes. Surely it was, really.

LW: The reason I ask is that, again, what is interesting in the Yorkshire paintings is their evocation of a very lived-in geography: the farms, the haystacks, the sense of human scale and habitation. Whereas the Grand Canyon, par excellence, is almost inhuman in its vastness: space and rock and little else. But at the same time, what is celebrated in your painting is the *human* capacity for perception. And, and the wonder of being alive before that kind of awe.

DH: A friend of mine looked at it and said he thought he was on the way to Heaven, as he put it. A very nice thing to say, really. My sister thinks space is God, and I like that.

LW: Which brings us back to Carl Sagan's insistence that we not be satisfied with puny Gods.

DH: Right, because his comment is actually about big space, isn't it?—how God must be even greater than we dreamed of. Much bigger. The universe, bigger. Grander. Vaster. More spacious. I thought that was marvelous.

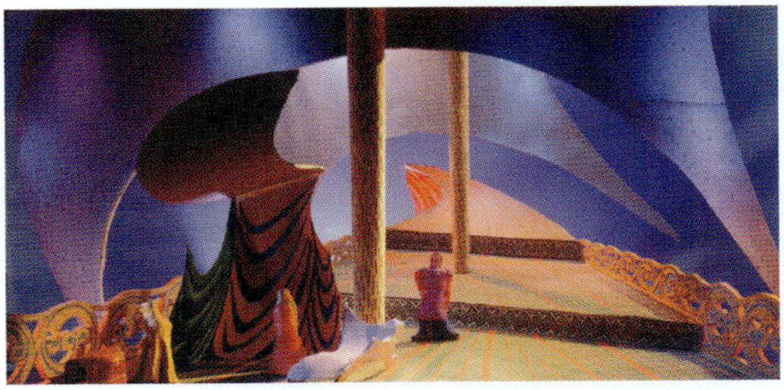

13 One-inch scale model, act 1 from *Tristan und Isolde*, 1987.

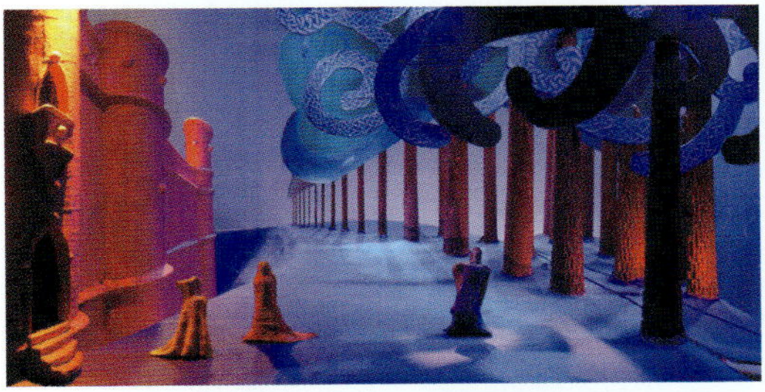

14 One-inch scale model, act 2 from *Tristan und Isolde*, 1987.

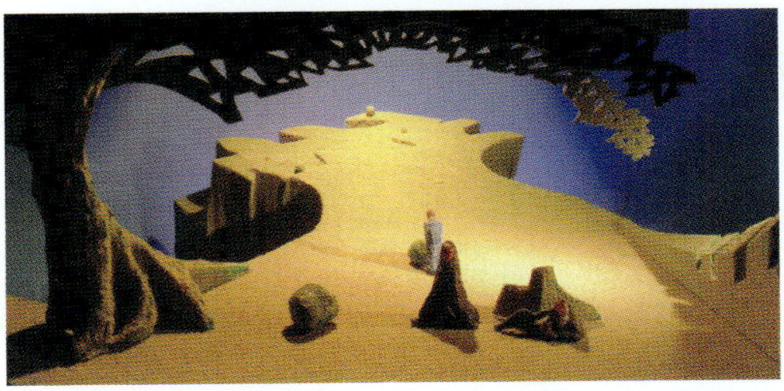

15 One-inch scale model, act 3 from *Tristan und Isolde*, 1987.

16 *Halaconia in Green Vase, 1996.*

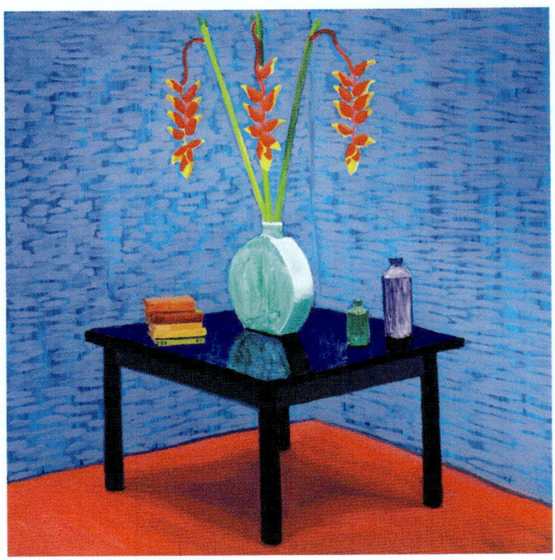

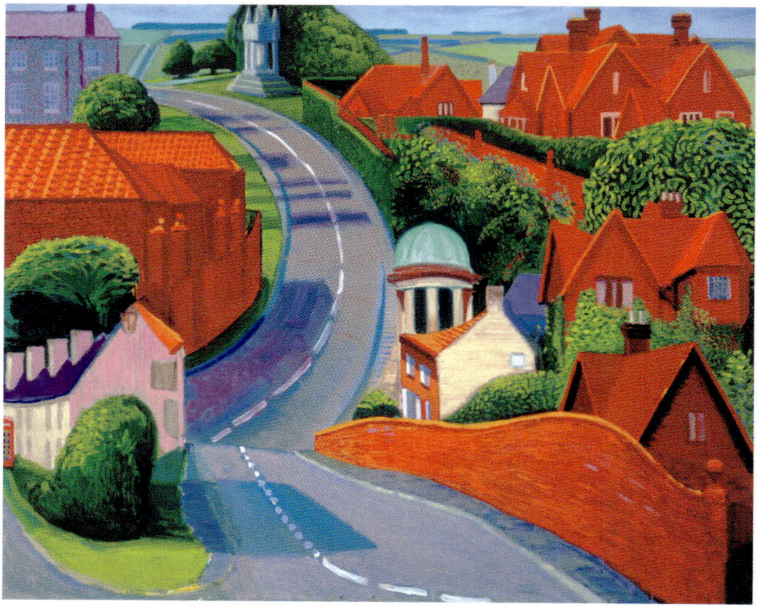

17 *The Road to York through Sledmere*, 1997.

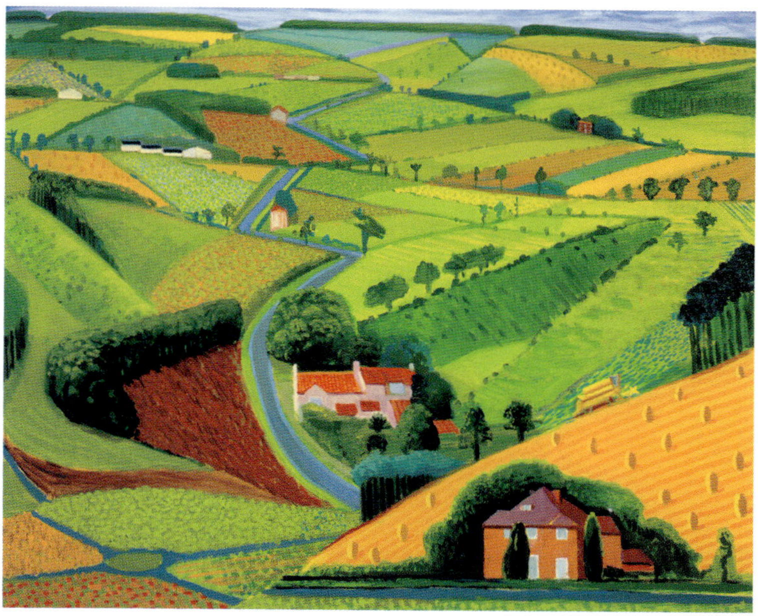

18 *The Road across the Wolds*, 1997.

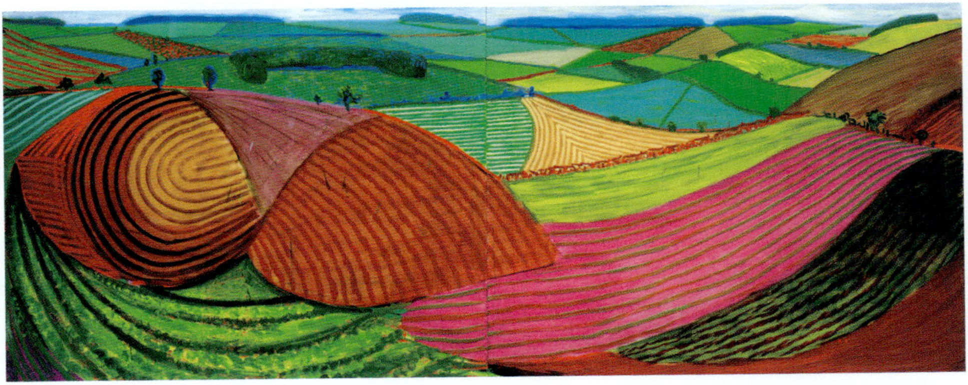

19 *Double East Yorkshire,* 1998.

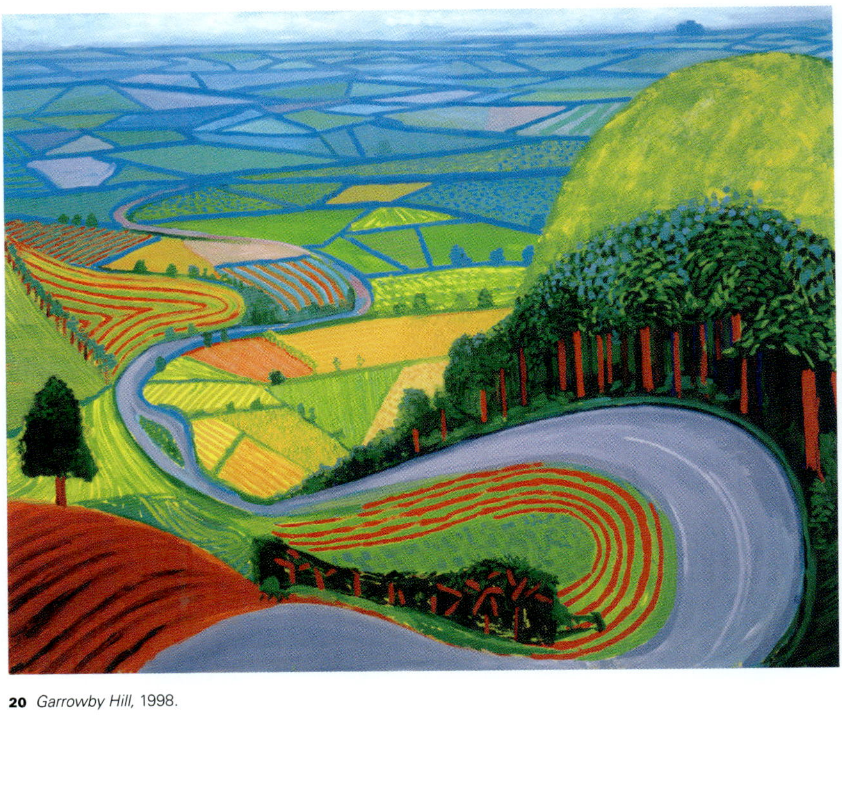

20 *Garrowby Hill,* 1998.

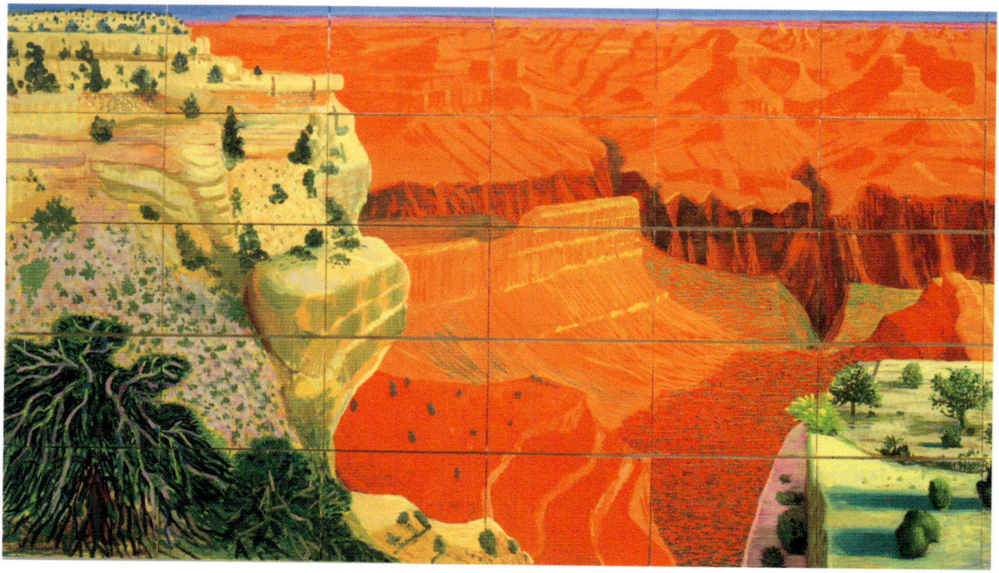

21 *A Bigger Grand Canyon*, 1998.

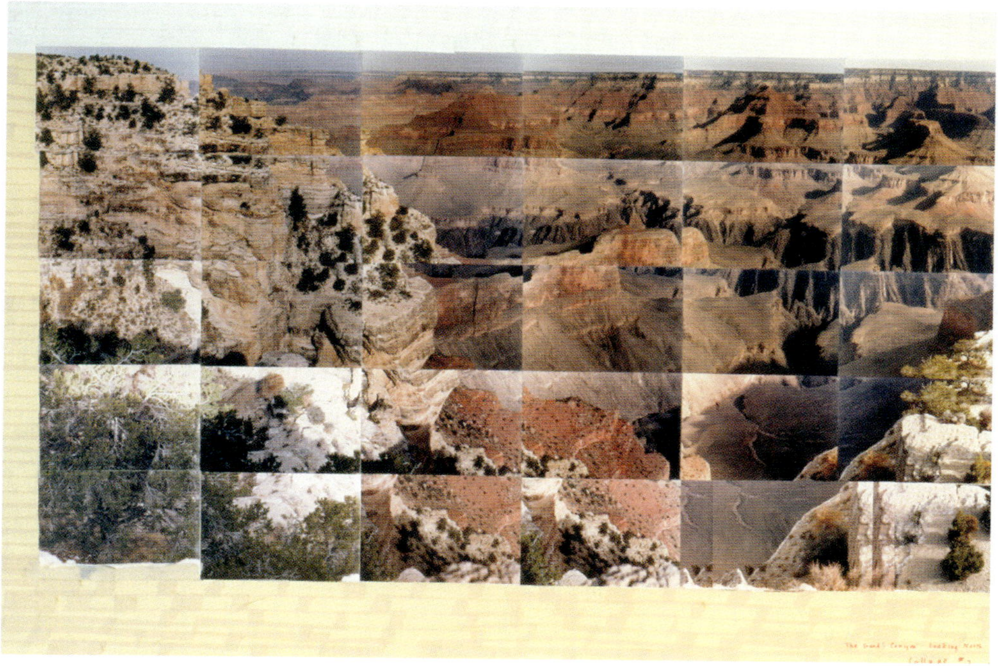

22 *Grand Canyon with Ledge, Arizona, Oct. 1982, Collage #2, Made May 1986.*

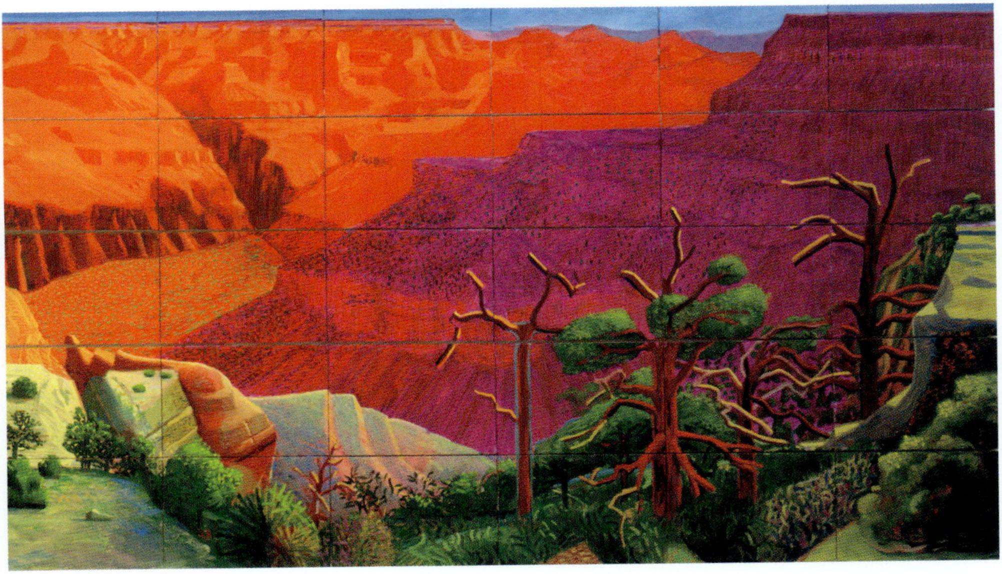

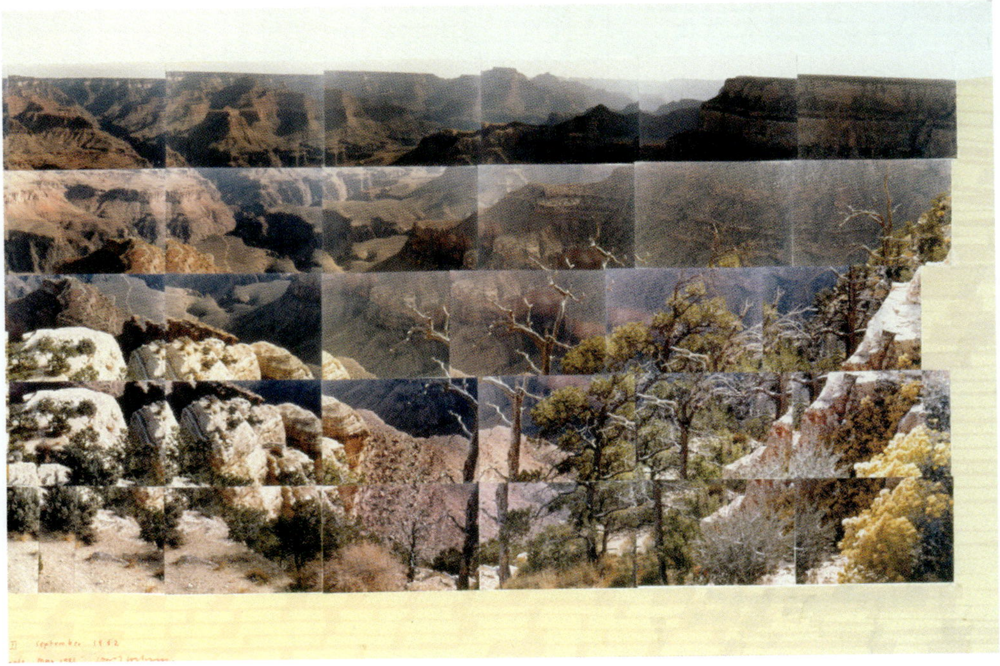

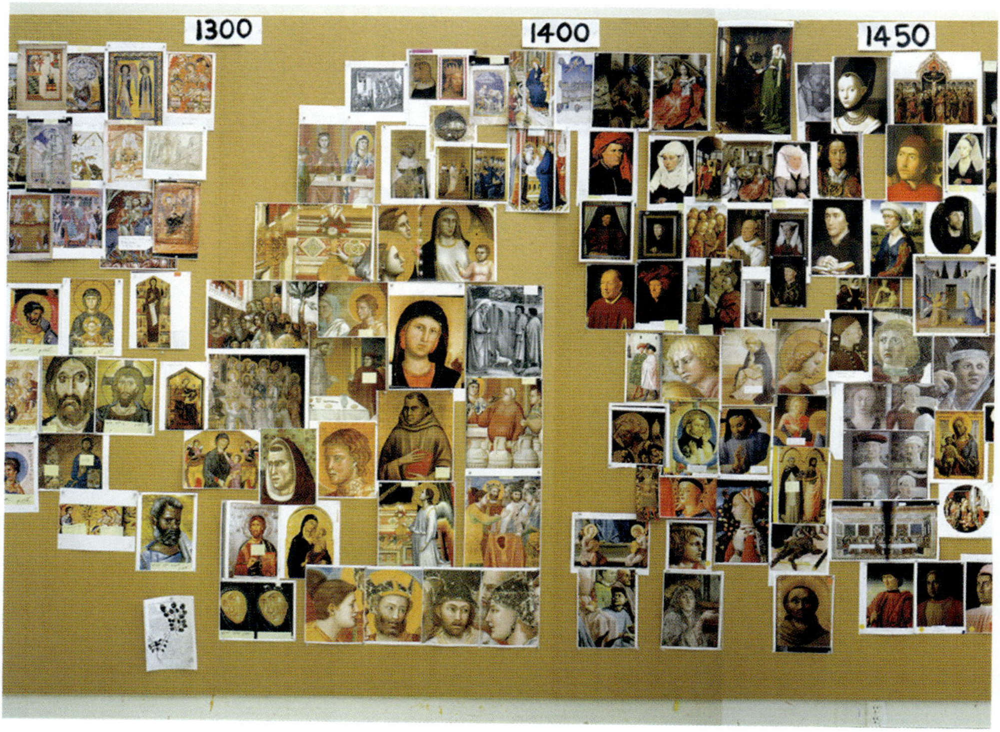

23 *The Great Wall* (detail), 2000.

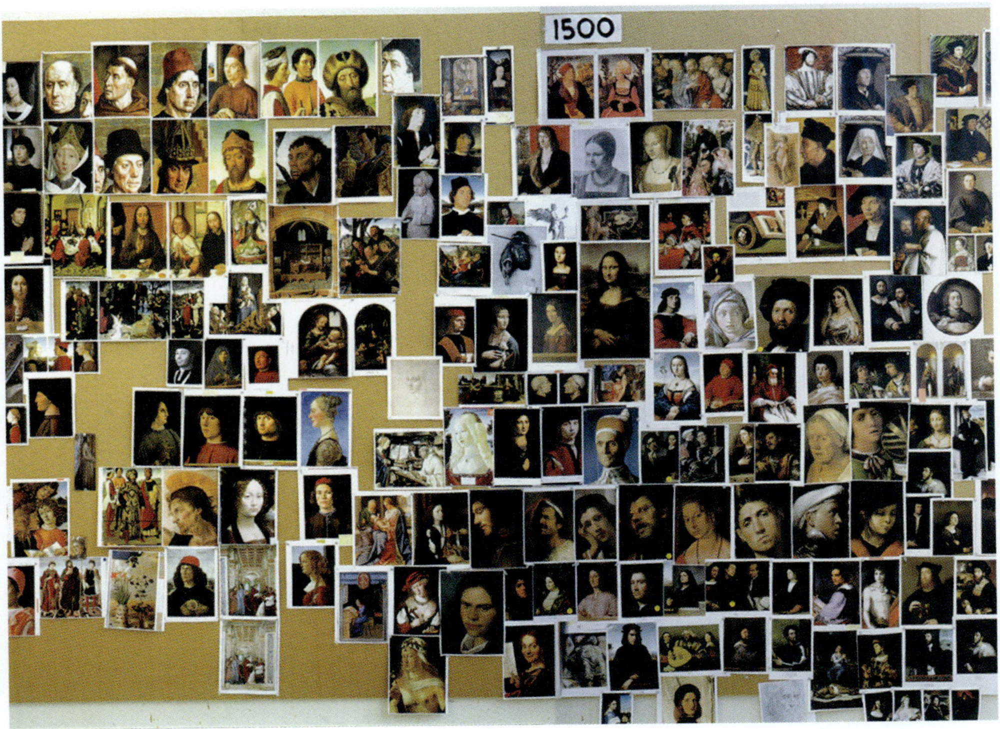
1500

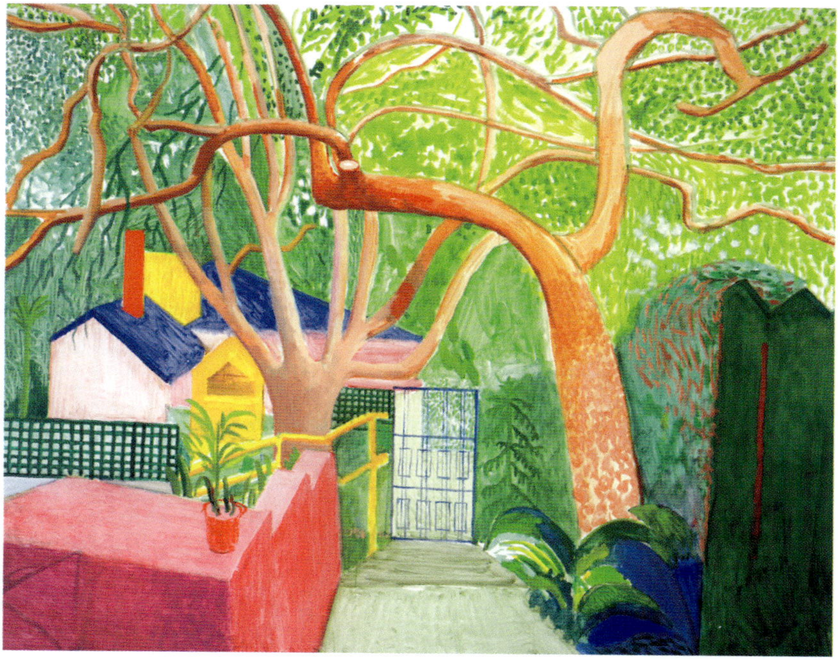

24 *The Gate*, 2000.

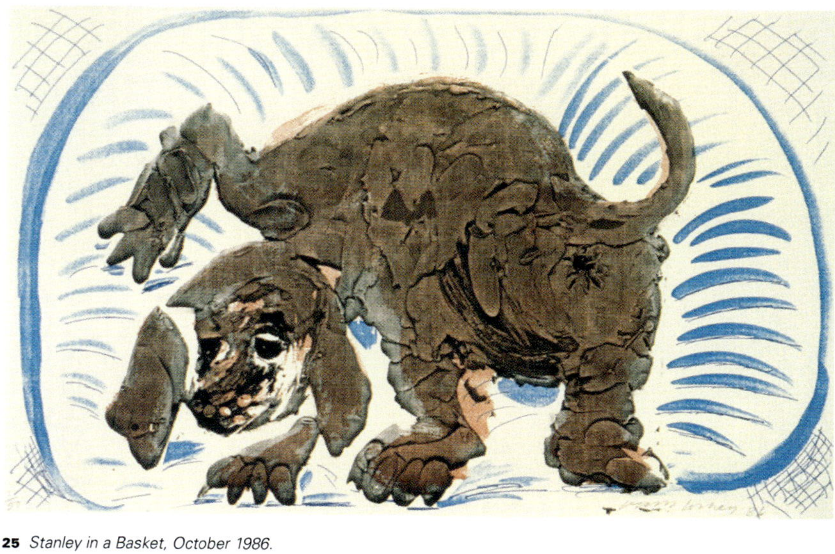

25 *Stanley in a Basket*, October 1986.

CHAPTER 5

the looking glass

ADVENTURES IN OPTICALITY

(1999)

Heads up! Watch out! Looks like Hockney's on another one of his perceptual-conceptual tears.

Or so I quickly came to realize several weeks back when I happened to be in Los Angeles and, as I usually do on such occasions, gave him a call to see how things were going. "Where are you?" Hockney demanded to know once, with no small difficulty in hearing, he'd finally managed to ascertain who I was. "Can you get up here right away? There's something I have to show you!"

Meeting me at the front door of his colorful home a few hours later, Hockney didn't even bother inviting me in for our usual tea, instead squiring me immediately up to the hillside studio, where the inside wall to the left of the entry was covered over with dozens of recent portraits of friends—or rather, on second glance, photocopied blowups of the lovingly rendered drawings whose originals had likewise been ranged along the perpendicular wall facing the studio entry (Fig. 35). Confronting such a remarkable array, I immediately thought of the death of Hockney's mother, at age ninety-eight, earlier in the year. As one of Hockney's studio assistants had commented to me in the wake of a similar eruption of the artist's impulse toward portraiture a few years back, immediately following the death of his beloved friend Henry Geldzahler, David tends to respond to such desperate losses by gathering his surviving friends yet closer around him in a sort of defiant inventory of the life that remains.

Hockney allowed me a few moments to admire the portrait walls, but rather quickly (uncharacteristically so) drew me away toward the wide worktable in the middle of the studio, which was covered over with art books, reference manuals,

---

A version of this essay originally appeared as an Onward and Upward with the Arts piece in *The New Yorker* of January 31, 2000.

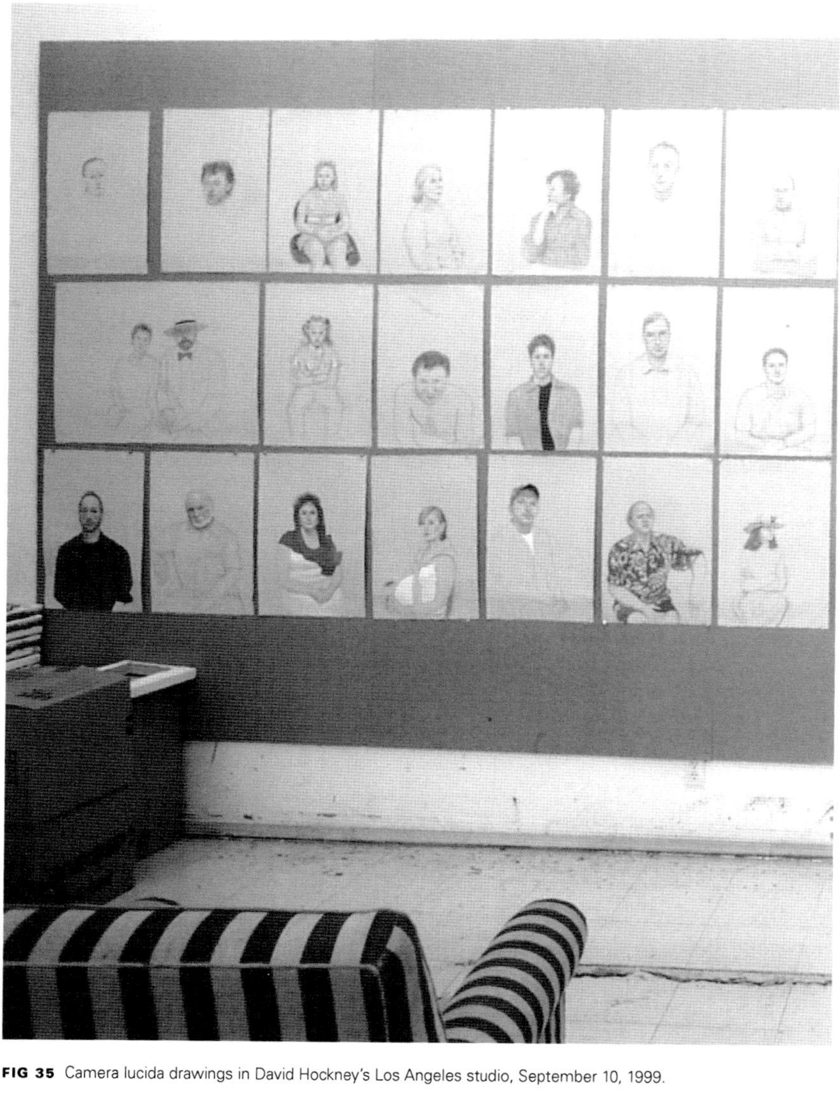

FIG 35 Camera lucida drawings in David Hockney's Los Angeles studio, September 10, 1999.

bulging folders, and hastily scribbled memos. One might have been excused for imagining Hockney to be gearing up for a full-frontal assault on the entire history of the Western painterly tradition; and, as it turned out, one would not have been far wrong.

"The past year, as you know, was an incredible one for art shows," Hockney now launched out. "The Pollock in New York, the Monet in London, and the Ingres, also, initially, in London. I spent hours at each, and each seemed to leave me more exhilarated than the one before. Especially the Ingres, which I went back to three times—the paintings, but, in particular, the drawings. Now, for someone like me, trained in the conventional Carracci tradition—you know, plumb line, the extended thumb, gauging relative proportions, and so forth—those pencil portraits of Ingres's were mind-boggling. For one thing, their size—how small they turn out to be, when you get to see them in person. The images are seldom more than twelve by eight inches, incredibly detailed and incredibly assured. If you draw at all, you know that's very rare and not at all easy. I bought the catalogue, brought it back here to L.A., studied it some more, read every word, blew up some of the drawings on the copier over there, and one morning, studying the blowups, I found myself thinking, Wait, I've seen that line before. Where have I seen that line? And suddenly I realized, That's Andy Warhol's line."

Hockney cited Studio Still-Lifes, a show of Warhol's at Paul Kasmin's gallery, in New York, the year before last. "Because Andy's is indeed the same kind of line: clean, fast, completely assured. Now, in Andy's case we know he was using a slide projector—Kasmin even had the original photos from which Andy had traced his images." Hockney reached for the Kasmin catalogue, opened the slim volume to a page featuring Warhol's 1975 arrangement of a bowl, a can opener, and a hand-held mixer (Fig. 36), and then opened his well-thumbed Ingres volume to the stunning 1816 portrait of Lady William Bentinck (Fig. 37).

"Look at that," Hockney said, "and now look at this, especially the clothes, the fall of the draped cloak, the ruffle around the neck, the gathered sleeve, and then her expression, its palpable freshness: the speed of the line, its boldness, its absolute confidence, no awkwardness, no hesitancy. Of course, Ingres wasn't using a slide

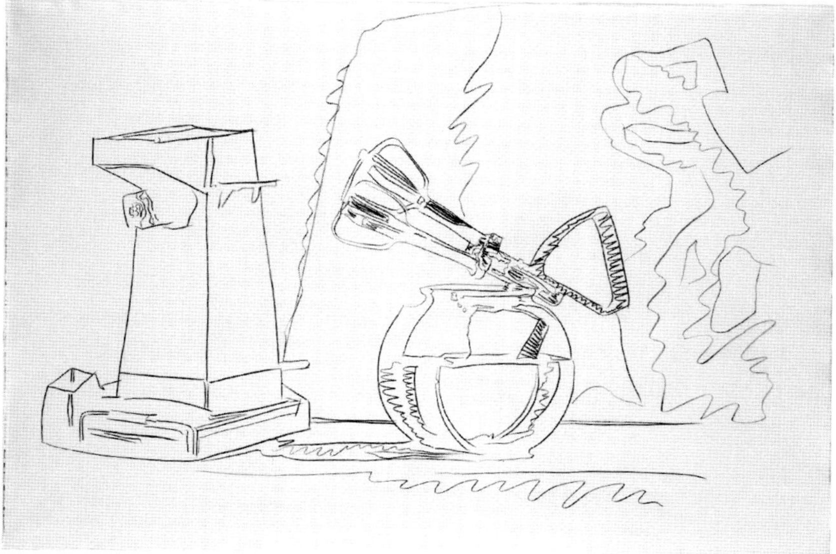

projector, but he might well have been using a camera, a refracting instrument of some sort."

Hockney reminded me that cameras and lenses long predated the invention of chemically fixed photography. For that matter, the things that happen to light as it passes through a pinhole are natural phenomena—"as omnipresent and wondrous as rainbows," Hockney said, and went on, "People have marveled over them literally for millennia, tinkering with ways to exploit the effects. And the more I looked at Ingres's drawings, the more convinced I became, on the basis of the optical evidence of the images themselves, that Ingres had to be using some sort of device based on those effects."

Hockney recalled how when he was in art school he'd been shown a camera lucida, a device invented in 1807. So now he sent his assistant down to an art supply shop to see if he could find one. "Turns out they're relatively rare nowadays and quite expensive: the one he found cost over two thousand dollars," Hockney said. "Anyway, I set up a little corner and—come here, I'll show you."

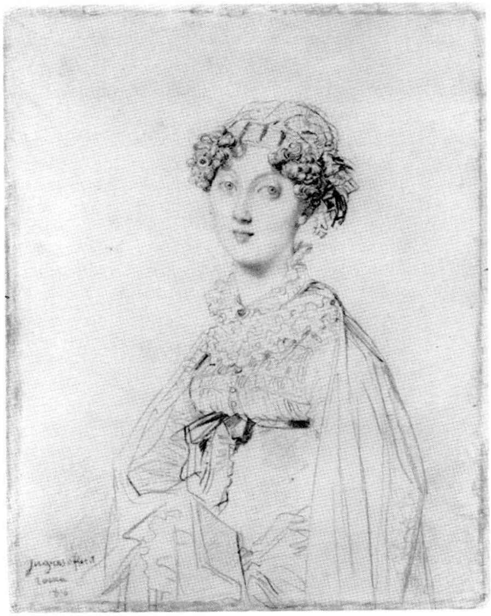

FIG 36 Andy Warhol, *Still Life*, 1975.

FIG 37 Jean-Auguste-Dominique Ingres, *Lady William Henry Cavendish Bentinck, née Lady Mary Acheson*, 1816.

Alongside the drawings wall, Hockney had erected an alcove, cordoned off with screens and curtains. This cozy little nook (I've often thought of Hockney, like Auden before him, as a sort of phenomenologist of the cozy) contained a comfortable chair propped before a flat drawing table, on which Hockney had installed his camera lucida—a tiny prism (barely wider than an eyeball) suspended, as if free-floating, at the end of a flexible metal rod. He showed me how when you looked down through the prism, the image of whatever happened to be before you seemed to be transposed onto the tabletop—or onto any blank sheet of paper that you might put there. The effect was illusory: no image was actually being cast on the page, as with a slide projector. But one could deploy the illusion to help capture a likeness (Fig. 38).

"Sit there," Hockney commanded, and then spent a few moments adjusting my pose. "Perfect," he said. "Stay like that." He fetched a sheet of Arches paper and a canister of sharpened pencils, laid the page beneath the prism, and set to work.

The first part of the session lasted about an hour, but Hockney used the camera

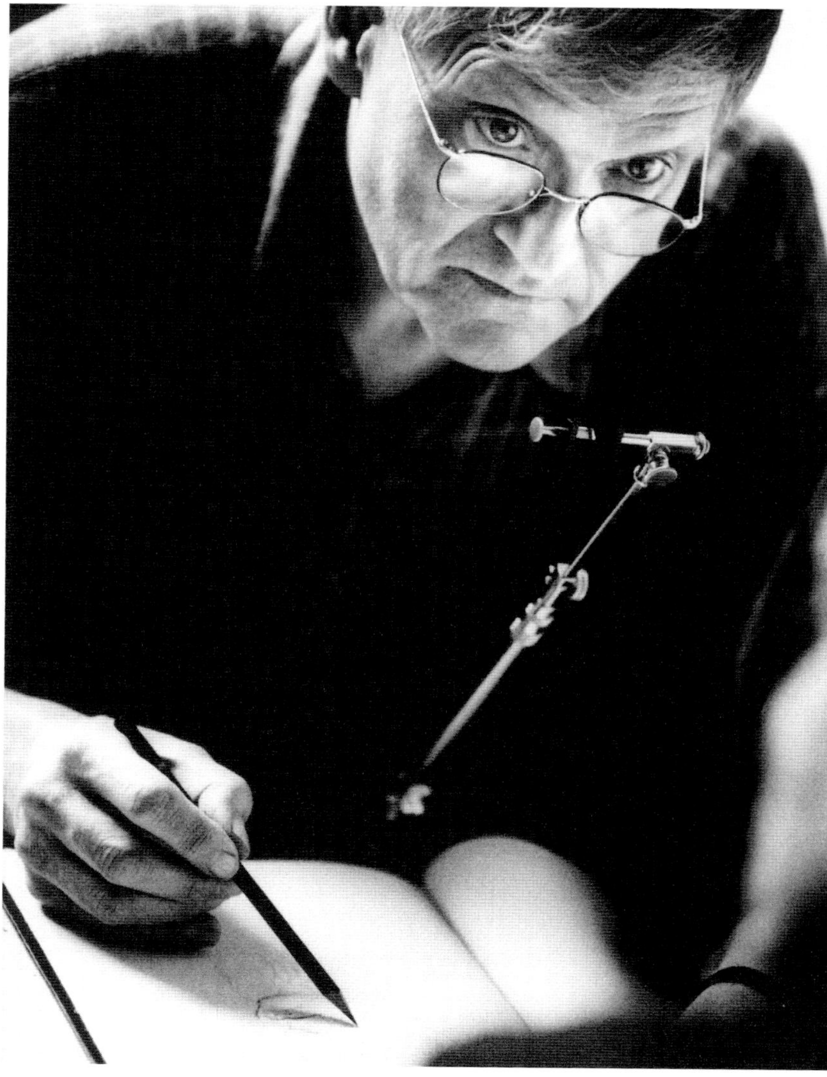

FIG 38 David Hockney drawing with a camera lucida, 1999.

lucida itself for only two or three minutes—quickly and, yes, with startling assuredness, sketching out the tangle of my hands, legs, and sleeves, and then, turning to my face, laying in the general shape of my head. Muttering, "This is the crucial part," he posited, with the faintest of pencil stabs, the coordinates of my pupils, the corners of my eyes, my nostrils, the lay of my glasses over my ears, the edges of my mouth. After that, he reverted to a more standard posture, gazing past the hovering prism, as if it weren't even there, and probing my face and then the page, back and forth. His own face was becoming increasingly scrunched up with concentration, so much so that at one point his earpiece began to screech (he plucked it out and set it aside); his tongue, animate, prehensile, lolled and darted from one side of his half-opened mouth to the other in evident syncopation with his drawing hand (it was as if he were thinking with his tongue). Only once or twice thereafter did he bother to look through the prism, for minor adjustments.

At length, we took a break, and Hockney reinserted his earpiece. The gist of the image was already well in hand. "Especially the mouth," Hockney said, tapping the page. "It's always the hardest to get right when you're just eyeballing it. Wasn't it Sargent who said, 'A portrait is a painting with something wrong with the mouth'? And a smile is hardest of all: it's not just the mouth but, rather, the precise fleeting relation of the mouth and the eyes, the crinkles around the eyes. I used to struggle for hours—days!—to get a proper likeness, revising and revising so as to transcend the drawing's inherent awkwardness, and, even so, if you look back, say, at those meticulously realistic drawings of mine from the early seventies, you'll notice how the sitters are hardly ever smiling: they're stiff, poised, still—*posed.*"

He reached once more for the Ingres catalogue. "Whereas here, look," he said, turning the page. "And this one here, see: absolutely no awkwardness. Not always; not every time. In some of the studies, especially early ones, he's laid in a traditional grid, and you can see his hand groping. But then you get another of those amazing pencil portraits he was doing in Rome, as a kind of sideline—visiting English gentry on their grand tours, people he was often meeting for the first time. He just dashes the images off, usually in a single sitting, with complete authority."

Hockney rifled among some of the other books and images spread about his table. "The thing is, once I started seeing it in Ingres, I began to notice lens- or

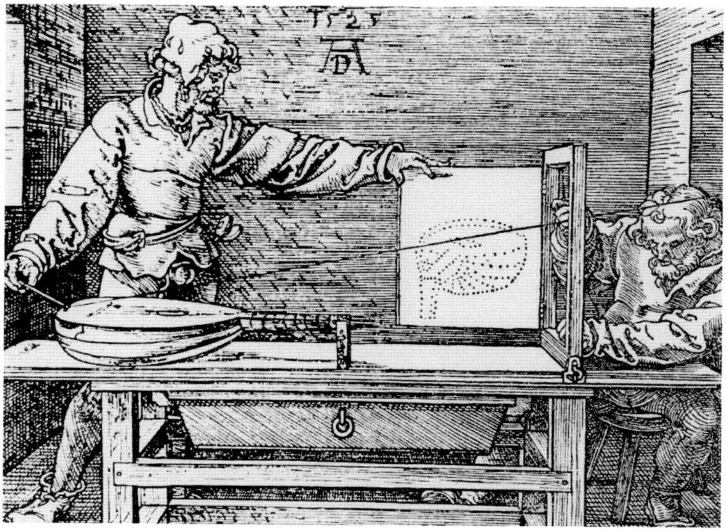

FIG 39 Albrecht Dürer, *Artist Drawing a Lute*, 1525.

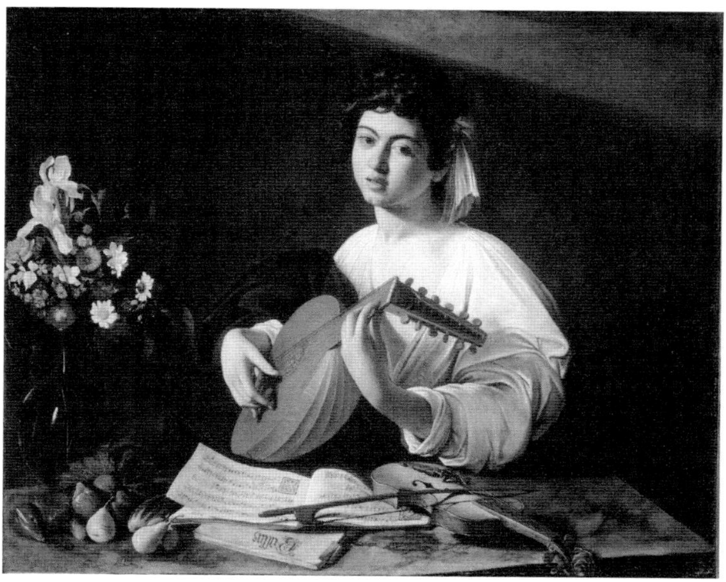

FIG 40 Caravaggio, *Young Boy Singing and Playing the Lute*, 1595.

mirror-based imagery, optically rendered imagery, in all sorts of other places, including before Ingres, and in fact well before. Hundreds of years before.

"Look here," he said, grabbing a photocopied image. "Most painters, most artists, are highly secretive about their methods. One of the few who were willing to divulge their secrets was Dürer, in the early sixteenth century. In this woodcut, he's showing how you drew a lute in perspective without, or maybe before the introduction of, lenses. Very complicated, very cumbersome. Takes two guys, an adjustable sightline, a slidable perpendicular grid, a page mounted on a hinged side panel that keeps getting swung into and out of position to note the precise spot where the moving sightline crosses the imaginary picture plane . . . Must have taken hours. That's—what?—that's 1525. And now look at this." Hockney pulled out a reproduction of Caravaggio's *Young Boy Singing and Playing the Lute.* "This is—what?—1595. Not only has Caravaggio rendered a lute in complex perspective, perfectly and seemingly effortlessly, with absolute authority, but he's thrown in a violin lying there on the table for good measure" (Figs. 39 and 40).

Back to Dürer, 1525. Hockney showed me another woodcut, this one portraying an artist using an intervening gridded glass plane to block out a portrait; the artist has to keep his eye steady, peering through an eyehole at the tip of a raised stick, and his subject is forbidden to move. "No wonder," Hockney was saying, "that when you paint like this you end up with faces like this." He showed me *Christ and the Fallen Woman,* by Cranach the Younger, a rendering from about the same period: stiff, impassive faces, mouths grimly shut, expressions stilled.

"Whereas just a few years later you get faces like these." Hockney began flipping through a nearby Caravaggio catalogue. Almost all the faces were vividly alive, openmouthed ("You try keeping your mouth open like that for more than a few moments, as one would have had to, using Dürer's gridded-glass method"), and characterized above all by fleeting, evanescent expressions—expressions, as Hockney put it, "captured on the fly."

He went on, "Notice the constant sense of assurance. And with no drawings, no sketches! There are no preparatory studies with Caravaggio. At any rate, none have survived. Or, for that matter, with Velázquez. Or Vermeer. Or Hals. Or Chardin. Hardly any." Hockney rustled through one reproduction after another. "Suddenly, they all seem to be able to render the image, just like that, onto the canvas itself. And it's not just the great masters." He showed me Dirck van Baburen's *Concert,* of 1623: a lute, a violin, one player grinning antically, another with his mouth open. Seemingly effortless.

Of course, the keyword there was "seemingly," for as Hockney went on to insist, "Optics don't make paintings; artists do. The lens can't draw a line, only the hand can do that, the artist's hand and eye in coordination with his heart. And, in any case, such optical devices are quite hard to use. You have to be a good draftsman to be able to take advantage of them at all. It took me a good several months to learn how to use that camera lucida. You look at somebody like Ingres, and it would be absurd to think that such an insight about his method undercuts the sheer marvel of what he achieves. Nobody can do it as well as he can—the subtlety of characterization, the inner life of the drawings—and the more I study him, my admiration just goes up and up and up. This whole insight about optical aids doesn't diminish anything; it merely suggests a different story, a more accurate one, perhaps—certainly a more interesting one."

With growing excitement, Hockney proceeded to lay out the broad contours of that story as he was beginning to understand it. Coming out of the Middle Ages, most painting, most rendering, he suggested, was a matter of "eyeballing," of "awkward, groping approximation," but the early Renaissance, especially in Italy, saw the rise of various mathematical systems of perspective and proportion—the transition, say, from Giotto (Fig. 41) to Piero della Francesca and Uccello, and then on through the glories of the High Renaissance, to Michelangelo and Titian. These systems of perspective were grounded in ever more elaborate intellectual superstructures, a virtual science of vision: tapering grids projected onto empty space, and then filled, according to rigorous rules, with the artist's idealized renditions of reality.

Hockney was becoming convinced, however, that during the sixteenth century, in different places and at different rates, an alternative way of proceeding started to emerge—one based on mirrors and lenses. It had been widely known since antiquity (Aristotle and Euclid both make much of the fact) that when light passes through a small hole into a darkened enclosure, a vivid if inverted image of the external world may appear on the far wall. The effect was much discussed, in tones of hushed and pious marvel, during the Middle Ages and went on to become a

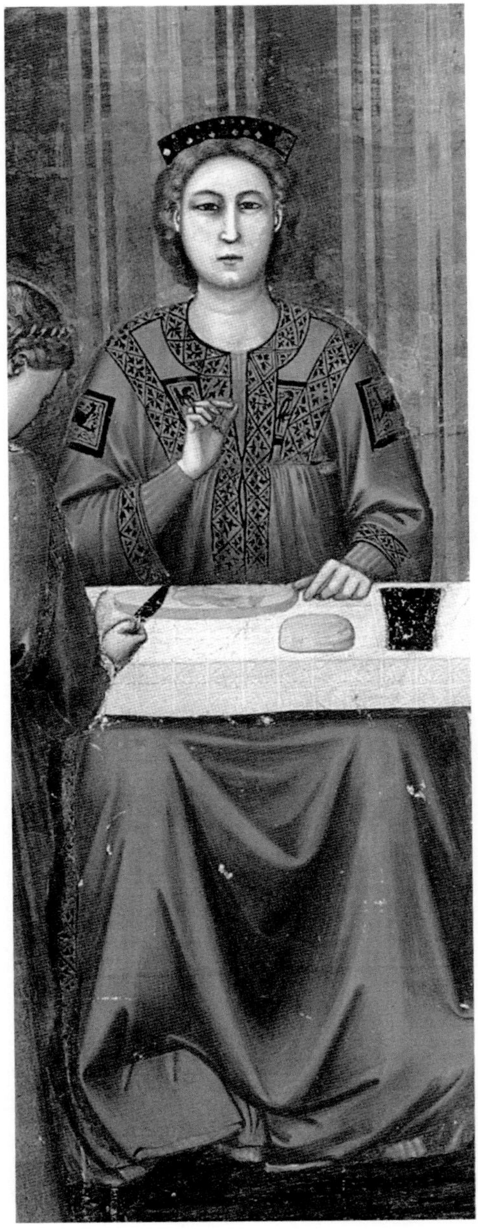

FIG 41 Giotto di Bondone, *Marriage at Cana* (detail), 1303–6.

central motif—the metaphor, that is, of the eye itself, and, for that matter, the mind, as a room receiving, through a pinhole and onto a blank wall, sense impressions from the outside world—in the epistemologies of thinkers ranging from Kepler and Newton through Descartes, Leibniz, Locke, and beyond. With the passage of time, the effect was deployed in a series of ever more sophisticated boxes—camera obscuras (literally, "darkened rooms")—with lenses to sharpen the projection and mirrors to reverse the inversion. Inevitably, such boxes drew the attention of artists; by the middle of the seventeenth century and into the eighteenth, the devices were in common evidence. Canaletto, for example, used them in his depictions of Venice.

But Hockney was increasingly coming to suspect that versions of lens-and-mirror technology (perhaps without the rigid confines of the camera obscura itself) were being used by artists long before that—initially, perhaps, in northern Europe (with Van Eyck and subsequently the Dutch landscape artists), but rather quickly spreading into northern Italy (and especially Caravaggio's Lombardy) as well.

The transition to lens-assisted artistic production was not without its controversies. Caravaggio, for instance, was regularly attacked by his more conventionally perspectival academic contemporaries, but, as Hockney now pointed out, "the attacks themselves were quite revealing." He reached for Howard Hibbard's 1983 monograph on the artist, which includes a generous sampling of such criticism. For instance, he cited Giovanni Pietro Bellori's slamming of Caravaggio for making "no attempt to improve on the creations of nature" and for lacking "*invenzione*, decorum, *disegno* or any knowledge of the science of painting." Bellori speaks of Caravaggio's need for models, "without which he did not know how to paint," and notes how older painters accused him of being able to paint only in cellars—which is to say, dark spaces—"with a single source of light and on one plane without any diminution." Nonetheless, Bellori goes on, "many artists were taken by his style and gladly embraced it, since without any kind of effort it opened the way to easy copying, imitating common forms lacking beauty."

"Well, maybe not that easy," Hockney concluded, putting the book aside. "I mean, few artists could do it as well as Caravaggio. But, still, it's clear from attacks like these that they must be talking about optical devices of some sort—devices whose use is further confirmed by the evidence of the paintings themselves. I mean, for instance, compare the mathematical foreshortening involved in one of the slain battle figures in a picture of Uccello's with the uncanny rendering of the Apostle Peter's outstretched arms in Caravaggio's *Supper at Emmaus,* with the near and far hands almost the same size—precisely the effect you'd get, incidentally, with certain kinds of telephoto lenses" (Figs. 42 and 43).

These optical techniques were increasingly dominant in the seventeenth and eighteenth centuries and became virtually ubiquitous during the first half of the nineteenth century, at which point, according to Hockney, "Suddenly something happens. And that, of course, is the invention of photography—or, to be more precise, the invention of various methods for chemically fixing the sort of lens-cast image that up till then had required the interposition of a human hand."

Hockney pointed out that photography grew directly out of the camera lucida. Rummaging around in his pile, he read from William Henry Fox Talbot's account of how, in 1833, by the shores of Lake Como, he'd been attempting to sketch with a camera lucida, though "with the smallest possible amount of success." For, Talbot went on, "when the eye was removed from the prism—in which all looked beautiful—I found that the faithless pencil had only left traces on the paper melancholy to behold. . . . The idea occurred to me . . . how charming it would be if it were possible to cause these natural images to imprint themselves durably, and remain fixed upon the paper!" By 1835 Talbot was experimenting with papers soaked in silver chloride, and by 1839 he was able to publicize his method; by 1841 he was using negatives to make multiple positives, a marked improvement on Louis Daguerre's method, developed around the same time, which could produce only a single image.

On first encountering a daguerreotype, Ingres's great rival, Paul Delaroche, declared, "From today, painting is dead." For his own part, as Hockney points out, Ingres himself increasingly turned to photos rather than the camera lucida in the years prior to his death in 1867. "His late self-portraits all have the tonality of photographs," he elaborated, turning once more to the catalogue. "Compare the forehead from his portrait of Monsieur Bertin, of 1834, here, with the forehead in that late self-portrait and you can see the effect on painting of the daguerreotype."

But it wasn't so much that photography killed painting, Hockney now went on to argue ("I mean, obviously not!"), as that it provoked a decisive rupture in the blending of painting and the sort of lens-based way of seeing that had dominated

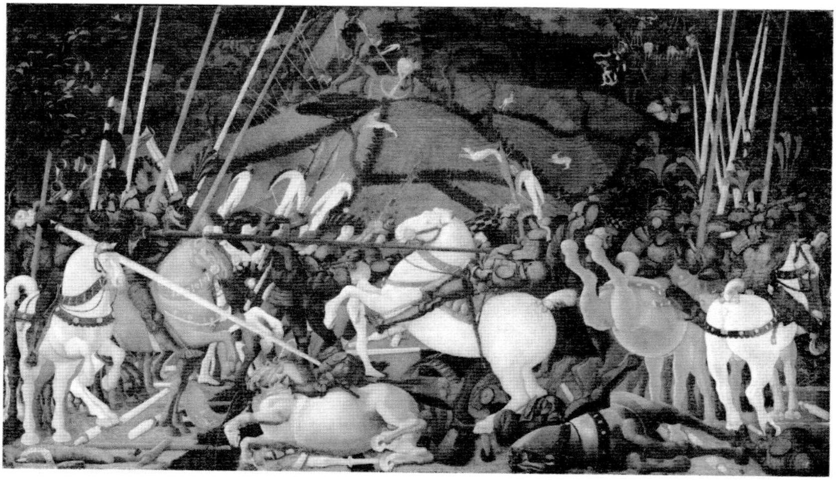

FIG 42 Paolo Uccello, *The Battle of San Romano*, ca. 1455.

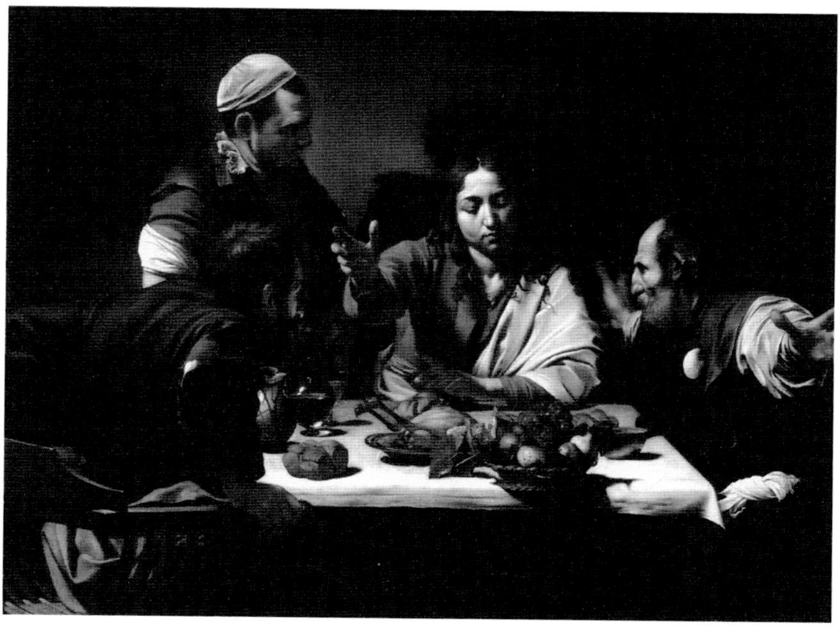

FIG 43 Caravaggio, *The Supper at Emmaus*, 1601.

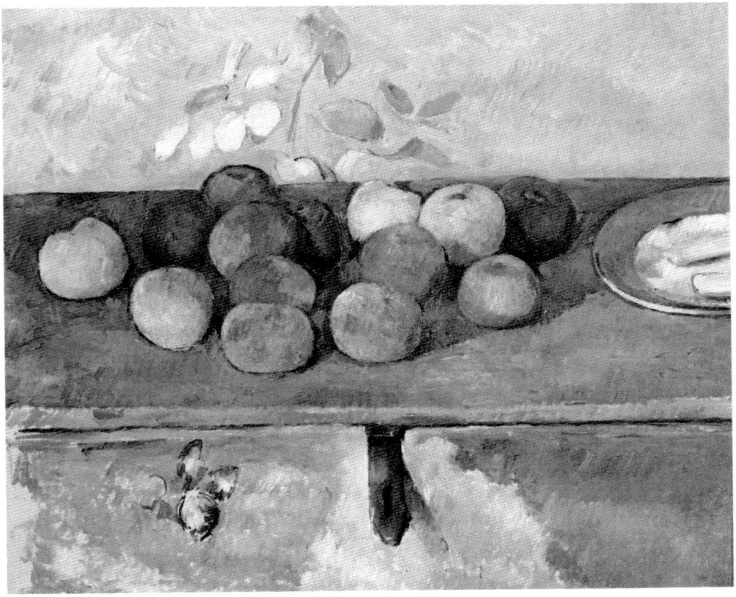

FIG 44 Paul Cézanne, *Apples and Biscuits*, ca. 1880.

it for more than three hundred years. "By 1870, the photograph had pretty much established itself as a cheap form of portraiture, and artists, for their part, started to fall away," he said. "Cézanne, for instance, starts to look at the apples before him with both eyes, opening one and then the other, and painting his doubts [Fig. 44]. Awkwardness returns to European painting, for the first time, really, since Giotto. Surely this is part of why the artists of Europe suddenly start turning toward Japan, and China, where the lens-based methodologies had never held sway.

"Soon cubism arises and, in this context, can be seen as an ongoing critique of monocular photography and, by extension, I suppose, of the entire lens-based tradition that preceded it. Painting would now endeavor to capture all the things a photograph or a single-lensed vantage could not: for example, time, duration, multiple vantages, the sense of subjectively lived reality. As the years passed, that rupture between painting and lens-based opticality widened, though at first, I'm convinced, it was a choice. Cézanne and his contemporaries knew about the various

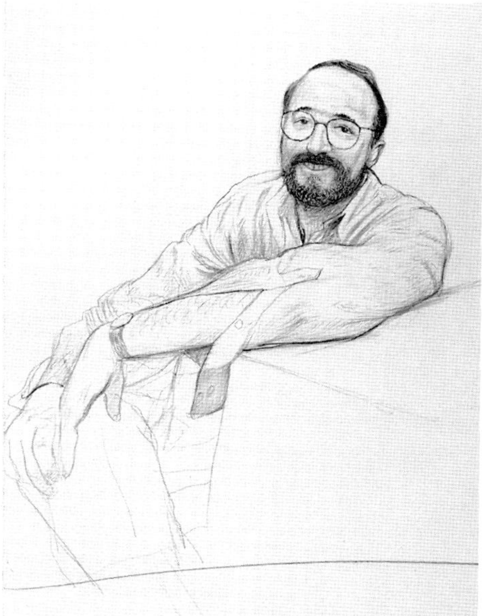

FIG 45 David Hockney, *Lawrence Weschler, Los Angeles, 20th September 1999.*

lens-based devices and chose not to use them. But within a generation or two the knowledge had been lost. And eventually you get to a generation like mine, going to school and looking back at Caravaggio and Velázquez and Ingres, and we honestly can't imagine how they were able to do it. The question itself doesn't even occur to us. They loom there like giants, preternaturally gifted, demigods, almost another species."

I was reminded of the way the peasants, deep in the Middle Ages, had gazed upon such antique relics as the Pont du Gard, the soaring Roman aqueduct outside Nîmes, stumped as to how fellow humans could have built such things, and convinced that a species of giant must once have strode the earth.

"Well, maybe we should finish that portrait," Hockney now said, smiling, as he straightened his books and pages. He escorted me back to the alcove, pulled out his hearing aids, and set to work. (It suddenly occurred to me that this surge of insights regarding the history of optical devices was flooding over an artist and thinker who happened to be finding himself more and more reliant on auditory ones—

sound lenses, as it were.) Over the next forty-five minutes, Hockney peered through his camera lucida another three or four times. The rest was steady gazing: my face and the sheet before him.

The likeness, once he'd concluded, was indeed striking, and the speed with which he'd rendered it even more so (Fig. 45). Oddest of all, though, was a strange distortion: my front arm seemed to bulge, as if in a convex mirror—much like that in Parmigianino's famous *Self-Portrait in a Convex Mirror* (from 1524).

"Precisely," Hockney said. "But look at the size of the image"—about twenty inches high. "If an artist wanted to avoid such distortions, he'd have had to have his subject stand further back, and the resultant image, in turn, would have been much smaller. Which, for that matter, is probably why those Ingres drawings are so small."

I'd noticed John Walsh's visage up on Hockney's portrait wall, not terribly well rendered (the face was still fairly stiff) but unmistakable nonetheless. I knew that Walsh, the erudite director over at the Getty Museum, had been a longtime admirer of Hockney's and had even helped to secure what was arguably the finest of Hockney's photocollages from back in the eighties—*Pearblossom Hwy.*—for the Getty's own collections. I figured I'd give him a call to see what he made of all this. (In another guise, Walsh is also a vastly knowledgeable art historian, especially steeped in Dutch art of the seventeenth century.)

"Well, I mean, it's quite remarkable, isn't it?" Walsh said, laughing, when I reached him by phone. "The sheer intensity of David's passion these days. David will often take a sound general observation—and not infrequently, like this, a surprising one, one that's long gone unnoticed—and then push and push it, way, way out to the very limit and beyond. Which is fine: it's what makes him an artist, that divine confidence of his. But in this latest discourse, marvelously suggestive as several of his notions are, I fear that David may well find himself sailing against the wind. For before the seventeenth century, where's the evidence? Where's the testimony of sitters or other contemporaries, or the treatises of the artists themselves? We have vast inventories, often compiled for inheritance purposes at the time of artists' deaths, every single brush accounted for—and where are all the lenses and other devices you'd expect to find listed, if David were right? It's pretty dicey."

Back in New York, I looked up Gary Tinterow, a senior curator of paintings at the Metropolitan Museum and one of the principal organizers of the Ingres show, which had been at the Met last fall. He had been through the exhibit several times with Hockney, and had even slotted the artist for an appearance at an all-day Ingres symposium scheduled for a few weeks hence.

We met in the galleries, and I found him a bit more receptive than Walsh. "Hockney's insights are potentially very important," Tinterow told me, "not only with regard to Ingres but maybe even more so with regard to some of the others, especially those painters for whom, as he notes, we don't have any preliminary sketches. But it will all depend on fact finding: our work as historians is now cut out for us, to find corroborating evidence. I mean, I think one can already say that Ingres's drawing style does undergo a noticeable shift after 1807, the year the camera lucida would have become available to him; and when I'm with David I can in fact see what he means by the Andy Warhol line, especially as it courses from one distinct garment, say, over onto another and then back again, seemingly oblivious of the separate volumes. Other times, though, by myself, I'm not so sure; that kind of skating over distinct volumes doesn't seem as evident to me.

"And, for instance, take this image here"—we walked over to one of the earliest pictures in the show, dated before 1806. "David would doubtless speak of its elongated foreshortening, how one is given to see more than one could ordinarily take in in a single glance—this kind of scooped-out concavity, from which David would infer that Ingres had to be looking through some kind of lens. Sounds great, sounds plausible, but we just don't *know* it to be the case. And the very same qualities, for that matter, could result from other factors. Perhaps Ingres is consciously quoting from earlier sources, and that's why you get these effects. Then again, maybe those earlier sources—Bronzino, Jacques-Louis David—were using optical devices of their own. As for the relative smallness of the drawings, perhaps, as David suggests, they result from Ingres's use of a camera lucida. On the other hand, Ingres's father was also a painter and, in particular, a miniaturist, and maybe it has something to do with that. Then again, as a miniaturist, maybe his father was likewise using lenses. It would be nice if we could find an account from one of Ingres's sitters—and there are many who left such accounts, who mention his easels and brushes and canvases—a sitter who described Ingres's use of such optical devices.

On the other hand, who's to say we won't yet come upon just such an account, especially now that we know what to look for?"

Such comments were typical of the hesitations raised by several (though not all) of the art historians I spoke with in the ensuing weeks—and several were far more bluntly dubious. Hockney was unfazed. "For one thing," he told me when I telephoned, "the paintings themselves are the evidence, if you know how to look at them—if you look at them, that is, as an artist would look at them. Many art historians regard themselves as too lofty—too concerned with the history of ideas, of iconography and so forth—to bother with questions about the mere craft of a painting's making. I must say, frankly, that I'm not all that interested in what sometimes passes for 'art history,' though I am intensely interested in the history of paintings.

"As for evidence," he went on, "if anything, it's the other way around: the burden is on them. If you say I'm wrong about the proliferation of lenses and optical devices, then you've got to explain how you could get Caravaggio's lutes just a few short decades after Dürer; how come those skills seem to rise up out of nowhere, spread everywhere, and then disappear just as quickly with the advent of the chemical process, some three hundred years later? How come awkwardness seems to disappear completely from western European art for three hundred years and then just as quickly reappear? It all just happens by itself? *That* would be the loopy theory."

But what about the apparent lack of testimony on the part of the artists or their sitters? "Artists are notoriously secretive about the specifics of their technique, always have been," Hockney replied, "and this would have been especially so in the early modern period, when the projection of such illusion was almost deemed a magical gift—though in many ways it's no less so today. Does anybody know exactly how Roy Lichtenstein created his effects? Or Morris Louis? Were they telling?

"As for the apparent lack of testimony, for example, by Ingres's sitters, the fact is—as you saw—the camera lucida is just a brief element of the entire process. It's tiny; if you didn't know to look for it, you might not even have paid it any attention. That may be one reason. More generally, the optical tools may just have been taken for granted by sitters as part of the artist's craft: nothing worth commenting on. If I asked you what it was like having your picture taken by some photo-portraitist today, you wouldn't reply, 'Well, he took this boxlike object with a bit of glass in the middle at the end of a stand with a cord he pressed.' You'd focus on other aspects of the experience, how he set you at your ease, made a nice cup of tea, chatted wittily, and so forth. And furthermore, for all we know, the sitters and witnesses have been commenting on the optical aspects all along; we just didn't know what words to look for. They may not have said optical device, or lens, or camera obscura . . . For instance, they may have used the word *glass*—as in *spyglass* for telescope, a *looking-glass* for a mirror—and up till now we weren't paying attention."

I could see why Hockney drove some art historians crazy. "He's a nimble thinker" is how John Walsh had parsed matters for me, his voice brimming with wry affection. "He's seldom at a loss for answers, even if those answers might seem to overlap in sometimes wildly contradictory ways."

"And anyway," Hockney was now saying, "who says there isn't already plenty of evidence of precisely the sort they seem to be demanding?" He noted how he'd recently begun a fax correspondence with Martin Kemp, the eminent art historian at Oxford University, whose massive 1990 study *The Science of Art: Optical Themes in Western Art from Brunelleschi to Seurat* was studded with suggestive leads. "And my friend David Graves, in London, has been spending time in the British Library, digging up all sorts of things. For instance, here"—I could hear him shuffling papers. "Right. This: from Giovanni Battista della Porta's 1558 four-volume treatise *Magiae Naturalis—Natural Magic*—by which was meant seemingly supernatural phenomena that could be explained scientifically. And here he's revealing what he calls the 'carefully guarded secret' of deflecting images onto a page. 'If you cannot paint,' he advises, 'you can by this arrangement draw (the outline of images) with a pencil. You have then only to lay on the colours. This is done by reflecting the image downwards onto a drawing board with paper. And for a person who is skillful, this is a very easy matter.' And so forth. So I really don't know what these historians are talking about: no evidence."

I began getting faxes on an almost nightly basis—part of a stream of such inspiration that Hockney seemed to be sending out to an ever-widening group of correspondents (Martin Kemp, David Graves, Gary Tinterow, and so on). The notes were invariably handwritten. Hockney—this great student of technical wizardry—has never learned to type, and hence shies away from e-mail. For that matter, the fax allows him to send reproductions of imagery, too.

One morning, I found a single sheet on which Hockney had included, side by side, a reproduction of *The Art of Painting,* by Vermeer (the artist in his silly dark pantaloons, seen from behind, seated at his easel, his model poised gracefully before him), and a witty *Triple Self-Portrait* by Norman Rockwell (the artist, likewise seen from behind, leaning over to peer, bespectacled, into a mirror as he completes the prettified self-image, without glasses, on the canvas before him). As Hockney subsequently remarked, both images manifestly fictionalized their own creative process; neither artist was in fact eyeballing the painting we see before us. Rockwell famously used photographs to develop his imagery, and Vermeer has been shown by the National Gallery of Art's Arthur Wheelock, among others, to have blocked out his canvases with the aid of a camera obscura.

Another morning, I woke to find yet another impromptu treatise on Caravaggio's method. "The more one looks into Caravaggio," Hockney wrote, the more "one can figure out his tool, which had to be a sophisticated lens." He went on to note that, as he'd suspected, there were contemporary written references to Caravaggio's "glass" ("I mention this for the historian of pictures who wants everything in writing so he doesn't have to look very hard at the pictures and deduce methods"), after which he set out, precisely, to deduce Caravaggio's possible technique:

> He traveled a lot, so the equipment has to be portable, not really very big. So I suggest a lens that is not much bigger than two cans of beans. Some lenses are more sophisticated than others. Today compare the results of a throwaway camera (cheap plastic lens) with exactly the same subject, lighting, and film, [taken] with a Leica. One will be fuzzy edges, all colors tending toward murky green; the Leica will be sharper and with richer and more varied colours. Common knowledge, you might say, but, again, I mention it for those who want it in writing, etc., etc.
>
> The lenses were all hand-made, hand-ground, etc. Caravaggio's would never have left his person, unless he was using it. In the highly competitive world of painters, no wonder he carried a sharp sword in those violent times.

> He worked in dark rooms—cellars. . . . He used artificial lighting, usually from the top left. He would use models from the street—who else would sit still for him very long?—and was known to work very fast. How long can you hold your arm outstretched even resting on a stand? Try it: you begin to ache under the arms.
>
> So the *Supper at Emmaus* was set up carefully in a cellar, lit carefully, and then he put his lens in the middle on a stand and hung a curtain (thick material in those days) around it. The room is now divided into a light part and a dark part. He is "in the camera" and the tableau is projected clearly with telescopic effect (notice again how the rear hand is almost bigger than the front hand nearer to you).
>
> He covers the canvas with a rich dark undercoat that, being wet, reflects light back. He takes a brush and with the wrong end draws guidelines for the figures in the composition, to enable him to get the models back in position after [breaks for] resting, eating, pissing, etc.
>
> He rapidly paints on the wet canvas, skillfully and with thin paint, knocking in the difficult bits, and then with his virtuosity he can finish by taking down the curtain, turning the canvas round and looking at the scene in reality.
>
> All this sounds perfectly plausible to me. So, say there's no lens; then give a reasonable explanation. Remember: there are no drawings, no notes.
>
> Goodnight, D. Hockney

Good night indeed: I noticed that the fax had been sent at two-thirty in the morning, his time.

I subsequently spoke with Gary Tinterow about this particular piece of Hockneyan speculation. We happened to be looking at one of the Met's own Caravaggios; he crouched at the side of the canvas and urged me to look up with him. "It's interesting about Caravaggio," Tinterow said. "Because the fact is that when you look at his paintings in a raking light like this, you can indeed still make out the marks made upon the canvas by the blunt end of the brush or a stylus as it traced out the contours of the various forms."

Thinking further about Hockney's scenario, I was reminded of the strange old performance tradition of tableaux vivants, in which society types would go to great lengths to gussy themselves up as figures in old-master paintings, painstakingly staging the costumed pose, lighting it just so, and then holding it like that, frozen, for minutes at a time before an admiring audience. For a moment, it seemed to me

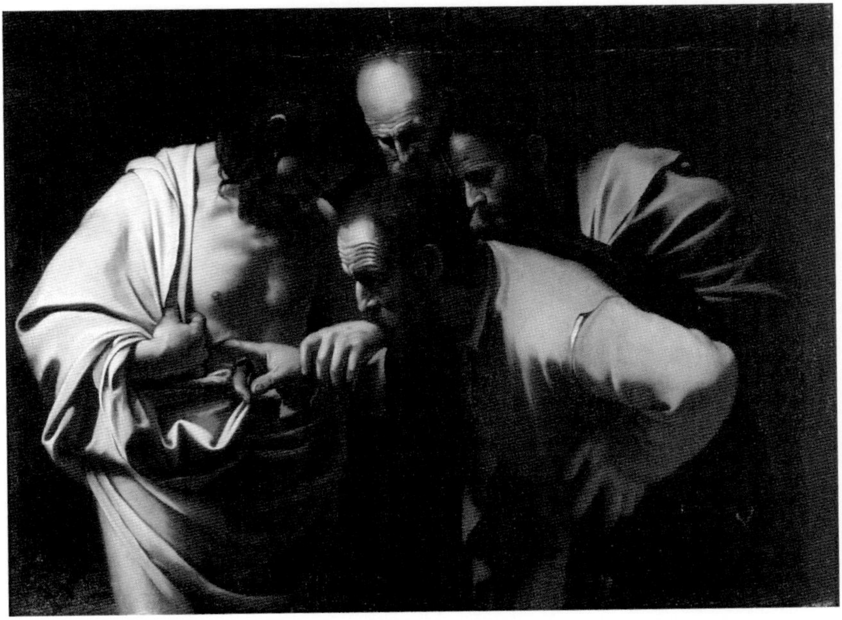

FIG 46 Caravaggio, *The Incredulity of Saint Thomas, 1601–2.*

that in such situations the canvas itself had been transformed into a sort of time prism, veritably projecting one group's frozen pose across the centuries onto another entirely different such group.

In a similar frame of mind, another afternoon, I was leafing through Hibbard's monograph when I came upon a reproduction of Caravaggio's astonishing rendition of *The Incredulity of Saint Thomas,* from the Staatliche Schlösser in Potsdam (Fig. 46). Christ stands to one side, gingerly pulling aside the cloth draping his torso so that a manifestly peasant Thomas, backed by two other street types, can literally poke his finger into the gash in the risen Messiah's flank. And for a fanciful moment I found myself wondering whether Caravaggio's composition might not contain a subliminal allusion to the dumbfounding hole-in-the-curtain methodology of the painting's very creation.

I tried such notions out on Hockney a few days later during another phone conversation, and the part he homed in on was this business of the evident street-class

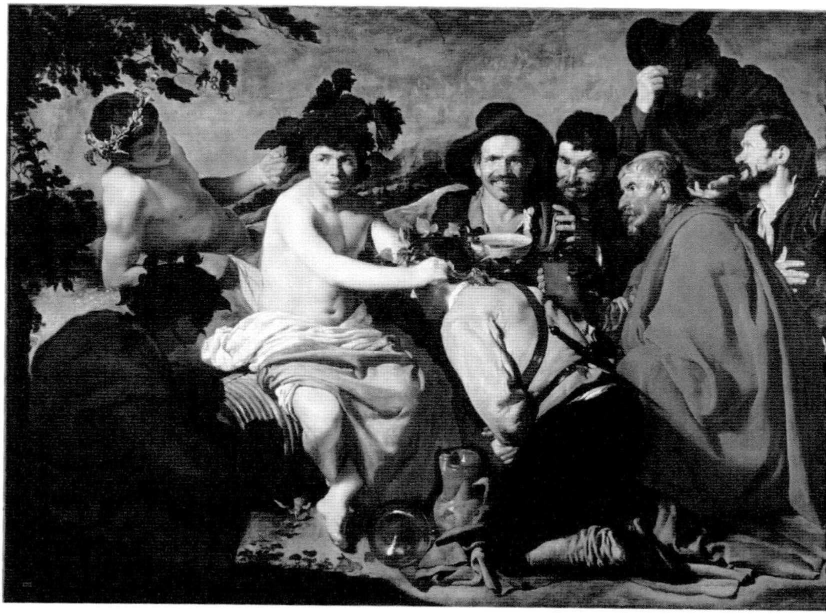

FIG 47 Diego Rodriguez Velázquez, *Triumph of Bacchus (Los Borrachos)*, 1628.

nature of Caravaggio's models. "Because, you see, that's the point," he said. "These methods have certain subjects and ways of treating them built into them. The street urchin down the lane becomes a god, an angel, an apostle, because he's the only one with the time and willingness to pose, or anyway the only one the painter can afford to pay. The well-scrubbed society types wouldn't bother—except maybe, years later, as a sophisticated form of divertissement. But that's why you now start getting these sorts of faces in such heightened contexts. It's exactly the same thing, some years later, with the early Velázquez: the same sorts of faces in the same sorts of contexts [Fig. 47]. And look at *those,* while you're at it: the fleeting expressions, the open mouths, the self-conscious grins. . . ."

About a week after I'd got Hockney's Caravaggio treatise, my phone rang me awake way before seven: there was a whistling on the line. "Oh, dear." Hockney's voice came rising through the whistle. "What time is it?" It turned out that he was calling from Canberra, Australia, where he'd gone to deliver an early version of these ideas as a lecture. Frank Stella, another Caravaggio enthusiast, was in attendance and, according to Hockney, he'd said to him afterward, "I'm sure you're right." Hockney apologized for waking me, but went on, "Listen, love, there's a book you have got to get. That Taschen book: *The Portrait.* Norbert Schneider. I picked up a copy this afternoon at the museum here, and it's incredible. The first page, in the introduction, Schneider writes—he's talking about the late fifteenth century—'It remains a source of continual astonishment that so infinitely complex a genre should develop in so brief a space of time, indeed within only a few decades.' *Continual astonishment:* he's talking about the arrival of the lens, and he doesn't even know it. But I'm absolutely convinced of it. The plates are amazing. Get the book and we'll talk later."

I did—it is a beauty—and that evening the phone rang again; it was Hockney, almost breathless with excitement. "You have the book?" he asked. "Good. Because I think Schneider's right. It happens before Dürer. Dürer is showing an *old* way in those woodcuts." He instructed me to turn to a page that featured a small color reproduction of Giovanni Bellini's portrait of the doge of Venice, circa 1500—an extraordinary painting (Fig. 48). Then he told me to turn to the opposite page, which was filled with a detail of the doge's face in black and white or, rather, sepia. "And there you can really see it," Hockney said. "Something about the sepia tonalities, perhaps, but the image looks for all the world like some antique 1870 photograph of an Indian raja."

The effect was indeed uncanny. Stripped of its color, recast in black and white, the image did indeed look exactly like a photograph, and the doge like our virtually immediate contemporary. (I was momentarily reminded of a similarly uncanny, if diametrically opposite, effect I'd experienced some years earlier on first gazing at a book of Sergei Mikhailovich Prokudin-Gorskii's 1909 color photographs for the czar: Count Tolstoy, a rug merchant, a beautiful young woman. How, I remembered thinking, stupefied, could they possibly ever have existed in color?)

"Look at the detail of the tight embroidering around the doge's cap," Hockney went on, "how precisely the pattern follows the contours of the cap—your eye thinks it's lying there perfectly. No way, absolutely no way that could have been eyeballed, no way mathematical perspective could account for such precision."

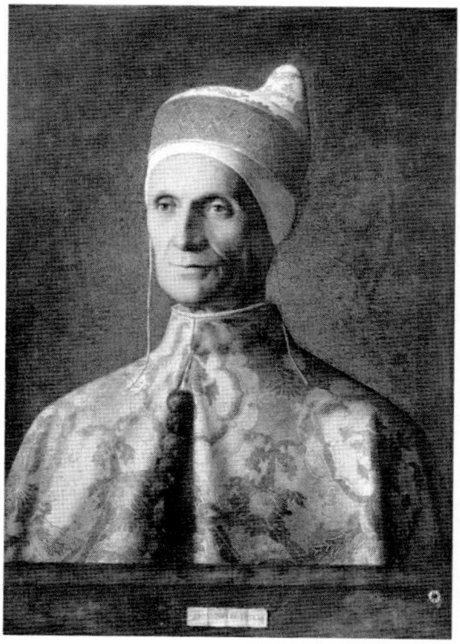

FIG 48 Giovanni Bellini,
The Doge Leonardo Loredano, ca. 1500.

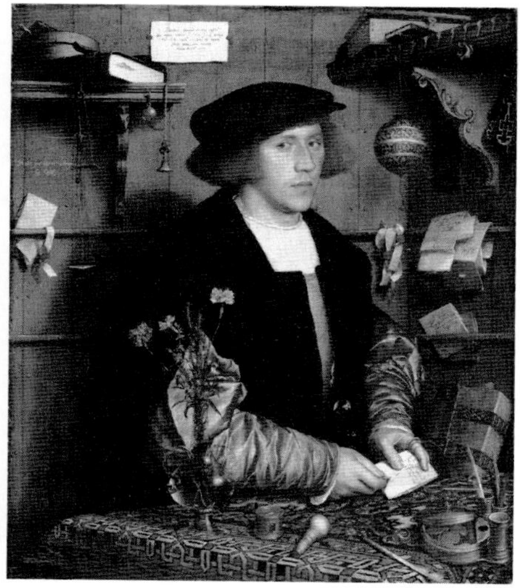

FIG 49 Hans Holbein the Younger,
The Merchant Georg Gisze, 1532.

Hockney then had me turn to a reproduction of Holbein the Younger's 1532 portrait of Georg Gisze. He pointed out the highlights on Gisze's sleeve, and how precisely the geometric pattern follows the rug as it falls over the edge of the tabletop. The glass vase, the pestle, both perfect, rest perfectly on the tabletop. "Your eye knows they're right," Hockney insisted, now guiding my attention to "that curious cylindrical brass canister on the table between them [Fig. 49]. Because something's wrong: I mean, itself it looks right, but something's wrong with how it's resting on the tabletop. It's as if it had been added as an afterthought, a separate projection, which didn't align quite right. Right?"

Hockney was warming to his theme. I realized that it must be six in the morning for him, and I wondered whether he'd slept at all. He directed me to turn to a Raphael painting, circa 1517, of Pope Leo X (Fig. 50). "Look at the thick brocade of his sleeve: perfect," Hockney said. "I was talking with a historian the other day about this picture, and he stopped me cold. What was I talking about? There couldn't possibly have been any lenses in 1518. Galileo doesn't happen till 1609, Leeuwenhoek is more like 1660. 'Oh yeah,' I countered. 'What do you think that is in the

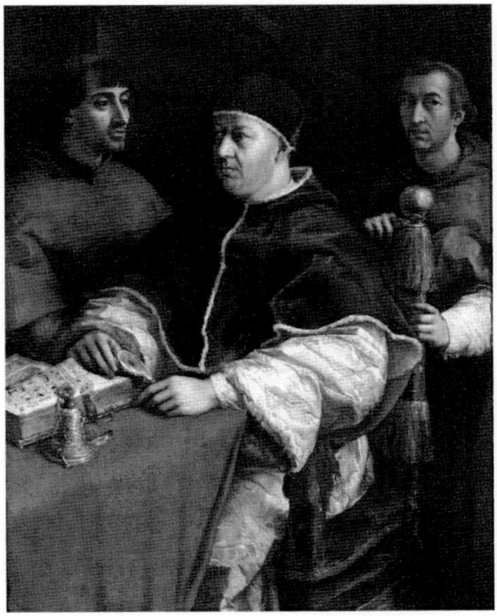

FIG 50 Raphael (Raffaello Sanzio), *Pope Leo X with Cardinals Giulio de' Medici and Luigi de' Rossi*, ca. 1517.

Pope's hand?'" Sure enough, Pope Leo was holding a magnifying glass. "And, of course," Hockney said, "it stands to reason that lenses would first have been prized by popes and kings, the wielders of power, and, in turn, their court painters—accurate portraiture being such an important aspect of their rule—and only later, maybe even much later, by scientists and academics and their lowly like."

He paused for air, but not for long. "And, by the way, look at which hand the Pope's holding his lens in." The left. "I was talking with another historian the other day, and he assured me that no left-handed person would ever have been allowed to become pope in those days: the left was the devil's hand. *Sinistra*. But that's the effect you would get, in the early days of lens projection, if you hadn't yet learned to compensate for the reversal caused by the lens. For that matter, look through the rest of the book: Lorenzo Lotto's *Man with a Golden Paw*, in which the paw in question is clearly being held in the guy's left hand. Doesn't it seem to you there are an inordinate number of left-handed people in this book?" He paused again before positively exulting, "I'm right. I'm right. I'm more certain of it every day." Whereupon he rang off.

A few weeks after that, Hockney was back in New York, addressing the Ingres symposium at the Met. His presentation was the last of the day, following public talks by such art historians as Thomas Crow (on Ingres and David), Jack Flam (on Ingres and Matisse), and Robert Rosenblum (on Ingres's progeny, from Gérôme to Picasso).

During his slide show, Hockney went over much of the material he'd been rehearsing with me and with others over the previous several weeks—Ingres, Warhol, Caravaggio, Bellini, Raphael—but he added some newer material as well. For instance, he devoted more time to Velázquez, Van Dyck, and Rubens (an oddly anomalous eyeballer). He'd developed a charming riff on early modern Spanish still lifes, especially the work of Juan Sánchez Cotán (1561–1627), a master of sliced melons ("the lutes of the vegetable world") and cabbage heads. "How long do you think a cabbage like that one would have lasted in those days, prior to refrigeration, in a strong light like that?" Hockney challenged his audience.

Later, during the question period, someone in that audience asked the historians what they made of Hockney's theory, a question that drew a long, somewhat embarrassed silence, though whether the embarrassment was for themselves (at never having noticed such a thing before) or for Hockney (how could anyone publicly champion such ridiculously grandiose claims?) was not immediately apparent. One of the historians hazarded the predictable "But there are no documents." To which Hockney responded with his growing arsenal of ripostes, culminating in the faux-modest "I mean, I'm only speaking from my experience as an artist, though surely that must count for something"—which brought down the house.

Hockney returned to Los Angeles, and his fax and phone updates resumed apace. "Heresy," he announced one evening over the phone. "It turns out that della Porta got himself arrested, playing with these effects. Earlier, in the thirteenth century, when Roger Bacon wrote to the pope about lenses, he was told to shut up and get himself back to Oxford. And, of course, Galileo. The Inquisition. Lenses were still dangerous things, highly suspect at the dawning of the scientific age. No wonder they aroused so much secrecy. No wonder there's so relatively little written evidence about them."

"America!" he announced on another occasion. "Doubtless it won't have been lost on you that the lens begins to proliferate across Europe almost simultaneously with the discovery of the New World, a discovery that, in turn, required its own breakthroughs in lenses and optical measuring and navigational devices of all sorts."

Then, just the other day: "But of course it's all coming back together again nowadays. I mean, the rupture between photography and modernist painting. What else is one to make of the news these days? All the revelations about the ease with which journalistic photo editors are regularly altering their digitally based images. The computer changes everything: pixels rather than negatives, the hand back inside the camera! That's what the *Guardian*'s picture editor must have meant when he got found out in one of those mini-tempests: 'Ah,' he said, 'we've been caught with our fingers in the electronic paint box.' From this day forward, one might want to say, paraphrasing Delaroche, chemical photography is over! The monocular claim to univalent objective reality is falling away once and for all, and we are being thrust back on ourselves, forced to take responsibility for the way we make and shape our realities, with eye and hand and heart. Who knows where it all will lead? But it's a very exciting time."

It had been an exciting couple of months for *me,* at any rate, trying to keep up with the pace of Hockney's rampaging discoveries. Sometimes I wasn't sure. Some of his arguments verged on the tautological: if the rendering was assured, the methodology had to have been lens-based; if it was groping or awkward, it couldn't possibly have been lens-based; therefore, assured rendering proved the presence of lenses. Weren't his claims perhaps too broad? I mean, *all* art over a three-hundred-year swath founded on lens-based techniques? Might it not, rather, have been a case of perceptual hegemony—that a lens-based look came to be deemed real, and that artists, through a variety of techniques, were now required to hew to that standard? And what of virtuosity? Mightn't certain artists who began by using lenses eventually have graduated beyond them, having got the proportions and the vantages into their very bones, so to speak? And couldn't one imagine visual prodigies, individuals who might never have required such aids? One speaks of a musician having perfect pitch, of certain readers having a photographic memory of everything they've ever read. Might not it likewise be possible for certain artists (say, Velázquez) to have a photographic memory, as it were, of everything they saw—so that, for example, it wouldn't matter if the cabbage rotted; they would have it whole in their minds and could paint it at their own slow sweet confident leisure?

At other times, however, such hesitations seemed like quibbles. It was as if Hockney had laid a camera lucida across five hundred years of art history, projecting the entire expanse in vividly novel detail. And who cared, finally, if Hockney's version of history was to actual history what Hockney's version of a pool is to an actual pool? Which would one rather look at?

One day, I asked John Walsh what he made of the general arc of Hockney's theory. "Oh, I don't know about vast historical arcs," he said. "Maybe there is such a thing. But it seems to me history is far more circuitous, filled with starts, stops, backsliding, lurches forward. In the end, though, none of that really matters, because in the end nobody is expecting a killer theoretical tome from Hockney. What one awaits, with ever mounting anticipation and excitement, is how he's going to interweave all these fresh insights into his own ongoing work—what fresh new art all this is going to provoke."

CHAPTER 6

through the looking glass

FURTHER ADVENTURES

(2001)

When a version of the preceding chapter first appeared in the January 31, 2000, issue of the *New Yorker,* it provoked a veritable Niagara of response. I write about all sorts of things—hell, I write about relations between Jews and Poles, for God's sake—so I'm used to getting letters. But I'd never found myself on the receiving end of anything like this. It turns out that the question of technical assistance may be the Third Rail of popular art history. Most people, it seems, prefer to envision their artistic heroes as superhuman draftsmen, capable of rendering ravishingly accurate anatomies or landscapes or townscapes through sheer inborn or God-given talent (talents, which in a corollary to this conviction, somehow seem simply to have dried up, for the most part, over the past hundred and fifty years). Back in the Old Days, I was repeatedly told, artists just knew how to draw—they wouldn't have needed, and certainly wouldn't have deigned sully themselves with, cameras or lenses or prisms. Hockney's observations were by and large dismissed as the self-serving rationalizations of an envy-addled latter-day midget—though sometimes in terms not quite so stark. Nor were professional historians, for the most part, any more open to Hockney's surmise. (In fact, theirs were some of the rudest ripostes.)

Granted, such revulsion was hardly universal. Maybe a third of the letters came from individuals who'd long harbored suspicions about this artist or that, without perhaps ever having been quite able to articulate them; or else from other individuals with this or that stray scrap of information, which suddenly made sense in the context of Hockney's wider puzzle; or from others still who were simply charmed and energized by Hockney's vaulting speculations. (And even a few historians numbered among this group.)

One of the more unusual dispatches of this latter sort came from a professor

This sequel to the preceding piece, from the *New Yorker,* ran on the Artkrush Web site, November 2001.

named Charles Falco, who introduced himself as chair of the condensed matter/solid-state physics program at the University of Arizona in Tucson. He averred no particular artistic expertise, or even that much interest, unless you included his thralldom to the aesthetics of motorcycles. Living out there in the desert, he'd compiled a superb collection of vintage bikes and was known for his spare-time expertise in that field—so much so that when the Guggenheim began assembling materials for its celebrated 1998 Art of the Motorcycle show, staff members there had initially come to ask him for advice and to borrow the odd bike or two and ended up marshaling his services as cocurator of the entire exhibition. One of his Guggenheim collaborators from those days had spotted my article and sent it on to him, and now Falco was contacting me to say that though his main scientific enterprise these days consisted of running an extremely high-tech lab (one of the most lavishly funded in the country, as I subsequently found out) devoted to figuring out (among other things) how to narrow the thickness of the layer of cobalt atoms arrayed on the surface of a silicon wafer from their current six hundred down to a single one (with the consequent increase in computer-chip efficiency such a breakthrough would entail), this work had forced him to become expert in quantum optics, which in turn had required his becoming proficient in standard optics as well. A proficiency, he went on to suggest, that might prove helpful to Hockney in his ongoing researches.

I put the two of them in contact with each other, and a few weeks later I flew out to L.A. to join Falco on one of his first visits to Hockney's studio. The two had hit it off immediately: and it turned out the ride was only just beginning.

Hockney, for his part, had hardly been standing still.

For one thing, he'd continued burrowing into his own series of camera lucida portraits, probing the medium (for both its promises and limitations) and honing his skill ("It's not that easy," he insisted. "The truth is, if you need the device in order to be able to draw, it won't be of much use at all. On the other hand, if you don't, it can be immensely useful.") Most of his subjects were friends and new fellow explorers (notably including Martin Kemp, the Oxford historian whose *Science of Art* is arguably the premier book in the field and who was to become a frequent fax correspondent in the months ahead), and by the spring he was mounting a show called Likenesses, of forty such works, at UCLA's Hammer Museum. Later that season, as his contribution to the millennial Encounters show at London's National Gallery, in which over twenty contemporary masters had been invited to perform riffs on particular masterpieces by their predecessors lodged within the museum's bounteous collection, Hockney chose to honor Ingres himself by performing a variation on that master's feat of capturing perfect likenesses of British aristocrats who'd visit his Rome studio for a single session in the midst of their European Grand Tours. Reversing the class polarities, Hockney had the museum select twelve guards, previously unknown to him, whose images he now endeavored to capture, likewise in a single sitting, and likewise (or so he insisted) through the initial deployment of a camera lucida. Although Hockney made no claims for the relative parity of the resultant images (Ingres, after all, being one of the greatest draftsmen of all time), the effect was nonetheless quite powerful: for one thing, visitors to the museum often got to witness Hockney's version side by side with the living models. (The guards, normally invisible watchers, were thus suddenly transformed into objects of intense scrutiny themselves—had that guard there been one of Hockney's subjects? how about that other one there? For that matter, forget the art; look at the density of that living face right over there! For a short period, strolling through the museum, one was invited to gaze upon passing faces with the same focused regard an artist might.) Beyond that, there could be no doubt as to the similarity of the "look"; and in fact, more uncanny yet, many of the guards turned out to a startling degree to look just like several of Ingres's own aristocrats, as Hockney, with his encyclopedic visual knowledge of Ingres's portraits, was able to demonstrate with a sly grid alignment of his own (Figs. 51 and 52).

In London, with the protean assistance of David Graves, his tall, lanky, and astonishingly competent aide, Hockney had likewise continued burrowing into libraries and archives for any further scraps of evidence they could muster. Back in his Hollywood home, with Graves still in tow, Hockney now cleared the long two-story-high wall of his hillside studio (the studio retains the general dimensions of the onetime tennis court over which it was built), installed a color photocopier in the middle of the space, and, drawing on his brimming private horde of art books and

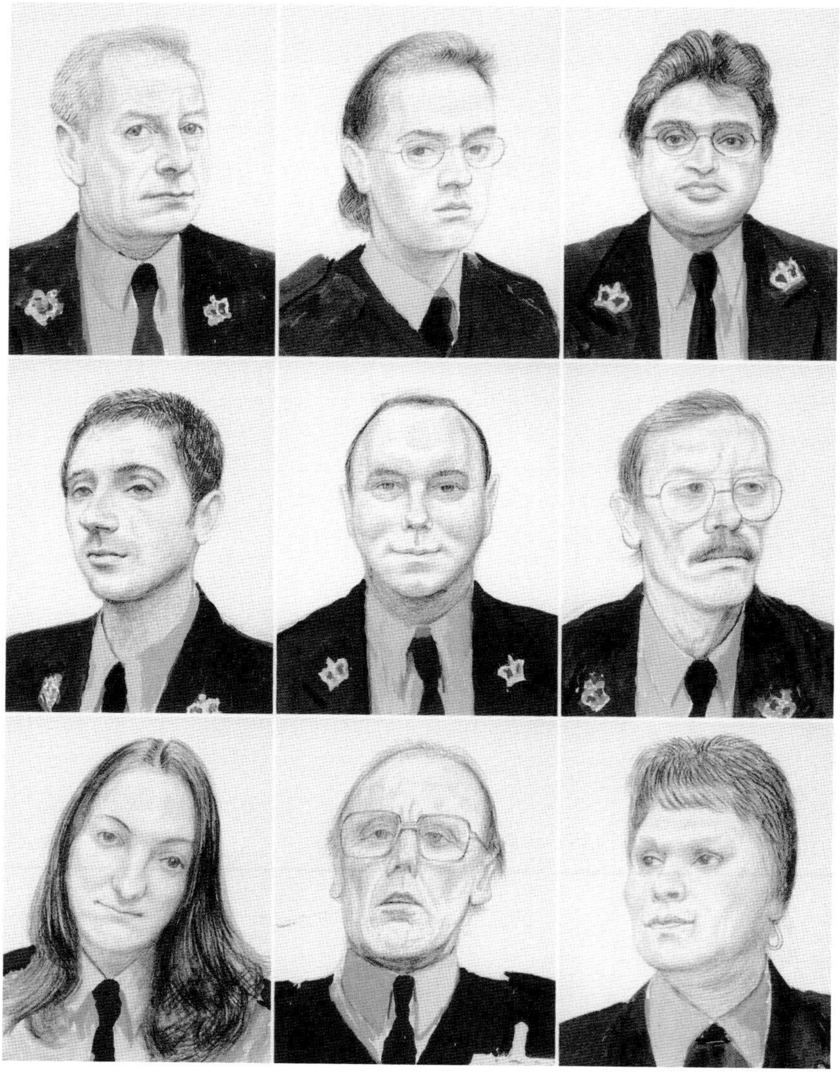

FIG 51 David Hockney, (top left) *Ron Lillywhite, London, 17 December 1999* (detail); (top center) *Devlin Crow, London, 11 January 2000* (detail); (top right) *Pravin Patel, London, 5 January 2000* (detail); (center left) *Jack Kettlewell, London, 13 December 1999* (detail); (center) *Graham Eve, London, 7 January 2000* (detail); (center right), *Ken Bradford, London, 20 December 1999* (detail); (bottom left) *Maria Vasquez, London, 21 December 1999* (detail); (bottom center) *Brain Wedlake, London, 10 January 2000* (detail); (bottom right) *Fazila Jhungoor, London, 18 December 1999* (detail).

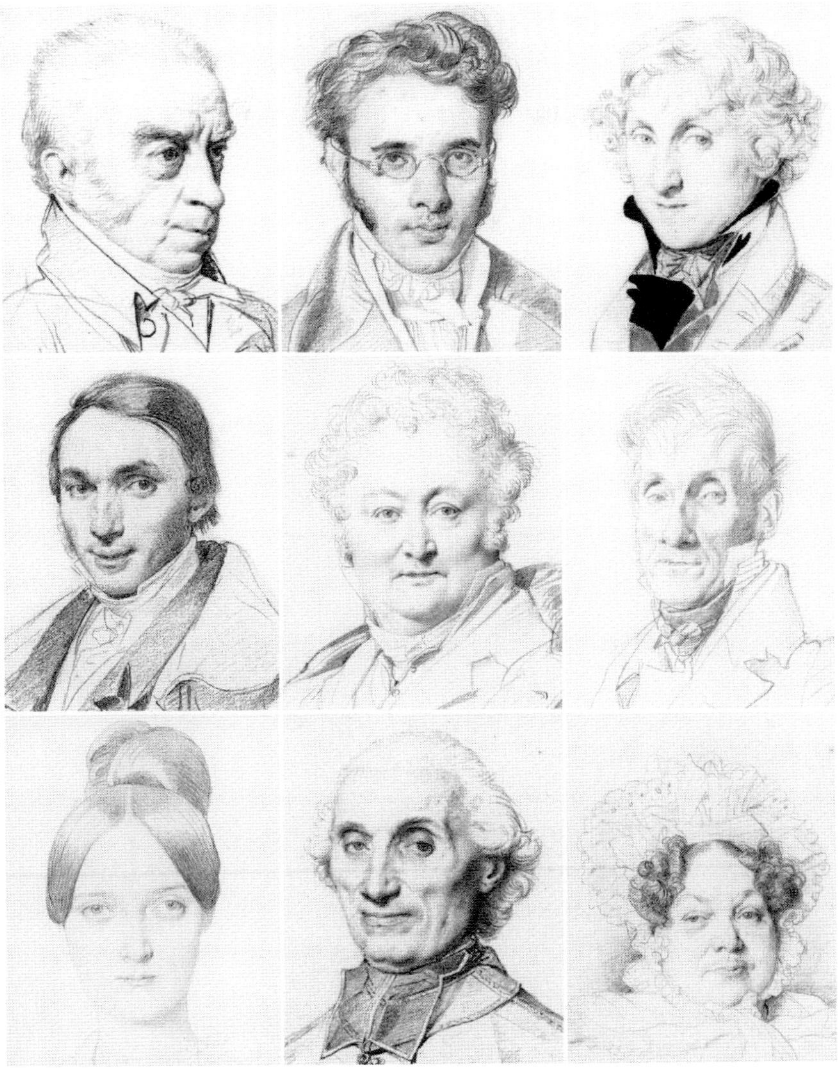

FIG 52 Jean-Auguste-Dominique Ingres, (top left) *Dr. Thomas Church* (detail), 1816; (top center) *André-Benoit Barreau, called Taurel* (detail), 1819; (top right) *Charles Thomas Thruston*, 1816; (center left) *Jean-François-Antoine Forest*, 1823; (center) *Guillaume Guillon Lethière* (detail), 1815; (center right) *Portrait of a Man, Possibly Edmé Bochet*, 1814; (bottom left) *Portrait of Madame Adolphe Thiers*, 1834; (bottom center) *Monsignor Gabriel Cortois de Pressigny* (detail), before end of May 1816; (bottom right) *Madame Louis-François Bertin, née Geneviève-Aimée-Victoire Boutard* (detail); 1834.

monographs, effectively proceeded to photocopy the entire history of European art, shingling the images one atop the next—the year 1300 to one side, 1750 to the far other, northern Europe on top, southern Europe below—a vast, teeming pageant of evolving imagery (and in some ways Hockney's most ambitious photocollage yet) (Plate 23).

When, he was asking, and where does that optical look first emerge? And with the procession of European art splayed out like that, the answer was as patent as it was unexpected: far before Caravaggio, and not even in Italy. Rather, in Bruges, where, basically across the single decade on either side of 1425, a group of Flemish masters (the Master of Flémalle, who was most likely Robert Campin; Jan van Eyck; Rogier van der Weyden) almost from one moment to the next, without any awkward groping toward proficiency, evinced a seemingly instantaneous mastery (as if one morning European painting had simply gotten up and put on its glasses)—and there it was, out of nowhere, the optical look, which would now spread rapidly and, as Hockney would indicate for visitors with a triumphant sweeping gesture, come to dominate European painting for the next four hundred years.

The claim was almost literally revolutionary, a turning of the traditional account on its head. Italy, after all, had long been deemed the font of the Renaissance, from which the rebirth of classical knowledge spread outward in the early 1400s, in particular owing to the (re)discovery and elaboration of a mathematically rigorous and idealizing one-point perspective. Van Eyck and his cohort were often referred to as "Netherlandish primitives" because they hadn't yet attained that new knowledge (they were only able to portray things as they were, went the traditional critique, not as they ideally ought to be). But here Hockney was (he'd lately taken to loping up and down the Wall, sporting a V-neck T-shirt emblazoned with the legend I KNOW I'M RIGHT!), both discounting the importance (and the pervasiveness) of Italianate one-point perspective and highlighting the countervailing spread of the northern optical look. "It's easy to see how the early art historians got it wrong," Hockney would cluck to visitors before the Wall. "Modern art history gets going more or less around the same time as the invention of chemical photography, in the middle of the nineteenth century, and by then, if you were a British or a German academic, where were you going to want to be spending your summers, in dilapidated industrial Bruges or amidst the golden rolling hills of Tuscany?" (He ought to know, this child of dreary Yorkshire who'd long ago transplanted *himself* to sunny Southern California.)

For all Hockney's certainty (and Graves's steadily mounting corroborating research), the theory was still subject to substantial qualms. Apart from the evidence of the pictures themselves (and Hockney's insistent claims that he could plainly make out a lens-based optical "look"), the corroboration was mostly circumstantial (for example, indications that lenses of a certain type might indeed have existed at such and such a moment, somewhat earlier than had been thought). Skeptics were quick to advance other possible theories, and meanwhile, there was precious little evidence that lenses had been in widespread use in Bruges, of all places, as early as 1420.

This was the state of play when Falco arrived on the scene early that March. Hockney had immediately led him up to the studio, and the two men had traipsed up and down the Wall, like a pair of generals reviewing their troops, with Falco on the lookout for a specific sort of image, a picture with a particular set of characteristics, an image like . . . like . . . like *this one here.* He'd speared a reproduction of a painting by the Venetian master Lorenzo Lotto, the Hermitage's *Portrait of a Husband and Wife,* dating from about 1543 (which is to say roughly a century after Van Eyck and three-quarters of a century before Caravaggio); he took it down and brought it over to the worktable (Fig. 53). "See," he'd explained, now repeating the explanation for my benefit, "the husband and wife are sitting on the far side of an intervening table and, as it happens, there's a Turkish carpet draped over the table, with that regular repeating triangular border pattern running along the edge facing us." Falco, a mustachioed dervish, may be the only person I've ever met who can even begin to approximate Hockney for sheer exalted enthusiasm. "Now, whether that's centimeters or inches, whatever, those triangles make up a regular repeating pattern, and the point is we can use their modular dimension as the basis for a series of measuring calculations." He whipped out a notepad and threw himself into a dizzying array of calculations, muttering merrily away about image size and subject size, lens-image distance, magnification, average spacing between the pupils of the sitters' eyes (though such calculations seemed entirely second nature to him, he was leaving even Graves in the dust), presently emerging with the claim that Lotto would most likely have been using a lens with a diameter of roughly

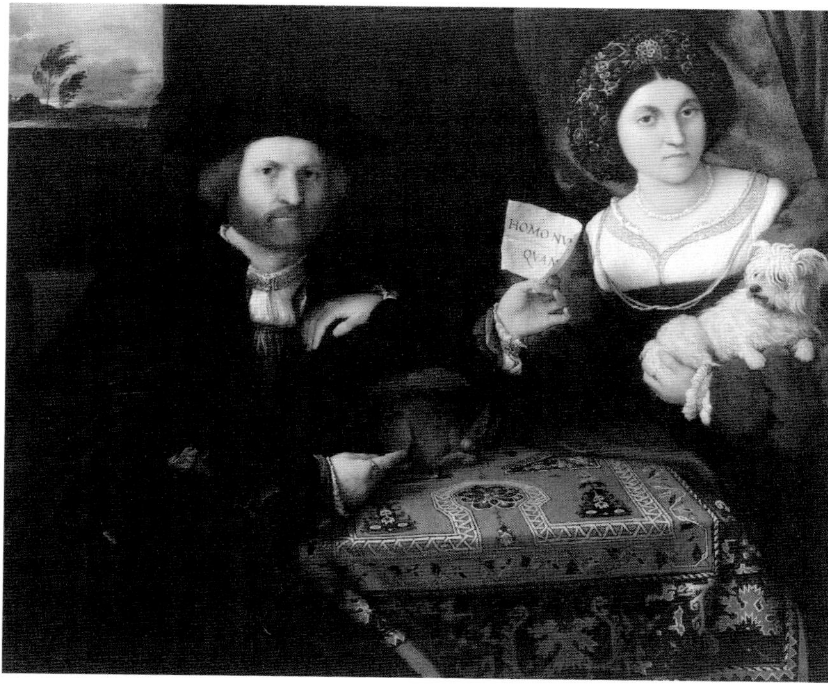

2.4 centimeters and a strength of, let's see, 1.86 diopters ("roughly the equivalent of a pair of reading glasses"), with a depth of field (the depth before the image went out of focus) of about 22 centimeters.

But what sort of claim was this? "Well," he went on, "it's a scientific hypothesis, which we'd now need to test against other details in the image. And see, here"—he jabbed his finger at the middle of the table—

"Yes," Hockney interrupted, "David and I already noticed that, too. The border pattern juts back into the middle of the table there in a sort of arch, but there at the back it goes *out of focus,* which would have been impossible for an artist to see, let alone replicate, without witnessing the effect projected onto a flat surface by some sort of lens. After all, the moment he would have tried to attend to that out-of-focus patch, it would have gone into focus for him. Whatever we look at is always by definition in focus as we look at it."

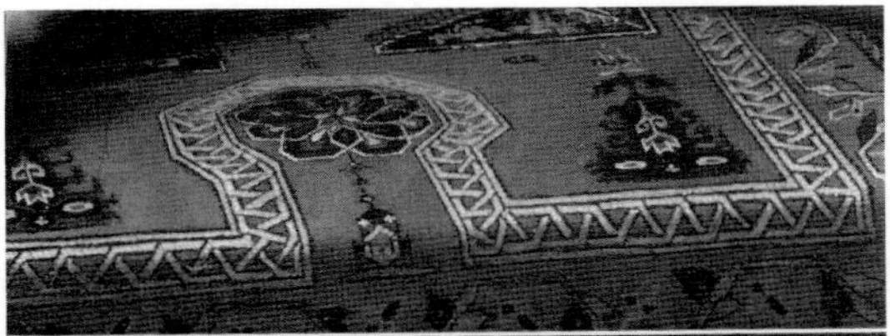

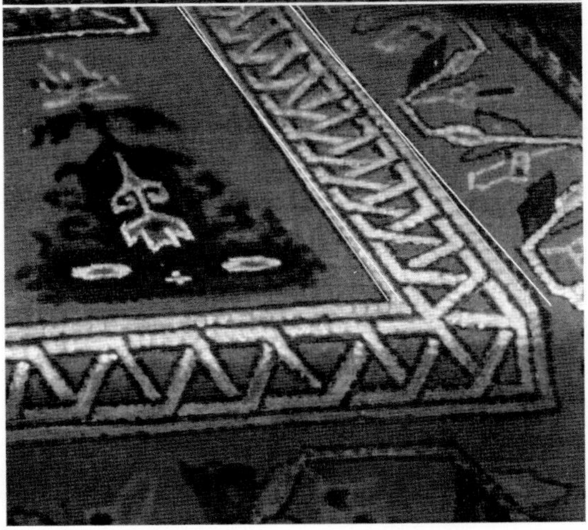

FIG 53 Lorenzo Lotto, *Portrait of a Husband and Wife,* ca. 1543.

FIG 54 Lorenzo Lotto, *Portrait of a Husband and Wife* (detail), ca. 1543.

Falco nodded. "Yes, and it goes out of focus at the right spot, according to our calculations, about twenty-two centimeters back. And furthermore, you'll notice that beyond that, the image is back in focus again, which means Lotto would have had to refocus his lens, either by moving the lens, or the canvas, or the table, but (think about what happens when you refocus a zoom camera, the lens telescoping either out or in) that would have subtly affected the magnification, the two parts would not quite have jibed, and you would expect furthermore"—he pulled out a ruler and traced the front part of the receding pattern, and then its back part (Fig. 54)—"and, yes, you get it: rays receding back to two entirely different vanishing points. This painting was obviously not accomplished according to some mathematical model. Assuming our hypothesis is correct, the same sort of thing should be happening elsewhere in the picture, for example here, on the right-hand edge of the table, where the receding triangular pattern at first seems to stay in focus all the way back; the band is narrower here on the edge than with that arch there in the middle of the table, and hence it would have been easier for Lotto to fudge. But if we take out our ruler, I bet you it will turn out that"—pen swipe, pen swipe—"yup, the vanishing points again differ for the front and the back, by the slightest but still an identifiable degree.

"That," he rose up, smiling, triumphant, "is what in science we refer to as a proof."

("You make a prediction," he would subsequently recount for me, as we discussed that first day and the Lotto painting which he'd taken to referring to as "our Rosetta Stone"—"you make a prediction, and then it holds true. We like that in science. It's strange," he went on, surveying what by then had already grown into several months of collaboration between him and Hockney, "but had either one of us maintained all of this on our own, nobody would have believed us. But together . . ." He let the thought trail off, breaking into another wide smile.)

Hockney and Falco were almost slaphappy with excitement at this point, and I hated to be the one to throw a damper on things, but, still somewhat skeptical, I broke in, "That's all fine and good, but what about back over here, with Van Eyck in Bruges? Isn't the problem that there's no good evidence of the existence, let alone widespread dissemination, of such lenses, at that place at that time?"

None of us was subsequently able to recall precisely what Falco said in response (as far as he was concerned, he was only repeating what every optical scientist would know, though, as I was subsequently able to determine, hardly a single art historian seemed to know it)—but somewhere buried in the subclause of a subclause of his response, he noted how, "Of course, a concave mirror has exactly the same optical properties as a lens"—a throwaway comment that veritably stunned Hockney and Graves.

Really?!

"Sure," Falco continued. "Try it yourself. In the morning, in the bathroom, take your shaving mirror—you know, the one that magnifies the image of your face—you may want to narrow the f-stop a little, for maximum effect, wrap a little bagel of cardboard around the outer circumference of the mirror—anyway, when it's bright outside and still dark on your bathroom's inner wall, aim the lens at the world outside the window so the gathered light bounces off the mirror and onto the darkened wall, move the mirror in and out till things cast there onto the wall come into focus, and what you'll get is a Technicolor perfect image of the world outside. Upside down, granted, but incidentally *not* right-left reversed, as would be the case with a lens."

As Falco had been expounding, we'd all drifted on over to the 1420 section of the Wall. "You mean," asked Hockney, "a mirror like this, or this, or this?"—he jabbed at one image after another, for almost simultaneous with the proliferation of the optical look there in Flanders, there had occurred a proliferation of mirrors in Netherlandish paintings.

"Well," Falco concurred, "those are all *convex,* which is to say bowed *outward* at the center. You'd need to turn them around but"—we'd come to Van Eyck's celebrated *Arnolfini Marriage* (1434) (Fig. 55), with its mirror dead center on the far wall, at the focal point of the entire painting, the master's ornate signature, "Johannes Van Eyck made this," immediately above it. "But once you did—and remember, in those days the back side of a mirror wasn't blackened; they just silvered the bottom of a globe of blown glass and sliced out the circular segment—you'd have a *concave* mirror, and in fact, a mirror quite like that one may well have been used to construct this image. Now, of course, such a mirror would only have had a sweet spot of around thirty centimeters"—a zone of focus, an invisible sphere or globe, as it were, 30 centimeters from side to side and front to back—"so that the artist would have had to move it around, refocusing, with the consequent multiple overlapping vanishing rays. I'm sure if we spent a little time studying this image we'd come upon all sorts of anomalous . . ."

And hence, I pointed out, the lack of unified one-point perspective which, as far as the Italianists were concerned, still rendered these images so "primitive."

"Whereas, in fact, the visual intelligence and sophistication involved here," Hockney countered, "the way in which the perspectives are layered, one upon the next, is of the very highest order. Not in the least bit primitive."

Up to that point, critics of Hockney's theory, especially its maximal Flemish claims, had been castigating him over the lack of evidence for the existence of the lenses or flat mirrors they'd imagined crucial to the process (after all, the Flemish seemed only to have had those reflection-warping convex mirrors, and what good could they possibly have been?), whereas it now turned out that it was the flat mirrors that would have proved useless, and only curved mirrors, with their

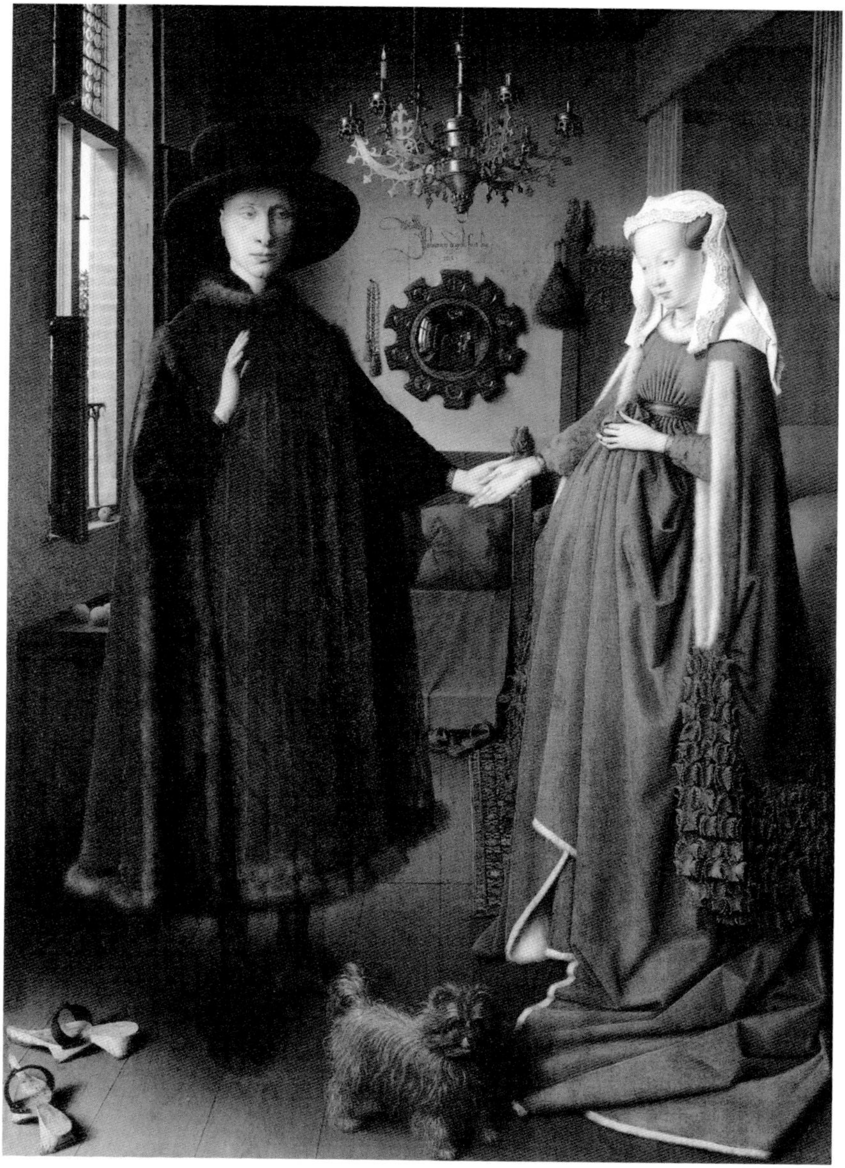

FIG 55 Jan van Eyck, *The Portrait of Giovanni(?) Arnolfini and His Wife Giovanna Cenami(?) (The Arnolfini Marriage)*, 1434.

ray-concentrating properties (the same properties, as Falco pointed out, that had led Archimedes to deploy them as burning lenses to defend Syracuse from besieging flotillas), that would have done the trick.[1]

"For example, look at that chandelier," Hockney now crowed (he'd immediately grasped the implications of Falco's throwaway comment about the concave mirror). "There's another one there, and there, and there"—he was pointing all about that 1420s Netherlandish region of the Wall. "There's no way anybody before that could have recorded such an astonishingly accurate and assured rendition of a chandelier." He pointed back at some earlier approximations, in Giotto and others. "Nor is there any way Van Eyck could have achieved it with one-point perspective, either. But here suddenly they're all doing it, almost as if to say, 'Commission me to do your portrait and I'll throw in that chandelier for free.'"

"And keep in mind who this is," Graves now interceded. (He seemed to have become as encyclopedically grounded in the history of fifteenth- and sixteenth-century art history as Falco was in the physics of curved mirrors.) "Mr. and Mrs. Arnolfini. He's an Italian merchant, resident in Bruges—Florentine, and in fact the representative on the scene of the Medici Bank. He could easily have taken the knowledge—"

"—one of the most valuable bits of knowledge of its time!" Hockney chimed in.

"Yes," Graves continued, "taken it back with him to Tuscany."

The sweet spot of Hockney's entire theory suddenly seemed to swim vividly into focus.

Falco left that evening, returning to Tucson—not a bad day's work—but the very next morning, Hockney and Graves and Hockney's California assistant Richard Schmidt were out alongside the outer wall of a guest cottage on the other side of the compound, building a little outhouse-size art-mirror shed: essentially darkness-enclosing walls with a crisp square outfacing window, and inside a standard shaving mirror mounted on an adjustable pedestal. They'd been studying a drawing Van Eyck had made on the occasion of Cardinal Niccolò Albergati's one brief visit to Bruges, in December 1431 (Fig. 56). It was a drawing that Van Eyck would use the following year as the basis for his celebrated painting of the cardinal (Fig. 57). "Look,"

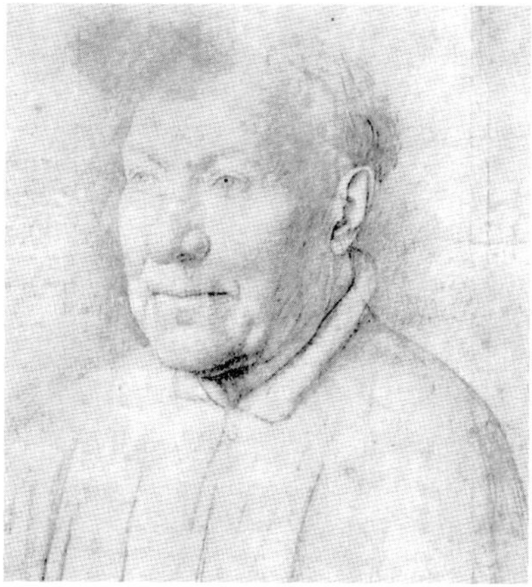

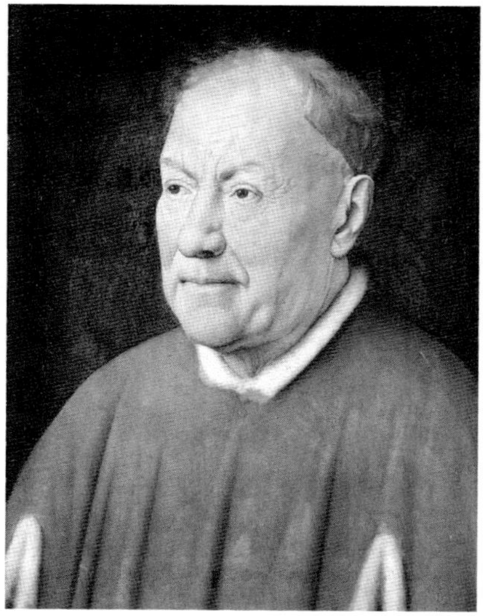

FIG 56 Jan van Eyck, *Cardinal Niccolò Albergati, 1431.*

FIG 57 Jan van Eyck, *Cardinal Niccolò Albergati, 1432.*

Hockney commented. "Look at the pupils: little pinpricks. Quite unusual, but exactly the contracted effect you'd get if you'd sat your subject outside in the bright sun." Graves, inside the shed and adjusting the mirror pedestal, pointed out that the Bruges artists had all been members of the Guild of St. Luke, which, as he now recalled from his researches, happened to be the guild of "painters and mirror makers." Hockney invited a visiting friend to sit for him outside, swathed the man in a red cape reminiscent of the cardinal's, climbed into the operator's cockpit inside the shed, adjusted the mirror—and it was exactly as Falco had foretold: A perfect upside-down image of the man outside was being cast onto the blank sheet of paper Hockney had affixed to the wall beside the window. He worked quickly, sketching out the contours of the man's face and noting the signposts, and then, pulling the page off the wall and flipping it right-side up onto an easel, simply polished off the man's likeness, in a process that was if anything even more straightforwardly efficient than the camera lucida.

Back up in the studio, a few hours later, marching up and down the Wall again, Hockney was pointing out the profusion of window-framed images that characterized the portraiture of the latter half of the fifteenth century and on into the sixteenth, initially in Flanders and then everywhere. "And usually with very pronounced shadows," he pointed out, "as if the sitter were outside, even when the sitter is being portrayed as if he's the one on the inside."

Presently he zeroed in on a marvelous interior scene, a teeming *Last Supper* by Dirck Bouts, the central panel of an altarpiece painted around 1466 (Fig. 58). "See," he said. "Another chandelier, and as with Van Eyck's in the *Arnolfini,* painted as if from head-on and not from below. In fact, the heads of each of the disciples gathered around Christ are painted as if close-up and from head-on, as, for that matter, are their feet—and actually, wait a second, wait a second: isn't that the same fellow seen over and over again, from different angles—Christ and that disciple and that other one over there? Bouts must not have had enough models to stage a full dozen. And then, look over here, the two men in the window looking in on the scene from outside, as if Bouts were providing us with a clue as to how he'd accomplished the whole composition. I recognize this technique, because in essence, it's the same way I built up my Polaroid collages back in the early eighties: close-up and one framed detail at a time, slowly building out to a sense of wider space. In many ways the opposite of the standard Italian one-point perspective, as in this one over here"—Andrea del Castagno's 1447–49 version (Fig. 59)—"which in turn mimics a standard single-snap photographic shot."

Meanwhile, on an almost hourly basis, Falco was chiming in by fax with his own fresh discoveries. (He subsequently told me that the session with Hockney had left him so energized that he'd found it impossible to sleep that night, and that at three in the morning he'd risen from bed, popped his contacts back in, and begun scouring the art books he had rapidly taken to collecting.) There were numerous carpet-draped tables—a Memling from fifty years before the Lotto, Holbein's portrait of Georg Gisze from 1532 (which had already been the focus of some of Hockney's most intensive earlier investigations; see Fig. 49)—exhibiting improbably multiple vanishing rays entirely incongruent with any mathematically perspectival approach. (On the lower right-hand side of the Gisze panel, as Hockney himself now noticed, the table just seemed to fall away completely: very odd. Graves, for his part, was becoming convinced that the curious little canister with the mysterious slot opening on the table in front of Gisze's forearm might itself be some sort of optical device: couldn't that little highlight inside the slot be the glint of a tiny mirror?)

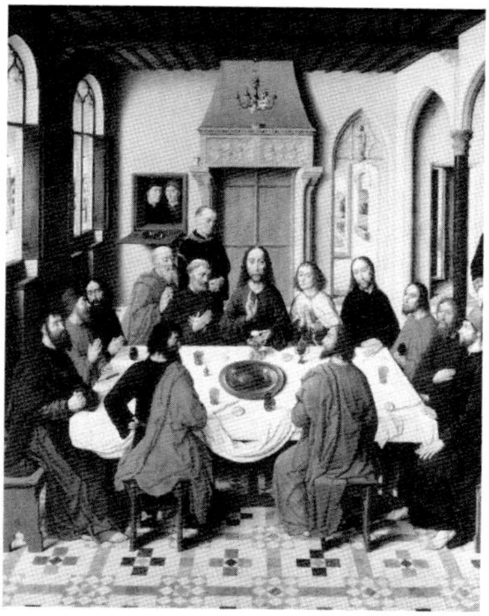

FIG 58 Dirck Bouts, *Last Supper*, ca. 1466.

FIG 59 Andrea del Castagno, *Last Supper*, 1447–49.

Furthermore, Falco had been researching the Cardinal Albergati drawing and its subsequent painting. It turned out that while the drawing was 48 percent of life-size, the final painting was 41 percent larger than the drawing, the sort of thing that gets obscured in art books (such as this one) that reproduce the two images side by side and at the same scale. And yet, Falco noted, if you make a transparency of the drawing and blow it up to scale and place it over the painting, the lines match up almost precisely—the forehead, the pupils, the nose, the lips—far more so than could be accounted for by mere eyeballing, and impossible to have accomplished by the pinprick-and-charcoal tracing method advanced by some art historians as the likeliest technique when the scale of the drawing and the painting is identical. (The drawing had in any case never been pinpricked.) No, Falco maintained, the likeliest scenario involved Van Eyck's having deployed some sort of prior-day epidiascope (or opaque image projector)—and if he'd used such a thing to transfer the image, why would he not have used a similar device to make the image in the first place, especially when he'd been granted so little time with his distinguished sitter? Furthermore, as Falco related in a subsequent note, the failure of the transparency of the drawing to line up perfectly with the painting was itself highly revelatory: the front half of the face did, but the ears and back of the head were off

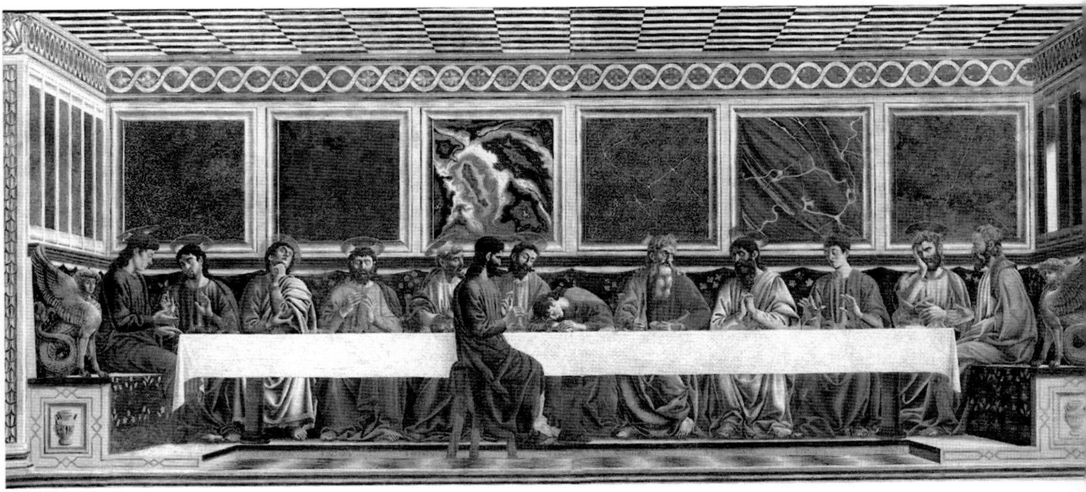

by a few degrees. If, however, you shifted the transparency left two millimeters and up four millimeters, the ears and the shoulder squared up perfectly (while the front of the face went out of whack). Wasn't it likely, Falco surmised, that Van Eyck or some assistant had simply bumped up against the mirror, or the easel, or the worktable, in the middle of the transferring process, therefore accounting for the barely perceptible double exposure?

Falco, like Hockney, proved a veritable logorrheic on the fax machine: his steadily accumulating dispatches, of which I was being sent copies, would come to fill two huge binders on my shelf (at times I felt as if I were eavesdropping on Freud and Fliess), with Hockney's to Falco and Kemp and others swelling another several folders. Of all Falco's myriad observations and calculations in the months ahead, one of my favorites would involve the famously elongated smear of a skull at the bottom of Holbein's 1533 painting *The Ambassadors,* another of Hockney's own most cited works (Fig. 60). Hockney had always admired the "marvelous accuracy of the foreshortening" in the anamorphic skull, rendered all the more palpable when subjected to computerized restoration. But Falco noted how the compressed version still "bothers me every time I look at it." And he'd now figured out what the problem was: "The back of the skull is far too big—and if you look at the top of the

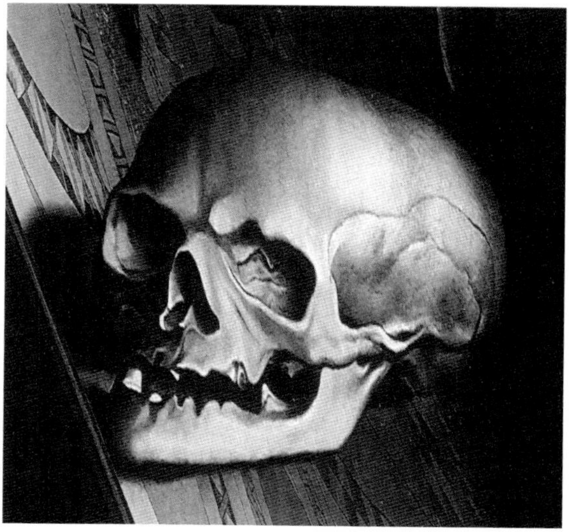

FIG 60 Hans Holbein the Younger, *Jean de Dinteville and Georges de Selve (The Ambassadors)*, (computer-manipulated detail), 1533.

skull, it's clear it's made of two curves. This happens at an appropriate depth into the scene for Holbein to have had to refocus, had he used a lens. If you slice the attached fax at this joint (that is, where I drew a vertical line) and slide the back portion of the skull to the left by one inch and up by a half inch, not only does the skull take on a much more human look, but several important lines and features Holbein painted on the two portions of the skull line up."

Forget Freud and Fliess. Other days, I imagined I was eavesdropping on the earliest days of plate tectonics theory.

During the weeks that followed, back home now in New York, I continued to listen in, mostly by way of cc'ed correspondence, on the ongoing investigation being conducted, principally, by Hockney, Graves, Falco, and Kemp. Graves passed along a curious engraving he'd come upon, the frontispiece of a 1572 Latin translation of the tenth-century Arab scholar Alhazan's *Optics,* which featured a panoply of illustrated optical effects: a rainbow, legs refracted in water, and down there at the bottom a very odd little man bouncing the image of his face off a concave mirror

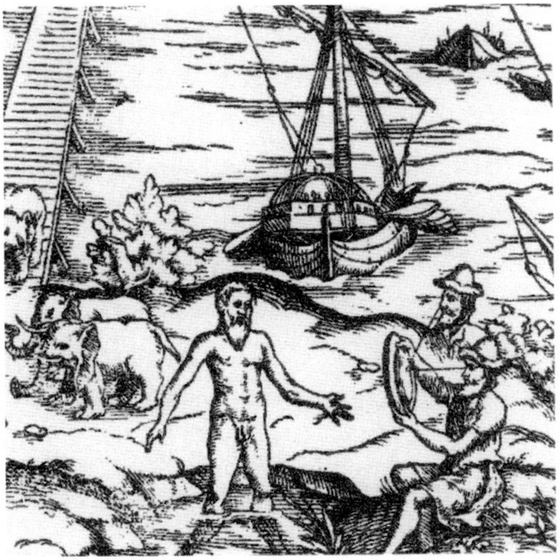

FIG 61 Alhazan, "Archimedes using burning mirrors to destroy the Roman fleet in Syracuse harbour."

(Fig. 61)! Hockney, meanwhile, zeroed in on the Mona Lisa, of 1503, which he said stood out on his Wall as the first instance of the softer focus one actually gets from an image projected (by either a mirror or a lens) into a darkened chamber. (Earlier artists had aspired to more exact measurements, but Leonardo seemed to be approximating the very cast of the projected image.) He also noted the bright light shining down from above (indicated by the deep shadows beneath the nose and lips)—at which point one of the others pointed out that Leonardo, at any rate, certainly knew of the optical properties of the camera obscura, mention of which occurs dozens of times in his notebooks (written in his secret-keeping reverse handwriting, of course). (*What didn't Leonardo know?* Hockney marveled in response.)

In a similiar vein, Hockney pointed out how one of the hardest things to master with collaged, multiple-vantage painterly composition was a believably realistic spatial relationship *between* figures. With Georges de La Tour, for example, for all the French master's splendors, the figures seem separately posed (as they probably were) and seem barely to inhabit the same space. They fail to make eye contact; the spaces between figures are subtly wrong. In *The Fortune Teller* (ca. 1630, Fig. 62), for example, the girl in the rear is bigger than the young man in the foreground.

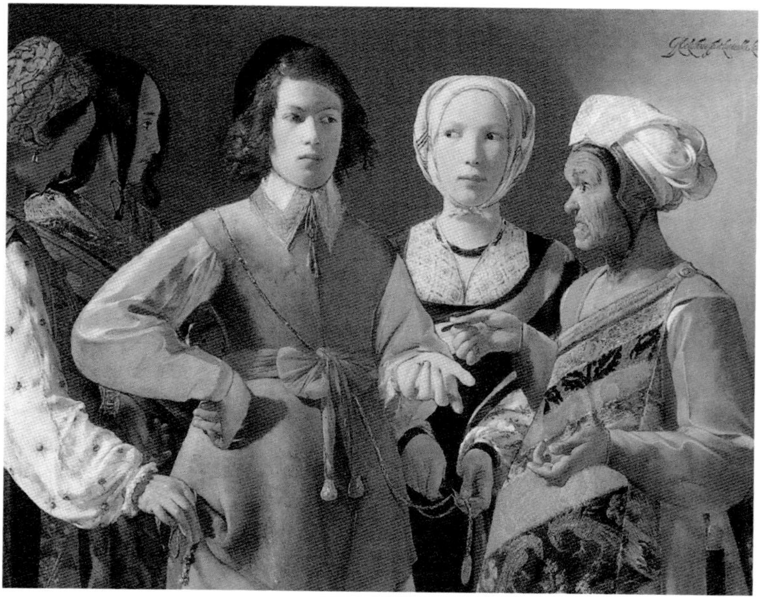

FIG 62 Georges de La Tour, *The Fortune Teller*, ca. 1630.

FIG 63 Frans Hals, *Young Man with a Skull (Vanitas)*, 1626–28.

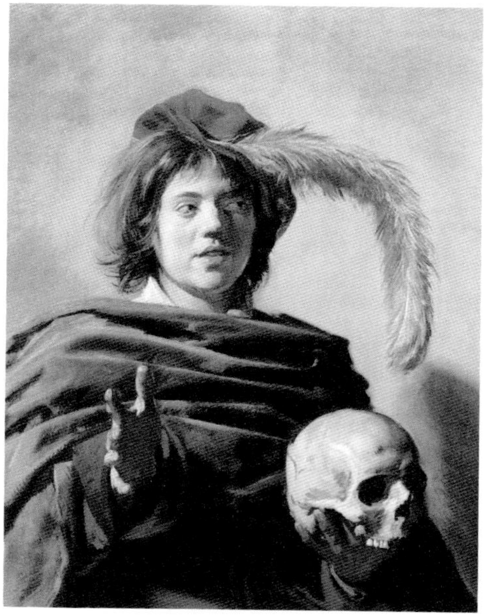

By contrast, Hockney came to see in the later Velázquez a virtual champion of the technique—again thanks to his softening of the atmospheric contours of the various figures, so that they indeed seem to stand side by side or one behind the other. (In fact, Velázquez's entire career can be seen as one of consistent progress toward such consummate mastery.)

Meanwhile, Frans Hals, of all people, began increasingly to consume Hockney's attention: strange, because he of all artists seems the most slapdash and spontaneous. Precisely, Hockney countered, but look, for instance, at the amazing foreshortening of the outthrust hand in his portrait of the boy with the red-feathered cap holding the skull, from 1626–28 (Fig. 63). How long could a model have been expected to hold that pose? Keep in mind, there is no charcoal underdrawing, yet the gesture retains an astonishing freshness. Could Hals merely have eyeballed this, Hockney wondered, or was some solid optical structure guiding the quick, fluid brushstrokes?

Presently, Falco invited Hockney to come out and visit him at his Tucson lab, and I decided to join them. On a sweltering, crystal-clear May afternoon, Falco picked us up in his arrest-me-red BMW and squired us over to his air-conditioned lab on the top floor of the university's ten-story Optical Sciences Center. (On the way, he pointed out that the pristine air and the desert stillness of the atmosphere accounted for the presence of more working telescopes within fifty miles of Tucson than anywhere else on earth.) Once at the lab, we were all required to don head-to-toe pillow-white ghostbuster outfits, complete with shower caps and booties, and then to subject ourselves to an invigorating air shower before breaching the inner sanctum. (Falco explained that some of the experimental chambers within were required to maintain vacuums ten thousand times purer than even the vacuum found in outer space.) We looked preposterous but endearing, I suppose: some while later a faxed photo of the touring group began circulating among us, to which somebody had affixed the hand-scrawled motto: "Fifteenth Century Art History: It's a Tough Job, but Somebody's Got to Do It."

Inside, multi-million-dollar contraptions assured the perfect gyroscopic stillness of platforms on which additional multi-million-dollar contraptions assured the yet more perfect stillness of various further million-dollar electron-scanning supermicroscopes. (Suddenly I could see where Falco might have gotten that idea about Van Eyck's inadvertently jiggling the Cardinal Albergati epidiascope.) "I always tell my students," Falco explained, "that there are two ways you can be better than everybody else. The first is to be smarter: not that easy; there are a lot of smart people. The second is to have better equipment."

"Same as Van Eyck," Hockney deadpanned, without missing a beat.

Falco had an assistant zero in with one of the video monitors hooked up to the microscope. "Let's see," he said. "As you can see, that's an array of eleven cobalt atoms lined up one beside the next." It was incredible: one could actually count them.

"I think artists and scientists have more in common with each other," Falco now hazarded, "than either do with the historians of their respective disciplines. For one thing," he continued, "scientists tend to be deeply visual, that's how they think, whereas I'm surprised to say that many of the art historians I've been talking with lately don't seem to be visual at all." Hockney concurred absolutely—this, after all, being one of his favorite stalking horses. (He tends to retain as straw man a stereotype of his art-historical interlocutors, as many of them do of his evolving and increasingly nuanced theory.) "They just don't get it," Hockney insisted. "They go on and on as if the artists of that time would have been too unsophisticated or too ashamed to have been using optical devices, whereas on the contrary, these weren't stupid people, they were keen to make pictures! They weren't art historians, for god's sake." He went on to note Kemp's comment to him that painters in an era when they hadn't yet divided off from scientists—we are speaking of a time before that artificial division—far from being ashamed, would have taken pride in their proficiency with optical devices; they'd have been ravenous to deploy any new aid. "And anyway," Hockney went on, "why is it that mathematical perspective is deemed acceptable as such an aid, but a camera obscura is somehow suspect? I'm sure that wasn't the case for them."

Falco noted how he'd been astonished at the relative scientific illiteracy he was encountering not just among the average folks to whom he was endeavoring to explain the team's optical discoveries, but among the tenured humanities professors as well. "It's not just that their eyes glaze over at the slightest whiff of an equation"—Hockney and I eyed each other sheepishly—"they don't even seem to understand the rudiments of scientific discourse. I was laying out our Lotto discoveries for one of the art history profs around here the other day, and he ended up saying, 'Well, that's your theory, I just happen to have a different one.' This isn't a theory, I just about shouted at him, *it's a proof!* It's *established fact.* He just shook his head at me, condescendingly. It was incredible."

The sheer exasperation of it all made us all hungry, so we decided to head out to get a bite to eat. As we left, I noticed a framed photo of Falco astride a veritable beast of a gleaming, souped-up motorcycle in the very middle of his lab. "How did you manage to—" I started to ask. "Long story," he said, "long story."

"What's their alternative theory?" Hockney now asked, as Falco drove us over to the restaurant: he was still fuming. "That one day all over Europe painters simply started receiving postcards saying, 'Hey guys, the Renaissance has started. Time to ramp up your drawing technique!'"

The conversation segued into a consideration of specific painters. Falco had been studying Petrus Christus, a Netherlandish painter from the generation following Van Eyck. "Historians credit him with being the first guy up there to transcend the so-called primitivist look and attain a one-point perspective, but I think they've got it wrong. I think he was just incompetent at moving the lens around."

We pulled into the restaurant parking lot—brief blast of furnace-hot air between two air-conditioned enclaves—and once inside, after we'd ordered, Hockney pulled out a sheaf of photocopied reproductions he wanted to go over with Falco. The first was a Van Dyck, a circa 1626 portrait of a seated Genovese matron with her son standing beside her: quite beautiful, quite convincing, until you gave it a second look (Fig. 64). "I mean," Hockney asked Falco, "if she were to stand up, how tall would she have to be?" Falco, who seldom allowed such challenges to pass as merely rhetorical, whipped out a pen and pocket ruler and began to make napkin calculations: "At least fifteen feet," he presently surmised. "Mothers weren't giants in those days," Hockney asked, "were they?"

He then pulled out another image, Chardin's *Silver Tureen* from the Met, a still life with a cat to one side, a couple of pears off to the other (Fig. 65). "Wonderful painting," he averred, right from the outset. "Incredible surfaces, truly exquisite rendering. But the pears are as big as the cat, which seems a bit strange—unless, of course, as with the Van Dyck mother and son, they were painted separately, off

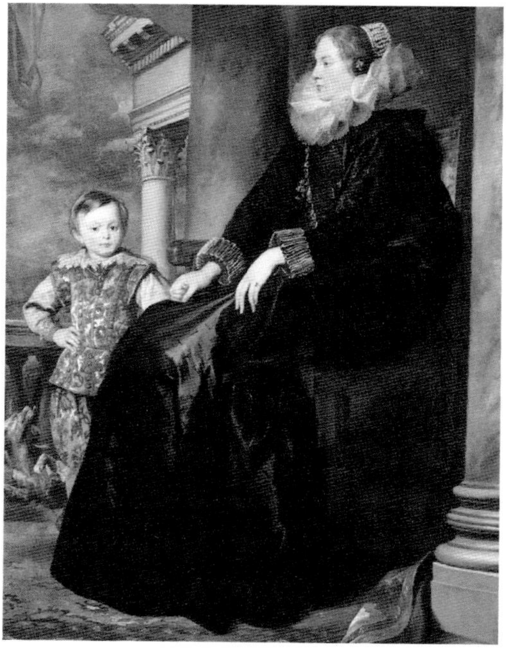

FIG 64 Anthony van Dyck, *A Genovese Noblewoman and Her Son*, ca. 1626.

FIG 65 Jean-Siméon Chardin, *The Silver Tureen*, ca. 1728.

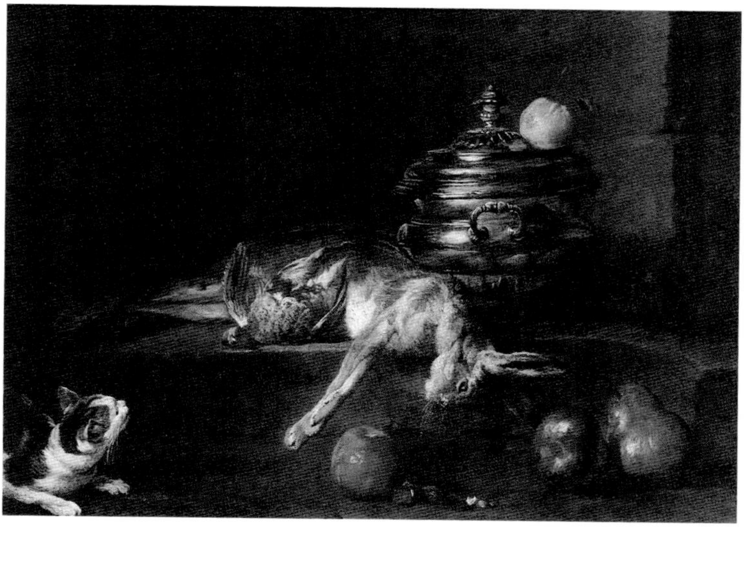

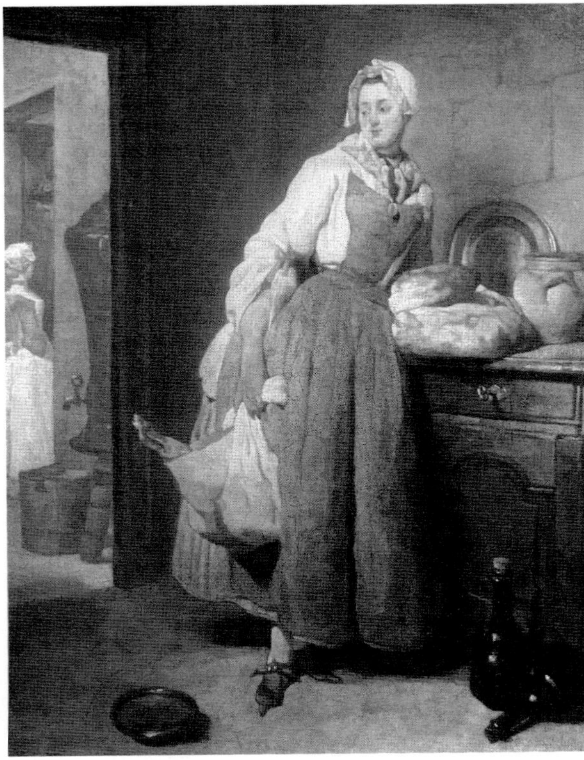

FIG 66 Jean-Siméon Chardin, *Return from the Market (La Pouvoyeuse)*, 1739.

separate projections." He pointed out that Chardin was another of those artists from whom precious few study drawings or underdrawings exist; and he was notoriously secretive about his techniques. "The marvelous thing, though," he continued, "is the way the viewer's eye compensates, the viewer's mind actively corrects so that it doesn't seem strange, partly because we too take the pictures in through a series of details, which we then configure into a seamless whole, and partly because we know this is a cat and that a pear, this a mother and that a son, we know their relative sizes, and we adjust for them accordingly. Our minds do that, the perceiving mind being perhaps the greatest wonder of all."

Hockney pulled out another, if possible still more lovely, Chardin, the sublime *Return from the Market* of 1739 (Fig. 66). "She's another tall one," he noted, and

Falco whipped out his pen and pocket ruler again. Following a few quick measurements and calculations, he concurred: "If the space between her pupils were the standard two and a half inches, then she'd have had to be approximately, let's see, umm, six foot eleven—she'd have had a hard time making it through that door jamb." Hockney noted that he and Graves had already ascertained that the composition featured at least two distinctly different vanishing points (the back wall rectangular stones and the chest of drawers receded to separate foci), consonant with at least two different projections, one for her lower body and a separate one for her upper half. "But look here," Hockney went on. "Where's her elbow? If you look at the picture from below, running up her exposed forearm, it's at one place. Whereas if you follow her shoulder down, it's somewhere entirely different. It's as if her arm has an extra middle bone. This is clearly bothering Chardin as well, because in two other versions of the same painting, he's still monkeying around with the elbow passage, trying to get it right."

Falco grabbed back the image and proceeded to hold it flat, extending the page straight out level from his squinting eye. "I'm looking at the door jamb. Yeah, you can see it, you can see the jog, at least one, there might be another. Here," he said, his finger on the spot as he brought the image back onto the table, "and maybe here as well. That's what we scientists call 'sighting along the data.' You do that sometimes when you've got a chart with a splatter of data points; you hold it up from the side and see if you can't make out a pattern that wouldn't otherwise be discernible."

"The point, though," Hockney went on, "is precisely that unless we focus on the disjunction, we don't see it. And who focuses on elbows? The lower arm seems fine, the upper as well, our mind makes the necessary elisions, and the painting as a whole feels seamless. Perfect."

Back at his campus office, later that afternoon, Falco pulled out a sheaf of his own, the working draft of a piece on their discoveries which he was coauthoring with Hockney and which they would soon be submitting for publication to the *Optics and Photonics News,* the prestigious monthly of the Optical Society of America, with subscribers in fifty countries (though probably not a single art historian among them). The two reviewed a few outstanding issues, after which Falco drove us to the airport for the flight back to L.A.

The next morning, before returning to New York myself, I went up to visit Hockney at his studio. For the first part of the visit we were joined by a distant neighbor of his, the sleight-of-hand artist and antiquarian historian of magic, Ricky Jay. After Hockney demonstrated the mirror shed for him with its upside-down projection, Jay pointed out how forgers too often preferred to work upside down. It made for a more accurate, less mind-filtered copying process. "Here," he said, grabbing my notepad, penciling a line down its length, and then handing the pad to Hockney: "Go ahead, sign your name underneath the line." Hockney did so and handed the pad back to Jay, who turned it upside down and, after flourishing his pencil hand a few times theatrically, proceeded to dash off (backwards) an uncannily precise simulation of Hockney's signature on the other side of the line. "Of course, I'd never dream of deploying such a skill to illicit purpose," he assured us, whereupon he took his leave.

The Wall, meanwhile, had wrapped itself clean around the entire studio, 1750 now continuing all the way around past the invention of photography up through about 1900, which kissed back up against the 1300 corner of the far wall. "Awkwardness," Hockney was saying, wheeling around, "the disappearance of awkwardness, the invention of chemical photography, and the return of awkwardness. The preoptical," he wheeled once more, "the age of the optical, and then the post-optical, which is to say the modern. And look here." He led me over to the corner where the two ends of the procession abutted. On the one wall he'd posited, as endpoint, Van Gogh's portrait of Trabuc; next to it, on the other, was a medieval Byzantine icon of Christ (Figs. 67 and 68). If anything, the overlapping effect was even more uncanny than that of Ricky Jay's paired signatures.

The photocopying machine had been pushed over to the side, and the center of the studio was once again teeming with Hockney's own painting efforts, and in particular a remarkable canvas portraying the view immediately outside the studio: the tree-covered path leading back down to the house. But this was no mere photo-optical approximation. On the contrary, the image, thrillingly precise, somehow was managing to convey not only what was directly before the viewer but what was wrapping up above and below and to the side; it even seemed to be beginning to include what was behind (Plate 24). This was no window, cut out and cut off: this was a world in the process of being entered, a space fully inhabited, enfolding,

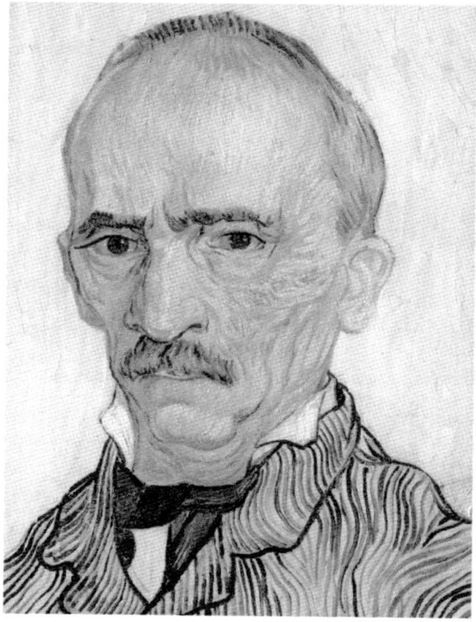

FIG 67 Vincent van Gogh, *Portrait of Trabuc,* September 5–6, 1889.

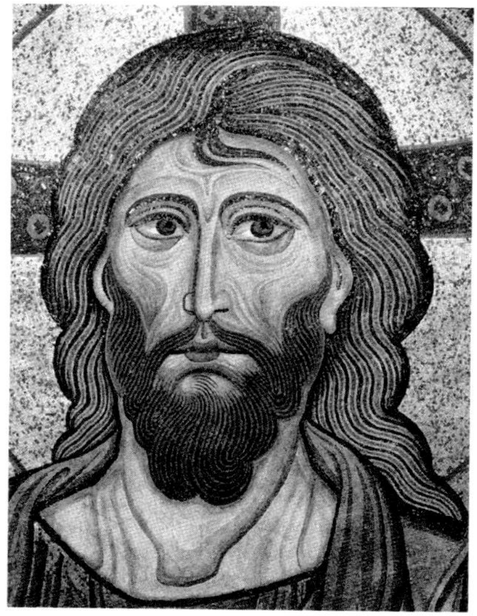

FIG 68 Christ Pantocrator, ca. 1150. Byzantine apse mosaic. Cefalù cathedral, Sicily.

and receiving: a sort of concave phenomenological bulge. I'd never seen anything quite like it. Next to it, leaning against another easel, was a similar view of the patio outside his London studio. "I wanted to paint that vista from memory," Hockney explained, "without the use of any photographic aids, only as I was able to reconstrue it in my mind's eye. And next month, when I get back to London, I'm going to attempt a similar series of views from my breakfast table here, gazing out toward the patch of valley in the distance. Again as a further way of evading the optical bias."

No more lenses, he seemed to be saying. Or rather, maybe, a different sort of lens: his very being reconfigured as a time lens.

A couple months later, when I happened to be passing through London on other business, I paid a call on Hockney at his Pembroke studio, and the L.A. vistas were indeed on his easels. (The July issue of *Optics and Photonics News* was likewise on his table, the *Arnolfini Marriage* splashed across its cover.) As it happened, Hockney's staging of Stravinsky's *Rake's Progress* was going to be receiving its twenty-fifth anniversary performance the next afternoon down in Glyndebourne, and Hockney invited me along.

Such celebratory productions are increasingly bittersweet affairs for Hockney, what with his continually encroaching deafness. He no longer participates in the actual staging, and is no longer taking on fresh projects. (Granted, he's not beyond using his auditory difficulties to maximum tactical effect. If he doesn't want to entertain objections to or hesitations about his theories, he simply doesn't hear them and plows on, oblivious. The deafness may account, at least in part, for what seems a narrowing of his universe, but it also allows for a sometimes awe-inspiring intensity of focus as well—seldom have such proliferating manifold perspectives been pursued with such monomaniacal passion—so it's a mixed bag.)

At any rate, the *Rake's Progress* the next day was as crisp and fresh as ever—a true evergreen staged in a setting of lulling pastoral ease (the grazing sheep on the meadows surrounding the manor bunched and drifting like earthbound clouds)—but the thing that most astonished me was how already, way back then, Hockney had been conceiving of the opera's Bedlam scenes. Virtually every other conception of an insane asylum I'd ever encountered (from the *Bell Jar* through *Cuckoo's Nest,* from Hogarth through *Sweeney Todd*) envisioned the madhouse as just that: mad. A tumultuous, roiling chaos. But for Hockney—and remember, this was twenty-five years ago, long before his various photocollage investigations or the more recent spate of theorizing—Bedlam was already a hell of receding one-point perspective, each inmate slotted into his tapering little foreshortening cell in the perfect vise of a cyclops's gaze (Fig. 69). Already back in 1975, this had been the prospect from which Hockney had clearly been endeavoring to escape.

Back in London the next day, as if in blithe and tonic compensation, Hockney was recalling for me the trip he and Graves had taken to Bruges a few weeks earlier: the paintings, even more lustrous than their most vivid reproductions; the light filtered through the leaded casement windows (pattern-gridded windows that almost forced one to look through multiple vantages); the wood-beamed interiors within which he and Graves had undertaken their own pocket mirror experiments. But the most enthralling experience of all, he went on, had been their side trip to

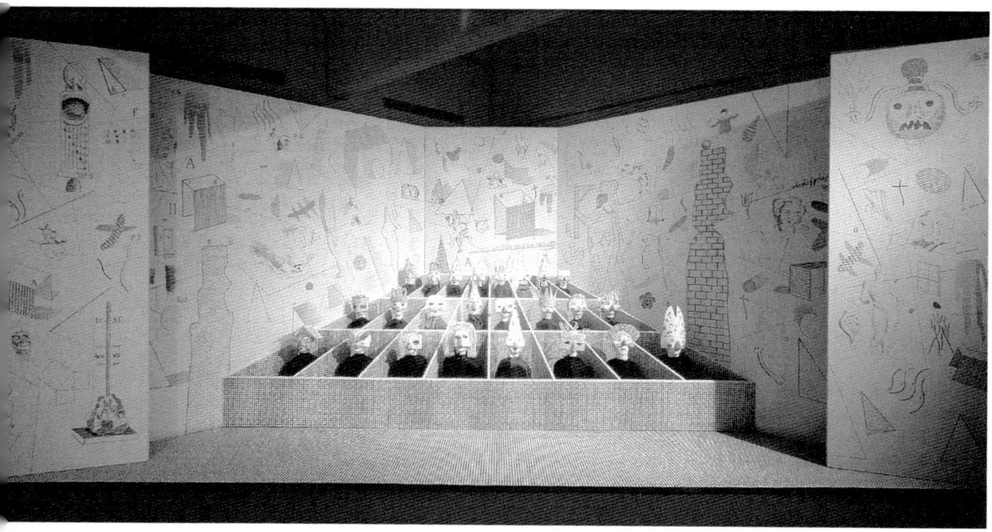

FIG 69 David Hockney, large-scale painted environment with separate elements based on Hockney's design for "Bedlam" from Stravinsky's opera *The Rake's Progress*, 1983.

neighboring Ghent to experience Van Eyck's magnum opus, the altarpiece, in person. "No amount of viewing of reproductions can prepare you for the experience," he assured me. "For one thing there were the colors: colors you never encounter in nature, and can't even reproduce on the page, but which we've been continually encountering in our own projections. I mean, I *recognized* that green. And then, there's the sheer scale. The central panel, with its marvelous *Adoration of the Lamb,* is almost twenty feet long and over twelve feet high—nothing like the miniature foldouts you get in most monographs." He nevertheless reached for such a foldout and showed me (Fig. 70). "The point is that such renditions necessarily betray the altarpiece's essential conceptual genius—the literally hundreds of separate detailed vantages—by homogenizing everything to a single one-point perspective shot. I've been talking with the people over at the BBC"—he'd agreed to host a series of documentaries on his new theories, to be aired this October in conjunction with the publication of a book laying out his argument, early galleys of which he'd also been showing me—"and I was telling them, there will simply be no way that they

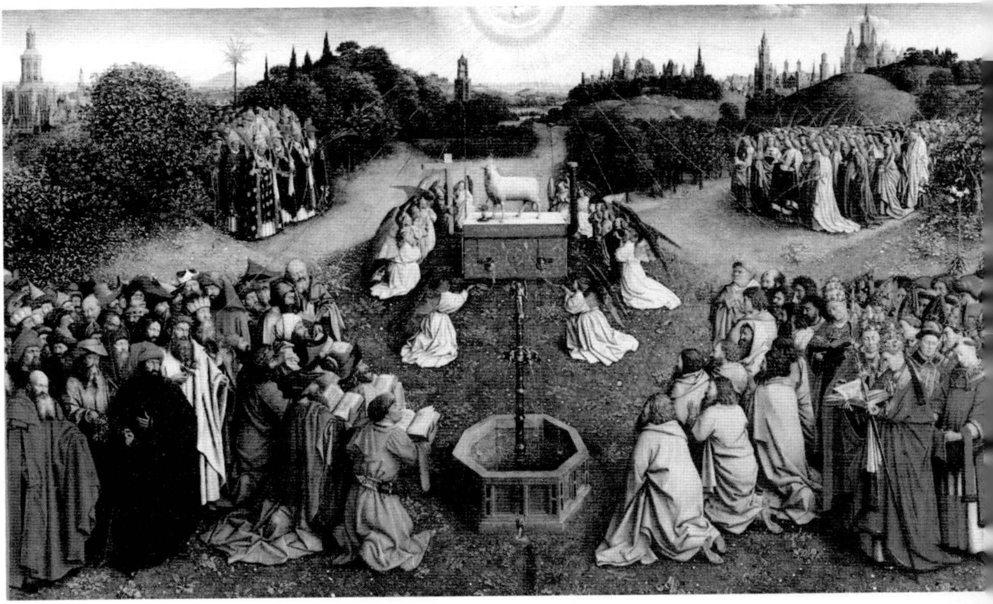

FIG 70 Jan and Hubert van Eyck, *Adoration of the Lamb*, panel from the Ghent Altarpiece, 1432.

will be able to engage the entire expanse of the *Adoration* within a single shot. They replied that that was all right, they'd just sweep across the panel in a series of slow panning takes, to which I replied, 'In other words, you'll be doing exactly what he did: hundreds of individual vantages, one after the next, bringing every detail up close.'

"Now, I may have been sensitized to this in advance," he went on, "because in a way, and again without in any way wanting to compare the quality of the final products, Van Eyck built up his *Adoration* exactly the way I built up my *Pearblossom Highway*"—one of the last and perhaps the most ambitious of his photocollage tableaus.

Hockney pulled out a catalogue of his own work and turned to a reproduction of the piece (see Plate 11). "Again, of course, reproductions distort a fundamental aspect of the work," he said, "but you can get an idea." The convergence was indeed startling—almost comically so: Compositionally, the center ditch and fountain pole of the *Adoration* echoed the median divider of *Pearblossom*—or, I guess, vice versa; the red platform of the former was mirrored in the stop sign of the latter; and so forth. "The point is," Hockney explained, "it took me two days out there at that intersection in the desert to photograph all of those details; I had to climb on a ladder, for example, to get the head-on shots of the stop sign, and for that matter to get the proper down-gazing vantages of the foreground asphalt. Those beer cans to the side, I had to get right up close to them and then photograph them from an angle which subsequently would meld with all the surrounding shots I was taking. And all of that is what accounts for the sense of immediacy, of closeness, of being right there, that you get with the final collage—especially if you compare it with a standard single snap of the same scene (see Fig. 29). And I'm convinced Van Eyck was doing something remarkably similar, pulling in close for each face in the crowd, for each clump of trees, for each flower, and then feathering all of those vanishing points one atop the next. After which, for all his trouble, he gets dismissed as 'primitive'!"

He paused, gazing over at the L.A. vistas on his easels, and from them, apparently, free-associated back over to his upcoming BBC documentary project. "It will have the same title as the book," he said, "*Secret Knowledge,* but I'm thinking of giving it its own subtitle: 'Four Picture-Making Cities: Bruges, Ghent, Florence, and Hollywood.'" He laughed and then grew more serious. "Because, actually, the history of picture making is continuous. Today's Hollywood epics grow directly out of the tradition of prior history painting: Abel Gance comes right out of David, DeMille directly out of Alma-Tadema, and David and Alma-Tadema, of course, directly out of what had come before: Poussin, Caravaggio, Van Eyck . . . Think of the very shapes and dimensions of the screens upon which movies were projected from the start, and then, conversely, of the lenses and other optical devices with which we've been showing that those earlier paintings were themselves created." I recalled how once, a few months previous, pointing to the deep shadows in a night scene of Velázquez's, Hockney had quipped, "Day for Night." Back in the Bradford of his youth, Hockney was now recalling, "My dad used to take us to 'the pictures,' that's what they were called, and they were playing at the Picture Palace. And in fact, looking at things again from the other way around, I think one of the most common misperceptions about the old masters is to imagine them as solitary freelancers, on the order of Van Gogh, for example—the great romantic myth of the artist as anguished and questing loner. Whereas, of course, it's not for nothing that Van Eyck and Van Dyck and Rubens and Velázquez were all said to have *studios.* Their studios were like nothing so much as the Hollywood studios of the Golden Age. They had lighting people and lens assistants, costume people and makeup artists, accountants and apprentices, and I'm sure Rubens had two flaming queens in the back in charge of all the hats." (Of course, one of the ironies here is that both the old masters and Hollywood were among the leading promulgators of that myth of the solitary questing knight.) "Caravaggio, in his cellar studio, arranging his models in their poses, draping the costumes over their shoulders, gauging the light, ducking behind the lens to study the image projected onto his wet blackened canvas, coming back out to rearrange the poses once again—his referent nowadays wouldn't so much be some other painter as, say, Zeffirelli."[2]

Caravaggio had probably been the principal focus of Hockney's interest, certainly after Ingres, in the earliest phases of his historical investigations, and now, during the latter part of 2000 and into the winter of 2001, the Lombard master seemed to wheel back into the center of Hockney's purview once again. This was in part owing to the sojourn of the dazzling Genius of Rome show at the Royal Academy in London; Hockney visited the exhibition repeatedly, often in the company of a new colleague-in-inquiry, John Spike, the seasoned Florence-based historian and author of a forthcoming Caravaggio catalogue raisonné. Spike subsequently recalled for me how he'd telephoned Hockney shortly after arriving in town for a few days' visit and Hockney had insisted that they meet at the exhibit right then, immediately—alright, fine, in twenty minutes. "He is definitely a man on a mission," Spike commented, "and he is definitely noticing things." He went on to describe, for example, how the two of them had stood for some time before Caravaggio's so-called Kansas City John the Baptist, and how Hockney had pointed out the absurd, anatomically impossible appearance of the youth's rippling abdomen. "The reason is simple," he told Spike. "It's another depth of field distortion. He was focusing his lens on the elbow in the foreground, such that the boy's torso went out of focus. An effect you couldn't possibly eyeball, but which you couldn't avoid using a lens projection." Spike was convinced, but now he returned once again to Hockney's passionate absorption. "At one point," he recalled, "a few moments later,

I noticed how a stooped old man had stationed himself behind us and was likewise gazing intently. Actually, he didn't seem to like this particular painting and was muttering under his breath. And you'll never guess who this was: Henri Cartier-Bresson, the great photographer! Hockney was too absorbed even to notice. Needless to say, it was an uncanny moment for me."

Back in L.A., later in the winter and into the spring, as Hockney and Graves completed work on their book version of the theory (due out from Thames and Hudson and Viking that coming October), they remained focused on Caravaggio, as I came to realize on another trip out, a few months ago, when Falco happened to be visiting as well. We converged on Hockney's hangarlike auxiliary studio space down on Santa Monica Boulevard, which had been converted into a vast optical lab.

"Look here," Hockney veritably crowed, as he drew us over to a black tentlike structure, with thick drapes hanging over a tall metal-pipe modular armature, an easel on the inside of the tent, a sliding lens-bearing contraption at its edge (where the drapes were pulled to the side) and a table on the outside, with a bank of daylight-simulating floodlights bearing down upon it. "Now, watch this." He placed a highly reflective armor breastplate on the table (remember, we were in Hollywood, after all), so blindingly reflective, in fact, that it was virtually impossible to make out any of its details. "Now, come in here," he said, pulling aside the drapes. Inside, an image of the armor was indeed being cast, upside down, onto the blank canvas, but with the blinding brilliance subdued, the colors and the composition subtly modulated into an enchanting compositional whole—one that looked, if you'll pardon the expression, exactly like a painting. Falco had whipped out his calculator and was pointing out that both the luminosity and the spectroscopy of the armor still life were being compressed by the lens—he tossed off a series of numbers. "Or try this," Hockney continued, scooting outside and replacing the armor with a tumbling swath of satin. Again, out in the bright glare of the floodlights, it was almost impossible to make out the glaring fabric—but inside (the cast image was lovely and deeply affecting) you could easily make out where each of the highlights belonged. "Same thing with wall maps," Hockney went on. "We were noticing the wall maps in the Vermeers at the recent New York show, for example the one behind the girl in *The Allegory of Painting*—and we did the experiment. With the naked eye, there'd be such an overload of information—the coastline, the marshes, the borders, and so forth—that it would be difficult to make out the creases and folds in the hanging map itself. But when you cast such a scene through a lens, creases and folds are just about the first thing you notice. . . .

"Now, come here." He drew us back out of the tent and over to a side wall onto which had been pinned a Hockneyesque pastiche of Caravaggio's *Supper at Emmaus* of 1601. "We figured out precisely how he did it. It's a bit more complicated than we thought before. Remember how before, I thought he set up the whole ensemble, all four of the sitters, and then he had them pose while, retreating behind his curtain, he sketched out the whole thing on his glistening wet and reflective canvas, incising the contours with the blunt end of his brush so that his models could take occasional breaks and then return to their positions. But we don't think it was quite like that anymore. Rather, here, look." He reached for a superb reproduction of the heartrending painting (see Fig. 43). "Look at Peter's extended left hand, here on the side, the one closest to us. It's roughly level with the fruit basket, in terms of depth, yet just about the same size as the fruit basket: those must be mighty tiny apples and positively minuscule grapes. Now, look at Peter's other hand, flung deep into the backdrop of the painting: it's the same size as the one closest to us—in fact if anything even bigger, and bigger certainly than Jesus's hand, which in turn is thrust way forward. Before, we used to think he must have been using some kind of telephoto lens. But no, this is what he did, we did the experiment." Hockney nodded over at his pastiche. "The lens stayed in place, but he posed the figures separately, one at a time. First, let's say, Peter. He moved his easel over so that the cast projection was falling on the canvas's right side. He had his model pose with his hands outthrust, and first he sketched in the hand closest to us, but the rest of the guy's body went out of focus. So when he'd finished with those notations, he had the sitter move forward, so that his head and torso fell into the sweet spot of the focus, adjusting the easel accordingly; and finally he had him move forward one more time, so that he could get the back hand which, being in the same sweet spot, was the same size as the front one. Note how Peter's gaze actually seems to fall on nothing—he's not making eye contact with a Jesus who literally wasn't there at the time he was painted. Okay, so now Caravaggio moved the easel again, so that the sweet spot fell on the center of the canvas, and he had the Jesus model sit in pretty much the same place and now he did him. After which, moving the easel again, he did the two other figures, one by one. Notice, by the way, the white tablecloth over the Persian rug. That solved the Lotto problem—and you'll notice by the way the same strategy being used by all sorts of artists around that time. You'll also notice," Hockney was now regarding his own pastiche, "this way you could even use the same models over and over again."

It occurred to me that in a sense Hockney had refined his Zeffirelli analogy yet further. Caravaggio had effectively built up his story through a series of close-ups and reaction shots. "Exactly," Hockney agreed. "For the people of those times, such paintings *were* motion pictures—their eyes were invited to move through the unfolding story."

It also struck me that this more supple version of the theory bore to the original version something of the relationship that Hockney's gridlike Polaroid collages bore to their more fluid and dynamic Pentax successors. For that matter, the entire theory had the feel of a lens being dragged across a vast swath of history as one detail after another fell into its sweet spot.

"This is what we now think happened," Hockney was holding forth, summing up. "It begins with the concave mirrors, most likely in Bruges around 1425 and spreading outward, but curved mirrors have got this problem: they can only project a zone of focus of about thirty centimeters diameter. Presently artists begin to notice that you can get the same and an even better effect with a lens, and that lenses are much more versatile. Della Porta is describing lenses projecting images through a hole into a darkened chamber as early as 1558. From 1570 or so till about 1660, we enter the era of the left-handed sitters—suddenly you see them everywhere, everybody's drinking or signaling or grabbing their swords with their left hands (you even get left-handed monkeys!), which is because the lens, unlike the mirror, not only turns the image upside down but reverses right and left. And the artists aren't able to compensate for that until flat mirrors become affordable, toward the last half of the seventeenth century. After that, artists become more and more adept, the lenses more and more sophisticated—Vermeer, Velázquez, and so on—and new variations arise (Reynolds's secret camera obscura that could collapse into the shape of a book and, thus disguised, be slotted onto a shelf; Ingres's camera lucida), up through the invention of chemical photography itself in 1839.

"Of course," he said, "that still leaves us with the problem of Brunelleschi."

Brunelleschi: a Florentine contemporary of Van Eyck's, widely regarded as the progenitor, actually about a decade prior to Van Eyck's breakthroughs, of classic Italian mathematical abstract perspective. The story of that astonishing innovation is one of the chestnuts of art history: how Brunelleschi—who would go on, as his greatest achievement, to mastermind the dome over the Florence cathedral—had earlier in his career contrived a spectacularly realistic pair of paintings, one of the octagonal Baptistery as seen across the square from the cathedral's deep portal, the other of the view across another nearby square. Both of these panels have since been lost, but their reputation lives on. So precise were they said to have been that Brunelleschi was able to bore a hole through the center of each of the panels and then have viewers stand precisely where he had stood in making them, bring the back side of the panel up to their faces, peer through the hole at the actual scene, and then extend a flat mirror at arm's length so they could gaze on the reflection of the painted panel itself—and there was no difference!

Hockney and Graves had long been wondering about those panels and that epiphanous moment. How would anyone who had never seen photos or optical projections of any sort ever have come up with the idea for one- or two-point perspective or any other system of mathematical abstraction? There are no medieval antecedents, and understandably so: We don't ordinarily suddenly find ourselves standing stock-still, storklike, closing one eye and freezing the other in its gaze, in order to gauge a scene. Rather (as cognitive psychologists have recently been showing ever more emphatically) vision as it is lived involves a stereoscopic vantage in continual motion, with the perceiving mind actively engaged in retrieving memory, projecting expectation, computing relative scales, compensating for seeming discrepancies, and so forth. How would the idea of doing it any other way ever have arisen?

The standard account (for example in Martin Kemp's *Science and Art*) has Brunelleschi extrapolating from the surveying skills and arts he had been perfecting in his ongoing study of antique ruins. But Hockney and Graves began to suspect that Brunelleschi himself had used an optical device, perhaps even a concave mirror. (Admittedly, were this the case, it might require a rethinking of the putative Bruges-to-Florence trajectory, though perhaps still with the Medici banker Arnolfini as the carrier.) In corroboration, Graves had dug up a remarkably suggestive description of a curved mirror being used to cast an image onto a wall "of things outside not in sight" in a text written in 1275 (!) by the Polish monk Witelo, who in turn seems to have based his hermetic suggestions on the writings of Roger Bacon and, before him, that eleventh-century Arab scholar Alhazan. Graves was also able to build up a fairly strong case for the simultaneous presence of Witelo manuscripts at the turn of the fifteenth century in libraries in both Florence and Ghent. Might not Brunelleschi and Van Eyck, omnivorously curious as both of them obviously were, have separately come upon the same reference? Thanks to contemporary accounts, we know that Brunelleschi staged his demonstration, particularly of the Baptistery panel, early in the morning; that he stood a few feet inside the darkened cathedral portal, facing out into the bright morning light, and that the panel he created was approximately thirty centimeters in length (precisely the dimension of a mirror projection's sweet spot). Mightn't he have used a mirror to make the image in the first place and then, instead of moving the lens around as the Flemish took to doing, mightn't he or his successors have noticed the way the three-dimensional world's parallel lines seemed, on the two-dimensional panel, to recede to specific vanishing points, and then gone ahead and extended those imaginary lines to create a mathematical perspective (as an alternative to the multiple-vantage method with all its attendant splicing problems)?

Hockney became more and more convinced that this was indeed the case. In late May, on the occasion of a gathering in Florence of scientists and historians exploring scientific issues in Italian Renaissance art, with both Spike and Kemp in attendance, Hockney arranged to have the cathedral's portals swung open at seven in the morning (a highly unorthodox procedure, for which he'd had to secure special ecclesiastical dispensation) so he could demonstrate what he thought Brunelleschi did. And it worked.

What its "working" meant was open to debate. This time he even left the normally enthusiastic Kemp somewhat cold (Kemp had devoted an entire appendix in his *Science and Art* to his more orthodox account, based on surveying): This was all just too speculative. "David sees the optical evidence everywhere," Spike, for his part, subsequently commented to me, "and that may be a problem. He attempts to explain too much. Caravaggio's Bacchus being left-handed, for example: that could have had an optical genesis, but it also might just be an iconographic decision, the left hand being thought of as notoriously lascivious. David leaves too many threads for the naysayers. And yet the overall thrust of his argument is quite powerful."

Spike's critique reminded me of an account I'd once heard of the nature of heresy in the Early Christian church—how a heresy in those days wasn't so much false in itself as an excavation of a long-suppressed aspect of the Truth which was then raised to the level of the Whole Truth and idolatrized as such. The trouble with such heresies (and one could easily substitute all manner of subsequent ones—the feminist heresy, the Afrocentric heresy, the Serbocentric heresy, and so forth, and maybe Hockney's as well) wasn't so much one of verity as one of proportion and right relation. (Another art historian once commented to me how she'd have thought that an artist of all people would have been the *most* suspicious of a Theory of Everything.)

But Hockney's a real shape-shifter in this regard. Suddenly he'll seem to double back: "It's not that everybody was necessarily using optical devices all the time," he commented to me that day beside his optical tent. "Rubens, Rembrandt, Titian, they often seem to be eyeballing things, whereas even those who clearly are using such devices may not be relying on them at every moment. But the devices established a standard, they dictated a look. In fact," he gestured back into the tent where the tumble of satin was still glowing on the blank canvas, "to see it *was* to use it. You see how overwhelmed everybody is by the sheer beauty of such projections even today—and we live in a world surrounded by movies and magazines and television. Imagine the impression that sort of projection must have made on them! And these were visually intelligent people; looking was what they did for a living. Surely they would have seen the implications. How *convincingly* a three-dimensional space could be laid across a two-dimensional plane. You think they would have thought twice about using it? And even if they themselves did, with everybody else using it, the optical look would have spread everywhere because they'd all have been studying each other's efforts."

In the meantime, I've been beginning to notice a subtle shift in the sorts of objections to Hockney's theory that I've been hearing. In the earliest days, when

I'd broach the theory with an art historian or a curator, I'd encounter the old bird-talking-back-to-the-ornithologist problem: What standing did a mere artist have even to be entering such charged and protected terrain? (All professions, as someone once said, are to a certain extent a conspiracy against the laity.) Hockney's speculations would be dismissed out of hand—not true, impossible, where's the documentary evidence, where are the written accounts or instruction manuals or references in ledgers and so forth? More recently, skeptical response has segued into variations on "Well, we knew that all along." Or somewhat more subtly, "But who cares how they made the paintings—that's not what matters. What matters is iconography, social context, market relations, the metahistory of representation"—whatever.

Hockney has been countering that the story of how artists saw and extended the possibilities of seeing is inherently fascinating, in and of itself. But in the end, that's not been his main concern. In the same way that during the early eighties, when he was taking literally hundreds of thousands of snaps across his photocollage passion, the celebration of photography itself had never been Hockney's principal intention (in fact the whole passion was being conducted as a massive *critique* of the claims of photography)—so, more recently, for all his immersion into the techniques and triumphs of the old masters, celebrating their optical achievement has never been his principal focus. How they made their paintings—the four-hundred-year optical hegemony over painting—matters to Hockney primarily because of what came after: his true passion has been the post-1839 assault on the optical waged by his real heroes—Manet, Van Gogh, Cézanne, and Picasso, artists who through great struggle threw off the cyclopean way of seeing and began looking at the world with *two* eyes, from a more realistically moving and lively vantage.

"Look," he said to me one day a few months ago as we gazed across the length of his studio at the 1750–1900 expanse of his Wall. "Look at that basket of fruit by Chardin over there on the left, and now at the same subject by Cézanne—see it there on the right? Chardin's version, for all its indisputable mastery and beauty, feels far away; it's a picture of fruit at the far end of an optical remove, receding into the picture, whereas Cézanne's, even from this far away, feels right up close; those apples feel close at hand, they feel *present to hand,* they come out to us. That's what you can achieve when you break from the tyranny of the optical.

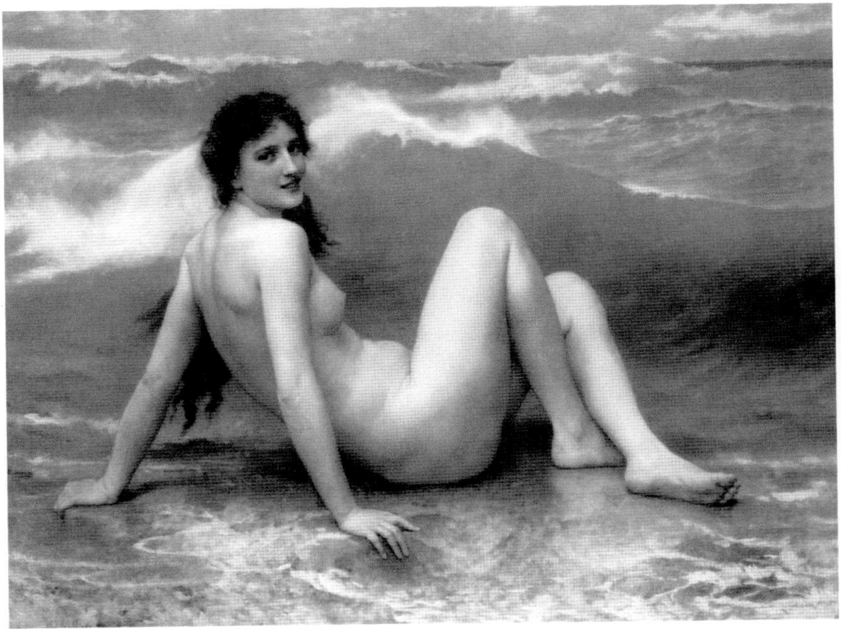

FIG 71 William-Adolphe Bouguereau, *La Vague*, 1901.

"And yet"—he now pulled me back across the room toward that section of the Wall—"for all the modernist achievement in that regard, it was the monocular optical vision that appears nevertheless to have triumphed. Compare those Cézanne bathers there with this Bouguereau nude, an academic work, which in effect continued the optical tradition in painting long after the invention of chemical photography [Fig. 71]. You can just see how Bouguereau was using projected photographs: the breaking wave is an entirely artificial backdrop, ludicrously unintegrated with the figure in the foreground, a flat; you can even make out the table the model must have been sitting on in the indentations of the sand. But this is the view that won and continues to hold sway to this day, in photojournalism, in advertising, on television (which is one great receding perceptual tunnel), in movies. David Graves came upon a great line in one of those thirteenth-century precursor texts he's been digging up, Arnold of Villanova's advocacy of secrecy about emerging esoterica:

'Some of this knowledge should not fall into the hands of showmen and fools.' Quite something to come upon," he laughed, "here in Hollywood on the far side of the millennium."

One morning I rose to find another of Hockney's occasional faxes dangling out from my machine. He'd photocopied two printed texts onto a page. The first, in boldface, read:

> 4. Thou shalt not make unto thee any graven image, or any likeness *of any thing* that *is* in Heaven above, or that *is* in the earth beneath, or that *is* in the water underneath the earth;

and the second:

> Islam tells us that on the unappealable Day of Judgment, all who have perpetrated images of living things will reawaken with their works, and will be offered to blow life into them, and they will fail, and they and their works will be cast into the fires of punishment.

Beneath these unsettling edicts, Hockney had scrawled:

I will try to send some better news later.

For all the humor of his dispatch, there's no question that Hockney feels he is playing for big stakes—that more, at any rate, is up for grabs than a mere reinterpretation of the history of painting. Falco, for his part, has been pushing his researches into almost revolutionary territory. He is convinced that his collaboration with Hockney has been leading him toward an entirely new way of conceiving the problem of computerized visual analysis, one of the holy grails of artificial intelligence research. So now he has yet something else to do on those mornings when he's not monkeying around with his bikes out in the garage.

The other day, reviewing my files as I prepared to write this piece, I happened upon a handwritten note Hockney had faxed me roughly midway through the adventure, when the stakes were beginning to come clear to him:

Dear Ren:

We move on, we have begun to understand the construction of the Van Eyck altar pieces—Dirk Boutes, Rogier van de Weyden, etc. It's not one window—like Alberti's perspective, but many windows—more like the Polaroids.

Nevertheless, this is not just about Art History—nor about artists "cheating," although we had in the process of all this to understand the use of optics.

The real problem, as I've said before, is when the lens joins with chemicals—photography. The hand has gone and we are then reduced to a mathematical point. "The pencil of nature" [as the new medium was being referred to in the 1840s] is a mad idea: you need a hand with the pencil. It won't do anything on its own.

I've thought this for a long time, as you know—but all this had to be done before others could begin to see what human vision means.

Images, Images, Images, they have taken over, and they are not human enough. Cezanne and cubism were right, but what has happened: Post-Modernism is Pre-Modernism, it accepts the chemical picture. Our job here is to make others see this, and the big pictures to come of the big beautiful world.

—No edges.

We are not mathematical points.

We are a dimension.

the 5th (?)

I don't know, but this is why all this was done.

Artists "cheating" is about the lowest level of all this—trivial and unimportant.

More later

Love life

David

Love life: this has been the way Hockney has been signing his dispatches of late—in fact for several years now. And it's not mere verbiage. In fact the defiant love of life—in the face of his encroaching deafness, of the way AIDS and cancer have been laying waste the community of his closest friends, of the death of his ninety-eight-year-old mother at the outset of this particular passion, and of his beloved dog Stanley, at age fourteen, in the very midst of it—that unshakable treasuring of life itself has been the leitmotif of Hockney's late career, and in many ways one of the most remarkable and heartening things about it.

CHAPTER 7

sometime make the time

YORKSHIRE WATERCOLORS

(2004)

"Look," David Hockney bade me see, a few weeks ago, as we sat in his spacious Hollywood Hills studio, after I'd brought up the question of a particularly ferocious attack on his optical theory that had appeared in a recent *Scientific American.*

Shortly after that last piece of mine had made its first appearance, over the net at a Web site called Artkrush.com, coming on five years ago now, Hockney's *Secret Knowledge* book was indeed published, and shortly after that, in December 2001, the New York Institute for the Humanities at New York University, of which I happened to be director, convened a veritable college of cardinals, a weekend-long public conference bringing together artists, critics, scholars, and scientists from all over the world to decide, as it were, whether Hockney ought be elected pope or rather burned at the stake. Passions ran high (lines coursed around the block), and in the end the verdict was mixed (though Hockney was at least permitted to go on living and promulgating his controversial convictions).

Curiously, though, some of the sharpest differences at that conference emerged among the scientists. (Even though common definitions, methods, and so forth might have been expected to elicit a certain consensus among them—or so many of the other participants had been hoping—this proved far from the case.) In particular, Falco butted horns with another optical scientist, David Stork (from Ricoh Systems and tangentially associated with Stanford). And indeed, in the months and years that followed, from one academic conference to the next (Ghent, Florence, etc.), Stork had been continuing to stalk Hockney and Falco with virtually Ahabian relish—marshaling mathematical arguments and counterexamples of his own, arguments Falco, for his part, just as quickly would parry and wrestle back

---

This essay was written for the catalogue to the Hand Eye Heart show of Hockney's East Yorkshire watercolors at the LA Louver Gallery in February 2005.

to the ground. The *Scientific American* piece in turn being Stork's latest return thrust.[1]

"But, look," Hockney was now saying, "I don't take those sorts of arguments very seriously. For one thing they are not addressing the essential point I was trying to make. I've never contended that all these artists were slavishly tracing every line in their projections, though I must say I always liked Richard Wollheim's observation that even tracing involves eyeballing, in other words requires consummate skill, some being better at it than others . . . At most I was arguing that these devices could be deployed as aids for measurement and notation of key points, after which the artist would revert to traditional eyeballing techniques, though even such limited deployments would result in an identifiably optical look. The main point to be made about optical projection, though, from an artist's point of view—especially back then in the early fifteenth century—was that *even just to see it* (the projection, that is, of three-dimensional reality onto a two-dimensional surface) was to use it. Artists would have been irresistibly drawn to the optical projection: how it harmonized color relations; how it allowed you to reach out and actually touch the edges, say, between the contour of a face in the foreground and the grove behind. The way—and this was critically important—you could move but the image cast onto the wall would stay fixed, *unlike any other experience you had ever had.* Suddenly, as a result of this phenomenon, for the first time in the history of painting, we encounter accurate renditions of reflected light on armor, or of highlights on satin, because on the projection they stay fixed in place even though your head bobs around observing them. In the real world, of course, they wouldn't: when your head would bob, so would they. And then, similarly, the projection yields up one-point perspective—*and nothing else does.* It's difficult nowadays, in a world saturated with television and photographs and billboards and movies, to recall how radically new one-point perspective would have appeared to those first exposed to it. That's not how the world presents itself to anyone moving through it, never does, though it is how the world presents itself and can't help but present itself through a one-point projection, be it a pinhole or a lens or a curved mirror. And the main point is, *pictures influence pictures*—it's as simple as that. Pictures frame how we then go on to see, and, thus seeing, to portray."

He paused, flicking a final dismissive gesture with his hand. "At any rate," he now resumed, "I've been getting bored with the whole controversy—by the beginning of this year I'd pretty much dropped out of the daily fray of it: I had other things I needed to be doing."

Like what?

"Like painting! I needed to be getting back to painting. For a short time, but only a very short time, I wondered if there were some way I could adapt optics to my new purposes. But I quickly realized that no, the trouble with optics is the trouble with photography: it's not *real* enough, it's not true enough to *lived* experience. The Chinese say that painting draws on three things: the eye, the heart, and the hand. And I longed to return to the hand."

For starters he dispensed with his cameras. He has dozens, and he hasn't picked one up in months, in coming on years. "*Like that,*" he says, "cold turkey. I consciously abandoned the camera. I don't want to look through it again. No more pinholes! Enough with those claustrophobically constricting edges!"

Instead he began packing a sketchbook—a series of dozens and presently hundreds of sketchbooks. "I experimented and found a certain size that was good. You could put it in your coat pocket, always have it with you. I sought out these new pens with brown inks that dry quickly and don't fade; I developed brush techniques. And I was constantly drawing, which in turn makes you look harder, look more, *see* more, remember more—it did me. And I realized, this is fun!"[2]

As usual with a fresh new passion, Hockney early on discovered—or rediscovered—a fresh master, in this instance, Rembrandt. He delved, ecstatic, back into his multivolume edition of the master's collected drawings.

And what, I asked, so captivated him in Rembrandt?

"The hand!" he replied instantly. "The evidence of a human hand moving. I could feel his elbow jutting, the way he balanced and rebalanced his pen between his fingers, adjusting and readjusting. Every mark, visible. The boldness, and yet the economy of means. The precision and yet the liveliness of gesture, of observed and rendered gesture. As in the great Chinese paintings of that same period—one of the high points of Chinese art, after all, was occurring during those very same years—and remember: they were not in thrall to the optical. No shadows in the Chinese art of that time, as there had to be in European optical painting with its necessarily strong illuminations. I'm sure Rembrandt would have been aware of

Chinese art—Amsterdam being a port city, seat of the Dutch East India Company, and so forth. . . ."

It turned out Hockney had been thinking about Rembrandt and the Chinese a good deal. As it happens, Chinese porcelain (covered over with calligraphically suggestive nature imagery) was pouring into Holland in stupendous quantities during the middle years of Rembrandt's life: such "chinaware" repeatedly shows up in the backdrops of Dutch still lifes of the period; and over the past few decades, salvaging operations on several wrecks from those years that have dredged up the contents of merchant frigates bound from China to Amsterdam have yielded tens of thousands of bowls, dishes, and other objects (and millions of dollars for the salvagers once these troves made their way to Christie's). When the Chinese porcelain industry momentarily foundered during a transitional civil war in the mid-1640s, the Japanese took up the slack. (And the Dutch themselves founded elaborate porcelain works of their own during this same time, hence the emergence of Delftware.)

The main point to be made here, though, in terms of Hockney's argument, is that the Chinese in Rembrandt's time were not yet hostage to the Western optical hegemony—no lenses, pinholes, or concave mirrors in China. The hand—and its robustly manifest trace—still reigned supreme. "Take a look at these three images," Hockney now suggested, reaching for a file (Figs. 72–74): a photograph of a seventeenth-century Chinese ceramic saucer dish from about 1625, covered over with renderings of branches and leaves; a Rembrandt drawing of an avenue of trees, from circa 1654 ("clearly rendered without recourse to any optical device"); and another tree drawing, this one a couple hundred years later, from 1836, by the Danish Golden Age master Christen Købke ("just as self-evidently rendered *with* the use of optical aids, a camera obscura maybe or a camera lucida"). As self-evidently as all that? "Well, yes," Hockney averred. "When you've been looking at images for several years with this question in mind, you begin to note the telltale signs. In this case, for instance, see how Købke is clearly tracing the exterior silhouette of the trees—much the same way, once again, that Andy Warhol did when he would trace from photographic slide projections. Simultaneously recording the contours of the object while effacing, as it were, to the extent possible, any trace of the hand doing the recording. It could have been done by a machine: within a few years it

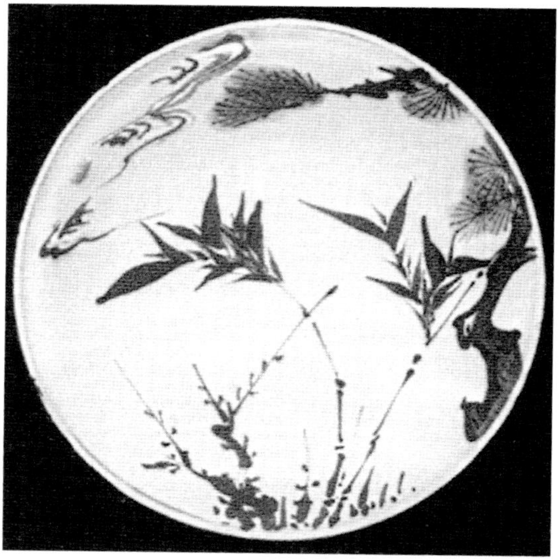

FIG 72 Saucer dish, Ming dynasty, Tianqi period, ca. 1625.

would be being done by a machine. The chemical fixative comes online just three years later.

"But now compare that with the Rembrandt, a drawing rendered, assuming we are correct, a good two hundred years into the European optical tradition but one which completely sidesteps that tradition. See how Rembrandt not only evokes the life force of the tree, how it is growing up out of the ground toward the light, but he recapitulates that force in his act of drawing, with his bold and lively up-and-out stroke. Almost calligraphic, and in that way reminiscent of the contemporaneous Chinese stroke. I'm not insisting that Rembrandt necessarily got that from the Chinese (although I'm sure he would have been fascinated by those Chinese imports)—only that both are examples of what can happen when you eschew the optical. And look what does result. You might think that work that calls attention to the gesture involved in laying in the mark—that continuously shimmers between the gesture and the image it is conveying—would lie flatter on the page: after all, it never tries to efface its origin as human mark on page. And yet, compare the Rembrandt with the Købke. The Købke is much flatter, precisely because what Købke

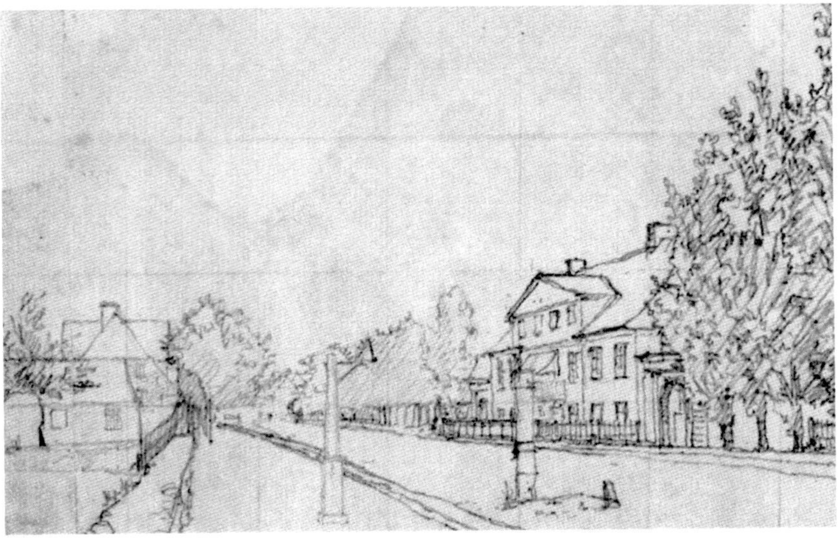

FIG 73 Christen Købke, *Parti af Osterbro I morgenbelysning*, 1836.

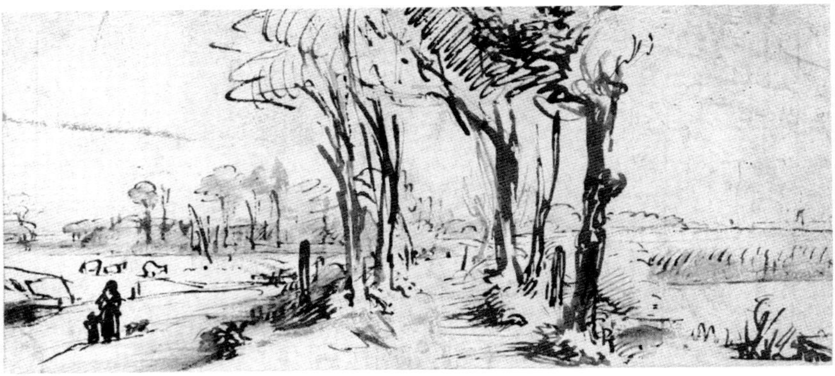

FIG 74 Rembrandt Harmensz van Rijn, *Avenue, on the Left a Woman with Child*, ca. 1654.

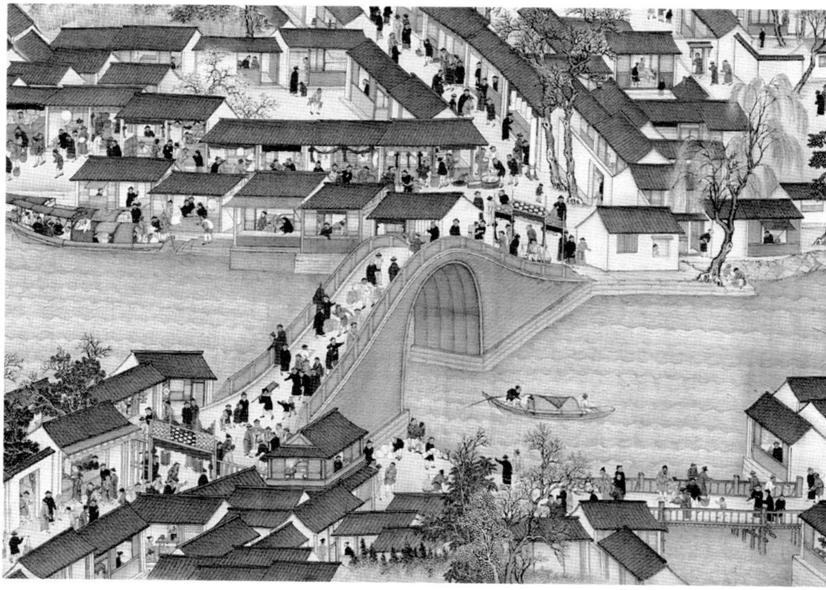

FIG 75 *The Kangxi Emperor's Southern Inspection Tour, Scroll Seven* (detail).

was portraying was *a flat projection!* He was looking down on a two-dimensional projection of the world and rendering that, whereas Rembrandt was attempting to capture the world itself, a world into which he was moving.

"Here," Hockney continued, reaching for another set of examples: a detail from a Chinese scroll by Wang Hui, *The Kangxi Emperor's Southern Inspection Tour,* from 1698, and a reproduction of Vermeer's sublime *Little Street* from circa 1658 (Figs. 75 and 76). "Now, the Vermeer is of course a masterpiece, one of the very pinnacles of the European optical tradition. I'm not trying to compare the relative merits of these two works of art, but rather their ways of seeing. Because the Vermeer takes part in that European trope of the canvas as a window, with us as viewers at a remove from the world we are being invited to view out there, in receding one-point perspective. Whereas, as we've discussed before, the Chinese never entertained that window vantage. In their scrolls in particular, the vantage, the perspective, is always moving—moving with the viewer as the viewer scrolls through the scroll,

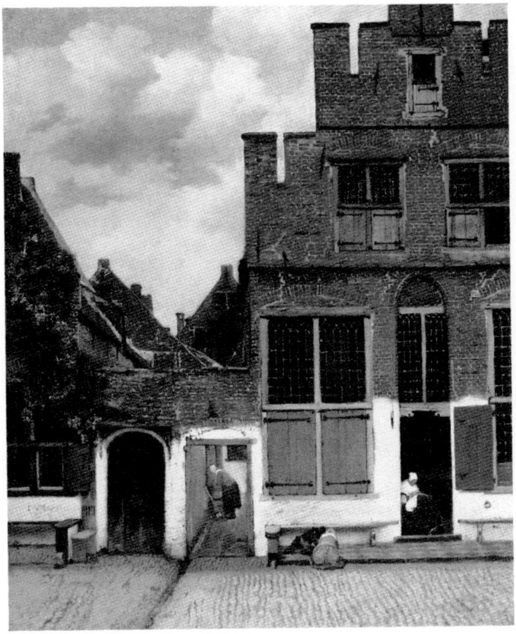

FIG 76 Johannes Vermeer, *The Little Street*, ca. 1658.

recapitulating the painter's own movement through the world. We, as viewers, are in that world, not outside it. See this little detail here, for example, which comes about midway through the seventy-foot scroll. Notice, for starters: no shadows (no need for bright projecting illumination, hence no chiaroscuro, as a way of depicting you never do get in Oriental art).[3] And then note how the bridge is seen from one side, as it would be by us as we first approach it, unspooling from the right side. But the town with its little streets—look how here the houses appear as they would from on top of the bridge, a different vantage, whereas these houses here look as they would from this whole other vantage over here. And yet it all coheres visually; it all makes sense. A different way of seeing, arguably more true to life."

Hockney paused for a moment, content, his eye drifting about the studio.

"Take that picture over there," he said, pointing over at a blowup of Figure 1466 from his Benesch edition of Rembrandt's collected drawings (Fig. 77). (He had similar blowups of the same image pinned to walls all around the house.) "The

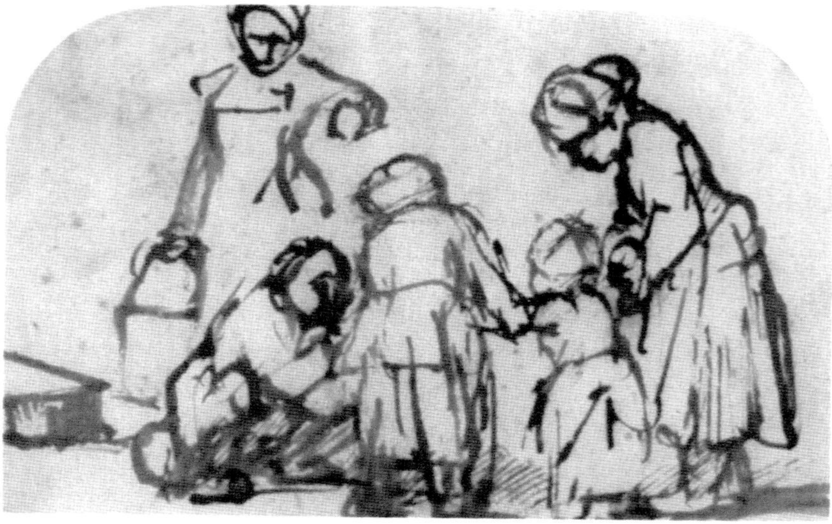

FIG 77 Rembrandt Harmensz van Rijn, *A Child Being Taught to Walk*, ca. 1660–62.

Single Greatest Drawing Ever Made," he declared flatly. "I defy you to show me a better one."

A family grouping: mother and older sister holding up a toddler boychild as he struggles to walk, tottering, toward the outstretched arms of his crouching father, a milkmaid ambling by in the background, balancing a brimming bucket.

"Look at the speed, the way he wields that reed pen, drawing very fast, with gestures that are masterly, virtuoso, not calling attention to themselves but rather to the very tender subject at hand, a family teaching its youngest member to walk. Look for instance at those whisking marks on the head and shoulders of the girl in the center, the older sister, probably made with the other side of the pen, which let you know that she is craning, turning anxiously to look at the baby's face to make sure he's okay. Or how the mother, on the other side, holds him up in a slightly different, more experienced manner. The astonishing double profile of her face, to either side of the mark. The evident roughness of the material of her dress: how this is decidedly not satin. The face of the baby: how even though you can't see it, you can tell he is beaming. This mountain of figures, and then to balance it all, the passing milkmaid, how you can feel the weight of the bucket she carries in the extension of her opposite arm. All of it conveyed, magically. But look at the speed, the sheer mastery. The Chinese would have recognized a fellow master."

A mother teaching her youngest to walk. One needn't be an analyst to recognize the resonances that particular image might have held for this artist at this particular juncture in his life, a few years after the death of his own mother. That, and then as well: Father Rembrandt teaching Baby David to walk.

To walk. Or rather, in this instance, to watercolor. For coming out of his *Secret Knowledge* passion, Hockney presently eschewed oils altogether in favor of the—as he saw it, for himself anyway—more challenging medium of watercolors.

"I'd done one or two watercolors a long time ago," he explained, "but never really explored the medium, and unless you truly explore a new medium like that, you don't really get into it. Watercolors are very difficult to use. Oil paint you can do almost anything with, because it doesn't dry quickly and you can always just wipe it off. But you can't do that with watercolors. Once the marks are down, they're there. They dry very quickly. Which was a bit forbidding, that and the fact that there's a long tradition of watercoloring, especially in England, with all its tricks and by now stylized techniques, all of which put me off the medium for a long time."

Nevertheless, he now did become interested. Why?

"The full-laden brush, I realized, was very effective. It's the most direct method of laying in a mark flowing from the eye, the heart, down the arm to the hand, through the tip of your instrument, everything flowing very quickly and seamlessly. Oil painting in a sense you have to push. Watercolor just flows, ink flows. Much more immediate and direct."

As opposed, for that matter, to the mediated fixity of the projected optical image?

"Precisely, it's more lively. The thing is it does take a while to master the techniques—having to work, say, from light to dark, because unlike with oils, you won't be able subsequently to daub a light color over a dark one. Everything has to be thought out in advance—and I realized it would take time to master all this. I had to ask myself, was I going to be willing to take six months to learn all this? Well, I was and I did, and it took even longer, mastering the medium, innovating new techniques, but by the end I'd broken into this looser, more immediate way of being present to my material."

At first he pretty much confined himself to working in his studio—still lifes and portraits—though increasingly the studio in question was proving to be the one he maintains in London. Shortly after his mother died, his beloved dachshund Stanley, back in California, also passed on. For over a decade, Stanley had to a certain extent kept Hockney contentedly anchored in California. (For one thing, one isn't allowed to bring dogs into England without a long period of quarantine.) With Stanley's death, that necessity no longer pertained. A few months later, one of his closest California friends, the marvelously witty and vital Jeff Berg (heir in some ways to the earlier roles played successively in his life by Geldzahler and Silver), also died, and there was still less to keep him in L.A. You couldn't even smoke any longer in public places;[4] and then, most perverse of all, following 9/11, one of Hockney's closest British friends, a regular long-term guest in his Hollywood Hills home, was suddenly being denied his standard reentry into the country on grounds that several years earlier he'd once overstayed his visa by two days.

And that was the last straw: in yet another triumph for Homeland Security, one of the most identifiable and beloved chroniclers of the light and life of California no longer felt at home in his adopted home state. His current visit, as a matter of fact, was his first in over a year, and it was going to last only a few weeks.

Back in England, he began experimenting with ways of taking his watercolors out of the studio and into the world. He would look out the window, gauge the weather and premix two or three colors accordingly, pour those admixtures into leakproof canisters (childproof pill bottles!), and slip the bottles into his pockets. He'd fill sketchbooks with his impressions, occasionally rushing back to the studio to cast larger renditions onto bigger sheets while the memory was still fresh.

And increasingly, he began returning to Bridlington and its environs.

In part he was again (as with his earlier Yorkshire suite of oil paintings) drawn by out-of-the-way, off-the-beaten-track East Yorkshire, which, unlike West Yorkshire, was in painterly terms largely virgin terrain. But he was also experiencing this virgin terrain, more forcefully this time around than before, in terms of his own *childhood* haunts. "I mean," he explained to me, "these were hardly my first forays into landscape painting. By contrast, though, in Norway, for example, or Iceland, or earlier, during my travels across the American West, I was always painting *views,* I was *sight*-seeing. Whereas there, around Bridlington, I was painting *the land,* land that I myself had worked. I had dwelt in those fields, so that out there, seeing, for me, necessarily came steeped in memory."

This sense of a return to origins somehow registers most palpably in some of Hockney's autumn- and winterscapes—this sense of returning in winter, perhaps, to the scene of one's own springtime. (Eliot again.) Furthermore, Hockney's mother's ashes were now scattered among those fields, so that the area around Bridlington had quite literally become his motherland. And yet a decidedly living and lively motherland.

"That was one of the things about spending weeks and weeks coursing along those roads," Hockney was now going on to explain. "Because you began to realize how *alive* the land is there. The agriculture is constantly changing; the land is constantly changing in colors and textures and feel. And the sky! Unlike in California, with its constantly blue sky, there in East Yorkshire clouds are continually racing past; and the moment you set yourself the challenge of painting that sky, you realize how fast *everything* is moving, how alive it all is."

Much as with Rembrandt's skies?

"Well yes. And of course it is almost the same sky—just across the sea. This part of England is just north of a district called New Holland—and the houses facing the Bridlington waterfront are markedly Dutch in style. You feel that."

At the same time, though, in another sense, the skies of East Yorkshire were reminiscent, as well, of those of the western United States—in their unexpected breadth and spaciousness. "I think that the area around Bridlington is one of the few areas in England where you regularly experience the sorts of wide vistas you get all the time in the American West. A lot of England has got these rather tall hedges girdling the roads, especially southern Cornwall, where you might be driving along, but you don't ever get to see very far."

As we have seen, the articulation of all that space, even more than that of "the views," had increasingly been the focus of much of Hockney's landscape work in the American West over the past fifteen years—think of his mammoth Grand Canyon grids or the giant *Pearblossom Hwy.* photocollage. At the same time, though, right alongside those efforts, Hockney had been engaged in a more intimate landscape project, the ongoing attempt to capture the changing feel of his own backyard garden. (Much like Monet at Giverny, Hockney would paint the garden, reconfigure the actual plants in the actual garden into more picturesque patterns, and then paint the new patterns, and so forth, in a continual process of revisitory recirculation.) The thing about East Yorkshire, though, what with its soft rolling hill-swells and its little cusped valley hollows, all beneath that wide, wide sky, was that it now afforded Hockney the opportunity to meld those two streams of his American landscape project through the evocation of passages, as it were, of *intimate spaciousness.*

"And some time make the time to drive out west / Into County Clare," Seamus Heaney launches out into his own masterful poem "Postscript," proceeding to evoke in positively virtuoso fashion the vivid autumn landscape whizzing by, the ocean to one side "wild / With foam and glitter," "a slate-gray lake" to the other "lit / By the earthed lightning of a flock of swans," until, at length, he concludes,

> Useless to think you'll park and capture it
> More thoroughly. You are neither here nor there,
> A hurry through which known and strange things pass
> As big soft buffetings come at the car sideways
> And catch the heart off guard and blow it open.

And indeed, such is precisely the sense one had gotten from Hockney's oil paintings of East Yorkshire in the last show. The sense of being on the move ("One is always nearer for not standing still," notes Thom Gunn in the first poem in his own early motorcycle sequence, *The Sense of Movement*)—the vantage being from the right-side driver's seat, nudging the middle of the surging road (in the case of Garrowby Hill, the uncanny sense that the front wheels of the car have just crested the top of the hill while the back wheels have yet to do so). "Useless to think you'll park and capture it more thoroughly," indeed. Yet that is precisely what Hockney is up to in this more recent set of watercolors (Plates 27–30). Again and again he has pulled over and parked to the left side of the road (this being England); he has opened the side door and, from the slightly lowered vantage of the passenger seat, he is gazing out and indeed capturing it more thoroughly, allowing his scrutinizing heart (and ours) to be blown wide open.

It's intriguing in this regard to compare the grid of sixty photographic snapshots that had accompanied the Looking at Landscape show of East Yorkshire oil paintings back in 1997 with the grid of thirty-six watercolor studies Hockney had arrayed along the far wall there in his Hollywood Hills studio the day I was visiting—in some ways, it seemed to me, the most vivid and engaging piece in the entire upcoming show (though Hockney was still trying to decide at that point whether it *was* one piece, or could be broken up and dispersed). The sense, time and again, of pause, immersive scrutiny, capture, and only then moving on. One is always nearer, Hockney seems to be saying, *for* standing still. "See the difference," Hockney was now commenting, having opened up the earlier catalogue. "For starters how much wider the vantages are in the watercolors than in the snapshots, and how the paintings allow your eyes to wander, side to side, foreground to background. There is less bullying: aim the camera, snap, and look at *that!* Indeed, with the watercolors there has been more looking, so there is more to see."

Hockney got up and shambled over to a side drawer, riffled about for a moment, and pulled out a moleskin sketchbook. "I was able to procure one of these Japanese-style sketchbooks, whose pages are attached and folded in one upon the other in such a way that—see?—they can accordion out into one long scroll. And I set out one day with my friend Jean Pierre driving. I was sitting in the passenger seat, and every few yards I'd have him pull over and stop so that I could sketch a particular stalk of grass or weed in the low roadside hedge. See? Each one quite distinct, quite different." A calligraphic cavalcade of things noticed, one upon the next. "The point being, the more you draw, the more you see and then you start seeing everywhere, order emerging from out of chaos, an order you can draw on the next time you take on the subject of an entire foreground hedge."[5]

Stop. Look. Look so you can draw. Draw so that you can see. See so that you can convey. More. More stuff. Wider vantages.

"Compare that grid," Hockney was now saying, turning back to the wall of watercolors, "with the furiously churning array of television monitors behind those floundering anchor people the other night during their presidential election coverage. For all the data streaming across those monitors, it was almost impossible to absorb anything. Hopeless. Look by contrast at how much sheer information, how much focused scrutiny, is held and delivered across that wall."

Striking in these images of the land, how often trees figure as the presiding presence, a further occasion for pause and scrutiny.

"Well, yes," Hockney concurred. "Trees are very, very beautiful. I've always felt that. They're the largest plant, which is one of the things I love about looking at them, probably everybody does. And another of the things about them is that you get to *see* the life force. That is, of course, if you are looking at them the way Rembrandt was rather than the way Købke did.

"There was a period a few years ago when I got very much into potted bonsai stands, you know, those little miniature trees. Remarkable subculture: tremendous body of expertise." It occurred to me that with these watercolor sketches, Hockney was casting full-size trees at precisely the scale of bonsai (just as he had been playing with scale in precisely the opposite direction in an earlier suite of watercolors of those bonsai). "My friend the Sheik even gave me one exactly my age," Hockney went on. "But the thing you notice with bonsai is that there are in fact two forces at work, the life force pushing up and out, and at the same time gravity pulling down, curling everything back toward the earth. You notice that with bonsai because with them this second force has to be artificially rendered through the use of pull wires. But you quickly learn to see how the contest between these two forces, gravity and the life force, plays out in an infinite variety of particular specific instances. Much too complicated to make up. You have to go out and look. Study. Record. Especially in winter when the skeletal form is most magnificently revealed. I would drive out and pull over and sketch the forms in my moleskins or onto pads, then take the sketches back to the studio and painstakingly transfer those studies into bigger formats. But always particular trees."

Hmm, I suggested: gravity as mortality. As the life force pulls us up and out, time is already pulling us down.

"Well, yes," said David. "Gravity will pull us all down as we finish. We all finish up in the earth, don't we? Dust."

Family trees. The more we live, the more living itself pulls us down?

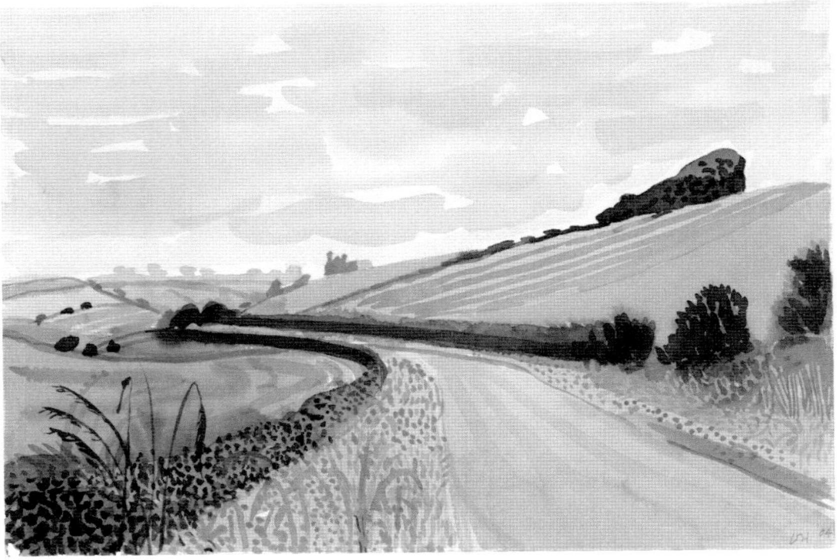

FIG 78 David Hockney, *Road and Farmhouse, East Yorkshire, July 2004.*

"Well, yes, of course," David replied. "*C'est la vie,* isn't it?" He paused before breaking into a wide smile. "I must say, though, I am very attracted to trees."

To trees, yes, but to the road as well. (Actually we speak of trunk roads—don't we?—and of the way side roads branch off.) At any rate, striking, too, in these images of the land, how often the road itself figures as a presence. And a paradoxical one at that. For a road receding toward the horizon constitutes a virtual archetype of relentlessly tapering one-point perspective. And yet these roads don't work like that: off center, shunted to the side, variously sloping downward or losing themselves in a stand of trees before reaching the horizon, if anything they seem to subvert that one-point hegemony (Fig. 78). They operate more like the road at the end of Chaplin's *Modern Times,* a figure for open-endedness. "Every character, real or invented," as Grace Paley puts it somewhere, "deserves the open destiny of life." Far from tapering, these roads just go on and on.

CHAPTER 8

a return to painting

(2007)

He is painting again. Aye, is he painting.

With a zest and a passion and a confidence I haven't witnessed in the coming on two and a half decades that I have been dropping over to visit with him, David Hockney has returned to the wide empty canvas and the oil-laden brush.

Granted, there have been moments, intermittent phases, over those twenty-five years when Hockney did dabble in oils (for the several decades before that his preferred and preeminent medium). There were, for example, the regular suites of portraits of his friends, including those lovingly rendered pet dachshunds; there were the cubist experiments such as the *Visit with Christopher and Don,* and the operatic still-life flower portraits; there were occasional vantages upon his homelife and the immediate surround, and several epic stabs at the Grand Canyon, and then likewise that thrilling (if somewhat short-lived) survey of some of the more intimate sweeps of the East Yorkshire of his youth.

But other passions always seemed to draw him away from such burgeoning reinvolvements with oil paint—toward the operatic stage, for example, or photocollage, or various photocopying technologies, or watercolor, or Chinese scrolls, or late Picasso, or high Rembrandt, and then, especially over the past several years, toward inspired speculative scholarship, pure and simple: that elaborately compounding (and compoundingly controversial) theory of his about the old masters and their lenses.

Throughout those years Hockney would insist that all the other work was just as valid and just as privileged as oil painting, that he really didn't give greater priority to any of the various media he was deploying in what he saw as a consistent path of inquiry and exploration. Yet still, as he concluded each fresh frenzy of alternative creation, he would seem to sigh with an exhalation that became almost a refrain: "Oh, dear," he would tell me once again, gazing upon a Cézanne or some other masterwork along some museum walk, "Oh, dear, I truly *must* get back to painting."

But now he has—almost with a vengeance—regularly, over the past few years, e-mailing his friends ever-vaster JPEG caches of fresh work: dozens, scores, and presently hundreds of enthrallingly vivid plein air landscapes, once again of the East Yorkshire vistas of his youth, pictures that, taken together, may someday, say fifty years from now (if there is a fifty years from now), command the same sort of scholarly interest and besotted devotion that Van Gogh's similarly concentrated renditions of the *paysages* around Arles do today.

Several months ago, on the train up from London to visit Hockney at what have now truly become his principal digs in Bridlington, I'd been riffling through a file of recent Hockneyana when I came upon Mark Johnson's March 17, 2006, *New York Times* review of the Hockney Portraits retrospective at Boston's Museum of Fine Arts, parts of which, clearly, he'd liked a whole lot and other parts of which he'd apparently liked a whole lot less:

> Around 1966, [Mr. Johnson began,] when Pop, Minimalism and Color Field painting were the preferred options for a serious artist, the British painter and Los Angeles resident David Hockney embarked on a daring exploration of what was then thought irretrievably retrograde: realist painting. Over the next decade, he created full-figure portraits of people, alone or in couples, that were as intimate as they were monumental and as poetically thrilling as they were visually lucid. The best of them can still be counted among the most memorable artworks of the postmodernist era.

Johnson went on to note how

> in the 70's, Mr. Hockney's realism intensified, but it never looked overworked, and though he used photographs as references, it did not turn into Photorealism. Nor did it ever appear stuffy or old-fashioned. Looking at the paintings of this period . . . , you get the exhilarating feeling of an artist on a roll who can do no wrong.
>
> Then, sometime after 1977, Mr. Hockney abandoned his time-consuming, painstaking commitments and, like a man recently divorced or released from prison, plunged into a period of restless promiscuity that has continued up to the present. The turn-

> ing point is marked by a 1979 portrait of the transvestite actor Divine. Painting in garish colors with a wide brush, Mr. Hockney achieved a cheery Fauvist immediacy but left behind the hallucinatory illusionism of the realist paintings. . . .

At length, Johnson concluded how, though Hockney had admittedly in the meantime been engaged in other sorts of enterprise as well, "Judging by this exhibition alone, it is difficult not to feel that sometime at the end of the 1970's, Mr. Hockney lost his way."

A few moments later, Hockney, there at the station to pick me up, noticed the clipping spilling from my folder and surprised me by judging *it* quite fine. "Not bad, that review," he declared, leading me over to his car and presently easing the car into the mild late afternoon traffic. "And he *is* onto something. I mean, I think he's wrong about the Divine portrait, because the thing you do see with that one is how, suddenly, it reads completely clearly from all the way across the room, you feel close even from far away, which hadn't been the case with the other, earlier, and more conventionally popular ones—you know, Celia and Ossie with Percy the cat, or Henry Geldzahler and Christopher Scott, or the Beverly Hills housewife Betty Freeman, or any of those sort.

"The fact is, though, that *Times* guy is right: I *did* reach a crisis with my painting there in the late seventies—partly one of sheer boredom: I mean, I knew how to paint that earlier kind of image, I'd cracked that code, and while I could have gone on quite happily making more images like that, and a lot of people, especially including a lot of dealers, would have been very happy if I had, they were no longer presenting a challenge to me. But the crisis was in fact more serious than that, because I began to notice that there was something wrong with those paintings, something which in retrospect I now realize had to do with the straitjacket asphyxiation brought on by the one-point perspective of their photographic source materials and the similarly optical vantage to which they themselves likewise aspired. This became devastatingly clear to me—We've talked about this—with that painting I kept trying to complete of the view across the street from my studio on Santa Monica Boulevard [see Fig. 23]: yes, precisely around that time, in the late seventies, the one I never was able to finish—because I couldn't seem to bring it alive. It kept feeling dead. Where that *Times* fellow is wrong, though, is in his notion that thereafter I was promiscuously flitting from one thing to another: on the contrary, the past twenty-five years for me have been a consistent struggle through all sorts of other media with that single fixed problem of how to depict an image in a lively way, one, that is, that is true to life . . ."

I reminded him, though, about the way he'd kept saying he had to get back to painting.

"Well, yes," he agreed, as, having parked the car in the courtyard, we'd entered the compound and were making our way upstairs to his airy attic studio, "and now, as you will see, I have, though I'll be the first to admit that it did take a bit longer than I thought it would."

This particular visit of mine was taking place in June 2006, and the current surge had started about a year earlier—in late July 2005 to be exact, when Hockney launched into a prodigious outpouring of three-by-two-foot canvases, revisiting the sites of many of the watercolors from his earlier sequence so as to recast the scenes in vividly luminous oils (Plates 31–38). Each vantage was fresh and clear and *fast* (he'd record the exact start and finish times of each painting's composition, and he seldom took longer than two hours to complete one), sometimes two or three a day, thirty-two of them that first month. Ripening wheat fields, lazy meadows, tree-lined country lanes, hollows falling away, hills rising up in the middle distance. Skies of crisp blue, cloud-mottled horizons, gauzes of lavender haze, the orange raking light of late afternoon. (In one particular bravura performance [see Plates 32 and 33], he'd painted a country lane receding into the early morning mist from 6:30 to 7:20 and then turned around and painted exactly the same scene from 7:30 to 8:30, this time, what with the mist's having burned off, in gleaming clarity, as if freshly minted.)

The frenzy of productivity had continued unabated into the fall, with images of the harvest being gathered in, puddle-rutted lanes after autumn squalls, and trees starting to shed their leaves. By early winter, when I went up to visit Hockney in Boston on the occasion of the opening of that Portraits show, he'd been showing me his latest innovation, two-panel combines, wider vistas of blustery skies and groves stripped bare, the trees gone all stark and skeletal.

All of which is to say that I had some sense, climbing the stairs to the third-floor studio that afternoon, of what to expect, but in the event, nothing quite prepared me for what, rounding the corner, now greeted my eyes. For over the past several weeks, Hockney had apparently made a further quantum leap, embarking on a series of yet vaster combines (bigger panels, three by four feet now, arrayed in grids of six at a time, allowing for vistas six feet by twelve)—wider and yet wider perspectives, indeed.

"I've been looking at Constable a lot recently," Hockney declared as he fumbled for a match to light his cigarette. "There was that show at the Grand Palais in Paris a few years back, and then just at the beginning of this month, the Tate opened its exhibit of his Great Landscapes. Superb. Wonderfully moving. I mean, Constable had already made a great impact on me back during my student days, freshly arrived in London from Bradford, as how could he not have? He was after all the first English painter ever to really engage the English landscape in an authentic manner. With Gainsborough, for example, by contrast, you merely get a generic backdrop. But Constable is clearly out there traipsing through the Suffolk countryside; you can almost sense the mud on his boots. Granted, he is not yet fully painting in the open air, though he is one of the first to go outside, painting with his little box. He was still having to make do, though, with paint bladders—remember, the collapsible tube doesn't come online till several years later. Let's see, Constable dies in 1837, just before the invention of chemical photography—for that matter, he and Turner constituted the last generation of English painters not to have to contend with the full onslaught of chemical photoreproduction—and collapsible tubes don't really start appearing until the 1850s. Without those tubes, impressionism, for example, would have been a lot more difficult, if not impossible—Van Gogh could carry the tubes with him out there into the fields around Arles, and with them all that pure color.[1] Constable, by contrast, would mainly sketch, working up a whole series of studies on-site before then returning to his studio to paint the actual canvases, especially of course those Great Landscapes.

"Even as a student, though, I think I was more struck by those studies, actually," Hockney continued, taking a drag on his cigarette. "With them you could see the work of his hand, the sweep of his arm, you could see him groping. No doubt at first, as he set out on each new painting, you would have been able to see those marks as well, although then, as was the fashion at the time, and for that matter as it had been for several centuries before, he'd apply that meticulous finish, effacing all signs of the labored mark, which is to say all sign of the history of his own working of the image. A few years later, Cézanne's paintings would allow you to see both—the mark and the scene that the mark was bringing into being, the two joined together as it were. Meaning you were deeply aware of the surface, which paradoxically then added to the illusion of spatial depth. Late Picasso was also working in that vein.

"Which in turn, in a way, is the opposite of what happens with a camera obscura. I realized this all over again last year when we went to Harewood House, very near to where I was brought up actually, to study how Thomas Girtin would have done it—I'd spotted one of his drawings of the house, from 1798, which I was fairly certain must have involved a camera, since it featured those two distinct vanishing points so characteristic of refocusing, and I wanted to check my hunch out. So we set up a camera obscura there, and then later we did the same thing at Sledmere House, closer to here.

"Incidentally, I'm sure that Constable there in Suffolk would likewise have been aware of camera obscuras. Remember: his father was quite a rich man, owned two big water mills, in fact steel mills, rather than wood. Constable is painting just before the invention of the steam engine; his is still the era of wind and water power, another reason perhaps that his countrysides look so much older than they actually are. Anyway, Constable was of a class that would regularly have been exposed to camera obscuras, and I'm sure he would have found the projected image fascinating.

"Because it *is*—I realized that all over again there at Harewood and Sledmere. You set up the apparatus, which can be fairly elaborate: the table, the lens housing above it in its armature, the thick black cloak draped over both the table and you there in your chair, with your back to the thing you are looking at, which in itself of course is very odd: you are sitting there with your back to what you will be drawing! And there in the dark this incredibly beautiful world swims into focus, the colors all harmonized—on top of which everything is moving! This would have been like cinema for them. It would have seemed the height of reality, especially at a time when such projections of nature were so relatively rare, whereas for us today in a world where we are surrounded by such projections, we tend to focus on their artificiality. But in either case, artificial or real, the point is that the moment you put your pencil down onto the page and you begin to draw, you realize your eyes are no longer looking through space but rather onto a flat surface. Afterwards, when you lift the curtain, any sense of space or spaciousness completely evaporates, something that becomes all the more evident when you now turn around and gaze back upon the actual place you have been attempting to capture.

"No," Hockney concluded, stubbing out his smoke, "in order to convey space and spaciousness, rather than mere surface—and this is what I have been realizing with greater and greater force these past several months—you have to be out there, in person, *en plein air,* facing out into all that space."

Meanwhile, he went on to explain, over the past few months he'd been nursing an ever more powerful hankering to be painting at scale—at the scale, that is, of Constable's paintings, a scale that could envelop the viewer, as it were, and draw him in. Although to do that was going to present problems. For starters, how might one transport a canvas that size out into the wild, and how then erect an armature solid enough so that the wide canvas expanse wouldn't start flapping about like a sail in the wind, and then how to transport the painting back to the protection of the studio between sessions, especially since the oils would now be wet and glistening? Beyond that, how would one be able to see past the expanse of canvas itself to all the plein air scenery one was attempting to capture? One would constantly have to be traipsing over to the side of the interfering canvas, catching a glimpse of subject matter, and then rushing back to the appropriate spot on the painting so as to lay it in (along with all that intervening sense of spaciousness) before it dissipated from consciousness.[2]

"It took a while to figure things out," Hockney now related. "On the way back from Boston, in Pembroke Studios in London, I'd had David Graves mount several of the earlier paintings, along with some of the two-panel combines, in a grid along our studio wall, and I got to thinking, hunh, maybe one could do it that way. Broken into panels like that, one could achieve a real sense of scale. I ordered up some larger canvases and, back up here, I had Jean Pierre mount a grid of six such blank canvases on the wall over there, and for several days I'd just come up here and stare at that grid, thinking about how we might do it. I'd drive out to that place in the Woldgate Woods, off the side of the paved road, where three paths converge, the place we call the Tunnel because of the way one of those paths slices perpendicularly across the road and seems to recede endlessly into the distance. I'd portrayed that spot several times in the single panels, so I knew it quite well, but I'd go look at it again, and then come back here and stare at the six empty panels. And then one day I got up and laid in the horizon line, approximating where the paths would go and some of the more defining trees. Then we packed those canvases into the car and went out there. This was still in winter so we premixed some of the paints we'd be using, we didn't want to be out there in the cold spending an hour mixing up the subtle grays—in any case I'd already developed the technique of anticipating colors like that with my watercolors. I had a pair of easels in the car, and we'd set them up, put them side by side, so as to be able to rejigger the cross-strut and lay one canvas above while leaning another below. That way we could have four up at once—sometimes, with a third easel, even all six (Plate 26)—though as time passed, I got to the point where I really only did one or two at a time. In any case, at first we had to go out with several cars so that returning, we could lay out the wet canvases on the back seats without smudging them. Eventually we built a sort of rack in the back of the van with six shelves, so we could transport all six canvases at once, even if all of them were wet. It's like I always say: You've really got to prepare if you're going to try to be spontaneous.

"Anyway, each night when I'd come home, I'd have Jean Pierre mount the six-panel grid once more, so that I could get a sense of the evolving whole. Sometimes I would have him take a digital photograph of the entire combine and then print that photo out on a piece of paper, upon which I could then trace over possible approaches to the next day's work, in any case using those photos as reference the next day when I was out in the field and had only one or another of the panels on the easel before me."

It occurred to me as Hockney described this process that his use of photography now was the exact opposite of what he had been doing thirty years ago, as for example in the case of those stacked photostudies of Peter Schlesinger for the painted figure by the painted pool (see Fig. 1). In those days he had taken a vertical series of photographic snaps as a way of preparing to paint a single figure. Now, by contrast, he was taking a single snap to encapsulate an entire grid of paintings. When I pointed this out to David, he replied, "Well, I've always said that the only thing a photograph is good at capturing faithfully is another flat surface."

Continuing, Hockney now averred that it had taken some time to get the hang of the process—that is, to get to the point where he could fashion a finished grid that didn't simply fall into a pell-mell jumble—and he'd had to draw on lessons from many of his other excursions from the past several decades. For example, the way he'd learned, with *Pearblossom Hwy.* (see Plate 11), to create a single overarching vantage out of a series of separately distinct mini-vantages. But like a boy on a trampoline, he got better and better, more and more self-assured, and now, pointing over to the side of the studio, he showed me the first of the ones he felt had really been working. A springtime gaze down that arboreal tunnel at Woldgate.

"And see, look," he now said, walking me over (Plate 39). "You can see the marks, and you can see how, whereas with the watercolors I was using my hand, and with the earlier oils I was using my arm, here I am painting from my shoulders, I am painting with my whole body. And the painting itself is addressing you in your entire body: it is big enough to be doing so. You can *feel* it. And that's the point: out there in the world but here as well, space is a *feeling.*"[3]

In addition to the feeling of space, the combine evinced a marvelous sense of the peripheral—another aspect of the experience of looking and seeing to which David had been attending for many years (all the way back, at any rate, to the *Luncheon at the British Embassy* photocollage from 1983—see Plate 10): the way that a tree trunk coursing down the far left side of the two leftmost panels was far and away the biggest single incident in the entire grid, taking up the most acreage, as it were, of paint yet almost disappearing completely from the viewing experience. That tree, although closest to us, wasn't what we were looking at; it was off to the side and experienced as such. Unless, turning, we now turned our attention to it, at which point the lovely surface textures in the rendering of the paint itself shone through.

"That's what I mean about surface mark and spaciousness," Hockney concurred when I said as much, as he now walked me over to the other grid along the central wall facing his easy chair, the one he was currently working on: this time the image, only recently mapped out and barely begun, of a farm field falling away into a hollow and rising back up in the middle distance—a cozy grand canyon. "And here's something else," he said. "You see this patch of grass over here to the lower left side, that and the hedgerow next to it? That's what I'm going to be working on tomorrow morning. Tomorrow we'll get up and drive out there, I'll take this lower left-hand canvas and spend a few hours working in the detail of that foreground patch along with the hedge, and when we come back in the afternoon, you'll see, working that in like that will have the effect"—he now ambled over to the other side of the combine grid—"of pushing back the sense of space all the way over here in the upper right-hand canvas. Without so much as my touching that part of the painting."

As would indeed prove right: he wouldn't and it would.

The next morning, Jean Pierre loaded up the van with easels, sliding the six canvases into their slat shelves, and the three of us piled in for the drive out to the hedge and the grass tuft overlooking the cozy grand canyon.

Backing out of the driveway, we were less than half a block from the edge of the bluff overlooking the North Sea, all spangly in the morning sun. I asked David if he ever thought about painting the sea. "I did paint the sea some once, in Malibu, but you can see for yourself how the land is so much more interesting."[4]

We banked inland and quickly out of town (Bridlington is a small town), the van's dark shadow racing headlong before us. "I love driving like this in the morning, the sun low behind us, for we are far north here, lighting everything ahead. The clouds racing by up above. You realize that Constable did stunning cloud studies. Now, clouds are difficult, especially in a place like England—small northern European island subject to barometric pressures on all sides. When you start trying to paint clouds, you quickly realize how much they're moving, how much the whole sky is moving—unlike in Southern California, say, with its strong, even light and barely ever a cloud anywhere in the vault above. Here, in painting the sky, you've somehow got to capture all that movement and changeability, so you have to work very fast—unlike in the San Gabriel Mountains, for example, where I often felt like I had all the time in the world. Wasn't it Cézanne, though, who said that you have to hurry up if you're ever going to see?"

Presently we arrived at the hollow and Hockney pulled the van over to the side of the road. Jean Pierre unloaded one of the easels, set it up by the grass tuft, and slid the appropriate canvas out of its shelf, along with a tray of paint tubes and brushes. Hockney pulled out a collapsible chair, positioned it just so overlooking the scene, checked his watch and the sun behind us, lit up a cigarette, and took a seat, steadying himself, taking it all in. A few minutes later, he set to work, laying in the grass, blade by blade.

We left him to it. Jean Pierre grabbed his laptop from the backseat of the van and motioned me over, and we sat on a little outcropping by the side of the road. Jean Pierre revved up the laptop and presently opened a file of digital snapshots. "Here, I'll show you something," he said. It turned out that while Hockney himself may have sworn off photography, vowing never again to squeeze his eye up to a viewfinder, his assistant appeared to have caught the bug in spades, and on several occasions he'd meticulously documented every stage of the coming-into-being of several of David's recent paintings, a snap seemingly every ten or twenty seconds—thousands of images, which he was in the process of editing and ordering into evenly paced slide shows. He tapped on one such file, and the show began to unfurl (Fig. 79). It proved uncommonly engrossing, in fact much more so than those famous movies, say, of Pollock slathering paint over an outspread canvas or Picasso whipping a flashlight about through the dark surround. This may have owed something to the advantages of the medium. With the even flow of most real-time movies featuring artists painting, the mind is given to wandering, slipping in and out of focus; whereas Jean Pierre's approach was more akin to something like Chris Marker's *La Jetée,* a film made up almost entirely of stills, stills upon which the mind is continually being required to refocus, reconstituting each new vantage as if from scratch. That formal advantage was no doubt enhanced by Jean Pierre's own inspired sensitivity, for he was hardly serving as mere docu-slave, his camera trained on the canvas alone. Rather his gaze would wander, from the canvas out onto the vista Hockney himself was surveying, back a few steps for a shot encompassing artist, canvas, and vista together. Some shots of a teacup, the paint tubes, the jar of brushes; back to the canvas; then out again to the vista. A remarkable thing would happen in the midst of the interplay between canvas and vista. You might be guided to look at the vista for a few seconds, then back to the canvas, where Hockney would make a stab at a particular detail, say a bush or a shack that you yourself had not noticed a few moments earlier when you had first surveyed the same scene, but now, when you surveyed it again, sure enough, there it would be, Jean Pierre homing in for a detail of his own. (Two intelligences were at work, and a third as well, if you counted your own as it too gradually became honed to these novel rhythms of awareness.) David and Jean Pierre had not yet decided what, if anything, they were going to do with these trills of images, but sitting there, I remember thinking how wonderful it would be to have been vouched similar documentation of Cézanne at work, or Van Gogh, or Constable. . . .

A couple hours had passed, and now another car pulled up, and out popped John (another regular from the Hockney compound, in fact the very young friend whose ridiculous American visa troubles had soured David on California in the first place, a few years back), bearing tea and sandwiches. David continued daubing for a few more minutes: the pelt of grass blades had now been worked well in, the hedge worked in as well, and Hockney was beginning to turn his attention to a tree in the middle distance. Presently he laid down his brushes and came over to join the rest of our *déjeuner sur l'herbe.*

"I've been looking at this landscape here in East Yorkshire, Bridlington and environs, for two years now rather closely, day in and day out, and I've never really done that before anywhere else," he said. "And I realize that you keep seeing more and more, actually. Because you see with memory. Meaning, when I'm looking out over this vista, well I was here last summer, in fact this is one of the first places I painted, but I hadn't yet seen it in winter. But now I have, and this time I am watching the summer with the winter in mind. For example, that tree I've just started working on. Trees are notoriously difficult to paint: they fall so easily into stylized generalization, and to combat that you have to be rigorously attentive, capturing the particular and individually specific nuances of each separate plant. Now, this one here, it's all filled out with leaves again, but back in winter, it was bare and I was able to study its structure more closely. For that matter, speaking more generally, in winter, things are so much more alive. The bare trees, you notice how the branches are all straining upward toward the light, up and up! Later, come spring and now the summer, the canopy of leaves will fill in and weigh the branches back down, but in winter you can grasp that life force full-on. A knowledge which in turn, preserved in memory, can't help but inform how you see the tree now."[5]

Hockney paused, reaching for another sandwich and refreshing his tea. "I'm sure this winter I will see more as well, informed as my memories will have been by yet another summer, and then the same for next summer. In fact, it's almost impossible to imagine truly painting landscape without staying put for a long while. Constable hardly ever left Suffolk, and just think of everything he saw!"[6]

Later that afternoon, on the drive back into Bridlington, Hockney was still

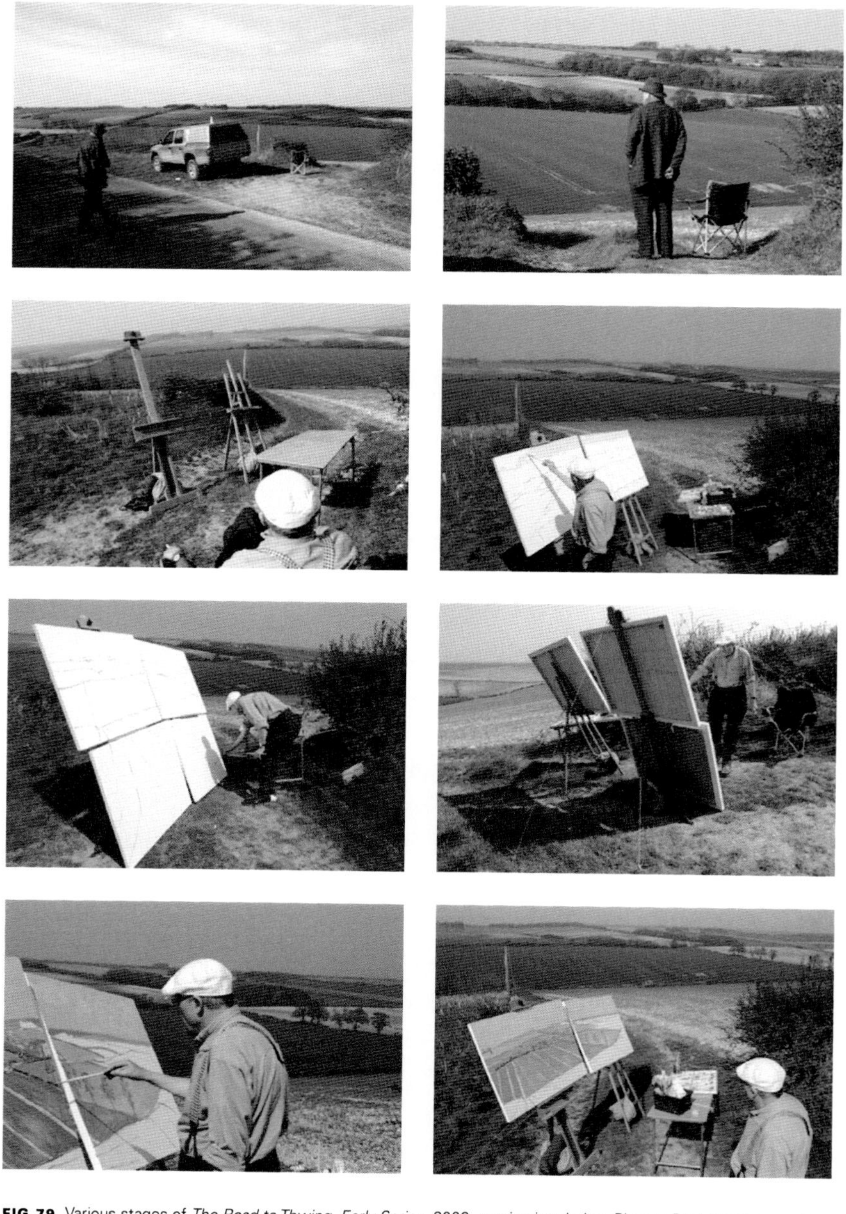

FIG 79 Various stages of *The Road to Thwing, Early Spring*, 2006, coming into being. Photos: David Hockney and Jean Pierre Goncalves.

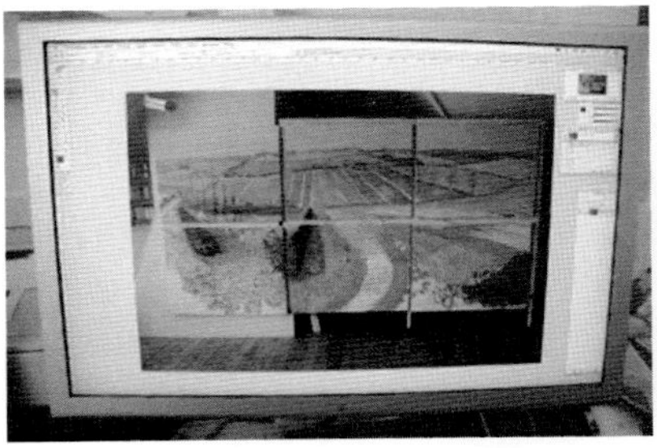
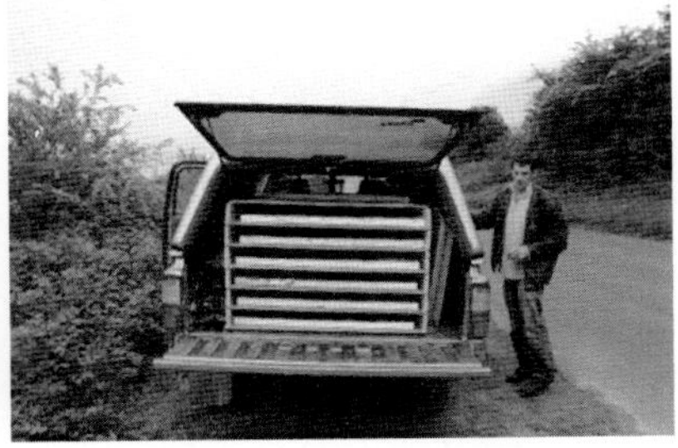
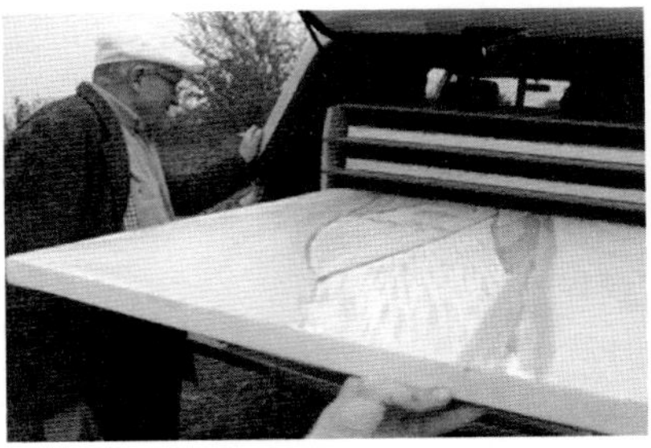
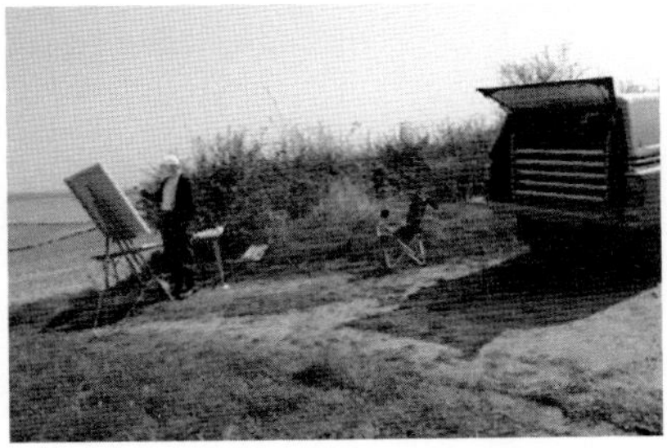
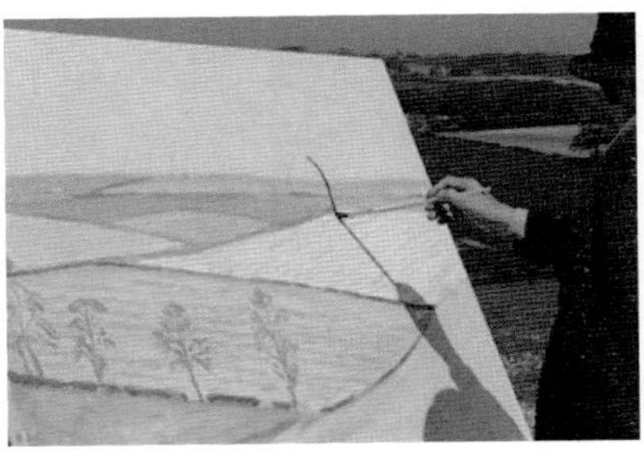
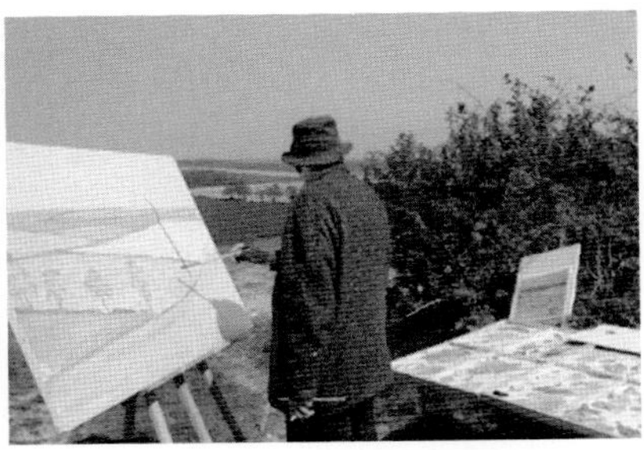
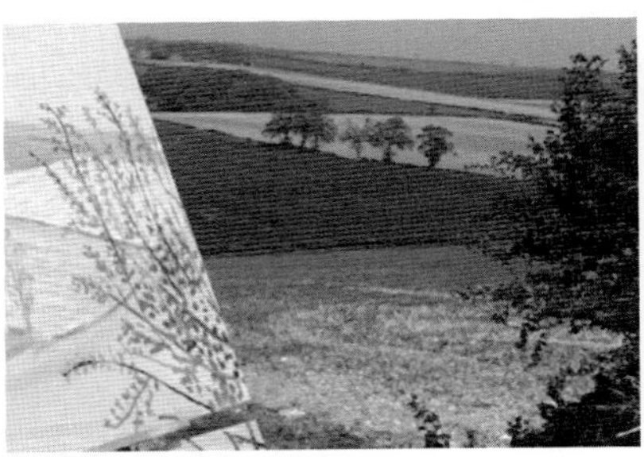
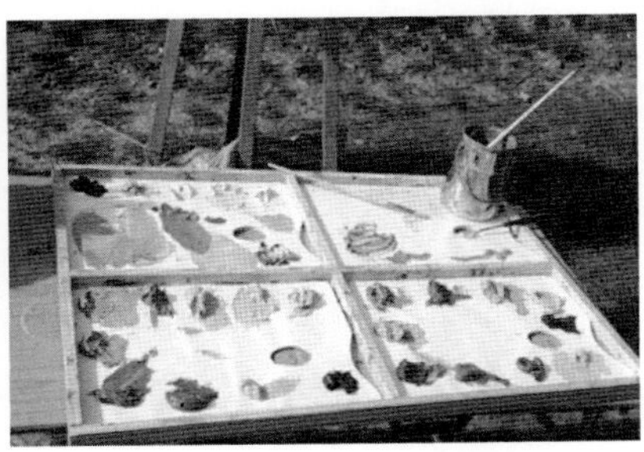

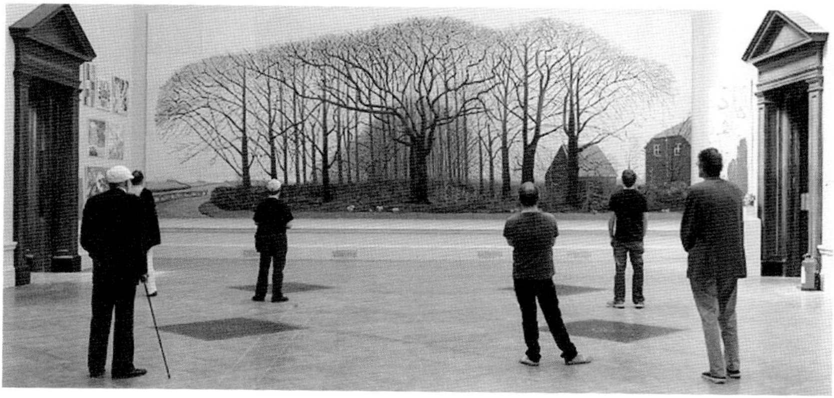

FIG 80 David Hockney and friends looking at *Bigger Trees near Warter,* at the Royal Academy of Arts, London, 2007.

rhapsodizing on the glories of winter. "One night last January," he recalled, "we watched from the window as snow was drifting straight down, which meant, no wind at all. After a few hours we loaded into the car and headed out into the forest, where, owing to the absence of wind, everything was coated just so in a layer of soft white, like you would never see it otherwise, completely magical, a crystal palace in the canopy. We came back home, warmed up some tea, and on the radio, the weatherman was describing it as 'a bad night.'"

I returned home the next morning. The months passed. The paintings kept coming. Presently eleven separate six-panel seasonal variations of that arboreal tunnel at Woldgate Woods, five of which would come to grace the great staircase at Tate Britain (stairs that in turn led up to an exhibition featuring Hockney's own selection from and commentary on the museum's holdings of Turner watercolors) (Plates 39–43). Elsewhere in London, the talk of the Royal Academy's riotously various summer 2007 exhibition was Hockney's *fifty*-canvas combine, his vastest ever, a staggering winterscape, *Bigger Trees near Warter,* which took up the entirety of the far wall in the long hall; indeed, when the rest of the show came down, Hockney's crew mounted a pair of uncannily precise, identically sized photocopies of the original combine to either side along the hall's flanking walls, and the confines of those walls seemed to vaporize completely, so commanding was the sense of airy space receding in all directions (Fig. 80).

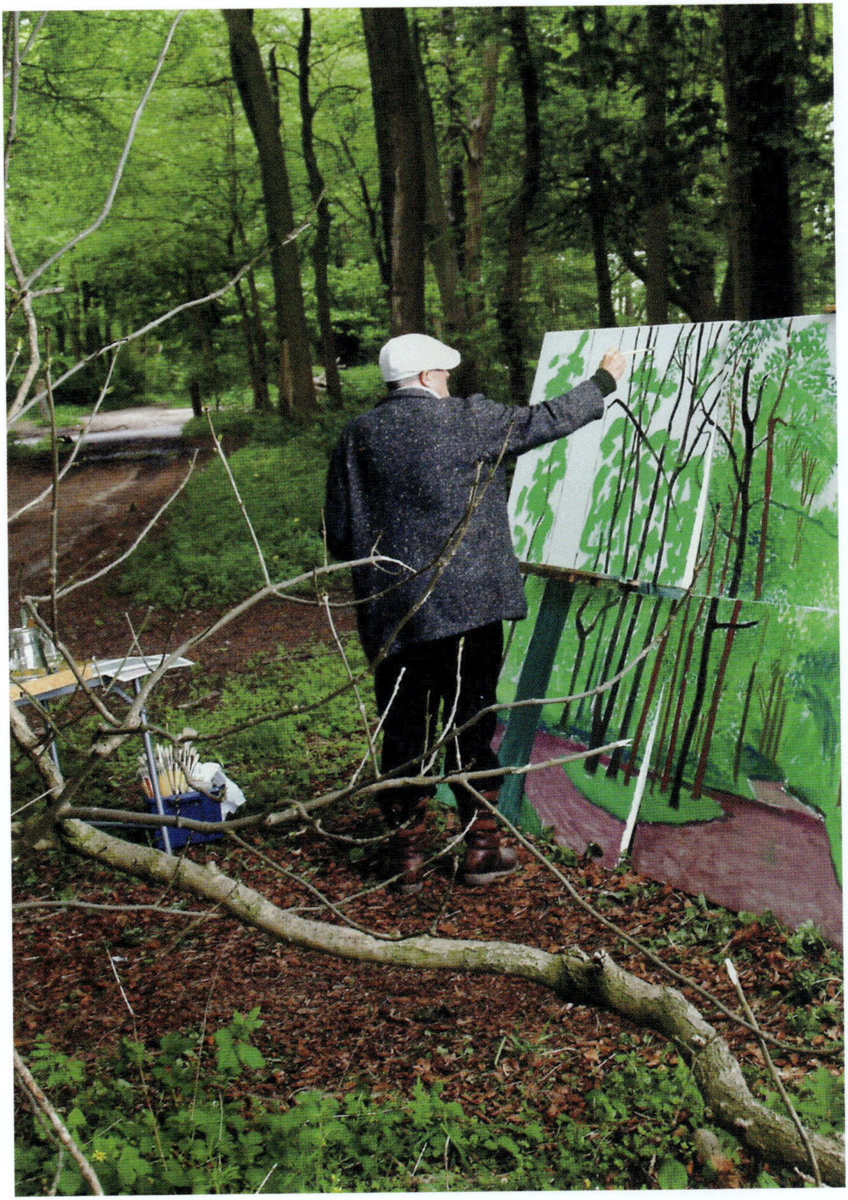

26 David Hockney painting, May 17, 2006, Woldgate Wood, East Yorkshire. Photo: Jean Pierre Goncalves.

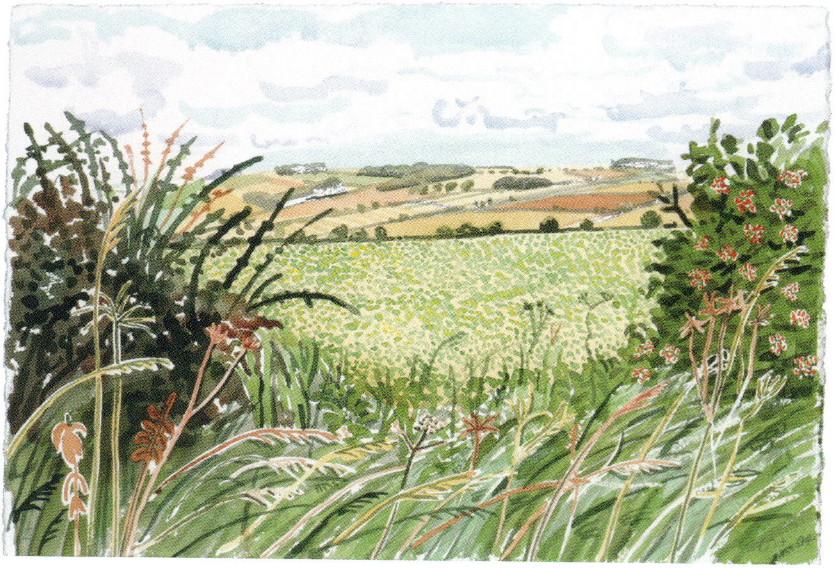

27 *A Gap in The Hedgerow*, 2004.

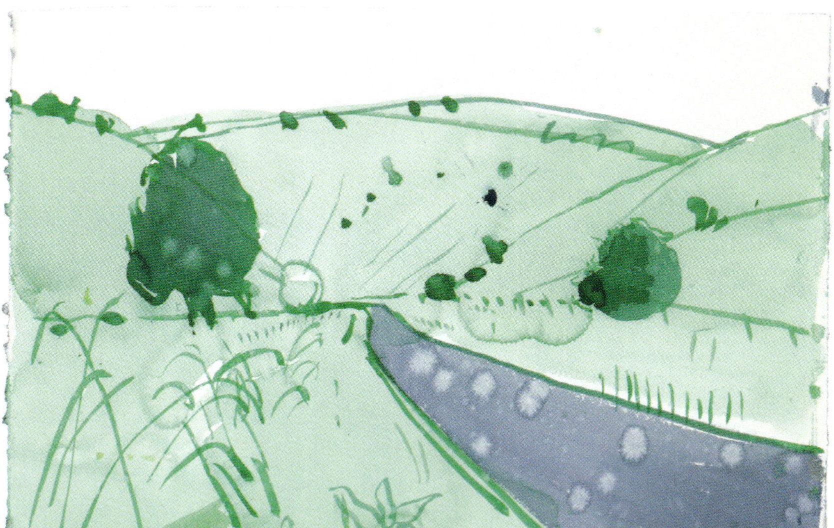

28 *Valley, Millington. E. Yorks.*, 2004

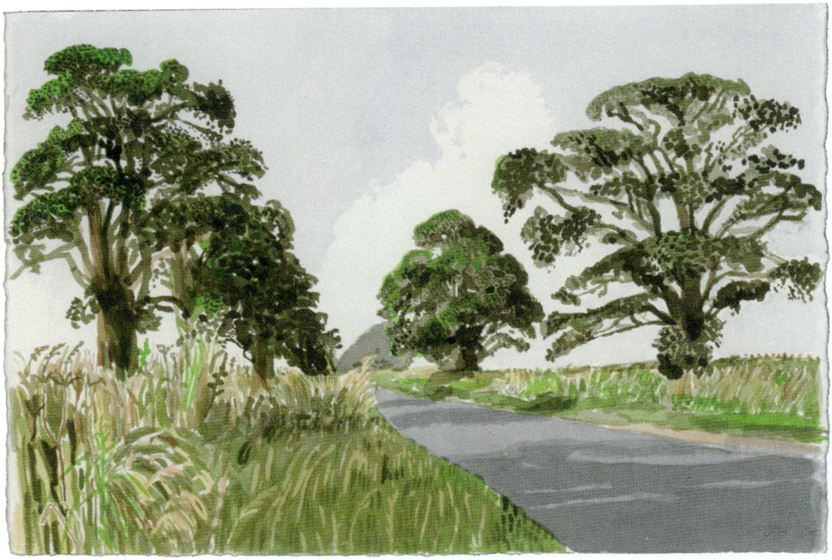

29 *Trees near Rudston*, 2004.

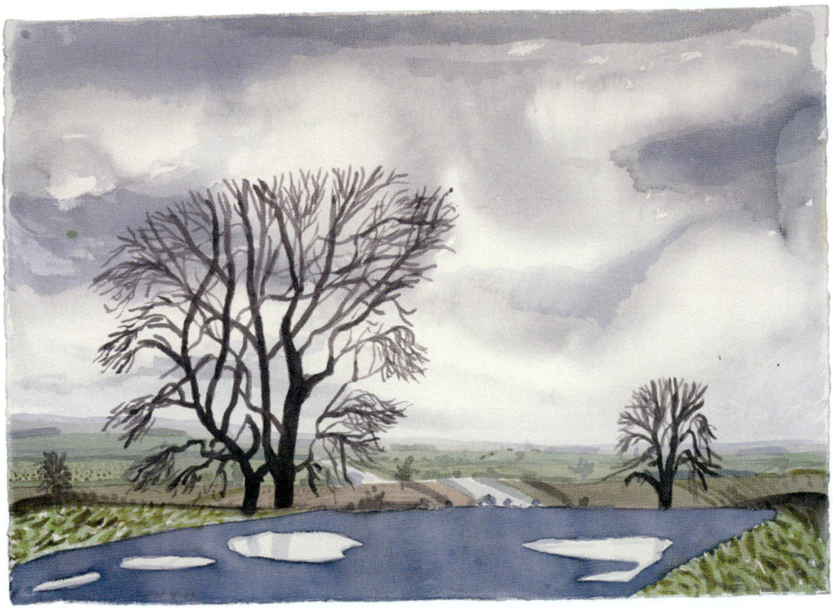

30 *Trees and Puddles, East Yorkshire*, 2004.

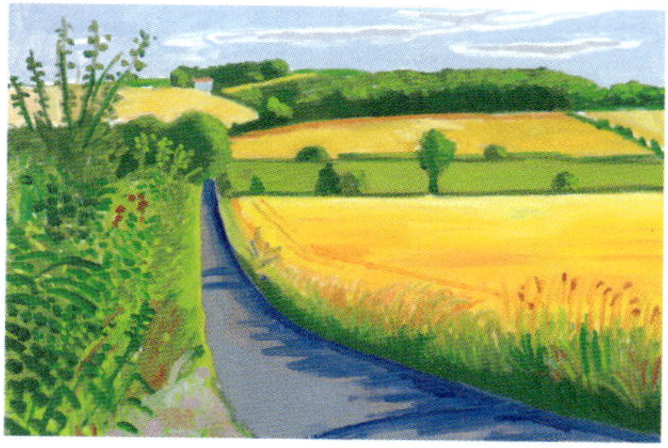

31 *Untitled Harvest*, 2005.

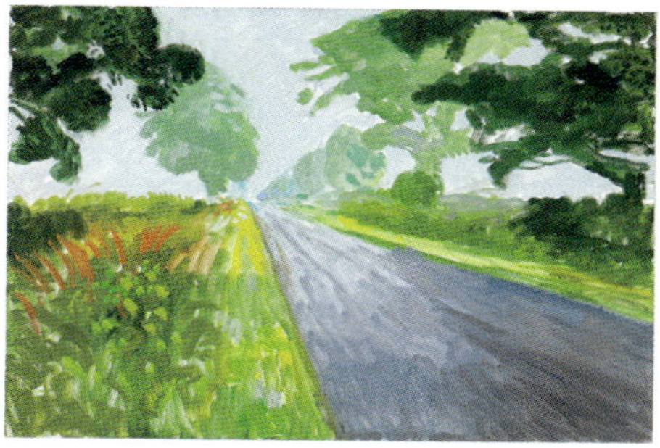

32 *Rudston Trees I, 29 July 2005.*

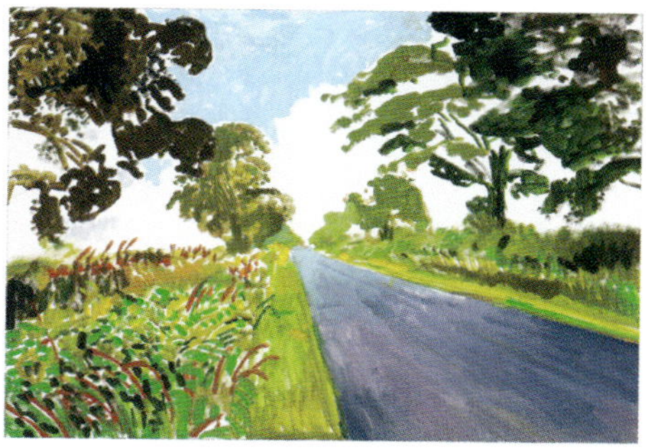

33 *Rudston Trees II, 29 July 2005.*

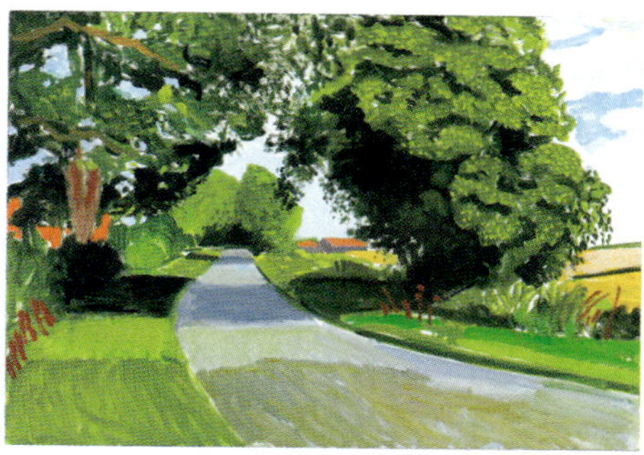

34 *Langtoft to Kilham, 31 July 2005.*

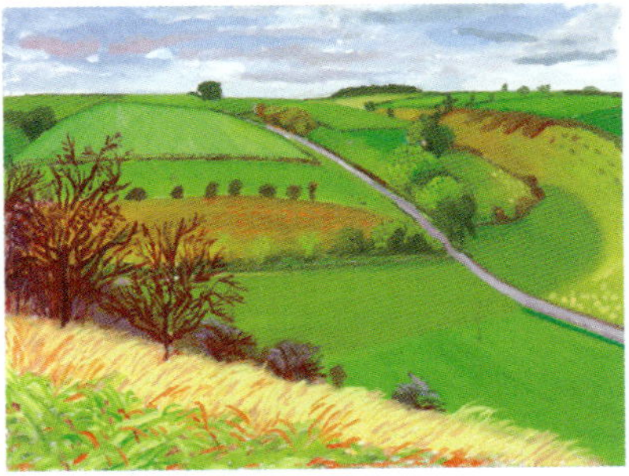

35 *Fridaythorpe Valley, 25 October 2005.*

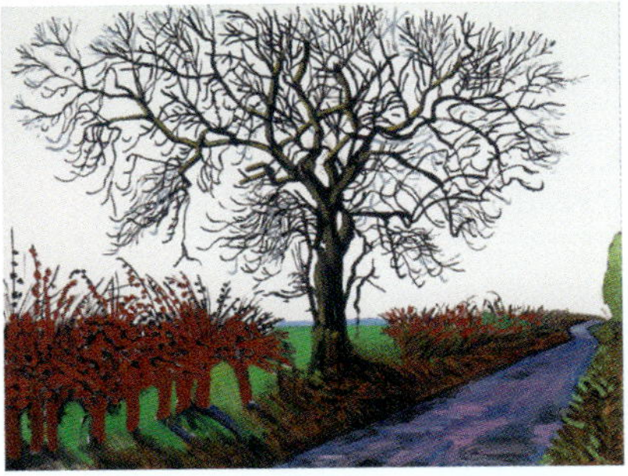

36 *Woldgate, 29 November 2005.*

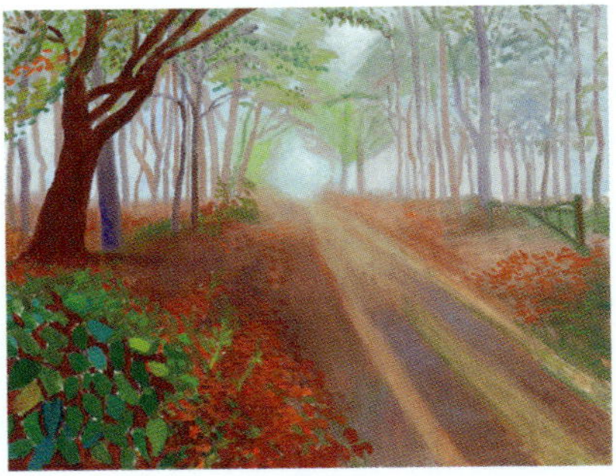

37 *Woldgate Mist, November 2005.*

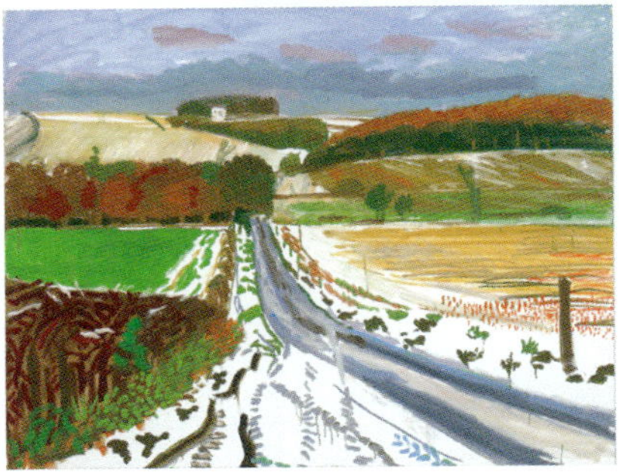

38 *Woldgate to Boynton (Snow),*
25 November 2005.

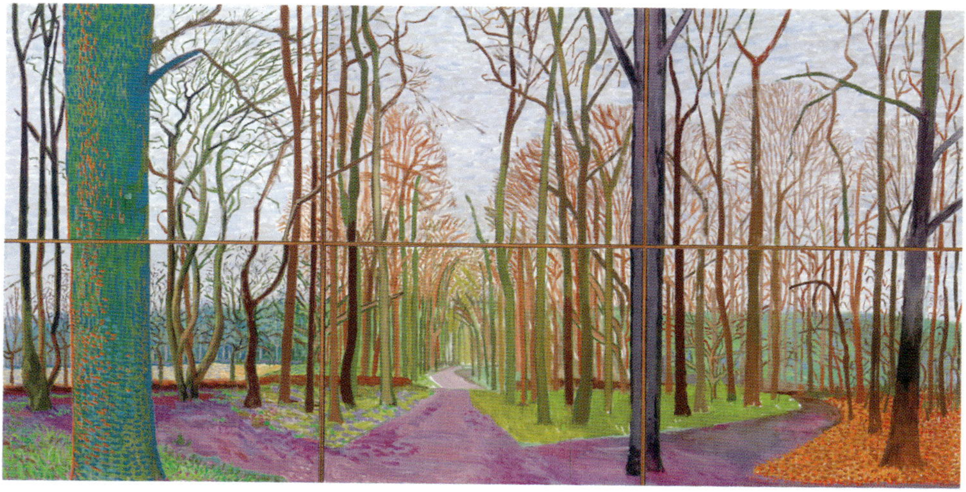

39 *Woldgate Woods, March 30–April 21, 2006.*

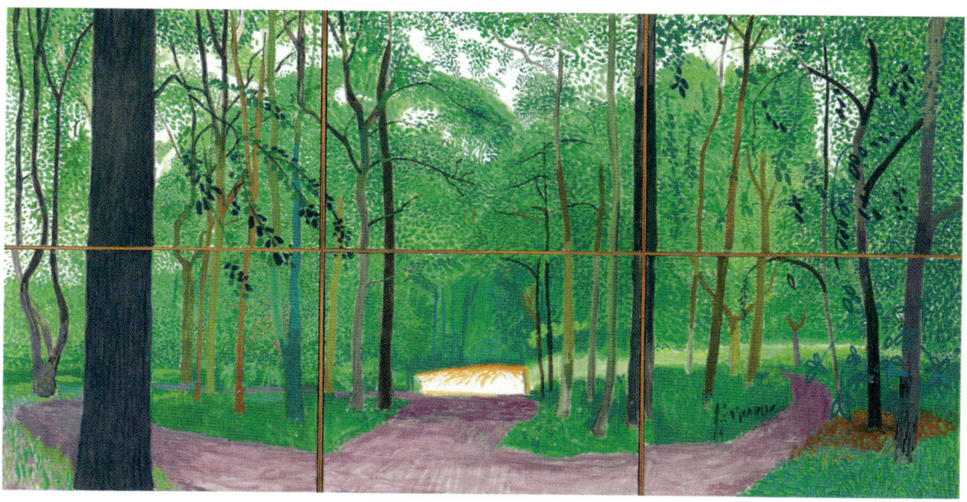

40 *Woldgate Woods, 26, 27 & 30 July 2006.*

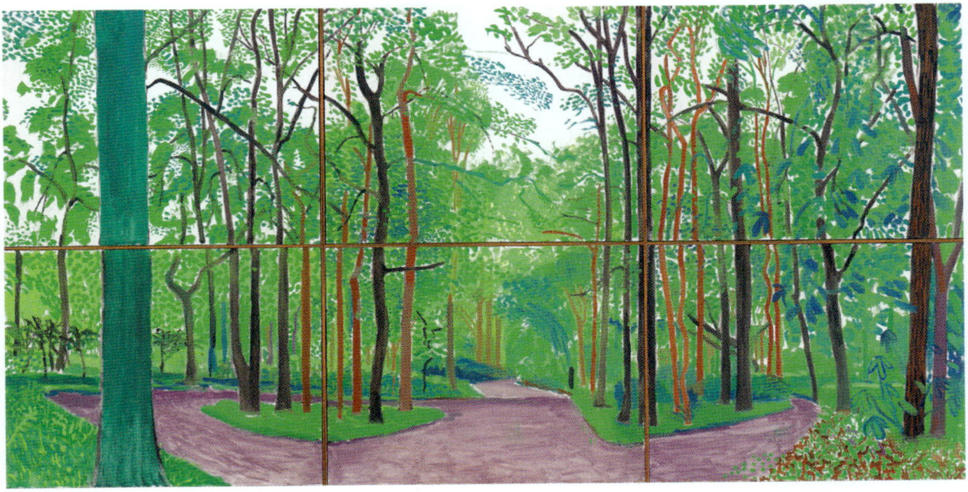

41 *Woldgate Woods III, May 20 & 21, 2006.*

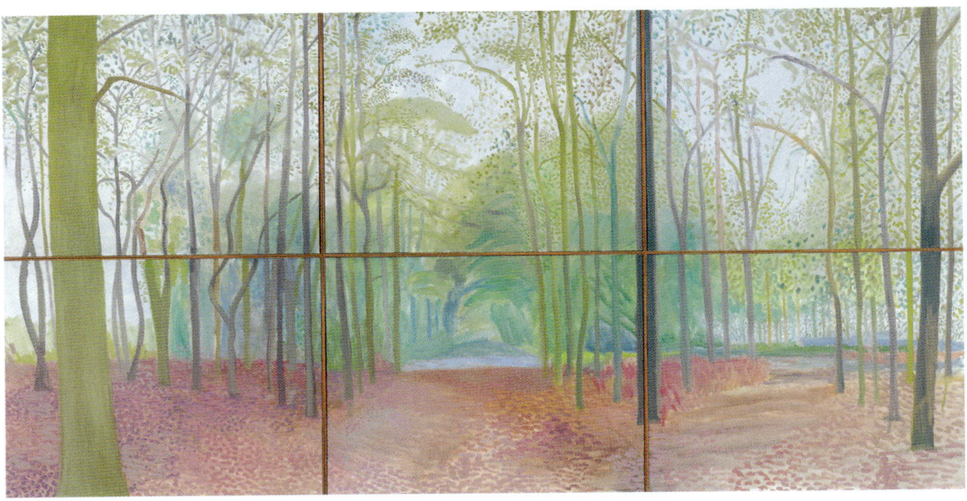

42 *Woldgate Woods, 7 & 8 November 2006.*

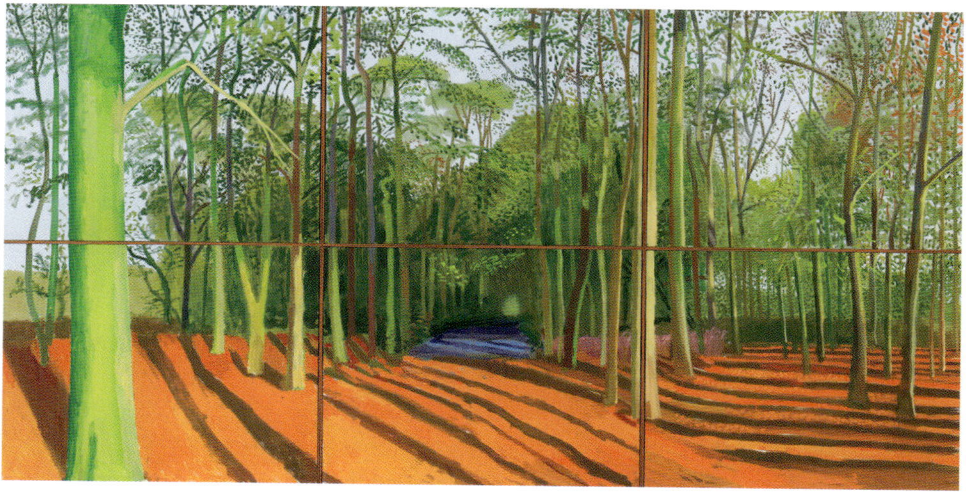

43 *Woldgate Woods, 6 & 9 November 2006.*

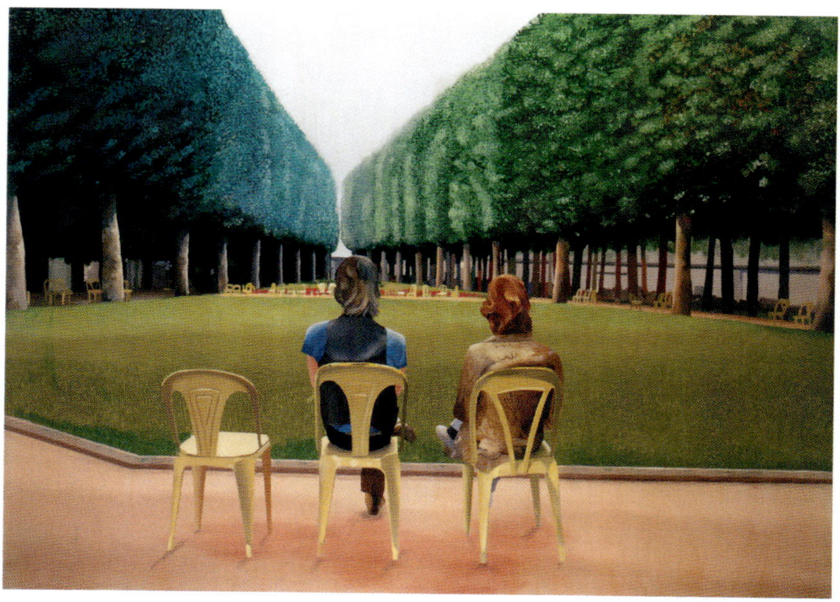

44 *Le Parc des Sources, Vichy,* 1970.

Standing there before the capacious spectacle on a return passage through London, considering once again the distance Hockney had been traveling over the past twenty-five years with his flight from the merely optical, and beyond that the stakes for which he still seemed to be playing, I was put in mind of a passage I'd recently encountered in Rebecca Solnit's marvelous *River of Shadows,* her meditation on the transformative significance, as the book's subtitle would have it, of "Eadweard Muybridge and the Technological Wild West." At one point, Solnit points out how during five years to either side of 1835, three great inventions—the train, the telegraph, and chemical photoreproduction—came online virtually simultaneously, to compoundingly reinforcing effect. That effect being *(and so it was seen at the time)* nothing less momentous than "the annihilation of time and space." Train, telegraph, and photography: everything since, Solnit suggests, has been mere commentary, an elaboration (albeit an increasingly frenzied elaboration) of that initial aspiration. For, as she herself elaborates:

> "Annihilating time and space" is what most new technologies aspire to do: technology regards the very terms of our bodily existence as burdensome. Annihilating time and space most directly means accelerating communications and transportation. . . . What distinguishes a technological world is that the terms of nature are obscured; one need not live quite in the present or the local.[7]

Surface supersedes space; immediacy supplants consideration. Whereas presence and the local, time and space—taking time, precisely, so as to be able to savor space—are with growing insistence and increasing assuredness what Hockney's recent work, and especially his buoyant return to painting, have been all about.

I crossed town to visit the Woldgate Woods seasonal variations banked along the stairwell of the Tate Britain one last time. They're all pretty terrific—leaf-lush greeny high springtime, pink-misty barren late fall—but the one that kept drawing me back was an especially vivid late afternoon scape from early November, tree trunk shadows diagonally zebra-scored across the orange forest loam, the arboreal tunnel receding into the far distance (see Plate 43). And here I was put in mind of an earlier signal achievement from Hockney's career, this one among the most brilliantly realized canvases from those years (so prized by Mark Johnson of the *New York Times,* among others) when he had been maximally in thrall to the optical—

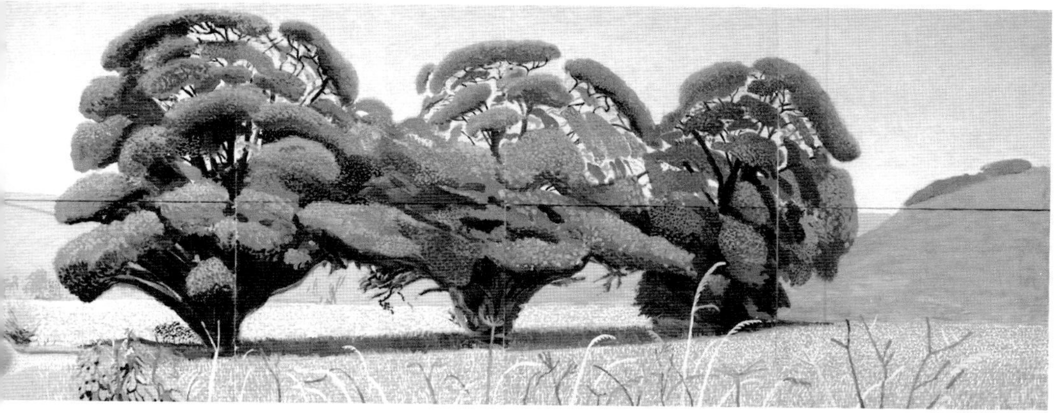

FIG 81 David Hockney, *Trees near Thinxendale* (August), 2007.

Le Parc des sources, Vichy (1970, Plate 44). Virtually the same image, come to think of it: trees receding relentlessly into the distance, though in the former instance, they'd done so as disciplined colonnades to either side of an impeccably manicured lawn, two men seen from behind seated on plastic park chairs (a third chair to their side, presumably Hockney's own, empty while he steps back to take in the scene), the two men gazing ahead, down the very barrel of the meticulous one-point perspective. The distance Hockney had traversed between the two compositions could hardly be more starkly revealing. The gazing gentlemen of the 1970 canvas seem straitjacketed, veritably squeezed in the vise of the composition's perspectival grip. (One is put in mind of the moment in *Star Wars* where Harrison Ford's embattled *Millennium Falcon* starcruiser suddenly vaults right out of its own skin, sucked into hyperspace—talk about the annihilation of time and space!) For my own part, now recalling that canvas, I was in turn reminded of Hockney's characterization several years ago of his drive through the twenty-three-mile tunnel under the St. Gotthard Pass (with the tunnel's opening a pinprick straight ahead in the far far distance) as what it must be like to live in "one-point-perspective hell."[8] The Woldgate Woods combine, by contrast, more accurately recalled Hockney's experience of his emergence from that St. Gotthard tunnel into the sudden heaven of reverse perspective, the viewer, no longer being sucked anywhere, free instead to lounge in the fullness

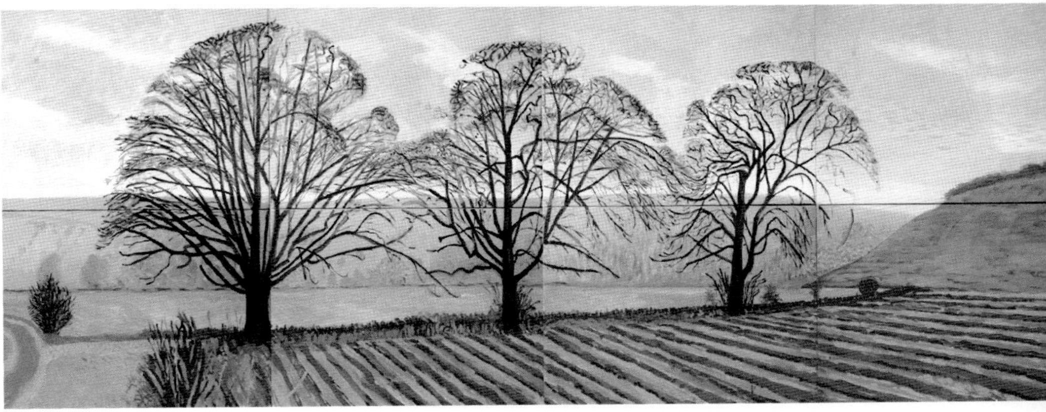

FIG 82 David Hockney, *Trees near Thinxendale* (December), 2007.

of being. Note how one can gaze at a side angle deep into the woods to either side of the main vista. Or look at those zebra shadow stripes cutting diagonally across the central arboreal tunnel (for that matter, recall suddenly how often Hockney himself has referred to this particular copse in the woods as "The Tunnel"): note how the shadows positively defy one-point perspective. Either our heads are moving, swiveling on their neck joints (no longer gripped in the straitjacket vise of the optical), or else the sun is progressively sinking behind us. Or maybe both. Time, at any rate, is passing: true to life and the living. And one thing's for sure: We are no longer experiencing the world from the point of view of that paralyzed cyclops for a split second.

I returned home, the JPEGs kept coming. A particularly sweet matching, later in the year, of the three trees in the middle of a farm field (spread this time across a rectangular grid of eight canvases), the first vantage in August, the trees like great breathing lungs, stripped to desiccated cross-section by the second, in December (Figs. 81 and 82).

Hockney himself, meanwhile, decided to take a break, climbing into his roadster for a jaunt through the Chunnel past Bruges and Ghent to Baden-Baden (where he and his friends spent a week taking the waters) and then down through Florence and Siena and onward to points further south. One afternoon he phoned to check in. He'd been spending that morning in Florence's Santa Maria della Novella church, transfixed before Masaccio's spellbinding (and, indeed, spell-weaving) *Crucifixion* of 1427–28, famously one of European art's earliest instances of deep perspectival artifice. "One can't help but notice," he pointed out, "how unusual and excruciating a form of execution crucifixion is. There is no action: no arrows pierce the air, no ax plunges toward the neck. In fact you die precisely because you are *prevented* from moving."[9] A few days later he called from Siena, positively crowing, "God how I love Sienese art, the painting when there was still light, when there was still space, before all the shadows came flooding in as Florentine perspective conquered all before it." A few days after that he was phoning from Palermo, recalling a canvas he'd seen a few days earlier in Naples: "A nineteenth-century painting of the archaeologists digging up Pompeii. I call it Nineteenth-Century Primitive. Where else you see that way of depicting space nowadays is on TV, flipping through the channels. The Simpsons are real, but then you flip the channel: more of that Nineteenth-Century Primitive."

The trip was beginning to wear on him, though. He'd reveled in all that fresh looking ("It was like traversing my Wall in reverse!") but it was time to be heading back to Bridlington so he could take up his oils once again. "I've taken to thinking of these recent canvases of mine as figure paintings." He waited two beats till I obliged him: "But they're all just landscapes," I pointed out. "There are no figures in them." "Ah," he corrected me triumphantly, "but *you* the viewer are the figure *in* them."[10]

He paused for a moment. "Instead of holding you relentlessly at a remove, as ordinary perspective pictures do, they draw you in. That's why I am so excited by all this. Really, it's completely rejuvenated me. I was seventy in July, but I feel thirty, frankly—or all right, maybe forty. In any case," he continued, "I know this is hardly the end of things. In fact, things are barely just beginning."

notes

1 : CAMERAWORKS

1. For a sly parodic counterargument to Hockney's contention that an ordinary photograph can't be viewed for more than thirty seconds, see Veronica Geng's Annotations piece in the November 1984 *Harper's,* "How Long Before You Black Out? Staring Down Photography Theory," in which Ms. Geng stares down an initially quite ordinary-looking snapshot, finding deeper and deeper layers of oddness and peculiarity during a long and increasingly bemused (albeit odd) absorption.

As for Hockney's specific observation about the inability to look at even erotic photography for longer than thirty seconds—how even those images quickly lose their sense of liveliness and lived reality (the observation that he suggests launched him out into this whole field of inquiry in the first place)—I find myself wondering about the counterexample of bondage photography. Bear with me here. For isn't it precisely the model's being forced to stand still (immobile, bridling against the restraints) that gives such images a sense of duration, of passing time, of lived reality, greater than that of other erotic imagery—the constrained subject's rhyming, as it were, with the constraints imposed on the viewer's gaze by the limitations of the photographic medium. We and she (he?) are yoked in an analogically parallel straitjacket.

Something similar might be said, if you will allow me one further vaulting association, about the wondrous effect of Vermeer's paintings. People often comment on how uncannily still Vermeer's paintings seem, which at one level, of course, is ridiculous: of course they are still; they are paintings! But there's something to the observation, for time and again Vermeer chooses to portray his women at moments when they themselves are forced momentarily to stand still (as they test the balance of these scales, or pour from that jug of milk, or assess this strand of pearls held against the neck, or pause, drop-jawed, to read that letter). We, coming upon them, are stopped in our tracks by their stoppage; we become hushed voyeurs, and time passes: life transpires. Duration unfurls. Oddly enough, it is precisely because we sense time passing that we think of the women as still (consider, by contrast, Napoleon astride a rearing horse in one of David's portraits, which we would never think of as still in this way). If anything, Vermeer is anticipating the movies. Look again at the milkmaid in the painting where nothing is moving except the milk, which you could swear is actually flowing. One has to experience the passage of time to experience the sensation of stillness. And Vermeer allows that.

Returning, finally, to Hockney's initial insight, about the inability to look on conventional erotic photographs for more than thirty seconds. Again, consider by contrast (which is to say in support of his theory) the conventional raincoat exhibitionist. The whole point of his activity is that he afflicts his victim with a quick peek and then covers himself up again—the sudden inappropriate revelation shocks us, whereas a longer exposure would simply devolve into ridiculousness. But note the language here: what is he doing? In keeping with the photographic roots of his vocation, we say he is exposing himself; we say he is *flashing.*

2. John Berger has written with exceptional clarity and insight about many of these same issues, notably in a 1981 essay entitled "Drawn to the Moment," in which he starts out by describing some drawings he'd recently made of his dead father and then goes on to consider some of the differences between drawing and photography. "In the nineteenth century," he writes, "when social time became unilinear, vectorial, and regularly exchangeable, the instant became the maximum which could be grasped or preserved. The plate camera and the pocket watch, the reflex camera and the wristwatch are twin inventions. A drawing or a painting presupposes another view of time. . . .

"A photograph is evidence of an encounter between event and photographer. A drawing slowly questions an event's appearance and in doing so reminds us that appearances are always a construction with a history. We use photographs by taking them with us in our lives, our arguments, our memories: it is we who *move* them. Whereas a drawing or a painting forces us to *stop* and enter its time. A photograph is static because it has stopped time. A drawing or painting is static because it encompasses time. . . .

"To draw is to look, examining the structure of appearances. A drawing of a tree shows not a tree but a tree being looked at. Whereas the sight of a tree is registered almost instantaneously, the examination of the sight of a tree (a tree being looked at) not only takes minutes or hours instead of a fraction of a second; it also involves, derives from, and refers back to much previous experience of looking. Within the instant of the sight of the tree is established a life experience. This is how the act of drawing refuses the process of disappearances and proposes the simultaneity of a multitude of moments" (Berger, *Selected Essays,* ed. Geoff Dyer [New York: Pantheon, 2001], pp. 419–24).

3. The English-language catalogue to the show is *David Hockney: Photographs* (London: Petersburg Press, 1982).

4. The choice of imagery for this first Polaroid collage was by no means random. Hockney was effecting a photographic replication of his then-most-recent oil painting, a triptych conceived in London well over a year earlier. At that time, Hockney, a bit depressed by the grim, gray London winter, decided to contrive a free-form remembrance of his California home—free-form in that he was working from memory (no photographs) and ostentatiously playing with color (transposing the bright, cheerful hues from his most recent work in stage designs). After he returned to California, he decided to recast the plain white walls of the house in the playful colors he'd invented for his London triptych. He even had the red brick windwall around the pool painted a brighter red! So that now, as he was snapping his Polaroids, he was contriving a photographic remembrance of a painting he'd made a year earlier that had helped to transform the house *it* was recalling into the house Hockney was now photographing.

5. David Hockney that morning was not the first person to take the artistic possibilities of the Polaroid camera seriously. His most famous precursor, perhaps, was Lucas Samaras, who confined himself, however, to working within individual Polaroid tiles, experimenting with the magical transformative capacities of the chemical pigments as they developed. At any rate, the Polaroid Corporation was for many years able to sustain an entire magazine devoted to the exposition and dissemination of new artistic work in the medium.

As it happened, a few photographers working at roughly the same time as Hockney were also experimenting with collagist deployments of Polaroid squares. (Hockney, who as a painter is not particularly current with contemporary photographic practice, became aware of these particular parallel projects only after his own Polaroids began being exhibited, in the summer of 1982.) In Belgium, for instance, a young artist named Stefan de Jaéger was fashioning figure studies in rectangular Polaroid grids, although in his versions the elongated figures seemed to float in empty space. (A plurality of the squares in his grids were made up of purplish white blank wall, a backdrop without incident.) The American Joyce Niemanas, meanwhile, was making lushly detailed studies, only she wasn't using a grid format. In her collages, the squares overlap one another at vertiginous angles, and a large part of the compositional delight comes from the jutting and jagging of white borderlines across the image, which in turn get integrated by the matching of lines and contours fairly exactly from frame to frame (as in the Hockney "joiners"). There was even an album jacket for a recording by the Talking Heads, produced in 1978 and conceived by David Byrne, which featured a grid of over five hundred Polaroids, but here again the image beyond the grid, if somewhat attenuated, was largely integrated.

Around the time of the first exhibition of the Hockney Polaroids, Henry Geldzahler commented, "Other artists have used Polaroid in a similar way, but other artists used the pencil before Ingres, and only Ingres found out how to make a certain kind of line" (as it happens, a particularly prescient example, as we shall see in the "Looking Glass" chapter of this book). It wasn't, however, just the highly personal line that distinguished Hockney's Polaroid collages from those of his colleagues; it was also the ambition—which, as we shall presently see, had to do with the exploration of cubist perception—that was distinctive to Hockney's efforts.

(Incidentally, none of these Polaroid collagists was the first to experiment with extended photographic composites. For a detailed survey of the history of prior efforts, see the exhibition catalogue *Target III: In Sequence: Photo Sequences from the Target Collection of American Photography,* ed. Ann Wilkes Tucker [Houston: Museum of Fine Arts, 1982].)

6. As with all the collages in his series, Hockney shot that interior without a flash. Indeed, he feels that the frequent resort to flash devices is yet another way in which conventional photography falsifies reality, providing viewers with scenes they would never glimpse in their ordinary experience (e.g., the uniformly bleached contrasts, the stark projected shadows). Hockney prides himself on his ability to keep his camera steady no matter how long the exposure, and he insists that "if it's bright enough to see it, it's bright enough to photograph it."

7. Memory and vision. Hockney has often noted in interviews the importance to his work of his frequent reading of Marcel Proust. Indeed, volumes from *The Remembrance of Things Past* often show up in his paintings, lying on laps or tables. While he was working on these photo collages Hockney was also reading the philosopher Henri Bergson (an important source author for Proust), as well as *Proust's Binoculars,* Roger Shattuck's study of memory, time, and recognition in *The Remembrance of Things Past.* Several passages from that book seem particularly resonant in a consideration of Hockney's photocollage work. For example, at one point Shattuck delineates "three basic ways of seeing the world—or of recreating it." The first is the *cinematographic* principle, which "employs a sequence of separately insignificant differences to produce the effect of motion or animation in objects seen" (Muybridge). The second is the *montage* principle, which "employs a succession of large contrasts to reproduce the disparity and contradiction that interrupt the continuity of experience" (Sergey Eisenstein). The third is in some ways the richest, and its development is one of Proust's greatest achievements: "The *stereoscopic* principle abandons the portrayal of motion in order to establish a form of arrest which resists time. It selects a few images or impressions sufficiently different from one another not to give the effect of continuous motion, and sufficiently related to be linked in a discernible pattern. This stereoscopic princi-

ple allows our binocular (or multiocular) vision of mind to hold contradictory aspects of things in the steady perspective of recognition, of belief in time." These comments, which refer to Proust's narrative technique, also suggest certain aspects of Hockney's drawing style, both in the Polaroid collages and, even more, in his later photocollage work (Shattuck, *Proust's Binoculars* [Princeton, N.J.: Princeton University Press, 1983], pp. 50–51).

8. See Christopher Knight's lovely exposition of this theme in his article in *Aperture,* no. 89 (1982), 34: "The charms of these spectacular 'drawings' is precisely their expansiveness, their nonexclusionary quality. The isolating eye of the camera segments the views, but the reassembled grid juxtaposes things of starkly different natures: the hard geometry of shelves abuts the softness of narrow chin and full lips. The grid is a rational structure for an exercise in intoxicating sensuality. The drab and insignificant become the singular and radiant."

9. Viewing cubist pictures, Hockney recently told me, is "very difficult, but tremendously rewarding. I mean, no cubist painting jumps off the wall at you—you have to go to it. There was recently a remarkable Essential Cubism retrospective at the Tate, curated by Douglas Cooper, and I spent hours and hours there during my last trip to London. That show *forced* you to slow down. If you just glanced quickly, you didn't see anything. But when you did slow down, the paintings just grew and grew: your eyes darted in and out, forward and back, just like in the real world. At times you almost forgot you were looking at pictures on a wall! Coming out of those galleries, it just happened that I was confronted with my own painting of Ossie and Celia and, next to it, a Francis Bacon triptych. The cubist paintings had been mainly still lifes, and here these ones of Bacon's and mine were fairly dramatic paintings of people. You'd have thought they would have stood up. But on the contrary, following the intensity of the experience of the cubist studies, these two paintings, based as they were on a pretty standard one-point perspective, seemed strangely distant, flat, and one-dimensional."

10. Excerpts from Hockney's lecture, "Major Paintings of the Sixties," are quoted from the tape transcript, Los Angeles County Museum of Art (January 1983).

11. "Poetic history," the literary critic Harold Bloom has written, "is . . . indistinguishable from poetic influence, since strong poets make that history by misreading one another, so as to clear imaginative space for themselves." Many of the insights in Harold Bloom's books on poetics, especially his *Map of Misreading* and *The Anxiety of Influence,* might well be brought to bear in considering Hockney's relationship to Picasso. Clearly theirs is no simple father-son relationship: of course, no father-son relationship is ever simple, but theirs is even more complex than usual. Here we have a son who has chosen his father, who has *claimed*

his father. He has declared Picasso the father of his inspiration, but at the same time he has to a certain extent distorted Picasso's meaning—or, at any rate, emphasized particular aspects of the master's legacy while ignoring others—precisely so as "to clear an imaginative space" for himself. This is not the place to analyze those distortions in detail. I would suggest that it is pointless to quibble that Hockney is misinterpreting Picasso, however, since in this passion "misinterpretation" and creation are simultaneous surges. For an important study of the Picasso-Hockney relationship, see the catalogue by Esther de Vécsey, *David Hockney: Sources and Experiments* (Houston: Sewall Art Gallery, Rice University, 1982).

One might also note, incidentally, how, if anyone is the true father of Hockney's vocation, it is not Picasso but Matisse (who has the same love of color and, like Hockney, consecrates lounging bourgeois pleasure), but Hockney hardly ever talks about him.

12. Dr. Oliver Sacks, the British neurologist working in New York, once published a remarkable book entitled *Awakenings,* in which he presents the case histories of several patients suffering from a post-encephalytic Parkinsonian condition so extreme that at one point he describes their situation as "an ontological emergency." One of the myriad symptoms with which these patients must occasionally contend is what Sacks calls "kinematic vision," the tendency to experience the ordinary world as if in a series of stills. "Sometimes," Sacks explains in describing the case of Hester Y., "these stills form a flickering vision, like a movie which is running too slow. Mrs. Y. and other patients who have experienced kinematic vision have occasionally told me of an extraordinary (and seemingly impossible) phenomenon which may occur during such periods, viz., the displacement of a still either backwards or forwards, so that a given 'moment' may occur *too soon* or *too late.* Thus, on one occasion when Hester was being visited by her brother, she happened to be having kinematic vision at about three or four frames per second, i.e., a rate so slow that there was a clearly perceptible difference between each frame. While watching her brother lighting his pipe, she was greatly startled by witnessing the following sequence: first, the striking of the match; second, her brother's hand holding the lighted match, having 'jumped' a few inches from the matchbox; third, the match flaring up in the bowl of the pipe; and fourth, fifth, and sixth, etc., the 'intermediate' stages by which her brother's hand, holding the match, jerkily approached the pipe to be lit. Thus—incredibly—Hester saw the pipe actually being lit several frames too soon; she saw 'the future' so to speak, somewhat before she was *due* to see it. . . . If we accept Hester's word in the matter (and if we do not listen to our patients we will never learn anything), we are compelled to make a novel hypothesis (or several such) about the perception of time and the nature of 'moments.' The simplest of these, I think, is to take 'moments' as ontological events (i.e., as *our* 'world-moments') and to assume that

we 'take in' several at a time (as a moving whale continually swallows a swarm of shrimps), or that we keep a small hoard of them 'in stock' at any given time, and in either case feed them into some internal projector, where they become activated or 'real' one at a time in their proper sequence. Normally, this proceeds correctly and easily; but in certain conditions, it would seem, our ontological moments may be fed to us in the wrong order, so that moments which are chronologically 'past' or 'future' get ectopically displaced and presented to us as utterly convincing (but inappropriate) 'nows'" (New York: Vintage Press, 2nd ed., 1976), pp. 142–43; (New York: Dutton Obelisk, 3rd ed., 1993), pp. 102–3.

13. *Aperture,* no. 89 (1982), 34. Interestingly, while I see these words of his as applying equally well to the new photocollages, Christopher Knight himself faults the newer pieces for not being more like the Polaroids. In a review in the *Los Angeles Herald Examiner* (July 13, 1983), Knight argued that "what's missing from the new pictorial representations is the wholly abstract structure that made the Polaroids so potent. In the place of the grid, the artist seems to have opted for a random visual scan of the scene: It is intensely focused in certain areas, abruptly halted in others, or it arbitrarily trails off in still others. Random scanning is indeed the way we see the world. One doesn't see in sequential and orderly units, but the grid format of the Polaroids provided the essential counterweight: It served to abolish any sense of hierarchy within the pictorial representations." Ironically it is precisely Hockney's success at rendering his newest studies in perception more lifelike that in Knight's view has begun to mitigate their impact as art.

14. William Carlos Williams, *Pictures from Brueghel and Other Poems* (New York: New Directions, 1962), p. 7.

15. In such comments as these Hockney appears either ignorant of or momentarily oblivious to the rich tradition of cubist-inspired avant-garde cinema—works by such artists as Man Ray, Fernand Léger, the early Luis Buñuel, René Clair, and more recently Stan Brakhage and Michael Snow—artists obsessed with many of the same issues as Hockney. In earlier comments in this text, Hockney seemed likewise to downplay the achievement of such cubist-inspired photographers as Stieglitz, Paul Outerbridge, or Harry Callahan. But here again we see how Hockney, like most artists, clears an open space for his own creative work by momentarily occluding prior tradition. Critics and academic historians can rush in to cite influences and antecedents—but such people are usually incapable of creating art themselves. (Too much knowledge of a certain kind can crowd out the possibility of independent creation—or at any rate, that knowledge must be suspended as creativity begins.) Hockney's account of the history of cubism is interesting not so much because of its technical accuracy in every detail as because it affords a vantage on his own creative process (how cubism-

for-Hockney made *Hockney's* photocollages possible); and even when Hockney's account fails to be 100 percent accurate vis-à-vis the history of prior achievements, his insights into the stakes involved in cubism and the drama of everyday human perception are remarkably suggestive.

2 : A VISIT WITH DAVID AND STANLEY

1. Hockney read the following passages from Pierre Daix, *Le Cubismo de Picasso* (Neuchâtel, Switzerland: Ides et Calendes, 1979), p. 184. The translation is from "Vogue par David Hockney," *Vogue* (Paris), December 1985–January 1986, 256:

> This transformation in painting should be related not to ephemeral fashions and short-lived schools, but to the long duration of changes in cognitive methods and mental attitudes. Perspective has lasted for some five hundred years. Cubism is the chance name given to the first emergence of a different art, or rather to the concretization of difference which suddenly became perceptible. . . .
>
> It is only now, in the last quarter of the twentieth century that we discover that Cubism was not only a revolution in pictorial space, but a revolution in our understanding of pictorial space. This was in all probability linked to the fact that physics was simultaneously destroying our three-dimensional space-time perception. Our discoveries in this field are only just beginning.

2. Here is the passage from which Hockney quotes (David Bohm, *Wholeness and the Implicate Order* [London: Routledge and Kegan Paul, 1980], pp. x–xi):

> It is clear that in reflecting on and pondering the nature of the movement, both in thought and in the object of thought, one comes inevitably to the question of wholeness and totality. The notion that the one who thinks (the Ego) is at least in principle completely separate from and independent of the reality that he thinks about is, of course, firmly embedded in our entire tradition. (This notion is clearly almost universally accepted in the West, but in the East there is a general tendency to deny it verbally and philosophically while at the same time such an approach pervades most of life and daily practice as much as it does in the West.) General experience . . . along with a great deal of modern scientific knowledge . . . suggest[s] very strongly that such a division cannot be maintained consistently. . . .
>
> Clearly, this brings us to consider our overall worldview, which includes our general notions concerning the nature of reality, along with those concerning the total order of the universe, i.e., cosmology. To meet the challenge before us, our notions of cosmology and of the general nature of reality must have room in them to permit a consistent account of consciousness. Vice versa, our notions of consciousness must have room in them to understand what it means for its content to be "reality as a whole."

The widespread and pervasive distinctions between people (race, nation, family, profession, etc.) which are now preventing mankind from working together for the common good, and indeed, even for survival, have one of the key factors of their origin in a kind of thought that treats things as inherently divided, disconnected, and "broken up" into yet smaller constituent parts. Each part is considered to be essentially independent and self-existent.

When man thinks of himself in this way, he will inevitably tend to defend the needs of his own "Ego" against those of others; or, if he identifies with a group of people of the same kind, he will defend this group in a similar way. He cannot seriously think of mankind as the basic reality, whose claims come first. Even if he does try to consider the needs of mankind he tends to regard humanity as separate from nature, and so on. What I am proposing here is that man's general way of thinking of the totality, i.e., his general worldview, is crucial for the overall order of the human mind itself. If he thinks of the totality as constituted of independent fragments, then that is how his mind will tend to operate, but if he can include everything coherently and harmoniously in an overall whole that is undivided, unbroken, and without a border (for every border is a division or break) then his mind will tend to move in a similar way, and from this will flow an orderly action within the whole.

3. The text of Samuel Y. Edgerton Jr.'s book *The Renaissance Rediscovery of Linear Perspective* (New York: Basic Books, 1975), pp. 164–65, from which Hockney read, went as follows:

It should not be overlooked that almost coincidental with the appearance and acceptance of linear perspective came Gutenberg's invention of movable type. Together these two ideas, the one visual, the other literary, provided perhaps the most outstanding scientific achievement of the fifteenth century: the revolution in mass communication. Linear perspective pictures, by virtue of the power of the printing press, came to cover a wider range of subjects and to reach a larger audience than any other representational medium or convention in the entire history of art. It is fair to say that without this conjunction of perspective and printing in the Renaissance, the whole subsequent development of modern science and technology would have been unthinkable. . . .

So far as science is concerned can there be any question that the special geniuses of Leonardo da Vinci, Columbus, and Copernicus were given a very special catalysis at this time by the new communications revolution of linear perspective? Indeed, without linear perspective, would Western man have been able to visualize and then construct the complex machinery which has so effectively moved him out of the Newtonian paradigm into the new era of Einsteinian outer space—and outer time? Space capsules built for zero gravity, astronomical equipment for demarcating so-called black holes, atom smashers which prove the existence of anti-matter—these are the end products of the discovered vanishing point.

Or are they? Surely in some future century, when artists are among those journeying throughout the universe, they will be encountering and endeavoring to depict experiences impossible to understand, let alone render, by the application of a suddenly obsolete linear perspective. It, too, will become "naive," as they discover new dimensions of visual perception in the eternal, never ultimate, quest to show truth through the art of making pictures.

4. From George Rowley, *The Principles of Chinese Painting* (Princeton, N.J.: Princeton University Press, 1947), p. 61:

> Chinese painting is an art of time as well as space. This was implied in the arrangement of the group by movement motif through intervals; in the extended relationship of groups, movement in time became the most memorable characteristic of Chinese design. . . . These early principles were later transformed and enriched until they reached their fulfillment in the supreme creation of Chinese genius—the landscape scroll. A scroll painting must be experienced in time like music or literature. Our attention is carried along laterally from right to left, being restricted at any one moment to a short passage which can be conveniently perused. This situation entirely alters the choice of design principles. . . . In the European tradition, the interest in measurable space destroyed the "continuous method" of temporal sequence used in the Middle Ages and led to the fifteenth century invention of the fixed space of scientific perspective. When the Chinese were faced with the same problem of spatial depth in the T'ang period, they reworked the early principles of time and suggested a space through which one might wander and a space which implied more space beyond the picture frame. We restricted space to a single vista as though seen through an open door; they suggested unlimited space of nature as though they had stepped through that open door and had known the sudden breathtaking experience of space extending in every direction and infinitely into the sky. Again, east and west look at nature through different glasses; one tries to explain and conquer nature through science, and the other wants to keep alive the eternal mystery which can only be suggested. Each seeks truth in its own way, and each has its strengths and weaknesses. The science of perspective achieved the illusion of depth and gave continuity and measurability to the spatial unit; however, perspective put the experience of space into a strait jacket in which it was seen from a single fixed point of view and was limited to a bounded quantity of space. The control of space might give measure to an interior figure scene but it was certainly harmful to landscape painting.

5. Hockney presently made a film of his Chinese scroll discoveries, with the director Philip Haas, entitled *A Day on the Grand Canal with the Emperor of China, or Surface Is Illusion but So Is Depth,* which remains available on DVD from Milestone Films.

3 : *LIEBESTOD*

1. Notwithstanding Hockney's protestations (and my great-grandmother's spectacularly vivid response), *Tristan is* a silly story, or anyway a peculiarly charged one—"Peculiar piece" being one of the first things Jonathan Miller said to me when I called to chat with him about his *Tristan* experience. Florid, fraught, wildly overwrought: susceptible to all manner of feverish associations across its capacious, deceptively static three and a half hours—for starters,

to the highly peculiar particulars of its own psycho-biographical origins, which in turn wend directly back to the composer's edgy anxieties about his *own* ambiguous origins.

Richard Wagner's father, Friederich, died a bare half year after the boy's birth, a victim of the typhus epidemic that engulfed their native Leipzig in the immediate aftermath of the Napoleonic Battle of Nations in 1813. The thing is, within only nine months of that, Richard's widowed mother married the dead father's closest friend and protégé, a young actor named Ludwig Geyer (for the first fifteen years of his life, Richard even went by the last name Geyer), under circumstances suspicious enough to eventually give young Richard cause to wonder whether the actor hadn't in fact been his own actual father all along. (This last surmise in turn was to become highly fraught, both for Wagner and for his subsequent Nazi enthusiasts, because Geyer may or may not have been part-Jewish.)

At any rate, throughout the rest of his turbulent life, Wagner seemed drawn into repeated reenactments of that inappropriate primal configuration, endlessly falling himself for the wives of his most steadfast patrons and ensnaring them in the most fetid, steamy, and overblown relations. Which, in turn, of course, stripped to its barest essentials, is what *Tristan* itself is all about: the inappropriate passion that flares up between a king's betrothed and his most loyal duty-bound knight. Wagner, incidentally, began writing the libretto while he and his own wife were the houseguests of a passionately devoted patron, a Zurich silk merchant with whose twenty-eight-year-old bride he presently struck up a feverish (though perhaps never quite consummated) affair.

Soon after completing the libretto, Wagner gave an intimate reading in the presence of only five listeners: his own wife, Minna; the silk merchant and his young wife; and his single most fervently supportive musical champion, the great conductor Hans van Bülow and *his* new bride, Cosima (the illegitimate daughter, as it happened, of the composer Franz Liszt). The occasion was so drenched in overwrought emotions that the silk merchant's bride went into a weeping fit during Wagner's reading of the final scenes and almost fainted. Who knows how the nineteen-year-old Cosima responded. Suffice it to say that within a few years, as Von Bülow embarked upon the long and arduous labor of mounting the premier production of the completed opera, Wagner himself (having long since tossed aside the silk merchant's pathetic wife) launched into a highly public affair with Cosima right under Von Bülow's nose.

Wagner even sired a child with Cosima, a baby girl, delivered as Von Bülow himself was engaged in the first day of the opera's orchestral rehearsals, whom they quickly named Isolde! ("Paging Ken Russell," a tiny voice constantly seems to squawk inside one's head as one meanders through any of the myriad of Wagner biographies; "paging Ken Russell: your services are *urgently* required on page 243.")

Several years after Isolde's birth, Richard and Cosima abandoned their respective spouses and were married—with Cosima eventually going on to preside over the master's festival shrine at Bayreuth right up until her own death, at age ninety-two, in 1930.

So that, at any rate, if, like me, part of you tries each fresh time to steel yourself against the sinuous blandishments of Wagner's music (you're not going to fall for such blatant, hyper-romantic manipulations, not this time, not yet again); and if each fresh time you fall for them nevertheless (for how can you not? the music *is* absolutely ravishing); if once again Wagner has his imperious way with you, leaving you (in the thrilling wake of Isolde's excruciating *Liebestod* and the orchestra's subsequent exalted final chord) an utterly spent, exalted dishrag of your former self, such that you find yourself muttering, amid your neighbors' thunderous applause, "The bastard, the god-damned bastard! How does he *do* that?"—the point is: *precisely,* you will have hit the nail on the head. For in at least one of its aspects, *Tristan* is in its essence an opera about the condition of bastardy and the bastard's desperately anxious lunge for legitimacy. With that final chord, Tristan and Isolde at last achieve in death the transfigured unification that had so eluded them in life: they live on, having indeed become the One they fervently aspired to be. And the One they've become (in psycho-autobiographical terms) is none other than Wagner himself, who, as the possible bastard progeny of precisely such a union, has ended up rendering the epic of his own procreation.

Or, anyway, that's one reading of the opera's unnerving power. There are others. For starters that it is just great, great music.

4 : WIDER PERSPECTIVES

1. Carl Sagan, *Pale Blue Dot: A Vision of the Human Future in Space* (New York: Random House, 1994), p. 52.

2. Maybe even, not to put too fine a point on things, as a version of his sick friend Jonathan's head (compare Fig. 32, p. 99).

6 : THROUGH THE LOOKING GLASS

1. On a visit to the library, I subsequently came upon an article in a 1982 issue of the *Art Bulletin,* the premier American academic art historical quarterly, in which a fellow named

David Carleton, focusing on this very painting of Van Eyck's, *The Arnolfini Marriage,* had suggested that its curious "elliptical optics" could be accounted for by the painter's deployment, in some unknown manner, of the convex mirror there on the wall in the back; the guy had been roundly ridiculed in subsequent articles in follow-up issues of the *Bulletin*—after all, how could a convex mirror have been of any use whatsoever? It occurred to me in retrospect how in that article Carleton had been something like Tycho Brahe, the great Danish sixteenth-century astronomer, who'd almost figured it all out: he'd determined that all the planets revolved around the sun, which in turn revolved around the earth. Close, so close, but no cigar.

2. Or perhaps the painter-turned-filmmaker Julian Schnabel rendering *Basquiat* (1996).

7 : SOMETIME MAKE THE TIME

1. For more on "Art and Optic," the December 2001 NYU/NYIH conference, see http://www.nyu.edu/fas/institute/nyih/public/archive.html.

As for the ongoing Falco-Stork controversy, both gentlemen have posted detailed Web sites summarizing their positions and providing profuse bibliographies. Falco's is at http://www.optics.arizona.edu/ssd/FAQ.html, and Stork's at http://www.diatrope.com/stork/FAQs.html.

Stork's "Optics and Realism in Renaissance Art" appeared in the December 2004 *Scientific American.* Hockney himself responded with a letter to the editor in the magazine's April 2005 issue.

2. Hockney's studio recently released a DVD featuring the complete contents of *Fifteen Sketchbooks: 2002–2003: London, Iceland, Norway, Los Angeles.*

3. Here again Hockney advances this notion of his that in China, because artists did not use camera/lens projections they never depicted shadows, or never, at any rate, deep chiaroscuro shading. (I once heard him even go so far as to suggest that in ordinary life we ourselves don't notice shadows, which is to say we watch someone moving along, and they may walk from sunlight into shade and back into sunlight, but we don't register the change as such unless, precisely, we are looking through a lens, at which point the shift makes all the difference in the world.) This idea of Hockney's seems paradoxically at odds with Jun'ichiro Tanizaki's short and much beloved treatise on ancient and traditional Japanese aesthetics, *In Praise of Shadows* (1933), wherein, for example, the great novelist notes:

> Whenever I see the alcove of a tastefully built Japanese room, I marvel at our comprehension of the secrets of shadows, our sensitive use of shadow and light. For the beauty of the alcove is

> not the work of some device. An empty space is marked off with plain wood and plain walls, so that the light drawn into it forms dim shadows within emptiness. There is nothing more. And yet, when we gaze into the darkness that gathers behind the crossbeam, around the flower vase, beneath the shelves, though we know perfectly well it is mere shadow, we are overcome with the feeling that in this small corner of the atmosphere there reigns complete and utter silence; that here in the darkness immutable tranquility holds sway. The "mysterious Orient" of which Westerners speak probably refers to the uncanny silence of these dark places. And even we as children would feel an inexpressible chill as we peered into the depths of an alcove to which the sunlight had never penetrated. Where lies the key to this mystery? Ultimately it is the magic of shadows. Were the shadows to be banished from its corners, the alcove would in that instant revert to mere void.
>
> This was the genius of our ancestors, that by cutting off the light from this empty space they imparted to the world of shadows that formed there a quality of mystery and depth superior to that of any wall painting or ornament. The technique seems simple, but was by no means so simply achieved. We can imagine with little difficulty what extraordinary pains were taken with each invisible detail—the placement of the window in the shelving recess, the depth of the crossbeam, the height of the threshold. But for me the most exquisite touch is the pale white flow of the shoji in the study bay; I need only pause before it and I forget the passage of time.
>
> (Trans. Thomas J. Harper and Edward G. Seidensticker [Stony Creek, Conn.: Leete's Island Books, 1977], pp. 20–21)

On the other hand, the paradox may only be apparent, for Tanizaki is writing of the Oriental lifeworld itself, as it were, whereas Hockney is talking about how that world came to be *depicted.* Indeed, it may even be the preternaturally heightened sensitivity to shadows in the actual world (with their "quality of mystery and depth superior to that of any wall painting or ornament") that allowed Japanese artists, anyway, to leave such shadows out of their imagery. (Viewers could be relied upon to read them into the image in any case, much as a love scene in a filmed romance can be all the more vividly evoked for being stylishly occluded and, as we say, "left to the imagination.")

4. Aye: don't get Hockney going on smoking! Or, hell, there's no point: he's going to get himself going in any case. For the past several years, perhaps the only thing that has exercised his rhetorical passions more than optics is the (as he sees it) relentless persecution of smokers, the progressive constriction of their innate civil rights, the run-amok prerogatives of the nanny state, etcetera, etcetera, etcetera.

Most visitors to his home become so inured to the ongoing rant that they hardly notice it anymore. But occasionally . . . I am thinking of a time recently when I'd brought my then-nineteen-year-old daughter along with me on a visit to Bridlington, and while awaiting the arrival of dinner at a nearby restaurant, David was once again getting all revved up on his second-favorite stalking horse, railing that the treatment of smokers in Blairite England was getting as bad as Stalinist . . . at which point my daughter suddenly interjected, "But David, *that's ridiculous!* What are you *talking about?*" All the rest of us around the table were momentarily stunned: not just that someone was having the temerity to challenge David but that someone was having the perseverance to actually listen to what he was saying in this regard and to respond in kind. (David for his part appeared—or rather, maybe, fashioned himself to appear—not to hear.)

Perhaps, though, these antismoking rants of David's shouldn't be taken all that seriously: they are like conceptual screen savers, the sound David's mind makes in idle while it gathers up energy for its next more serious intellectual onslaught.

5. Compare a similar moment, or at any rate a similar sudden passion, in Robert Irwin's career, from near the outset of Chapter 22 of my *Seeing Is Forgetting*, the companion volume to this book (regarding Irwin's preparations for his work on the Getty Garden):

> As things developed, it turned out to be the latter of these two passions that had set us on this particular wild-goose, or maybe I should say wild-grass, chase, for after about an hour's drive Irwin eased the Cadillac off the road and onto a dusty embankment so that we could gaze upon precisely that—a tuft of wild grass. "Amazing, isn't it?" Bob marveled, and it was, though I'd otherwise never have given it a glance. He proceeded to tell me how he had had his eye on that particular tuft for almost a year now—auditioning it, as it were, in different lights, across different seasons. "Some grasses," he explained, "you can come upon them in high season, when they're really on their game, and they're just humming. But you go back a couple of months later and they're simply gone. Or else they've fallen apart completely—a real mess. But then there are others, like this one, that even when they're down, the dry seedpods are still beautiful. The stalks can get this haunting, graceful, quite striking quality." He got out of the car, crouched in front of the dried tuft, ruffled its stalk spray, palmed its feathery plumes. "Yup," he said, smiling, as he climbed back into the car and negotiated a happy U-turn. The tuft seemed to have passed muster—it, along with more than a thousand other plant types that, Irwin now explained, he'd been subjecting to similarly rigorous seasonal inspections over the past several years as he ever so gradually, ever so painstakingly, pulled together the horticultural components of his garden palette.

8 : A RETURN TO PAINTING

1. This would prove one of Hockney's few recent citations of Van Gogh, amid a veritable raft of invocations of Constable and, to a lesser extent, Turner—this, perhaps, being another instance of that anxiety of influence I inferred earlier with regard to how Hockney

keeps talking about Picasso when Matisse, whom he barely mentions, might seem a more proximate antecedent.

2. Velázquez is of course playing with some of these same paradoxes in *Las Meninas* by rendering himself craning out for a moment from behind the huge canvas he is painting—the very one, he may cheekily imply, that we are looking at. (On second thought, however, that surely can't be right: maybe, rather, he is portraying himself portraying the king and queen whose reflection we make out in the distant mirror behind him, but in that case, why then the huge canvas? For that matter, at that scale, could he, painting away like that, hope even to reach much higher than their knees?)

3. "Painting," Constable once wrote his friend John Fisher, "is another word for feeling."

4. I was indeed reminded of a little painting of David's from those days when he'd kept a Malibu beach house: the churning blue ocean taking up the entire backdrop, with a dainty little porcelain tea set resting demure on a glass tabletop in the foreground, snug indoors behind a thick plate glass window.

Meanwhile, Hockney's response, somehow quintessentially English, reminded me as well of a few paragraphs from Jonathan Raban's *Passage to Juneau,* where the author anatomizes the first interactions, in the straits off what would become British Columbia, between the age-old natives and arriving white colonists:

> Two worldviews were in collision; and the poverty of white accounts of these canoe journeys reflects the colonialists' blindness to the native sea. They didn't get it—couldn't grasp the fact that for Indians the water was a place, and a great bulk of the surrounding land mere undifferentiated space.
>
> The whites had entered a looking-glass world, where their own most basic terms were reversed. Their whole focus was directed toward the land: its natural harbors, its timber, its likely spots for settlement and agriculture. They traveled everywhere equipped with mental chainsaws and at a glance could strip a hill of its covering forest (as Vancouver does again and again, in his *Voyage*) and see there a future of hedges, fields, houses, churches. They viewed the sea as a medium of access to the all-important land.
>
> Substitute "sea" for "land" and vice versa in that paragraph, and one is very close to the world that emerges from Indian stories, where the forest is the realm of danger, darkness, exile, solitude, and self-extinction, while the sea and its beaches represent safety, light, home, society, and the continuation of life.
>
> (Jonathan Raban, *Passage to Juneau: A Sea and Its Meanings*
> (New York: Pantheon 1999), p. 103)

5. "You see with memory." I am not unaware how this postulate of David's would seem to run diametrically counter to Robert Irwin's entire aesthetic, summed up as it is in my bi-

ography's title *Seeing Is Forgetting the Name of the Thing One Sees.* Which is to say that to truly see something, one need forget everything about it, right down to its very name.

On the other hand, with the passing years, Irwin's own thinking has likewise become more supple in this regard. See, for example, our extended conversation about trees and other plants in our collaborative book, *Robert Irwin Getty Garden.*

6. Viz., Søren Kierkegaard, in his guise as the aesthete "A," *Either/Or,* vol. 1, trans. David Swenson and Lillian Swenson (Garden City, N.Y.: Anchor Doubleday, 1959), pp. 287–88:

> My own dissent from the ordinary view is sufficiently expressed in the use I make of the word "rotation." This word might seem to conceal an ambiguity, and if I wished to use it so as to find room in it for the ordinary method, I should have to define it as a change of field. But the farmer does not use the word in this sense. I shall, however, adopt this meaning for a moment, in order to speak of the rotation which depends on change in its boundless infinity, its extensive dimension, so to speak.
>
> This is the vulgar and inartistic method, and needs to be supported by illusion. One tires of living in the country, and moves to the city; one tires of one's native land, and travels abroad; one tires of Europe, and goes to America, and so on; finally one indulges in sentimental hope of endless journeyings from star to star. Or the movement is different but still extensive. One tires of porcelain dishes and eats on silver; one tires of silver and turns to gold; one burns half of Rome to get an idea of the burning of Troy. But this method defeats itself; it is plain endlessness. And what did Nero gain by it? Antonine was wiser; he says: "It is in your power to review your life, to look at things you saw before, from another point of view."
>
> My own method does not consist in a change of field, but rather resembles the true rotation method in changing the crop and the mode of cultivation. . . . Here we have at once the principle of limitation, the only saving principle in the world. The more you limit yourself, the more fertile you become in invention.

How telling, in turn, that Hockney himself becomes aware of this truth precisely by observing the changing seasons across the farmers' fields of his native Yorkshire.

7. Rebecca Solnit, *River of Shadows: Eadweard Muybridge and the Technological Wild West* (New York: Viking, 2003), p. 11.

8. For those who might rather pursue a more psychologically tinged interpretation of Hockney's *Le Parc des sources,* compare it instead with some of Courbet's "source" paintings, such as *La Source de la Loue* or *Le Puits noir* and then of course all the way back to the source of all source paintings, *The Origin of the World*—another instance, among other things, of symmetrically flanked recession to a vanishing point. See Michael Fried, *Courbet's Realism* (Chicago: University of Chicago Press, 1990), pp. 209–16.

9. Forcing Hockney's point a bit, one might well wonder to what extent the perpendicular axis of the crucifixion (and its replication in all sorts of ways throughout medieval

Europe, in church architecture, for example) might have prepared the ground for the arrival of perspectival vision with Masaccio and his contemporaries. A similar question haunts the generation of Descartes's axial geometry two hundred years later, and with it the near vanishing point of the Cartesian cogito, that other great progenitor of modern technological disembodiment.

10. Robert Irwin could hardly have parsed things better: *You are the figure.* And with this insight, it seems to me, Hockney's and Irwin's seemingly divergent projects converge about as closely as one can possibly imagine—whether or not the two are talking to each other.

acknowledgments

When it comes to acknowledgments in a book like this, I feel a bit like David with a deck of Polaroids in my hand, getting set to splay out the pattern—only, in this case the deck of names spreads out over decades, and the patterns turn in and in on themselves: a four-dimensional kaleidoscope.

For starters, of course, there are the remarkable assistants and more-than-assistants from Hockney's own shop: majordomos Karen Kuhlman, Julie Green, and Gregory Evans; the photographers Richard Schmidt and Jean Pierre Goncalves; the ever hospitable and cheerful Elsa Duarte; and house intellectual (and master detective) David Graves, ever teeming with fresh hunches and insights.

And then, especially during the Looking Glass passion, where would any of us have been without the University of Arizona's optical wizard Charles Falco? Similarly, time and again I found myself turning for guidance and perspective to the Getty's John Walsh; the National Gallery's Arthur Wheelock; and Gary Tinterow and Mike Hearn at the Metropolitan.

I boggle at the number of editors who over the many years have lent their sage counsel to this evolving project, starting at the *New Yorker* with William Shawn and followed by all three of his successors as editor in chief (Robert Gottlieb, Tina Brown, and David Remnick), as well as my own editors there over the years: John Bennet, Pat Crow, and Jeffrey Frank. I've lost track of which particular fact checkers there shepherded which particular piece, but I salute the entire incomparable kennel! In addition, I am happy to be able to thank Raymond Foye at the Petersburg Press and Mark Horowitz at *Los Angeles Magazine*.

At the LA Louver Gallery, Peter Goulds and Elizabeth East were wry and steadfast and always wonderfully supportive.

At the University of California Press, editor Stephanie Fay and her crack troubleshooter Eric Schmidt lavished steadiness, humor, and grace on what developed into an improbably complicated publishing process, and Sandy Drooker proved as marvelously resourceful a designer as she had been on the Irwin project on which we first collaborated almost thirty years ago (as hard as that is for either of us to credit).

Parts of this book have come into being under the protection of each of my three agents—Flip Brophy, Deborah Karl, and now Chris Calhoun—and I am more than glad to be able to doff my cap to each of them here.

My endlessly forbearing and put-upon bride, Joasia, forbore all with never-less-than-bemused good cheer, and our daughter, Sara, veritably grew from infancy into adulthood lapped along by these dialogues, the smartest of us all, and the funniest.

And then finally, of course, there's David. My subject and my teacher and in the end my friend. This book owes all to his brimming generosity of spirit and insight, and to his inextinguishable love of life.

index

DESIGNER : SANDY DROOKER
TEXT : 10/14 ADOBE GARAMOND
DISPLAY : UNIVERS
COMPOSITOR : INTEGRATED COMPOSITION SYSTEMS
INDEXER : ANDREW JORON

Neurosurgery for Junior Trainees

Neurosurgery for Junior Trainees

Fourth Edition

Edited by

Reuben D. Johnson

LLB(Hons), BSc(Hons), MB ChB, DPhil(Oxon),

AFRACMA, FRCS (Neurosurgery), FRACS, FACLM

and

W. Adriaan Liebenberg

MB ChB (Stellenbosch), MMed Neurochirurgie (Stellenbosch),

FCS (Neurosurgery) (SA)

OXFORD
UNIVERSITY PRESS

OXFORD
UNIVERSITY PRESS

Great Clarendon Street, Oxford, OX2 6DP,
United Kingdom

Oxford University Press is a department of the University of Oxford.
It furthers the University's objective of excellence in research, scholarship,
and education by publishing worldwide. Oxford is a registered trade mark of
Oxford University Press in the UK and in certain other countries.

First Edition published in 2004
Second Edition published in 2010
Third Edition published in 2018
Fourth Edition published in 2026

Published in the United States of America by Oxford University Press
546 Fifth Avenue, New York, NY 10036, United States of America

British Library Cataloguing in Publication Data
Data available

Library of Congress Control Number: 2026939229

ISBN 978–0–19–889363–9

DOI: 10.1093/med/9780198893639.001.0001

Printed and bound by
CPI Group (UK) Ltd., Croydon, CR0 4YY

This book is dedicated to Drs Neil and Susan Johnson, whose love and passion for medical publishing made this book possible.

Foreword

Neurosurgery has evolved exponentially in the new millennium and the authors have remained attuned to its progress through various editions of this book. Application rates into residency programmes would suggest the specialty also remains attractive and highly competitive amongst medical students and resident doctors keen to pursue neurosurgery as their career.

While access to knowledge has become relatively easy for the new generation, having the right information in the right proportion could be a challenge. This well-crafted and much-loved book has been meeting this challenge since its first edition in 2004.

Because of their own extensive training and diverse practice settings, the authors have tried to distil the knowledge base essential not only for those seeking admission to this specialty but also for residents in training looking to brush up on their fundamentals.

I congratulate the authors for providing this comprehensive pocketbook covering the salient questions pertaining to neurosurgery in its wider context in a way that can make it a true companion. The latest edition benefits further from a chapter on skull-base surgery to complement previously addressed subspecialities of spinal and paediatric neurosurgery.

I am expecting this book on the desk of every resident neurosurgeon.

Pragnesh Bhatt
MS, MCh, FRCS (Edinburgh, England and Glasgow), FEBNS, FFSTEd, FACS
AO Spine Global Diploma, Global Neuro Trauma Diploma
Consultant Neurosurgeon—Aberdeen, Scotland, UK
Honorary Clinical Senior Lecturer—University of Aberdeen
Electives Convener—MBChB
Council Member—SBNS/SSHM
Ex-Regional Director for Scotland—RCS England
Dy. Director—FST—RCS Edinburgh
Member SSB in Neurosurgery—RCS Edinburgh
Member, Editorial Board—eBrain, IJNT, JOSS, BIDA
GMC Associate

Contents

Abbreviations

A&E	Accident and Emergency
AANS	American Association of Neurological Surgeons
ABC	Airway, Breathing, and Circulation
ABCDE	Airway maintenance with cervical spine protection; Breathing and ventilation; Circulation with haemorrhage control; Disability/neurological assessment; Exposure and environmental control (or Airway, Breathing, Circulation, Disability/neurological assessment, Everything else)
ACA	Anterior cerebral artery
ACDF	Anterior cervical discectomy and fusion
Acomm	Anterior communicating artery
ACTH	Adrenocorticotrophic hormone
ADC	Apparent diffusion coefficient
ADH	Antidiuretic hormone
AF	Atrial fibrillation
ALIF	Anterior lumbar interbody fusion
AMT	Abbreviated Mental Test
ASDH	Acute subdural haemorrhage
ATLS	Advanced Trauma Life Support
AVM	Arteriovenous malformation
AVPU	Alert, Responds to Voice, Responds to Pain, Unresponsive
BA	Basilar artery
bd	*bis in die* (twice daily)
BIH	Benign intracranial hypertension
cACA	Contralateral anterior cerebral artery
CBV	Cerebral blood volume
CCP	Cerebral perfusion pressure
CDSH	Chronic subdural haematoma
CEA	Carcino-embryonic antigen
CMR	Cerebral metabolic rate
CNS	Central nervous system
CODE	Clotting, Opiates, Dextrose, Electrolytes
CPA	Cerebellopontine angle
CPC	Choroid plexus coagulation
CPP	Cerebral perfusion pressure
CSDH	Chronic subdural haematomas
CSF	Cerebrospinal fluid
CSW	Cerebral salt wasting
CT	Computed tomography

CTA	Computed tomography angiogram/angiography
CTV	Computed tomography venography
CVA	Cerebrovascular accident
DDAVP	1-d-amino-8-D-arginine vasopressin (desmopressin)
DI	Diabetes insipidus
DIND	Delayed ischaemic neurological deficit
DIPG	Diffuse intrinsic pontine glioma'
DNET	Dysembryoplastic neuroectodermal tumour
DNT	Dysembroplastic neuroepithelial tumour
DPTS	Delayed post-traumatic seizures
DSA	Digital subtraction angiography
DTI	Diffusion tensor imaging
DVTs	Deep-vein thromboses
DWI	Diffusion-weighted imaging
DWM	Dandy–Walker malformation
EAM	External auditory meatus
ECF	Extracellular fluid
ECG	Electrocardiogram
EDH	Extradural haemorrhage
EEG	Electroencephalogram
EICA	Extracranial internal carotid artery
EMG	Electromyography
ENT	Ear, nose, and throat
EPTS	Early post-traumatic seizure
ESR	Erythrocyte sedimentation rate
ETV	Endoscopic third ventriculostomy
EVD	External ventricular drain
FBC	Full blood count
FLAIR	Fluid-attenuated inversion recovery
fMRI	Functional MRI
FRT	Fractionated radiotherapy
FSH	Follicle-stimulating hormone
G+S	Group and save
GBM	Glioblastoma multiforme
GCS	Glasgow Coma Scale
GH	Growth hormone
GOS	Glasgow Outcome Scale
Gy	Grey
Hb	Haemoglobin
HDU	High-dependency unit
IAC	Internal auditory canal
ICA	Internal carotid artery
ICP	Intracranial pressure
ICU	Intensive care unit

IIH	Idiopathic intracranial hypertension
INR	International normalized ratio
IMRT	Intensity-modulated radiotherapy
ISAT	International Sub-Arachnoid Aneurysm Trial
IV	Intravenous
IVH	Intraventricular haemorrhage
LAICA	Left anterior inferior cerebellar artery
LFT	Liver function tests
LH	Luteinizing hormone
LICA	Left internal carotid artery
LP	Lumbar puncture
LPICA	Left posterior inferior cerebellar artery
LR	Lindegaard ratio
LVA	Left vertebral artery
MAP	Mean arterial pressure
MCA	Middle cerebral artery
MI	Myocardial infarction
MMSE	Mini-Mental State Examination
MRA	Magnetic resonance angiography
MRC	Medical Research Council
MRI	Magnetic resonance imaging
MRS	Magnetic resonance spectroscopy
NAA	N-acetyl aspartate
NAI	Non-accidental injuries
NF1/2	Neurofibromatosis type 1/2
NICU	Neuro-intensive care unit
NPH	Normal pressure hydrocephalus
NSAID	Non-steroidal anti-inflammatory drug
OGM	Olfactory groove meningioma
OLIF	Oblique lateral interbody fusion),
OPLL	Ossification of the posterior longitudinal ligament
PCNSL	Primary central nervous system lymphoma
Pcomm artery	Posterior communicating artery
PE	Pulmonary embolism
PEEP	Positive end expiratory pressure
PET	Positron emission tomography
PICU	Paediatric intensive care unit
PLIF	Posterior lumbar interbody fusion
PNET	Primitive neuroectodermal tumours
PR	per rectum
PSA	Prostate-specific antigen
PTC	Pseudotumour cerebri
PXA	Pleomorphic xanthoastrocytoma
qds	*quater die sumendum* (four times daily)

RICA	Right internal carotid artery
RPCA	Right posterior cerebral artery
RSCA	Right superior cerebellar artery
RTA	Road traffic accident
RVA	Right vertebral artery
SAH	Subarachnoid haemorrhage
SDH	Subdural haemorrhage
SEGA	Subependymal giant cell astrocytoma
SHO	Senior house officer
SIADH	Syndrome of inappropriate antidiuretic hormone secretion
SM	Spetzler–Martin
SNUC	Sinonasal undifferentiated carcinoma
SOS	Site of surgery
SRS	Stereotactic radiosurgery
TBI	Traumatic brain injury
TCD	Trans-cranial Doppler
TEDs	Thromboembolic-deterrent stockings
TLIF	Transforaminal lumbar interbody fusion
TORCH	**TO**xoplasmosis, **R**ubella, **C**ytomegalovirus, **H**erpes simplex
U&E	Urea & electrolytes
VA	Ventriculoatrial
VP	Ventriculoperitoneal
VS	Vestibular schwannomas
WCC	White cell count
WFNS	World Federation of Neurological Surgeons
WHO	World Health Organization
WI	Weighted image
XLIF	Extreme lateral interbody fusion
XR	X-ray

Contributors

Campbell Baguley, *Consultant Otolaryngologist, Wellington Regional Hospital, Newton, Wellington, New Zealand*

Selena E. Briggs, *Vice Chair, Department of Otolaryngology, MedStar Washington Hospital Center; Professor, Department of Otolaryngology, Georgetown University, Washington DC, USA*

Jonathan G. Bull, *Consultant Neurosurgeon, St Bartholomew's Hospital, West Smithfield, London, UK*

Adel Helmy, *Associate Professor, NIHR Brain Injury MedTech Co-operative, Department of Clinical Neuroscience, University of Cambridge, Cambridge, UK*

Sabrina M. Heman-Ackah, *Neurosurgery Chief Resident, Department of Neurosurgery, University of Pennsylvania, Philadelphia, PA, USA*

Reuben D. Johnson, *Consultant Neurosurgeon and Clinical Lead, Wellington Regional Hospital, Newton, Wellington, New Zealand*

Timothy Lawrence, *Consultant Paediatric Neurosurgeon & Craniofacial Surgeon, Nuffield Department of Clinical Neurosciences, John Radcliffe Hospital, Oxford, UK*

W. Adriaan Liebenberg, *Neurosurgeon, Private Practice, Founder of The Health Collective/ Founder and Director of The Pain Collective, Cape Town, South Africa*

Sean Martin, *Nuffield Department of Surgical Sciences, John Radcliffe Hospital, Oxford, UK*

James Moore, *Consultant Anaesthetist and Intensive Care Physician, Head of Trauma Services, Wellington Regional Hospital, Newton, Wellington, New Zealand*

Simon Robinson, *Otrolaryngologist, Wakefield Specialist Centre, 99 Rintoul Street, Newton, Wellington, New Zealand*

Saurabh Sinha, *Consultant Neurosurgeon, Department of Paediatric Neurosurgery,Sheffield Children's Hospital, Sheffield, UK*

Agadha Wickremesekera, *Consultant Neurosurgeon, Wellington Regional Hospital, Newton, Wellington, New Zealand*

Yuhan Wei, *Neurosurgeon, Neurosurgical Offices, Auckland City Hospital, Auckland, New Zealand*

1

Duties and Responsibilities of the Junior Neurosurgical Trainee

Yuhan Wei, Sean Martin, and Timothy Lawrence

CONTENTS

OVERVIEW AND GENERAL DUTIES

Junior posts in neurosurgery are generally filled by two groups of doctors: the first is the career neurosurgeon, a trainee who has successfully entered a competitive neurosurgical training programme; the other group is of rotational trainees who may or may not have an interest in neurosurgery as their desired future career path. The terminology for the latter varies by region: for example, the term senior house officer (SHO) may be used in the UK, senior resident in Australia, or house officer transitioning to junior registrar in New Zealand. We will circumvent this problem by using the terms 'junior neurosurgical trainee', or simply 'neurosurgical trainee'.

Regardless of career aspirations, neurosurgery represents an invaluable learning environment for motivated, hard-working individuals. Neurosurgical trainees will leave the job having developed vital skills in caring, on the ward and in the neuro-intensive care unit (NICU), for complex patients with a variety of both surgical and medical problems. There will be exposure to some of the most exciting advances in medicine in a specialty that is rapidly developing with new technology and scientific discovery.

Neurosurgical pathology is extremely diverse and is often affected by other body systems, and often affects them in turn. A sound understanding of systemic disease is, therefore, essential. A well-organized junior team will have plenty of opportunities to go to theatre and to outpatient clinics, and it is in these places that a full appreciation of neurosurgery is achieved. Attending theatre, rounds on the NICU and inpatient wards, and follow-up clinics reveal the whole scope of neurosurgical practice, and what can be achieved in the short, medium, and long term for conditions affecting the nervous system.

The duties of the junior neurosurgical trainee centre mainly around the inpatient wards. This includes taking care of the patients before and after surgery, both elective and emergency, ensuring that they are fit for their operations, and responding quickly to any changes in their condition. Neurosurgery registrars spend a large amount of their time in the operating theatre, in clinic, or running the on-call service, and so the safety and care of the patients on the ward is very much in the hands of the more junior trainees. The importance of the junior trainee's position in the working day cannot be overstated: they are the critical team member who ensures that patients make it to the operating theatre safely and are cared for appropriately afterwards.

Neurosurgery is, understandably, often a life-altering event for patients and their families, for whom the junior trainee is usually the first point of contact; this is a responsibility that should not be underestimated, but it is also a privilege that is extremely rewarding if treated accordingly.

Occasionally, when the on-call registrar is busy, it may be necessary for the junior trainee to carry the receiving bleep. This can be daunting at first, but it is an excellent opportunity to learn the essentials of managing an acute neurological service. A short section on how to take neurosurgical referrals is included at the end of this chapter.

ORGANIZATION OF THE WORKING DAY

Clearly, there will be variation in practice and organization of the working day between different units, but below we have laid out a framework that should be broadly recognizable as a usual day's work in any neurosurgical service.

The day usually begins with a morning handover meeting attended by the on-call teams from the previous day and the current day, together with a variable number of consultants and trainees, and other allied specialties (such as neuroradiology). The format differs between units, but usually will consist of the junior trainees and registrar on call presenting the new admissions and referrals from the previous day, discussing outstanding emergency or urgent operations, and clinical priorities on the ward. The presenting doctors are often asked detailed questions by the consultants on the history, examination and scans of the previous day's admissions and referrals, and questions usually follow on the management options.

This is an excellent forum in which to learn about neurosurgery, and the opportunity should be taken to ask questions of the consultants, especially on more controversial issues. It is worthwhile presenting patient history and examination findings before presenting the scan in order to allow others to localize lesions and formulate a differential diagnosis on the basis of history and examination alone.

After the meeting, the morning round will probably begin on the NICU, and will be led by the neurosurgical registrars, consultants, and the intensive care team. Often, the junior trainees will be expected to present formally the patients and their progress over the last day, allowing the registrars and consultants to make decisions regarding further management. As the trainee will probably be bleeped during the day to deal with problems that may arise, it is essential that they understand these patients' clinical status, management plans, and what is happening with the patient. Care should be taken to document the following:

- Members of the team present.
- Diagnosis.
- Any surgery undertaken so far and number of days post-op.
- Neurological status.
- Sedation or use of other specialized drugs.
- Cardiorespiratory status and vasoactive drugs.
- Wound review and evidence of any infection.
- Presence of drains; outputs and prescriptions.
- Advice for the patient's care for the day.
- Head of bed and mobility restrictions.
- Prophylaxis of venous thromboembolism.
- Steroids and anti-epileptics.
- Management plan for the day.

Neurological status will be indicated by the Glasgow Coma Scale (GCS) score (which should be descriptive rather than just numbers!). The pupillary response and any focal deficits must be noted. The usage and details of sedative or other specialized drugs include, for example, propofol, midazolam, and anti-epileptics; reporting of cardiovascular status will mention use of inotropes, type of respiratory support, fraction of inspired oxygen, etc., and specific advice concerning the day's care of the patient will deal with matters such as wound drain, external ventricular drain, and lumbar drain. The management plan should be a clearly numbered list; for example: (1) computed tomography (CT) scan tomorrow; (2) if no changes on CT, wean sedation and reassess neurology; (3) keep intracranial pressure (ICP) <20 mmHg until sedation weaned.

The round will progress to the ward and ideally the juniors should present each patient, that is, name, age, diagnosis, procedure, progress, and current plan. Nursing staff should be given the opportunity to raise any issues. Check-lists for each type of patient are given in the later chapter on the *Ward Management of Neurosurgical Patients* (Chapter 8). However, it is worth bearing a few matters in mind at this point. It is essential to check wounds frequently for signs of infection or cerebrospinal fluid (CSF) leak. Obviously, up-to-date blood results should be available for the round, and particular attention should be paid to reporting daily sodium levels for patients with subarachnoid haemorrhage (SAH) and for patients after pituitary surgery who may also require paired daily blood and serum osmolalities. For patients with tumours, steroids should be reviewed each day to ensure that there is a plan in place for their discontinuation. Patients are rarely discharged on steroids, though a small maintenance dose may be given to tumour patients until they are seen by the oncologist, or to pituitary patients until they are seen by the endocrinologist. We make no apologies for repeating the point: never allow a patient to leave the unit without a plan to stop their steroids, and ensure that follow-up is in place for another clinician to review it at a suitable date. Gastroprotection should be concurrently prescribed for patients on dexamethasone to prevent peptic ulcers. A clear plan should also be made for new or changed prescriptions of anti-epileptic drugs: prophylactic courses should have an end date, and it should be noted whether a patient has had a seizure, as this has implications for driving restrictions. It is advisable to be up to date on histology results and know when they are due, and to ensure that there are dates available for oncology or endocrinology review.

Following the round, the ward jobs tend to consist of ordering scans and referring patients to other specialties (e.g. neurology, ophthalmology, etc.) or back to their local hospitals if the neurosurgical part of their treatment has been completed. Some units allow letters to be dictated, whereas in others, letters will have to be typed. It is best if the junior trainees can find an efficient way of organizing referrals back. Valuable information often goes missing so, if possible, document the name of the consultant who referred the patient to the neurosurgical unit early on. Letters to the local hospital should include a summary of the presentation, details of the procedure, progress so far, a brief note about expected prognosis, details of medication (including plans to stop steroids, and antiepileptics), a plan for removal of staples or sutures, and arrangements for follow-up. Remember that many tumour biopsies are taken in the neurosurgical unit to provide a diagnosis so that definitive treatment can be planned and administered elsewhere.

Repatriating patients to their local hospital is one of the most important jobs that a junior trainee has to do: it should be completed in a timely fashion and the bed manager should be informed once done—if there is no movement of patients out of the unit, there is no space for new patients to come in for emergencies or for elective cases; neurosurgical beds are at a premium in every unit.

Once all the ward jobs have been completed (hopefully by mid-morning!) the rest of the day will consist of covering the ward and NICU, seeing any new admissions, and attending theatre, outpatient clinic, or pre-operative assessment clinic. If there is no afternoon round by the registrar on call, it might be useful to get together with your team before the end of office hours to check that all results are back and acted upon. Ensure that any scans ordered have been completed and reviewed, and management decisions made or agreed by the registrar or consultant. It is the responsibility of the person who signs the request form to make sure that the scans are reviewed, so if you sign it make sure you see the scan and show it to someone who can make a decision. You should ensure that medicines and fluids required overnight are prescribed before you go home (you know your patients better than the night on-call doctor does), and that all patients on tomorrow's list are ready to go to theatre and have relevant blood results and scans available.

Pre-operative assessment clinics are much the same as in other specialties. Assessments are made for fitness for surgery and relevant investigations or specialist reviews organized. It is essential to ensure that anticoagulants and antiplatelet agents are discontinued in good time before most neurosurgical procedures. Most consultants prefer patients to be off all forms of non-steroidal anti-inflammatory drug (NSAID) for at least a few days prior to elective surgery, particularly for intradural procedures, whether cranial or spinal.

In neurosurgery, junior trainees generally do not carry their own receiving bleep, are not asked to go to the Accident and Emergency (A&E) department, and are usually only required to attend a few outpatient clinics. However, in some centres the job is still extremely busy, with hours stretching far beyond those quoted on the rota.

The neurosurgical post demands a high level of responsibility and knowledge. The junior trainees form the basis on which a busy department can function safely and effectively. A good junior trainee will be aware of the complexity of disease in neurosurgical patients, how rapidly a patient's condition may deteriorate, and how vital the junior doctors are to the successful care of their patients. It is essential that the junior trainees work as a team: this is the only way everyone will get a chance to carry the registrar bleep or go to theatre.

TAKING NEUROSURGICAL REFERRALS

Taking neurosurgical referrals is unlike taking referrals in most other surgical specialties you will have worked in. You will not always be able to walk down to the A&E department to see what is going on because frequently the patient will be miles away in another hospital—you are completely reliant on the examination and history-taking skills of the referring doctor, which is also worth remembering if you are ever on the other end of the phone and are referring a patient to neurosurgery. Despite this, you may find that once you have been phoned, the person making the referral will assume you have taken over the care of the patient! There is also often an assumption that all you need is to see the scans. Never accept a referral of the type: 'Have you seen Mr Thompson's scans? Are you going to take him?' Assume that in such cases, Mr Thompson has fixed dilated pupils, a massive diffuse head injury, a clam-shell thoracotomy (but no intravenous access), bilateral open femoral shaft fractures, and has not had any cervical spine films. While this may seem obvious, the importance of obtaining as much of the relevant information as possible at the time of the first call cannot be overemphasized. If the person referring cannot answer all your questions, make sure they understand that advice can be given only when all the information is available.

Remember to be polite—neurosurgical cases can be quite frightening, especially to the uninitiated, and we can all forget things in a crisis. By all means have a look at the scans and present them to your registrar, but make it clear that the referring team is gathering all the facts. The following is the minimum amount of information that should be obtained from the referring team. Don't accept anything less!

DETAILS OF THE REFERRING TEAM

- Name of the referring doctor.
- Contact number of the referring doctor.

- Name of the consultant in charge of the referring team.
- Name of the referring hospital.

These details are essential. It is all too easy to put the phone down after obtaining a great history only to find you don't know which hospital the patient is in. Beware the 5 p.m. referral—the referring doctor might be going off duty. Make sure to ask whether this is the case, and if it is, that you *also* ask for the contact details of their replacement who will be taking over the patient's care.

PATIENT DETAILS

- Name.
- Age.
- Sex
- Date of birth.
- Location (emergency department/ward).
- Unique identifier (NHS number/hospital number/CHI number).

Remember that A&E departments can be quite big, busy, and overcrowded. If a patient is comatose in A&E don't just assume they are in the resuscitation bay!

HISTORY

- Sequence of events.
- Past medical history.
- Drug history.
- Social history.
- Time of the patient's last meal.

Obtain a concise sequence of events and begin to formulate a picture in your mind as to what sort of pathology you may be dealing with (see Chapter 5 on *Neurosurgical History and Examination*). Tailor questions according to pathology: for example, if the history suggests spinal pathology make sure to enquire about sphincter dysfunction. When the history is equivocal, always enquire regarding a history of trauma (e.g. SAH can be traumatic as well as spontaneous). If there is trauma, are there any other significant injuries? In the case of the comatose patient ask about medically reversible causes (e.g.

seizures, blood sugar level, and toxicology). If there was an ictus, ask for details of prodrome, the event, and post-ictal state. Progress after the event should be sought in detail—an eyewitness account can be helpful.

Past medical history and drug history are very important. If a patient has a tumour on their scan it is vital to know whether they have a known primary; similarly, if they have had an acute subdural haemorrhage (ASDH) it is useful to know that they have atrial fibrillation (AF) and are on anticoagulants. It is essential to know about any medicines that may affect blood clotting if there is bleeding or if an operation may be required; remember to ask specifically about warfarin, novel oral anticoagulants, heparin, anti-platelet agents, NSAIDS, and sodium valproate (which can also affect platelet function): a blood count and coagulation screen should be obtained, including relevant drug-specific tests, such as the thrombin clotting time for dabigatran. A brief social history should be obtained, including details about mobility; for example, 'Mrs Jones lives in a warden-controlled residential home, uses two sticks to walk, but is otherwise independent and takes the bus to go shopping'.

EXAMINATION

- ABCDE and other injuries.
- Current GCS.
- Any fluctuations in GCS.
- Pupils: size and reaction to light.
- Cranial nerve abnormalities.
- Peripheral deficits: power and sensation.
- Tone, reflexes, signs of spasticity.
- Cerebellar signs, gait.
- Sphincter dysfunction.
- Observations (obs).

Do not assume that the patient has been assessed and stabilized from other medical issues other than just the neurosurgical one referred to. Enquire specifically about the basic ABCDE assessment (**A**irway maintenance with cervical spine protection; **B**reathing and ventilation; **C**irculation with haemorrhage control; **D**isability/neurological assessment; **E**xposure and environmental control) and any adjunctive investigations (such as eFAST chest, spine, pelvis, and long-bone X-rays) and any other injuries or problems.

After the primary survey, a detailed neurological examination should then be sought. Certain parts of the GCS may be more relevant than others: for example best motor response, which bears prognostic value in severe brain injury (see Chapter 5 on *Neurosurgical History and Examination*). Always make sure that the person referring can break down the GCS into all its components, and ask them what they mean—do not accept 'E1V3M4'! You need to ask them to tell you in words what the eyes, speech, and motor response actually are—after all, the GCS in its truest form does not have any numbers in it. Ask about fluctuations in the GCS: it might be 13 but it might also keep dropping to 5.

Pupil size and reaction need to be documented even if the GCS is 15, as pupil dilatation due to tentorial herniation can occur in the awake patient. Focal neurological deficits can help to localize the lesion: ask about the cranial nerves, power, sensation, proprioception, tone, signs of spasticity, cerebellar function, and gait. Sphincter assessment again is mandatory if a compressive spinal lesion is suspected. Always take a note of the observations to include heart rate, blood pressure, haemoglobin oxygen saturation (sats), respiratory rate, and temperature.

Always be thinking about whether or not the examination findings are consistent with the history, and question any inconsistencies. For example, a history of fits and confusion is unlikely to fit with a GCS of 15.

MANAGEMENT IN THE REFERRING HOSPITAL

- Current location of the patient, and level of care.
- ABCDE assessment and Advanced Trauma Life Support (ATLS).
- Investigations.
- Treatments implemented.
- Plan and documentation.
- Most senior doctor/consultant's opinion.

Enquire about the location of the patient and level of care. Remember that at this stage you are only taking a referral and are not managing the patient. However, if it sounds as though the patient needs to be in a high-dependency area, then suggest that this is discussed in the referring hospital. As touched on in the above section on examination, the ABCDE assessment should be completed and acted upon, and a full ATLS protocol should be carried out for trauma patients. If you are not assured, ask: for example, are you happy with the airway? If a patient has a low conscious level, suggest that the referring team needs to speak to the anaesthetist in their hospital as intubation might be appropriate. Do not insist dogmatically on intubation on the basis of a GCS score, unless it is obvious that the patient will need transferring to NICU or theatre. Remember—the patient may have had a pre-terminal event and intubation may be entirely inappropriate.

Enquire about what investigations have been undertaken (e.g. cervical spine films or a trauma pan-scan; magnetic resonance imaging (MRI) brain and CT chest–abdomen–pelvis for suspected metastatic malignancy; ophthalmology and endocrinology reviews for a pituitary tumour) and what is being sent to you. Make sure you determine what treatments have been initiated in the referring hospital, such as anticoagulant reversal, blood pressure management, hyperosmolar therapy, steroids, anti-epileptics, etc.

PLAN

You should always discuss the plan before you put the phone down, and document it clearly on your referral card/book/online system. The consultation may be completed at the first phone call, or the plan might be that you will discuss the case and scans with your registrar or consultant and get back to the referring team. However, the referring team may also need to conduct further investigations, or consultations with other specialties, or to arrange for an anaesthetist to be involved, before discussing further.

WRITE IT DOWN!

If you have only jotted notes during the consultation, make sure that it is then formally documented before handing over to your colleagues. Your documentation may be the only evidence of the advice that you have given. You should always date and time these entries, that is, when the information was given to you, and also when you gave advice, if it was not at the same time.

2 Overview of Neurosurgical Patients

Jonathan G. Bull

CONTENTS

INTRODUCTION

Neurosurgery, like other specialties, is divided into subgroups and it is helpful to have some understanding of these. Boundaries between subspecialties may appear arbitrary and there is considerable overlap between them. In the past, an individual's practice would evolve during their Consultant career. Increasingly, as trainees undertake subspecialty fellowships, their practice is becoming more defined. In some units, for example, a surgeon's practice may be entirely spinal, and perhaps even resigning from general emergency on-call duties.

There have also been significant changes in the scope and nature of many surgical specialties. Neurosurgery is no exception, and surgeons now work very much within multidisciplinary teams. This aids decision-making, typified by an epilepsy surgery service where a single surgeon requires a large team of neurologists, neurophysiologists, neuropsychologists, and specialist nurses to ensure that the most appropriate patients are selected for surgical treatment.

This approach has developed in response to the evolution of new treatment modalities, particularly in vascular neurosurgery. For example, the

International Sub-Arachnoid Aneurysm Trial (ISAT) demonstrated significant benefits, in some cases, of endovascular coiling of an aneurysm over surgical clipping. Interventional neuroradiologists are fully involved in discussions over treatment of these patients, and in many units many aneurysms will be treated by the neuroradiology team, leaving the more challenging for surgery: not ideal training cases, and hence the need to undertake subspecialty fellowships.

VASCULAR NEUROSURGERY

Vascular neurosurgery remains a subspecialty associated with the management of often very ill patients, the mainstay being patients with subarachnoid haemorrhage (SAH) and associated aneurysms and entailing the non-operative management of SAH. Treatment decisions are undertaken in conjunction with interventional neuroradiologists and investigation by computed tomography angiogram (CTA), magnetic resonance angiography (MRA), and/or formal catheter angiogram (with or without coiling). Vascular abnormalities, such as arteriovenous malformations (AVMs) and dural arteriovenous fistulas, may be managed by operative or interventional means. Increasingly, some cases are managed by stereotactic radiosurgery. Cavernomas may be managed through watchful waiting, the key role of the surgeon being to give reassurance and thought as to the correct time for treatment: the literature has disparate views on the re-bleed risk. Surgeons are also carrying out bypass surgery (external to internal carotid) and carotid procedures (endarterectomies).

PITUITARY NEUROSURGERY

This encompasses the surgical treatment of hormone-secreting pituitary adenomas in cases where medical therapy has failed, or of space-occupying non-hormone-producing adenomas with the aim of preventing blindness and of reducing compression of brain tissue. Surgery is typically undertaken trans-sphenoidally, and more so endoscopically utilizing the access through the sphenoid sinus, although an intracranial approach may be necessary in some cases. Pituitary lesions are managed by a multidisciplinary team with endocrinologists and specialist nurses providing pre- and post-operative reviews of hormonal supplementation.

SKULL-BASE NEUROSURGERY

This is a specialty embracing the treatment of tumours of the clivus, dorsum sellae, cerebello-pontine angle, around the third ventricle, foramen magnum, and parasellar area. The skull-base subspecialty has evolved dramatically since the first successful resection of a vestibular schwannoma in Edinburgh in 1896. Procedures are often undertaken with ENT surgeons (translabyrinthine approach), though the subspecialty is shrinking in terms of operative intervention, as cases are increasingly treated by using stereotactic radiosurgery. The cases that remain are more challenging, again necessitating subspecialty training. A large group of patients exists where the surgeons and patients elect for a watch-and-wait approach with often lengthy pre-operative observation and post-operative follow-up.

SPINAL NEUROSURGERY

Spinal neurosurgery encompasses more than half of neurosurgical practice, with significant overlap with orthopaedic spinal surgery. Spinal neurosurgeons manage a great range of pathologies: degenerative conditions managed by decompression of the spinal cord and nerve roots by means of laminectomies, discectomies, and foraminotomies posteriorly. Anterior approaches may be undertaken, commonly in the cervical spine and less so in the thoracic and lumbar spine, necessitating thoracotomy or laparotomy. Furthermore, in patients with spinal instability, fusion of the vertebral column with instrumentation is often undertaken. The practice of fusion for back pain is increasingly coming under scrutiny. In the lumbar and thoracic spine, pedicle screw fixation or inter-body fusion techniques are employed. Complex spine procedures, which were previously common in rheumatoid patients, have decreased with the advent of efficacious medical management. In addition, spinal neurosurgeons may be involved in the treatment of developmental abnormalities and deformities of the spine, including scoliosis surgery.

PAEDIATRIC NEUROSURGERY

Paediatric neurosurgery is increasingly a separate specialty, necessitating subspecialty training. Nonetheless, paediatric neurosurgeons treat pathologies like those in adult patients in addition to the developmental abnormalities seen in children (see Chapter 14, on *Paediatric Neurosurgery*). Specifically, cases associated with spinal and cranial dysraphisms, CSF circulation problems, and oncology form the bulk of the work load. Some paediatric neurosurgeons undertake subspecialty work such as craniofacial work with plastic and maxillofacial surgeons. The number of purely paediatric neurosurgeons is growing. Surgeons may cover paediatric emergencies on call, which most commonly involve shunt problems, subsequently handing on specific cases for urgent, rather than emergency, treatment.

FUNCTIONAL NEUROSURGERY

Functional neurosurgery is a fascinating and rapidly evolving subspecialty. Surgeons working in this area undertake the surgical treatment of chronic pain, movement disorders, neuropsychiatric disorders, and epilepsy. This is usually undertaken in association with neurophysiologists and neurologists. Pre-operative planning for deep brain stimulation procedures is complex, and the surgery may be undertaken with the patients awake during the stereotactic insertion of stimulators (depth electrodes). Follow-up and adjustment of the devices is often done by neurophysiologists and specialist nurses.

Intractable dysaesthetic pain following failed back surgery or trauma can be treated with spinal cord stimulators, posterior rhizotomies, or stimulation/ablation of the periaquaductal grey area or areas of the thalamus. Functional neurosurgeons may also be involved in the placement of spinal cord stimulators to treat chronic pain, and of baclofen pumps to treat spasticity.

Neurosurgeons involved in the management of epilepsy patients will carry out procedures to place intracranial electrode grids to help establish an epileptic focus prior to any subsequent ablation or resection procedures. Epileptic patients may also be treated with vagal nerve stimulators and deep brain stimulation.

PAIN NEUROSURGERY

Some neurosurgeons treat neurovascular compression syndromes, such as trigeminal neuralgia and hypoglossal neuralgia. Surgery is considered once medical treatment has failed or when side-effects can no longer be tolerated. A variety of methods is used, ranging from short-term local anaesthetic injections when patients are in extremis, to ablative procedures such as radiofrequency rhizotomies. Microvascular decompression surgery to treat trigeminal neuralgia is again typically performed by a limited number of surgeons in a unit.

TRAUMA NEUROSURGERY

Trauma neurosurgery, currently considered part of the role of the general neurosurgeon, is evolving, with large units having subspecialists who are interested in the non-operative and post-operative management of patients. Patients with head injuries will be admitted and treated in the first few hours by a general neurosurgeon and in such units referred to the subspecialist. The use of intracranial pressure monitors and probes for cerebral oxygenation and temperature as well as microdialysis are aiding treatment development in this field. Trauma neurosurgery encompasses intracranial injuries, such as traumatic haemorrhage (subdural, extradural, intracerebral haematomas), and diffuse axonal injury, skull fractures, and spinal trauma.

RADIOSURGERY

Oncologists and some neurosurgeons treat patients with external radiation. The Linac accelerator, which works with conventional radiation beams, and the Gamma knife (Cobalt 60 source) and Cyber knife, are focused external radiation sources that can be concentrated on localized areas of the brain, minimizing the effect on surrounding structures. The scope of these treatments has extended to include treatment of AVMs, skull-base tumours, and also some cases of neuralgia such as trigeminal neuralgia where surgery is not appropriate or will not be tolerated. The time to determine successful effect is longer, with patients treated for AVMs having to wait up to 2 years for conclusions with regard to the treatment outcome. This area of treatment is increasingly replacing open neurosurgical techniques.

ONCOLOGICAL NEUROSURGERY

Oncological neurosurgery is a large field and has generally constituted part of the general neurosurgical remit. However, there is an increasing demand for neurosurgeons who subspecialize in neuro-oncology. Neuro-oncological surgery involves biopsy and resection of tumours both the spine and the brain. Neuro-onclogy is a multidisciplinary subspecialty and surgeons collaborate closely with oncologists in determining the appropriate management of these patients. There are currently many avenues of research into radiological methods of determining the nature of tumours, with the potential to diminish the need for biopsy.

GENERAL NEUROSURGERY

The ambit of the general neurosurgeon is usually taken to include spinal, trauma, oncology, CSF diversion, and posterior fossa and peripheral nerve surgery. Typically, most neurosurgeons will cover these cases on call but may hand on more complex cases subsequently. Most surgeons are now appointed with a subspecialty interest, providing general neurosurgery cover on call.

3

Neurosurgical Pathology

Cranial Disorders

W. Adriaan Liebenberg

CONTENTS

MANIFESTATIONS OF CEREBRAL DISEASE

As neurosurgeons, we deal mostly with either compressive or destructive lesions. The history usually gives an accurate idea of the type of pathology involved, and this usually is indicated by the length of the history and the progression. Patients who have sudden acute episodes with associated headache and immediate deficit or loss of consciousness have usually had a vascular type of incident, whereas people who present with progressive mental dysfunction, speech difficulties, and progressive limb deficits usually have a tumour of some description. Sometimes patients present with seizures alone, and this is quite typical usually of low-grade tumours, or arteriovenous malformation, although this is not exclusively true. When presented with a patient who has a history of dysfunction and has clinical signs on examination it is important to localize the lesion to the part of the CNS from which it originates. Specific lobes of the brain have specific functions.

FRONTAL LOBES

The frontal lobes are concerned with personality, the cortical control of micturition, and conjugate eye movement. The main function of the frontal lobes, however, is motor function, and the whole motor strip is found in the posterior aspect of the frontal lobe, in front of the central sulcus. Penfield's homunculus demonstrates which part of the cortex is responsible for which part of the body. A lesion on the convexity on the lateral side will cause dysfunction of the facial muscles, whereas lesions parasagittally in midline will cause dysfunction of the legs. Speech is also controlled by the lower part of the motor strip, the so-called Broca's speech area, and lesions here result in an expressive dysphasia. Seizures are common with frontal lobe lesions.

PARIETAL LOBES

The parietal lobes are quite small; located behind the central sulcus, they are mostly concerned with recording sensory information and spatial orientation. Speech is relayed via the supramarginal and angular gyri. The other important part of the parietal lobes is the visual association area, governing awareness of the images recorded in the occipital lobes. Lesions in the parietal lobes therefore lead to cortical sensory loss, dysphasia in a dominant hemisphere lesion (speech is usually located in a dominant hemisphere), and dyspraxia (inability to move limbs appropriately because of a loss of spatial orientation) in a non-dominant hemisphere. A parietal lesion would also lead to a homonymous hemianopia or an attention hemianopia (see Chapter 5, on *Neurosurgical History and Examination*).

OCCIPITAL LOBES

The occipital lobes are truly small and are mainly concerned with visual function. Lesions in the occipital lobe lead to blindness in the contralateral eye with sparing of the pupillary reflex, which, as we shall see, loops only as far back as the brainstem.

TEMPORAL LOBES

Once again, seizures are a large part of the manifestation of temporal lobe pathology, and, as we shall see, a contralateral upper quadrant hemianopia is seen when the fibres of Meyer's loop are affected. The centre for receptive speech discrimination—Wernicke's area—is located in the superior temporal gyrus, and lesions in this area lead to receptive dysphasia. Bilateral lesions in the temporal lobe can also cause memory deficit.

SUMMARY

- Frontal lobes
  - Motor function
  - Speech
  - Micturition
  - Conjugate eye movements
  - Personality
  - Higher mental function
- Parietal lobes
  - Sensory awareness
  - Spatial awareness (non-dominant hemisphere)
  - Speech (dominant hemisphere)
  - Visual tracts
- Occipital lobes
  - Vision
- Temporal lobes
  - Vision
  - Receptive speech

TYPES OF CENTRAL NERVOUS SYSTEM (CNS) PATHOLOGY

Following a full clinical evaluation and after localizing the pathology to a particular region of the nervous system, special investigations are ordered to confirm the presumptive diagnosis. Following the results of the special test, a firm diagnosis may be made in some instances, and in some instances the clinician may be left with a differential diagnosis of the most likely pathologies. This is impossible without understanding the pathology of the CNS. The main types of CNS pathology that concern neurosurgeons are malignancy, infection, inflammation, vascular abnormalities, and abnormal CSF flow patterns.

INTRACRANIAL MALIGNANCY

There are many ways of classifying CNS tumours. Pathologically, these tumours can be classified according to cell type, for example glial tumours or tumours of neuroepithelial origin. However, it can be extremely useful to consider tumours according to their anatomical site of origin in the CNS. In the forebrain and cerebellum, there are tumours that are inside the parenchyma of the brain and tumours that are outside the parenchyma of the brain but still inside the cranium. The first group are known as intra-axial tumours, and the second group of tumours are called extra-axial tumours. What follows here is a discussion of the types of tumour that most commonly occur in different parts of the intracranial compartment. This is not a dry and formal description of pathology per se. Rather, it is a more general discussion which aims to include some insights into the particular problems different tumours present to the patient and clinician. Spinal tumours are considered later.

The AANS (American Association of Neurological Surgeons) classification is the most user-friendly of the many classifications in use today.

I. Primary tumours of the brain
  A. Gliomas
    Lowest-grade tumours
      Pilocytic astrocytoma
      Subependymal giant cell astrocytoma
      Protoplasmic astrocytoma
      Ganglioglioma
      Xanthomatous astrocytoma
      Subependymoma
    Lower-grade malignancies
      Fibrillary (gemistocytic, protoplasmic) astrocytoma
      Ependymoma
      Oligodendroglioma
      Mixed oligo-astrocytoma
      Optic nerve glioma
    Higher-grade malignancies
      Anaplastic astrocytoma

- Anaplastic oligodendroglioma
- Anaplastic mixed glioma
- Highest-grade malignancies
    - Glioblastoma multiforme
    - Gliosarcoma
    - Gliomatosis cerebri

B. Meningioma
- Benign
- Atypical
- Malignant

C. Primitive neuroectodermal tumours (PNET)
- Medulloblastoma
- Ependymoblastoma
- Pineoblastoma

D. Pituitary tumours
- Pituitary adenoma
- Pituitary carcinoma
- Craniopharyngioma
- Rathke's cleft cyst

E. Pineal tumours
- Pineal cyst
- Pineocytoma
- Pineoblastoma
- Germinoma
- Mixed germ cell tumour
- Pineal gliomas
- Pineal teratoma

F. Choroid plexus tumours
- Choroid plexus papilloma
- Choroid plexus carcinoma

G. Other, more benign primary tumours
- Neurocytoma
- Dysembroplastic neuroepithelial tumour (DNT)
- Lipoma
- Hemangioblastoma
- Hamartoma
- Teratoma

H. Tumours of nerves and/or nerve sheaths
- Neuroma

Schwannoma
Neurofibroma

I. Cysts
    Colloid cyst
    Arachnoid cyst
    Dermoid
    Epidermoid
    Rathke's cleft cyst
    Pineal cyst

J. Other primary tumours, including skull base
    Chondroma
    Chordoma
    Sarcoma
    Gliosarcoma
    Chondrosarcoma
    Rhabdomyosarcoma

K. Primary central nervous system lymphoma (PCNSL)

II. Metastatic brain tumours and carcinomatous meningitis

INTRA-AXIAL TUMOURS

The most common intra-axial tumours are metastatic tumours that have spread mostly from the lung in males and breast in females (but also from the skin, kidney, and prostate). The second most common intra-axial tumours are glial cell tumours and are known as gliomas.

Metastatic tumours

Metastatic tumours are sometimes treated by surgical excision. However, they are frequently multiple, and treating the cerebral metastases does not remove the primary tumour. The exception is in patients with fully treated primary tumours and single superficial metastases; these patients are quite often offered surgery, plus adjuvant therapy.

The main aim in patients with metastatic tumours is tissue diagnosis; chest X-ray, breast examination in females, and computerized tomography (CT) scanning of the abdomen are indicated to try to find a more accessible lesion from which to obtain a tissue diagnosis. If the hunt for the primary is unsuccessful, the clinician would then offer a stereotactic biopsy of one of the lesions which is thought would be the most accessible and least likely to lead to complications.

Glial tumours (gliomas)

Tumours are graded according to their histological characteristics, and four features are searched for: mitosis, nuclear polymorphism, neovascularity, and necrosis. Tumours which have only mitotic features or nuclear polymorphism are usually graded lowest grade and lower grade, whereas where there is evidence of new blood vessel formation the tumours are usually classed as higher grade. Tumours where the tissue growth is so rapid that the tissue outstrips its blood supply, and therefore undergoes areas of necrosis, are defined as highest-grade tumours, also called glioblastoma multiforme. Because glial tumours are made up of brain tissue, they frequently appear as irregular bits of brain on CT scans before the administration of contrast, and in cases of low-grade tumours there is no enhancement with contrast. The one exception to this rule is the juvenile pilocytic astrocytoma, which enhances vividly, although it remains a lowest-grade tumour. The usual reason for enhancement of a tumour is because of the new blood vessels forming inside the tumour, and enhancement with contrast denotes a high-grade tumour. If there is added necrosis, it then becomes a fairly obvious diagnosis of highest-grade tumour. We therefore find that most irregular-looking enhancing tumours are either metastases (since these also have neovascularity) or higher-grade/highest-grade gliomas. Both these tumours carry a grim prognosis and more than 70% of patients with these diagnoses pass away within 9 months.

These malignancies unfortunately are untreatable and palliation is the only option. The decision to offer a debulking procedure usually hinges on the patient's age, general condition, and Karnofsky score (a score derived from the patient's ability to function in everyday life—see Chapter 15, Table 15.7). Patients who present at an advanced age with malignant tumours carry the worst prognosis. This is due to the fact that they are medically less fit, and also because these tumours are usually much more aggressive biologically than tumours that present in younger patients. The basis of treatment of these malignant tumours is a debulking procedure without damage to normal brain, followed by radiotherapy. Only a single treatment of radiotherapy can be given to any one patient, and therefore regrowth after radiotherapy leaves only the option of further debulking and chemotherapy. Most patients, as noted earlier, do not survive very long, but there are a few notable exceptions, and therefore if patients have good Karnofsky scores and wish to have their tumours treated, they should be offered treatment.

OLIGODENDROGLIOMAS

Another type of primary brain tumour is the oligodendroglioma, which is made up of oligodendrocytes. This is a slow-growing tumour, which enhances irregularly with contrast, just like the malignant tumours, but is usually found in the frontal lobes and may have lots of calcification in it.

Because calcium is hyperdense like bone, tumours of this type are usually hyperdense on CT scan before contrast and are relatively easily diagnosed. They are more benign than the malignant gliomas, and patients have been known to survive a long time with these tumours. Debulking and chemotherapy is usually indicated in the anaplastic variant, with these tumours being very chemo-sensitive.

NON-HODGKIN'S B-CELL LYMPHOMA

Another tumour which is hyperdense before contrast, but less intensely so, and usually located in a periventricular location, is non-Hodgkin's B-cell lymphoma. Because the brain does not have a lymphatic system, all these are theoretically metastatic tumours, although there is a distinct difference between patients with a known systemic lymphoma and patients in whom the tumour appears to function as a primary brain tumour. These tumours are particularly common in patients with HIV-AIDS. They enhance with contrast quite uniformly. They carry quite a grim prognosis and usually need multimodal therapy.

INTRAVENTRICULAR TUMOURS

Intraventricular tumours are fairly rare, and the differential diagnosis would be tumours arising from the arachnoid cap cells (meningiomas), from the choroid plexus (papillomas or carcinomas), from the subependymal lining (subependymal giant cell astrocytomas), and from the ependyma (ependymomas). Another benign intraventricular lesion is a colloid cyst, a hyperdense cystic lesion in the third ventricle, which obstructs the foramina of Munro and can lead to sudden death. Midline tumours in the pituitary fossa and pineal region can also invade and extend into the ventricular system because of its close proximity. These are, however, extra-axial tumours.

POSTERIOR FOSSA TUMOURS

In adults, an intra-axial posterior fossa tumour is either a metastatic tumour, a haemangioblastoma, or more infrequently, a glioma. Haemangioblastomas are benign tumours, which consist of a largely cystic component and a small mural module. They can usually be excised quite successfully with surgery. In a small number of cases, a posterior fossa haemangioblastoma can be part of von Hippel Lindau syndrome. This syndrome is typified by the presence of two or more of the following:

- A positive family history of von Hippel Lindau (autosomal dominant inheritance)
- Posterior fossa haemangioblastoma
- A retinal haemangioma
- Renal cysts or carcinoma
- Pancreatic cysts or carcinoma
- Epididymal cysts
- A phaeochromocytoma.

A small number of patients also suffer from increased red blood cell production secondary to excess erythropoietin secretion.

EXTRA-AXIAL TUMOURS

Meningiomas

Meningiomas arise from the arachnoid cap cells in the dura and are mostly benign tumours. They arise from the covering of the brain and cause symptoms and signs by compressing the brain just as an extra-axial collection of subdural or extradural blood would. They have also been called dural warts due to their appearance. These tumours are peripherally located and are diagnosed by the fact that they always have dural attachments. They are frequently very vascular and the distinguishing sign on CT scanning is that they enhance vividly with contrast. Surgery on these lesions can, therefore, frequently be quite tricky, with great blood loss. To try to prevent this they are often embolized pre-operatively to reduce their vascularity.

Pituitary region tumours

Brain tumours in the pituitary region are also extra-axial, and the differential diagnosis for tumours in the pituitary region would be pituitary adenoma, metastasis, meningioma, vascular cerebral aneurysm, epidermoid tumours, germ cell tumours, arachnoid cysts, or craniopharyngiomas.

Pituitary adenomas

Pituitary adenomas are either functional (secreting hormones) or non-functional (non-hormone secreting). The more usual hormone-secreting adenomas are prolactinomas, which may be micro-adenomas (<1 cm), mesoadenomas (1–2 cm), or macroadenomas (>2 cm). There are also cortisol-producing adenomas (usually micro-adenomas), growth hormone-producing adenomas, or thyroid-stimulating hormone-producing adenomas.

Prolactinomas

Prolactinomas cause the clinical picture of galactorrhoea and amenorrhoea in women, and impotence and hypogonadism in men. Cortisol-producing adenomas cause Cushing's disease and growth hormone-producing adenomas produce acromegaly in adults and gigantism in children.

Craniopharyngiomas

Craniopharyngiomas are benign lesions which take a long time to grow but cause problems because of compression of the hypothalamus and obstruction of CSF flow. These tumours are thought to arise from remnants of Rathke's cleft, and are classified as adamantomatous or papillary. The adamantomatous type is found in children and is more aggressive; the papillary type is found in adults and is less aggressive. These tumours have an epithelial lining and enlarge slowly by the shedding of this epithelium into the cavity. The resulting keratin and cholesterol crystals cause this tumour to be different on imaging from a macroadenoma. On CT scanning, they usually have multiple areas of calcification and enhance with contrast; on magnetic resonance imaging (MRI), they have a variable appearance but are frequently hyperintense on T1 and T2, indicating not just the fluid content but also fat content due to the cholesterol crystals. Children will usually present with growth retardation, other pituitary deficiencies, and visual defects. Adults are more likely to present with visual field defects and pituitary dysfunction.

Aneurysms

Aneurysms can present like tumours with mass effect, and, if they are large, they are visible on CT scanning and enhance with contrast, just as tumours would do. Taking a biopsy from an aneurysm unfortunately leads to drastic consequences and one must take care not to fall into this trap. Angiography is, therefore, a useful investigation if there is any doubt.

Pineal region tumours

Tumours in the pineal region (just posterior to the third ventricle) are either made up of the substance of the pineal gland (pinealomas and pinealoblastomas), or are germ-cell tumours. Pinealomas are tumours with fairly good prognosis. Pinealoblastomas are very aggressive tumours. Germ-cell tumours are either germinomas or teratomas, and they can frequently be diagnosed by doing serum markers for human chorionic gonadotrophin (β-HCG), fetal alkaline phosphatase, or alpha-fetoprotein. They are usually extremely radiosensitive and there is also great controversy over whether they should be resected, biopsied, or whether they should undergo radiotherapy without any form of surgery.

Cerebellopontine angle tumours

Tumours in the cerebellopontine angle are either acoustic neuromas (vestibular schwannomas), meningiomas, metastases, arachnoid cysts, or epidermoid tumours.

Vestibular schwannomas are nerve sheath tumours arising on the vestibular nerve; they are slow-growing, benign tumours and frequently are associated with neurofibromatosis type 1 (NF1, von Recklinghausen's disease) and neurofibromatosis type 2 (NF2). The gene for NF1 is located on chromosome 17q11.2 and codes for the protein neurofibromin. Although more than half of NF1 cases are due to an inherited autosomal dominant mutation, there is a significant proportion of sporadic new mutations. NF2 is due to inactivation of the schwannomin gene located on chromosome 22q12.2. Clinical manifestions of NF1 include neurofibromas (commonly on skin), skin abnormalities (café au lait spots), axillary freckling, and Lisch nodules (neurofibromas on the cornea). A small number of these patients also have optic gliomas. Skin abnormalities are less common in NF2 patients, but the presence of bilateral acoustic neuromas is pathognomonic.

Vestibular schwannomas usually present with tinnitus and hearing loss; facial nerve dysfunction is, however, infrequent, even though these tumours usually compress and splay the anterior-located seventh nerve during growth. In tumours smaller than 3 cm, radiosurgery can be quite successful. Patients with larger tumours usually need surgery and most surgeons will monitor small tumours for growth before planning surgery.

One controversy surrounding acoustic neuromas relates to whether they should undergo radiosurgery or open surgery. Situations where radiosurgery might be beneficial include:

- Lesions <3 cm
- Where hearing preservation is important
- Medically unfit patients
- Patients who request it.

Surgery is preferred in patients who are medically fit with large lesions, smaller tumours that are growing, or for patients who have indicated that they would prefer surgery. Another controversy is whether one should aim for a posterior fossa approach, or a translabyrinthine approach. Hearing may be lost whichever approach is used, though it is normally preserved when the posterior fossa approach is undertaken, or when the tumour is very small and a middle fossa approach is undertaken. A middle fossa approach is uncommon in the UK. In the proper hands, these tumours carry a very good prognosis. The main complications are post-operative facial nerve palsies, other cranial nerve damage, and CSF leaks.

Epidermoid tumours

Epidermoid tumours are inclusion tumours and they consist of epithelium. They are enclosed at the time of neural tube folding during embryogenesis and are similar to craniopharyngiomas, in the sense that they slowly enlarge because of epithelial cell desquamation. They are benign tumours but, like the craniopharyngiomas, are impossible to remove totally; luckily, however, they have a very slow growth pattern. Craniopharyngiomas and epidermoid tumours can be treated only with surgery since radiotherapy has little effect on them.

INTRACRANIAL VASCULAR DISORDERS

Bleeding into the cranial space frequently has disastrous consequences. Bleeding can either be intraparenchymal, or can occur in the ventricular, subarachnoid, subdural, or extradural spaces. The mechanism can either be traumatic or spontaneous. It should also be borne in mind that intracranial vascular abnormalities may present without bleeding, due to their compressing local CNS structures.

SPONTANEOUS BLEEDS

Cerebral aneurysms

Spontaneous bleeds are due to abnormal vasculature, and in cases of cerebral aneurysms this is due to weakness and out-pouching of the tunica interna and media through deficient external layers of the blood vessels. This is thought to be a flow-related mechanism and is usually found at vessel bifurcations at the site of the greatest flow. Because the blood vessels are located in the subarachnoid space, aneurysms usually lead to subarachnoid bleeds. There is, however, a percentage of aneurysmal bleeds that either also have a parenchymal component or are completely intraparenchymal with no subarachnoid component. Usually there has been a previous leak which has caused some fibrosis between the fundus of the aneurysm and the parenchyma, so that when this ruptures, instead of leaking into the subarachnoid space, it leaks straight into the parenchyma of the brain, presenting like a cerebrovascular accident (CVA) with a deep blood clot in the brain tissue. Aneurysms are classified according to their size, that is, small (<10 mm), large (>10 mm), giant (>25 mm), or their location, that is, which blood vessel they arose from (internal carotid bifurcation, anterior communicating artery, middle cerebral artery, basilar artery, posterior cerebral artery, posterior inferior cerebellar artery, etc.).

Making the diagnosis of SAH is critical, and there are two components to it. The first is identifying the blood on a CT scan, and the second is demonstrating the breakdown products of blood by spectroscopy. CT scans are 98% sensitive in the first 12 h after the ictus for detection of SAH, but decline in sensitivity after that to about 70% by day 3. It is, therefore, quite possible to miss the diagnosis if CT scans are used as the only diagnostic modality. If blood enters the CSF, the red cells lyse and oxyhaemoglobin is liberated. This is then converted to bilirubin, a process which takes 12 h; this can only happen *in vivo* since the enzyme is found only in the brain itself. CSF in a test tube will therefore produce oxyhaemoglobin secondary to lysis of red blood cells, but not bilirubin because of the absence of the enzyme. The presence of bilirubin can have only one explanation: that there has been blood present in the subarachnoid space for at least 12 h, thus confirming the diagnosis of SAH. This underlies the extreme importance of waiting 12 h before doing the lumbar puncture (LP). If it is done before 12 h it will be negative for bilirubin and may allow blood to be introduced into the subarachnoid space, therefore making any further testing a futile exercise. Doing the LP more than 12 h after the ictus will make the diagnosis successfully in 100% of cases for 2 weeks. The steps involved in making a diagnosis of SAH are summarized in Figure 3.1.

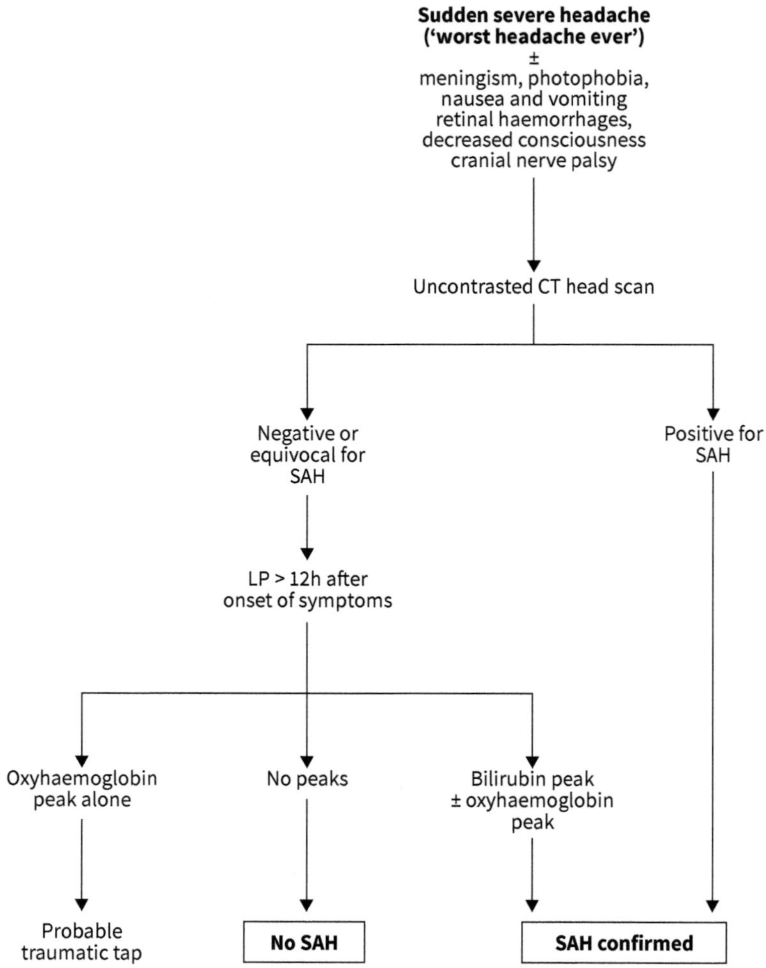

Figure 3.1 Flow-chart demonstrating the decision-making process in the diagnosis of subarachnoid haemorrhage.

Arteriovenous malformations

In an AVM (arteriovenous) there is a short-circuit between the arterial and venous systems without an intervening capillary system; this leads to a shunt. Patients with these conditions may present with a bleed due to the stresses placed on the fragile venous system, with epilepsy secondary to brain irritation, or with a steal phenomenon (where there is cranial dysfunction of certain parts of the brain which are starved of blood supply because of the short circuit). Around 80% of AVMs will have haemorrhaged by the time the patient has reached the age of 50 years, and there is an increased incidence of bleeding during the third and fourth decades. AVMs are classified according to the Spetzler–Martin (SM) grading system, which has a 1–5 grading. Points are given for size, eloquence of brain, and the depth of the draining veins. The size is subdivided into lesions smaller than 3 mm, between 3 and 6 mm, and larger than 6 mm. Location depends on whether the lesion is in an eloquent area (motor/speech area, visual cortex, etc.), and the venous draining system depends on whether it drains superficially or into the central deep veins of the brain. A maximum of 3 points will be given for size, and an extra point added for eloquence or deep-draining vein, giving a maximum score of 5. Small AVMs less than 2 mm can be treated with radiotherapy, but these lesions can take several years before they completely obliterate. Lesions larger than 2 mm that are located superficially in non-eloquent brain can be treated surgically. Other lesions can be treated with a combination of endovascular treatment and surgery, or with endovascular treatment alone. SM grades 4 and 5 are not surgically curable in most instances and it may be safer not to treat.

Cavernous angiomas

Cavernous angiomas are bundles of sinusoidal capillaries which have no arterial supply or venous drainage and have a propensity to bleed. Whereas AVMs can be diagnosed with either conventional, CT, or magnetic resonance angiography, these lesions cannot be demonstrated by angiography and have to be searched for with conventional MRI scanning. They are thought to be surgically treatable if superficial.

Venous angiomas

Venous angiomas are just coils of veins and can be seen as abnormal areas of veins on angiography and usually do not require any treatment. Venous angiomas, AVMs, and cavernous angiomas bleed into the parenchyma and should be searched for in patients who are in their first 6 decades and have had spontaneous bleeds.

STROKES

Strokes can be occlusive or haemorrhagic. Occlusive strokes are due to either venous or arterial occlusion and can have secondary haemorrhagic transformation. Haemorrhagic strokes are usually found in the region of the internal capsule and caudate nuclei where the lenticulostriate branches of the middle cerebral artery are found. This is usually because of micro-aneurysms forming on these arteries, secondary to hypertension. Cerebellar hypertensive bleeds are also common, and, less frequently, hypertensive bleeds can be seen in other areas in the different lobes of the brain (lobar hypertensive haemorrhage). Strokes usually occur in older people and are in deep inaccessible brain, and therefore are usually not treated with surgery. The exceptions would be patients who have a cerebellar hypertensive bleed, who are deteriorating secondary to hydrocephalus because of obstruction of the fourth ventricle, and in young patients with non-dominant hemisphere lobar bleeds which are close to the surface of the brain.

TRAUMATIC BLEEDS

Trauma can lead to haemorrhage, either because of direct impact or because of the secondary effects of rotation. Very high velocity impact, like being struck by a baseball bat, is dampened quite successfully by the immersion of brain in CSF and leads only to focal damage. This usually manifests as skin lacerations and subepidermal and subgaleal haematomas, or skull fractures which can lead to tears in the arteries on the dura, such as the middle meningeal artery which can, in turn, lead to extradural haematomas. We also sometimes see subdural haematomas following focal impact. Slower impact and rotational movements, like being involved in a car accident or falling down stairs, lead to the brain's being shaken around inside the skull. This leads to diffuse brain injury; in a mild form, it leads to concussion, and in a severe form, it leads to the patient remaining vegetative, secondary to diffuse white matter damage. As the brain gets shaken around, tearing of the axons takes place and, on a microscopic basis, the diagnosis of diffuse axonal injury can be made. There are three grades of diffuse axonal injury (Grade 2 and Grade 3 patients carry a poorer prognosis):

- *Grade 1.* Patients who suffer injury with the appropriate mechanism and have point bleeds through the parenchyma of the brain on CT scanning.
- *Grade 2.* The presence of point bleeds in the parenchyma and point bleeds in the corpus callosum.
- *Grade 3.* Point bleeds in the dorsolateral brainstem.

Patients with acute subdural haematomas usually have a component of diffuse brain injury, and the subdural haematomas usually result from rotational movement and tearing of the bridging veins between the brain and the dura. Patients with extradural haematomas frequently do not have intrinsic brain damage, but become symptomatic because of external compression of the brain, and, if treated promptly, usually carry a good prognosis. In patients with acute subdural haematomas, the bleed is a manifestation of a more serious underlying brain injury, and the response to treatment is variable. In practice, we usually see a mixture of focal and diffuse brain damage. Smaller pin-point contusions are frequently interspersed with larger bleeds in the parenchyma, called haemorrhagic contusions. These are usually found at the tips of the temporal lobes where the brain tissue comes into contact with bone, and also the inferior frontal lobe, as the brain moves over the rough orbital ridges of the cranial floor. Finding subarachnoid and intraventricular blood indicates that there has been a severe diffuse brain injury.

Because subdural haematomas are caused by blood vessel disruption and, in severe cases, parenchymal disruption, it follows that the mechanism of injury leading to diffuse brain injury (and, on a microscopic level, axonal injury) is tailor-made to cause subdural collections. Diffuse brain injury and subdural collections are, therefore, frequently found together, carrying a grim prognosis. Point bleeds may enlarge to become haemorrhagic contusions. Trauma can also lead to intraparenchymal bleeds: these are usually close to the cortex or come to the surface of the brain.

Extradural collections are caused by focal trauma. Due to the fact that the underlying brain is frequently undamaged, they carry a good prognosis if evacuated promptly before brain herniation sets in. Mixed pathology, resulting in both a diffuse injury and a focal injury, is seen, for instance, in cases where a patient's head hits the windscreen during a road traffic accident (RTA), followed by the car rolling and subjecting the patient to rotational movements and diffuse injury. Contact and focal injuries also frequently lead to *coup-contracoup*-type injuries where soft tissue swelling and skull fracture denotes the site of impact clinically and on CT scan, and an intraparenchymal haematoma or haemorrhagic contusion in the opposite part of the brain denotes contact injury which occurred when the accelerating brain came into contact with the skull.

DISORDERS OF CSF FLOW

CSF is actively produced by the choroid plexus and ependyma, and is passively absorbed by the arachnoid villi. The ventricular system in the adult contains approximately 150 ml of CSF and approximately 20 ml/h (nearly 0.5 litres per day) is produced. It follows that if there is no resorption, the intracranial cavity will be rapidly overinflated with CSF. The irreversible consequence of this is death. Overinflation with CSF leads to dilatation of the ventricular system (ventriculomegaly).

OBSTRUCTIVE (NON-COMMUNICATING) HYDROCEPHALUS

Ventriculomegaly due to an obstruction of CSF flow between the ventricles is characterized by some of the ventricles being over-inflated whilst the others, being downstream of the obstruction, remain of normal proportion. This type of ventriculomegaly due to an obstruction is called obstructive hydrocephalus or non-communicating hydrocephalus. Obstructive (non-communicating) hydrocephalus can be caused by external compression of the ventricular system by bleeds or tumours, or by intraventricular obstruction by tumours or bleeds. Obstruction within the body of the lateral ventricles will lead to only a portion of that ventricle being dilated. Obstruction at the foramen of Munroe will cause the whole lateral ventricle to dilate (anterior horns, body, posterior horns, atrium, and temporal horns). Obstruction at the level of the third ventricle obstructing both foramina of Munroe will lead to both lateral ventricles becoming dilated, and lesions at the level of the aqueduct will cause dilation of the lateral ventricles as well as the third ventricle, with the fourth ventricle being of normal calibre. In the cases of aqueduct stenosis, the pressure can be relieved by making a small hole in the floor of the third ventricle with an endoscope during a third-ventriculostomy. Ventriculo-peritoneal shunting is a very successful treatment of obstructive hydrocephalus.

COMMUNICATING HYDROCEPHALUS

Hydrocephalus can also occur from failure of CSF absorption by the arachnoid villi. The arachnoid villi can be damaged by infection, SAH, high protein states, and increased venous pressure (e.g. sinus thrombosis). Because there is free communication between the ventricles, this type of ventriculomegaly is known as communicating hydrocephalus. Communicating hydrocephalus can frequently be managed by serial lumbar punctures. If the condition does not clear up, shunting may become necessary.

Hydrocephalus is an excellent demonstration of the Monro-Kellie doctrine which states that because the cranium is rigid, the three tissues contained (brain, blood, and CSF) have an inverse relation to each other, such that an increase in one leads to a decrease or compression of the other two.

NORMAL PRESSURE HYDROCEPHALUS

Normal pressure hydropcephalus is a term used to describe communicating hydrocephalus in the elderly. It is a misnomer, as the intracranial pressure (ICP) is usually raised intermittently. Young people usually have small ventricles and so diagnosing hydrocephalus is quite easy in them. In older people, it can be quite difficult. As we get older our brain atrophies, and in keeping with the Monroe–Kellie doctrine this creates more space for CSF, since the blood flow, which is the third intracranial component, does not increase. CSF is, therefore, seen to fill the spaces created by the shrinking brain and this translates on a CT scan to large ventricles, or ventriculomegaly, and enlarged sulcal and cisternal spaces. This is a normal state of affairs. When the ventricles enlarge disproportionally to the cisternal and sulcal spaces, this is called ventriculo-sulcal disproportion and points to a high pressure within the ventricular system. The diagnosis is then suggested of communicating hydrocephalus in the setting of relatively normal intracranial pressure, or normal pressure hydrocephalus. The pathology behind this is thought to be a reduced absorption of CSF due to obliteration of subarachnoid spaces and arachnoid villi dysfunction. The key to diagnosis rests on the clinical picture, which consists of Adam's triad of dementia, ataxia, and incontinence, as well as the demonstration of a relative increase in CSF pressure of around 20 cm H_2O on LP. The absolute confirmation comes from an improvement in the symptoms (especially gait) following the removal of 30–50 ml of CSF via LP. This then confirms that the symptoms of dementia, ataxia, and incontinence are not due just to a normal ageing process. It follows, therefore, that if fluid could be permanently drained off via a ventriculoperitoneal shunt, a resolution of symptoms might be expected. The principle is that the shunt, having a valve which opens at a certain pressure, would not allow the pressure to rise above that level. The shunt can have either a fixed valve which has a predetermined pressure or a programmable valve which can be adjusted by an external magnet; the second situation allows the valve to be adjusted in the outpatient department to titrate CSF flow, and so obtain the optimum clinical benefit for the patient.

BENIGN INTRACRANIAL HYPERTENSION

Another type of CSF absorption dysfunction which leads to a rise in intracranial pressure is thought to be caused by increased venous sinus pressure and is called benign intracranial pressure or pseudotumour cerebri. This is seen predominantly in young, overweight women and is sometimes due to venous sinus thrombosis. There is certainly nothing benign about this intracranial hypertension despite the name. Due to the decreased absorption of CSF there is a general brain swelling and this diffuses down the length of the optic nerve causing venous stasis in the optic nerve and optic nerve swelling. The main complaints are severe high-pressure headaches and peripheral field deficits. There is no ventriculomegaly (hydrocephalus) in these cases and the ventricles are usually slit-like. Once again, the diagnosis is made by demonstrating high pressures in excess of 20 cm H_2O on LP and demonstrating a decrease in symptoms following drainage of 30–50 ml of CSF. Most cases are managed medically with weight loss, diuretics, and sometimes steroids. The visual symptoms can sometimes be alleviated by optic nerve fenestrations done by the ophthalmologists. The headaches and the optic symptoms can frequently be improved by CSF diversion by a shunt. Because the ventricles are usually quite small, and therefore difficult to cannulate, these patients usually have a lumboperitoneal shunt put in; this consists of a catheter that runs from the intraspinal space at level L3/4 to the peritoneum, running under the skin of the flank.

CAUSES OF SHUNT FAILURE

Many patients with hydrocephalus are treated with a shunt. Most commonly these are ventriculo-peritoneal shunts. However, the distal catheter may drain to a variety of body cavities. Shunts are mechanical devices and so may malfunction, resulting in the return of symptoms of hydrocephalus. Shunt dysfunction may be due to infection, blockage, or mechanical failure.

Blockage due to infection within the first 3 months is usually due to infection with organisms implanted during surgery. *Staphylococcus epidermidis* and *Staphylococcus aureus* are the main culprits with *S. epidermidis* three times more prevalent than *S. aureus*. The predeliction for this organism in shunt infection is due to the fact that it produces a layer of slime under which it hides and which prevents antibiotics and immune cells from entering. That, coupled with the fact that it lives on the skin of both the patient and the theatre staff, makes it the number one suspect.

Shunts should be done by senior staff in daylight hours with the minimum staff in theatre, masks should be worn by all present, the shunt should only be handled with instruments and not hands, and contact between the shunt and the patient's skin should be prevented at all times. Shunt infection can present with meningitis-type symptoms (fever, malaise, headache, photophobia, nausea and vomiting), with raised inflammatory markers, or with symptoms of raised intracranial pressure. Patients may have only raised ICP without external signs of sepsis but with elevated inflammatory markers. The only definite proof of shunt infection is a positive gram stain and culture. It is necessary, therefore, to obtain a CSF sample. This can be done either by tapping the reservoir of the shunt or during open revisional surgery for blockage. We need continually to drain CSF, and therefore we need a catheter to drain the ventricle. Leaving the shunt in and giving antibiotics alone is one possible method of treatment if the shunt is not blocked. However, this only has a 20–30% chance of success. In the still-functioning shunt, removing the distal end to let it drain into a drainage bag whilst giving antibiotics is another option. The CSF collected in the bag is tested from time to time; when the CSF clears of organisms for a good 24–48 h the old shunt is removed and replaced with a new one. This appears to be a very successful way of treating infection of a patent shunt system. In the case of shunt blockage, the best option is to remove the shunt and use an external ventricular drain (EVD) draining into a drainage bag to allow the CSF to clear (as in the option above, where the functioning shunt was externalized distally). Another option is to replace the infected, blocked shunt straight away with a new one. Many neurosurgeons find this option less desirable, however, as placing a piece of plastic into an environment with an abundance of organisms puts the new the shunt at high risk of being colonized and infected (remember the slime layer of *S. epidermidis*). A further discussion on the management of shunt problems can be found in Chapter 8 on *Ward Management of Neurosurgical Patients*.

CONGENITAL DISORDERS PRESENTING IN ADULTHOOD

AQUEDUCT STENOSIS

This is an infrequent cause of obstructive hydrocephalus. Aqueduct stenosis due to congenital anatomic abnormality is not as common as aquired aqueductal stenosis due to external compression.

CHIARI MALFORMATIONS

Chiari (Arnold–Chiari) malformations are divided into four subtypes: patients with types III or IV usually die shortly following birth, so only types I and II, therefore, will be seen in clinical practice. It is important to note that

Chiari malformations are sometimes referred to as hindbrain hernias for reasons that are evident from the following descriptions.

Chiari I

Chiari I is the adult type and usually presents in the 4th decade of life with a mean presentation at 38 years. The deficit is thought to be due to a large foramen magnum, small posterior fossa and possibly perinatal anoxia. The cerebellar tonsils herniate through the foramen magnum and become compressed. On MRI scanning this is seen as tonsils protruding beyond a line drawn from the anterior to the posterior rim of the foramen magnum. Clinically these patients present with cough headaches, myelopathy and tetraspasticity, vertigo, downbeat nystagmus, and the symptoms of syringomyelia. The cough headaches are thought to result from CSF being forced past the tonsils into the posterior fossa. This may also be the cause of an associated syringomyelia. In syringomyelia there are cystic spaces within the spinal cord leading to dysfunction of the sensory modalities, especially spinothalamic sensation, as well as motor dysfunction (spastic paresis being the most common abnormality). Treatment consists of an occipital approach and enlarging the bony rim of the foramen magnum as well as incision of the dura, and duraplasty. Some surgeons do not open the dura as they not only feel that doing so may increase the risk of complications but believe that not doing so does not reduce the success rate of the procedure.

Chiari II

As in Chiari I, the cerebellar tonsils are herniated through the foramen magnum, but in Chiari II the 4th ventricle and medulla have also herniated beyond the line connecting the anterior and posterior rims of the foramen magnum. Chiari II usually presents in infancy with hydrocephalus and respiratory distress (see Chapter 14, on *Paediatric Neurosurgery*). It is usually associated with myelomeningocoele.

INTRACRANIAL INFECTION

Introduction of infection into the nervous system can be by several routes. Direct inoculation can occur during penetrating trauma or during surgery (the infected planes can either be extradural, subdural, or intraparenchymal, depending on the extent and site of the inoculation). Haematogenous spread may occur from more distant pathology. This is frequently the case in patients with infected granulations on their heart valves, poor dental hygiene, or abscesses at other sites. The usual presentation is that of intracranial abscesses. Direct spread may occur from nearby paraspinal abscesses or infected cranial sinuses. This usually leads to the formation of an extradural or subdural empyema.

Patients with fever accompanied by convulsions should be assumed to have intracranial sepsis until proven otherwise. It is as easy as that. This is a condition with a great morbidity and mortality. Urgent CT scanning with contrast administration is required to demonstrate the infection and, if this is negative, MRI scanning should be considered since this is more sensitive. Aggressive treatment with high-dose antibiotics and emergency surgical drainage is indicated. Long-term antibiotics should be administered intravenously for 6 weeks and oral antibiotics continued until all inflammatory markers and imaging have returned to normal. In some cases this may take months. This is especially true for intracranial abscesses since the protective abscess capsule can be resistant to antibiotic penetration. It is important to appreciate that an abscess can take up to 2 weeks to develop a capsule. The earliest stage of intracranial abscess formation consists of a patchy infection of the parenchyma, known as cerebritis.

4

Neurosurgical Pathology

Spinal and Peripheral Nerve Disorders

W. Adriaan Liebenberg

CONTENTS

SPINAL DISORDERS

There is a bewildering variety of pathology that affects the human spine. The main types of spinal pathology in which the neurosurgeon becomes involved include tumours, degenerative disease, infection, and, more rarely, bleeds. In addition, there are developmental deformities that may require correction. There are various spinal cord syndromes that result from spinal disease, and it will be useful to become familiar with these. These are, therefore, discussed at the end of this section on spinal pathology.

TUMOURS

Tumours of the spine are located in one of three anatomical compartments: the extradural compartment; the intradural, extramedullary compartment; or the intramedullary compartment.

Extradural compartment

Primary tumours

Bony tumours *Osteoid osteoma.* This is a benign skeletal neoplasm presenting in young people but rarely in children younger than five. The salient clinical feature is pain that is worse at night and is relieved by small doses of salicylates. On imaging, the lesion presents as a small island of sclerotic bone with a radiolucent centre that is usually less than 1.5 cm in diameter. Radionuclide scans are a good way to locate the tumours. The tumour sometimes involutes spontaneously. Treatment is with surgical excision or radiofrequency ablation and the aim is complete ablation or resection of the tumour, which is curative.

Osteoblastoma. This is a benign tumour that is closely related to the osteoid osteoma and is differentiated by the ability of the nidus to grow larger than two centimetres. Patients usually present in the first three decades of life. Osteoblastoma has to be differentiated from the aggressive osteosarcoma. On imaging, the lesion usually presents as a well-circumscribed radiolucent lesion with a thin rim of new bone that separates it from the surrounding soft tissues. Osteoblastomas that are more aggressive display local resorption of the cortex, destruction of bone, and extension into surrounding soft tissues. For tumours that remain subcapsular local resection is acceptable. More aggressive types with extracapsular extension require resection with a wide margin, which is usually curative.

Osteosarcoma. This malignant tumour usually presents in the lumbosacral spine in the fourth decade of life and has a male preponderance. These tumours present with pain and local mass effects. On imaging, this is usually a tumour of the vertebral body that extends into the soft tissues and may incorporate the posterior elements. The tumour is usually intensely hyperdense and the vertebrae have been called ivory vertebrae. There is frequently a loss of height of the vertebrae. Despite wide surgical resection and adjuvant chemotherapy and radiotherapy, the diagnosis is poor with life expectancy usually less than two years.

Cartilaginous tumours *Osteochondroma.* These are benign tumours presenting in the third and fourth decades of life. They involve the cervical spine mostly (especially C2) and are usually located in the posterior elements. On imaging the lesion presents as an exostosis with a cartilaginous cap. In adults this cap should be less than 2 cm; if it is not, malignant transformation to chondrosarcoma should be suspected. Complete surgical resection is usually curative.

Chondrosarcoma. These are malignant tumours presenting mostly in men in the fifth decade of life and most commonly in the thoracic spine. They present on imaging with a characteristic matrix arranged in the form of rings and arcs, and in approximately 30% extend through the disc spaces into adjacent levels. Complete cure can be achieved with total excision and a wide margin. Adjuvant chemotherapy may be used to reduced tumour mass. These lesions have the potential to metastasize (mostly to the lungs) and lesions that are not resected with a wide margin mostly recur.

Lymphoproliferative tumours *Multiple myeloma.* This is a systemic disease of middle-aged people caused by malignant plasma cells that produce elevated levels of immunoglobulins. This is the most common primary bone tumour and presents with local bone destruction. Diagnosis is confirmed by detecting immunoglobulins with protein electrophoresis in the patient's serum and urine. The mainstay of treatment is radiation therapy and chemotherapy with surgical stabilization of destructed and unstable levels.

Solitary plasmacytoma. These are also caused by malignant plasma cells but are solitary lesions that occur in younger people and have a better prognosis. Radiation therapy and surgical stabilization as above are the mainstay of treatment. These lesions can transform into multiple myeloma and it is important to follow up patients lifelong.

Lymphoma. This can either be primary lymphoma of the bone or secondary deposits of both Hodgkin and non-Hodgkin lymphomas (cranial lymphoma is non-Hodgkin). These patients present with local compressive effects due to tumour growth. On imaging, lymphoma appears as a large soft tissue mass extending from the bone, is homogenous and hypointense on T1 WI images, and enhances strongly with contrast. Technetium bone scans are very sensitive in detecting these lesions. The mainstay of treatment is radiotherapy, with surgery reserved for cases requiring decompression and stabilization.

Tumours of notochordal origin *Chordoma.* These tumours arise from a notochord remnant (the notochord evolves into the nucleus pulposus of the intervertebral discs). These are large soft tissue masses and have associated vertebral destruction. More than half demonstrate calcification on imaging and they are hypointense on T1 WI and hyperintense on T2 WI since they have high water content and enhance with contrast administration. Surgical resection with adjuvant chemotherapy and radiotherapy is the treatment of choice. Sacrococcygeal tumours have 8–10 year survival and tumours at other sites have 4–5 year survival. These lesions may metastasize but death is usually due to the local effects of the tumour.

Round cell tumours *Ewing sarcoma.* These malignant tumours occur in children and mostly in the sacrococcygeal region. Diffuse sclerosis is usually evident on imaging and these lesions are usually located in the vertebral bodies with soft tissue extension. Treatment consists of radiotherapy and chemotherapy and this achieves nearly 100% local control with nearly 90% long-term survival. This is less true for sacral tumours since they are usually larger at presentation.

Metastatic tumours

The tumours that most commonly metastasize to the spine are carcinoma of the prostate, breast adenocarcinoma, lung adenocarcinoma, renal cell carcinoma, and gastric carcinoma. Treatment is based on several factors including the general status of the patient, status of the systemic disease, amount of neural compression, and the presence of intractable pain. Metastatic tumours cannot be cured by local excision of the metastasis and the treatment is aimed at local decompression of the tumour. Concurrent stability procedures are aimed at preserving anatomical integrity and for pain relief. The mainstay of treatment for metastatic tumours of the spine is radiotherapy.

Intradural, extramedullary compartment

Nerve sheath tumours

Neurofibromas and schwannomas are derived from a common Schwann cell origin. Neurofibromas are made up of fibrous tissues as well as nerve fibres. In neurofibromas there is a fusiform enlargement of the nerve and it is not possible to distinguish between the nerve tissue and the fibrous tissue. Schwannomas are round or ovoid masses that are suspended from the nerve and are made up of bipolar cells that are either arranged in a palisade formation, called Antoni-A or are loosely arranged, called Antoni-B. The latter is less common. These tumours occur between the fourth and the sixth decade, arise mostly from a dorsal nerve root, and are mostly intradural. Some extend through a neural foramen as the classical dumbbell tumours, and rarely they are entirely extradural. These are benign tumours and the treatment is excision with excellent prognosis.

Meningiomas

Both these and the nerve sheath tumours make up 25% each of intradural tumours. They arise from the arachnoid cap cells on the dura at the edge of the root sleeve and are therefore found mostly in a lateral position. There is a female preponderance and they arise mostly in the thoracic spine. These are also mostly benign lesions, just like their cranial counterparts, and treatment is complete excision with excellent prognosis.

Filum terminale ependymomas

Nearly half of spinal canal ependymomas arise in the filum terminale. There is a slight male preponderance and these tumours tend to occur in the third to fifth decade of life. The histological arrangement is myxopapillary and consists of tumour cells surrounding a core of hyalinised and poorly differentiated connective tissue. These are benign tumours for the most part and the treatment is excision.

Intramedullary compartment

Ependymomas

These benign tumours, making up 55% of all intramedullary tumours, occur mostly in men in the fourth decade. They can occur throughout the spine but a specific type, the myxopapillary ependymoma, arises in the conus and filum terminale. These tumours are homogenous and well circumscribed, discrete and cause their symptoms by intrinsic compression of the spinal cord rather than infiltration. They are hypointense on T1 WI, enhance strongly with contrast and are hyperintense on T2 WI. Resection results in prolonged survival. Some lesions may undergo malignant transformation, infiltrate, and metastasize within the CNS.

Astrocytomas

Low-grade astrocytomas and pilocytic astrocytomas, together making up 30% of intramedullary tumours, are slow growing, usually have cleavage planes, and may be totally or nearly totally excised. Residual tumours may be treated expectantly although the treatment of these residual tumours is controversial. Anaplastic glioma and glioblastoma multiforme are rare but lethal. Resection of these malignant tumours is not possible and life expectancy is generally less than 2 years.

Other tumours

Generally these tumours have the same imaging characteristics of their cranial counter parts. Intramedullary oligodendrogliomas are rare, the optimal management is not yet known and chemotherapy sensitivity, unlike the cranial type, is unproven. Dermoid cysts, epidermoid cysts, and lipomas are inclusion tumours that are slow growing. The aim of treatment is total resection with prolonged survival in dermoids and epidermoids but lipomas are frequently difficult to excise completely. Haemangioblastomas can be cured by complete removal. They are vascular, and piecemeal removal is risky. Gangliogliomas are more common in childhood, are benign, and the aim of treatment is total resection with prolonged survival. Subependymomas are rare lesions and experience with their management is limited but total resection is the main aim of treatment.

DEGENERATIVE DISEASE

Neural compromise due to compression is usually due to the bony compression of spinal stenosis or to disc degeneration and prolapse. The areas where the stable segments of the spine (the thoracic and sacral spines) join the more mobile segments of the spine (the cervical and lumbar spines) is where the most stress is placed and disc degeneration and prolapse occurs. The most usual segments for this are C5/6, C6/7, and C7/T1 in the cervical spine, and L4/5 and L5/S1 in the lumbar spine. Thoracic disc disease is more unusual.

Patients who present with disc prolapse usually do so in the first four decades of their life, and there is usually a precipitating event, such as a fall or picking up a heavy object. The disc is composed of a central soft part, the nucleus pulposus, and a tougher outer fibre layer, the annulus fibrosis. Damage to the annular fibres leads to damaged disc material herniating through into the spinal canal.

There are various ways in which the separate stages of disc prolapse can be described. In our opinion, the following four terms provide a useful descriptive classification.

1. *Disc bulge:* annular damage with the disc material bulging but still contained by the annular fibres.
2. *Disc protrusion:* the disc fragments protrude through the annular fibres.
3. *Disc extrusion:* the disc material has completely migrated outside the anatomical boundaries of the disc space. On an MRI scan this is seen as a fragment bulging into the spinal canal.
4. *Sequestered fragment:* a piece of disc has broken off and lies loose within the canal.

The single all-encompassing term for the above is *disc prolapse*. The usual initial symptom from disc prolapse is back pain followed by radicular (nerve root) pain. Radicular pain is pain that is caused by nerve root compression and the pain manifests in the dermatome supplied by that specific nerve root.

It is important to understand the anatomy of the spine and the relation of the nerves to the surrounding structures, and to tie that in with the anatomy of the dermatomes. The nerve root of a corresponding segment leaves under the pedicle of the vertebra of that segment. Thus the L5 nerve root leaves under the pedicle of L5 which is opposite the L5/S1 disc space. The nerve root of L5 thus lies quite lateral in the anatomical area opposite the L5/S1 disc space and will be compressed by a disc prolapse which is off the midline in the lateral recess and neural foramen. A disc prolapse in the midline will compress the S1 nerve root on its way to the nerve root foramen under the pedicle of S1. Therefore, at any one given level, a lateral disc herniation will compress the nerve root of that level, while a central disc herniation will compress the nerve root of the level below. Compression of a nerve root leads to numbness and paraesthesia, pain, and muscle weakness. We can work out from the sensory symptoms and the dermatomes which nerve root is being compressed. The other diagnostic tool is myotome dysfunction, for example a central L4/5 (compression of L5 nerve root) disc prolapse will lead to weakness of ankle dorsiflexion and toe dorsiflexion, whereas a L5/S1 disc prolapse (compression of S1 nerve root) will lead to weakness of ankle eversion and plantar flexion with a dropped ankle reflex.

Cervical disc disease causes neck pain, radicular symptoms, and myelopathy. Because of the presence of spinal cord in the cervical area (rather than nerve roots as in the lumbar region), central disc herniations will compress the cord and lead to a myelopathy with spasticity in all four limbs. A lateral disc herniation will compress the nerve root and lead to radicular symptoms with pain, numbness, paraesthesia, and weakness. A broad central disc herniation can cause both a myelopathy and a radiculopathy, and patients are said to have a radiculomyelopathy. We can once again identify the level according to the dermatomes and myotomes. Spinal stenosis is a disease of general wear and tear and usually occurs from the 5th decade onwards. In the cervical area, this leads to slowly progressive myelopathy and sometimes to acute paresis following a sudden extension injury, such as a fall following a slip in the bathroom. The critical diameter of the cervical cord is about 13 mm and compression beyond that leads to symptoms of myelopathy and weakness.

Spinal stenosis in the lumbar area leads to claudication. Unlike arterial claudication, which can occur at rest, neurogenic claudication usually follows walking, and, in severe cases, just standing. The pain is in the calf and is relieved by flexing the hips and standing bent over or sitting down. This leads to less strain on the nerve roots and usually relieves the pain. Spinal claudication is therefore posture related and the pulses are readily palpable, denoting an adequate vascularity. Spinal stenosis is thought to begin with disc degeneration, leading to excess mobility. This is thought to lead, in turn, to facet joint hypertrophy and ligamentum flavum hypertrophy, with resultant autobony fusion, as the body tries to negate this mobility. Eventually, there is a decrease in spinal canal diameter and the patient becomes symptomatic due to compression of the neural structures. Spinal stenosis is treated surgically by decompressive laminectomy. Surgery for a disc prolapse is in the form of a discectomy. However, it is important not to forget that conservative management of disc prolapse can be very successful. Discectomies can be via a number of approaches, including microdiscectomies (via a small bony opening of only a part of the lamina), hemilaminectomies, full laminectomies, or via lateral approaches to the exit foramina for laterally-placed disc prolapses. More complicated surgery of the spine is used in cases where the nerve root compression as well as mechanical spinal pain are due to degeneration in the intervertebral disc and facet joint arthrosis. Spinal instrumented fusion with or without anterior cage placement is used in these instances.

INFECTION

Infection of the spine follows the same basic pathological principles as in the brain, and three mechanisms—metastatic spread, direct extension, and direct inoculation—are responsible for infection. Metastatic cancer spreads to the vertebral bodies, whereas metastatic infection spreads to the disc space causing discitis with severe local back pain, pressure tenderness over the affected segment, fever, and raised white cell count and inflammatory markers. Discitis frequently leads to extradural empyema with compression of the thecal sac and the spinal cord contained within the upper spine and the cauda equina contained in the lower part of the lumbar canal. These patients are not only toxic but also have neurological deficits. Extradural empyema is a feared complication of epidural anaesthesia, and discitis can follow discectomy. Treatment of discitis involves strict bed rest and a long course of intravenous (IV) antibiotics (usually >6 weeks). Extradural empyema requires emergency surgical drainage, followed by bed rest and antibiotics.

SPINAL CORD SYNDROMES

It is helpful to split these syndromes according to whether they occur in the upper or lower parts of the spinal canal.

SYNDROMES OF THE UPPER SPINAL CORD

Anterior spinal cord syndrome

This is due to dysfunction of the cord tissue supplied by the anterior spinal artery and can follow occlusion or damage to this artery, or it is due to anterior compression. It is manifested by muscle weakness below the level of the injury as the motor fibres have an anterior course in the spine. Usually, soft touch (carried anteriorly) and pain and temperature sensation (carried laterally) are also involved. This is an extensive lesion with usually only proprioception (carried posteriorly) intact, and carries a poor prognosis.

Central cord syndrome

This is usually due to hyperextension injury in the elderly where an already critically narrowed diameter of a spinal canal leads to cord compression. The motor fibres in the spinal cord are arranged with the lowest fibres—the legs—being outermost and the fibres of the arms being innermost. A central cord syndrome therefore damages the inner fibres more than the outer fibres, leading to arm weakness that is greater than leg weakness. There is usually a variable amount of sensory deficit as well.

Bell's cruciate paralysis

This is seen in victims of trauma who have intact function of their legs but weakness in their arms. This is because the arm fibres cross higher in the spine than do the leg fibres, and a focal injury of the central spinal cord at the point of decussation leads to this phenomenon.

SYNDROMES OF THE LOWER SPINAL CORD

Remember that, in the lower part of the lumbar canal, beyond the conus, there are only nerve roots (cauda equina).

Conus medullaris syndrome

This is due to compression of the conus, which is at L1/2 level. This is the origin of the cauda equina, and compression leads to both spinal cord compression (myelopathy with spastic weakness and sensory deficits) and nerve root compression (radiculopathy with pain, paraesthesia, and lower motor neurone flaccid weakness as well as sphincter disturbance).

Cauda equina syndrome

This is frequently seen as a neurosurgical emergency due to sphincter dysfunction. Compression of the roots leads to the usual radicular symptoms of pain, paraesthesia, and weakness, but the more sinister component is the compression of the sacral nerve roots that supply perianal, perineal, rectal, and bladder sensation as well as sphincter control of both the bladder and the rectum, and erectile function in males. Emergency surgery to remove the compressive element is needed within 24 h of the onset of urinary incontinence/retention or rectal incontinence to save sphincter function. Saddle anaesthesia is usually a warning symptom of pending catastrophe.

PERIPHERAL NERVE DISORDERS

Peripheral nervous system pathology is predominantly the territory of the neurologist. However, there are various peripheral nerve compression syndromes that are amenable to treatment by neurosurgeons.

Compression of the median nerve under the flexor retinaculum leads to pain in the median distribution, as well as to paraesthesia. This is known as carpal tunnel syndrome. Patients frequently wake from sleep with a severely painful hand which improves with elevation. The history is distinctive and tapping over the flexor retinaculum can elicit the symptoms in severe cases (Tinnel's sign), as can holding the wrist fully flexed for >60 s (Phalen's sign). The diagnosis is confirmed with electromyography (EMG) studies and surgical treatment includes carpal tunnel decompression.

Ulnar nerve compression can occur in the forearm at the wrist (Guyon's canal) or at the elbow, leading to pain, paraesthesia, and paralysis in the ulnar distribution. Surgical release can be quite successful, for example ulnar nerve transposition at the elbow.

Peripheral nerve dysfunction may also be caused by peripheral nerve or nerve sheath tumours.

5

Neurosurgical History and Examination

Reuben D. Johnson and W. Adriaan Liebenberg

CONTENTS

INTRODUCTION

Taking a good history and performing a competent neurosurgical examination requires a basic level of knowledge and understanding of the various types of neurosurgical pathology. It is for this reason that this chapter follows the overview of neurosurgical pathology. You should endeavour to use the history and examination to produce a fairly reliable working diagnosis and to localize pathology. Bear in mind non-neurosurgical pathology (e.g. acutely ischaemic legs can mimic a cauda equina lesion), so make sure to enquire about vascular symptoms and feel (and document!) for relevant pulses. The history and examination discussed here are focused on patients who are alert enough to be on the ward.

HISTORY

This is the most important of all. *Listen carefully and allow patients sufficient time to speak.* There is no such thing as a 'poor historian'—rather it is a reflection of a lack of skill on our part as history-takers.

Have a diagnosis in mind when you have finished, or at least a differential diagnosis; otherwise ask more probing questions to help yourself. Be able to verify which part of the nervous system the pathology is most likely to be located in, and roughly what type of disease process you are expecting. For instance, in the patient who has difficulty walking, it is important to appreciate, and to differentiate between, spinal and cranial pathology, and equally important to distinguish between the different types of pathology—vascular, degenerative, oncological, etc. Be sure to find out, therefore, whether the history is progressive or of sudden onset. You should by now have some appreciation of the significance of different types of headache, for example early morning headaches (raised intracranial pressure), sudden onset occipital headache (subarachnoid haemorrhage (SAH)), cough- or strain-related occipital headache (hindbrain hernia). Relevant associated symptoms should be inquired about, for example fevers, photophobia, alterations in vision, urinary and faecal continence. Be sure to ask about relevant risk factors and associations; for example in patients with SAH ask about smoking, family history, and polycystic kidney disease.

HISTORY CHECK-LISTS

It may be useful when you start out in neurosurgery to write down a series of check-lists to be covered for different types of patient. Write down the key questions that need to be asked of each patient and perhaps any questions you feel may help in distinguishing between the differential diagnoses. The following are examples of how question check lists can be helpful.

Headaches

Common causes of headache in neurosurgical patients include vascular causes (subarachnoid haemorrhage, AVM), CSF problems (hydrocephalus, CSF leak), tumours, infection, and trauma. Key features in the history will help differentiate between the causes.

1. Onset: sudden (vascular) or gradual (tumour, hydrocephalus, infection).
2. Location, nature, duration, course (episodic or progressive).
3. Associated signs or symptoms. Whilst nausea and vomiting may be non-specific signs with any cause of raised intracranial pressure, other features, such as swallowing problems, may be associated with Chiari malformations.
4. Exacerbating and/or relieving factors. Whilst hydrocephalus may be associated with worsening headache in the supine position, CSF leak may be associated with increased headache on standing.

Facial pain

The most likely reason that patients with facial pain will be seen in a neurosurgery ward is because of trigeminal neuralgia. The history should be focused on ascertaining whether or not the pattern of pain fits the criteria for trigeminal neuralgia.

1. Is it paroxysmal (seconds to <2 min)?
2. What is the distribution of the pain (which divisions of the trigeminal)?
3. What is the severity of the pain?
4. Are there any triggers (wind, shaving, eating, brushing teeth)?
5. Are there any associated neurological deficits (there should not be with trigeminal neuralgia)?
6. Has it been relieved by medication (e.g. carbamazepine)?

Spine patients

In all spine patients accurate information needs to be ascertained from the history regarding patterns of pain, motor function (can the patient walk?), sphincter function (bowel and bladder), and sensory loss (spinal levels). In patients with back pain be certain to try to ascertain some idea about the aetiology of the pain. Remember that although back pain is common in degenerative spines, it can also be caused by discitis and tumours. In addition, there are certain questions which it is useful to ask for specific cases. For example, in patients with cervical myelopathy it is revealing to ask about function: can the patient do up their buttons/shoe laces? Can they run to catch a bus? Another feature to ask about is shooting pains down the arms and legs (Lhermitte's sign). In sciatica patients it is important to ascertain whether the pains pass below the knee or to the foot, and whether or not there is any foot drop (foot dragging).

Pituitary patients

It is useful when taking a history from a pituitary patient to think about the symptoms that may arise due to the mass effect of the lesion and those that may arise as a result of endocrine dysfunction. Expansion of a pituitary lesion can cause visual field defects (compression of optic nerve), diplopia, or facial pain. Endocrine sequelae will depend upon the type of endocrine disturbance. Female prolactinoma patients may have menstrual irregularities. Panhypopituitary patients may complain of loss of libido, worsening memory, fatigue, and hair loss (often not needing to shave). Acromegalic patients may notice enlargement of their hands when their wedding ring gets tight, or of their feet when their shoes become too small. Cushing's patients may report weight gain, diabetes, mood swings, and joint pains.

Movement disorders

Patients with movement disorders can be challenging for neurosurgical trainees as these patients are predominantly managed by neurologists. However, with the increasing number of functional neurosurgery units, these patients are commonly seen on neurosurgery wards. It may be helpful to think about symptoms according to anatomical regions. Ask about basal ganglia region symptoms (tremor, rigidity, bradykinesia, dystonias). For tremor and rigidity it is important to ascertain which limbs are affected, whether tremors occur at rest or with purposeful movement, and whether there are any precipitating or relieving factors (e.g. alcohol). Ask about walking and whether it is difficult to get going or to stop. Ask whether there are any uncontrolled movements of the face, trunk, or limbs (dystonias). For Parkinsonian patients ask about on/off periods and the side effects of medications. Ask patients about cerebellar symptoms (ataxia, nystagmus). Patients may have numerous problems in these complex disorders and so it can be very helpful to determine which symptoms they are most bothered by, and which they would change if they could.

EXAMINATION

The awake patient

The following overview of the intricacies of neurological examination is by no means comprehensive or detailed. It attempts, however, to give broad guidelines and background that would be useful in everyday practice. Being pleasant and open in your approach helps patients to settle down quickly and be more compliant. It is very important always to have a system. There are several approaches and the following is a comfortable one. Remember always to introduce yourself and explain to the patient what you are doing.

General observation

Take your time to observe the patient, otherwise important signs such as a Horner's, facial weakness, or abnormal movements may be missed. Look for scars, particularly in patients who have had previous neurosurgery. Key areas to check include:

- Behind the ears (cerebellopontine angle surgery).
- The front and back of the neck.
- The arms (neural compression syndrome surgery).
- The vertebral column.
- The chest and abdomen (shunt patients).

In patients with shunts *in situ*, be sure to follow a shunt from the top to the bottom and feel for any breaks in the shunt tubing. Some patients may not recall where their shunt is placed, so do not assume that a shunt is always peritoneal as it may be placed in the atrium of the heart or the pleural cavity.

General observation is particularly important in pituitary patients. Acromegalic patients may have large hands, coarse features, and a large tongue. Cushing's patients may have the classic moon face and acne. Panhypopituitary patients may have smooth skin with little hair.

Mental function and orientation

A quick assessment can be made by asking patients a series of questions about themselves and their surroundings. The questions below constitute the Abbreviated Mental Test (AMT) score which is given out of 10 (1 point for each question). A common mistake is to refer to this as the Mini-Mental State Examination (MMSE). However, the MMSE takes longer to do, includes drawing tests, and is scored out of 30.

1. What is your age?
2. What time is it (to the nearest hour)?
3. Can you remember this address—42 West Street (recall at end of test)?
4. What year is it?
5. Where are you now (name of hospital)?
6. Can you tell me who these people are or what they do (recognition of two people, e.g. a nurse, a doctor)?
7. What is your date of birth?
8. What year did the First World War start?
9. Can you name the present monarch?
10. Can you count backwards from 20 to 1 in threes?

More detailed assessment of higher cerebral function should measure orientation, attention, memory (short and long term), and some testing of cerebral lobes: calculation (parietal); abstract thought (frontal); spatial awareness (occipital).

Cranial nerve function

CN I

The olfactory nerve is rarely dysfunctional, except in cases of subfrontal tumours, like meningiomas, or in trauma with an anterior skull-base fracture. Smell function can be tested with a pinch of coffee, each nostril being examined separately whilst pinching the opposite nostril. Intact olfactory function can more conveniently be verified by asking the patient whether they can smell their food.

CN II

We are mostly interested in compression of CN II and the dysfunction resulting from it. The optic nerves run in close proximity to the carotid artery and the cavernous sinus, as they extend backwards to the chiasm in front of the lamina terminalis, which is the anterior margin of the 3rd ventricle. From there, they pass around the brainstem to the lateral geniculate body, from where the optic radiations emerge, going to the calcarine cortex in the occipital lobes.

The visual pathways and the defects produced by various lesions in the pathways are summarized in Figure 5.1. Images are transmitted from the retina backwards via the optic nerves, with the nasal fibres crossing over and the temporal fibres continuing straight backwards. The lower retinal fibres cross anteriorly (upper temporal visual field) and the upper retinal fibres cross posteriorly in the chiasm (lower temporal field). As the fibres reach the lateral geniculate body, the fibres fan out in an optic radiation, the fibres serving the lower nasal retina (upper temporal field) dipping into the temporal lobe: this part of the optic radiation is known as Meyer's loop. It thus follows that a lesion in the left temporal lobe will cause a deficit in the information carried by the fibres originating on the right nasal retina (upper temporal field). The fibres originating in the left lower temporal retina on the left-hand side also pass through Meyer's loop and a lesion here therefore results in a right-sided upper quadrant homonymous hemianopia. The fibres then reach the calcarine cortex of the occipital lobe where images are recorded, and we become aware of them as the occipital cortex has relays to the visual association areas in the parietal lobes bilaterally. The contralateral relay is much weaker than the ipsilateral relay, and this is the basis for inattention hemianopia. Although a lesion in the right parietal lobe means the patient should not have awareness of an image recorded in the occipital lobe, the patient is nevertheless aware of the image because of contralateral relay to the opposite visual association area. If, however, at the same time, there is an image in the right visual field, which will relay to the left occipital cortex, the ipsilateral input to

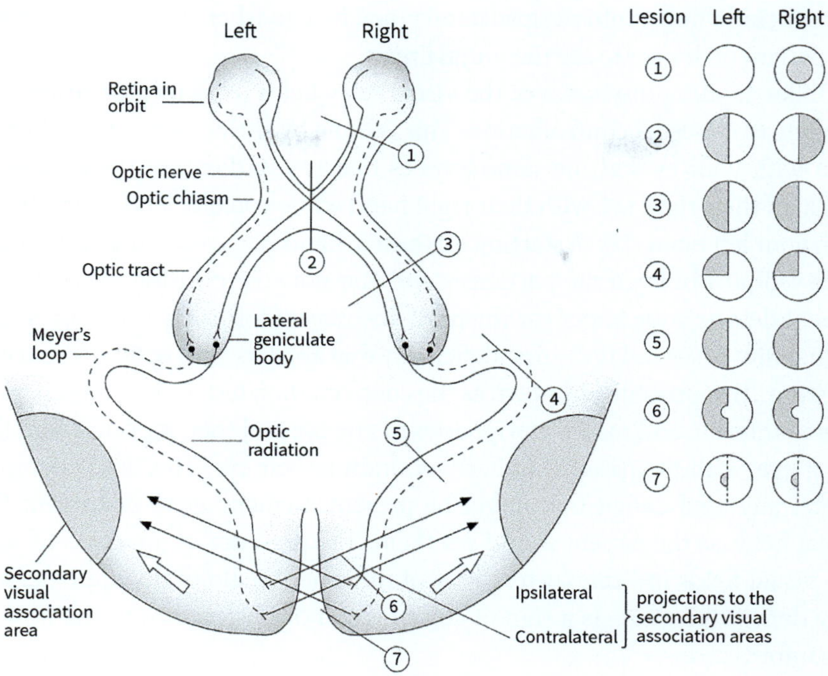

Figure 5.1 Diagrammatic representation of the visual pathways from the retina to the cerebral cortex. The visual deficits shown are due to the lesions indicated: (1) right optic nerve; (2) optic chiasm; (3) right optic tract; (4) right Meyer's loop; (5) right optic radiation; (6) right calcarine cortex; (7) tip of right occipital lobe. Note that the outer part of the visual field may be spared in an early compressive lesion of the optic nerve. The secondary projections to the ipsilateral and contralateral visual association areas are also shown (note that the contralateral projection is much weaker). These are important to understanding the basis of attention hemianopia. If there is a lesion in the right parietal visual association area (serving the left visual field), the contralateral (left parietal) area will allow vision, provided that there is no concomitant input to the left side from the right visual field. This reflects the weakness of the secondary contralateral projections compared to the ipsilateral inputs to the visual association areas. Clinically, attention hemianopia is demonstrated by asking the patient to identify two fingers moving in each side of the visual fields. If the patient can identify fingers moving in one side of the field when they are moved alone but not when fingers in both sides are moved, then they have attention hemianopia.

the left visual association area will obliterate the weaker contralateral input from the right occipital area and the patient will no longer see the image in the left visual field.

We can demonstrate this in practice by testing visual awareness with a finger placed in the contralateral visual field to where the lesion is, and showing that introducing a finger into the ipsilateral visual field to where the lesion is causes the patient no longer to see the initial finger.

Understanding the basics of the visual relay helps us to locate a lesion accurately from visual confrontation. This is done by sitting opposite to the patient with your eyes at the same level as theirs; you then ask the patient to block off their right eye with their right hand while you block off your left eye with your left hand. Then, starting on the left-hand side, you bring your finger (or a red pin) in from the periphery and you note the position in which the patient detects your finger (or the pin). The reason for using a red pin is that an inability to see red is the first deficiency that appears with optic nerve compression. This procedure, known as the confrontation test, is done in superior, lateral, inferior, and medial peripheries of one eye and then repeated with the other eye, with the patient similarly occluding their eye. This easily demonstrates any field deficit that might be present. Remember to document the visual fields as the patient would see them. The presence of intact vision and full visual fields indicates a free flow of information along the optic nerves. Any deficit, therefore, is a sign of compression or obstruction to the flow of this information.

The four typical lesions that we find are:

- *Type 1.* A lesion of a single optic nerve before it reaches the chiasm: this will result in loss of vision in a single eye. Therefore, a compression, or loss of function, of the left optic nerve will result in left eye blindness.
- *Type 2.* A lesion compressing the chiasm: this will initially compress only the nasal fibres which cross over, because the temporal fibres, which do not cross over, are more laterally situated. This lesion will lead to a loss of vision in both temporal visual fields.
- ·*Type 3.* A lesion in the temporal lobe: this will, as described previously, lead to a contralateral upper quadrant homonymous hemianopia.
- ·*Type 4.* A lesion in the parietal or occipital cortex: this will lead to a contralateral homonymous hemianopia of both the upper and the lower quadrants.

Assessing visual acuity is also an intrinsic part of testing the function of the optic nerve, although people can have near complete obliteration of their optic field and still have intact visual acuity. Visual acuity is tested with an eye chart at a distance of 6 m. The vision is documented as a fraction of 1; a value of 1 indicates normal vision, that is, an ability to read the 6 m line with the chart placed at 6 m (denoting the ability to see the same size letters as a person with normal vision would be able to see at 6 m). The patient with the worst recordable vision would be one who could see at 6 m only letters of a size that a person with normal vision would be able to see at 60 m; therefore it is recorded as one-tenth of normal vision, or 6/60.

The third and last step of testing the optic nerve is by doing fundoscopy. It is, perhaps, the case that never have more lies been told in medicine than in the reporting of fundoscopic results. There is frequently general confusion about fundoscopy, and the skill to diagnose papilloedema comes only with repeated examinations of different normal fundi. The term 'papilloedema' means bilateral disc swelling and should be reserved for that. It is best to note down whether optic disc swelling is left-sided or right-sided. Papilloedema takes 10–14 days to develop, and is thus unlikely to be present in acute neurosurgical pathology. It is therefore important to realize that lumbar puncture in a patient with intracranial pathology might be hazardous, even though the fundoscopy is normal. There are four very easy-to-remember stages in the development of papilloedema.

- *Stage 1*. The back pressure in the optic nerve leads to decreased ability of the veins to drain, and therefore there is an increase in venous calibre and tortuosity. It is also possible, with experience, to see a decreased venous pulsation.
- *Stage 2*. Because of the swelling, the optic disc changes from its normal pale colour to pink, and starts to swell, causing the vessels that usually plunge into the disc to stop abruptly at its margins.
- *Stage 3*. The disc margins have now become indistinct and blurred.
- ·*Stage 4*. The disc now is elevated, pink, and swollen, and it is quite common to see haemorrhages around the veins.

Fundoscopy is useful, therefore, for detecting papilloedema that is usually present in cases of long-standing tumours or hydrocephalus, but it is also useful for detecting haemorrhages. In SAH we do see—albeit infrequently—retinal and vitreous haemorrhages (Terson's syndrome) and subhyaloid haemorrhages (bleeding beneath the subarachnoid membrane).

CN III, IV, VI

Examination of the oculomotor nerve has two components. The third cranial nerve works together as a team with the second cranial nerve to constrict the pupil, and works together with the fourth and sixth cranial nerves to move the eye around in the orbit. A light-stimulated impulse travels back in the optic nerve to reach the lateral geniculate body; then, in the brainstem at the level of the superior colliculus, fibres are given off bilaterally to the Edinger–Westphal nuclei. From the Edinger–Westphal nuclei a parasympathetic pathway passes through the brainstem, quite close by an area called the conversion centre, into the third cranial nerves of both sides. Both the Edinger–Westphal nuclei and both oculomotor nerves are thus activated by input from a single side, and we therefore have a bilateral, consensual reaction to a unilateral input (see Figure 5.2). As the impulse travels down the oculomotor nerves, it reaches the ciliary ganglion from where the short ciliary nerves serve the sphincter pupillae to cause a pupillary constriction. The fibres of the oculomotor nerve that mediate sphincter constriction lie on the surface of the nerve on the dorsal aspect and are, therefore, usually involved quite early on in compression of the third nerve. Pupil constriction is therefore a parasympathetic function, mediated by the third nerve following activation of a parasympathetic nucleus by the second cranial nerve. Damage to the afferent pathway (retina, optic nerve, chiasm and optic tract) leads to a pupillary response known as the Marcus Gunn pupil. This is elicited by swinging a flashlight in a pendulum motion between the two pupils. As the light falls on the unaffected eye, both pupils will constrict fully because of the afferent input on both Edinger–Westphal

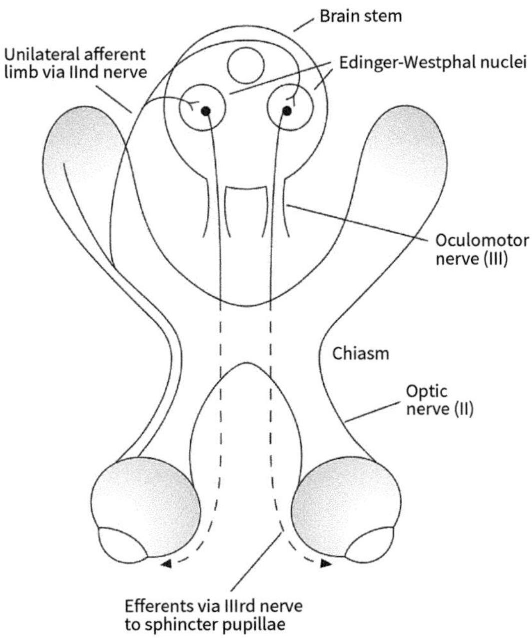

Figure 5.2 Diagrammatic representation of the afferent and efferent limbs of the pupillary reflex. Note that the afferent limb conveys impulses from a single eye to both Edinger–Westphal nuclei. This is the basis of the consensual light reflex where light shone into one eye causes bilateral pupillary constriction.

nuclei. As the light falls onto the affected eye, instead of constricting, the affected pupil will slightly dilate because of the decrease of afferent input due to afferent pathway damage. Efferent pathway lesions lead to a loss of constriction and therefore to dilatation of the pupil served by the oculomotor nerve, which denotes dysfunction caused either by intrinsic mechanisms or by extrinsic compression. The fact that the pupilloconstrictor fibres lie superficially on the third nerve is an important distinguishing factor between medical dysfunction of the third nerve and a surgical (compressive) lesion. Third nerve dysfunction where there is involvement of the pupil is usually compressive. The third nerve also carries some sympathetic fibres which innervate the superior and inferior tarsus muscles of Müller which assist eye opening. The first component of a third nerve compression is therefore dilatation of the pupil, and the second is ptosis.

Pupillary dilatation is brought about by sympathetic activity, which is initiated in the hypothalamus and then descends down into the spinal cord to the level of T1. At the level of T1, the white rami of the nerve roots of C8 and T1 pass to the cervical sympathetic ganglion and from here sympathetic nerves enter the cranial cavity on the surface of the carotid artery, and are delivered to the pupil via a branch of the ophthalmic nerve. Dysfunction of this system leads to ptosis (because of decreased supply to the tarsus muscles), myosis (loss of mydriasis), and anhydrosis (loss of sweating)—the so-called Horner's syndrome.

The second main function of the third cranial nerve is movement of the eyeball, in conjunction with the fourth and sixth cranial nerves. The third cranial nerve supplies all the muscles of the eyeball, except for the superior oblique and lateral rectus muscles: this can be remembered easily using the formula, $(LR_6SO_4)3$, where: LR = lateral rectus (muscle); $_6$ = 6th cranial nerve; SO = superior oblique (muscle); $_4$ = 4th cranial nerve; and 3 = 3rd cranial nerve. A patient with a full third nerve palsy will, as we have discussed before, have a dilatation of the pupil, as well as a ptosis. They will also have a pupil which is looking downwards and outwards. This is because of the unopposed pull of the lateral rectus and superior oblique muscles. The lateral rectus muscle causes the eyeball to look towards the outside, and the superior oblique muscle, which hooks around a trochlea, causes the eye to look inferiorly. It follows that lateral rectus palsy causes an inability of the affected eye to look laterally. It is difficult (and quite rare) to find an isolated fourth nerve palsy: when it does occur, it usually presents with diplopia on looking outward and downward because of superior oblique dysfunction. This can best be conceptualized by recalling that the superior oblique pulls the eye down and medially, whilst the inferior rectus pulls the eye down and laterally. In a patient with a fourth cranial nerve palsy, downward gaze results in the unopposed action of the inferior rectus pulling the affected eye down and out. Downward gaze, therefore, precipitates or worsens diplopia.

CN V

The three branches of the trigeminal nerve traverse the cranial cavity in three separate places: the mandibular nerve enters through the foramen ovale; the maxillary nerve enters through the foramen rotundum; and the ophthalmic division through the superior orbital fissure. The trigeminal nerve is mostly sensory and supplies sensation to the whole face. The mandibular nerve carries the motor part and this supplies the muscles of mastication. Examination of the trigeminal nerve primarily tests the sensation of the first, second, and third division, as well as the corneal reflex (which is part of the first division). Power of muscles of mastication, as well as the jaw jerk, which are part of the evaluation of the trigeminal nerve, are of lesser clinical significance.

It is important to recall that the third, fourth, and sixth cranial nerves, as well as the first division of the trigeminal nerve, run through the cavernous sinus and can be compromised by lesions there. Patients with intracavernous aneurysms, tumours, or arteriovenous fistulae frequently have palsies of the third, fourth, and sixth cranial nerves, and of the first division of the trigeminal nerve on the ipsilateral side.

CN VII

The facial nerve is almost purely motor, and supplies all the muscles involved in facial expression. It also has a sensory component to the external auditory canal and conveys taste from the anterior two thirds of the tongue via the chorda tympani. Clinical evaluation of the seventh cranial nerve hinges on the understanding that there are two separate components to facial nerve function: the first is the supranuclear innervation of the muscles of facial expression, and the second is mainly concerned with reflex eye closure and does not have a cortical component. Both eyes will shut if there is any danger to either individual eye, and therefore there is dual innervation of both sides of the forehead. This leads to the finding of intact upper face function in patients who have had a hemispheric incident, such as a stroke.

The fifth, seventh, and eighth cranial nerves are located in a space between the pons of the brainstem, the cerebellum, and the cranial base, in an area called the cerebellopontine angle.

CN VIII

The vestibulocochlear nerve really consists of two nerves, with the cochlear nerve relaying hearing from the cochlea, and the vestibular nerve relaying information from the apparatus of balance (the semicircular canals and otolith organs). Acute events, such as trauma and infection, cause decreased hearing as well as balance problems. Chronic compression leads to a decrease in hearing, though balance remains intact due to compensation by the contralateral vestibular function. Hearing can be crudely tested by rubbing your fingers together at the side of the patient's ear and determining whether or not the patient can hear the movement. Webber and Rinne testing can be extremely useful to distinguish between conductive and sensorineural deafness. If more information is needed about hearing function, a patient should be referred to an audiologist.

CN IX, X, XI

The ninth, tenth and eleventh cranial nerves are usually tested together. The reason for this is anatomical. These three nerves share the same motor nucleus, the nucleus ambiguus, in the medulla (although the accessory also has a spinal nucleus) and they all exit the skull by the same route (through the jugular foramen). This close anatomical association within the confines of the skull means that it is unusual for centrally located pathology to produce isolated lesions of these cranial nerves.

The glossopharyngeal nerve (IX) is the main afferent path of the gag reflex, supplies some sensation around the external auditory canal, and conveys taste from the posterior third of the tongue. The only clinically significant aspect is the afferent part of the gag reflex. The vagus nerve (X) also helps to convey sensation from the ear but is the main afferent pathway for the gag reflex. The vagus nerve is also motor to most of the muscles of the palate. Testing the ninth and tenth cranial nerves thus consists of testing the gag reflex, which demonstrates an intact afferent pathway (ninth cranial nerve) and efferent pathway (tenth cranial nerve) and also testing palatal function by asking a patient to open their mouth and say 'aah'. If there is a palsy, the muscles that are intact on the unaffected side will pull the palate in that direction and therefore demonstrate the palsy.

The spinal accessory nerve (XI) originates in a nucleus in the spinal cord, leaves the spinal cord through cervical branches, and then goes on to supply the sternocleidomastoid and trapezius muscles on the ipsilateral side. This nerve is unusual in that the higher control is not crossed and a right-sided lesion will therefore lead to a right-sided nerve dysfunction. The function of the eleventh nerve is tested by asking the patient to lift the ipsilateral shoulder up against resistance to test power in the trapezius muscle; the patient is then asked to turn his head away from the side being tested whilst pressure is applied to the head while the patient is looking in the contralateral direction, and the sternocleidomastoid muscle is palpated to check for a good muscle action and bulk. A right sternocleidomastoid and right eleventh nerve function is therefore tested by asking the patient to look towards the left against resistance and palpating the muscle on the right-hand side.

CN XII

The hypoglossal nerve (XII) supplies the motor fibres of the tongue and is tested by asking the patient to open their mouth and let the tongue lie loosely in the mouth. Fasciculations are noted at this point, and the patient is then asked to stick his tongue out and move it from side to side. If there is a palsy, the stronger and intact side will push the tongue over towards the weak side.

Cranial nerve testing

It is extremely important to develop a quick and efficient manner of testing the cranial nerves. Usually, the first cranial nerve is not tested except when there is a clinical suspicion; the second cranial nerve is tested by doing acuity visual confrontation fields and fundoscopy; the third, fourth, and sixth cranial nerves are tested together by checking the movements of the eye; the fifth cranial nerve is checked by noting the sensation in the face; the seventh cranial nerve is tested by asking the patient to move their face in a grimace, to whistle, and to wrinkle their forehead; the eighth cranial nerve is tested by rubbing your fingers together close to the patient's ear; and the lower cranial nerves are testing by examining the gag reflex, looking at palatal function, checking shoulder and neck movements, and finally by looking at movements of the tongue. If practised, this can be done quickly and in sequence within a few minutes.

After noting down the history and asking a few pointed questions to ascertain the patient's mental function, and when the cranial nerves are fully tested, it is time to move on to the rest of the neurological examination.

Motor system

As we know, motor function is controlled contralaterally in the cerebral hemisphere, and there can be dysfunction anywhere from the motor cortex, corona radiata, internal capsule, the decussation in the medulla, to the spinal cord, and peripheral nerves. These are the so-called pyramidal pathways. Motor function is also dependent on the extrapyramidal system and upon the modulation supplied by the cerebellum. Table 5.1 summarizes myotomes and dermatomes.

Even minor dysfunction can be demonstrated by forcing a patient to rely on both the pyramidal system (intact power) and extra-pyramidal system (positional feedback and proprioception). This can be done by asking a patient to hold their arms outstretched in front of them and asking them to make a piano-playing movement in the air. Alternatively, you can ask them to close their eyes and stand with their arms outstretched, palms facing up. Inability to do piano-playing movements, or a drift towards the inside (pronator drift), indicates mild weakness. This is useful for testing patients who have cranial dysfunction. Power is noted on a scale of 1–5, with 5 being normal power, 4 being mildly reduced power, 3 indicating anti-gravity power, 2 indicating movement which is not able to defy gravity, and 1 indicating a flicker. The Medical

Table 5.1 Summary of myotomes, dermatomes, and root values of common reflexes.

Nerve root	Myotome (muscles supplied)	Action	Reflex	Dermatome
5	Deltoid	Shoulder abduction	Biceps jerk	Lateral forearm
	Biceps	Elbow flexion		
C6	Biceps	Elbow flexion	Biceps jerk	Thumb
	Brachioradialis	Elbow flexion	Brachio-radialis jerk	
C7	Triceps	Elbow extension	Triceps jerk	Middle finger
C8	Flexors digitorum	Finger flexion	—	Little finger
T1	Intrinsic muscles of the hand	Finger abduction and adduction	—	Medial forearm
L1	Hip flexors	Hip flexion	—	Anterior thigh & inguinal area
L2	Hip flexors	Hip flexion	—	Anterior thigh
L3	Quadriceps	Knee extension	Knee jerk	Anterior thigh
L4	Quadriceps	Knee extension	Knee jerk	Anteriormedial thigh
	Tibialis anterior	Ankle dorsiflexion and foot inversion	—	—
L5	Extensor halluces longus	Big toe extension	—	Lateral leg
S1	Ankle	Plantar flexion	Ankle jerk	Posterior lower leg and lateral side of foot
S2	Ankle	Plantar flexion	—	—

Research Council (MRC) scale is summarized in Chapter 15 (Table 15.6), which deals with scoring systems in neurosurgery.

The pyramidal system

Trying to decide the location of the dysfunction causing a power deficit can be confusing, but if we stick to a few simple rules it should be fairly obvious. If there is abnormal power, there has to be a dysfunction at some point between the brain and the muscle. In neurosurgery, we do not usually get to deal with muscle abnormalities, and will therefore ignore those. Lesions of the brain pathways or the spinal cord will cause weakness, but will also decrease the higher modulation of reflex activity in the spinal cord. This will cause patients to have overactive reflexes and therefore to appear spastic.

It is important to realize that the lower part of the lumbar spine does not contain spinal cord, but only the cauda equina, and so only lesions above the level of L1/2 will lead to spasticity; a lesion from L3 downwards cannot lead to spasticity. Above L3, the rule that governs the level of dysfunction is different. At the level of the lesion you may find lower motor neurone signs, and therefore weakness without spasticity (decreased reflex), while at the level below that you will find weakness with increased reflexes and spasticity. Thus, a cord lesion at C5 will lead to decreased power in the biceps and a reduction in the brachioradialis reflex, but spastic reflexes in the fingers and in the lower limbs.

The basis for finding the origin of weakness is the absence or presence of spasticity and the level of that spasticity. For instance, a patient with compression in the thoracic cord will have spastic legs, but normal tone and reflexes in the arms; a patient with compression of the brain or the cervical cord will have both spastic arms and legs. Patients with lumbar disc disease can never be spastic due to their disc. A patient with both facial weakness and a hemiparesis most likely has an intracranial cause for their neurological deficit.

Reflexes should be noted as absent, present with reinforcement, present, increased, increased with non-sustained clonus, or increased with clonus.

The extrapyramidal system

The cerebellum is the main modulator of movement, and integrates proprioceptive feedback from all over the body to modify and change motor signals to our muscles. As a general rule, lesions of the cerebellar vermis will lead to truncal ataxia and an inability to stay upright whilst sitting in bed. Hemispheric cerebellar lesions tend to cause ipsilateral limb ataxia. A left cerebellar lesion thus causes ataxia in the left arm and left leg.

A patient with cerebellar disease will usually be hypotonic on the side of the lesion, reflexes will be decreased, and nystagmus is common. Limb ataxia in the upper limbs can be elicited by asking a patient to touch their nose and then to touch your finger which is held about 60 cm or so away from the patient's nose; the movement is then repeated rapidly to and fro. The patient will frequently not be able to touch your finger, and will point past it. There will also be a shaky and unsteady movement of the hand. It is also not possible for the patient to keep their hands outstretched and do piano-playing movements (this will already have been picked up in the screening test for motor dysfunction).

The lower limbs can be tested for ataxia by asking the patient to run the heel of one foot up and down the shin of the other leg, starting at the knee and returning to it. This will usually be a very shaky and uncoordinated movement if there is ataxia present. The final test to confirm the ataxia is to ask the patient to do rapid and alternating movements, such as tapping his foot on the floor or tapping the back of one hand with the other hand as fast as he can. An inability to do this is termed dysdiadochokinesis.

Evaluation of gait is an often neglected but important part of neurological examination. Patients with severe lower back and radicular pain will have an antalgic type of gait where they put less pressure on the affected side. In patients with cerebellar disease, there is a general unsteadiness due to limb ataxia. In patients with a cerebrovascular accident (CVA), there is usually fixed flexion of the upper limb and a straight, outstretched leg with plantar flexed foot, which causes them to walk by circumducting the affected leg (swinging the stiff, outstretched leg out and around before placing it down). Patients who are myelopathic have a stiff and spastic gait and frequently shuffle along.

It is, therefore, quite obvious that a lot can be learned from observing a patient's gait. Romberg's test depends on our need for at least two out of three senses (proprioception, middle ear, vision) to be able to stand unaided. Therefore, closing the eyes will cause patients to fall over backwards or forwards if they have either middle ear pathology or decreased proprioception. As can be imagined, this is not a very specific test, and has little clinical value.

Sensory system

When testing sensation, you basically have to test four modalities: light touch, pain, temperature, and joint position sense.

Light touch is tested by lightly touching the patient's skin, either with your finger tips or with cotton wool, down the whole length of the body and comparing results between each side of the body.

Pain sensation is tested with pin-prick and this is usually quite successful in delineating sensory level. It is important to compare normal with abnormal and also to compare the two sides of the body. If you think that a patient has a sensory lesion at the T4 level, it is useful to compare sensation in the face with sensation on the trunk; sensation on the face would probably be normal. Be careful not to fall into the 'C4–T4 trap': these dermatomes are very close on the trunk and it is possible to misdiagnose a C4 lesion as a T4 lesion. We then also have to compare left to right. It is usually unnecessary also to test temperature sensation, since the two modalities, pain and temperature, are closely related physiologically (fibres for both modalities run together in the spinothalamic tracts).

Two-point discrimination is reliable only when tested on the fingertips where discrimination of 3–5 mm should be sensed by a normal patient. Joint position sense should be tested in both hands and both feet, and is quite a reliable indicator of abnormal function of the sensory cortex. There is no specific clinical significance in testing vibration sense.

When testing sensation, we really want either to indicate a level at which sensation changes or ends, or to show a hemispherically located decrease in recorded sensation, when comparing the two sides. Sensation testing is an aid in localizing pathology.

THE COMATOSE PATIENT

Competent assessment of the comatose patient requires accurate assessment of the score on the Glasgow Coma Scale (GCS) and searching for focal deficits by evaluating pupillary responses and motor function.

Glasgow Coma Scale

The GCS is an excellent tool (Table 15.1). Unfortunately, there are too many people who do not fully understand it and seem frightened to use it. Being awake does not equate to a GCS of 15/15, and being difficult to rouse does not mean that the patient is confused. The GCS score is a very biological measurement; it is not a measure of a patient's alertness so much as of their ability to defend and look after themselves. This can be seen when the three components of the GCS are considered in turn.

The motor response

This is prognostically the most valuable part of the GCS. A full mark is 6/6 and the worst mark is 1/6.

6/6	Being able to follow commands which need a rather sophisticated train of events in the nervous system.
5/6	Aware of, and being able to localize, a painful stimulus (pain) in order to defend oneself (called purposeful flexion or localizing to pain).
4/6	Aware of, and flexing to, but unable to find, the threatening stimulus (reported as non-purposeful flexion).
3/6	Decortication, when the arms are spasmodically fully flexed next to the body (this can be thought of as an action that has no reliance on the cognition of the cortex—decortication).
2/6	Decerebration, when the arms are spasmodically extended on either side of the body, the legs also are spastic and extended (think of a stage of spinal reflex that does not rely on the cerebrum at all—decerebration); this and the previous stage are called posturing, and have a grim prognosis.
1/6	No motor response.

Speech

A full mark is 5/5. This can sometimes be misleading, as a lesion in the speech area might be small but sufficient to cause a person to lose speech, and thus lead to a score of only 1/5 in the speech component, thereby dropping the total GCS total score to 11/15.

5/5	Fully orientated with regard to place, time and person (orientation).
4/5	Confused speech without full orientation (confusion).
3/5	Words.
2/5	Sounds.
1/5	No sounds.

Eye opening

A full mark would be 4/4 and the lowest mark 1/4. Being able to see a threat is crucial to an organism's ability to defend itself.

4/4	Spontaneously has eyes open.
3/4	Will open eyes to speech or sound and is aware of surroundings.
2/4	Only a painful stimulus makes the patient aware of a threat; unaware of surroundings: it has been proposed that pressure—on the bed of the finger nail, the trapezius muscle, and the supraorbital notch—should replace pain as a stimulus to eye opening (see Teasdale et al., 2014).
1/4	No stimulus is enough to make the patient open his/her eyes.

Teasdale, G., Allen, D, Brennan, P. et al. The Glasgow Coma Scale: an update after 40 years. *Nursing Times* 2014;110:12–16.

Total score

The total GCS score is 15. The lowest GCS is 3/15 and this is true in patients who are fully sedated, those who are only functioning on their brainstem or those who have even lost this primal function and who are thus brain dead. See Chapter 9 (*Neuro-intensive Care*) to see how to test for brainstem function. It is now recommended that the scores on the three components of the GCS should be reported in addition to the total score.

Focal deficits

Pupillary function

Pupillary dilatation is a symptom of herniation and increased intracranial pressure (ICP) and it is an important warning sign. This is tested as one of the brainstem reflexes.

Motor function

It is important to establish whether there is a hemiparesis (weakness) or hemiplegia (no function). A comatose or confused patient's examination is usually restricted to the GCS, pupillary response, and presence or absence of a paesis.

6

Interpretation of CT Head Scans

Reuben D. Johnson

CONTENTS

INTRODUCTION

Identifying neurosurgical abnormalities on computed tomography (CT) head scans need be no more difficult than interpreting a chest X-ray. Similar principles apply.

- Confirm the patient details and date of the scan. This also helps you to put the scan up correctly since to read the patients details the scan must be the right way up and not back-to-front.
- Identify whether the scan is with or without contrast.
- Work through the scan in an ordered and systematic fashion.
- If there is an obvious abnormality, describe all its features, that is, site, shape, density, and homogeneity, and whether or not it enhances.
- Ensure that you go back and check all your review areas to make sure you don't miss anything.

To be able to do all these things, you need to have a system of working through the scan, and to know how to identify the gross anatomical structures on a CT scan so that you can localize the lesion. You will also need to know the terms that are used to describe cranial CT lesions. It will be useful to have a simple mnemonic to ensure you have checked everything.

CRANIAL ANATOMY ON CT SCAN

You need to able to identify the following areas: spaces (ventricular system, cisterns); parenchyma (lobes of hemispheres, cerebellum, brainstem, basal ganglia); dural folds (tentorium, falx); sinuses (sagittal sinus). Figures 6.1a, 6.1b, 6.1c, and 6.1d show the main features of a normal axial CT head scan.

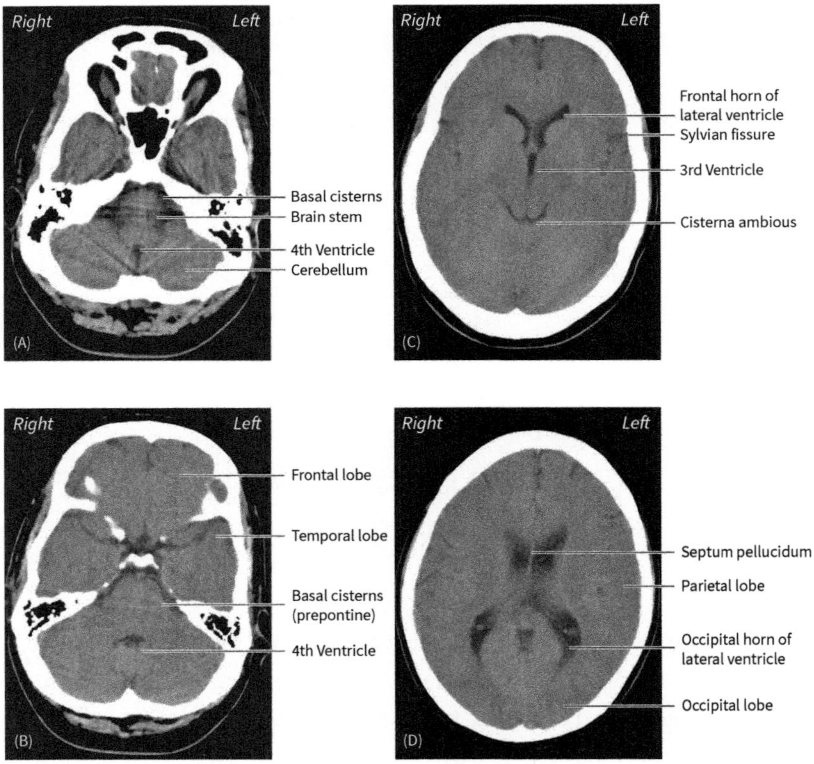

Figure 6.1 Features of a series of normal axial CT head scans from caudal (A) to rostral (D). The key features that should be identifiable on a CT head scan are annotated. Note that the location of the right and left side of the patient reflects the radiological convention of looking at scans from a caudal viewpoint.

DESCRIBING LESIONS

Describing lesions is very important. You should be able to describe a scan over the phone to a senior colleague. It is essential to use a system and terms that everyone is familiar with and understands. The following features of a lesion should be covered when describing them on scans.

- *Site:* anatomy (see previous section); is the lesion intrinsic (within the parenchyma) or extrinsic (arising outwith the parenchyma, but may be pushing into it)?
- *Shape:* diffuse or well-circumscribed; smooth or irregular edge.
- *Density:* hyperdense (whiter than brain), hypodense (darker than brain), or isodense (same density as brain).
- *Homogeneity:* homogeneous or inhomogeneous density.
- *Enhancement:* enhancing (regularly, irregularly, or ring-enhancing) or non-enhancing; the significance of enhancement is that it indicates that the blood–brain barrier has been breached, or that there is neovascularity.
- *Associated features:* for example surrounding oedema, dural origin, calcification.

A SYSTEM OF REVIEW

Start at the bottom of the head and work up through the axial slices.

CSF SPACES

Ventricular system

The ventricular system comprises the 4th ventricle, the aqueduct, the 3rd ventricle, and the lateral ventricles. The aim here is to identify hydrocephalus and, if it is present, to determine whether it is communicating or obstructive. Note in particular the temporal horns (see Figures 6.10, 6.12, 6.13, 6.20, and 6.22 later in this chapter). These are not normally visible in younger people and their presence indicates that there is hydrocephalus. Once hydrocephalus has been identified, see whether there is any obvious level of obstruction. For example, if the 4th ventricle is of normal size but the ventricles above (3rd and lateral) are dilated then there must be obstruction at the level of the aqueduct. See Figure 6.13 for a good example of obstructive hydrocephalus due to blood in the 4th ventricle and Figure 6.22 for an example of hydrocephalus secondary to obstruction at the level of the 3rd ventricle.

Basal cisterns

Reviewing the basal cisterns is particularly important as it can help in determining whether or not intervention is required. For example, if an elderly man with a small chronic subdural haematoma has no midline shift and his basal cisterns are widely open, then he may not require intervention as he has room to compensate for the mass effect of the haematoma. On the other hand, if the basal cisterns are completely obliterated in a diffuse head injury then it may be that intervention will not alter the outcome as the patient has already coned. The basal cisterns also communicate with the subarachnoid space and are therefore one of the commonest sites in which to identify subarachnoid blood—see the features of subarachnoid haemorrhage (SAH), below.

SYMMETRY OF BRAIN SUBSTANCE AND TISSUES

Work up from the foramen magnum through the cerebellum, basal ganglia, and internal/external capsule to the hemispheres. Look for any asymmetry as this indicates that something is wrong somewhere. If there is shift to one side, examine the contralateral side carefully for any space-occupying lesions. Look in particular at the sulci and Sylvian fissures. They may be effaced if there is a compressive lesion.

It is useful to look at the skull and the extracranial tissues as any asymmetry due to fractures or scalp swelling can give clues to the presence of intracranial lesions. If anything abnormal is seen, try to identify which part of the brain it is in. Does the location of the lesion conform to the history? A useful tip is that if you can see the falx in the midline, then you are above the tentorium.

CONSISTENCY OF SCAN AND HISTORY

It is essential to confirm that the scan is consistent with the history. For example, if a patient has a history of a gradual onset, right-sided weakness and a scan shows a small, right-sided, acute, basal ganglia bleed, this does not add up. In this case it would be necessary to look for left-sided pathology, such as infarct or subdural haematoma, or it might be necessary to consider spinal pathology.

Also, a scan might look horrendous even though the patient might actually be better clinically. In this case, ensure that you have the correct patient's scans and check the date of the scans.

Consider carefully the sequence of events. For example, consider a patient who fell off their bike and has subarachnoid blood on the scan. Did they have a spontaneous bleed from an aneurysm and then fall off their bike, or were they knocked off by a car, in which case they may have had a traumatic bleed?

A CHECK-LIST MNEMONIC

The following mnemonic (CT SCAN) provides a useful check-list to ensure that you have not missed anything.

- C CSF flow: ventricular system
- T Tissues: symmetry of intracranial, cranial and extracranial tissues
- S Sulci and Sylvian fissures
- C Cisterns
- A Abnormal blood: look for SAH, extradural haemorrhage (EDH), subdural haemorrhage (SDH)
- N Never forget the history! Is the scan consistent with the history?

CT FEATURES OF COMMON NEUROSURGICAL CONDITIONS

To formulate a differential diagnosis you need to know the features typical of common neurosurgical conditions. These conditions have characteristic patterns in terms of site, shape, density, homogeneity, enhancement, and any additional features.

It was pointed out earlier that, in very broad terms, neurosurgical pathology can be divided into haemorrhage and tumours. It is useful, therefore, to consider typical CT features of common conditions under these headings. In addition, we will consider CT features of other neurosurgical conditions, namely abscesses, diffuse head injury, common cysts, and infarction.

HAEMORRHAGE

It is useful to remember the different appearances of extravasated blood on CT scans. Acute blood (<72 h) is hyperdense (white), subacute blood (72 h to 1 week) is isodense, and chronic blood (>1 week) is hypodense.

Traumatic bleeds

Extradural haematoma *(see Figures 6.2 and 6.3)*

- Between skull and brain.
- Biconvex (inner convexity pushing into brain) due to the fact that the dura is being stripped away from the bone.
- Hyperdense.

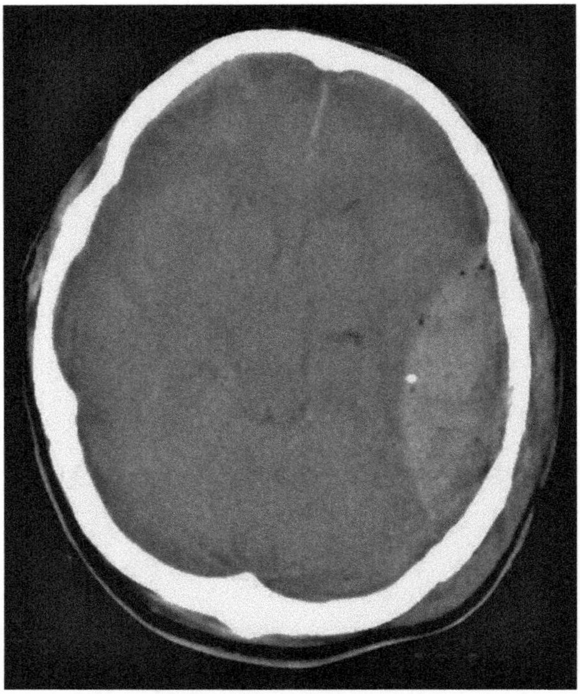

Figure 6.2 Axial CT head scan showing a large, left-sided, parietofrontal extradural haematoma. Note that the haematoma is biconvex and hyperdense. This haematoma is probably due to rupture of the left middle meningeal artery. There are also some hyperdense areas at the frontal poles that may represent contusions from a contracoup injury. The presence of extracranial soft-tissue swelling on the left side is further evidence that the blow is likely to have been to the left side of the head.

Subdural haematoma *(see Figures 6.4–6.9)*

- Between skull and brain.
- Crescentic (follows contour of brain).
- Hyperdense (acute), isodense (subacute), or hypodense (chronic).

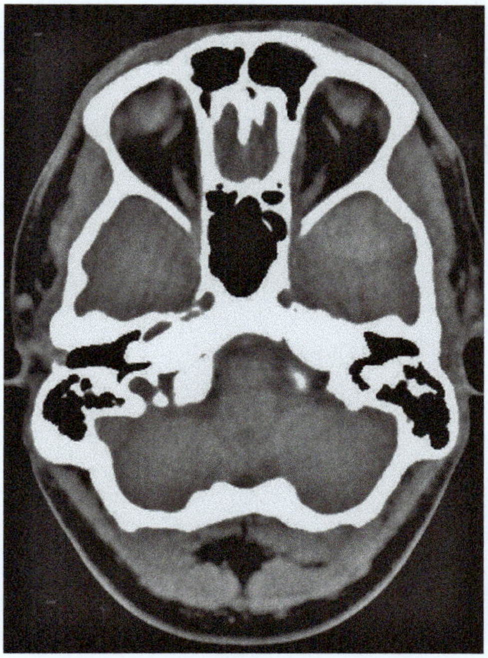

Figure 6.3 Axial CT head scan showing a left-sided temporal haematoma. Note the classic crescentic shape and hyperdense appearance.

- Loculation and membranes may be visible in chronic subdural haematomas (CSDH).

Spontaneous bleeds

Subarachnoid haemorrhage *(see Figures 6.10–6.14)*

- Subarachnoid space.
  Basal cisterns: circle of Willis aneurysms.
  Sylvian fissure: internal carotid, posterior communicating artery (Pcomm), or middle cerebral artery (MCA) aneurysms.
  Interhemispheric fissure and anterior flame-shaped intraparenchymal haemorrhage: anterior communicating artery (Acomm) aneurysm (the most common aneurysm).
- Diffuse streaks following surface of brain.
- Hyperintense—but after 1 week may not be visible due to dissipation by CSF flow. (CT scans are 98% sensitive in the first 12 h for SAH, but sensitivity declines to 70% by day 3).

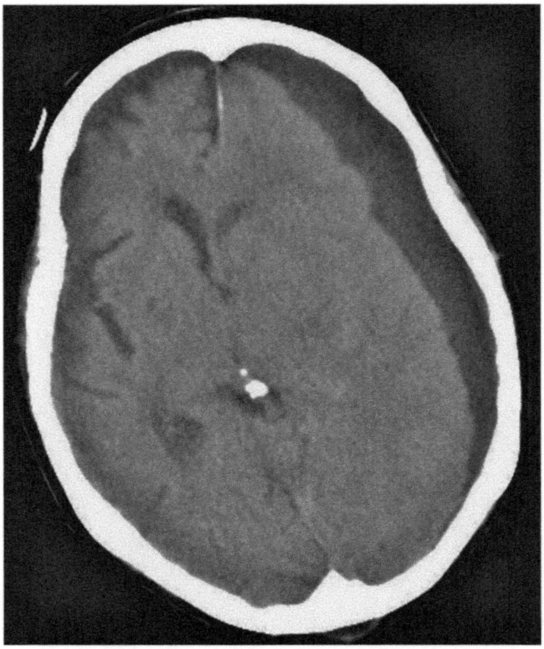

Figure 6.4 Axial CT head scan showing a large, left-sided, chronic subdural haematoma covering the convexity of the whole hemisphere. There is significant midline shift (>1 cm) with distortion of the ventricular system. The haematoma is crescentic and hypodense. Note that the sulci over the left hemisphere have been effaced. In smaller haematomas this may be the only sign indicating the presence of subdural blood, especially if the blood is subacute and isodense (see Fig. 6.6).

Hypertensive bleeds

- Most commonly basal ganglia and cerebellum, but can be a lobar intraparenchymal cerebral bleed.
- Vary in shape.
- Hyperdense in acute phase.
- Hypodense area may surround clot due to oedema.
- Usually elderly hypertensive patient, but not exclusively so.

Arteriovenous malformation (AVM)

- Similar features to hypertensive bleed but more cortical location and more likely to occur in normotensive younger patients.
- Frequently have an underlying 'salt and pepper' appearance with the mass of underlying vessels faintly visible on an uncontrasted scan and vividly visible following the administration of contrast.

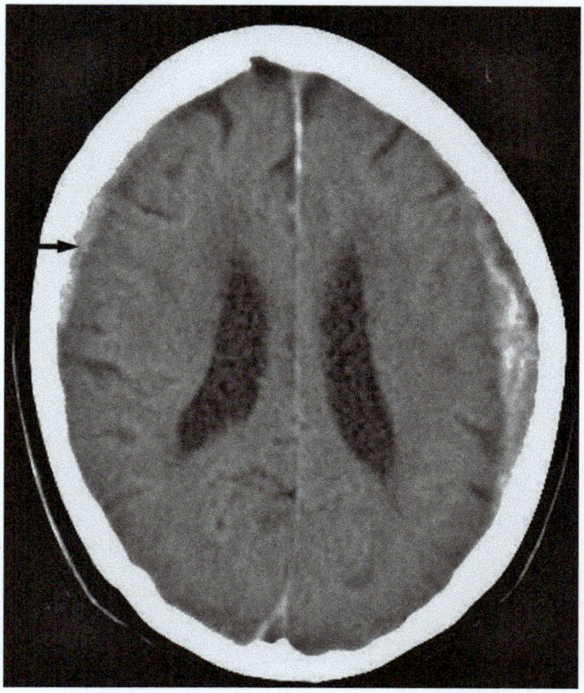

Figure 6.5 Axial CT head scan showing a left-sided, frontoparietal, acute subdural haematoma. The haematoma is crescentic and hyperdense. Note that there is also some acute subdural blood on the right side (arrow).

TUMOURS

Metastases (see Figure 6.15)

- Intraparenchymal (intrinsic) and may be multiple.
- Well-circumscribed.
- Mixed density.
- Inhomogeneous.
- Enhancing: either inhomogeneously or ring-enhancing and can have central necrotic areas.

Gliomas

Low-grade *(see Figure 6.16)*

- Intraparenchymal (intrinsic).
- Regular shape but poorly defined edges.
- Hypodense or isodense.
- Homogeneous.
- Non-enhancing (except for juvenile pilocytic astrocytoma).

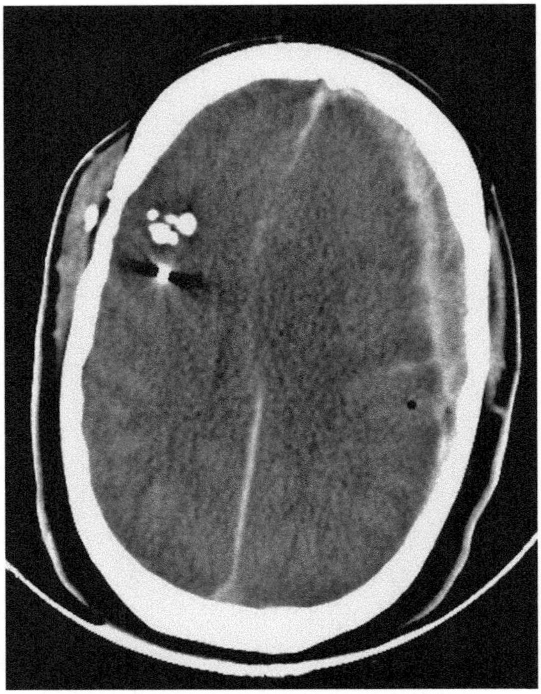

Figure 6.6 Axial CT scan showing a left-sided, frontoparietal, subdural haematoma (crescentic and hyperdense). Note that there are also some hyperdense areas in the right hemisphere with some associated scatter effect. This is usually seen with radio-opaque foreign material. There are also a couple of hypodense areas within the parenchyma suggesting the presence of intracranial air. Swollen parenchyma is also contributing to the shift to the right side. Unfortunately, this patient was shot at close range through the head with a low-calibre weapon. The foreign bodies in the right hemisphere are the remnant of the bullet and/or fragments of bone.

High grade *(see Figure 6.17)*

- Intraparenchymal (intrinsic).
- Irregular and may be diffuse.
- Mixed density.
- Inhomogeneous.
- Strongly enhancing (in an inhomogeneous fashion) with central necrosis in the highest grade—glioblastoma multiforme (GBM).

Meningiomas (see Figure 6.18)

- Extrinsic—although appearing parenchymal they will always have a dural origin.

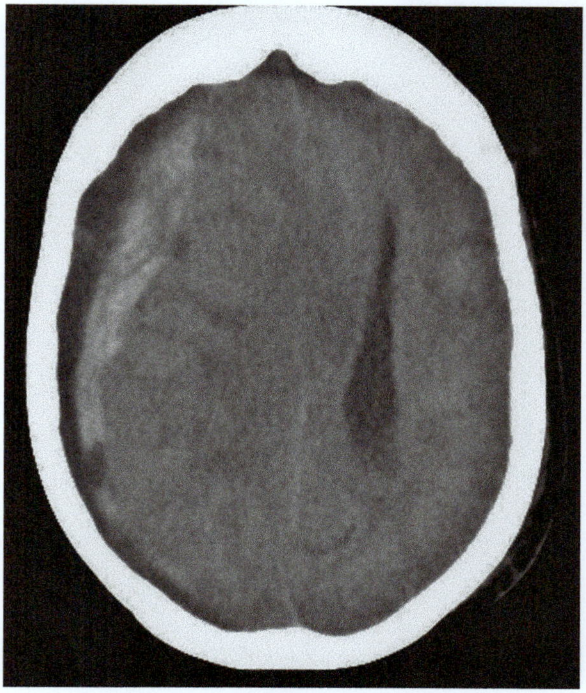

Figure 6.7 Axial CT head scan showing a right-sided, acute-on-chronic, subdural haematoma covering most of the right hemisphere. Note the crescentic shape and the mixture of hypodense and hyperdense areas indicating, respectively, old and new blood.

- Well-circumscribed smooth or lobular.
- Hyperdense.
- Homogeneous.
- Enhance homogeneously (they light up like a light bulb).
- Skull changes—associated with skull erosion and thought to be a malignant feature. Other meningiomas are associated with hyperostosis, much like fibrous dysplasia.

Oligodendrogliomas (see Figure 6.19)

- Commonly in the frontal and temporal lobes.
- Calcification is almost invariably present.
- Inhomogeneous appearance.
- Inhomogeneous enhancement.

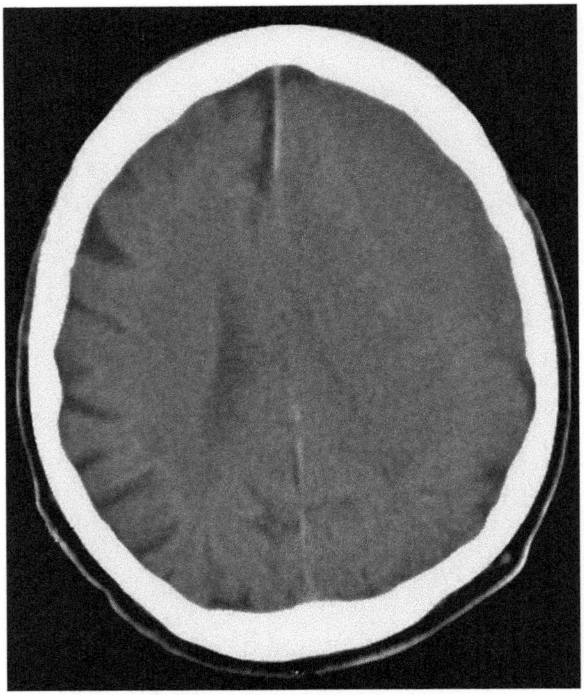

Figure 6.8 Axial CT head scan showing a large, subacute, left-sided, subdural haematoma. The haematoma is beginning to turn hypodense. However, the clear asymmetry seen in the scan is more evident because of the absence of obvious sulci in the left hemisphere.

Primary CNS lymphomas (PCNSL)

- Periventricular intraparenchymal (intrinsic).
- Irregular.
- Hyperdense with surrounding hypodensity (oedema).
- Homogeneous.
- Enhance homogeneously.
- Disappear with steroids ('ghost tumours').

Haemangioblastomas (see Figure 6.20)

- Posterior fossa.
- Regular, well-circumscribed cystic.
- Hypodense but with isodense mural nodule.
- Mural nodule may enhance and become more clear.

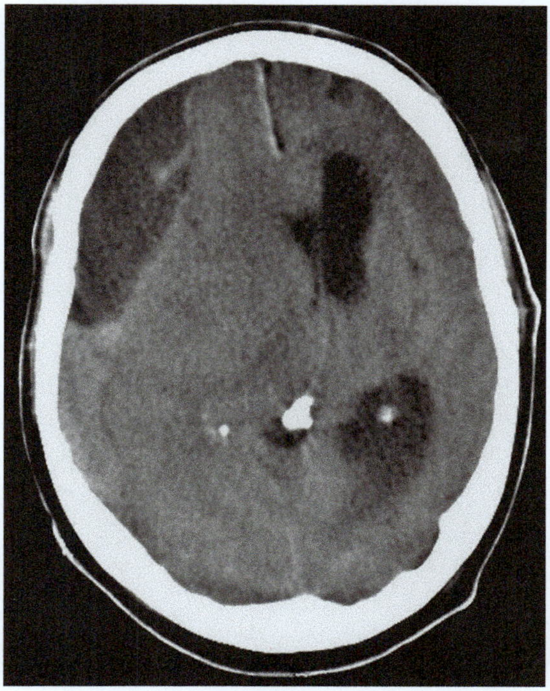

Figure 6.9 Axial CT head scan showing a large, right-sided, chronic, subdural haematoma with massive midline shift. Note that there is a horizontal level demarcating the upper hypodense area from a lower hyperdense area. It is possible that the hyperdense area represents a further acute bleed separated by membranes from the chronic component. However, it is more likely that this is simply sedimentation of an old bleed.

Medulloblastomas

- Children.
- Posterior fossa, midline.
- Regular, well-circumscribed.
- Isodense.
- Homogeneous.
- Enhance homogeneously.

Ependymomas

- Mostly in children in the posterior fossa.
- Also in adults, and can appear anywhere in the brain.
- In the posterior fossa they usually arise from the foramina of Luschka and Magendie.
- Usually enhance uniformly.

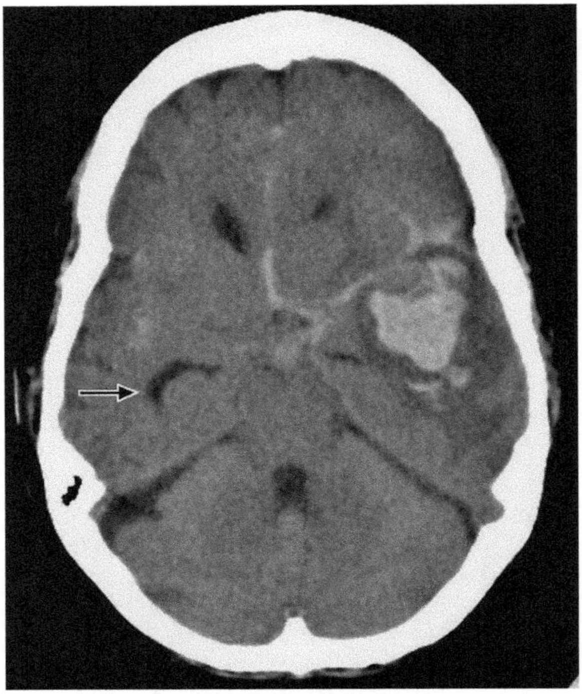

Figure 6.10 Axial CT head scan showing the presence of acute subarachnoid blood. There is also a large left temporal intraparenchymal haematoma (hyperdense). Interestingly, the middle cerebral artery aneurysm responsible for this bleed can be seen silhouetted against this haematoma. The hypodense area around the haematoma reflects the swelling in the surrounding parenchyma. The other noteworthy abnormality is the enlarged right temporal horn (arrow) indicating the presence of moderate hydrocephalus.

Cerebellar gliomas

- Usually in children, and form the main differential diagnosis of posterior fossa tumours along with ependymomas and medulloblastomas.
- The same imaging characteristics are true as in the cerebral gliomas and they are usually not midline tumours.

Primitive neuroectodermal tumours (PNET)

- Found in the cerebrum in children.
- Have the same characteristics as medulloblastomas.

TUMOURS BY INTRACRANIAL LOCATION

It is extremely helpful to have some appreciation of how the intracranial location of the tumour can help determine what type of tumour it is. In adults,

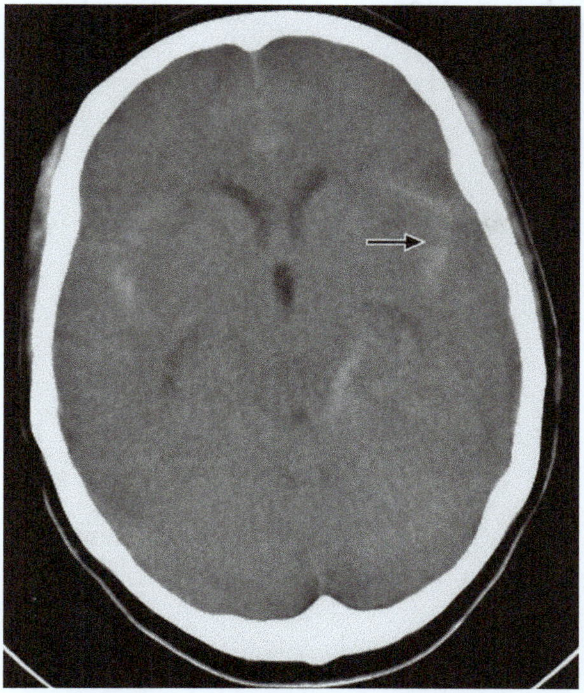

Figure 6.11 Axial CT head scan showing the presence of subarachnoid blood (hyperdense). Note in particular the presence of blood in the left sylvian fissure (arrow).

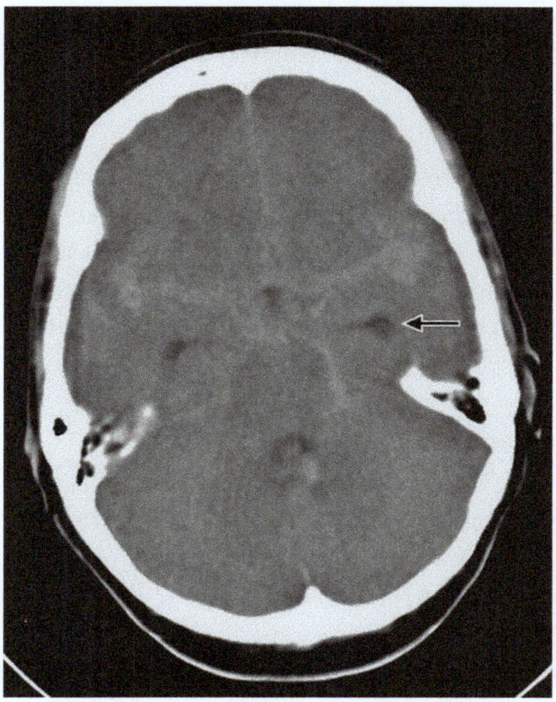

Figure 6.12 Axial CT head scan showing diffuse subarachnoid blood (hyperdense). Note that the temporal horns are slightly enlarged, indicating the presence of hydrocephalus (arrow indicates left temporal horn).

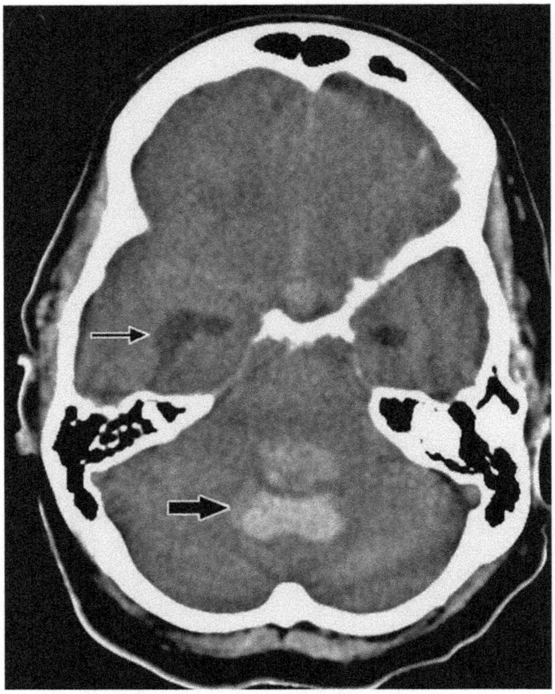

Figure 6.13 Axial CT head scan showing the presence of subarachnoid blood and a large collection of blood in the 4th ventricle (thick arrow). This obstruction of the 4th ventricle is causing hydrocephalus, as evidenced by the enlarged temporal horns on this scan (thin arrow).

for example, a posterior fossa lesion or parenchymal lesion is most likely to be a metastasis, but a haemangioblastoma should be considered if the lesion is cystic with a mural nodule. In children, posterior fossa lesions are much more likely to be primary brain tumours such as medulloblastomas and pilocytic astrocytomas. Some of the locations which help in the identification of tumour types are listed below.

Intraventricular tumours

- Ependymomas.
- Subependymoma is the only non-enhancing intraventricular tumour.
- Neurocytoma (lobulated, adjacent to septum pellucidum or foramen ovale, hyperdense on CT).
- Pineal tumours.
- Choroid plexus tumours (prominent enhancement): most common in 4th ventricle in adults, but more common in lateral ventricle in children.
- Meningiomas (prominent enhancement).

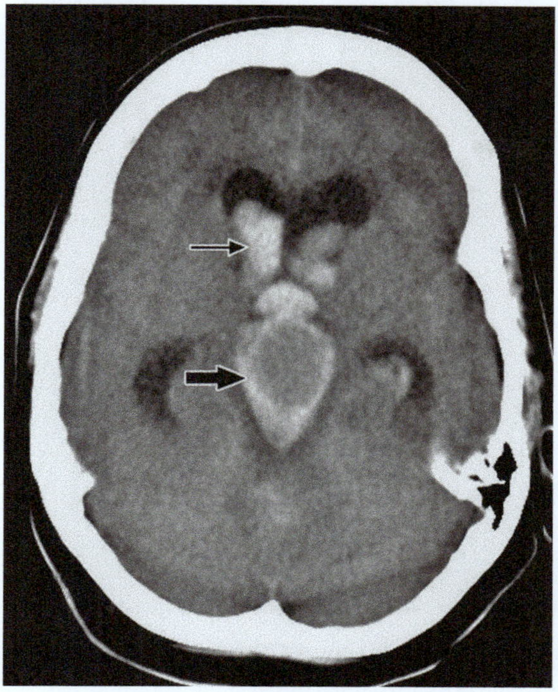

Figure 6.14 Axial CT head scan showing a large, intraventricular bleed. Blood can be seen in the 3rd ventricle (thick arrow) and frontal horns of the lateral ventricles (thin arrow). The presence of ventriculomegaly confirms the presence of obstructive hydrocephalus.

Paraventricular tumours

- Subependymal giant cell astrocytoma (SEGA): associated with tuberous sclerosis (cortical tubers, subependymal nodules along lateral ventricles, benign foci of dysmyelination in deep white matter); often arise from the caudate; hypo/isodense on CT.
- PCNSL (see earlier).
- 75% in contact with ependyma/meninges hence 'pseudomeningioma pattern' (but no calcifications and usually multiple).
- 'Ghost tumour' as may disappear radiologically with steroids.

Temporal lobe tumours

- Dysembryoplastic neuroectodermal tumours (DNETs): variable density with variable enhancement.
- Ganglioglioma: cystic; calcified with isodense mural nodules; rarely enhance; rarely associated with oedema; clinical picture is often a child with a seizure.
- Pleomorphic xanthoastrocytoma (PXA): cystic; discrete mural enhancing nodule; presentation in teenage years/early twenties.

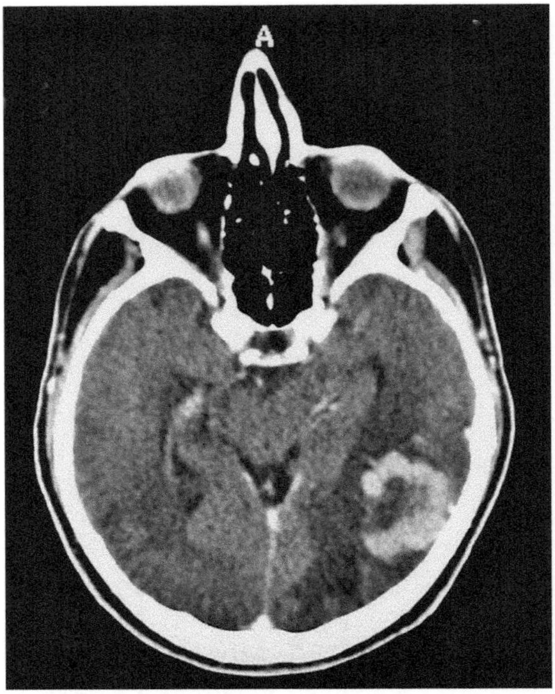

Figure 6.15 Axial CT head scan with contrast, showing a metastasis in the left parietal lobe. Note that the lesion is well-circumscribed, enhancing, and of mixed density. There is probably some central necrosis.

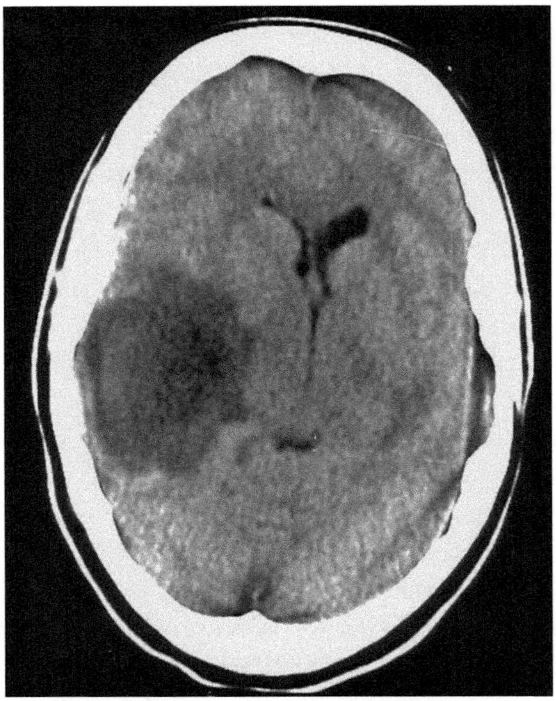

Figure 6.16 Axial CT head scan of a large, low-grade glioma of the right parietal lobe. The lesion is hypodense and virtually homogeneous.

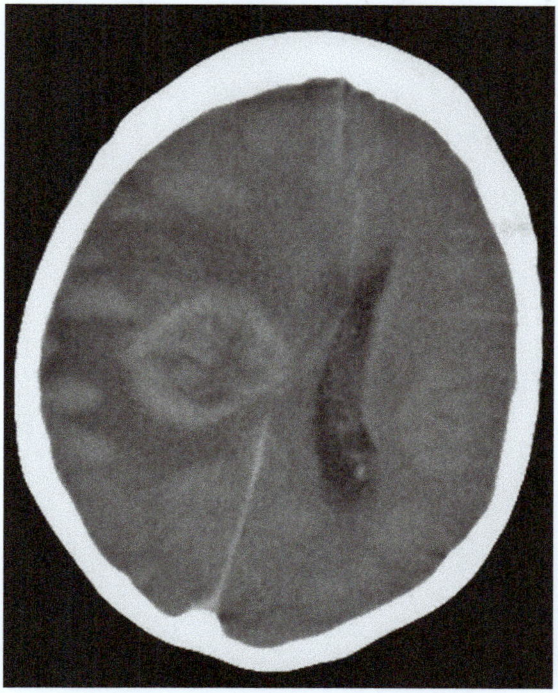

Figure 6.17 Axial CT head scan with contrast, showing a large, right-sided, enhancing, parietal space-occupying lesion with surrounding oedema (hypodense area) and midline shift. The centre of the lesion is inhomogeneous. This is a high-grade glioma with a necrotic centre.

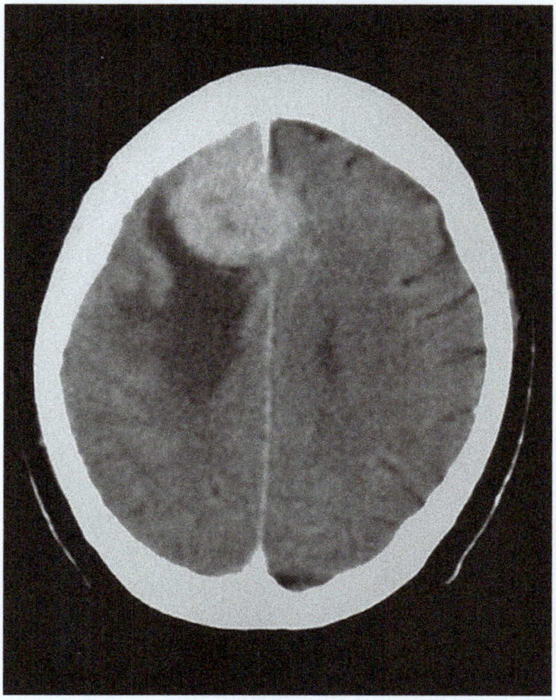

Figure 6.18 Axial CT head scan with contrast, showing a right frontal meningioma. The lesion is enhancing and homogeneous with a dural attachment.

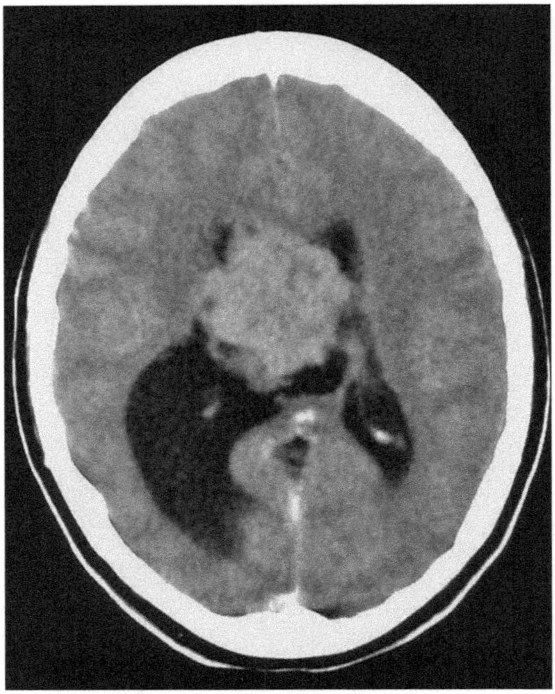

Figure 6.19 Axial CT head scan with contrast, showing an inhomogeneous, intraventricular oligodendroglioma.

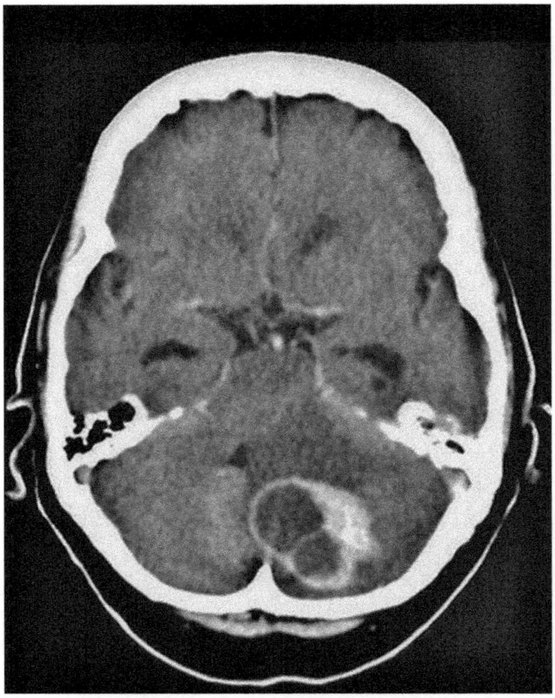

Figure 6.20 Axial CT head scan with contrast, showing a ring-enhancing, cystic, space-occupying lesion in the posterior fossa (cerebellum). Note the effacement of the 4th ventricle and the presence of obstructive hydrocephalus as evidenced by distended temporal horns. This is a haemangioblastoma.

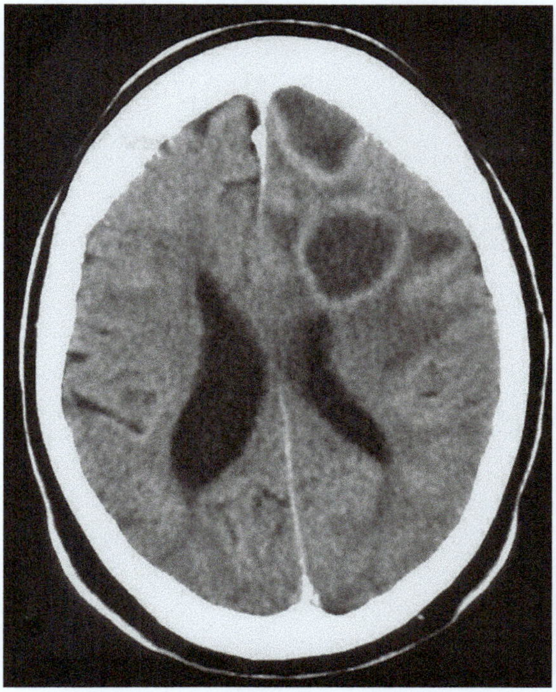

Figure 6.21 Axial CT scan with contrast, of two cerebral abscesses located in the left frontal lobe. The lesions are hypodense and ring-enhance with contrast.

INFECTION (CEREBRITIS AND ABSCESS)

(See Figure 6.21)

- Encapsulated abscess: takes 2 weeks to develop from cerebritis.
- Cerebritis: normal scan or poorly defined hypodense area (may enhance).
- Abscess: well-defined rounded hypo/isodense lesion which 'ring-enhances' with contrast, with the capsule tending to be thinner on the side of the ventricle, and the side of the convexity being thicker.

CORTICAL INJURY

Diffuse axonal injury

- In acute stages, CT may be normal.
- Hyperdense spots (petechial haemorrhages) in white matter—see the description of the three grades in Chapter 3, *Neurosurgical Pathology*.

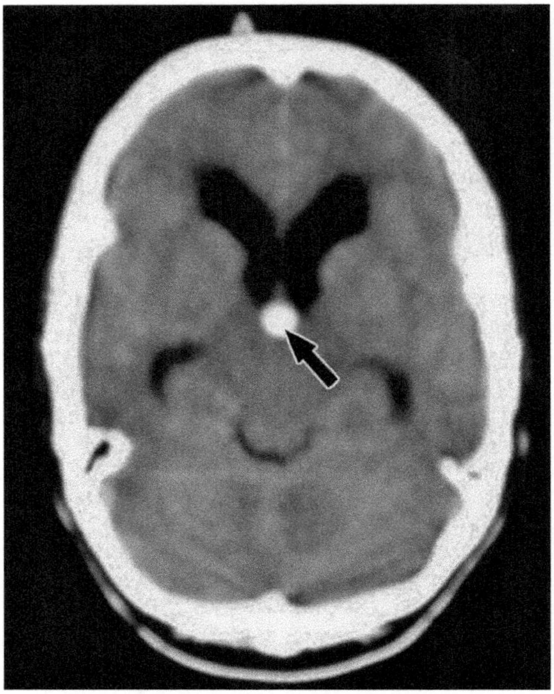

Figure 6.22 Axial CT scan showing a hyperdense colloid cyst in the anterior 3rd ventricle obstructing the foramen of Munro (arrow). Obstructive hydrocephalus is confirmed by the presence of distended anterior and temporal horns.

Cortical contusions

- Patchy areas of hypodensity with sporadic hyperdense spots (petechial haemorrhages) in acute phase.
- Later, more hyperdense areas develop as bleeding continues and there is more associated hypodense oedema and mass effect; these lesions develop into haemorrhagic contusions, particularly between days 5 and 7, with maximal swelling and re-bleeding occurring then.
- Temporal lobe and frontal lobes most commonly affected.

INFARCTION

- Normal scan in acute phase.
- Later, areas of low density develop and shape will depend on cause of infarction, for example, wedge-shaped infarct with MCA occlusion, but more diffuse areas with infarction after vasospasm associated with SAH.

SOME COMMON CYSTS

Arachnoid cyst

- Well-defined, hypodense extra-axial lesions (same density as CSF).
- Frequently found in the area of the pituitary fossa and cerebellopontine angle, but can be found anywhere.

Colloid cyst (see Figure 6.22)

Small, round, hyperdense midline lesion in the anterior part of the 3rd ventricle.

7

Overview of Neurosurgical Investigation and Monitoring

Sean Martin and Timothy Lawrence

CONTENTS

INTRODUCTION

Many of the major recent advances in neurosurgery have resulted from developments in imaging and monitoring techniques, and this continues to be a rapidly evolving field. There are many investigations utilized in order to aid diagnosis and facilitate localization of surgical anatomy, and to help in neurosurgical treatment. It is therefore paramount that the junior trainee has at least a basic understanding of what these modalities are best used for and how the images are obtained. A brief overview follows some of the more important investigations that you will come across.

PLAIN RADIOGRAPHS

The plain X-ray (XR) remains a common and useful imaging technique in neurosurgery, where it is most heavily relied upon in spinal surgery; it is, however, beginning to be replaced by more advanced imaging techniques, including intraoperative CT and neuronavigation systems. Static and dynamic (i.e. flexion, extension, weight-bearing, etc.) images of the spine may be utilized prior to surgery in order to check stability, and may help to plan parts of the operation. Intraoperatively, the image intensifier is a portable C-arm XR tube that can be used in theatre to obtain images, and it is most commonly used to check the operative level in spinal surgery, or to check screw position.

The plain XR is also often used, in combination with a CT scan, in the investigation of a cerebrospinal fluid (CSF) shunt. In this setting, fluoroscopy of the skull, neck, chest, and abdomen (anteroposterior and lateral abdomen to show depth as well as position) is obtained to follow the shunt tubing from its insertion point in the brain to its end point, ensuring it is continuous and has not become disconnected or fractured.

Clearly, abdominal XRs are not necessary in cases of shunts that do not end within the abdominal cavity. The skull XR should be obtained orthogonal to a programmable shunt valve in order to show the setting of programmable valves, when comparing the image with the manufacturer's shunt setting card—which is easily obtained from the Internet, though it is essential you know the type of valve (this should be documented in the patient's notes, and always on the operation record).

COMPUTED TOMOGRAPHY (CT)

The development of computed tomography revolutionized investigation and diagnosis in neurosurgery. It has now become the standard form of imaging and one with which the junior trainee needs to be very comfortable and familiar. Multiple rotating beams of X-rays pass through tissue. The degree of absorption of each beam is measured by a circular array of detectors. Standard CT allows for 3–5 mm slices; however, a helical CT will allow for finer slices of 1–2 mm and for faster scanning times. Fine slices allow for multi-planar reconstruction of images, essentially allowing the viewer to look at the image as a 3D model, and can look at areas of interest in any plane. Manipulation of the different window settings allows better examination of tissues of varying density. Neurosurgeons are often interested in bony windows and soft tissue windows, allowing for identification of fractures, bony abnormalities, intracranial masses, blood, ventricular shape and size, and so on. Much like XR, tissues with higher density allow fewer XR beams to pass through, and so show up more 'white' on CT. 'White' areas are described as displaying high attenuation—on the basis of the amount of X-ray absorbed by

Table 7.1 Most commonly seen tissues from high to low attenuation.

Metal > bone > calcified tissue > fresh blood (i.e. clot) > contrast medium > brain > old blood (fibrinolysed) > CSF > fat > gas

the tissue: denser tissue attenuates more X-ray (Table 7.1 shows the most commonly seen tissues from high attenuation to low attenuation).

CONTRAST-ENHANCED CT

Contrast administration helps provide additional information about abnormalities picked up on plain scan, such as tumours, vascular abnormalities, and infection. This works by injecting iodinated contrast and then performing a CT scan. Regions with local disruption of the blood–brain barrier will show up as regions of higher attenuation than the surrounding brain: for example, within or around the periphery of some tumours, around or within a focus of infection (e.g. abscess, empyema, infected collection), or in a post-surgical cavity. This is described as 'contrast enhancement', and the pattern may be characteristic or suggestive of certain pathologies.

CT ANGIOGRAPHY (CTA)/CT VENOGRAPHY (CTV)

These are contrast-enhanced CT series in which the period between contrast injection and image acquisition is carefully timed in order that the contrast is within mainly the brain arteries (CTA) or venous sinuses (CTV) when the images are taken.

CTA is usually the first diagnostic test undertaken following a confirmed diagnosis of subarachnoid haemorrhage (SAH). Modern multi-slice CT scanners with advanced 3D reconstruction are able to generate very detailed images of the cerebral vasculature and are now highly sensitive for identifying aneurysms which are the most common cause of spontaneous SAH.

PERFUSION CT

This is less commonly used in clinical practice, though it is used routinely in some centres. Perfusion CT scans are ordinary CT scans where contrast is administered and a software package calculates the perfusion in the different areas of the brain according to the flow of contrast through it. Other perfusion scans use the administration of xenon gas to calculate blood flow; these can demonstrate regional hypoperfusion states and allow us to modify our therapy.

MAGNETIC RESONANCE IMAGING (MRI)

The physics behind magnetic resonance imaging is complicated. What follows is a highly simplified version of how MRI and some sequences work, but allows a helpful framework for thinking about what you are looking at.

Essentially, a magnetic field aligns the spin of protons (hydrogen nuclei of molecules of water within tissue)—this alignment is important as the resting state for T1. Proton spin alignment is then displaced by a superimposed electromagnetic pulse, which also induces the protons to spin 'in phase' with one another—the resting state of 'out of phase' spinning is important for T2. As the pulse switches off, the tissues return to their resting state. Different tissues return to a resting state at different speeds, and indeed, show different proton densities. By changing the radiofrequency pulse sequences, and measuring the time taken to reach resting state, as well as employing computed algorithms, a variety of different image types can be generated that show up different tissues on the basis of their magnetic properties.

There are many different MR sequences that are used to visualize different tissue types—detailed descriptions of these is beyond the scope of this chapter, but a short overview of the more clinically relevant and common sequences is laid out below. The 'whiteness' of an image in MRI is described as 'signal intensity' in an analogous way to attenuation as described for CT imaging. Comparison of signal characteristics of the same tissue through different sequences gives the radiologist clues as to what the most likely components of an abnormality might be, and therefore, may help to infer potential diagnoses.

T1 SEQUENCES

These are sequences that are based upon the time taken for the protons within a given tissue to realign their spin axis with the constant magnetic field following displacement by the radiofrequency pulse. A prolonged T1 relaxation time gives hypointensity and so appears darker—water and therefore CSF appear as black on T1-weighted sequences.

On T1-weighting, hyperintense lesions (compared with normal brain) prior to contrast administration include fat, subacute blood, melanin, and proteinaceous fluid. Most other tissues are hypointense to brain, and include bone, most tumours, ischaemia, and demyelination.

T1 sequences are very good for demonstrating contrast enhancement, since paramagnetic substances greatly shorten the time taken to return to resting state, and so tissues that these contrast agents leak into (i.e. localized damage to the blood–brain barrier) show marked enhancement of the signal intensity in these regions. Plain T1 images should be compared with T1 sequences following contrast administration (gadolinium is most often used—a paramagnetic substance) to highlight areas that enhance.

T2 SEQUENCES

These are sequences that are based upon the time taken for the protons within a given tissue to return to their 'out of phase' spinning state following the radiofrequency pulse. A prolonged T2 relaxation time gives high signal intensity—water, and therefore CSF, appear as white on T2-weighted sequences.

In T2 sequences, tumours are usually hyperintense as well, reflecting the presence of fluid from cystic and necrotic areas as well as from neovascularization and tumour-associated oedema. These sequences are particularly useful when looking at spinal pathology since the white CSF makes a good contrast and backdrop to any pathology. Tumours or disc herniations can usually be seen to displace the normal white areas. Cranially, T2 sequences tend to overestimate the size of tumours, as the lesion seen is the tumour plus the surrounding oedema.

A variation of T2 is the fluid-attenuated inversion recovery (FLAIR) sequence, which essentially nullifies the signal from fluid, and so is good for demonstrating lesions close to the normal anatomical CSF collections (i.e. periventricular, or at the peripheries).

DIFFUSION-WEIGHTED IMAGING

Diffusion-weighted imaging (DWI) MRI has been increasingly used in recent years. In simple terms, DWI reflects the rate of water diffusion: changes in cellular density can affect the extent to which water can move by random

Brownian motion. The impedance of water diffusion is quantified as the apparent diffusion coefficient (ADC).

As a general rule, restricted diffusion is represented on imaging by density opposite to that of CSF, since CSF is essentially water: for example, if CSF is black then areas of restricted diffusion will be white—and there should be a corresponding area of black on the ADC map. The presence of restricted diffusion on DWI can help differentiate between a tumour (which has water-rich fluid) and an abscess (water molecules will not move around as readily in thick pus as they will in less viscous fluids), but can often look similar on conventional CT or MRI (e.g. ring-enhancing, with perifocal oedema). These are not fixed rules, but in context with clinical findings they may help aid diagnosis and treatment planning.

DIFFUSION TENSOR IMAGING

Diffusion tensor imaging (DTI) is also becoming more commonly used, particularly in oncological neurosurgery, for resection of tumours around critical white matter fibre tracts such as the corticospinal tract. This works in a similar fashion to DWI, but is vectorized and so includes directionality of flow of water molecules. Bundles of axons arranged in fibre tracts within the brain 'encourage' the diffusion of water molecules along their path, since diffusion will follow the path of least resistance along white matter tracts.

These sequences give the surgeon information regarding proximity, infiltration, deviation, or destruction of lesions around important tracts. When combined with volumetric images and neuronavigation, these can be used intraoperatively to allow the surgeon to visualize and avoid critical structures when working close to them.

MAGNETIC RESONANCE ANGIOGRAPHY (MRA)

Sequences can be designed to detect the different signal intensities generated by rapidly flowing protons (i.e. in blood vessels) compared with those that are stationary. By selecting different flow velocities, arteries or veins can be targeted. As the technology improves, the sensitivity for detection of abnormalities is approaching that of traditional angiography; however, it is not there yet, and does not afford the therapeutic opportunities that an invasive angiogram does.

HIGH-, ULTRA-HIGH-, AND LOW-FIELD MRI

As with most technologies in medicine, there is always a push to develop more powerful equipment. Standard clinical MR scanners are typically 1.5 Tesla (1.5T), and 3T scanners are now widely available. Values such as 1.5T and 3T refer to the strength of the constant magnetic field that aligns the proton spin, as discussed earlier.

Increasing magnetic field strength offers greater spatial resolution, determined by signal-to-noise ratio, which is proportional to nuclear spin polarization which scales linearly with magnetic field strength: hence the greater the magnetic field, the higher the signal-to-noise ratio, and the better the spatial resolution.

In the research arena, there are 7T scanners being used to scan human brains *in vivo*, and even more powerful ones yet are in operation (up to nearly 12T, which is a more powerful magnetic field than used in the Large Hadron Collider), though they are not in standard clinical usage: these offer exquisite spatial resolution.

At the other end of the spectrum, low-field MRI is likely to become an area of more interest in medical diagnostics. The use of smaller, cheaper, safer scanning, employing low magnetic fields and new techniques to ensure that the signal-to-noise ratio remains adequate, is likely to become an attractive option in future.

MR SPECTROSCOPY

MR spectroscopy (MRS) can be useful for differentiating between inflammatory conditions, metabolic diseases, tumours, radiation necrosis, and abscesses. MRS provides information about the chemical composition of a lesion. For example, N-acetyl aspartate (NAA) is a neuronal marker which is usually decreased in pathological CNS conditions (breaking down to glutamate and aspartate). Choline, on the other hand, is increased with plasma membrane turnover and hence shows increased levels in tumours.

FUNCTIONAL MRI

By measuring blood oxygenation, functional MRI (fMRI) infers brain activity by brain oxygen usage. This works on the premise that haemoglobin and oxyhaemoglobin have different magnetic characteristics. 'Activation' of areas of brain can then be measured during testing—for example by showing a patient a visual stimulus.

IMAGE-GUIDED SURGERY (NEURONAVIGATION)

Usage of neuronavigation systems is now standard practice in neurosurgery. The basic premise is that a high-resolution 3D volumetric brain scan can be uploaded to the navigation software and displayed on a screen in front of the surgeon in the operating theatre. The surgeon then tells the system where fixed points on the patient's head are, and the software is able to match this against the same points on the uploaded scan. This means that navigation pointers can be used on the real patient, and this is then pin-pointed to the relative point on the scan and displayed in real time on the screen. This is particularly useful when planning a craniotomy for a lesion, since the lesion can be seen on the screen and therefore marked out on the scalp/skull using the navigation equipment. It is also very useful for placing catheters into the ventricles of the brain, since the burr-hole and then the trajectory can be preplanned.

The most commonly employed systems work using either an optical system or an electromagnetic system. Optical systems work by having the patient's head pinned in position relative to a reference array which must remain fixed. The coordinates of the navigation pointers are then calculated relative to the reference array and then shown on the screen.

Electromagnetic systems do not require the patient to be pinned, but are less precise. These calculate the position of navigation pointers relative to a sensor placed on a fixed position on the patient's head. Metal instruments also interfere with these systems, though improvements are being made to minimize this.

It is likely that your local radiology department will not do navigation-compatible CT or MRI scans as standard, and so you should remember specifically to request these if it is likely that neuronavigation will be used in the case for which a scan is being obtained.

DIGITAL SUBTRACTION ANGIOGRAPHY

Conventional digital subtraction angiography (DSA) is the gold standard for the detection of vascular abnormalities. New advances have been the ability to treat these abnormalities endovascularly and, potentially, to treat complications of subarachnoid haemorrhage (SAH), such as vasospasm. There is a small but definite risk attached to this procedure, therefore it is not used as a routine screening test but only in cases where there is good reason to suspect underlying vascular abnormalities.

You should know the basic anatomy on an angiogram and what to look out for in order to be able to diagnose an AVM or aneurysm. There are usually several views done and they are marked in the top corner usually as LICA (left internal carotid artery), RICA (right internal carotid artery), and posterior circulation. There are anteroposterior and lateral views for LICA, RICA, and posterior circulation. See Figures 7.1, 7.2, 7.3, and 7.4) for examples of standard angiogram views.

Make sure that you can read the patient's name and that you have the two LICA and two RICA as well as the two posterior circulation sets together. There will also be an oblique or spin view of the LICA and RICA: ignore them for now.

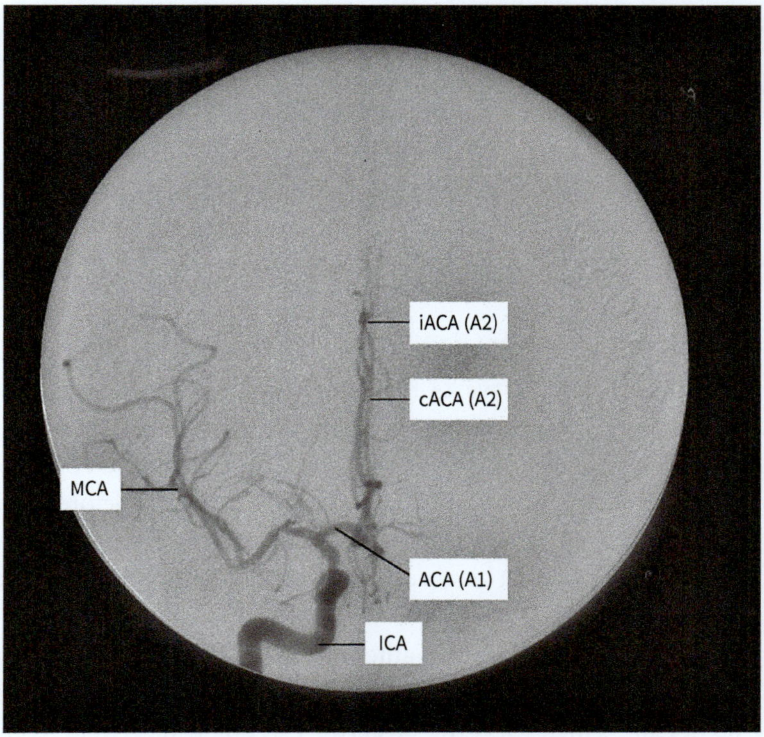

Figure 7.1 Right internal carotid angiogram sequence (posterior-anterior view). The vessels are annotated as follows: middle cerebral artery, MCA; internal carotid artery ICA; anterior cerebral artery A1 segment, ACA(A1); ipsilateral anterior cerebral artery A2 segment, iACA(A2); and contralateral anterior cerebral artery A2 segment, cACA(A2).

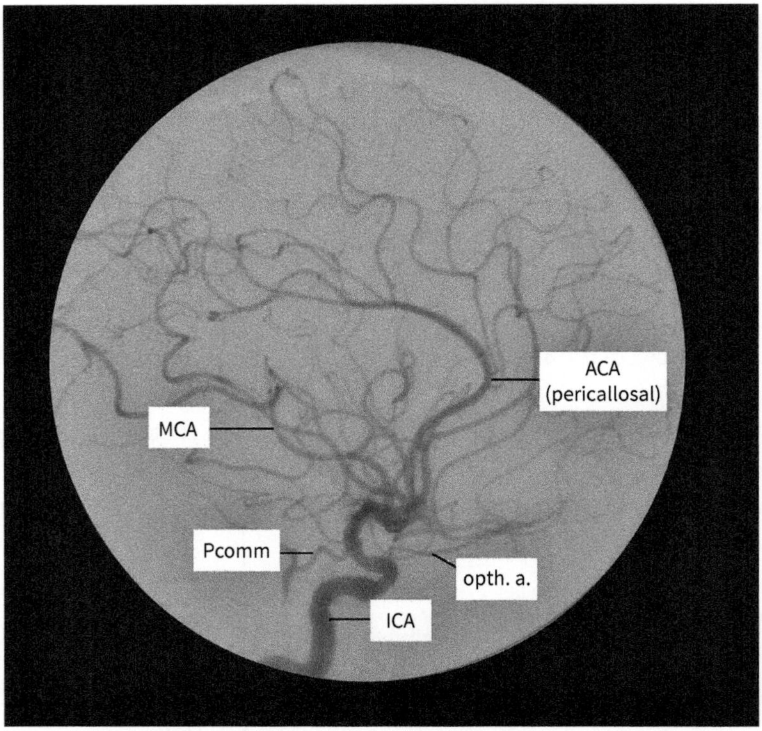

Figure 7.2 Right internal carotid angiogram sequence (lateral view). The vessels are annotated as follows: internal carotid artery, ICA; ophthalmic artery, ophth. A; posterior communicating artery, Pcomm; middle cerebral artery, MCA; anterior cerebral artery, ACA.

It is important to practise looking at the different arteries in the different views. The internal carotid passes through the petrous bone and has several twists and turns before passing through the cavernous sinus and exiting through the foramen lacerum into the cranial space. It then has an ophthalmic segment, communicating segment, and a choroidal segment, before it divides into the middle cerebral artery (MCA) and anterior cerebral artery (ACA). The names of these segments are derived from the branches that leave the carotid.

The ophthalmic artery runs in an anterior direction and is the first branch seen. This is followed by the posterior communicating artery (Pcomm) slightly higher up, which joins the posterior cerebral artery. The Pcomm is usually slightly larger than the ophthalmic artery, but sometimes it is much larger and this is then called a foetal Pcomm. In the foetus, the posterior circulation is fed by the anterior circulation via the Pcomm, and only later in foetal development is the posterior circulation fed by the vertebral arteries and the

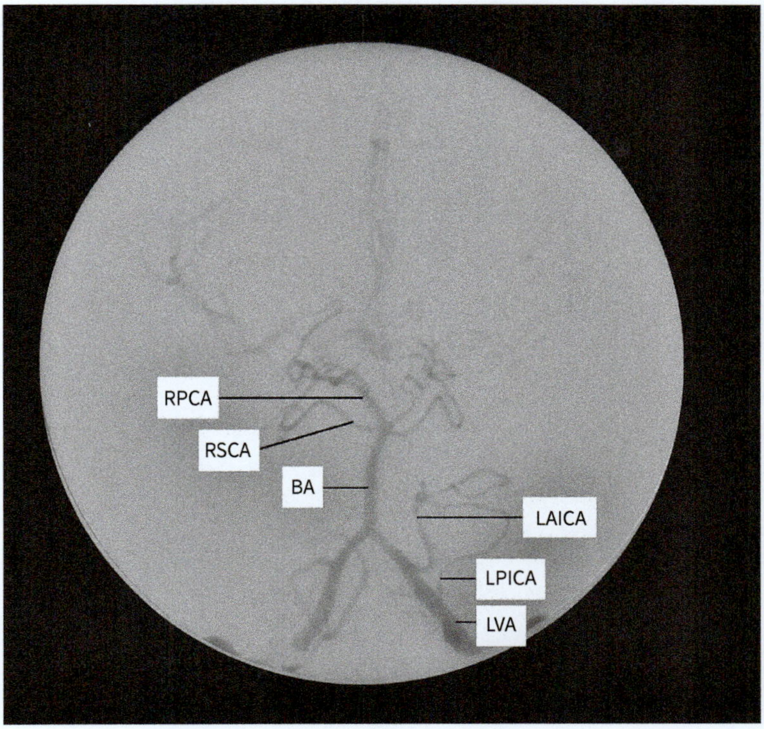

Figure 7.3 Left vertebral artery angiogram sequence (anterior view). The vessels are annotated as follows: left vertebral artery, LVA; left posterior inferior cerebellar artery, LPICA; left anterior inferior cerebellar artery, LAICA; basilar artery, BA; right superior cerebellar artery, RSCA; right posterior cerebral artery, RPCA. Note that all these are paired, bilateral vessels, apart from the single midline basilar artery.

basilar artery. If this state persists, the Pcomm is hypertrophied and important in the supply of the posterior cerebral artery territory (occipital lobes).

The next artery is the anterior choroidal artery which is usually within 4 mm of the bifurcation of the carotid and also extends posteriorly. Aneurysms are flow-related phenomena and thus are usually seen at the origin of these arteries rather than distally. Therefore, if you carefully follow the carotid up to the bifurcation, looking at the origins of the ophthalmic, posterior communicating, and anterior choroidal arteries, you will not miss aneurysms (looking like round or irregular outpouchings) on these arteries. Do this for both the left and the right sides.

On the lateral views there are two areas to look at now. One is the very busy area where the branches of the MCA are coming directly at us and are quite bundled together on the image, and the other is the area of the ACA, which curves anteriorly and around the corpus callosum, and

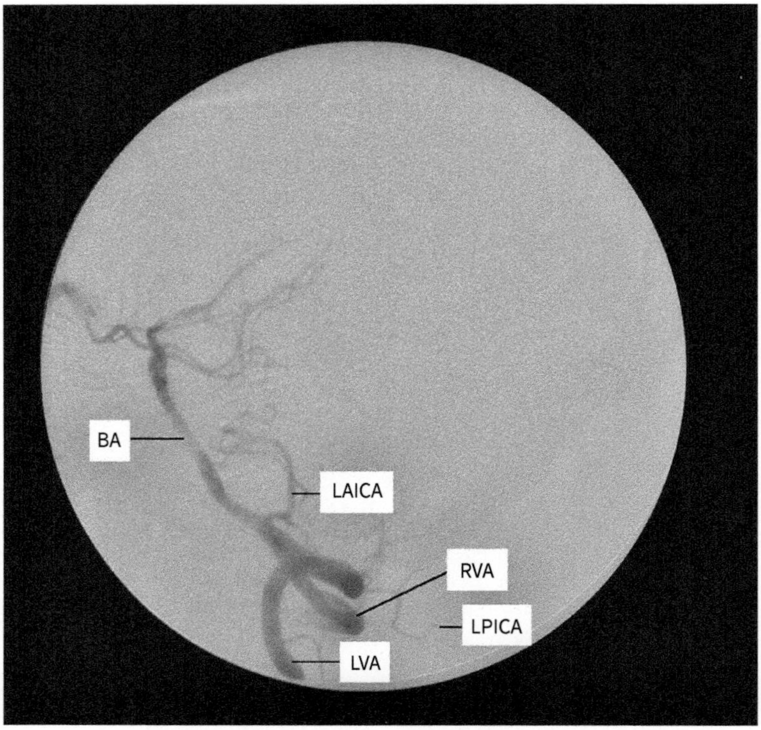

Figure 7.4 Left vertebral artery angiogram sequence (lateral view). The vessels are annotated as follows: left vertebral artery, LVA; right vertebral artery, RVA; basilar artery, BA; left posterior inferior cerebellar artery, LPICA; left anterior inferior cerebellar artery, LAICA.

allows easy identification of the branches as they are seen on their lateral aspect. The ACA has a pre-communicating segment, a communicating segment, and a post-communicating segment. The pre-communicating segment is short and extends from the origin of the ACA to the anterior communicating artery (Acomm) which connects the two ACAs. Most aneurysms are found around the Acomm as this is where the most turbulent flow occurs as the arteries change direction. Distal to the communicating segment there are several branches: the frontopolar, callosomarginal, and pericallosal arteries. It is unusual for aneurysms to occur in these branches.

On the anteroposterior view, the MCA artery can be visualized properly and it has two bifurcations where aneurysms usually form: one proximal and the other more distal. This view will also demonstrate which ACA is the dominant artery and whether it flows across to the other ACA via the Acomm. This is important, since we usually approach an Acomm aneurysm from the non-dominant hemisphere.

The posterior circulation should be filled by both vertebral arteries during angiography, and an anteroposterior view and a lateral view are used to demonstrate aneurysms. Identifying AVMs can take some experience. Angiography is a dynamic process and there will be several images of the same view on one film. This is to demonstrate the filling of the arteries; the last images are the venous phase and start to show up the veins into which the arteries drain. Seeing a vein earlier than expected would mean a shortcut between the arterial and venous system and therefore an AVM. A blush of arteries and veins together can be quite easily seen, and this also denotes an AVM. It is sometimes necessary to demonstrate not only the two internal carotid arteries (ICAs) and two vertebral arteries (four-vessel cerebral angiography) but also the two external carotid arteries (six-vessel cerebral angiography) when there is a suspicion that the arteries supplying the dura contribute to an AVM.

POSITRON EMISSION TOMOGRAPHY

Only a very few centres have positron emission tomography (PET) as it requires a cyclotron. PET scans are functional scans which can detect radioactive isotopes administered to patients. Oxygen uptake and glucose delivery can demonstrate biological activity and, for instance, differentiate between a tumour or post-radiation necrosis, a distinction which is notoriously difficult to make by other means.

INTRACRANIAL PRESSURE MONITORING

Intracranial pressure (ICP) can be measured from three anatomically distinct locations: subdural, intraparenchymal, and intraventricular. Subdural sensors are the most frequently used and the least sensitive, but carry the lowest risk of infection. Placing the sensor into the parenchyma increases the sensitivity and accuracy of the measurement but increases the risk of infection. Intraventricular monitoring via an extra ventricular drain (EVD) is the most reliable and allows the option of draining CSF off when there is an increase in ICP. However, this carries the greatest risk of infection. The sensors are attached to a monitor and the pressures are recorded continuously. CSF pressures differ from person to person, but a normal pressure is considered to be between 10 and 20 mmHg. Pressure of more than 20 mmHg usually warrants treatment. Looking at the pressure waves on the monitor also provides important information.

Sustained rises in ICP are thought to correlate with secondary brain damage and are therefore an important indicator of deterioration and consequently of the need for intervention. If patients are awake, then clinical examination is used to gauge neurological status. This is not possible when the patient is asleep, and ICP monitoring therefore provides vital information about progressive intracranial injury. In cases where there are short transient increases in ICP the clinical effect is usually not severe. If there is a continuous increase or a plateau in ICP, it becomes important to treat, as these are usually malignant increases. By measuring the ICP and mean arterial pressure (MAP) we are able to calculate cerebral perfusion pressure (CPP).

$$CPP = MAP - ICP$$

This allows manipulation of blood pressure in order to optimize cerebral perfusion. Pressure monitoring is most commonly used in traumatic brain injury, but some centres also use it in other intracranial pathology such as SAH. See the section in Chapter 10 (*Basic Neurosurgical Procedures*) for the insertion of an ICP monitor.

DUPLEX DOPPLER

This is a velocity measurement of blood flow, and is used to provide evidence of vasospasm (arterial narrowing that may or may not cause a focal ischaemic neurological deficit following SAH). The MCA is usually targeted through the thin squamous temporal bone, but the Doppler technician can also target other intracranial arteries. If the blood flow exceeds 200 ml/s in the MCA, it is indicative of vasospasm. In the awake patient, deterioration is usually the hallmark of clinically relevant vasospasm but duplex Doppler can diagnose vasospasm in the awake and comatose/sedated patient. It is therefore a valuable tool in the treatment and monitoring of SAH patients.

JUGULAR VENOUS OXYGEN MONITORING

Continuously monitoring the amount of oxygen in the venous blood as it returns from the brain can help to tell us what the oxygenation of the brain parenchyma is like, and this procedure is used in some centres. The aim is to stop the oxygenation from dropping below 60% by manipulating the blood pressure and ventilation requirements. Few units use it routinely.

8

Ward Management of Neurosurgical Patients

Reuben D. Johnson

CONTENTS

INTRODUCTION

Individual Consultants and different neurosurgical units will undoubtedly have their own preferences as to how to manage patients on the ward. However, it is unlikely that the management will differ drastically from that described below. This chapter is designed to give you an overview and an insight into what you are trying to achieve while managing patients on the ward. It cannot be overemphasized how important your input is on the ward. The whole unit is built around the nursing staff and the surgical trainees. The calibre of the current batch of surgical trainees is evidenced by how well the unit functions. You should take pride in owning the unit and consider the Registrars and Consultants as mere infrequent visitors—it should never be possible for them to know more about your patients than you do! Good peri-operative care really does equate with good outcome.

ADMISSIONS

Most neurosurgical units are busy with a large number of elective and emergency admissions every day. It is essential to be aware of patients who are going to be admitted under your care, so that you can organize your time and prioritize appropriately. There is much that can be done to pre-empt problems and facilitate care before patients arrive on the ward.

EMERGENCY TRANSFERS

Most units will have a list of patients due to come in from other hospitals. Make sure that, at the beginning of each day, you find out from the on-call Registrar which patients are due to come in and what the plan of action for each is. For some patients the plan may be to see and assess, whereas for others it may be that going to theatre is a near certainty unless the patient's condition is radically different from that described by the referring team.

It is recommended that you contact a member of the team looking after each patient in the referring hospital and check up on the patient's situation. A patient might have been on the list for some days and things could have changed considerably. It is useful to ascertain an update on the patient's clinical state and find out what treatment has been initiated. Has the patient with the subarachnoid haemorrhage (SAH) been started on adequate IV fluids? Has the patient with the brain tumour been started on steroids? Has aspirin been stopped on the patient with the posterior fossa tumour, who is due for theatre tomorrow? Has the international normalized ratio (INR) been checked on the patient with the subdural haematoma? Has the sodium been checked recently on the SAH patient?

For a patient being transferred as an emergency, it might be possible to arrange for cross-matched blood to be sent with the patient. For every patient who is transferred, it is imperative that copies of their scans are available. In most cases this will be via an image link facility, but if this is not available a CD of the scans (or, if need be, hard copies) should be sent with the patient. This is extremely important as it will prevent delays in going to theatre—in neurosurgery, time is life.

The following is a good check-list for a sure and safe transfer:

S *Scans:* have hard copies been sent with the patient?
U *Update:* has the patient's condition changed?
R *Rx:* what treatment has the patient received so far?
E *Electrolytes:* are all blood results available?
&
S *Steroids:* have steroids been given (dose and duration)?
A *Aspirin:* if necessary, has aspirin been stopped?
F *Fluids:* has an appropriate fluid regime been commenced?
E *Extra investigations:* CXR? Coag screen? PSA/ESR?

ELECTIVE CASES

It is advisable to make yourself aware of the operating list well in advance. For each patient on the list, make sure they have had a full medical clerking and that bloods have been taken. Patients who have not been assessed in pre-admission clinic may need to be admitted early for a full medical work-up. Make sure you have checked their clotting function and platelet count, and that any blood thinning agents have been stopped. The guidelines for stopping anticoagulants vary according to the indication for their use and the operation to be performed. In general, aspirin should be stopped 10 days before surgery, warfarin should be reversed on admission 1–2 days before surgery, and low molecular weight heparin stopped 48 h before surgery. However, it is essential to know why the patient is on anticoagulants and to liaise closely with the medical team that normally manages the patient. This is particularly important in the case of cardiology patients who may have eluting stents. Find out whether the patient needs any blood saved or cross-matched.

An electrocardiogram (ECG) should generally be performed in all patients with a cardiac history (including hypertension) or who are over the age of 60 years. A pre-operative chest X-ray (CXR) should be performed in patients with cardiorespiratory disease (with no CXR in the last 6 months), acute respiratory tract signs or symptoms, malignant disease, and in patients who have resided in a tuberculosis-endemic area. Alert the anaesthetist to any problems.

Find out whether your patient requires any specific pre-operative imaging. The neuroradiology department will appreciate knowing this well in advance. Make sure the patient's images are available for the Consultant to view the day before the operation, and that these are also made available in the operating room.

You should ask your Registrar or Consultant whether a Neuro-Intensive Care Unit (NICU) bed may be required post-operatively, and, if so, give the NICU department plenty of notice as they are usually very short of beds.

The following is a useful check-list for what needs to be done in working up elective admissions:

1. History and examination.
2. Blood—FBC, U&E, clotting, G + S or X-match.
3. ECG, CXR (if required).
4. CT/MRI images on the computer system.
5. Pre-operative and intra-operative imaging pre-arranged (if required).
6. HDU/ICU bed pre-arranged (if required).
7. Anaesthetist review.
8. Consent + site of surgery (SOS) marking by Registrar/Consultant.

GENERAL PRECAUTIONS

In neurosurgery, there are a few basic precautions to keep in mind during your daily tasks, such as prescribing fluids and analgesia. In general, intravenous dextrose solution should be avoided, as it can alter the plasma osmolality and increase swelling at the site of intracranial pathology. Normal saline should therefore be used as first-line IV fluid, and in neurosurgery you are allowed to prescribe more than one litre of normal saline in 24 h. You should, however, keep a close eye on the patient's sodium levels, particularly if their renal function is impaired.

Neurosurgical patients are also at higher risk of developing abnormalities of sodium due to cerebral salt wasting, the syndrome of inappropriate antidiuretic hormone secretion, and diabetes insipidus (DI), so most patients should have a blood test at least two to three times weekly, unless the patient has suffered an SAH, in which case electrolytes should be checked daily.

When prescribing analgesia, you should avoid non-steroidal anti-inflammatory drugs (NSAIDs) if possible, particularly if the patient is going to theatre, as this may affect their platelet count. If you are monitoring a neurosurgical patient's level of consciousness you should prescribe opiates cautiously, as they can make patients feel drowsy and thereby mask any decrease in the level of consciousness due to the underlying intracranial pathology.

Finally, ensure that bleeding risk is minimized as much as possible during surgery. This means that you should routinely check that clotting function tests and platelet counts are up to date and clearly documented in the notes, and that any potential blood thinners are avoided in all patients going to theatre. You won't go very wrong if you adhere to the simple CODE of neurosurgical practice:

C *Clotting:* avoid blood thinners before surgery; keep clotting function tests up to date.
O *Opiates:* avoid if monitoring GCS.
D *Dextrose:* avoid in neurosurgical patients; prescribe 0.9% saline.
E *Electrolytes:* watch the sodium!

PERI-OPERATIVE CARE

CEREBRAL TUMOURS

Patients with cerebral tumours tend to present with a progressive history of headache, focal neurological deficit, or seizures. Patients with signs of raised intracranial pressure or focal neurology will usually benefit from a course of steroids. A loading dose, for example 10 mg dexamethasone IV, can be given, followed by 4 mg dexamethasone (oral or IV) qds. This can be gradually reduced after surgery in most instances. If a patient deteriorates while on steroids, due to further mass effect of the tumour, it is often worth trying another loading dose of 8–10 mg dexamethasone IV. However, in all cases of neurological deterioration, repeat neuro-imaging must be considered on an urgent basis. Particularly post-operatively, patients are at risk of deteriorating due to increased cerebral oedema or haematoma.

If you think the patient's Glasgow Coma Scale (GCS) score has dropped even a point you should inform your Registrar after stabilizing the patient and discuss arranging a post-operative CT scan. It is important to be overcautious with steroids, and to check with the Registrar what the exact management plan is. Some patients may have their steroids reduced and stopped, while others may be left on a maintenance dose of 2 mg dexamethasone bd orally, at least until seen by the oncologist. Patients cannot be left on steroids indefinitely, and, as a general rule, patients are not usually discharged on steroids unless there is an express instruction from a senior to do so. Steroids have serious side effects, including psychosis and intracranial or intraspinal sepsis. All patients on steroids need to receive some form of protection against gastric ulceration, for example ranitidine or lansoprazole.

In patients with tumours without a tissue diagnosis it is essential to ensure that basic investigations have been performed to rule out a primary lesion outside the central nervous system (CNS). This means that a full history needs to be taken. For example, has the patient:

- coughed up any blood?
- had any change of bowel habit?
- passed any blood in the stool?
- had difficulty passing urine?

A full clinical examination needs to be performed, including a breast examination in women. A chest X-ray to look for an obvious lung primary is a minimum requirement. Basic blood work should include a urea and electrolytes (U&E), full blood count (FBC), liver function tests (LFTs), erythrocyte sedimentation rate (ESR), and clotting studies in the form of an INR. Tumour markers may also be useful in certain patients, and include alpha-fetoprotein (testicular cancer), carcino-embryonic antigen (CEA) (colorectal, pancreatic, breast cancers), CA-125 (breast cancer), S-100 (melanoma), and prostate-specific antigen (PSA) (prostate cancer). Below is a checklist for cerebral tumours.

Check-list for cerebral tumours

Pre-op

1. Full Hx and Ex for primary tumour.
2. Bloods: FBC, U&E, LFTs, CRP, ESR, clotting studies, tumour markers.
3. CXR.
4. Steroids: loading dose (10 mg dexamethasone) and maintenance (4 mg dexamethasone qds).
5. CT scans: done and available on the ward.
6. Operative plan: biopsy/debulk.

Post-op

1. Review steroid plan: reduce and stop, or continue maintenance dose.
2. Oncology referral, and liaise with neuropathology regarding histological diagnosis.

SUBARACHNOID HAEMORRHAGE

The ward management of subarachnoid haemorrhage (SAH) is a fine balance and also extremely important. A good operation is not the only surgical factor that determines a good outcome in SAH. A large part is due to your diligence and meticulous care on the ward. In an ideal world, all SAH patients would be best managed in a high-dependency environment. However, resources being what they are, many patients of good grade on the World Federation of Neurological Surgeons (WFNS) grading scale (see Chapter 15, Table 15.3) will, of necessity, be admitted to the neurosurgical ward prior to angiography and surgical treatment. It is important to have a clear idea of the risks these patients face and of what you are trying to achieve peri-operatively.

Patients face the greatest risk of a devastating re-bleed in the first 24 h and the risk of re-bleed is as high as 20% in the first 2 weeks following the initial event—with 4% re-bleeding on the first day and 1.5% per day for the next 2 weeks. There is an 80% mortality with a re-bleed. Blood often enters the ventricular system at the time of the initial bleed, and patients may develop obstructive hydrocephalus due to blockage of CSF flow within the ventricular system (e.g. aqueduct or outlet of 4th ventricle) or communicating hydrocephalus due to blockage of reabsorption through the arachnoid granulations (this usually occurs at a later stage).

If there is a large intraparenchymal blood clot, patients may deteriorate due to the mass effect. SAH patients are at high risk of developing vasospasm, which is one of the major causes of neurological deficit and morbidity in this group (see Chapter 15, Tables 15.4 and 15.5). The greatest risk of vasospasm after the initial bleed occurs around 1 week, especially days 4–7; the risk is low in the first 3 days and later than 2 weeks.

Electrolyte abnormalities are common in SAH patients—in particular, hyponatraemia due to cerebral salt wasting. There is also a small but not insignificant risk of seizures developing following SAH. In summary, therefore, you need to be aware that patients admitted with SAH are specifically at risk of:

1. Re-bleeding.
2. Hydrocephalus (usually obstructive in acute phase).
3. Vasospasm/delayed ischaemic neurological deficit (DIND).
4. Hyponatraemia.
5. Seizures.

Your peri-operative care is aimed at preventing these complications by reducing the risk of their happening. Measures that need to be taken to prevent re-bleeding include preventing excessive rises in blood pressure. This has to be balanced with preventing an excessive drop in blood pressure which might exacerbate vasospasm. In general, most neurosurgical units will aim to maintain a systolic blood pressure in the range of 120 mmHg to 150 mmHg in patients with an unsecured aneurysm. This may be difficult to achieve, however, and you may need to seek the help of the NICU team.

The patient should be nursed in as quiet and calm an environment as possible, and usually on strict bed rest. Be careful not to put patients in a corner of the ward that is quiet because it is not readily visible—when these patients do deteriorate you will need to act quickly. Patients may be better with 30° head up as, at least in theory, this may help in maintaining CSF flow, reduce intracranial pressure (ICP) due to increased venous return, and prevent chest problems in the more elderly patients. Remember that placing patients on bed rest increases their risk of developing deep-vein thromboses (DVTs), so thromboembolic-deterrent stockings (TEDs) should be prescribed.

Medication is important in preventing large increases in blood pressure, and adequate analgesia should be prescribed, for example a codeine phosphate infusion which can be titrated against the clinical response and helps to guard against a precipitous drop in blood pressure associated with some forms of intramuscular analgesia regimes. Antiemetics, and laxatives such as lactulose, help prevent the blood pressure changes associated with nausea and constipation, and should be prescribed. Oral nimodipine has been shown in randomized controlled trials to reduce delayed ischaemic deficits associated with vasospasm. The regime that should be used is 60 mg of nimodipine orally every 4 h, and this should be continued for 21 days after the initial bleed. If patients are unable to take oral medication then an IV infusion can be used instead. However, the evidence is only for oral nimodipine given 4-hourly, and not for IV regimens. The efficacy of calcium antagonists might not be as clear-cut for patients with established ischaemia or with a poor initial grade of SAH. Further studies may reveal improved dosing regimens, and consider the efficacy of calcium antagonists other than nimodipine.

SAH patients should be well hydrated with oral or IV fluids as this is thought to reduce the risk of vasospasm. At least 3 litres of fluid per day should be given; if this is done intravenously, saline is preferable. Hydration is one of the three Hs of 'triple-H' therapy for vasospasm. Daily electrolytes should be monitored, with a close eye on the sodium to identify hyponatraemia early. Routine blood work should include coagulation studies in the form of an INR and group-and-save (cross-match at least 4 units if the patient is going to have an aneurysm clipped).

The following is a useful checklist for the management of subarachnoid haemorrhage:

Check-list for subarachnoid haemorrhage

1. Strict bed rest.
2. Oral nimodipine 60 mg 4-hourly.
3. 3 litres fluids/day.
4. Analgesia—for example codeine phosphate.
5. Antiemetics
6. Lactulose 10 ml bd.
7. U&E, FBC, INR, X-match (daily Na+).
8. Hourly neuro-obs minimum.
9. CT scans available on ward.
10. Results of lumbar puncture (if done) written in notes.
11. CT angiogram or cerebral angiography requested.

Although the administration of prophylactic anticonvulsant medication has been accepted practice for aneurysmal surgery for many years, the benefits of these medications need to be balanced against the risk of adverse reactions. A retrospective study published in 1995 found that the incidence of seizures following craniotomy for aneurysm repair was low, and it was concluded that the administration of prophylactic phenytoin was necessary only for the first 7 days post-operatively. There seems to be a paucity of strong evidence for the prolonged use of prophylactic anticonvulsants in SAH.

HEAD INJURIES

You will see many patients with head injuries during your time as a neurosurgical trainee. In general, if a patient needs admission to a neurosurgical unit then the head injury is severe. Some patients will arrive and go directly to theatre for evacuation of a traumatic bleed (extradural or acute subdural haematomas) or exploration of depressed skull fractures. Others may be unconscious due to diffuse axonal injury or cerebral contusions and will be admitted to the NICU for ICP monitoring and care. There will also be a subgroup of patients with contusions or small intracranial haematomas who are considered at high risk of further deterioration and are, therefore, admitted to the neurosurgical unit for ICP monitoring and observation. If the condition of these patients deteriorates they will need rescanning and either theatre or ICU care.

The principles of head injury care are the same for all patients, and while all should have been assessed according to the Advanced Trauma Life Support (ATLS) protocol in the referring hospital, it is nevertheless essential that on a patient's arrival in the neurosurgical unit, you reassess each patient according to the ATLS protocol, as the patient's situation may have changed.

If a patient is intubated and ventilated, check pupillary response. If bilaterally fixed, dilated pupils are found, it may not be appropriate to undertake surgery. If the patient arrives unventilated, then your assessment might determine the need for intubation. Remember: GCS less than 8 = intubate! If you are not happy with the safety of the airway, speak to your Registrar or the anaesthetist and ask about high dependency unit (HDU)/ICU care.

Ensure that, if the neck is not immobilized, the patient has had adequate C-spine clearance in the referring hospital. Find the C-spine films and determine whether they are adequate or not. If the patient is not sufficiently awake for clinical assessment of the C-spine do not be afraid to put a collar on the C-spine, even if the neck films are normal. The patient's neck can be reassessed when they are more alert, or by further imaging.

Ensure that you are happy with your primary survey before moving on to the secondary survey. If a full trauma series has not been undertaken then ensure that this is done. Check the notes for blood results—bloods may have been taken but perhaps not checked before transfers. Ensure that you have a sample of blood for cross-match.

Document your neurological assessment clearly to include GCS and pupil reactions. If a patient has deteriorated neurologically at any time, reassess everything again and discuss with the Registrar before sending the patient for another scan. Ask for a minimum of hourly neuro-obs from the nursing staff. Examine the scalp for wounds and see what management and care they have received. All wounds need to be cleaned properly. If there is an underlying depressed skull fracture, proper surgical exploration and debridement will be required in theatre. Check specifically for CSF leak from the nose and ears and document it.

There are several controversial issues in the management of head injuries. Should prophylactic antibiotics be given in the presence of CSF leak? Are steroids of any benefit in head injury? Are anticonvulsants indicated to prevent epilepsy?

Antibiotics

The use of antibiotics in neurosurgery is widespread yet remains controversial due to the paucity of a solid evidence base. This reflects the difficulties in gathering data in this area of neurosurgery. For example, although in skull fractures with associated CSF leak the incidence of infection may be as high as 25%, the actual incidence of CSF leak is very low. This means that it is extremely difficult to undertake a proper prospective study to compare prophylactic antibiotic regimens with acute treatment of frank infection. The rationale for recommendations regarding the use of prophylactic antibiotics in neurosurgery tends to be based on assessments of the risk of infection, the likely organisms involved, and the penetration of the antibiotic to the site of infection (e.g. CSF penetration across the blood–brain barrier, or penetration of tissues in the surgical field). Prophylactic antibiotics are not always given. If a patient is septic, however, then antibiotics are usually indicated, although ultimately the use of antibiotics or not will be decided on a case-by-case basis. If there is an open skull fracture then it is arguable that antibiotics should be given to prevent osteomyelitis. Discuss with your Registrar regarding choice of antibiotic, and never perform a lumbar puncture (LP) without first clearing it with a senior.

Steroids

Steroids are sometimes given in patients with head injuries, although there is scant evidence for the value of doing so. A comprehensive review of randomized trials on the use of steroids in head injury (Alderson and Roberts, 1997) found that even when all patient data from trials up to 1997 were combined, the numbers of patients involved was only a little over 2000, and there seemed to be only a statistically non-significant 2% reduction in mortality with steroid use. Nevertheless, a 2% reduction in mortality would represent a large number of lives saved in view of the millions of deaths from severe head injury that occur each year. This was the incentive for a subsequent randomized placebo-controlled trial (the CRASH trial) of intravenous steroids in adults with head injury (Edwards et al., 2005). This trial, involving 9673 patients, was completed in 2005; the 6-month outcomes showed a significantly higher risk of death, and a non-significantly higher risk of death or severe disability, with corticosteroids than with placebo. The investigators concluded that corticosteroids should not be routinely administered in the treatment of head injury.

Anticonvulsants

The situation is no more clear-cut for anticonvulsants, but their use, and that of phenytoin in particular, is widespread practice with patients who suffer seizures following traumatic brain injury. More controversial, however, is the use of phenytoin prophylactically to prevent seizures occurring, especially when one has to balance the potentially harmful adverse effects of medication. Up to 50% of patients suffering a penetrating brain injury will develop seizures. Of these, approximately 10% will show seizures in the first week following injury, and by 2 years around 80% of those who are going to fit will have done so (Pruitt, 2001). A seizure occurring in the first week is referred to as an early post-traumatic seizure (EPTS); seizures occurring after this period are referred to as delayed post-traumatic seizures (DPTS). When considering the use of anticonvulsants to prevent DPTS it is important to note that, according to available evidence, 95% of patients suffering penetrating brain injury will remain seizure-free if they have not suffered a seizure in the first 3 years (Weiss et al., 1986).

Where trials have been conducted there is considerable disagreement regarding the validity of the methodology, and disparity in the results, with one body of opinion suggesting that phenytoin is effective in reducing EPTS but not DPTS (Temkin et al., 1990), while another body of opinion holds that phenytoin is lacking in efficacy in both situations (Young et al., 1973). The evidence so far seems to suggest that if there is any benefit from phenytoin it will be only in EPTS, and so administration for a longer period of time would not be necessary. However, individual Consultants working side-by-side within the same neurosurgical unit may differ in their practice with regard to prophylactic phenytoin, and it is an interesting exercise to enquire as to their reasons, as they will have a wealth of clinical experience which will have shaped their practice. So far, there is little evidence concerning the degree to which the nature of penetrating brain injury influences the risk of post-traumatic seizure, for example the site of cortical injury, the presence of a foreign body, or infection. This does not mean to say that such factors are not relevant but only that there just has not been a study big enough to find any answers.

There is a growing trend to use levetiracetam instead of phenytoin; this is because regular level checks are not needed, and also because in certain Asian populations phenytoin can cause severe skin reactions (e.g. Stevens–Johnson syndrome and toxic epidermal necrolysis).

Thiopentone

The use of barbiturates, such as thiopentone, to control ICP remains controversial, particularly because their administration prolongs the stay of severely brain-damaged patients in the NICU, without necessarily improving their clinical outcome. Although it has been shown that the administration of barbiturates is effective in lowering ICP (Shapiro et al., 1979), and it is widely accepted that control of ICP is likely to improve survival and outcome in severe head injury, there is conflicting evidence that the use of high-dose barbiturates achieves this aim (Rea and Rockswold, 1983; Ward et al., 1985).

Check-list

The following check-list summarizes the actions to be taken in patients admitted with head injury.

Check-list for head injury

1. On arrival in unit, reassess according to ATLS guidelines.
2. If the patient's condition has changed determine whether they need to be in a HDU/ICU.
3. If the patient is stable, ensure secondary survey complete, including all appropriate radiology (spine cleared?—up to 30% of severe head injuries have associated spinal injuries), and ensure all blood work has been done.
4. Document neurology and ensure regular neuro-obs performed.
5. Antibiotics not normally given prophylactically but if there is CSF leak or open skull fracture discuss with Registrar or Consultant.
6. Phenytoin may be given prophylactically, but again discuss preferences with Registrar or Consultant.
7. Steroids probably not indicated.
8. Bloods, including group-and-save, done.

SHUNT PATIENTS

CSF shunt problems are a common cause of admission to the neurosurgical unit. The commonest problems will be under-shunting of CSF (e.g. due to disconnection or blockage) and infection, although some patients will present with low-pressure headaches due to over-shunting. Patients present in a variety of ways: for example headaches, deterioration in level of consciousness; confusion, focal neurological deficit, sepsis, or seizures. Assessment of patients with a shunt problem requires detailed inquiry regarding the history of the shunt itself. What was the indication for the shunt? When and where was it put in? Has it ever needed to be revised, and, if so, which end was revised? Does this episode feel like any previous episodes of shunt problems?

Patients usually know if they have a shunt problem: when the patient is a child, always believe the parents—they are almost always right. Enquire about symptoms of raised intracranial pressure (headache, nausea and vomiting, fatigue, ataxia), sources of sepsis (urinary tract infections, respiratory tract infections), and any seizures.

When examining the patient be sure to inspect and palpate the shunt along its entire length, looking particularly for obvious gaps in the shunt and for areas of inflammation. Examine for signs of raised intracranial pressure (papilloedema, 4th nerve palsy, upward gaze palsy, bulging fontanelles in infants). Pumping and tapping of shunts is best left to the Registrar until you have been taught how to do these. A CT scan needs to be performed and, if possible, old scans should be obtained for comparison. A shunt series of plain films should be requested, as this provides information about the location of the distal catheter and may identify any obvious disconnections. Blood work should include white cell count (WCC) and inflammatory markers to look for evidence of an infective process.

Check-list for shunts

1. Full Hx & Ex (history & examination).
2. CT scan + old films if available.
3. Shunt series.
4. WCC, ESR, CRP.
5. Shunt tap (never do this without discussing with Registrar/Consultant).

PITUITARY PATIENTS

To understand the peri-operative care of patients with pituitary tumours it is helpful to consider briefly the effects these tumours may have. The mass effect of pituitary tumours can cause compression of: the optic chiasm, causing visual field defects; the pituitary gland, causing hypopituitarism; and the cavernous sinus, causing compression of cranial nerves III, IV, V_1, V_2, and VI.

Pituitary tumours may be functional, secreting a variety of hormones, for example prolactin, adrenocorticotrophic hormone (ACTH), growth hormone (GH). It is essential, therefore, to examine and document visual fields and cranial nerves thoroughly. Formal visual field testing by an ophthalmologist is often organized pre-operatively and should always be booked post-operatively. Blood work must include endocrine evaluation. Most Consultants will insist that the results of these endocrine investigations are documented in the notes. It is useful to discuss the appropriate blood tests with an endocrinologist early on in your job. Most Consultants will work in liaison with a particular endocrinologist, and getting to know them will greatly facilitate the care of your patients. In general, all pituitary patients will need pre-operative assessments of prolactin and growth hormone levels, IgF1, testosterone, follicle-stimulating hormone (FSH), luteinizing hormone (LH), and other profiles, to assess their adrenal, gonadal, and thyroid axes. Inducing the pituitary to produce cortisol with an ACTH stimulation test (short synacthen test) will indicate any occult deficiencies in the pituitary secretion of cortisol which might therefore be inadequate during a stress response. These patients need a low maintenance dose of cortisol. There is obviously also a high risk of disrupting pituitary function at surgery, and all patients will need steroid cover post-operatively. An example regime is 100 mg hydrocortisone IV at induction of anaesthesia, followed by 50 mg IV 8–12-hourly post-operatively, reduced gradually to 20 mg mane and 10 mg nocte, both orally, before discharge. Remember to give gastric cover with ranitidine or lansoprazole. Watch carefully for the development of DI by monitoring urine output and daily sodium levels (see below for management of DI). All pituitary patients need a follow-up endocrinology appointment, and this should be booked and documented in the notes. Prophylactic antibiotics (amoxicillin and flucloxacillin) are commonly given in pituitary surgery as there will be contact of CSF with the nasal cavity. If a CSF leak is detected post-operatively, observe the patient carefully for the development of meningitis and discuss with the Registrar/Consultant about the need for CSF diversion, for example lumbar drain.

Check-list for pituitary patients

Pre-op

1. Formal visual field assessment and documentation of cranial nerve examination.
2. Pre-op endocrine assessment discussed with endocrinologist and results documented in notes.
3. Steroid cover from induction and reduced to maintenance post-op.
4. Antibiotic prophylaxis—watch for CSF leak and development of meningitis.

Post-op

1. Monitor urine output and daily Na + post-op.
2. Ophthalmology appointment booked.
3. Endocrinology follow-up booked and documented in notes.
4. Monitor for CSF leak.

SPINAL PATIENTS

You will manage a range of spinal patients on the neurosurgical ward, including those with spinal injuries or acute compression syndromes, and patients admitted electively for laminectomies and discectomies. Patients with spinal injuries should be managed in a similar fashion to that described for head-injured patients, with a full reassessment on admission according to ATLS principles. If in doubt about C-spines, ensure that hard collars and sandbags are used. Spinal injury patients are at risk from aspiration and hypotension, so ensure that you are happy with the airway and pay close attention to the blood pressure (minimum IV line with saline infusion). Document the results of a detailed neurological examination, paying particular attention to motor and sensory levels. Document sacral sensation and sphincters (check anal tone and ask whether the patient can feel you pulling gently on their catheter).

Steroids may have a role to play in spinal trauma and several clinical trials have been done to evaluate this. However, this treatment modality remains controversial, and practice differs between clinicians and centres; too few studies have been conducted in this area for definitive conclusions to be reached. Although a meta-analysis (Bracken, 2000) of three trials showed some apparent benefit for methylprednisolone, the methodology of these trials has been questioned: improved outcome in motor function was seen at 1 year, provided that treatment was given within 8 h of injury and in the following regimen: (1) 30 mg/kg bolus of methylprednisolone; (2) after a 45-min pause, an infusion of 5.4 mg/kg/h for a further 23 h. Treatment with methylprednisolone should therefore take this form, and possibly be continued for a total of 48 h; the meta-analysis referred to above showed that further motor improvement may occur if infusion is continued for this length of time, particularly if started >3 h after injury. A review in 2003 (Spencer and Bazarian, 2003) found that, although neurological improvement was seen with methylprednisolone, there was no effect on overall mortality.

If a patient needs a fracture stabilized surgically, be sure to check with the operating surgeon regarding instructions for mobilization, for example to see whether any check films are required first.

Patients with spinal stenosis or disc prolapse may be admitted electively for surgery, or as an emergency if there is rapidly progressive motor weakness, a cauda equina syndrome or intractable pain. Again, it is important to document neurology, including the presence or absence of saddle anaesthesia and sphincter disturbances.

Steroids, in the form of dexamethasone, are advocated in cases of spinal cord compression by some, but not all, neurosurgeons.

In the post-operative period it is imperative to document any change in neurology and to check wounds regularly for CSF leak. In patients who undergo anterior approaches through the neck to cervical discs, keep an eye out for haematoma formation as there is a risk of airway compromise with haematomas in the neck.

Spinal tumours should be managed in an analogous way to cerebral tumours and these patients will benefit from steroids (dexamethasone).

COMPLICATIONS

If at all possible, it is recommended that you try to attend a course on the management of critically ill surgical patients, as this provides you with a systematic approach to all surgical patients with complications on the ward. The principles are the same for neurosurgery, but it is helpful if you are aware of, and understand, some of the complications which are specific to, or common in, neurosurgical patients.

"MRS JONES HAS DIPPED"

This is perhaps the commonest reason you will be called to the ward—because a patient has 'dipped'. Be sure to ascertain what is meant by 'dipped'. It usually refers to a drop in the GCS score, or to a deterioration in focal neurology. Go and assess the patient and remember to use an ABCDE approach, as neurosurgical patients need system support and can deteriorate as a consequence of cardiorespiratory problems, such as myocardial infarctions (MIs), pulmonary embolisms (PEs), and chest infections, as much as any other surgical patient. While you are giving oxygen and putting in your lines, find out about the patient's diagnosis and treatment and try to have a list of reasons why a neurosurgical patient might 'dip' neurologically. The following is a useful check-list:

Post-op craniotomy

1. Haematoma—EDH, ASDH, intraparenchymal.
2. Cerebral oedema.
3. Seizures.
4. Na + abnormalities.
5. Infection—meningitis/abscess.
6. Hydrocephalus.

Cerebral tumour patients

1. Further mass effect and oedema.
2. Seizures.
3. Bleed associated with tumour.

SAH patients

1. Re-bleed.
2. Hydrocephalus.
3. Vasospasm.
4. Na + abnormalities.

Patients with shunts or EVDs

1. Shunt/EVD failure.
2. Meningitis.
3. Seizures.

Head injuries

1. Blossoming of contusions.
2. Further bleeding—EDH, ASDH.
3. Seizures.
4. Meningitis.
5. Na^+ abnormalities.

Remember to consider rapidly reversible causes, such as low blood glucose and seizures. Patients who have fitted may be postictal. Do not be afraid to use lorazepam to control patients who are actively fitting, but beware of using sedatives in patients who are postictal. If in doubt, there is little harm in loading patients with phenytoin (15–18 mg/kg loading dose over at least 30 min to prevent cardiac dysrhythmias; maintenance is 5–8 mg/kg/day in a single night-time dose or in divided doses over the day). Once you are happy that a patient is stable from a cardiorespiratory perspective (this may mean asking the anaesthetist to intubate) then the patient will need some

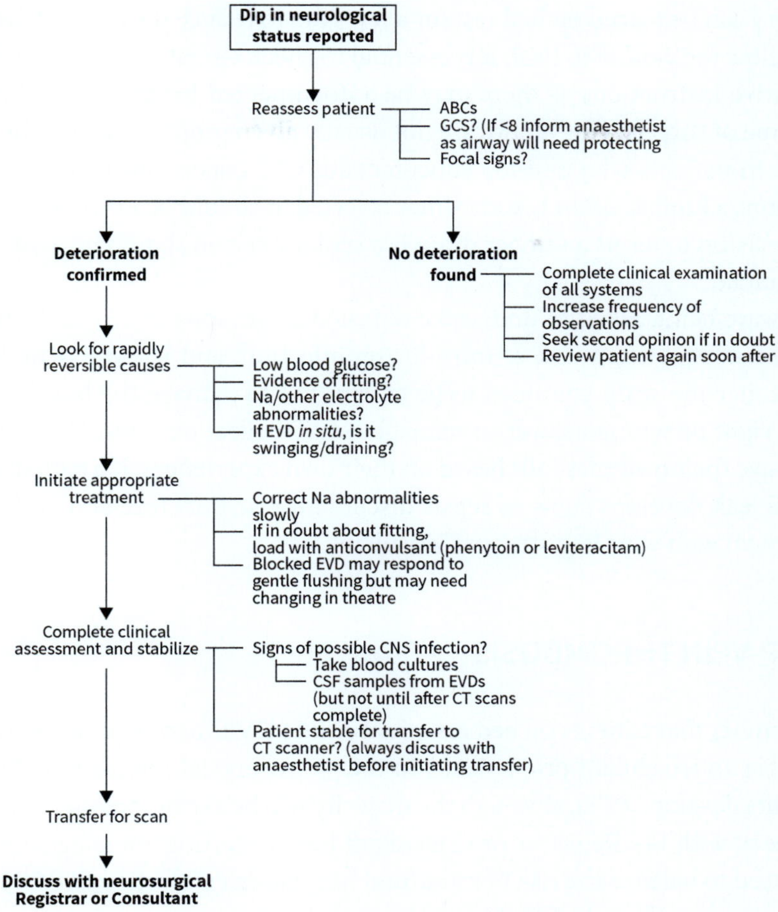

Figure 8.1 Examples of the sequence of actions in a patient who 'dips' on the ward, that is, a deterioration in neurological status is reported. Although there is no single correct sequence of events, this chart highlights various essential points, including the need to consider and, if necessary, treat reversible causes of neurological deterioration before sending a patient to the CT scanner.

form of repeat imaging, probably in the form of a CT scan. Always inform the Registrar on-call about patients who 'dip' as they may require theatre urgently. Figure 8.1 summarizes the sequence of actions in a patient whose level of consciousness drops on the ward.

CSF LEAKS

CSF leaks may occur after trauma or surgery. CSF leaks from surgical wounds may stop with an extra stitch or two. Patients with CSF leaks following spinal surgery can be placed on bed rest for a few days to reduce the effect of gravity and allow the wound to heal. It is essential to check operative notes and postoperative instructions as there may be a documented breach of the dura at the time of surgery. Antibiotics are not usually given prophylactically for CSF leaks. In patients who develop subcutaneous CSF collections following craniotomy, a lumbar drain is sometimes inserted: it should be emphasized that the decision to insert a lumbar drain is a senior one and should be made by a Consultant.

Beware being asked to undertake repeated aspirations of CSF collections. There is a significant risk of introducing infection, and if there is no bone flap under the scalp you need to be careful not to damage the brain. There is no right or wrong answer in managing CSF collections, and Consultants will have their own methods based on their own experiences. If a patient with a CSF leak develops signs of sepsis discuss lumbar puncture and antibiotic treatment with your Registrar or Consultant.

DEEP-VEIN THROMBOSIS

Remember that patients on bed rest are at risk of DVTs and require TEDs and possible anticoagulant prophylaxis. In the neurosurgical population, 30% of patients develop DVTs, although the majority will be asymptomatic.

Check with the Registrar or Consultant before starting anticoagulants, as you need to balance the risk of intradural haematoma with risk of DVT. Most Consultants will be comfortable with anticoagulants more than 48 h after surgery but some may prefer them to be prescribed even sooner. The use of perioperative thromboprophylaxis varies from department to department. Also, there are many individual patient factors that need to be taken into account, and peri-operative anticoagulants should be used only in direct consultation with the patient's Consultant.

SODIUM ABNORMALITIES

There are several conditions which are frequently seen in neurosurgical patients and which cause abnormalities in serum sodium. You need to be able to recognize them and be familiar with their treatment.

Raised serum sodium is seen in DI, and reduced sodium is seen in cerebral salt wasting (CSW) and the syndrome of inappropriate antidiuretic hormone secretion (SIADH). It is particularly important to understand the differences between CSW and SIADH because, although both produce hyponatraemia, they have different effects on extracellular fluid volumes and are treated differently. Remember that all abnormalities of sodium, particularly low sodium, need to be corrected slowly and cautiously due to the risk of central pontine myelinosis. There is an increasing trend for endocrine teams and NICU teams to be involved in the treatment of sodium abnormalities in ward patients.

Diabetes insipidus

Reduced ADH secretion is known as neurogenic DI, whereas renal resistance to ADH is known as nephrogenic DI. Neurogenic DI is the type you are most likely to encounter in neurosurgical patients and may be the result of trauma, tumours, infection, or surgery. Patients at particular risk are those with severe head injury involving damage to the pituitary, after pituitary surgery, or with lesions pressing on the pituitary (e.g. craniopharyngiomas or anterior communicating artery aneurysms).

It is important to appreciate that DI may be transient, especially after pituitary surgery. Because of the reduction in ADH there is production of a large volume of dilute urine (>200 ml/h, urine osmolality <200 mosm/L); as a consequence the serum sodium rises (>145 mmol/L, with plasma osmolarity >295 mosm/L). In conscious patients this will result in a thirsty patient who classically craves iced water. The volume of fluids taken in may be enough to match losses and keep serum sodium within the normal range: this is where most cases of DI are missed, because it is assumed that the high urine output is due to polydipsia. The key issue, therefore, is whether or not the kidneys are concentrating urine. A quick bedside test is to dip the urine to test specific gravity. Urine in DI will have a specific gravity <1.005; if it is >1.010, then the patient almost certainly does not have DI. In patients with suspected DI always check specific gravity, and serum and urine sodiums and osmolalities. If DI is mild, patients may be able to keep up with fluid losses by taking fluid orally. If DI is more severe, or if the patient is not able to drink because of reduced conscious level, then IV fluids will need to be administered. In this situation dextrose is preferable to saline as the serum sodium is likely to be high. In transient DI, chasing fluid losses until the episode resolves is the best management. However, when it is proving difficult to keep up with losses the ADH analogue 1-d-amino-8-D-arginine vasopressin (DDAVP) may need to be given. This should be used cautiously and only with senior supervision. There is a danger that if DDAVP is given inappropriately in too high doses, urine output can dry up, with resultant renal shut-down and no urine production, leading to brain swelling and a serious situation. Although the subcutaneous dose is 1–4 μg, we usually start at a lower dose of 0.5 μg or even less.

Cerebral salt wasting

CSW can be defined as renal loss of sodium secondary to intracranial disease. The pathophysiology of renal sodium loss remains elusive, but there appears to be an initial renal sodium transport defect that leads to sodium loss. CSW results in hyponatraemia and is also associated with loss of water. This is in contrast to SIADH (see below), in which there is hyponatraemia-associated retention of water due to excess ADH. CSW is seen particularly in patients with SAH. It is essential not to mistake CSW for SIADH in this setting, as fluid restriction (treatment for SIADH) in patients with SAH can precipitate or worsen vasospasm. To differentiate CSW from SIADH look at the patient's hydration (dry in CSW), central venous pressure (low in CSW), and serum osmolality (normal or high in CSW, low in SIADH). CSW is treated by replacing fluid losses with salt-rich fluids: 0.9% or hypertonic saline. A very effective alternative or adjunctive is fludrocortisone, a mineralocorticoid which may need to be given to stimulate renal reabsorption of sodium: this should, however, be a senior decision, as complications of pulmonary oedema, hypokalaemia, and hypertension may occur.

Syndrome of inappropriate antidiuretic hormone secretion

SIADH can occur with a variety of neurosurgical pathologies: tumours, head injury, post-craniotomy, meningitis. Inappropriate secretion of ADH results in hyponatraemia due to water retention. Serum sodium and serum osmolalities are therefore low, but there is no detectable abnormality in renal function. Fluid restriction to <1 L/day is the first-line treatment. The use of hypertonic saline with diuretics should be reserved for refractory cases and undertaken only with senior advice. Remember the warning given above about confusing SIADH and CSW in patients with SAH.

SEIZURES (FITS)

Seizures are a common complication in neurosurgical patients, and patients in status epilepticus need to be stopped from fitting. The basics of managing a fitting patient are summarized in Figure 8.2.

It is imperative to consider what the cause of the seizure may be, as a patient may have developed a post-operative haematoma that may need surgical evacuation. In status epilepticus, attention must be given to the airway and oxygen administered. Protocols for seizure control vary between hospitals; however, lorazepam 4 mg IV over 2 min can be given for adults actively fitting.

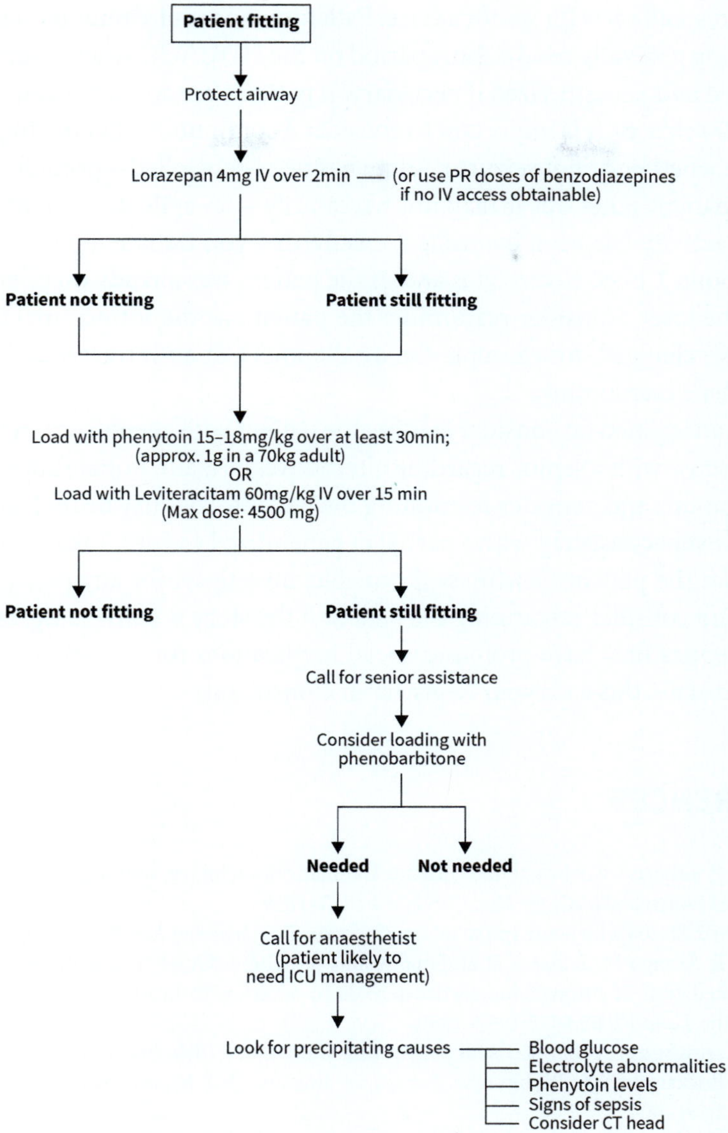

Figure 8.2 Example of management of the fitting patient—doses and protocols may vary locally (NB: doses will be different for paediatric patients—see Chapter 14).

If there is difficulty in obtaining IV access then per rectum (PR) benzodiazepines may be administered. Patients may be loaded with phenytoin 1 g IV, even if the lorazepam/diazepam stops the fitting. If fitting still does not stop after phenytoin, consider other agents, including phenobarbitone. In all cases of seizures, call early for senior advice. Patients who require multiple agents to stop fitting generally need a short period on the HDU/ICU where they can be intubated and anaesthetized if necessary. If patients are anaesthetized to control their seizures, it is important to consider a continuous EEG tracing to determine whether or not seizure activity has been controlled—propofol might keep a patient quiet but it may not necessarily stop epileptic activity. Once seizure activity has been controlled, ensure that you initiate the relevant investigations. Check electrolytes and, if the patient was already on phenytoin, check the level. Consider rescanning the patient, as the intracranial picture may have changed, for example the development of an intracranial haematoma after a craniotomy.

With an isolated fit, consider loading the patient with agents such as phenytoin (discuss with a senior regarding alternatives). Again, initiate appropriate investigations and consider rescanning the patient. You may be told about an isolated event consistent with a partial or generalized seizure. Take a good history from the patient or witness if possible, investigate for any precipitating cause, and consider rescanning the patient if the story is convincing. Starting antiepileptics may have profound social implications for the patient, so you should discuss this with your Registrar or Consultant.

REFERENCES

Alderson P, Roberts J. Corticosteroids in acute traumatic brain injury; systematic review of randomised controlled trials. *Br Med J* 1997;314:1855–1859.

Bracken MB. Steroids for acute spinal injury. *Cochrane Database Syst Rev* 2000; 2: CD001046.

Edwards P, Arango M, Balica L et al. Final results of MRC CRASH, a randomised placebo-controlled trial of intravenous corticosteroids in adults with head injury—outcomes at 6 months. *Lancet* 2005;8475:1957–1959.

Pruitt BA. Antiseizure prophylaxis for penetrating brain injury. *J Trauma* 2001;51:S41–S44.

Rea GI, Rockswold GI. Barbiturate therapy in uncontrolled hypertension. *Neurosurgery* 1983;12;401–404.

Shapiro HM, Wyte SR, Loeser J. Barbiturate augmented hypothermia for reduction of persistent intracranial hypertension. *J Neurosurg* 1979;40:90–100.

Spencer MT, Bazarian JJ. Are corticosteroids effective in traumatic spinal cord injury? *Ann Emerg Med* 2003;41:410–413.

Ward JD, Becker DP, Miller JD et al. Failure of prophylactic barbiturate coma in treatment of severe head injury. *J Neurosurg* 1985;62:383–388.

Weiss GH, Salazar AM, Vance SC et al. Predicting posttraumatic epilepsy in penetrating head injury. *Arch Neurol* 1986;43:771–773.

Young B, Rapp RP, Norton JA et al. Failure of prophylactically administered phenytoin to prevent early posttraumatic seizures. J *Neurosurg* 1983;58:231–235.

9

Neuro-Intensive Care

Adel Helmy and James Moore

CONTENTS

INTRODUCTION

The intensive care unit (ICU) is a vital component of any neurosurgical service and it is important that all members of the neurosurgical team have an insight into what goes on there—even junior trainees! It may seem a daunting place at first, but a methodical approach and a few key principles go a long way to dispelling any of the mystery. The exact role that the basic trainee takes varies from unit to unit; nevertheless, every opportunity should be taken to familiarize yourself with the ICU environment. While this chapter cannot turn you into a neuro-intensivist, hopefully it will go some way to allowing you to assess patients, understand the key principles, and communicate effectively with your senior colleagues or other specialty teams.

APPROACH TO THE NEURO-ICU PATIENT

There are many approaches to the ICU patient; however, for the assessment of the neurosurgical patient the following ABCDE (Airway, Breathing, Circulation, Disability/neurological assessment, Everything else) approach is an easily remembered method.

AIRWAY

Is the patient's airway protected? As a rule of thumb, patients with a Glasgow Coma Scale (GCS) score of <9 (and particularly those that are not localizing) usually require intubation and ventilation in order to protect their airway. If the patient's clinical state is improving, perhaps this is the time to consider extubating the patient. In the longer term, a patient who cannot maintain their airway may require a tracheostomy. Your ICU colleagues are usually best placed to make these decisions, but it is important for the neurosurgical team to take an active part in this process. Are you expecting the patient to get better or worse? What is the surgical plan for this patient? For example, there is little point in extubating a patient who is expected to go to theatre later the same day.

BREATHING

In the awake, spontaneously ventilating patient this assessment is the same as on the ward. In the intubated patient it is important to look at the blood gases and the ventilator—particularly the fraction of inspired oxygen (F_iO_2). Is the patient's oxygenation improving (F_iO_2 coming down) or is it deteriorating (F_iO_2 going up)? For example, patients subjected to trauma may have unrecognized chest injuries and patients who have been intubated for some time may develop a ventilator-associated pneumonia. These factors may prevent a patient from being extubated: usually an F_iO_2 of 0.4 or less is required before extubation is considered. Look carefully at the partial pressure of carbon dioxide (P_aCO_2) on the arterial blood gas result. As we shall see, P_aCO_2 has an important effect on intracranial pressure (ICP).

CIRCULATION

The mean arterial blood pressure (MAP) is an important parameter to check. This pressure is required to perfuse the brain with blood and it may need to be manipulated with fluids and vasoactive drugs in patients with raised ICP or vasospasm. The pulse rate can be affected by many factors, such as pyrexia, pain, and drugs; however, in the context of trauma, a tachycardia is always indicative of blood loss until proven otherwise. Patients with high spinal injuries may have low blood pressure without the normal tachycardic response. This is sometimes called 'neurogenic shock', and it occurs when the sympathetic outflow from the spinal cord is interrupted by spinal cord injury above T6 as sympathetic outflow to the lower limb and abdominal vasculature exits at thoracic and lumbar levels.

DISABILITY/NEUROLOGICAL ASSESSMENT

In the pharmacologically paralysed patient, the reaction of the pupils may be the only neurological assessment you can make. This is because neuromuscular blocking drugs act at the nicotinic acetylcholine receptor, while pupillary constriction is controlled by the parasympathetic nervous system via the muscarinic acetylcholine receptor. You should always note both the pupil size (in mm) and reactivity to light. In patients who are not sedated and paralysed, an assessment of the GCS should be made. It is the most important measure of how patients are progressing. In particular, the motor component of the GCS is the most prognostically important element. A formal neurological examination can be made if the patient is awake and cooperative; however, a simple assessment of arm or leg movement can be made even in the most uncooperative patient.

EVERYTHING ELSE

Intensivists are fond of amusing acronyms and recommend that you give every ICU patient a 'FAST HUG' every day:

F **F**eeding
A **A**nalgesia
S **S**edation
T **T**hromboprophylaxis
H **H**ead up
U Stress **U**lcer prophylaxis
G **G**lucose control

This is where FAST HUG comes into its own, to remind you of all the other aspects of managing critically ill patients. Specifically, in the neurosurgical patient, make sure you check their blood glucose, serum sodium, temperature, and inflammatory markers. This is not, of course, to say that all the other blood tests are not also important.

SPECIAL TOPICS IN NEURO-ICU

ICU is a very different environment from the ward and there are some things you may never have come across before. This section provides an outline of some of the most important.

COMMUNICATION IN ICU

Critically ill patients, such as trauma patients, have pathologies that affect multiple organ systems. This means that many medical teams are involved in their care. At the very least, you will be involved with patients who are jointly under the care of an ICU team and a neurosurgical team.

Communication is absolutely paramount to looking after these complex patients successfully. It avoids conflict and duplication of effort, and it makes the working environment much more pleasant! In ICU, the senior nurses have a wealth of experience and are much better at working things like ventilators and monitors than anyone else. Always hand over any neurosurgical-specific instructions to the nurse looking after the patient, document the plan legibly, and include a date, time, and signature.

Family meetings are a key component of intensive care practice. A detailed discussion on how to communicate effectively in a family meeting is beyond the scope of this text, however there are a few key things to consider. Regular scheduled family meetings are very useful to keep family members (and the patient, if conscious) updated on progress and next steps. It also allows family members the opportunity to ask questions and clarify potential areas of confusion. Although brief bedside catch-ups have a role to play, organized family meetings should generally be held away from the bedspace in a quiet, private environment. Giving advanced notice of the time of the meeting allows key family members to ensure that they can be present. From a medical perspective it is important to include representation from the key groups involved in the patients care, including neurosurgery, ICU, nursing, and any other medical teams that are closely involved. In advance of meeting with the family, it is important for the medical teams to agree on the 'agenda', or the scope of what is planned on being discussed. Previous meeting records should be reviewed to ascertain the scope of what has previously been communicated to the family. Although the medical teams may at times have differing perspectives on vexed issues such as prognostication, it's important to present a united view to the family—on issues where there is disagreement, this needs to be presented in a respectful way that doesn't damage the trust or relationship the family has with the treating teams. Further, most circumstances where there is disagreement are those where there is uncertainty, and family are generally very accepting that the situation might not yet be clear, and that time is required, as long as this is presented in an open and honest manner.

In conducting family meetings, it is useful to identify who is going to lead the meeting, and ensure that everyone present has the opportunity to introduce themselves and their role—including family present and their relationship to the patient. The meeting should generally not proceed if a key person such as the patient's spouse or next-of-kin is not present, unless this has been agreed in advance. Ensure that everyone present has had the opportunity to communicate, including the nursing staff. Following the meeting, a written record of what was discussed should be entered in the patient's notes.

SEDATION AND PARALYSIS

Sedative and analgesic drugs have many important effects, such as reducing pain, anxiety, and agitation, and allowing the patient to tolerate a tracheal tube. Together with neuromuscular blockade, sedation helps to increase tolerance to mechanical ventilation and can stop the patient coughing or gagging. More specifically, a wide range of sedative agents reduce neuronal activity. This has the knock-on effect of reducing cerebral metabolism, cerebral blood flow (a phenomenon called flow–metabolism coupling), and intracranial pressure. For these reasons, sedation is widely employed in ICU.

The major limitation of sedation to the neurosurgeon is the inability to assess clinically a patient's neurology in order to establish a prognosis or to monitor for deterioration. For this reason, in sedated patients, monitoring techniques such as ICP monitoring may be used as an adjunct to provide early warning of secondary intracranial insults.

VENTILATION

A detailed discussion of ventilation and mechanical ventilators is outside the scope of this text, but the following principles are important to bear in mind.

Oxygenation

The brain is exquisitely sensitive to hypoxia, and a key requirement in every critically ill patient is to maintain oxygen delivery to the brain. In some patients with associated lung pathology, mechanical ventilation is required to improve oxygenation. In many circumstances, neurosurgical patients require intubation and mechanical ventilation because of their reduced level of consciousness, which means they may fail to protect their airway. In simple terms, there are three methods for improving oxygenation on a mechanical ventilator.

- ***Increase the FiO2:*** this increases the diffusion gradient across the alveolus.
- ***Increase positive end expiratory pressure (PEEP):*** this keeps alveoli from collapsing at the end of expiration and increases the alveolar surface area available for gas exchange.
- ***Increase the inspiratory time:expiratory time ratio:*** this works by increasing the time available for gas exchange.

Ventilation (carbon dioxide clearance)

There are many factors that control the calibre of the cerebral blood vessels. One of the most important is the P_aCO_2. In normal circumstances, as a part of the brain increases its activity and metabolism, it consumes more oxygen and generates more carbon dioxide. In response to the increase in PCO_2 the cerebral arterioles relax, dilate, and increase the cerebral blood flow. This compensatory mechanism allows an increased delivery of oxygen and metabolic fuels as well as removing more carbon dioxide.

This relationship between P_aCO_2 and cerebral-vessel calibre is very important in patients with high ICP. When the P_aCO_2 goes up and the blood vessels dilate this causes an increase in the cerebral arterial blood volume and in ICP. For this reason P_aCO_2 must be kept within tight limits that allow the blood vessels to deliver sufficient oxygen and fuel to the brain without causing too big a rise in ICP.

The P_aCO_2 is proportional to the 'minute volume'. This is defined as the amount of gas that moves in and out of the lung in 1 minute, and is calculated as tidal volume multiplied by respiratory rate. Increasing either the tidal volume or the respiratory rate (or both) will have the effect of reducing the P_aCO_2. The lungs can be injured by overzealous ventilation however, particularly due to excessive tidal volumes (volutrauma) or ventilatory pressures (barotrauma). Modern ventilators are designed to help ensure safe ventilation, but it is important to use a lung-protective ventilation strategy, which generally involves limited tidal volumes (around 6 mL/kg of ideal body weight).

Tracheostomy

A tracheostomy is a tube that is inserted directly through the anterior neck between the upper tracheal rings and into the trachea. They come in many types (e.g. cuffed, fenestrated, dual lumen). In Neuro-ICU they are most commonly used in patients unable to protect their airways for a long period of time, and to aid weaning from mechanical ventilation. Patients often require suctioning of secretions from the tube, and occasionally the tube can be obstructed by these secretions. Many units use an inner cannula which can be easily removed and washed if obstruction from secretions occurs.

It is important to know what to do if the tracheostomy is displaced in an emergency. Most units will have an emergency protocol which the staff are trained in. Because Neuro-ICU patients generally have a patent upper airway, if the tracheostomy tube is displaced, the stoma can be quickly covered with an occlusive dressing, and the airway managed 'from above', via the mouth and nose, as you would with a regular patient. If the tracheostomy has been recently placed, the stoma will close quickly; attempting to re-insert the tracheostomy in this situation can easily result in malposition and airway obstruction. However, if the tracheostomy has been in a more than 10–14 days, then it may be possible to carefully replace the tube through the existing stoma. It is essential to be aware of the potential for a false passage to occur if the tracheostomy is reinserted in this fashion—if the patient is not moving air via the re-inserted tracheostomy, it should be removed and the airway managed via the mouth and nose instead.

INTRACRANIAL PRESSURE MANAGEMENT

A key part of the management of neurological injuries is the prevention of secondary brain injury. Different monitoring techniques are used to identify these potential secondary injuries in an effort to prevent them. There are many specialized forms of monitoring that may be available on the ICU, such as intracranial pressure, jugular venous oximetry, brain tissue oxygen, EEG (electroencephalogram), microdialysis, transcranial Doppler, and near infrared spectroscopy, to name a few (Table 9.1). Understanding the technicalities of using these monitors, what they measure, and how to correct the monitored values when things go wrong, are among the most interesting aspects of managing patients on ICU.

The only monitoring that will be discussed in detail here is intracranial pressure as it is the most common and arguably the most important. ICP can be

Table 9.1 Specialized forms of monitoring in the management of neurological injuries.

Monitor	Technique	Uses
Jugular venous oximetry	Oxygen saturation in blood sampled from a catheter in the jugular bulb	Measure of balance between supply and demand of oxygen to the brain
Brain tissue oxygen	Clark electrode inserted into the brain substance	Direct measure of brain partial pressure can be used to titrate hyperventilation
Electro-encephalography	Panel of surface electrodes on the scalp surface	Used continuously or intermittently to exclude seizures
Microdialysis	Flexible tube with semipermeable membrane at the tip to sample metabolites from the brain extra-space	Lactate/pyruvate ratio (LPR) is a measure of the balance between aerobic/anaerobic metabolism; lower LPR indicates more aerobic metabolism
Transcranial doppler	Doppler ultrasound probe used to measure the flow velocity in vessels at the base of the brain	Increased velocity can indicate spasm in vessels
Near infrared spectroscopy	Differential absorption of near infrared lasers used to measure The percentage of oxygenated haemoglobin in the brain	A measure of the adequacy of the supply of oxygen to the brain

monitored with a dedicated pressure transducer inserted into the skull cavity or via an external ventricular drain. The shape and amplitude of the waveform can provide useful information, but it is the mean ICP that is most often used as a goal-directed measure.

ICP monitoring is most commonly used in patients with severe traumatic brain injuries. It serves two important roles. First, it is a monitor for potential deterioration in patients who cannot be assessed clinically because they are sedated and/or paralysed. Second, it acts as a goal-directed target, together with cerebral perfusion pressure (CPP). There is discussion in the literature as to the ideal target for ICP and CPP, but the current consensus is that ICP should be kept below 22 mmHg and CPP should be kept between 60 mmHg and 70 mmHg. It is absolutely essential to know that these values are for adults, and that the values for babies, infants, and young children are completely different (normal intracranial pressure is much lower in a baby than in an adult: see Chapter 14, *Paediatric Neurosurgery*). It is imperative, therefore, to liaise with your senior colleagues in neurosurgery and in ICU regarding the appropriate values of these parameters for younger patients.

Interpreting ICP properly requires some practical knowledge of the relationship between ICP, CPP, and MAP:

$$CPP = MAP - ICP$$

In practice, this means that blood pressure (MAP) is manipulated using fluid therapy and/or vasoactive drugs to maintain the CPP, and a number of measures, discussed below, are used to control the ICP. Some neurosurgeons advocate ICP monitoring in other clinical circumstances, but the evidence for this is less clear-cut than for traumatic brain injuries. The following sections discuss the different strategies for controlling ICP. For many of these strategies there are limitations and complications that have to be borne in mind. Balancing the benefits of controlling ICP and the risks of complications from these techniques is difficult in individual patients. Many units use an ICP protocol to help to standardize treatment.

General measures

It is important not to forget simple measures for controlling ICP. The head of the bed should be raised by 30° to aid venous drainage, and endotracheal tube tapes should not be too tight. Where possible the cervical spine should be cleared early with appropriate imaging, but in situations where a cervical collar is required due to injury, it should be carefully fitted to avoid compression of the neck veins. Fever should be treated with antipyretic agents such as paracetamol, or by active cooling if necessary. In addition, any seizures should be treated with an antiepileptic agent.

Sedation and paralysis

As already discussed, sedation reduces neuronal activity, cerebral blood flow, and cerebral blood volume. Paralysis stops the patient from 'fighting' the ventilator and this reduces intrathoracic pressure. Intrathoracic pressure is transmitted to the intracranial cavity via the venous system, and can increase ICP. These two interventions are very effective, however prolonged deep sedation may make the patient prone to chest complications, particularly respiratory tract infections, and prolonged paralysis can lead to muscle wastage resulting in prolonged ventilatory weans and ICU stay.

Hyperosmolar agents

Hypertonic saline or mannitol are used when it is necessary to control ICP rapidly, for example when a patient develops a fixed, dilated pupil. Traditionally, the explanation for their action is that they cannot get across the blood–brain barrier and therefore exert an osmotic gradient across the blood-brain barrier which draws fluid from the brain. Although this is undoubtedly true, they act too quickly on ICP for this to be the only mechanism involved. Other theories regarding the mechanism of action include improvement of the rheology (resistance characteristics) of blood by causing a transient increase in blood volume, or dehydration of red blood cells and a reduction in their volume, thus allowing them to pass through the microcirculation better; in addition, mannitol may have a free radical effect.

The limitation of hyperosmolar agents is that they cause a progressive increase in serum sodium concentration and osmolarity. Mannitol, which is a diuretic, can also cause severe hypokalaemia. The major practical difference between hypertonic saline and mannitol is that hypertonic saline is a volume expander and mannitol is a diuretic. In patients with polytrauma, hypertonic saline is the more useful agent, because it avoids exacerbating hypotension that can be induced by mannitol.

Surgical management of ICP

It may seem obvious, but in patients with high ICP any intracranial mass lesions should be considered for evacuation. Mass lesions include haematomas (extradural, subdural or intraparenchymal) and contusions. In addition, there are two other surgical methods for reducing ICP: extraventricular drainage of CSF and decompressive craniectomy.

An extraventricular drain (EVD) can be useful because some patients will develop hydrocephalus following a head injury; however, even if there is no hydrocephalus present, draining any residual intracranial CSF will reduce ICP. Some centres use continuous drainage of CSF and some use intermittent drainage, but the principle is the same. The disadvantage of using this technique is that the patient is subjected to a surgical procedure and the risk of EVD infection, particularly if the drain is kept in for more than 5 days. There is some evidence that aggressive EVD drainage may increase the need for a shunt because of fibrosis of the normal CSF absorption pathway in the arachnoid granulations.

Decompressive craniectomy is an alternative approach and involves removal of a large section of the skull vault to increase the volume of the intracranial space. This can be done laterally, bifrontally, or over the posterior fossa, and is often combined with an operation to remove any intracranial mass lesion. It is a very effective method for controlling ICP but has the risks of a craniotomy, and sometimes there are problems with kinking of cerebral veins at the edge of the craniectomy where the brain bulges out. In addition, if patients survive, many will request a cranioplasty in order to correct the defect, with the risks of a further operation. Two recent trials have explored the role of decompressive craniectomy in traumatic brain injury (TBI). The DECRA trial explored early decompressive craniectomy and could not show any benefit to surgery. The RESCUEicp trial explored late decompressive craniectomy when all standard medical therapies, other than barbiturates, were already employed and it showed mortality almost halved, but at the expense of an increased number of patients left in a vegetative state or with severe disability. The decision whether to undertake decompressive craniectomy is therefore difficult and needs to be needs to be individualized to the patient, and informed by discussions with next-of-kin and family.

Hyperventilation

As discussed in the section on ventilation, the P_aCO_2 is a major determinant of cerebral vessel tone and therefore of ICP. There is a trade-off between keeping the P_aCO_2 low to decrease ICP and keeping it high enough to maintain adequate cerebral blood flow and thus stop the brain from becoming ischaemic. In most patients, the P_aCO_2 is kept in the low-normal range (4.5–5 kPa, or 35–38 mmHg) unless there is a particularly refractory ICP, where it may be reduced as low as 4 kPa (30 mmHg). Such hyperventilation is not recommended outside the setting of specialist Neuro-ICUs, where monitoring, such as jugular oximetry or brain tissue oxygen, can be used to make sure that hyperventilation is not making the brain ischaemic.

Therapeutic hypothermia

Hypothermia reduces neuronal activity, cerebral blood flow, cerebral blood volume, and ICP. However, it can also inhibit cardiac and renal function and it makes patients more susceptible to infection. For this reason, active cooling is used with caution and generally only as a rescue intervention, targeting a temperature of 35°C.

Barbiturates

The barbiturate class of drugs (e.g. thiopentone or pentothal) are powerful sedatives. They are not usually used as first-line sedative drugs because they can inhibit cardiac function and cause problems with potassium homeostasis and infections due to impaired monocyte function. They are, however, effective at reducing ICP and may be used occasionally as a rescue therapy for refractory intracranial hypertension.

MANAGEMENT OF VASOSPASM

Vasospasm refers to constriction of the cerebral blood vessels which most commonly occurs following aneurysmal subarachnoid haemorrhage (SAH). However, it can occur following any cause of SAH, including trauma. It typically begins 4–7 days following SAH and can present with any number of neurological deficits, from a focal deficit to a global reduction in GCS. Although vasospasm was first described as a phenomenon of the large cerebral vessels seen on cerebral angiography, the neurological deficits following SAH do not always coincide with angiographic vasospasm. The pathophysiology of the clinical syndrome which is commonly referred to as vasospasm is, therefore, more accurately referred to as a delayed ischaemic neurological deficit (DIND). This term reflects the fact that the underlying pathophysiology is likely to be more complex than simple spasm of the large cerebral arteries, including thrombosis in the microvasculature, oedema within the brain substance, and cortical spreading depression. Nonetheless, vasospasm is the most commonly used term to refer to DIND and so these terms will be used here interchangeably. The pathophysiology of vasospasm relates to the blood load within the subarachnoid space: vasospasm is more common as the blood load increases. The severity of blood load as seen on a CT scan has been graded by Fisher (see Table 15.4 in Chapter 15, *Commonly Used Scoring Systems in Neurosurgery*) and a Fisher grade 3 has the highest risk of vasospasm at ~70%. Vasospasm is a significant cause of morbidity and mortality in patients who survive the first few days following an SAH. All patients admitted with a diagnosis of SAH are kept on oral nimodipine 60 mg 4-hourly for 21 days, to reduce the risk of vasospasm (British Aneurysm Nimodipine Trial). It is important to avoid hypovolaemia—patients should be kept euvolaemic and this may require IV fluid supplementation.

Diagnosis and investigation

Even with prophylaxis, a proportion of patients will still develop a DIND. In order to clinch a diagnosis of vasospasm three things are required: (1) a consistent clinical picture of an unexpected clinical deterioration 4–20 days following SAH; (2) exclusion of alternative diagnoses; and (3) ideally, evidence of hypoperfusion of the relevant cortical area. Alternative diagnoses may include hydrocephalus, re-bleed, electrolyte disturbance (especially hypo- and hyper-natraemia), seizures, sepsis, and hypoglycaemia. Typical investigations are CT head scan, a full set of bloods, EEG (if available), and a thorough clinical assessment. There is no single foolproof investigation for diagnosing vasospasm. The best investigation is cerebral angiography, but it is invasive, resource heavy and carries a risk of complications. Modern CT angiogram images are often of sufficient quality to demonstrate a reduction in vessel diameter, which can lend weight to the diagnosis. It is important to note that vessel calibre changes can be commonly seen on CT angiogram, so the diagnosis of vasospasm requires clinical correlation, rather than being purely based on imaging. Trans-cranial Doppler (TCD) is a method for assessing the velocity of blood flow in a major branch of the Circle of Willis, usually the anterior or middle cerebral arteries. The principle behind its use is that the narrower the vessel calibre, the higher the absolute velocity of blood within the vessel. This velocity does not take into account the flow within the vessel: if the flow increases then the velocity of blood flow will increase without a change in vessel diameter. To correct for this the Lindegaard ratio (LR) is used: this is the ratio of flow velocities within the middle cerebral artery (MCA) and the extracranial internal carotid artery (EICA):

$$\text{LR} = (\text{flow velocity within the MCA})/(\text{flow velocity within the EICA})$$

An LR ratio of >3 is used for the diagnosis of vasospasm. TCD is useful in the unconscious patient, where it can be repeated on a daily or twice-daily basis. With repeated measurements, the trend of TCD measurements is most informative. Newer imaging techniques, such as perfusion CT scan, are being used increasingly to demonstrate the hypoperfusion associated with vasospasm. On perfusion CT a number of derived measures ('maps') are calculated based on how quickly a bolus of contrast passes through the cerebral circulation into the brain tissue and the arterial wave form. The easiest maps to interpret are cerebral blood flow, which is expected to be reduced if there is ischaemia, and cerebral blood volume, which is increased if the brain tissue has infarcted, but is normal if it is ischaemic.

Treatment of vasospasm

Blood pressure augmentation (hypertensive therapy) is the mainstay of treatment. It can be used only in patients who have their aneurysm secured, as clearly hypertension can increase the risk of aneurysmal re-bleed. In practice, the patient has a central venous catheter for drug administration, and arterial line inserted for close haemodynamic monitoring. Again, it is crucial to ensure the patient is euvolaemic.

Typically, the MAP can be pushed up to 100–120 mmHg using an infusion of a vasoactive drug such as noradrenaline. You should assess the response in the patient's neurology to this change in pressure. If this does not work, some authors recommend raising the MAP further. There is also interest in the addition of other vasoactive drugs, such as the 'inodilator' agent, Milrinone which increases cardiac output as well as having a vasodilating effect. Hypertensive therapy can precipitate cardiac ischaemia and should be used with caution in the elderly or in those with a previous history of ischaemic heart disease.

Rescue angiographic therapy with the use of intra-arterial injections of vasodilating drugs such as calcium channel blockers, or balloon angioplasty may be an option for resistant vasospasm, where the neurological deficit persists despite hypertensive therapy. Long-term outcome benefit for these therapies is not yet proven.

BRAIN HERNIATION SYNDROMES

The definition of a hernia from general surgery is 'the protrusion of a viscus through the wall which normally contains it, into an abnormal situation'. An analogous situation can happen in the intracranial compartment. In this circumstance, the dural leaves making up the tentorium cerebelli and falx cerebri divide the skull cavity into left and right supratentorial compartments and the posterior fossa. If there is a localized increase in pressure in any of these compartments, brain tissue can be forced out. When any cerebral herniation occurs, three things need to be considered:

- What is herniating?
- Where is it herniating?
- What is compressed?

Knowing what is compressed will tell you what the clinical consequences will be. Compression of a cerebral artery leads to ischaemia or infarction in the relevant vascular territory. A summary of herniation syndromes is presented in Table 9.2.

In transtentorial herniation, compression of the midbrain leads to a fixed, dilated pupil (third nerve nucleus), hemiparesis (cerebral peduncle), and coma

Table 9.2 Common cerebral herniation syndromes.

Herniation	What	Where	Compressed
Subfalcine	Cingulate gyrus	Below the falx cerebri between the two supratentorial compartments	Anterior cerebral artery
Transtentorial	Uncus of the temporal lobes	Through the tentorial incisura	Midbrain posterior cerebral artery
Tonsillar	Cerebellar tonsils	Through the foramen magnum	Medulla oblongata

(periacqueductal grey). The lateralizing signs are usually ipsilateral to the side of the compression, but occasionally the entire midbrain is pushed over and is compressed at the tentorial incisura on the other side, leading to contralateral clinical signs. The eponym for the tentorial incisura is 'Kernohan's notch' and for this reason the phenomenon of contra-lateral signs with transtentorial herniation is called 'Kernohan's phenomenon' and is said to occur in 10% of cases. Transtentorial herniation can also be of the cerebellar vermis upwards through the tentorial incisura if there is a posterior fossa mass. Tonsillar herniation is a rapidly fatal event, as the cardio-respiratory homeostatic centres are within the medulla.

Cushing's phenomenon is bradycardia and hypertension associated with tonsillar herniation. It is a consequence of medullary ischaemia, causing a surge of sympathetic activity with a reflex bradycardia mediated by the parasympathetic nervous system. It is not a clinically useful sign of raised intracranial pressure in adults as it occurs very late and, by this time, the patient is inevitably in deep coma. However, in babies and young children, with hydrocephalus for example, bradycardia and apnoeic episodes can indicate raised intracranial pressure.

BRAINSTEM DEATH

Brainstem tests are a sequence of clinical tests to evaluate brainstem function. In the UK, if a patient meets the criteria for brainstem death on this basis they are legally dead. This has particular relevance to neurosurgeons as there are many cerebral pathologies that are irrecoverable but will allow a patient's heart to continue beating while they are on a ventilator. There is also an implication for transplant surgeons as a proportion of organ donors will come from these unfortunate patients, so-called beating heart donors. This is of great value to transplant recipients as the organ's ischaemic time is minimized. The legal situation differs in other countries; for example, in the USA, EEG and angiographic findings may also be used.

For a patient to be pronounced brainstem dead two sets of criteria need to be met, as discussed below. The tests themselves must be carried out by two experienced doctors of at least 5 years standing. Usually they are carried out by intensive care and neurosurgical Consultants. The tests must be done by each of the doctors, but this can occur at the same time. If there is a period of time between the two tests it is the time of the first set of tests that is taken as the legal time of death, although this cannot be verified until the second set of tests. The patient's friends and relatives need to be counselled carefully regarding brainstem death as it is a difficult time for them and the purpose and legal implications of the tests can seem confusing.

Prerequisites

Before the actual brainstem tests are carried out, a number of prerequisites must be met. Specifically, the patient must:

1. not be under the influence of any sedative or paralysing drugs;
2. not have any systemic disturbance that could cause coma;
3. be normothermic;
4. have normal serum biochemistry;
5. have a GCS of 3, despite persistent stimulus in the dermatome of the trigeminal nerve (usually over the supra-orbital notch);
6. be apnoeic: this is tested by pre-oxygenating the patient and passing a tube carrying high flow oxygen down the endotracheal tube to maintain oxygenation. The ventilator is then switched off to allow the P_aCO_2 to rise. The patient is closely observed to identify any respiratory effort. Before the test is completed a blood gas must be taken to ensure that the PCO_2 has reached at least 8 kPa. This level of hypercarbia should stimulate the respiratory centres.

Brainstem tests

To meet the criteria for brainstem death the patient must also have no brainstem function. The tests summarized in Table 9.3 are designed to test the brainstem. You should think of each of these tests in terms of the afferent and efferent limbs, and the part of the brainstem in which the relevant cranial nuclei reside.

Table 9.3 Summary of brainstem tests.

Test	Afferent limb	Efferent limb	Site of brainstem nuclei
Pupillary light reflex	II	III	Midbrain
Corneal reflex	Va	VII	Pons
Doll's eye reflex	VIII	III/VI	Pons/midbrain
Caloric reflex	VIII	III/VI	Pons/midbrain
Gag reflex	XI/X	XI/X	Medulla

The criteria indicative of brainstem death are:

- *Pupillary light reflex:* the pupils must be fixed, dilated, and unresponsive to light.
- *Corneal reflex:* the patient must not blink when a wisp of cotton is drawn across the cornea.
- *Doll's eye reflex:* the eyes are held open and the head is turned from side to side. The patient's eyes must not move. This is also called the vestibulo-ocular reflex.
- *Caloric reflex:* otoscopy is carried out to ensure that the external auditory meatus is free of any obstruction. Ice-cold water is slowly instilled into the outer ear. This procedure leads to convection currents within the semi-circular canals which normally lead to the eyes deviating towards the ear in which the water is instilled. No response is seen if the patient is brainstem dead.
- *Gag reflex:* the endotracheal tube is pulled or a suction catheter is placed down the tube to stimulate the pharynx. No cough or gag should be seen.

10

Basic Neurosurgical Procedures

Reuben D. Johnson

CONTENTS

INTRODUCTION

As a junior neurosurgical trainee you will have the opportunity to see a multitude of complex and dramatic operations. However, you are unlikely to play a large role in them in your early training. In spite of this, some commonly performed procedures may be classified as 'basic', such that junior trainees should be familiar with their principles and performance. They are not minor or easy; rather, they constitute the cases you will repeatedly see on the ward.

This chapter summarizes them, and you should endeavour to see them undertaken early in your post, thus maximizing your chance of actually performing at least some of them. Even if your career goal is not neurosurgery, understanding them will be of benefit when managing patients whom you refer to, or accept from, neurosurgery, as you will do in orthopaedics or general surgery.

Neurosurgery involves a significant amount of out-of-hours operating for potentially life-threatening conditions, which are often amenable to basic interventions—specifically: diversion of CSF flow using external ventricular drains (EVDs) and shunts; evacuation of chronic subdural haematomas

(CSDH); acute subdural haematomas (ASDH) and extradural haematomas (EDH); and spinal decompression. These are often the cases that you will manage from admission, and their frequency will provide ample opportunity to familiarize yourself with them.

CRANIAL PROCEDURES

SOME BASIC SURFACE ANATOMY

Opening the cranium requires an appreciation of basic surface anatomy and its relationship to deeper structures. When incising the scalp, appreciation of the location of scalp vessels ensures preservation of scalp flap vascularity. Generally, it is a highly vascular structure, but ideally, to minimize the risk of necrosis, major vessels should not be sacrificed.

There are five arteries bilaterally supplying the scalp. Anteriorly are the supratrochlear (medial) and supraorbital (lateral) arteries which arise from the ophthalmic branch of the internal carotid artery (ICA). More posteriorly are branches of the external carotid artery: the superficial temporal artery, the posterior auricular artery, and the occipital artery. Plentiful anastomoses exist, but there is a risk of ischaemia unless flaps are based upon one of these arteries. Perhaps the branch most relevant to the junior trainee is the superficial temporal artery, the pulsation of which can be palpated just in front of the tragus. When making the incision for the trauma craniotomy described below, it is prudent to palpate for this artery and begin your incision posterior to it. Another rule to adhere to is to make sure that the bottom half of the flap is never less than half the length of the top edge.

The nerve supply of the scalp itself is of less concern to the neurosurgeon; however, the temporal branch of the facial nerve can be damaged by an injudiciously placed incision, resulting in a palsy of the frontalis muscle. The temporal branch passes from within the substance of the parotid gland and crosses above the zygomatic arch about 2.5 cm anterior to the tragus—hence incisions in the zygomatic area are kept behind this point and above the zygomatic arch.

For the purposes of the procedures described here, the next most important structures to be aware of are the dural venous sinuses and the motor strip. Provided that burr-holes are placed well away from these areas, the risks will be kept to a minimum. The sagittal sinus runs in the midline, and so burrs are cut over 2.5 cm from the midline. It is important, when draping patients, to make sure that you can still confidently identify the midline. Other sinuses, such as the transverse sinus, should be well away from your drill, as you should not be cutting near the posterior fossa. The motor cortex is located about 3 cm behind the coronal suture which, with practice on yourself, should be easily palpable through the scalp. Alternatively, the position of the superior aspect of the motor cortex can be estimated by following a vertical line up through the external auditory meatus. An oft-quoted method is to use a tape measure (or piece of string that can be halved by folding) to find the midpoint of the arc extending from nasion to inion (external occipital protuberance): the motor cortex is 2 cm posterior to this point. Figure 10.1 summarizes these three methods for estimating the position of the motor strip. The transverse sinus can be marked out by drawing a line from the tragus to the external occipital protuberance.

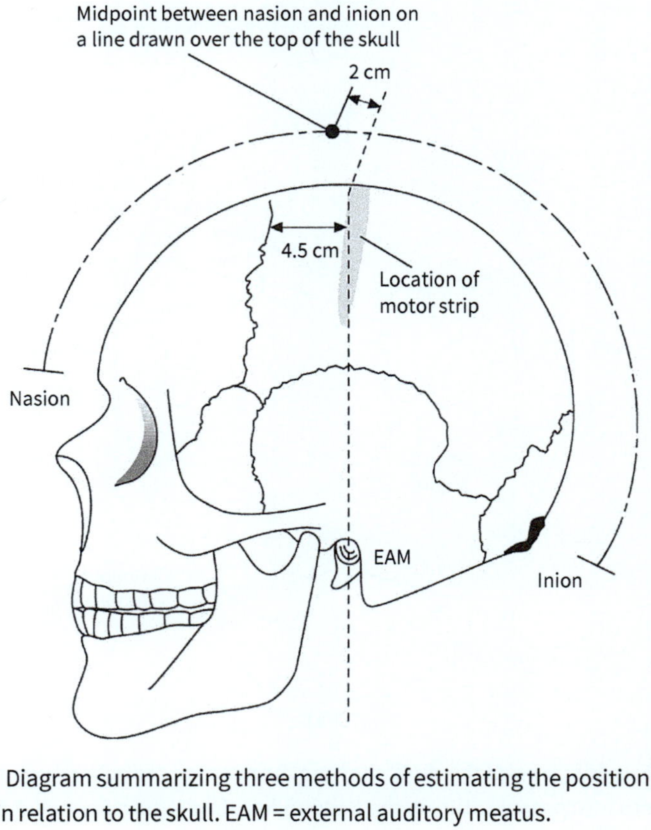

Figure 10.1 Diagram summarizing three methods of estimating the position of the motor strip in relation to the skull. EAM = external auditory meatus.

INSERTION OF AN ICP BOLT

Insertion of ICP bolts may be done in the intensive care unit (ICU) to monitor the intracranial pressure (ICP) in patients with diffuse head injury. If a patient goes to theatre, then insertion of ICP-monitoring devices is ideally performed at the time of surgery. If performed in the ICU, it is imperative that the procedure is carried out in as sterile a manner as possible.

Ideally, the surgeon will be positioned at the head of the patient, who is lying supine. Identify, shave, and mark Kocher's point, which is 1 cm anterior to the coronal suture in the midpupillary line, which is about 2.5 cm from the midline (see Figure 10.2).

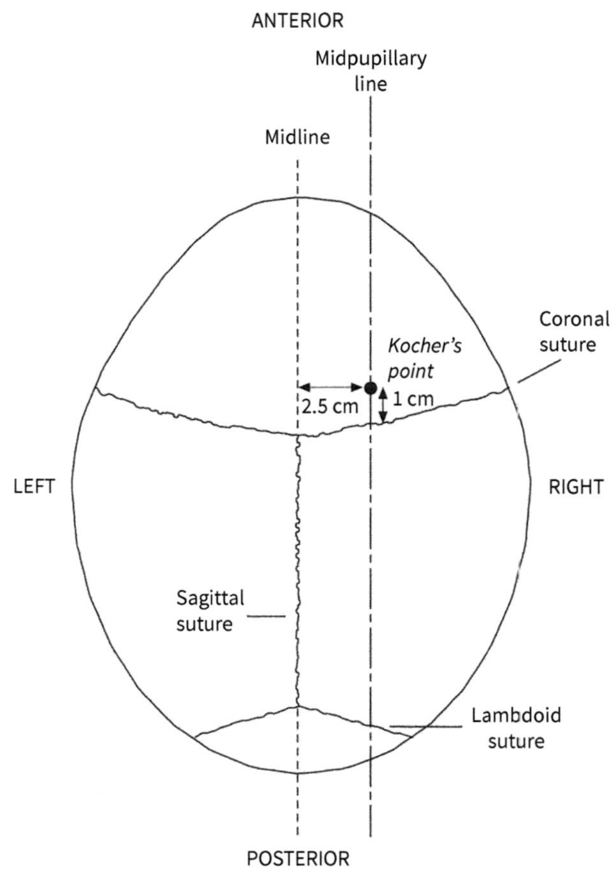

Figure 10.2 Superior view of the skull, showing the position of Kocher's point, which is 1 cm anterior to the coronal suture in the midpupillary line (approximately 2.5 cm from midline).

After cleaning the area and injecting some local anaesthetic (e.g. 2 ml lignocaine with adrenaline) make a small vertical stab incision (no more than 0.5 cm long) with a small blade, down to the skull. A twist drill is used to penetrate the skull. There should be a spur or shoulder on the drill to prevent plunging it into the brain. Once the skull has been breached, a small cylindrical tap is screwed into the hole to allow for passage of the ICP catheter (some ICP kits do not have this and the wire is then passed directly through the hole). It is advisable to calibrate the ICP monitor at this point before opening the dura. The exact procedure for calibration will differ between makes of machine, and the ICU staff will usually be familiar with the one they keep in stock (it usually involves obtaining a zero reading while the monitor wire is in sterile water, and writing down a reference number).

The dura is opened by pricking it with a blunt-ended probe placed down the cylindrical tap. The probe will be provided by the manufacturer, and will usually have a right-angle on it to prevent its going too far or being lost inside the cranium. A small back-flow of CSF is usually seen as the probe passes through the dura. The ICP monitor wire can now be passed down the tap (it should not exceed the inner surface of the cranium by more than 0.5 cm) and then screwed securely. Before attaching the ICP monitor wire to the monitor, make sure that it is securely fastened so as to reduce the chances of its being pulled out.

BURR-HOLE DRAINAGE OF A CHRONIC SUBDURAL HAEMATOMA

The drainage of a subdural haematoma can usually be achieved through one or two burr-holes. Two may be helpful, as this allows the washing of saline from one burr-hole through to the next. The location of the burr-holes will depend upon the location of the haematoma as determined by CT scan. However, the general principle is that burr-holes should be located along the same line as the incision of a trauma flap so that if there are any problems it is relatively easy to proceed to a trauma craniotomy. The procedure can be performed under local anaesthetic, but until you are more experienced, and unless the patient is likely to tolerate the procedure awake, it is best done under general anaesthetic.

The patient is positioned supine on the operating table with the head placed on a ring. Check the side of the haematoma on the scan at this point and double-check with a colleague. For burr-holes, the head can be kept straight or slightly angled to the side contralateral to the haematoma. It should be borne in mind that if it is necessary to proceed to craniotomy, the head will need to be rotated further laterally (see below). Once the head is positioned, the hair can be shaved and the skin incisions marked out (approximately 2–3 cm in length). The incisions should be placed along the line of an appropriate craniotomy, such as the question mark-shaped temporoparietal craniotomy described below. Ensure that your incisions are located so that the burr-holes will overlie the subdural haematoma. It is essential, therefore, to look at the scan again and decide the height of the haematoma in the cranium and its anteroposterior extent. Prep and drape the patient so that you can still locate the midline and can feel relevant landmarks, such as the glabella and external auditory meatus. Inform the anaesthetist, and infiltrate local anaesthetic with adrenaline into the sites of your incision. Before picking up the scalpel, check the side one more time. If the site of your incision is above the superficial temporal line (which it most probably will be), you will be able to cut directly through skin down to bone. Use the handle of the knife, or the handle of a periosteal elevator, to push the periosteum away from the skull. If you are using two burr-holes, prepare the second site before drilling. Insert a self-retainer to hold the wound open and expose the skull. You will find that the self-retainer will control most bleeding points from the scalp edges, but use bipolar diathermy to control any obvious bleeders.

You are now ready to use the drill. Make sure that you are comfortable, and hold the drill in both hands. Make sure that the patient's head is well supported by your assistant. You will be taught how to use the drill, but the following points must always be remembered: apply a constant firm pressure but without leaning your body weight on the drill; the drill will stop automatically once the cranium is breached and, when it does, take your foot off the drill pedal (and not before, as the clutch will disengage and it will not be possible to start it again) and withdraw the drill. Never restart the drill in the burr-hole once the drill has stopped. You should now be able to see dura and, if the burr-hole is properly located, you will see the dark blue of the subdural haematoma underneath. Control any bleeding from the bone with bone wax, and remove any fragments of remaining bone with a blunt hook and fine-toothed forceps. Now use the diathermy to scorch the whole area of exposed dura.

Open the dura by making a cruciate incision with an appropriately sized knife and sharp hook. It is safest to make a small incision to begin and then use the hook to lift the dura towards you. Once the dura has been incised in this way there will be four triangular leaves of dura. Shrink these back to the bone by grasping them with the bipolar and coagulating them. If the membranes around the CSDH have not burst by this point then scorch it with the bipolar and open it with a blunt instrument like a Macdonald. Alternatively, hold the bipolar tips close together and advance them into the membrane and allow them to open up (again, scorch the membranes as you advance). Once through, you will find that the dark brown fluid that constitutes a CSDH will drain out. Wash the subdural space through carefully with saline. Some surgeons insert soft catheters into the subdural space to wash it out, but it is important to avoid damage to the brain and using only a syringe can be a safer option in the junior surgeon's hands. You will see the surface of the brain and you should try to allow it to expand towards the cranium. This may happen spontaneously or you might ask the anaesthetist to induce a Valsalva manoeuvre to speed things up.

Before closing the wounds ensure that you have filled any gaps between the brain and skull as much as possible with saline. You may either leave the burrholes empty or fill them with Surgicel™, Spongistan™, or beeswax. The scalp is closed with 2/0 or 3/0 Vicryl™ to the galea, and clips to the skin.

FRONTOTEMPOROPARIETAL TRAUMA CRANIOTOMY (DRAINAGE OF ASDH AND EDH)

The reason for describing this craniotomy is that the most common site for an ASDH is the surface of the frontotemporoparietal cortex. Also, this incision can be used to evacuate an EDH which has formed in the classic temporal location due to bleeding from the middle meningeal artery.

The patient is positioned supine, with the head rotated to the side contralateral to the clot. The idea is to position the patient in such a way that there will be an optimal view under all edges of the craniotomy. Generally speaking, you should aim to have the side of the head as horizontal as possible. This is facilitated by the placement of sandbags under the ipsilateral shoulder. The head is best fixed with a three-point head fixator.

Shave the side of the head affected, all the way to the midline. Mark out a question mark-shaped incision which begins at the zygomatic arch no more than a finger's breadth in front of the tragus. Remember to palpate for the superficial temporal artery and avoid it. The line of the incision is a curve back around the top of the ear and then a curve towards the midline. From here it runs parallel to the midline anteriorly to the hairline (Figure 10.3). Prep and drape the patient.

Make an incision through the scalp along the line described above. This is a large incision and bleeding needs to be adequately controlled. This is achieved by direct pressure either side of the incision with the fingers on mastoid swabs. After every 5 cm or so of incision apply Raney scalp clips over the scalp edges

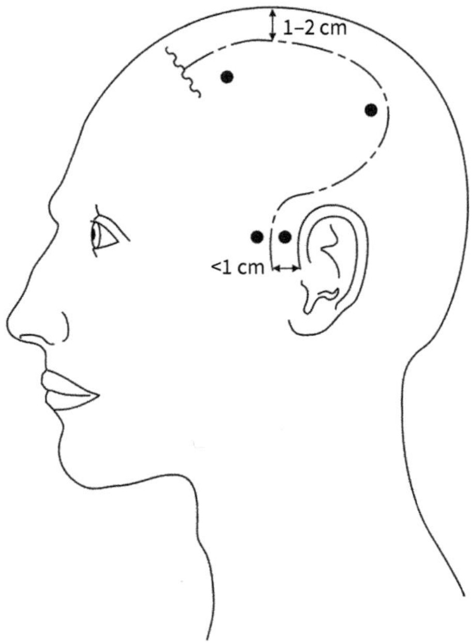

Figure 10.3 Diagram showing the location of a typical skin incision for a frontotemporoparietal craniotomy. Note that the location of four burr-holes is also shown: one frontal, one parietal, and two temporal. It is important to place the two temporal burr-holes low down in order to decompress temporal extradural haematomas.

to include the mastoid swabs. This should be an efficient, smooth process so as not to delay proceeding to the life-saving part of the operation. Part of your incision may take you directly down to bone, but in the temporal area it will overlie the temporalis muscle. You will need to sweep the scalp forward over the surface of the muscle using a wet swab and the back of the scalpel blade to expose the muscle. Wrap the scalp flap in a wet swab and anchor it forward out of the way with rubber bands.

Cut through the temporalis muscle down to bone with the monopolar diathermy. The line of incision is just inside your skin incision in an inverted 'U' shape. Remember that when you come to use the craniotome you need to be about 3 cm from the midline so as to stay away from the sagittal sinus. Leave the lowermost neck of temporalis intact. Sweep the periosteum clear with the periosteal elevators along the line of the incision.

Place four burr-holes: two temporal (one being at the pterion), one frontal, and one parietal. Connect the burr-holes with the craniotome. Use bone elevators to lift the bone flap gently away from the dura, taking care not to tear the dura as you do so. You are now left with either of two situations, depending on the indication for the operation: you will see either a bright red EDH overlying the dura or a dark blue ASDH underneath the dura.

In the case of an EDH, you have already performed the life-saving procedure by opening the bone. There remains only to evacuate the haematoma by sucking away at it, and then placing dural hitch stitches to attach the dura to the edges of the craniotomy. This is to prevent the EDH from re-accumulating. Use a non-cutting needle and 3/0 Vicryl™, taking care not to tear the dura or cause subdural bleeding by making sure that the needle passes only through the outer layer of the dura. It can be useful to slip a single layer of Surgicel™ between the dura and the bone to help haemostasis. When sucking away the haematoma, identify and control any bleeding points. Look under the edges of the craniotomy and remove any clots found.

In the case of a subdural haematoma it is necessary to incise the dura to evacuate the underlying clot. Beware opening the dura too widely as the brain may swell and herniate out of your incision, risking laceration on the sharp dural edges. This is true for cases where it is obvious from the CT scan that there is a lot of brain swelling and mass effect from the haematoma, and in these cases it is safer simply to fenestrate the dura with small slit lacerations and suck out the clot gently. This allows clot evacuation while minimizing brain herniation. The bone flap can be replaced and either fixed back with screws or bioplates, or allowed to ride free. Riding free may help control the ICP post-operatively. The scalp is closed with 2/0 or 3/0 Vicryl™ to the galea, and clips to the skin. This is a large flap and so a drain may be needed. When removing the Raney's, ensure that you take care to diathermy any bleeding points as there can be profuse bleeding at this stage. In the very acute situation, especially with an EDH, only the lower part of this exposure need be used. For example, in the case of a temporal EDH the first 5 cm or so of the incision can be made and the temporalis incised down to bone. A self-retainer is inserted and a temporal burr-hole made. This can be enlarged quickly using bone-clippers or rongeurs. This allows for extremely rapid decompression of the clot and can be life-saving.

INSERTION OF AN EXTERNAL VENTRICULAR DRAIN

Insertion of a catheter into the frontal horn of the lateral ventricle is a life-saving procedure in acute hydrocephalus, and familiarity with the technique is essential.

The patient is positioned supine with the head secured either on a ring or with a foam cushion. If the head is kept in the neutral position it is easier to coordinate catheter trajectory later on. Shave the right frontal area (the non-dominant side is usual for catheter placement, unless there is a contra-indication; e.g. underlying lesion).

Identify and mark Kocher's point which is 1 cm anterior to the coronal suture in the midpupillary line (approximately 2.5 cm from midline). This is the point at which the burr-hole will be made and the catheter inserted. Mark out a 2–3 cm incision centred on this point in a sagittal plane. Incise the scalp and fashion a burr-hole as described above. In this instance the dura does not need to be opened widely but just sufficiently to allow passage of the catheter. Scorch the pial covering of the cortex with the bipolar diathermy and use the tip of a sharp blade to ensure that it has been breached.

The next step is the most difficult part—placement of the catheter into the frontal horn of the lateral ventricle. There are numerous stereotactic methods described in the books and each is slightly different. The key is to have one method in mind, learn it, and stick to it. Basically, if you pass the catheter perpendicular to the surface of the skull to a depth of 5 cm (less in the presence of hydrocephalus) you will enter the frontal horn of the lateral ventricle. There are 5-cm and 10-cm markings on ventricular catheters. To help you ensure that the catheter is perpendicular you can check your position in the coronal and sagittal planes. In the coronal plane the catheter should be pointing towards the medial canthal line of the ipsilateral eye. In the sagittal plane the catheter should be pointing towards the external auditory meatus, or just anterior to it. When the catheter enters the ventricle you should feel a subtle 'give', and when the trocar is withdrawn you will drain CSF. Note that if you do not hit the ventricle after two passes, then call for help (from a senior colleague). Now advance the catheter with the trocar withdrawn. At this point it is imperative not to let the catheter move in relation to the skull. Hold the catheter with a pair of non-toothed forceps held flush to the skull while you tunnel the distal end of the catheter under the scalp to an exit point a few centimetres away from the skin wound. You would be well advised to secure the catheter in place with a few overlying sutures before closing the scalp incision. Attach your external ventricular drainage system and set it to a fixed setting, for example 10 cm H_2O (I recommend four stay sutures).

Close the scalp incision, taking care not to perforate the drain with your needle. Ensure that you secure the drain with a further series of sutures, as EVDs have a tendency to 'fall out' when patients are transferred.

INSERTION OF A VENTRICULOPERITONEAL SHUNT (OCCIPITAL CATHETER)

The patient is supine with a sandbag under the ipsilateral shoulder to allow good rotation of the head away from the site of insertion. The aim is to position the patient so as to provide as straight a line as possible from the occipital site of insertion distally across the neck and thorax to the abdominal site of insertion. Mark out the following:

(1) the site of the occipital burr-hole (6 cm superior to the external occipital protuberance and 3 cm from the midline);
(2) an incision around the burr-hole so that the incision does not lie over the top of the shunt site; and
(3) an abdominal incision.

Prep the whole area all the way from head to abdomen. Drape to expose the whole shunt path. It may be necessary to staple drapes in the neck area to ensure that they are flush with the skin.

Stop, and go through in your mind the sequence of events:

1. Open scalp and drill burr-hole—do not open dura.
2. Open abdomen—clip, but do not open peritoneum.
3. Tunnel, and pass distal catheter (and valve, if attached to catheter).
4. Open dura and pass proximal catheter.
5. Connect proximal catheter to valve (in the case of separate shunt-valve kits).
6. Check CSF flow through shunt.
7. Open peritoneum and pass distal catheter.
8. Close wounds.

Before proceeding, prepare the shunt by taking it out of its packaging and priming and soaking it in gentamicin. Make a curved scalp incision around the planned site of the burr-hole. The site of the burr-hole is 6 cm up from the inion (external occipital protuberance) and 3 cm lateral to the midline. Take great care with haemostasis at this stage (you can use monopolar once you are through the skin, if you prefer). It is useful to have forceps and mastoid swabs in one hand and diathermy in the other. Remember that water runs downhill, so start at the top of the wound and work down, otherwise your view will always be obscured by bleeders higher up. Also, cut vessels have two ends, so always check the other side of the wound if you find a big bleeder on one side. A useful tip is to develop scalp layers so that the aponeurosis can be separated and flipped back. This can be sutured over the proximal catheter later, adding strength to the proximal catheter.

Use scissors to develop a plane distally for receipt of valve and catheter: place the scissors in closed, then open them up and withdraw. Make the burr-hole. Cover the proximal wound with Betadine™-soaked swabs. Take care never to touch the edges of wounds.

Now go to the abdomen and open it up. This is similar to an appendix incision, except that it is in the upper part of the abdomen: knife to skin; Langenbecks through fat; scissors through muscle; clips to peritoneum (do not open yet). Leave the clips on the peritoneum and cover the wound with Betadine™-soaked swabs.

You are now ready to tunnel and pass the distal shunt. It is advisable to change gloves at this stage. Place clean swabs over the abdomen so that the shunt end can remain as sterile as possible once passed. It is academic whether you tunnel in a distal-to-proximal direction or vice versa. Bend the guide to the correct shape first (use the surface of the patient as a guide). Take care to advance over the clavicle and not to burrow into the neck. Remove the central trocar and pass the shunt through.

Now open the dura with diathermy in the centre of the burr-hole and pass the tip of the knife through. Use diathermy to extend the hole slightly and then buzz the surface of the brain only slightly. Pass the proximal catheter directed towards the glabella to a depth of 4 cm (or check the distance on the scan) and feel for entry into the ventricle. Remove the trocar to check for CSF flow and advance the catheter. Place the bulldog clip on the catheter to control the CSF flow and cut the catheter to the length required (i.e. almost flush with the skull—be careful not to lose the proximal catheter inside the cranium at this stage!).

Connect the two parts of the shunt system and tie securely with 2/0 Vicryl™. Take care not to pull the proximal catheter out at this stage. Remove the bulldog clip and check for CSF flow distally; aspirate if necessary.

Close the head wound with 2/0 or 3/0 Vicryl™ and clips to skin (it is best to use clips, as needles risk perforating the shunt). Remember that if you developed the scalp layers the aponeurosis can be flapped over the proximal catheter for extra protection.

Open the peritoneum by holding up the attached clips and checking with thumb and forefinger for the bowel before opening with the scissors. Introduce the distal end of the shunt into the peritoneal cavity. There is no need to suture the peritoneum unless you have made more than a very tiny incision. Close the aponeuroses and muscle with 3/0 Vicryl™ and use subcutaneous Vicryl™ to skin.

SPINAL PROCEDURES

LUMBAR PUNCTURE

The patient is positioned on their side with their knees curled up towards the chest. The back, straight or flexed anteriorly, should be close to the edge of the bed. As the spinal cord ends at L1/2 (continuing as the cauda equina below) the ideal intervertebral space to aim for is L4/5. This can be identified easily, as the highest point of the iliac crest is located on a level with the spinous process of the 4th lumbar vertebra. Feel for the space between the L4 and L5 spinous processes and mark the spot. It is helpful to ensure that, when the area has been cleaned and draped, it is possible to feel the iliac crest without contaminating the hands: this allows the level to be rechecked. Local anaesthetic is injected down to bone and below the skin. The spinal needle is advanced slowly in the midline in the L4/5 interspace in a slightly rostral orientation. The needle will be felt to 'give' when the dura is breached, and a backflash of CSF will be seen when the trocar is withdrawn. The central trocar should now be removed and a manometer attached to measure the opening pressure (this should always be done). A three-way tap attached between the manometer and spinal needle will allow CSF from the manometer to be taken for analysis. If the L4/5 interspace is not encountered the first time, then further attempts can be made with the same needle, provided that the tip is not withdrawn from the skin between passes. Always make sure that the patient is as comfortable as possible, and enquire expressly about nerve root pain in the legs (withdraw the needle if pain is felt).

LUMBAR DRAIN PLACEMENT

The procedure to place a lumbar drain is similar to that for a lumbar puncture, except that a larger needle is used which has an angled opening at the tip. This allows a drain to be inserted and guided into the vertebral canal. Care should be taken to orientate the bevel so that the sharp cutting edge runs parallel to the nerve roots. This reduces the risk of severing the root on insertion. Once in the canal, the needle can be rotated 90° to direct the passage of the drain into the canal.

LAMINECTOMY

The most common laminectomies that are encountered are lumbar and cervical, although thoracic laminectomies will also be seen. The positioning and techniques will differ for each, but the basic principles are the same for all three regions. Patients undergoing cervical laminectomy will be prone, and their heads will be fixed firmly, for example with a Mayfield; this is described as the Concorde position, as the neck is in flexion. It is important to ensure that the face of the patient is not pressing on anything that may cause injury, and that the anaesthetist is happy with the airway. In patients undergoing lumbar laminectomy it is important to ensure that the abdomen is not under any pressure, as this would result in increased venous pressure and excessive bleeding in the surgical field. Pressure can be reduced with the use of a pillow under the pelvis and one higher up at the level of the thorax.

There are several ways of determining the spinal level for the laminectomy. Spinal needles and the image intensifier are often used before the incision is made. However, it is good practice to confirm the level once the bone is exposed, using a metal marker (e.g. an artery clip—see below) fixed to the bone. Once the levels have been marked, an appropriate midline incision can be marked out. After infiltration of local anaesthetic, a midline incision is made down to the spinous processes. If the incision is truly in the midline then there will be minimal damage to the paravertebral muscles.

The muscles are detached from the spinous processes with cutting diathermy. Care should be taken regarding the depths of the wound to ensure that the diathermy is not pushed through the interspinous spaces into the spinal canal. The muscle is then stripped away from the laminae with a retractor and mastoid swabs. The rectangular mastoids are inserted vertically into the wound parallel to the spinous processes. The cob is then used to sweep the mastoids laterally out along the laminae, thus lifting the paravertebral muscles away from the bone. A self-retaining retractor system can now be used to hold the wound open. The spinous processes and the laminae should now be clearly visible. It may be necessary to take some time to clean any remaining tissue from the bone. The spinal level should be checked again at this point, using artery clips as markers and visualising with the image intensifier.

The relevant spinous processes are removed by using a Leksell bone rongeurs to break them away from the laminae. The Horsley's can be used in 'Herring bone' fashion to remove the remaining bases of the spinous processes. It is now fashionable to use the high-speed drill to perform a laminectomy, but you should ensure that you have received meticulous training in using the drill in the lumbar spine.

The ligamentum flavum is breached with a blunt implement to enter the spinal canal and the opening is extended using a 1–2 mm Kerrison punch carefully placed under the edge of the laminae. The first bites should be done with caution and the punch should never be forced into a space. If there is any doubt, probe carefully again with a blunt instrument. With diligence and persistence an opening will eventually be made and the spinal canal can be opened. The opening can be increased gradually by taking bites from alternate sides and working up the canal (using a larger 3–5 mm punch, provided that it fits). Care must be taken not to puncture the dura or to take bites out of the nerve roots. As a general rule, work upwards when removing bone and downwards when removing ligamentum. Knowledge of the anatomy of the spinal cord and vertebral canal is essential for this to be done safely. Remember: unless the surgeon knows which parts of the procedure are risky, it is not safe to proceed.

The canal is opened over a given number of predetermined vertebral levels. If the procedure is for decompression of a stenosis, then the canal is widened until the dura is free and not compressed. Otherwise the canal is opened only so far as is required, for example for the removal of an extradural abscess or tumour.

The wound is closed with several layers of deep Vicryl™ suture. The surgeon's preference will determine the skin suture.

11

Hydrocephalus and Shunt Systems

Reuben D. Johnson

CONTENTS

INTRODUCTION

Hydrocephalus, a condition in which there is abnormal enlargement of the ventricles due to an excessive accumulation of cerebrospinal fluid (CSF) resulting from a disturbance of its flow, absorption, or—less commonly—secretion, occurs in approximately 1 per 1000 live births; the incidence of adult-onset hydrocephalus is unknown. Paediatric hydrocephalus is discussed in Chapter 14, *Paediatric Neurosurgery*. The pathological basis of hydrocephalus is covered in Chapter 3, *Neurosurgical Pathology*, and its brief recapitulation here is a prelude to the discussion of shunt systems later in this chapter.

CSF PHYSIOLOGY

CSF production occurs predominantly in the choroid plexus, with a small proportion being produced by the ependyma and brain parenchyma. In an average adult, CSF is produced at a rate of about 0.4 ml/min (i.e.

approximately 500 ml/day), the total volume varying with age, being 100–150 ml, out of which 15–25 ml are contained within the ventricular system.

CSF flows from the lateral ventricles into the 3rd ventricle through the foramina of Monro and then, via the aqueduct of Sylvius, into the 4th ventricle. From the 4th ventricle it then flows through the foramina of Lushka and Magendie into the basal cisterns and the subarachnoid space. CSF bathes the basal cisterns and the spinal subarachnoid space and then flows over the cerebral hemispheres. It is largely absorbed by the arachnoid villi of the dural sinuses.

CLASSIFICATION OF HYDROCEPHALUS

There are several ways in which hydrocephalus may be classified, though probably the most useful of these is the dichotomous one which divides hydrocephalus into obstructive (or non-communicating) and communicating types.

OBSTRUCTIVE HYDROCEPHALUS

Hydrocephalus of this type arises when there is an obstruction, caused either by external compression or by intraventricular mass lesions, which prevents the CSF from flowing into the subarachnoid space and results in dilatation of the ventricular system proximal to the site of the obstruction.

Congenital hydrocephalus is usually of the obstructive type (see Chapter 14,). Consult Chapter 6, *Interpretation of CT Head Scans*, and look particularly at Figures 6.10, 6.12, 6.13, 6.14, 6.20, and 6.22, all of which demonstrate features associated with obstructive hydrocephalus.

Sites of obstruction in obstructive hydrocephalus are listed below.

- *Foramina of Monro:* linking the lateral ventricles to the 3rd ventricle. Obstruction may lead to dilatation of one or, if the obstruction is sufficiently large (e.g. in colloid cyst) both lateral ventricles.
- *Aqueduct of Sylvius:* linking 3rd and 4th ventricles. Obstruction by any one of a number of congenital or acquired lesions (e.g. atresia, ependymitis, haemorrhage, or tumour) causes dilatation of both lateral ventricles, as well as of the 3rd ventricle.

- *4th ventricle:* Obstruction of the 4th ventricle (e.g. by a posterior fossa tumour) produces dilatation of the aqueduct and the lateral and 3rd ventricles.
- *Foramen of Magendie:* linking the 4th ventricle and the subarachnoid space. Obstruction may be due to congenital failure of opening (e.g. Dandy–Walker malformation).
- *Foramina of Luschka:* on the left and right of the 4th ventricle, linking this to the subarachnoid space. As for the foramen of Magendie, obstruction may be due to congenital failure of opening.

It is essential to seek senior advice if lumbar puncture is to be considered, as this is generally contraindicated in obstructive hydrocephalus.

COMMUNICATING HYDROCEPHALUS

Communicating hydrocephalus occurs in the absence of any obstruction of CSF flow between the ventricles and subarachnoid space, being caused instead by impairment of CSF reabsorption. It has been postulated that this is a consequence of functional impairment of the arachnoid granulations, which are located along the superior sagittal sinus.

Various neurological conditions may result in communicating hydrocephalus; these include subarachnoid/intraventricular haemorrhage, meningitis, Chiari malformation, and congenital absence of arachnoid granulations. Prevention of CSF reabsorption causing diffuse ventricular dilatation can also result from scarring and fibrosis of the subarachnoid space, following infectious, inflammatory, or haemorrhagic events. Rarely, communicating hydrocephalus is caused by over-secretion of CSF, as in the case of choroid plexus papilloma.

CLINICAL FEATURES

The major presenting features of hydrocephalus are signs and symptoms of raised intracranial pressure, for example headache, vomiting, papilloedema, and deterioration of conscious state. Impairment of upgaze is often seen, resulting from pressure of the dilated 3rd ventricle on the superior colliculus of the tectum. Hydrocephalus may also present as slowly progressive deterioration in the form of headaches, failing mental function, memory loss, and behavioural disturbances.

The most important techniques for investigating hydrocephalus are computed tomography (CT) and magnetic resonance imaging (MRI) of the brain. A contrast CT scan or MRI will help to determine the cause of the hydrocephalus. Where indicated, lumbar puncture confirms high CSF pressure; senior advice should first be sought if this is considered. An intracranial pressure (ICP) monitor may be useful to record CSF pressures over a period of time.

The following entities are those which a neurosurgical trainee is likely to encounter during training.

NORMAL PRESSURE HYDROCEPHALUS

In 1965, normal pressure hydrocephalus (NPH) was first described as a clinical entity in a group of elderly patients showing a classic triad of dementia, ataxia, and incontinence; radiological studies in these patients revealed the presence of hydrocephalus even though lumbar CSF pressure was normal.

Although lumbar pressure is, by definition, normal in patients with NPH, continuous ICP monitoring will nevertheless reveal abnormal wave formation, especially at night. In some centres, a CSF infusion study via lumbar puncture is routinely performed in order to estimate the values of various parameters, including CSF outflow resistance, as an aid to identifying those patients who would benefit from a ventriculoperitoneal (VP) shunt procedure.

Another term to remember is hydrocephalus *ex vacuo*. This refers to enlargement of the cerebral ventricles and subarachnoid spaces, a condition which is usually due to brain atrophy as it occurs in dementias with small vessel ischaemia, post-traumatic brain injuries, and even in some psychiatric disorders, such as schizophrenia. Unlike the forms of hydrocephalus resulting from an excessive accumulation of CSF, and the consequent increase in CSF pressure, this condition is a compensatory enlargement of the CSF spaces in response to brain parenchyma loss. It is not the result of increased CSF pressure.

IDIOPATHIC INTRACRANIAL HYPERTENSION

Idiopathic intracranial hypertension (IIH), also known as benign intracranial hypertension (BIH) or pseudotumour cerebri (PTC), is a neurological disorder characterized by an increased intracranial pressure in the absence of ventriculomegaly, intracranial mass, infection, or hypertensive encephalopathy. This is a diagnosis of exclusion and some authorities also exclude patients with dural sinus thrombosis.

The majority of patients with IIH are young, obese females, the peak incidence being in the 3rd decade. The primary symptoms are headache, nausea, and vomiting, as well as visual symptoms which may include visual field loss (if untreated, IIH can progress to blindness). This condition is associated with menstrual irregularities or with taking the oral contraceptive pill. Although it has been suggested that an endocrine disturbance may be involved, careful studies have failed to find significant endocrine abnormalities.

Diagnosis of IIH is confirmed by demonstrating raised CSF pressures on lumbar puncture and a decrease in symptoms following drainage of 30–50 ml of CSF. Most patients are managed medically with weight loss and diuretics, for example acetazolamide. Sometimes the visual symptoms can be alleviated by optic nerve fenestrations carried out by ophthalmologists. It is essential to image the venous dural sinuses (e.g. using MR venography) so as to rule out the presence of venous sinus obstruction which may require a sinus stenting procedure by interventional neuroradiologists. It is necessary in some patients for a CSF diversion procedure in the form of a lumboperitoneal shunt or VP shunt to be carried out.

TREATMENT OF HYDROCEPHALUS

HISTORICAL BACKGROUND

The treatment of hydrocephalus has a long history. It was treated surgically even in the time of Hippocrates (460–370 BC) who described the use of trepanation and 'lemnisci' (bands of bark which were twisted around the skull and inserted into the trepanned openings in the skull). Vesalius gave the first full description of hydrocephalus in post-renaissance Europe, observing that in adults, hydrocephalus could occur without any external signs. Robert Whytt (1714–1766) is credited with giving the first full description of hydrocephalus as a disease entity; he experimented with numerous pharmacological remedies without success. Alexander Monro (Secundus) (1733–1817) described the use of a lance to puncture the ventricle directly: it is thought likely that this was a treatment already in practice at the time. Subsequently, prominent neurologists and neurological surgeons, including Carl Wernicke (1848–1905) and William Keen (1837–1932), also turned their attention to the treatment of hydrocephalus by external drainage of CSF. Possibly the first account of the diversion of CSF to another location within the body was given by Johann von Mikulicz (1850–1905) who described the use of nail-shaped glass wool which passed from the ventricles to the subgalea. Cushing described the use of lumbar-peritoneal CSF diversion, and Dandy performed a third ventriculostomy in 1920. It was, however, the development of the Spitz–Holter valve, in 1955, which led to the popularization of ventriculoperitoneal shunting.

The treatment of hydrocephalus has thus progressed from external CSF drainage to internal CSF diversion, with or without a shunt system, and almost every body cavity and space has been utilized to absorb the diverted CSF. Modern shunt systems are designed to optimize the process of CSF diversion while at the same time minimizing the risks of complications of these procedures.

TREATMENT STRATEGIES

Acute deterioration

In acutely deteriorating hydrocephalus, the treatment procedures include:

- External ventricular drain (EVD).
- Lumbar puncture (communicating hydrocephalus).
- Endoscopic 3rd ventriculostomy (obstructive hydrocephalus).
- Ventriculoperitoneal shunt.

Gradual deterioration

When deterioration is gradual, treatment is by means of the following procedures:

- Ventriculoperitoneal shunt.
- Lumboperitoneal shunt.

TYPES OF SHUNT

The three main categories of shunt are:

- Ventriculoperitoneal (most commonly used).
- Ventriculoatrial.
- Lumboperitoneal.

Apart from being placed in the peritoneum or right atrium, distal catheters can also be placed in the pleural cavity and, rarely, in the gall bladder, ureter, or urinary bladder.

COMPONENTS OF A SHUNT

There are four components of a shunt:

(1) *proximal catheter:* (ventricular/lumbar).
(2) *reservoir:* (permits CSF aspiration for analysis).
(3) *valve:*
  (a) fixed pressure (Heyer–Shulte, Hakim);
  (b) flow regulated (with antisiphon device, e.g. Delta, Orbis, Sigma);
  (c) programmable (e.g. Medos, Sophy): the advantage of this type is that the settings can be changed non-invasively following shunt procedure; it is important to note that settings may spontaneously alter following MRI magnetic exposure.
(4) *distal catheter.*

SHUNT TECHNIQUE

Shunt surgery requires meticulous attention to detail. Patients should have routine bloods pre-operatively, including coagulation screen and group-and-save. If possible, shunts should be performed in daylight hours, with a minimum number of staff in the theatre and masks worn by all. It is advisable to handle shunts with instruments and not hands, and contact between shunt and skin should be avoided. It is strongly recommended that antibiotics should be administered at the time of shunt induction, and haemostasis should be addressed with great care throughout the procedure.

Position

With the patient under general anaesthesia, the head is rotated to the side opposite the shunt placement, and the neck extended so that there is almost a straight line between scalp and abdominal incisions. Placing a sandbag under the ipsilateral shoulder allows good rotation of the head to the other side. Hair is clipped in the operating theatre.

Mark the sites of (a) burr-hole and the curved incision around it, and (b) the abdominal incision.

Burr-hole sites

Posterior parietal approach

For a posterior parietal approach the burr-hole is located at Keen's Point 3 cm posterior and 3 cm superior to the pinna.

Frontal approach

For a frontal approach Kocher's point is used—3 cm from the midline and 1 cm anterior to the coronal suture in the mid–pupillary line. This is particularly helpful if neck rotation is restricted and parieto-occipital exposure is difficult.

Occipital approach

For an occipital approach, the burr hole is located on the flat of the occiput, 3–4 cm from the midline along the course of the lamdoid suture.

Shunt induction

Ensure that the skin is meticulously prepped from the head to the abdomen, and adhesive drapes are used to cover the patient, being placed so as to expose the whole of the shunt path. At this stage, prepare the shunt by removing it from its packaging. It is an option at this stage to secure the valve to the proximal end of the distal catheter. The shunt system is primed and is left to soak in gentamicin solution.

A small scalp incision is adequate, and a pocket for the valve must be created distal to the scalp incision. A burr-hole is made using a perforator or twist drill. The dura is not opened at this stage, and the wound is left covered by a betadine-soaked swab.

The abdominal incision may be sited as vertical upper midline, transverse paraumbilical, or subcostal. The abdomen is opened in layers, and one has to be certain that the peritoneum is truly opened, with clips left on the peritoneum for identification. Some apply a purse-string suture to the peritoneum to prevent the omentum from herniating. Again, the wound is covered with a betadine-soaked swab.

It is advisable to change gloves before tunnelling. Care must be taken while tunnelling, especially over the clavicle. If the tunneller goes too deep, injury can be caused to neck structures, or potentially the chest can be entered! On the other hand, if tunnelling is too superficial, skin laceration can occur. Once tunnelling has been completed, the trocar is removed and tubing is passed through.

The dura is now opened and a ventricular catheter used to cannulate the ventricle. The ventricular catheter trajectory is determined according to external landmarks and available imaging. The ventricular catheter can usually be felt to pop once the ependyma has been breached, and there is a gush of CSF.

The system should be connected to the valve using a tie and the valve tucked into the pocket that has been created; the shunt system is then secured to the pericranium. Ensure that there is CSF flow distally before placing the tube in the peritoneal cavity.

Close the scalp and abdominal wounds in layers, paying meticulous attention to haemostasis.

See Chapter 10, *Basic Neurosurgical Procedures*, for further discussion of the insertion of a ventriculoperitoneal shunt using the occipital approach.

Complications

The main complications of shunt placement are:

- Infection.
- Subdural haematoma.
- Low pressure state.
- Shunt obstruction.
- Bleeding.
- Intra abdominal complications.
- Other complications.

Infection

Infections may include ventriculitis, meningitis, peritonitis, or inflammation along the subcutaneous channel. In patients with a ventriculoatrial (VA) shunt, bacteraemia may lead to shunt nephritis. *Staphylococcus epidermidis* or *Staphylococcus aureus* are usually involved. If there is already an established infection, it is advisable to remove the shunt and to reinstitute antibiotic treatment as per microbiology advice.

Subdural haematoma

This can be caused by shunt over-drainage.

Low pressure state

A state of low pressure may be manifested by headache and vomiting while sitting or standing. This requires rehydration and gentle mobilization. If this is not adequate, insertion of an anti-siphon device or conversion to a high-pressure valve is required.

Shunt obstruction

The intermittent or persistent recurrence of symptoms may indicate that the shunt system has become blocked with choroid plexus, debris, omentum, or blood clot.

Bleeding

There is the potential for bleeding (e.g. intraparenchymal or intraventricular) to happen anywhere along the shunt path.

Intra-abdominal complications

Intra-abdominal complications (e.g. bowel obstruction, bowel or viscus injury) can happen during the operation; occasionally, peritoneal tubing can cause erosion into bowel or viscus at a later stage.

Other complications

These include shunt fracture, displacement, seizures (rare), and risks from general anaesthesia.

Further discussions of the causes of shunt system failure, and of the ways in which these problems may be managed, are to be found in Chapters 3 (*Neurosurgical Pathology: Cranial Disorders*) and 4 (*Neurosurgical Pathology: Spinal and Peripheral Nerve Disorders*), and 8 (*Ward Management of Neurosurgical Patients*).

12
Skull-Base Neurosurgery

Sabrina M. Heman-Ackah, Selena E. Briggs, Campbell Baguley, Simon Robinson, Agadha Wickremesekera, and Reuben D. Johnson

CONTENTS

INTRODUCTION

Skull-base surgery is a subspecialization of neurosurgery which involves treating pathologies that affect the anterior, middle, and posterior fossae—structures which are juxtaposed to the brainstem, exiting cranial nerves, and major blood vessels supplying the brain parenchyma. While most neurosurgical trainees gain exposure to skull-base neurosurgery during the senior years of training, those wishing to dedicate a significant component of their practice to this field often pursue an additional year of fellowship subspecialization in skull-base surgery. Traditionally thought of as open/vascular versus endoscopic fellowships, the field has moved towards a focus on offering comprehensive training in 360° approaches to the skull base to provide the practitioner with the ability to offer the safest approach to a patient's pathology while minimizing the risk of traversing neurovascular structures. Importantly, given the surgical corridors and commonly affected structures of the skull base, neurosurgeons working in this field are one component of an interdisciplinary team often including rhinologists, neurotologists, audiologists, head and neck surgeons, ophthalmologists, plastic surgeons, neuro-oncologists, radiation oncologists, neuro-intensivists, and neuro-interventionists. There are myriad pathologies which affect the cranial base, and a comprehensive review of these is beyond the scope of this chapter. Rather, the goal is to provide a brief introduction to the interdisciplinary nature, overall clinical decision-making, most common pathologies of the anterior middle and posterior fossae, and the pitfalls of treating these, such that you are able to help catch and rescue complications and have a basis for further exploration into this incredible field should you choose to pursue it further.

PRINCIPLES OF SKULL-BASE NEUROSURGERY

KEY DECISION-MAKING

When encountering a skull-base lesion, the first and perhaps most important decision is whether to observe, radiate, or operate. Skull-base lesions are often discovered incidentally when cranial imaging is undertaken for unrelated reasons. Patients are then referred for neurosurgical evaluation. A thorough neurological examination, including detailed assessment of the cranial nerves, is a critical tool in assessing such patients and determining the next best course of action. When visual or hearing changes are discovered, or occasionally when the anatomic proximity to CN II (the optic nerve), or the CN VII/VIII complex (the facial/vestibulocochlear nerve complex) dictates, a patient may be referred for formal visual assessment with optometry and/or ophthalmology or hearing test with audiology. When no neurological deficits are detected, patients are often observed with serial imaging at an interval determined by the natural history of the pathology (usually every 3–6 months up to annually). On these serial assessments, lesion and neurologic stability are reassuring.

If a skull-base lesion is observed to grow over time or a patient develops neurological deficits which are attributable to the lesion, a more nuanced discussion of whether, when, and how to treat, as well as the associated risks of treatment, becomes important. While this discussion will necessarily be individualized to a particular patient, considering both their pathology and their goals, the general approaches to treatment of skull-base tumours will involve radiation, surgery, or a combination thereof. Skull-base tumours are rarely malignant, and consequently there is little emphasis on chemotherapy as a viable treatment option. Key considerations for radiation are tumour control and proximity to vulnerable structures. Table 12.1 compares typical radiation dosing for glioblastoma, the most common intraparenchymal tumour, to that for sellar/parasellar tumours, vestibular schwannomas, and meningiomas of the skull base. Note the significantly lower radiation doses, which are limited by the maximum dosing to the nearby optic apparatus, cochlea, and brainstem

Table 12.1 Radiation delivery method and dosing, considering nearby structures.

Tumour Type	Delivery Method	Radiation Dosing	Structure(s) at Risk
GBM (initial therapy)	FRT	59.4 Gy (33 fractions × 1.8 Gy)	Variable
GBM (recurrence)	FRT	>100 Gy (30–42 Gy fractions)	Variable
Sellar/parasellar tumours	IMRT, SRS, proton beam	12–25 Gy	Optic nerve (>10–12 Gy)
Vestibular schwannoma	SRS	12–14 Gy	Cochlea (>4 Gy)
Meningioma (skull base/posterior fossa)	SRS	13.6 Gy	Brainstem (>12.5 Gy)

FRT (fractionated radiotherapy); GBM (glioblastoma multiforme); IMRT (intensity-modulated radiotherapy); SRS (stereotactic radiosurgery); Gy (grey)

that can be delivered before deficits are incurred. In many cases, tumour control cannot be achieved by radiation alone and surgery becomes the primary treatment modality. This will be the focus of the remainder of this chapter.

CONSIDERATIONS OF SURGICAL APPROACHES

The primary goal of surgical approaches to skull-base lesions is to maximize the extent of resection, while minimizing the risk of injury to nearby critical neurovascular structures. Broadly, skull-base lesions are thought of as residing in the anterior, middle, and/or posterior fossa, and the approaches to each of these is subdivided into open or endoscopic. Often open and endoscopic approaches are combined to enable the greatest extent of resection without instrumenting across at-risk structures. Novel surgical corridors in keeping with this goal are constantly under development, and thus we by no means intend to present a comprehensive list here. However, it may be helpful to place patients undergoing these approaches in clinical context by reviewing the chart in Table 12.2.

PITFALLS AND COMPLICATIONS

Cerebrospinal fluid leak

Cerebrospinal fluid (CSF) leak is the most common complication after skull-base surgery. It is important to understand that the surgical corridors created for access to skull-base tumours also serve as conduits for CSF egress

Table 12.2 Common skull-base approaches based on lesion site.

	Anterior Fossa	Middle Fossa	Posterior Fossa
Endoscopic	Endoscopic endonasal transcribriform, transplanum, transtuberculum Transsphenoidal, Endoscopic keyhole supraorbital	Endoscope-assisted middle fossa	Endoscopic endonasal transclival Endoscope-assisted retrosigmoid
Open	Bifrontal Pterional Orbitozygomatic	Middle fossa Subtemporal/Kawase Transpetrosal (transchochlear, translabyrinthine, retrolabyrinthine)	Retrosigmoid Far lateral Suboccipital

after surgery. On a typical neurosurgical ward, this will most commonly be encountered after endoscopic endonasal transsphenoidal surgery (i.e. for pituitary tumour resection) and following retrosigmoid craniotomy (i.e. for vestibular schwannoma resection). In the case of retrosigmoid craniotomies, identifying clear fluid leaking through an incision should raise suspicion of a CSF leak. In patients who have undergone endoscopic endonasal transsphenoidal surgery, clear fluid may visibly leak from the nose, or patients may complain of a salty or metallic taste at the back of their throat and a sensation of postnasal drip. Sinus precautions—avoiding nose blowing, excessive coughing or sneezing, use of drinking straws—is commonly used as a precaution for those undergoing endoscopic endonasal transsphenoidal surgery. In both cases, when CSF leak is encountered, bed rest in a recumbent position of 30° or lower is an essential first step in management. When this is not sufficient to stop CSF leak, wound revision and/or CSF diversion with a lumbar drain or external ventricular drain may be necessary. When unrecognized, CSF leak can be a source for meningitis which can be fatal: thus, neurosurgical trainees play a crucial role in the post-operative examination and management of these patients.

Skull-base emergencies

True emergencies are rare in skull-base surgery. However, pituitary apoplexy is one such example which can cause permanent neurologic deficits and be rapidly fatal if missed. Apoplexy refers to the condition in which a large pituitary tumour acutely haemorrhages. This can result in acute visual loss secondary to tumour compression of the optic nerve or chiasm and acute hormone insufficiency which can lead to fatal haemodynamic instability. Rapid assessment of vision and hormone levels, as well as hormone replacement, can be life-saving for these patients, who typically also require urgent surgical decompression.

Diabetes insipidus (DI) is a disorder of water and salt regulation, which may occur following pituitary surgery. This is because the posterior pituitary gland is responsible for secretion of antidiuretic hormone (ADH). Under physiological circumstances, ADH acts on the distal collecting tubule of the kidney to promote water re-uptake from urine in response to rising serum sodium levels. However, the posterior pituitary may be transiently disrupted by pituitary surgery, leading to an inability to secrete appropriate amounts of ADH. Ultimately, this results in loss of water through urine, despite rising sodium levels. In patients, this manifests as excessive urination and thirst. When patients are alert and able to drink to quell thirst, this is the best approach to management of DI. However, maintain a high level of suspicion for DI in patients who are drowsy or otherwise impaired—these patients are at risk of fatal complications associated with severe hypovolemia and hypernatremia. When urine output exceeds the patient's capacity to drink to maintain volume and physiological Na levels, desmopressin (commonly referred to as DDAVP) may be supplemented to replace the action of ADH. Another life saved by a neurosurgical trainee!

ANTERIOR FOSSA SKULL-BASE SURGERY

SELLAR LESIONS

The most common tumour of the sella is the pituitary adenoma. Pituitary adenomas typically appear as diffusely enlarged, contrast-enhancing masses contained within the sella turcica. They may be functioning (60%, hormone secreting) or non-functioning (40%). The most common functioning pituitary tumour is the prolactinoma, which produces an excess of the hormone prolactin resulting in galactorrhoea, infertility, menstrual changes, and loss of libido in women, and gynecomastia, infertility, erectile dysfunction, and loss of libido in men. Acromegaly in adults and gigantism in children may result from functioning growth hormone-secreting tumours, and Cushing's disease by pituitary tumours secreting an excess of cortisol. Surgical management of pituitary adenomas may be considered for any of the above, or for non-functioning tumours, when the tumour causes compression of the optic nerve or chiasm, resulting in visual changes.

The endoscopic endonasal transsphenoidal approach has been widely adapted for the treatment of pituitary lesions. This involves traversing the nasal cavity to enter the sphenoid sinus, identifying the sella medially and optico-carotid impressions superolaterally at the posterior sphenoid sinus. The sellar bone is traversed either by drill or rongeur, revealing the underlying sellar dura which is incised to enable resection of the pituitary adenoma. This is considered a minimally invasive approach which makes use of natural corridors and results in fewer complications and faster healing than historical open approaches to the pituitary gland.

Post-operative evaluation should include visual assessment, and as previously mentioned, close monitoring for DI. Other pathologies that should remain in the differential diagnosis for initial evaluation of a sellar lesion include craniopharyngiomas and Rathke's cleft cysts.

ANTERIOR FOSSA LESIONS

Meningiomas are the most common primary brain tumour accounting for more than 30% of all intracranial tumours. Olfactory groove meningiomas (OGMs) account for 34% of anterior cranial fossa meningiomas. Meningiomas are thought to originate from arachnoid cap cells, and are commonly benign and slow growing, though higher-grade lesions may display more malignant behaviour. OGMs often cause a loss of olfaction, and if large enough they may compress optic nerves and/or chiasm resulting in visual loss. Importantly, OGMs may also be associated with significant frontal lobe oedema, with variable impact on patients' cognition and executive functioning capacity.

Whether an open or endoscopic approach is best for OGMs remains controversial. The most common open approaches for OGMs are the bifrontal transbasal and pterional approaches. The endoscopic endonasal transcribriform approach offers several surgical advantages—most notably, since OGMs arise from the cribriform plate, this approach allows direct access via the natural corridor to the tumour, minimizing brain retraction and manipulation of neurovascular structures to obtain adequate exposure. In cases of lateral extension and involvement of the paranasal sinuses, combined approaches may be considered.

Post-operative evaluation should include serial visual assessments. There is no expectation for olfaction to return following resection of an OGM.

Other pathologies that should remain on the differential diagnosis of a newly identified anterior fossa lesion include aesthesioneuroblastoma and sinonasal undifferentiated carcinoma (SNUC).

POSTERIOR SKULL-BASE SURGERY

CEREBELLOPONTINE ANGLE LESIONS

Vestibular schwannomas (VS, formerly known as acoustic neuromas) are the most common tumour of the cerebellopontine angle (CPA), appearing as well-circumscribed, contrast-enhancing tumours involving the internal auditory canal and CN VII/VIII complex. VS may arise sporadically or as part of a genetic syndrome, the most common being the autosomal dominantly inherited, completely penetrant, neurofibromatosis type 2 (NF2) in which bilateral VS ravage hearing in young patients. VS are slow-growing, benign tumours with no known metastatic potential. However, given their location, they may cause local compression of the brainstem, and the nearby cranial nerve VII (facial nerve) and VII (vestibulocochlear nerve). Interestingly, although the facial nerve may be severely compressed by tumour growth, facial palsy is an uncommon presentation, with patients more commonly demonstrating symptoms of vestibular dysfunction or brainstem compression. The facial nerve is, however, at risk during treatment regardless of modality, and facial palsy is a morbid iatrogenic complication with significant effects on patient quality of life and social stigmata, which must be discussed with patients and factored into treatment considerations.

VS may be treated surgically via retrosigmoid, translabyrinthine, or, rarely, middle fossa approaches. For entirely intracanalicular tumours, or for patients who have lost serviceable hearing on the side of their VS, a translabyrinthine approach provides an excellent corridor to the internal auditory canal (IAC), enabling the surgeon to identify the facial nerve laterally and increasing rates of preservation. For tumours located entirely within the CPA and for whom hearing remains a surgical goal, the retrosigmoid craniotomy offers a direct surgical corridor for tumour access, although with notably higher rates of CSF leak and post-operative headache. The middle fossa approach is rarely used to access small tumours (<1.5 cm) for patients in whom hearing preservation remains a surgical goal, although radiotherapy is an equivocal option for tumour control in patients with tumours of this size.

Post-operative evaluation should include detailed assessments of CN VII and VIII, including grading based on the House–Brackmann scale (see simplified version in Table 12.3 and refer to literature for a detailed description) as well as wound inspection for CSF leak, particularly in patients who have undergone retrosigmoid craniotomy.

Table 12.3 House–Brackmann scale, simplified.

House–Brackmann Grade	Definition
I	Symmetrical
II	Asymmetric, but with complete eye closure
III	Asymmetric, complete eye closure with effort, symmetrical mouth with max effort
IV	Disfiguring weakness, incomplete eye closure, asymmetry of mouth with max effort
V	Barely perceptible movement
VI	No movement

Non-VS tumours of the CPA which should remain in the differential diagnosis while evaluating new lesions in this region include meningiomas and epidermoid cysts. Meningiomas may share many imaging characteristics with VS, and may involve the IAC—however, IAC-sparing should raise suspicion of a meningioma. Epidermoid cysts are distinctive on imaging, as they are non-contrast-enhancing and diffusion restricting due to their high water content.

CLIVAL LESIONS

The most common tumours of the clival region are chordomas, slow-growing neoplasms that originate from remnants of the primitive notochord. Chordomas appear in roughly equal distribution in the skull base (32%), spine (33%), and sacrum (30%) and typically appear as well-circumscribed contrast-enhancing masses with lytic bone destruction and calcifications. Chordomas are relatively radio-resistant, though proton beam radiation has been shown to improve local control and overall progression-free survival after subtotal resection. Gross total resection remains the mainstay of treatment.

Because clival chordomas are midline lesions, displacing the neuroaxis dorsally or dorsolaterally, they were historically approached through extensive open procedures, including extended frontal/transbasal, transmaxillary, midfacial degloving, and transoral approaches. However, as expanded endoscopic endonasal approaches have been explored and techniques for their safe implementation developed, these lesions are more commonly approached through the endoscopic endonasal transclival approach, resulting in reduced morbidity associated with craniotomy and brain retraction. Larger clival lesions with significant lateral extension still require combined approaches, thus there remains a significant role for open approaches in the management of clival lesions.

Post-operative evaluation of the patient undergoing endoscopic endonasal transclival approach should include a detailed cranial nerve examination with attention to CN VI, which runs superiorly over the posterior surface of the clivus from the brainstem to exit Dorello's canal. In addition, examination for CSF leak through the nose is essential.

Other pathologies that should remain on the differential diagnosis of a newly discovered midline clival lesion include chondrosarcomas and meningiomas.

MIDDLE FOSSA SKULL-BASE SURGERY

PETROCLIVAL LESIONS

The most common petroclival lesion is the petroclival meningioma. Petroclival meningiomas, comprising 2.5% of all intracranial meningiomas, continue to present a formidable challenge for skull-base neurosurgeons given their deep-seated location and encasement by critical neurovascular structures. Gross total resection is frequently accompanied by permanent cranial nerve deficits increasing morbidity and mortality; thus, subtotal resection combined with stereotactic radiosurgery (SRS) is increasingly implemented.

The preferred surgical approach to petroclival meningiomas remains controversial but may involve any of the aforementioned approaches to the anterior or posterior cranial base, as well as the anterior transpetrosal (Kawase), posterior transpetrosal (retrolabyrinthine, translabyrinthine, transcochlear), or combined transpetrosal approaches. The choice of approach is dependent on the location of the tumour and the goals of surgery. The anterior transpetrosal (Kawase) approach is best suited to petroclival meningiomas medial to the IAC, without extensive involvement of the posterior fossa. The retrolabyrinthine approach is best suited to cases where anterior exposure of the brainstem is unnecessary and preservation of CN VII and VIII remains a goal of surgery. The translabyrinthine approach provides increased access to the anterolateral brainstem and inferior clivus at the expense of the labyrinth and thereby sacrificing hearing. The transcochlear approach provides maximal exposure to the anterior surface of the brainstem and the petroclival surface at the expense of hearing and possibly facial nerve function. Overall, consideration of the anatomical relationships of the tumour (middle fossa alone versus posterior and middle fossa, and relative to the IAC), the goal of hearing preservation, the individual patient's goals and the experience of the skull-base team, are key considerations guiding the approach to treatment of a petroclival meningioma.

Post-operative evaluation should include serial, detailed cranial nerve examinations with particular attention to CN IV, V, VI, VII, and VIII which may have been manipulated within the surgical corridor.

13
Spinal Neurosurgery

Reuben D. Johnson

CONTENTS

INTRODUCTION

All neurosurgeons will undertake spinal surgery as part of their training. However, the number and complexity of spinal procedures they undertake as Consultants depend on their subspecialty interests. It is not possible in this chapter to give a comprehensive overview of all spinal surgery, but it is my hope that I can highlight some of the complexities in the decision-making process and pass on some useful insights. Of course, before deciding on whether an operation is indicated you need to understand the natural history of the pathology you are treating and the benefits which are offered by surgery in ameliorating that natural history. I have deliberately not focused on that aspect (this is not a textbook per se), although some points have been covered in previous chapters. Suffice it to say that the art of patient selection is just as important as the art of performing the operation.

In this chapter I have included a few examples based on real cases in order to offer some insights into the art of selecting the right operation in the cervical spine. These insights just scratch the surface of the nuances of deciding on the right operation. There will be other surgeons who will have different opinions about which operation to do in these cases. However, I offer them as an insight into some of the thinking that goes on before offering surgery.

During your training it is important to glean as much as possible from your trainers as to why they offered one operation instead of another.

There are two pitfalls that are commonly seen in spinal neurosurgery which I outline below and which I would encourage you to avoid. Spinal surgery is still evolving and is an extremely rewarding subspecialty.

PITFALL NO. 1. SIMPLE VERSUS COMPLEX SPINE

You may hear the term 'simple spine', which refers on the whole to cervical and lumbar discectomies and laminectomies without instrumentation. The term 'complex spine' is used to refer to more involved procedures that require instrumentation or deformity correction. However, these terms should be obsolete as there is no such thing as a 'simple spine' operation. There has been a paradigm shift in the way that we think about spinal pathology, and whenever a 'simple spine' procedure is done, it is necessary to ask 'what will happen next?' Spine patients often need another operation in the future and a so-called simple spine case rapidly becomes a difficult complex spine case. So by approaching every spinal patient with a 'complex spine' mindset we may avoid unnecessary second procedures (or even third and fourth procedures).

PITFALL NO. 2. 'IN MY HANDS I WOULD . . .'

In spinal surgery, perhaps more than in any other area of neurosurgery, there is a tendency for surgeons to offer patients procedures that they can do and are comfortable doing. This is understandable, because as surgeons we learn various techniques during our training and the art of surgery is working out which methods work best 'in my hands'. However, whereas this approach is fine when it comes to different methods of cervical discectomies for example, it becomes more problematic if it is extended to decisions on whether to instrument or not, or whether to undertake an anterior or posterior approach to the cervical spine for decompression. A surgeon should not recommend a 3-level cervical laminectomy without fusion because 'in their hands' it is the best operation they can do and because they only do posterior approaches. If the patient has a kyphotic C-spine deformity and there is some evidence of instability then consideration should be given to additional posterior instrumentation to prevent worsening of the deformity/instability, or perhaps one should consider a multilevel anterior cervical discectomy and fusion to decompress and correct the deformity.

It is my recommendation to think only of what the best operation is likely to be and to discuss cases with other colleagues if it looks as though the case is complex, or is likely to become complex if the wrong first operation is done. There is no problem teaming up with another spinal colleague to do the best operation. Think complex, get another opinion, and do what is best in '*our collective* hands' not just 'in *my* hands'. You will get better outcomes and sleep better. Also, you will continue to learn and expand your repertoire of surgical expertise in the process.

CERVICAL SPINES

In order to highlight some of the different considerations for cervical spines I have shown four different cases, each of which is outlined below. These four cases show some of the nuances of decision making for cervical spine surgery.

CASE A

This is the case of a 59-year-old man with left C6 radiculopathy (arm pain and some sensory disturbance in the C6 distribution) because of a small left-sided (C5/6) acute disc prolapse (Figure 13.1a). Despite conservative measures, including physiotherapy and a C6 steroid nerve root injection, the symptoms are ongoing. The indication for surgery is to treat the arm pain and prevent neurological deterioration. The options in this case include an anterior cervical discectomy and fusion (or disc replacement) or a posterior cervical foraminotomy (Figure 13.1b). Either operation will adequately decompress the nerve root. There is no cervical deformity and no evidence of instability (assessed by flexion-extension X-rays). This is what many people refer to as a 'simple spine'.

CASE B

This is the case of a 59-year-old man who presents with symptoms of cervical myelopathy (poor balance, loss of fine movements of the hands, hyperreflexia) due to cord compression from an acute disc prolapse (Figure 13.2a). His myelopathy has progressed so that he has become wheelchair-bound due to global limb weakness. This case differs from Case A in that the acute disc prolapse is central and is resulting in cord compression rather than exiting

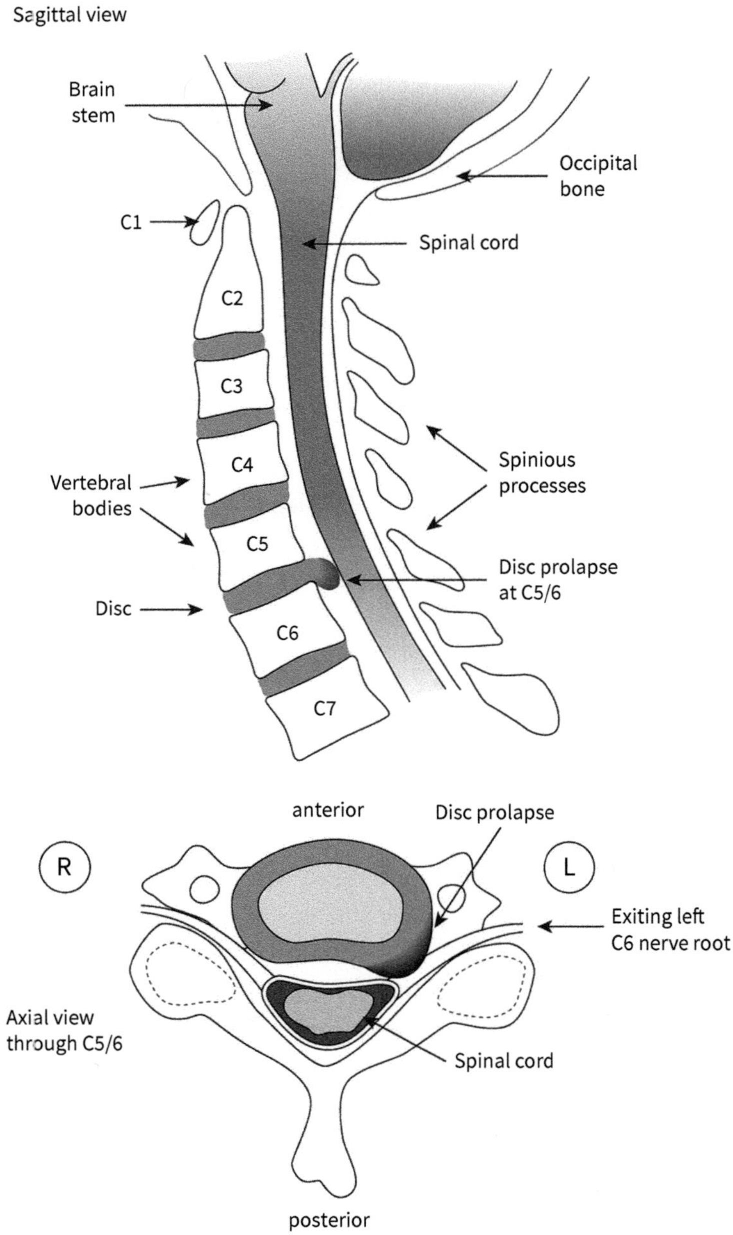

Figure 13.1a *Case A.* A small, left-sided (C5/6) acute disc prolapse.

nerve root compression. Also there is neurological compromise (limb weakness) rather than pain. The indication for surgery is to prevent further neurological deterioration (and hopefully gain some neurological improvement) by decompressing the spinal cord. In this case, a posterior approach, such as a

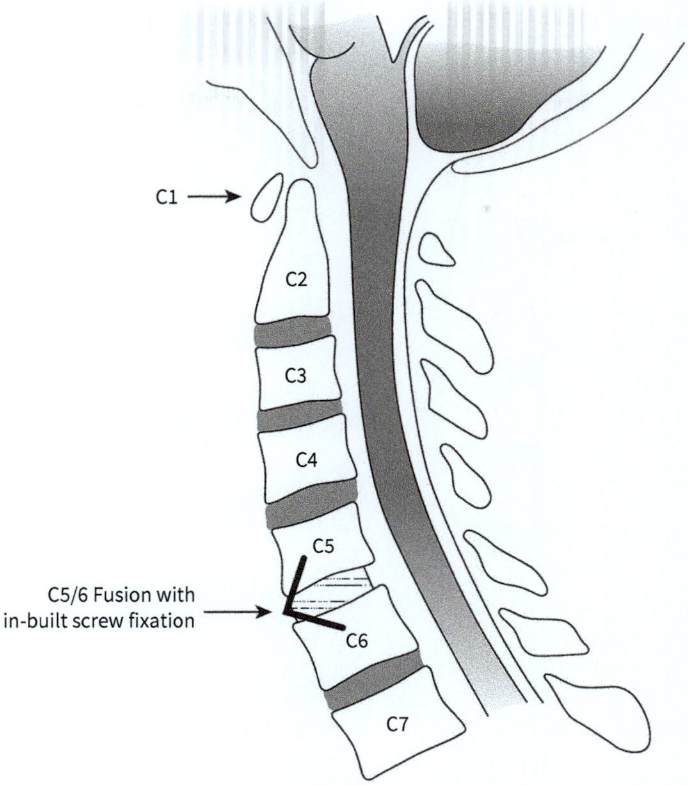

Figure 13.1b *Case A.* Surgical treatment with an anterior cervical discectomy and fusion.

cervical laminectomy, is not going to solve the problem, as the compressive pathology is anterior. A cervical discectomy and fusion is an option. However, if you look carefully, the disc prolapse has moved down behind the vertebral body around the corner from the disc space. Although this fragment might be retrieved with a single-level discectomy, the surgeon has to be prepared to carry out a vertebrectomy in order to gain access. Indeed, in this case a vertebrectomy was carried out. The patient became ambulant again within days of surgery (Figure 13.2b).

CASE C

This is the case of a 59-year-old man who has cord compression from what appear to be multilevel level disc protrusions, and again the patient is myelopathic with reduced mobility (Figure 13.3a). At first glance, a multilevel anterior

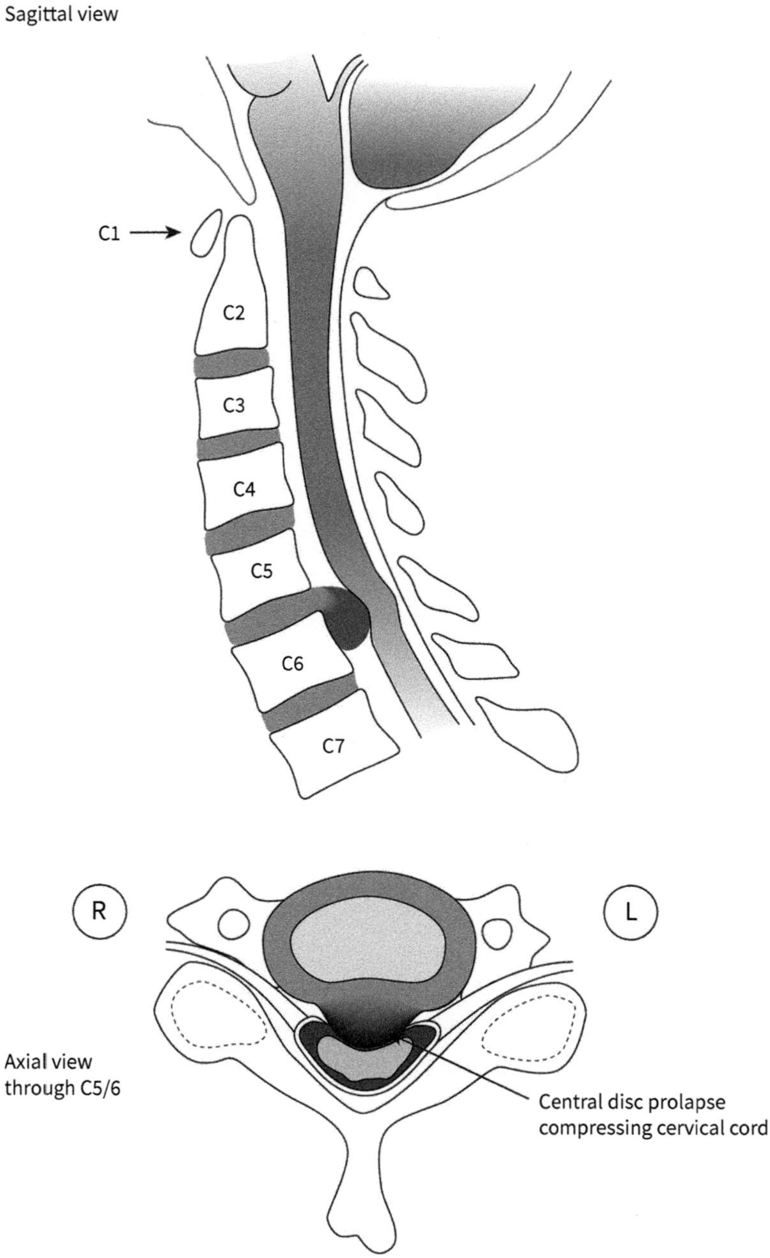

Figure 13.2a *Case B.* Cord compression from an acute central prolapse which is extending behind the vertebral body of C6.

cervical discectomy and fusion (ACDF) appears appropriate. However, a CT scan reveals that this patient has ossification of the posterior longitudinal ligament (OPLL). This is a condition that is more common in certain ethnic groups including Polynesians (as in this case). In order to decompress the

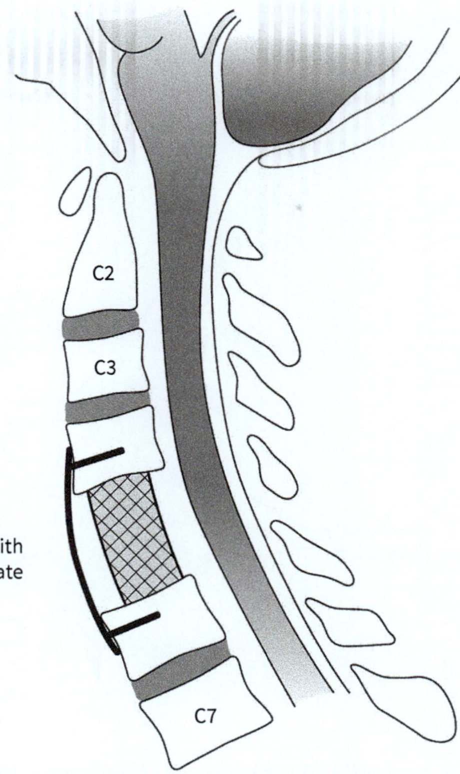

Figure 13.2b *Case B.* A discectomy and vertebrectomy was carried out.

cord adequately the options include a multilevel cervical corpectomy or a posterior cervical laminectomy.

In this case, a posterior cervical laminectomy was performed without instrumentation, as it was felt that there was no instability and no significant kyphotic deformity (although the normal cervical lordosis has been lost already). Furthermore, removal of an ossified posterior longitudinal ligament is associated with not insignificant risks. The ossified ligament can be adherent to the dura and removal can result in an anterior CSF leak, or, in severe cases, a vascular injury to the anterior spinal cord, with devastating consequences. With this in mind, a posterior approach was chosen with a good clinical result (Figure 13.3b).

However, it should be kept in mind that in the long term, further surgery may be required if there is progressive kyphotic deformity resulting in neurological compromise, and some surgeons would have recommended posterior lateral mass screws at the time of the laminectomy. It is prudent to follow the patient both clinically and radiologically quite cautiously.

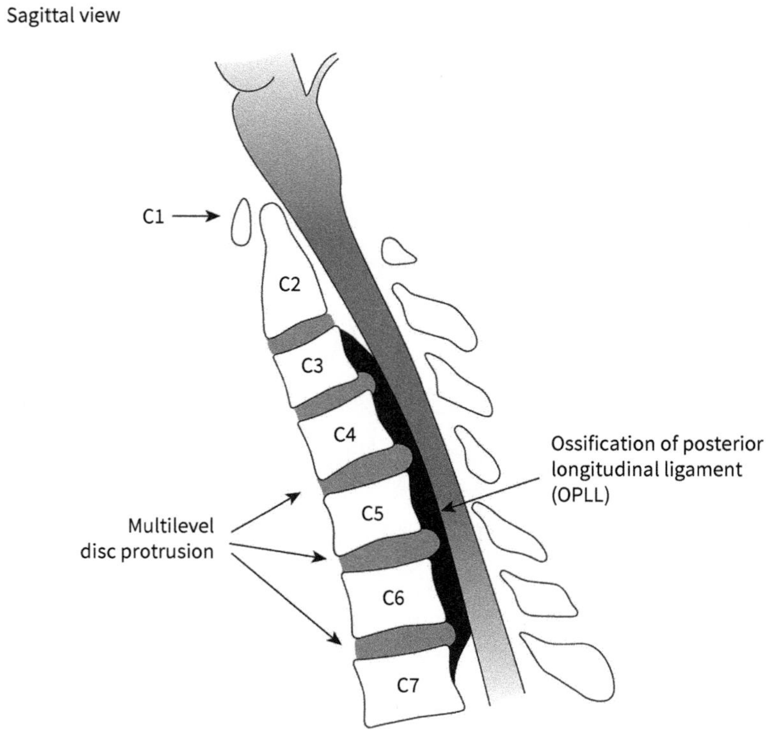

Figure 13.3a *Case C.* Cord compression from what appear to be multilevel disc protrusions, although CT revealed associated ossification of the posterior longitudinal ligament (OPLL).

CASE D

This is the case of a 75-year-old lady with severe cord compression due to progressive kyphotic deformity as a result of rheumatoid arthritis. The patient had previously had a posterior cervical laminectomy and instrumented fusion of the C4–C6 levels to treat cord compression and instability. You can see that the patient has developed critical stenosis and cord compression at the C2/3 level (Figure 13.4a). Surprisingly, the patient is asymptomatic from this, and the stenosis was an incidental finding. However, there is signal change in the cord.

In the absence of symptoms or progressive neurology a conservative non-operative course could be undertaken; nevertheless, in view of the severity of the cord compression, decompressive surgery was offered. However, decompression of the C2/3 level with a C2/3 laminectomy poses a risk of further instability without extension of the previous fusion. The options for instrumentation include extending the fusion with posterior screws up to C2, or extending all the way up to include the occiput, that is, an occipitocervical fusion.

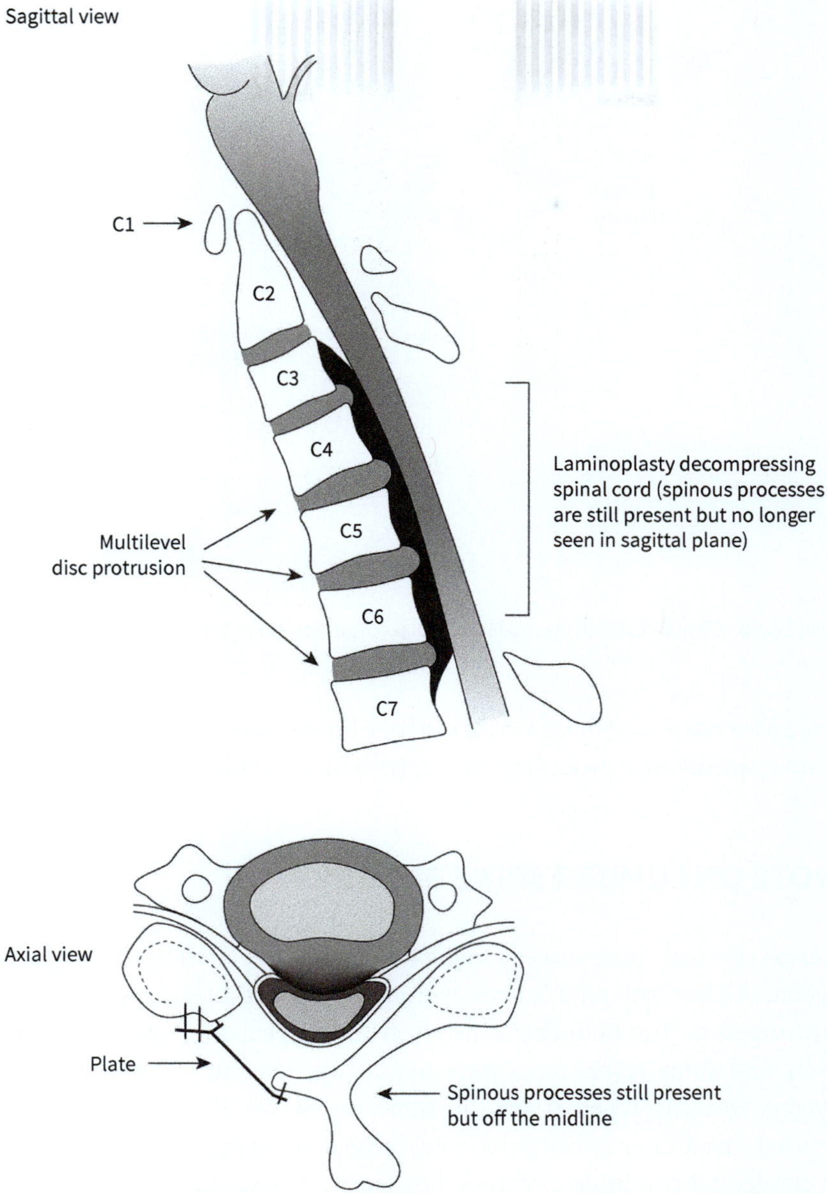

Figure 13.3b *Case C*. A posterior laminoplasty was performed without instrumentation.

However, this patient did not want to have her skull fused to her spine because of the significant reduction in neck movement that would be likely following this. In the end, a C2/3 laminectomy was done with serial imaging (yearly C-spine flexion/extension views) to check for instability (Figure 13.4b) There was no instability over the following 5 years and no neurological deficits. Although

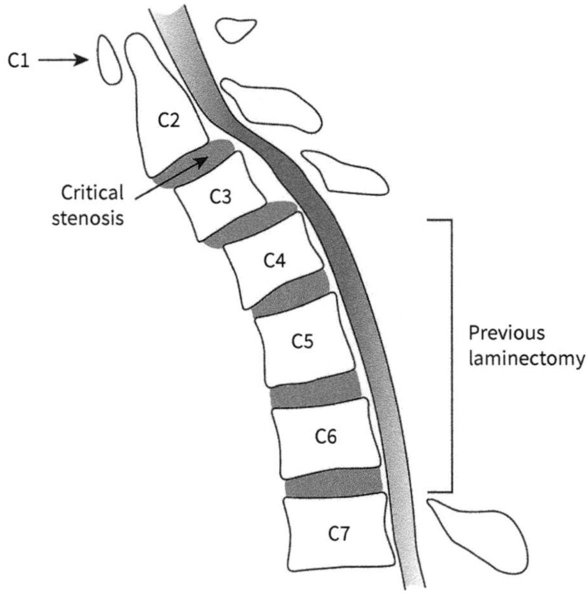

Figure 13.4a *Case D.* Critical stenosis and cord compression at the C2/3 level.

this is a fortunate outcome, it would not have been unreasonable to have undertaken a more invasive procedure with extension of the fusion.

A NOTE ON LUMBAR SPINE SURGERY

Whereas cervical spine surgery tends to be more the territory of the neurosurgeon, the lumbar spine is operated on by both orthopaedic surgeons and neurosurgeons. The boundaries between these specialties are disappearing rapidly and some spinal units have neurosurgeons and orthopaedic spinal surgeons working together on the same roster. On the whole, neurosurgeons have traditionally restricted their lumbar spine surgery to degenerative and congenital conditions, with orthopaedic surgeons undertaking surgery for back pain and lumbar deformities, for example degenerative scoliosis. Philosophically the approaches have been different, with neurosurgeons focusing on decompression of the neural elements rather than bony fusion operations for back pain. However, most neurosurgeons will fuse for instability (or the potential for future instability).

There are various approaches to the lumbar spine for fusion surgery and you will come across terms such as TLIF (transforaminal lumbar interbody fusion), PLIF (posterior lumbar interbody fusion), XLIF (extreme lateral interbody

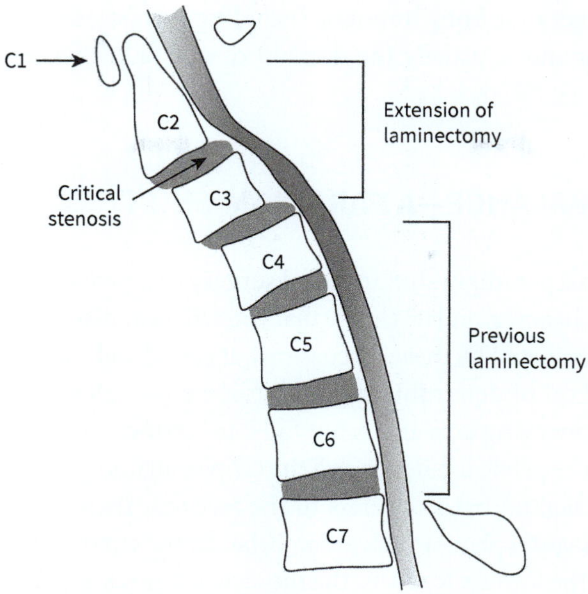

Figure 13.4b *Case D.* Treatment was with a C2/3 laminectomy.

fusion), OLIF (oblique lateral interbody fusion), and ALIF (anterior lumbar interbody fusion). There are a multitude of reasons for using one method over another and various advantages and disadvantages for each approach.

My advice is that early on in your training you understand first of all the indications for the lumbar surgery that the patients in your unit are undergoing. Is it because they have back pain, leg pain (sciatica or lumbar claudication), or neurological deterioration (cauda equina syndrome)? And try to understand why, in each case, a particular operation has been chosen over another. Also, ask your seniors whether there were other operations which could have been undertaken. This way you will very quickly develop your own views on lumbar surgery and get involved in the discussions early on.

Try to understand the basics of lumbar decompressive surgery, including lumbar laminectomy and lumbar discectomy (including micro-discectomy) and then build your knowledge from there.

A NOTE ON THORACIC SPINE SURGERY

In most neurosurgical units most thoracic spine surgery will be for spinal tumours, including intramedullary tumours or intradural extramedullary tumours. You may also see thoracic disc surgery, and some neurosurgeons will undertake surgery for bony tumours, including metastases. The surgery can be challenging and is usually the domain of one or two surgeons within a department.

SAGITTAL BALANCE—A PARADIGM SHIFT

There has been a paradigm shift in spinal surgery in recent years with the concept of sagittal balance, and it is likely that you will hear discussions about this. Do not be intimidated by these discussions. It can sound like a very daunting scientific method of determining the best operation. However, sagittal balance is still an evolving area and is not fully understood. You will hear people talking about the pelvic incidence and the C7 plumb line.

In essence, sagittal balance refers to the fact that there are several spinal curves in the sagittal plane which are in balance: the curve of the pelvic spine (the sacrum), the lumbar lordosis, the thoracic kyphosis, and the cervical lordosis. If there is disruption of one of these curves the other areas of the spine may compensate, but only up to a point, and after this there are extra stresses put on the spine which can be detrimental.

Sagittal balance measurements usually involve lateral standing X-rays of the whole spine. Measurements can be used to help determine whether corrective surgery is needed to increase lumbar lordosis or reduce thoracic kyphosis, for example. If you are in a unit where sagittal balance is used on a regular basis then I would recommend reading a short review on the subject (e.g. Johnson et al. 2013).

CONCLUSION

When you start working in a neurosurgical ward the first priority is to understand how to assess and look after these patients in the peri-operative period. However, if you take an interest in the different types of surgery and their rationale, then you will find that spinal neurosurgery is a fascinating and very fulfilling part of neurosurgical practice.

REFERENCE

Johnson RD, Valore A, Villaminar A, Comisso M, Balsano M. Sagittal balance and pelvic parameters—a paradigm shift in spinal surgery. *J Clin Neurosci.* 2013;20:191–196.

14

Paediatric Neurosurgery

Saurabh Sinha and Reuben D. Johnson

CONTENTS

OVERVIEW OF PAEDIATRIC PATIENTS

While it is beyond the remit of this book to deal with the entire topic of paediatric neurosurgery, there are important aspects that can be highlighted. For many trainees in surgical specialties, there may have been little or no contact with paediatric patients. We have therefore included a brief overview of some important physiological aspects at the beginning of this chapter. We have then given our view of how paediatric patients may best be evaluated. It is essential to remember that in the care of any critically ill child, the mandatory management involves optimization of airway, breathing, and circulation (ABC) prior to any attempts at definitive care. In the later parts of this chapter we will consider several aspects of clinical paediatric neurosurgery with which we feel new trainees should be familiar, including hydrocephalus, head injuries, and paediatric brain tumours.

The management of children is complicated by their differences from adults, and also by their own diversity. Some of the main ways in which these differences occur are discussed below.

WEIGHT

A child's weight increases most rapidly during the first year of life. At birth, the average weight is 3.5 kg and this rapidly rises to 10 kg at 1 year. The rate of increase slows until puberty when there is often another rapid rise. Fluid and drug therapies as well as blood volume in children are guided by weight, and therefore an accurate weight is essential for optimal management. An estimated weight can be obtained using the following formula:

$$\text{Weight (kg)} = 2 \times (\text{age in years} + 4)$$

FLUIDS

- Circulating blood volume = 80 ml/kg (60 ml/kg in adults).
- Fluid bolus for resuscitation = 20 ml/kg crystalloid.
- Transfusion of packed cells = 10 ml/kg.
- Transfusion of whole blood = 20 ml/kg.
- Maintenance fluids (24 h) = 100 ml/kg (first 10 kg); 20 ml/kg (next 10 kg); 10 ml/kg after that.

ANATOMY

The proportion of head to body size is significantly increased in infants in comparison with adults. The infant brain reaches approximately 75% of its adult size by 18 months of age and accounts for just over 10% of total body weight. Children lose a significant proportion of heat from the head and the increased head-to-body ratio (19% of body surface area at birth) can lead to a rapid loss of heat and leave them prone to hypothermia.

PHYSIOLOGY

Children are born with a small cardiorespiratory reserve and an immature immune system. Infections such as meningitis are, therefore, more of a concern in babies than in older children. Maternal antibodies crossing the placenta provide some protection, but this diminishes over the first 6 months. The physiological changes that occur as children grow mean that there are significant changes in heart rate, blood pressure and respiratory rate with age (Table 14.1).

The presence of open fontanelles and their subsequent closure, as well as the increase in CSF production as children grow, leads to differences in their intracranial pressure (ICP). The ICP in infants is approximately 3–8 mmHg, rising towards 15 mmHg after the fontanelle closes.

With the associated changes in blood pressure (mean arterial pressure in the newborn is around 50 mmHg rising to 80 mmHg in mid-teens), cerebral perfusion pressure (CPP) may only be 40–50 mmHg in infants, and nearer to 70 mmHg in teenagers.

Table 14.1 Change in vital signs with age.

Age (years)	Heart rate (beats/min)	Systolic blood pressure (mmHg)	Respiratory rate (breaths/min)
<1	110–160	70–90	30–40
1–2	100–150	80–95	25–35
2–5	95–140	80–100	25–30
5–12	80–120	90–110	20–25
>12	60–100	100–120	15–20

PSYCHOLOGY

Communication can be a difficult problem with infants and young children. The lack of complex language function often prevents description of their symptoms and may require help via non-verbal information. Older children will have a better understanding, and anxiety can be eased by appropriate communication. Fear and anxiety often accompany illness and injury in children, and can significantly alter their cardiorespiratory indices, making clinical assessment difficult. Providing them with age-appropriate information can help to allay some of their fears and to establish a rapport.

TAKING A PAEDIATRIC HISTORY

It is always useful to take as much information from the child as possible. Often they will tell you important features that family members may not have noticed, especially if the symptoms are chronic in nature. It also helps to establish a relationship with the child; this often eases any anxiety in both the child and the parents. The key aspects of a paediatric history are as follows:

- ***Pregnancy and delivery.*** Infections and illness during pregnancy and complications during delivery can lead to a variety of neurological insults. Prematurity increases the risk of intraventricular haemorrhage and subsequent hydrocephalus.
- ***Development/schooling.*** Inability to attain developmental milestones, or new difficulties with schoolwork, may be the only indications of an ongoing neurological problem.
- ***General behaviour.*** Young children with raised intracranial pressure may present with altered sleeping patterns, worsening temper, and 'head-banging.'

- ***Siblings.*** Developmental milestones in siblings may allow comparison with the affected child.
- ***Developmental milestones.*** The developmental milestones are shown in Table 14.2.

Table 14.2 Developmental milestones.

Age	Motor skills	Language skills	Social skills	Concerns
6 weeks	Pull to sit. Head lags	Vocalizes	Smiles responsively	Failure to fix/follow visually
	Fixates and follows to 90°	Quiets or startles to sound		No response to sound
				Doesn't smile
				Asymmetric reflexes
3 months	Follows object (180°)	Turns head to sound	Laughs	—
	Grasp object placed in hand	Squeals with delight		
6 months	Rolls	Babbles	Mouthing	—
	Sits up		Feeds self with biscuit	
	Reaches for objects			
9 months	Pulls self to stand	Understands 'No'	Stranger anxiety	Unable to sit
	Simple pincer grip			Hand preference
				Limited 'babble'
12 months	Stands alone	One/two words with meaning	Waves 'bye-bye'	—
	Walks with support	Understands simple phrases	Plays 'peek-a-boo'	
18 months	Gets up/down stairs	More words	Feeds self with cup/spoon	Unable to walk/ stand unsupported
	With support	Points to objects wanted		Inability to understand simple commands
	Handedness			No spontaneous vocalization
				No pincer grip
24 months	Runs	2–3 words into sentence	Puts on shoes	—
	Kicks a ball	Uses 'you' and 'me'	Dry by day	

(continued)

Table 14.2 Continued

Age	Motor skills	Language skills	Social skills	Concerns
	Makes a tower of several cubes		Plays near other children	
3–5 years	Stands on one foot	Counts to 10	Plays with others	Unable to speak in short sentences
	Skips	Names colours	Dresses/ undresses	Unable to colour match
	Hops	Knows age	Dry by night	

GENERAL EXAMINATION

Examination of older cooperative children is essentially similar to that of adults. In younger children, it is not always possible to carry out a full neurological examination, and varying strategies may need to be adopted to obtain a useful assessment. Don't forget the role of the parents: it may be more reassuring to the child to be examined on their parent's lap. As with adult patients, general inspection provides essential information, and the following list of questions should go through your mind during the examination:

- Are there dysmorphic features?
- Are there significant cutaneous features?
- Is the child alert/playful/interactive/easy to handle?
- Is the anterior fontanelle soft and pulsatile or tense and bulging?
- Are the scalp veins distended or flat?
- Is there failure of upward gaze ('sun-setting')?

DYSMORPHIC FEATURES

Craniofacial dysmorphism may suggest a diagnosis of craniosynostosis.

CRANIOFACIAL SIGNS

Cutaneous signs can give important clues to the underlying diagnosis, for example *café-au-lait* spots and neurofibromas are seen in neurofibromatosis, and facial port wine stains in Sturge–Weber syndrome. Don't forget to examine the midline! Midline deformities such as a sacral dimple and cleft palate may also provide important clues to underlying pathology.

IRRITABILITY AND EASE OF HANDLING

Children with acute neurological disturbance are often irritable and difficult to handle. This may be the only feature that a parent notices.

ANTERIOR FONTANELLE

A tense, bulging fontanelle is suggestive of raised intracranial pressure, especially if it remains as the head is raised.

SCALP VEINS

The presence of distended scalp veins is a further feature suggestive of raised intracranial pressure.

UPWARD GAZE

Failure of upward gaze, also known as 'sun-setting', is another feature suggestive of raised intracranial pressure often secondary to hydrocephalus, and is due to pressure on the tectal plate. It can, therefore, also be seen with tumours in this region, for example pineal tumours.

KEY ASPECTS OF THE NEUROLOGICAL EXAMINATION

LEVEL OF CONSCIOUSNESS

In critically ill children it is often important to obtain a quick overview of the problematic systems after the primary resuscitation. The AVPU scale allows for a rapid brief assessment of the overall level of consciousness.

- A Alert
- V Responds to Voice
- P Responds to Pain
- U Unresponsive

Table 14.3 Key differences in the paediatric GCS from the adult GCS.

Eyes	Verbal	Motor
Unchanged	5—smiles, coos, babbles	6—spontaneous or purposeful movements
(as for	4—cries, irritable but consolable	2—moans to pain, inconsolable, agitated
adult GCS)	3—cries to pain, occasionally consolable	1—none

If a more formal assessment is required, the Glasgow Coma Scale (GCS) can be used in its modified paediatric form. The key differences are shown in Table 14.3.

TONE AND REFLEXES

It is often easier to assess power and coordination by observing the child 'playing'. Ask the child to skip/hop/jump/run. Not only does this provide useful knowledge but it makes the examination fun for the child, thereby diminishing their anxiety about future visits. Young children are always keen on trying to copy their favourite characters; for example girls love to pretend to be Angelina Ballerina and will attempt to carry out complex twirls.

Generalized reflexes are usually elicitable after 33 weeks gestation. Although there are some differences in both tone and reflexes in children, the lack of symmetry should alert you to a potential neurological disorder.

Hypertonicity in the flexors of the elbow, hip, and knees is not abnormal in the first few months. The tone in the ankles may be markedly reduced while remaining normal in other joints. Children <2 years have an extensor response (Babinski) in their great toe and this is a normal feature. Some of the primitive reflexes are shown in Table 14.4.

PAEDIATRIC HYDROCEPHALUS

CSF PHYSIOLOGY

Cerebrospinal fluid (CSF) is considered a part of the transcellular fluids. It is contained in the ventricles and the subarachnoid space, and bathes the brain and spinal cord. The CSF is contained within the meninges and acts as

Table 14.4 Primitive reflexes.

Reflex	Description
Grasp reflex	Present until about 6 months
Moro reflex	Also known as the 'startle' response, this reflex is present until about 4 months
Landau reflex	In the prone position, with the abdomen supported, the head should extend and the hips flex (if no lower limb abnormalities)
Rooting reflex	Stimulation around the mouth should lead to turning of the head to the stimulated side

a cushion to protect the brain from injury resulting from position or movement. The CSF is formed by modified ependymal cells in the choroid plexus and directly from the walls of the ventricles. It is absorbed by the arachnoid villi and directly into cerebral venules.

There is experimental evidence to suggest that CSF may also flow along the cranial nerves and spinal nerve roots, allowing it into the lymphatic channels; this flow may play a role in CSF reabsorption in neonates, in whom there are few arachnoid granulations.

In adults and older children the total volume of CSF is 150 ml. The daily production is approximately 500 ml/day so the CSF turns over about three to four times per day. Experimental evidence suggests that CSF production in infants is approximately 125 ml/day, rising to about 320 ml/day by the age of 2 years.

The CSF has a composition identical to that of the brain extracellular fluid (ECF), but this is different from plasma. The major differences from plasma are:

- ***PCO2:*** higher (50 mmHg), resulting in a lower CSF pH (7.33).
- ***Protein content:*** normally very low (0.2 g/l), resulting in a low buffering capacity.
- ***Glucose concentration***: lower.
- ***Chloride concentration***: higher.
- ***Cholesterol content***: very low.

There are no lymphatic channels in the brain, and CSF fulfils the role of returning interstitial fluid and protein to the circulation. The CSF is separated from blood by the blood–brain barrier. Only lipid-soluble substances can easily cross this barrier, and this is important in maintaining the compositional differences.

CONGENITAL HYDROCEPHALUS

Hydrocephalus is the most common reason for admitting children to a neurosurgical unit. Hydrocephalus in children, as in adults, can be communicating or non-communicating (see Chapter 11, *Hydrocephalus and Shunt Systems*).

It is important to have some knowledge of the different causes of congenital hydrocephalus. The commonest causes are listed below, followed by an account of the different causes of congenital hydrocephalus:

- *Post-haemorrhagic* (premature infants, intraventricular haemorrhage).
- *Post-infective* (usually after meningitis).
- *Aqueductal stenosis.*
- *Dandy–Walker syndrome.*
- *Chiari malformation* (usually associated with spina bifida).
- *In association with tumours* (e.g. posterior fossa, choroid plexus, 3rd ventricle, pineal).

Myelomeningocoele

Approximately 80% of patients born with a myelomeningocoele have an associated problem with hydrocephalus. Although the initial concern is with the spinal defect, following closure the majority of these children will require treatment for hydrocephalus. Magnetic resonance images (MRI) of the neural axis should be obtained when the child is well, as these children commonly have an associated Type II Chiari malformation.

Aqueduct stenosis

This condition accounts for approximately 10% of congenital hydrocephalus. It can be secondarily acquired due to gliosis around the periaqueduct following intrauterine infections or haemorrhage. Four variants exist, all of which cause some form of narrowing of the aqueduct: gliotic variant, with narrowing caused by proliferation of subependymal astrocytes; forking variant, with several channels separated by normal tissue (associated with spina bifida); septal variant, with a septum across the aqueduct; and true narrowing, in which the aqueduct is histologically normal but has a narrow diameter.

Intraventricular haemorrhage

Approximately 35% of premature infants who have suffered an intraventricular haemorrhage (IVH) will go on to develop hydrocephalus. The increased survival of very premature infants with improvements in neonatal care make this

Table 14.5 Intraventricular haemorrhage (IVH) severity scale.

Grade	Features
I	Germinal matrix haemorrhage without extension into the ventricle.
II	IVH involving up to 50% of ventricular area and not dilating the ventricle.
III	IVH involving greater than 50% ventricular area and dilating the ventricle.
IV	Intraparenchymal component outside the germinal matrix region.

an increasingly important cause of congenital hydrocephalus. Haemorrhage usually occurs in the germinal matrix within the first 3 days of life. The four grades and their associated features on the IVH severity scale are shown in Table 14.5.

The underlying pathophysiology is not entirely understood. However, in the premature neonate, the walls of blood vessels in the germinal matrix region lack certain structural elements present in more mature vessels. Furthermore, the germinal matrix is the site of origin for cortical neuronal and glial cells. The blood vessels in this region are therefore required to provide sufficient blood for these rapidly dividing cells. These fragile vessels are exposed to significant changes in arterial and venous pressures in the premature infant, and this can lead to rupture and haemorrhage.

X-linked hydrocephalus

This is an inheritable form of aqueductal stenosis found only in male children. It constitutes fewer than 4% of all cases and accounts for 8–15% of primary hydrocephalus in boys. The underlying genetic anomaly is the presence of an abnormal gene located on Xq28, leading to a deficiency of the L1 cell adhesion molecule. It is commonly associated with mental retardation, corpus callosum hypoplasia, adducted thumbs, and lower limb spasticity.

Dandy–Walker malformation

Dandy–Walker malformation (DWM) accounts for approximately 2–4% of congenital hydrocephalus. It is characterized by atresia of the foramina of Lushka and Magendie, partial or total agenesis of the cerebellar vermis, and cystic dilatation of the 4th ventricle with a subsequent enlargement of the posterior fossa. Hydrocephalus develops in 70–90% of patients with DWM. The condition is often associated with other developmental anomalies including cranial and spinal dysraphism, dysgenesis of the corpus callosum, and cardiac anomalies. Hydrocephalus treatment in DWM involves shunting of the 4th ventricle +/– lateral ventricles. Standard ventricular-peritoneal shunting may lead to upward herniation and should not be used in isolation. A formal cardiac assessment is required prior to surgical intervention. The long-term prognosis is dependent on the absence or presence of other anomalies. When DWM is present in its mildest form, patients may remain undiagnosed until much later in life.

MANAGEMENT OF PAEDIATRIC HYDROCEPHALUS

Presenting features

Older children may present with the usual features of raised intracranial pressure: headache (usually worse in the morning or on lying down), vomiting, and double/blurred vision. More subtle presenting features include a deterioration in schoolwork and behavioural changes. Parinaud's syndrome (failure of upward gaze, light-near dissociation) and papilloedema may be seen. Younger children may present with an increasing head circumference, developmental delay, poor feeding and/or failure to thrive, irritability and poor handling, or sleep disturbances. A bulging fontanelle, distended scalp veins, occipito-frontal circumference >98th centile, and 'sun-setting eyes' may be seen.

Treatment

Don't forget: the treatment of *all* critically ill children starts with ABC!

General work-up

- *U&Es:* vomiting leads to electrolyte imbalance and dehydration.
- *FBC:* signs of infection.
- *Coagulation screen:* if presenting with haemorrhage.
- *Group-and-Save.*
- *TORCH screening:* in the newborn: TOxoplasmosis, Rubella, Cytomegalovirus, Herpes simplex are infections that can get passed from mother to fetus and can lead to focal cerebral calcification and hydrocephalus.
- *IV cannulation and fluids:* bolus 10 ml/kg if dehydrated.
- *CT scan:* to assess ventricular size and anatomy, haemorrhage and space-occupying lesions.
- *MRI:* allows better demonstration of ventricular anatomy, including relationship of the floor of the 3rd ventricle and the basilar artery if

considering endoscopic third ventriculostomy (ETV) (see below). It is also the imaging of choice in children to assess the entire neuro-axis in cases of spinal dysraphism and tumour pathology.

Specific treatment

- *Fontanelle tap:* in infants/neonates the anterior fontanelle provides immediate access to the ventricular system to allow reduction in ICP (which can be life-saving if the infant is in extremis) and also to allow CSF to be sent for analysis if infection is suspected. 10–20 ml/kg of CSF can be removed by this method, but the acute fluid loss in these infants needs to be replaced ml for ml intravenously.
- *External ventricular drainage:* external ventricular drainage (EVD) allows for a temporary diversion of CSF to an external collection bag. This provides a short-term solution and is used following acute haemorrhage (acute blood will block a shunt) or in the presence of infection. It can also be used to instil intra-thecal drugs (e.g. vancomycin). Usage beyond 10 days increases the risk of ventriculitis.
- *Shunt placement:* ventricular-peritoneal shunts (pleural and atrial shunts are used less commonly) are the mainstay of hydrocephalus treatment. They allow a permanent diversion of the CSF into the peritoneal cavity. Use of pressure (or flow) valves allows regulation of the amount of CSF that is removed. Lumbo-peritoneal shunts can be used in older children, but only in the presence of a communicating hydrocephalus.
- *Endoscopic third ventriculostomy (ETV):* ETV is a procedure that uses the endoscope to create a new channel via the floor of the 3rd ventricle to allow passage of CSF. Its role is predominantly in the treatment of an obstructive hydrocephalus where the CSF pathway between the 3rd and the 4th ventricle is compromised (e.g. aqueduct stenosis, pineal region, and posterior fossa tumours). The endoscope can also be used at the same time to biopsy tumours within the 3rd ventricle/pineal region/aqueduct or to allow introduction of an aqueductal stent.
- *ETV and choroid plexus coagulation (ETV/CPC):* ETV/CPC is increasingly being used as a treatment in communicating hydrocephalus. This procedure not only involves an ETV but then coagulation of the choroid plexus in the lateral ventricles and temporal horn bilaterally. This should lead to a decrease in the amount of CSF production and improve the chances of being shunt-free in such cases.

HEAD INJURY

Children's heads are disproportionately larger than those of adults in relation to their overall body size; this, together with the reliance on ligamentous stability, predisposes them to certain types of brain and cervical spine injury following trauma. Unmyelinated brain has a higher water content than the more developed brain, which makes it softer and more prone to acceleration–deceleration injury. Cerebral water content decreases with age, and thus shear-type forces cause greater harm to the child's brain than is produced by the equivalent force in adults. The presence of an open fontanelle in infants increases their tolerance to raised intracranial pressure in the early stages. A similar 'escape valve' allows slightly older children with open sutures to cope initially with rising pressures. Sutural diastasis is also a common feature in children with fractures. Whereas contracoup injuries are more commonplace amongst adult head-injured patients, coup injuries are more common in children. The increased compliance of the paediatric cranium leads to direct impaction on the underlying brain following trauma. The scalp is a very vascular region and profuse bleeding can occur from any open wound. It should be remembered that the circulating blood volume in a child is only 80 ml/kg and that haemorrhage from such wounds can lead to hypotension and shock in infants and small children. Similarly, intracranial haemorrhage can be significant enough to cause circulatory distress prior to neurological deficits. Two aspects exclusive to children are in birth and non-accidental injuries (NAI). The presence of a cephalhaematoma or depressed skull fracture may be seen following instrumented delivery. Subdural haematomas may develop in either type of injury. Following birth injury, they can manifest as seizures, pupillary abnormalities, or respiratory distress, and may develop within a few hours. The presence of a subdural haematoma without any signs of significant trauma or in the absence of a plausible history should raise concerns about NAI.

GOALS OF MANAGEMENT

The goals of management in children with head injury remain no different from those in adults. Primary brain injury occurs at the time of impact and is irreversible. However, further neuronal damage is caused by hypoxia and hypoperfusion. Head injury leads to raised ICP, reduced CPP with loss of autoregulation, and to neuroexcitotoxicity which accentuates these problems.

Management should therefore be aimed at preventing secondary brain injury by early treatment of these adverse factors. It is likely that the severely injured child will require standard traumatic resuscitation in accordance with APLS/ATLS guidelines. Airway management with cervical spine control, breathing, and circulatory resuscitation should all be addressed prior to neurological evaluation and specific treatment. In cases of severe injury, management will take place in the paediatric intensive care unit (PICU); the underlying basis of management in 'ward-managed' head-injured children is, however, no different. The goals remain to protect the airway, adequately oxygenate and correct any hypovolaemia and hypotension. The following sections will discuss the rationale behind the management strategies, before considering how patients should be managed on the ward.

AIRWAY AND VENTILATORY MANAGEMENT

In the presence of a severe traumatic brain injury where protection of the airway is essential, urgent consultation with the local PICU team should be sought. The goals of airway management are to provide a safe airway to allow optimization of ventilation, to prevent hypoxaemia, and to maintain normocapnia.

In the past, ventilatory strategies involved prolonged hyperventilation, as this had been shown to decrease ICP, albeit transiently. However, the associated vasoconstriction and decreased cerebral blood flow (CBF) caused more harm from cerebral ischaemia than protection from ICP. In consequence, normocapnia is now the aim, with short transient episodes of hyperventilation used only to treat an 'ICP crisis'. Several studies have shown that hypoxaemia is a significant predictor of morbidity; therefore, maximizing oxygenation is another essential prerequisite. These two factors are equally essential, even in the ward management of those children with a less severe brain injury. Remember the following three principles:

1. *Airway protection:* is the child able to cough and maintain a clear and safe airway? If the child is excessively drowsy consider PICU involvement at an early stage.
2. *Maximize oxygenation*: monitor saturations and give supplemental oxygen as required.
3. *Monitor respiration:* decreased respiratory rates (e.g. drowsiness, opioid drugs) will lead to hypercapnia and increases in ICP. Tachypnoea leads to hypocapnia and the problems addressed above.

CIRCULATORY SUPPORT AND FLUID MANAGEMENT

Cerebral blood flow averages 55–60 ml/100 g brain tissue/min in normal adults and is known to be higher in children. It is not known what the critical values of CBF are, below which cerebral ischaemia occurs. The most significant factor determining CBF at any time is the cerebral perfusion pressure (CPP). This can be calculated from mean arterial and intracranial pressures (MAP and ICP) by the formula:

$$\text{CPP} = \text{MAP} - \text{ICP}$$

$$(\text{MAP} = 2/3 \text{ diastolic pressure} + 1/3 \text{ systolic pressure}).$$

It therefore follows that maintaining an adequate CPP can be achieved by maintaining an adequate blood pressure, and by reducing any factors that increase ICP. Evidence has shown that improved outcome is inversely proportional to the number of hypotensive episodes, and thus falls in CPP. In the PICU setting, the use of invasive monitoring (arterial and central venous lines) allows for a comprehensive circulatory assessment. Inotropic support can be given to aid falling blood pressure, if required. Again, this important aspect of treatment also needs addressing in ward managed patients. Remember the following five principles:

1. Monitor pulse and blood pressure.
2. Check haemoglobin (Hb).
3. Keep normovolaemic.
4. Avoid dextrose solutions.
5. Avoid hyperglycaemia.

Pulse and blood pressure

Tachycardia may be the first sign of hypovolaemia and needs urgently to be addressed. Has adequate fluid been given during the resuscitative period? Is there another potential bleeding source (e.g. abdominal or long bone injuries)? Bradycardia may be a sign of an expanding intracranial mass lesion but can also be a sign of circulatory failure. Urgent consultation with PICU is again essential.

Haemoglobin

Low Hb values diminish the oxygen-carrying capacity of the blood and may suggest significant blood loss. Circulating blood volume in children is approximately 80 ml/kg and therefore even small losses can lead to significant hypotension.

Normovolaemia

Keeping a child normovolaemic is important, because there is an increased risk of hypotensive episodes if the child is kept 'dry'.

Dextrose solutions

Dextrose-containing fluids can lead to a decrease in plasma osmolality and hyponatraemia. This combination leads to an increased osmotic drive into the neuronal cells, leading to increased brain oedema. NaCl solution (0.9%) should be used in preference.

Hyperglycaemia

Hyperglycaemia can also lead to an increase in neural injury (glucose is metabolized to lactic acid and the subsequent fall in tissue pH leads to worsening metabolic injury). Insulin sliding-scale regimens may be required.

INTRACRANIAL PRESSURE MANAGEMENT

Controlling ICP is an important factor in managing patients with head injury. ICP is maintained within normal limits within a reasonable range of increased intracranial volumes. Efflux of CSF and/or venous blood forms a major part of this compensatory mechanism. However, as any intracranial mass lesion expands this compensation is overcome, and a rapid rise in ICP is seen, even with very small increases in intracranial volume. The Monro–Kellie doctrine, proposed in the early part of the nineteenth century, provides a formula for calculation of intracranial volume and a procedure by which it may be treated.

$$V_{\text{intracranial}} = V_{\text{brain}} + V_{\text{CSF}} + V_{\text{blood}} + V_{\text{mass lesion}}$$

A reduction in any of the four factors on the right-hand side of this equation will lead to a decrease in intracranial volume, and therefore to a drop in ICP. Various methods are available to achieve this, including:

- Head-up posture.
- Early clearance of spinal injury.
- Drainage of CSF.
- Mannitol.
- Sedation/paralysis.

- Barbiturate therapy.
- Surgery.
- Seizure management.

Head-up posture

Maintaining a head-up posture helps reduce ICP by increasing venous return, reducing V_{blood} and therefore increasing CPP. Elevation beyond 30° leads to a more significant decrease in CPP and thus limits the amount of head up recommended.

Early clearance of spinal injury

Cervical collars reduce venous return and can lead to a rise in ICP. In the absence of spinal injury, not only can the collar be removed but the patient can be sat up, which can help ventilation and prevent CO_2 retention.

Drainage of CSF

Insertion of an EVD will allow drainage of CSF, reducing V_{CSF} and thus ICP. Unfortunately, in cases of traumatic brain injury, the ventricles are usually small and CSF cannulation may not be possible.

Mannitol

Mannitol acts as an osmotic diuretic leading to 'dehydration' of neuronal cells which will decrease V_{brain} and thus reduce ICP. Its effect is short-acting and therefore is best used in the treatment of an ICP 'crisis'.

Sedation/paralysis

ICU management may involve not only ventilatory support but also medical treatment in reducing ICP. Sedative drugs, for example propofol, as well as paralytics (e.g. atracurium) reduce pain, agitation, and shivering, thereby reducing cerebral metabolic rate (CMR) and thus ICP.

Barbiturate therapy

Barbiturates are used in the treatment of refractory raised ICP. They are used to induce a barbiturate coma with a view to reducing CMR, cerebral blood volume (CBV), and ICP. They can also act as anticonvulsants.

Surgery

The presence of an intracranial haematoma (subdural, extradural, contusions) is an indication for surgery if there is significant mass effect or there is evidence of its expanding. It is vital that, prior to surgery, any 'ABC' abnormalities are corrected; in infants and small children, a large intracranial haematoma may cause a significant drop in haemoglobin and may be the predominant cause for the child's critical status.

Seizure management

Neuroexcitotoxicity is not uncommon following head injury and can lead to seizures. This leads to an increase in cerebral metabolic rate and rises in ICP. Post-traumatic seizures are more commonly seen in children than in adults, with up to 10% being affected. The role for prophylactic anticonvulsants in children remains questionable. Studies in adults have shown that prophylactic anticonvulsants reduce the incidence of early seizures (within 1 week), but have no long-term benefit. Various surgical options are available, including:

- ICP monitoring.
- EVD placement.
- Craniotomy for haematoma.
- Decompressive craniectomy.

ICP monitoring

Insertion of a pressure transducer to monitor ICP can easily be carried out via a twist drill procedure. Several transducers are available and can be placed in any of the intracranial compartments, although intraparenchymal monitors are the most commonly used.

EVD placement

Insertion of an EVD can also be performed via a (usually right frontal) burr-hole. This is only feasible if the ventricles are not effaced, and allows drainage of CSF to help control ICP.

Craniotomy for haematoma

A standard trauma craniotomy can be used to evacuate a significant extradural, subdural, or contusional injury. Burr-hole drainage can be used in more chronic haematomas but is not usually indicated in the acute period.

Decompressive craniectomy

Removal of the bone flap to increase the potential space for cerebral swelling (and, in essence, reduce the effect of V_{brain}) remains a controversial area. It is usually reserved for cases when the raised ICP has become refractory and is no longer manageable by medical therapies. At present there is very little evidence that it improves outcome: a single study in Australia suggests there may be a benefit from early decompression in children. The decision to undertake decompressive craniectomy is still taken on a case-by-case basis.

WARD-BASED MANAGEMENT

It is important to obtain a history outlining the nature and severity of the head injury, for example height of fall, speed of car, use of seatbelts, etc. This will also give an indication of whether other organs may also have been injured and need addressing. Often, this history has to be obtained from witnesses. The initial cardiorespiratory and neurological condition can best be obtained from members of the paramedic crew (the importance of whom should not be underestimated!). It is important to document the presence of seizures, length of any amnesic periods, and any episodes of loss of consciousness. An immunization history, especially a tetanus status, should also be obtained. A full systemic examination is required, especially in cases where it has not been possible to obtain a history. If the preceding history does not support the examination findings consider the possibility of NAI and seek expert help from senior staff and the paediatric service.

General work up

- *U&Es:* vomiting leads to electrolyte imbalance and dehydration.
- *FBC:* even small blood losses in young children can cause significant falls in Hb.
- *Coagulation screen:* risk of disseminated intravascular coagulopathy in trauma patients.
- *Cross-match blood:* at least 2 units.
- *IV cannulation and fluids.*
- *CT scan:* to assess presence of intracranial haematomas, cerebral swelling, midline shift, mass effect, sulcal effacement, and bony injuries.

Further treatment

The majority of ward-based head-injured children can be managed conservatively. It is important to monitor them closely so that their cardiorespiratory status can be optimized as mentioned above. Adequate analgesia should be provided as pain leads to increases in metabolic rate and also raises ICP. Fever causes a similar reaction and pyrexial events should therefore be investigated early and treated appropriately. Early discussions with PICU should occur in relation to any child in whom there is any cardiorespiratory or neurological compromise. While an expanding mass lesion may be the cause of an acute deterioration, electrolyte imbalances, particularly hyponatraemia, can also lead to neurological dysfunction—don't forget to check the bloods!

PAEDIATRIC BRAIN TUMOURS

Brain tumours are the commonest solid paediatric tumour and comprise 20% of all childhood cancers, being second only in incidence to leukaemia. Although paediatric brain tumours are predominantly infratentorial (approximately 60%), the location of tumours is highly dependent on age. Children under 6 months of age are more likely to have a supratentorial tumour (approximately 75%). The nature of the tumour is also dependent on its location and on the age of the child. While in the infratentorial compartment there is a relatively equal incidence of medulloblastoma, brainstem gliomas, and pilocytic astrocytomas, in the supratentorial region astrocytomas are significantly more common. Congenital tumours presenting in neonates are more likely to be neuroectodermal in origin, with teratomas being most common, while in older children astrocytomas, medulloblastomas, and ependymomas predominate. Some glial tumours, such as mixed gliomas, are unique to children; they are most frequently located in the cerebellum (67%) and are usually benign.

The World Health Organization (WHO) has recently reclassified brain tumours to introduce molecular parameters in addition to histology to aid diagnosis and treatment. This has had a significant impact in the nomenclature of paediatric tumours with the removal of the terms 'primitive neuroectodermal tumour' (PNET) and 'diffuse intrinsic pontine glioma' (DIPG). The new classifications are beyond the scope of this chapter and require further reading (see Louis et al., 2016).

PILOCYTIC ASTROCYTOMA

Juvenile pilocytic astrocytomas occur more often in children and young adults than in older adults. They are the most common astrocytic tumours in children, accounting for 80–85% of cerebellar astrocytomas and 60% of optic gliomas. They comprise about 33% of all posterior fossa tumours in children, and represent about 25% of all paediatric tumours. Juvenile pilocytic astrocytomas usually arise in the cerebellum, brainstem, hypothalamic region, or optic pathways, but they may occur in any area where astrocytes are present, including the cerebral hemispheres and the spinal cord. There is an association with neurofibromatosis: optic nerve gliomas are common tumours in patients with this condition and may present bilaterally. Patients with optic pilocytic astrocytomas associated with neurofibromatosis type 1

(NF1) usually have better outcomes than other patients with juvenile pilocytic astrocytomas.

Pathophysiology

These tumours are usually discrete, indolent lesions associated with cyst formation. The cysts may be unilocular or multilocular, with an associated tumour nodule. The nodular portion of the lesion usually demonstrates homogeneous contrast enhancement. Calcification is present in 10% of juvenile pilocytic astrocytomas. Histologically, the tumour contains fibrillary astrocytes with associated Rosenthal fibres (intracellular, eosinophilic, rod-shaped bodies). The tumour is named after the 'hair-like' bipolar (piloid) astrocytes. Features more typically seen in higher-grade gliomas can be seen (nuclear atypia, mitoses, endothelial proliferation, and necrosis), but they have no proven prognostic significance.

Epidemiology

The peak incidence is in patients of 5–14 years of age with no sex predilection.

Treatment

Posterior fossa pilocytic astrocytomas are typically treated with surgery and completely resected whenever possible. Optic nerve tumours can often be managed conservatively, surgery usually being indicated in an attempt to preserve vision in the unaffected eye.

Outcome

Patients with juvenile pilocytic astrocytoma have a better prognosis than do patients with most other types of astrocytomas. If gross total resection is possible, the 10-year survival rate is as high as 90%. After subtotal resection or biopsy, the 10-year survival rate is as high as 45%. Morbidity is related to the location of the tumour and to the associated complications of tumour resection.

MEDULLOBLASTOMA

Medulloblastomas originate from undifferentiated cells in the subependymal region in the foetal brain. Arising in the inferior medullary velum, they grow to fill the 4th ventricle, infiltrating the surrounding structures. They are the most common malignant posterior fossa tumour in the paediatric population.

Characterized by their tendency to seed along the neuro-axis, following CSF pathways, they can rarely metastasize to extra-neural tissues. Evidence of 'drop-mets' will be seen in 10–30% of patients at the time of diagnosis. Extra-cranial metastases (involving bone, liver and lymph nodes) account for 5% of cases.

Pathophysiology

Medulloblastomas are highly cellular, vascular tumours with a deeply basophilic nucleus and multiple mitoses ('small blue cell tumour').

Epidemiology

Medulloblastomas have a bimodal age distribution peaking at 5–9 years of age, with a smaller peak at 20–30 years, and a male:female ratio of about 3:1.

Treatment

Gross surgical excision, followed by craniospinal irradiation, remains the ultimate goal in these patients. However, any attempt to remove tumour from the floor of the 4th ventricle can lead to significant morbidity. Up to 30% of tumours will have invaded the ventricular floor, and care must be taken not to damage this very eloquent region.

Outcome

The newer classification of medulloblastoma categorizes these tumours into five different genetic sub-types and 13 different integrated diagnoses with differing outcomes in each category. Overall, children with non-disseminated medulloblastoma, and old enough to have radiation therapy have a 5-year survival rate of about 70%. In the presence of dissemination, adjuvant chemotherapy can be given, but the survival rates are significantly lower. Neurological, endocrine, and cognitive deficits are not uncommon in this latter group.

EPENDYMOMA

Ependymomas are derived from ependymal cells and occur most commonly in the ependymal lining of the ventricles. These tumours can also arise in the conus (myxopapillary) and spinal canal. The majority of ependymomas are located in the posterior fossa, with a predilection for the 4th ventricle. Extension through the foramina of Luschka and Magendie is not uncommon.

Approximately 10% of patients will have spinal metastases at the time of diagnosis, although this is more common with the anaplastic variants. Tumours presenting supratentorially are more common in adults than in children, and are usually located in the trigone of the lateral ventricles.

Pathophysiology

Ependymomas are usually benign tumours which present as solid mass lesions. Histologically, they are composed of uniform ependymal cells forming true rosettes and perivascular pseudo-rosettes. It is not uncommon to have associated calcification, cysts, and haemorrhage.

Anaplastic ependymomas tend to have histological features of a higher-grade tumour with vascular proliferation and necrosis.

Epidemiology

The female:male ratio is approximately 2:1. Presentation has a median age in the second decade, but is bimodal, with the younger peak at about age 5 years.

Treatment

Gross total surgical excision where possible, with adjuvant radiotherapy, is the treatment of choice.

Outcome

Combined treatment leads to a 35–60% 5-year survival rate. Although adults have an increased tendency to anaplastic variants, their survival rate is better than in children. This is most likely due to the fact that craniospinal radiation therapy is limited to children over the age of 5 years due to the adverse effects on the developing nervous system.

CHOROID PLEXUS PAPILLOMA AND CARCINOMA

Choroid plexus papillomas and carcinomas represent 0.4–0.6% of all intracranial tumours. They represent approximately 3% of childhood brain tumours, and are most likely to occur in the lateral ventricle. Although these tumours can occur in the 4th ventricle, this is a feature that is more commonly seen in adults. Symptoms are usually due to hydrocephalus, which is likely to be due to the presence of increased protein and xanthochromia within the CSF, causing diminished absorption. Overproduction of CSF is not uncommon, but does not explain the persistence of hydrocephalus after tumour removal.

Pathophysiology

Although macroscopically choroid plexus papillomas appear as reddish solid tumours, histologically it can be difficult to differentiate them from normal choroid. As with the other malignant variants of tumour, the presence of nuclear atypia, mitoses and necrosis is suggestive of carcinomatous change.

Epidemiology

Approximately 85% of these tumours present in children under 5 years.

Treatment

Surgical resection results in a cure for benign papillomas. These tumours are very vascular and, in the presence of carcinoma, preoperative chemotherapy may have a role in shrinking tumour size and reducing vascularity in order to aid surgical resection.

Outcome

Five-year survival rates of about 80% have been described. The main morbidity arises from persistent subdural collections due to a ventriculo-subdural fistula.

BRAINSTEM GLIOMAS

Overall, brainstem gliomas constitute 15% of all brain tumours. In children, however, brainstem gliomas represent 25–30% of all brain tumours. Most brainstem gliomas are low-grade astrocytomas and can be conservatively managed. Surgical debulking is reserved for exophytic portions of tumour.

As with medulloblastoma, the recognition of different genetic aspects of these tumours allows them to be separately categorized from the adult equivalents. The combination of a specific genetic mutation, diffuse pattern of growth ,and a midline location now provides a diagnosis of diffuse midline glioma and replaces the previous DIPG. Identification of these genetic variants should allow directed therapies against the mutations and may lead to a change in prognosis in the future.

CLINICAL FEATURES OF PAEDIATRIC BRAIN TUMOURS

Mass lesions in children may present in one of three ways: raised ICP, focal neurological signs, and seizures. Pituitary tumours and craniopharyngiomas may present with either neurological deficit (visual loss) or endocrine dysfunction.

MANAGEMENT OF PAEDIATRIC BRAIN TUMOURS

Remember ABCs!

General work up

As for hydrocephalus (see Chapter 11, *Hydrocephalus and Shunt Systems*).

Specific work up

- MRI of brain and spine.
- Tumour markers.
- Endocrine assessment.
- Ophthalmology/visual fields.

MRI of brain and spine

It is preferable to carry this out prior to any surgical intervention, as it is useful to assess suitability for endoscopic managements (e.g. ETV, biopsy) and allows better evaluation of the tumour and its relation to eloquent structures. Furthermore, it allows for assessment of any spinal disease (e.g. drop metastases).

Tumour markers

Tumour markers are obtainable from CSF and serum; they are essential for optimizing management of pineal region tumours.

Endocrine assessment

This is required in the case of pituitary and craniopharyngioma patients (who may need pre-operative hormone replacement).

Ophthalmology/visual fields

Ophthalmic and visual field examination is most commonly required for pituitary patients, but should be assessed in any child with a tumour along the visual pathway.

Treatment options

In most cases, treatment for symptomatic hydrocephalus is carried out first. This has the advantage of rapidly improving symptoms such as headache and vomiting, but also allows investigation of CSF markers. In the presence of an aqueductal stenosis due to an offending tumour, an initial endoscopic approach may be used to create a 3rd ventriculostomy and to biopsy the tumour at the same sitting. Surgical excision is carried out wherever tumour location makes it possible. Unlike in adults, the free use of chemo- and radiotherapy is not possible. Children under the age of 5 years have a significant long-term morbidity with whole brain (+/– spine) radiotherapy. Outcomes are improved in children over 5 years old at diagnosis with no evidence of disseminated disease and maximal surgical resection. Brainstem and optic tract gliomas are usually low-grade astrocytomas, and are predominantly managed conservatively.

Follow-up imaging

MRI within the first 24 h after surgery provides a baseline for further follow-up and for optimizing any adjuvant therapy. The artefact produced from surgical intervention makes radiological assessment of residual tumour after 48 h exceptionally difficult, and therefore, if imaging cannot be performed within this time period, it should be deferred for at least 6 weeks.

REFERENCE

Louis, DN, Perry, A, Reifenberger, G et al. The 2016 World Health Organization classification of tumors of the central nervous system: A summary. *Acta Neuropathol* 2016;131:803–820.

15

Commonly Used Scoring Systems in Neurosurgery

Reuben D. Johnson and W. Adriaan Liebenberg

CONTENTS

THE GLASGOW COMA SCALE

Table 15.1 is a modified version of the Glasgow Coma Scale (GCS). See also the discussion of the GCS in Chapter 5 on *Neurosurgical History and Examination*.

Table 15.1 The Modified Glasgow Coma Scale.

Score	Eye opening (max = 4)	Verbal response (max = 5)	Motor response (max = 6)
6	—	—	Obeys
5	—	Orientated	Localizes
4	Spontaneous	Confused	Withdraws
3	To speech	Inappropriate	Flexion (decorticate)
2	To pain	Incomprehensible	Extension (decerebrate)
1	None	None	None

Teasdale G, Jennett B. Assessment of coma and impaired consciousness: a practical scale. Lancet 1974; ii: 81–84.

THE GLASGOW OUTCOME SCALE

Table 15.2 is a modified summary of the Glasgow Outcome Scale (GOS), which was designed for the assessment of outcome in head injuries. The GOS is a valuable and established research tool. When critically evaluating new treatment modalities for head injury that reportedly produce improvements in the GOS, it is necessary to consider exactly what that means for the patient. For example, a treatment modality might be shown to improve the GOS in 90% of patients, but if the improvement equates to changes from a GOS of 1 to 2, that is, from death to a persistent vegetative state, then it is worth considering the implications for the patient. Is death always the worst outcome?

Table 15.2 The Glasgow Outcome Scale (modified).

Score	Description of patient
5	Normal life
4	Mild disability, able to perform basic activities of daily life independently, but not able to resume previously normal life
3	Severely disabled and dependent
2	Persistent vegetative state
1	Death

Jennett B, Bond M. The assessment of outcome after severe brain damage: a practical scale. Lancet 1975; i: 480–484.

WFNS GRADE OF SUBARACHNOID HAEMORRHAGE

The World Federation of Neurological Surgeons (WFNS) grading scale (Table 15.3) is a six-point (0 to 5) scale for rating the effects of subarachnoid haemorrhage in terms of GCS score and the presence or absence of focal deficit.

Table 15.3 The World Federation of Neurological Surgeons (WFNS) grading scale for subarachnoid haemorrhage.

WFNS grade	GCS	Focal deficit (aphasia, hemiparesis)
0 (unruptured aneurysm)	—	—
1	15	None
2	13–14	None
3	13–14	Present
4	7–12	None or present
5	3–6	None or present

Drake CG. Report of World Federation of Neurological Surgeons Committee on a universal subarachnoid haemorrhage grading scale. J Neurosurg 1988; 68: 985–986.

FISHER GRADE OF CT FINDINGS IN SUBARACHNOID HAEMORRHAGE

A poor Fisher grade (Table 15.4) correlates with increased risk of vasospasm.

Table 15.4 The Fisher scale for grading CT findings in subarachnoid haemorrhage.

Fisher grade	Blood on CT
1	None detected
2	Diffuse or vertical layers[a] <1 mm thick
3	Localized clot or vertical layer >1 mm thick
4	Intracerebral or intraventricular clot

[a] Vertical layers refers to subarachnoid spaces, e.g. intrahemisphere fissure.

Fisher CM, Kistler JP, Davis JM. Relation of cerebral vasospasm to subarachnoid haemorrhage visualized by CT scanning. Neurosurgery 1980; 6: 1–9.

MODIFIED FISHER GRADE OF CT FINDINGS IN SUBARACHNOID HAEMORRHAGE

The original Fisher scale (Table 15.5) has been modified for patients with thick cisternal blood and concomitant intraventricular or intraparenchymal haemorrhage. The higher the modified Fisher grade the greater the risk of symptoms.

Table 15.5 The Modified Fisher Grade of CT findings in subarachnoid haemorrhage.

Fisher grade (modified)	Subarachnoid haemorrhage	Intraventricular haemorrhage	Symptomatic vasospasm incidence (%)
0	None	None	0
1	Thin[a] focal or diffuse	None	24
2	Thin focal or diffuse	Present	33
3	Thick[b] focal or diffuse	None	33
4	Thick focal or diffuse	Present	40

[a] Thin subarachnoid haemorrhage is <1 mm thick.

[b] Thick subarachnoid haemorrhage is >1 mm thick.

Frontera JA, Claasen J, Schmidt JM et al. Prediction of symptomatic vasospasm after subarachnoid haemorrhage: the modified Fisher scale. Neurosurgery 2006; 59: 21–27.

MRC SCORE FOR MUSCLE STRENGTH ASSESSMENT

The MRC Score for Muscle Strength Assessment is detailed in Table 15.6.

Table 15.6 The MRC scale for grading muscle strength.

Grade	Strength
0	No contraction
1	Flicker
2	Moves if gravity eliminated
3	Gravity overcome
4	Moves against resistance
5	Normal strength

KARNOFSKY SCORE

The Karnofsky score (Table 15.7) was devised as a clinical and research tool to grade functional status in cancer patients. The maximum and best score is 100, which implies normal functioning. Lower scores imply varying degrees of symptomatology, disability, and sickness. The lowest score is 0 and implies death.

Table 15.7 The Karnofsky performance score.

Condition and score	Comments
A. *Able to carry on normal activity and to work. No special care needed.*	
100	Normal, no complaints, no evidence of disease.
90	Able to carry on normal activity, minor signs or symptoms of disease.
80	Normal activity with effort, some signs or symptoms of disease.
B. *Unable to work. Able to live at home, care for most personal needs A varying degree of assistance is needed.*	
70	Cares for self. Unable to carry on normal activity or to do active work.
60	Requires occasional assistance, but is able to care for most of own needs.
50	Disease may be progressing rapidly. Requires considerable assistance and frequent medical care.
C. *Unable to care for self. Requires equivalent of institutional or hospital care.*	
40	Disabled. Requires special care and assistance.
30	Severely disabled, hospitalization is indicated although death is not imminent.
20	Hospitalization necessary, very sick, active supportive treatment necessary.
10	Moribund, fatal processes progressing rapidly.
0	Dead.

Karnofsky DA, Burchenal JH. The clinical evaluation of chemotherapeutic agents in cancer. In: Macleod CM, ed. Evaluation of chemotherapy agents. New York: Columbia University Press, 1949: 191–205.

www.acsu.buffalo.edu/~drstall/assessmenttools.html

Appendix

Further Reading

Crockard A, Hayward R, Hoft JT, eds. *Neurosurgery: The Scientific Basis of Clinical Practice*, 3rd edn. Blackwell Science, 2000.

Greenberg MS. *Handbook of Neurosurgery*, 8th edn. Thieme, 2016.

Jennett B, Lindsay KW. *An Introduction to Neurosurgery*, 5th edn. Butterworth Heinemann, 1994.

Kaye AH. *Essential Neurosurgery*, 3rd edn. Blackwell Publishing, 2005.

Kranzler LI, Hobbs J, eds. *The Greenberg Rapid Review: A Companion to the 8th Edition.* Thieme, 2017.

Lindsay KW, Bone I, Fuller G. *Neurology and Neurosurgery Illustrated,* 5th edn. Churchill Livingstone, 2010.

Moore AJ, Newell DW, eds. *Neurosurgery: Principles and Practice.* Springer Verlag, 2005.

Patten J. *Neurological Differential Diagnosis*, 2nd edn. Springer Verlag, 1996, corr. 2nd printing 1998.

Rengachary SS, Ellenbogen RG. *Principles of Neurosurgery*, 2nd edn. Mosby, 2005.

Shah RS, Cadoux-Hudson TA, Van Gompel JJ, Pereira EAC. *Neurosurgery Self-assessment: Questions and Answers.* Edinburgh: Elsevier, 2017.

Tindall GT, Cooper PR, Barrow DL, eds. *The Practice of Neurosurgery.* Lippincott, Williams & Wilkins, 1996

Winn HR, ed. *Youmans and Winn Neurological Surgery*, 7th edn. W. B. Saunders, 2016.

Index

For the benefit of digital users, indexed terms that span two pages (e.g., 52–53) may, on occasion, appear on only one of those pages.

Note: tables and figures are indicated by an italic *t* and *f* following the page number.

R